Criminology and Penology

Criminology and Penology

RICHARD R. KORN

New York University

AND

LLOYD W. McCORKLE

Director, Division of Administration
Department of Institutions and Agencies, Trenton, N. J.
and Rutgers University

HOLT, RINEHART AND WINSTON

NEW YORK – CHICAGO – SAN FRANCISCO
TORONTO – LONDON

To our fathers
Louis Korn and James Henry McCorkle

January, 1967

Preface

THIS BOOK IS DESIGNED TO FULFILL THE NEEDS OF THE STANDARD
course in Criminology and Penology. It discusses and evaluates the
available data from these fields and outlines the more important
theoretical frameworks that have sought to contain these data. It also
explores the problems encountered in the quest for scientific knowledge
about crime and criminals.

Although there is no shortage of both professional and lay opinion
concerning the problems of crime causation, treatment, and prevention,
the foundations for a science of criminology and penology remain inadequate. Our organization and weighting of topics has therefore been
conditioned to a great extent by the need to explore the groundwork
of these foundations.

The student is first introduced to the body of recorded criminological data and to the requirements of a social science. These are brought
together in a discussion of crime statistics and the nature of the conclusions that can be validly drawn from them. The two essential functions of any science—the gathering of empirical evidence and the logical
ordering of this evidence in relation to explanatory conceptions—are
then illustrated by a discussion of the law both as a political and social
process and as an instrument of social control.

The third section consists of an analysis of the various classifications of crime and the criminal and of the implications of these classifications. Finally, we describe the different theories of causation from
the standpoint of their underlying frames of reference and conclude
with a suggestion as to the steps necessary to achieve a workable consensus for the clarification of criminological theory.

The discussion of penology rests upon our basic supposition that
many of the inmate's problems arise from the problems confronting the

agents of society appointed to deal with him. We indicate that a neglect of the interdependence of these two sets of problems, or a moralistic and emotional approach to them, results in a distorted and in many ways socially harmful picture of the convicted criminal, unrealistic to a degree unique in the social sciences.

In an attempt to correct this distortion we have provided a directly empirical analysis of three facets of correctional behavior and practice: the prison community, employing the techniques of the social psychologist; the problems of treatment, from the point of view of the offender as well as the treatment staff; and the problems of institutional adjustment, on the basis of direct participation in the prison community. The final sections of the text are devoted to issues of prevention and treatment in the community at large.

The number of people who have contributed to this volume in different ways is so large that we will not attempt even a partial listing of their names. When they read it they will recognize the imprint of their ideas and suggestions, for which we shall be ever grateful.

New York City and Trenton, N. J.   R. R. K.
May, 1959   L. W. McC.

Contents

PART TWO

PENOLOGY

SECTION I · PAST AND PRESENT MODES OF PUNISHMENT

SECTION II · APPREHENSION, ADJUDICATION, AND DISPOSITION

SECTION IV · CORRECTIONAL TREATMENT: TRENDS AND ISSUES

Criminology

PROBLEMS OF METHOD

An Introduction to the Data
of Criminology

The Extent of Lawbreaking in Modern Society

EVERY YEAR IN THIS COUNTRY APPROXIMATELY TWO AND A HALF million major crimes—give or take a hundred thousand—are reported to the Federal Bureau of Investigation. In round figures, this comes to one major crime reported for every sixty men, women, and children in the population. If one deducts from the total population those people who are almost never involved in lawbreaking—the very old, the very young, the sick or incapacitated—the ratio rises to approximately one offense for every forty persons old enough and well enough to walk around by themselves. And there is reason to believe that this figure represents only a fraction of the actual extent of lawbreaking that annually occurs in this country.

In the first place, the estimate is made solely on the basis of *crimes known to the police.* A great many offenses are never officially reported. Secondly, a comparable number is probably unknown either to the victim or to the offender himself. It would be difficult to estimate, for example, how often one is the victim of the felony of slander, and equally, if not more, difficult to determine how often one commits this offense oneself. The intoxicated driver is usually unable to estimate the extent of his drunkenness. For every petty thief who deliberately steals, there are probably several "borrowers" who never get around to returning what they borrowed—largely because they never intended to return it in the first place. The volume and value of goods appropriated by employees as "legitimate graft" is impossible to determine—but more than one large department-store owner has complained that he missed more items through "breakage" and "inventory losses" than he missed at the hands of shoplifters. Nevertheless, unless these "losses" get out of hand, they are not defined as thefts.

Surveys of Lawbreaking among the General Public

Until recently the study of crime was almost exclusively concentrated on those offenders who had already become involved in the legal process. During the last two decades, however, the growing realization of the wider extent of lawbreaking has stimulated research on crime among members of the general population. In 1946 in Fort Worth, Texas, a survey was made comparing the offenses admitted by a sample of college students with offenses charged against boys brought before the juvenile court. The violations admitted by the college boys, students of Texas Christian University, exceeded those charged against the juveniles both in number and seriousness.[1]

In 1947 James Wallerstein and Clement Wyle published the responses of a sample of adult New York residents to a questionnaire detailing forty-nine common offenses. Of the 1,020 men and 678 women answering the questions, 91 per cent admitted committing felonies and misdemeanors that might have resulted in imprisonment. The responses are summarized in Table I.[2]

When compared with nation-wide statistics of persons arrested for crimes, the results of the Wallerstein-Wyle study are particularly significant with respect to sex ratios. Of the 68,195 persons arrested for larceny in 1953, the ratio of men to women was approximately 6 to 1.[3] As against this, the ratio of men to women admitting larceny in the Wallerstein-Wyle study was almost equal: 89 per cent to 83 per cent. The ratio of men to women admitting burglary to Wallerstein and Wyle was approximately 4 to 1. But according to the *Uniform Crime Reports*, 46 men

[1] Austin L. Porterfield, *Youth in Trouble* (Fort Worth, Texas: The Leo Potishman Foundation, 1946).

[2] James S. Wallerstein and Clement J. Wyle, "Our Law-Abiding Law-Breakers," *Federal Probation*, 25:110, April 1947.

[3] *Uniform Crime Reports*, 24, No. 2 (1953), p. 113.

TABLE I

INDICTABLE OFFENSES ADMITTED BY ADULT NONCRIMINALS

	Per cent	
Offense	Men	Women
Malicious mischief	84	81
Disorderly conduct	85	76
Assault	49	5
Auto misdemeanors	61	39
Indecency	77	74
Gambling	74	54
Larceny	89	83
Grand larceny (except auto)	13	11
Auto theft	26	8
Burglary	17	4
Robbery	11	1
Concealed weapons	35	3
Perjury	23	17
Falsification and fraud	46	34
Election frauds	7	4
Tax evasion	57	40
Coercion	16	6
Conspiracy	23	7
Criminal libel	36	29

were arrested for burglary for every single female arrested for this offense in 1953.[4] Four times as many men were arrested for fraud and embezzlement;[5] the ratio of men to women admitting fraud and falsification was 4 to 3. The ratios for disorderly conduct are especially interesting because of the unusually wide discretionary powers of the policeman. For every 8 men admitting behavior definable as disorderly, 7 women made comparable admissions. But policemen were 5 times readier to insist that gentlemen were unmannerly than they were to charge the ladies with being unladylike.[6] The statistics for assault reveal a discrepancy in the reverse direction—either the policemen were being less gallant, or the ladies less candid. Only 1 woman for every 9 men in the Wallerstein-Wyle study admitted assaulting anyone. The F.B.I. figures reveal 1 female for every 5 men arrested for aggravated assault.[7] (In cases of less serious assault, gallantry apparently reasserts itself: only 1 woman was arrested for every 10 men.)[8]

Evidence of widespread crime by persons never—or only rarely—

[4] *Ibid.*
[5] *Ibid.*
[6] *Ibid.*
[7] *Ibid.*
[8] *Ibid.*

involved with the law is available from an increasing number of sources. In a notable series of studies, Edwin Sutherland called attention to extensive law-breaking among business and professional groups. Fraud and violation of trust, misrepresentation in advertising and restraint of trade were among the violations he noted.[9] Congressional and senatorial investigations of fraud and misrepresentation among companies holding government contracts during the war uncovered extensive collusion and profiteering. Only a relative handful of the violators were subjected to criminal prosecution. As Sutherland pointed out, the absence of organized public resentment against these groups tends to grant them a greater immunity than is enjoyed by the ordinary criminal.

The accumulating evidence of widespread but officially unrecognized crime by persons and groups in the general population suggests the following conclusions:

1. Estimates of crime based solely on the data of arrested or convicted criminals are biased and incomplete.

2. The data derived from these sources are less directly related to actual lawbreaking than they are to patterns of differential law enforcement.

3. Large numbers and groups of persons who commit criminal violations are protected from detection and prosecution by factors tending to prevent the official definition of their behavior as criminal.

Crime as a Matter of Definition

This question of definition—and of *who does the defining*—is crucial. The restaurant owner who catches one of his cooks going home with a few sirloins may reprimand him, fire him, or report him to the police as a thief. There is no doubt about the objective facts—neither the cook nor his employer has any difficulty in defining what took place. However, unless the owner shares this definition with the police by pressing a charge, the event never becomes criminologically significant; it remains merely a personal matter between a worker and his employer. This tolerance by the victim is often paralleled—and sometimes exceeded—by the police. Should the owner become angry enough to call a policeman, the chances are that he will have "cooled down" enough

---

[9] Edwin H. Sutherland, *White Collar Crime* (New York: The Dryden Press, 1949). See also his "White Collar Criminality," *American Sociological Review*, 5:1–12, February 1940, and "Is 'White Collar Crime' Crime?" *American Sociological Review*, 10:132–139, April 1945.

before the officer arrives to take a less severe view of the incident. Whether he has or not, by the time the policeman has pointed out the trouble the owner will have to go through in order to obtain justice—coming to the station house to press the charge, appearing before the magistrate to testify—the owner is likely to think twice about the matter. Finally, should this appeal to self-interest fail, there is always the possibility of an appeal to the victim's humane feelings. After the kindly officer has finished explaining the consequences of the arrest for the thief—getting fingerprinted, having a police record to explain for the rest of his life—the employer may begin to have doubts about who is really more guilty, he or the cook.

The incident just described is one of the commonplaces of the daily routine of law enforcement. It illustrates something of the informal, almost casual way in which large numbers of offenders-in-fact are protected by the ordinary citizen's general reluctance to get involved in legal routines—and by the parallel reluctance of the policeman to become indignant when the victim is not. There is evidence to suggest the existence of other factors that operate more systematically to produce the same result.

One of the more clearly authenticated of these is the socioeconomic status of the offender. Studies have shown that members of the middle and upper classes are considerably more immune to official police and court action than are members of the lower classes. In their studies of the social life of a modern New England town, W. Lloyd Warner and Paul S. Lunt found that the two lowest classes of the population accounted for approximately 90 per cent of all arrests, the two middle classes for approximately 10 per cent, and the two upper classes for less than 1 per cent.[10]

These and similar statistics suggest either that the poor commit proportionately more crimes than the rich or that the rich are in a better position to intimidate, corrupt, or otherwise manipulate law-enforcement agents. There will be little argument with the suggestion that a rich man is in many ways better able to defend himself from the difficulties of life, including the legal ones. Nor is there likely to be any dispute about the fact that money and pressure can corrupt and intimidate. Nevertheless, the unqualified assumption of official corruption in every case ignores other possibilities closer at hand. Policemen and judges are members of

[10] William L. Warner and Paul S. Lunt, *The Social Life of a Modern Community* (New Haven, Conn.: Yale University Press, 1941), pp. 373–377.

the same society that rewards the higher classes with prestige. As such, they are not immune to the unconscious operation of the general social bias.

Consider a fairly typical concrete illustration: Some young men from college go out on the town; they drink a little, "raise a little hell," and end up by smashing the plate glass window of a store. The local police come along, take the young men in tow, and turn them over to the university police. They are suspended for two weeks, instructed to pay the cost of replacing the window, and given a sharp lecture on the behavior appropriate to scholars and gentlemen. Two other boys, not from the college, do the same thing. They are haled into court on charges of drunken and disorderly conduct, convicted, and given a suspended sentence—if they are lucky.

Why the different treatment? Nobody has tried to bribe the police. Nobody has brought any explicit pressure to bear on the people involved in the judicial process. No one, in fact, has said a word. The point is that exactly the same behavior is defined in quite different ways, depending on the social background of the offender. In one case, the illegal activity is merely "high spirits," "wild oats"—regrettable but not wicked. In the other case, the illegal activity is "wanton vandalism."

This official tolerance of criminal behavior has its limits, but it is clearly present and operative. There are certain occupations that are more or less "sacred"—these include clergymen and doctors, among others. In doubtful situations, the balance usually tips in their favor— again, without any overt pressure necessarily being exerted. As has already been indicated, women, in general, are treated more leniently than men. The very young offender is treated more leniently than the older offender; this differential treatment is, in fact, built into the law. Whites are more leniently treated than Negroes, although it has been claimed that in the South and in large northern urban centers, many known crimes among Negroes are ignored so long as they do not touch the white world. (This "leniency" is, perhaps, more related to uncon- cern with the Negro victim than it is to any special consideration toward the Negro offender.)

Offenders in certain relationships to their victims derive consider- able protection from traditional social attitudes toward their role. The policeman who will arrest a person for assaulting a stranger will often take the role of peacemaker in a case of wife-beating: there is a long- standing aversion to washing the family linen in the criminal court.

Conventional Crime

Offenses by ordinary citizens, although well within the purview of criminology, still remain outside its main focus. This situation is little more than a reflection of the limited focus of law enforcement, which, in turn, inevitably reflects the attitudes of the general public. Socrates once said, "All men are liars." If he was correct, it would follow that, in a community of liars, it takes more than common everyday lying to make men angry. The professional criminal insists that all men commit crimes, and he is probably at least technically correct. Nevertheless, to the public at large, *being a criminal means something more than simply breaking the law.* This "something more" seems less difficult to recognize or illustrate than it is to describe or explain. It is certainly something more than being destructive, malicious, untrustworthy, or harmful to others. In attempting to describe it, commentators have spoken of the process of *stigmatization* and have used analogies suggesting a kind of social exiling, a mutual withdrawal of fellow-feeling between the criminal and the ordinary citizen. However this process works, its effects seem highly consistent and recognizable. When an ordinary citizen learns that another ordinary citizen has been discovered in some misbehavior that may lead to criminal prosecution, his reaction is likely to include elements of shock, sympathy, and dismay; it seems almost as if he were reacting to a misfortune that might have befallen himself. Should the ordinary citizen hear of the same misbehavior committed by a person already identified as a criminal, his reaction is likely to be the reverse. He is usually unsympathetic and not shocked at all; it is as if he expected no better in the first place. Interestingly, the character of the offender's previous criminality appears to have little effect on the reaction. His record may have been limited to a few petty thefts, or it may have included a variety of serious felonies. In either case, the public reaction is generally the same. *Apparently, once the stigma of criminality has for any reason been attached to an individual, virtually any form of misbehavior might be expected of him.* In recognition of this source of bias, English criminal procedure requires that any knowledge of the defendant's previous criminal record be concealed from both judge and jury until *after* the verdict.

At the beginning of this chapter, it was suggested that official estimates of offenses tend more to reflect the actual extent of law enforcement than to reveal the true extent of law breaking. But we have now reached a point at which this discrepancy loses much of its apparent significance. Faced with evidence that large numbers of persons commit actual violations for which they are never prosecuted, we are led to the further conclusion that the *actual, objective extent of law breaking may, in itself, be an unreliable index of criminality.* This conclusion is suggested by the recognition that criminality itself (as contrasted with law-breaking) is a matter of social stigmatization and official action in the first place. Now, since the official statistics more or less accurately reflect the true operation of this socio-legal process of enforcement in all its vagaries, we may return to our original point of departure: the two and a half million crimes reported each year. These offenses comprise the totality of crimes officially known and acted upon; collectively, they may be referred to as *conventional crimes.*[11] For better or worse, they form the raw data of criminology.

The Anatomy of Conventional Crime in the United States

The crimes reported in the *Uniform Crime Reports* cover twenty-seven separate classes of law violation. In view of the multiform definitions of crimes used by the various states and localities, this classification represents an impressive achievement in synthesis; without it, an over-all estimate of crime rates would be impossible. Because of their importance in providing standardized definitions of the different types of crime, the descriptions used in the *Uniform Crime Reports* are reproduced verbatim below.

Part I Offenses

1. *Criminal homicide.*—(*a*) Murder and nonnegligent manslaughter includes all willful felonious homicides as distinguished from deaths caused by negligence. Does not include attempts to kill, assaults to kill, suicides, accidental deaths or justifiable homicides. Justifiable homicides excluded from this classification are limited to the following types of cases: (1) The killing of a felon by a peace officer in line of duty; (2) the killing of a holdup man by a private citizen. (*b*) Manslaughter by negligence includes any death which the police investigation estab-

---

[11] Since criminality is itself a matter of convention, the term *conventional crime* seems well chosen. Modern writers have tended to become critical of the traditional emphasis on conventional crimes in criminology. Though this criticism is based on the increasing awareness of nonprosecuted violations—"unconventional crimes"—the fact remains that an act of actual lawbreaking does not become criminal in any realistic social or legal sense until and unless it is conventionally defined and officially acted upon.

lishes was primarily attributable to gross negligence on the part of some individual other than the victim.

2. *Rape.*—Includes forcible rape, statutory rape (no force used—victim under age of consent), assault to rape, and attempted rape.

3. *Robbery.*—Includes stealing or taking anything of value from the person by force or violence or by putting in fear, such as strong-arm robbery, stickups, robbery armed. Includes assault to rob and attempt to rob.

4. *Aggravated assault.*—Includes assault with intent to kill; assault by shooting, cutting, stabbing, maiming, poisoning, scalding, or by the use of acids. Does not include simple assault, assault and battery, fighting, etc.

5. *Burglary—breaking or entering.*—Includes burglary, housebreaking, safecracking, or any unlawful entry to commit a felony or a theft, even though no force was used to gain entrance. Includes attempts. Burglary followed by larceny is included in this classification and not counted again as larceny.

6. *Larceny—theft* (except auto theft).—(*a*) Fifty dollars and over in value; (*b*) under $50 in value—includes in one of the above subclassifications, depending upon the value of the property stolen, thefts of bicycles, automobile accessories, shoplifting, pocket picking, or any stealing of property or article of value which is not taken by force and violence or by fraud. Does not include embezzlement, "con" games, forgery, worthless checks, etc.

7. *Auto theft.*—Includes all cases where a motor vehicle is stolen or driven away and abandoned, including the so-called joy-riding thefts. Does not include taking for temporary use when actually returned by the taker, or unauthorized use by those having lawful access to the vehicle.

Part II Offenses

8. *Other assaults.*—Includes all assaults and attempted assaults which are not of an aggravated nature and which do not belong in class 4.

9. *Forgery and counterfeiting.*—Includes offenses dealing with the making, altering, uttering, or possessing, with intent to defraud, anything false which is made to appear true. Includes attempts.

10. *Embezzlement and fraud.*—Includes all offenses of fraudulent conversion, embezzlement, and obtaining money or property by false pretenses.

11. *Stolen property; buying, receiving, possessing.*—Includes buying, receiving, and possessing stolen property as well as attempts to commit any of those offenses.

12. *Weapons; carrying, possessing, etc.*—Includes all violations of regulations or statutes controlling the carrying, using, possessing, fur-

nishing, and manufacturing of deadly weapons or silencers and all attempts to violate such statutes or regulations.

13. *Prostitution and commercialized vice.*—Includes sex offenses of a commercialized nature, or attempts to commit the same, such as prostitution, keeping bawdy house, procuring, transporting, or detaining women for immoral purposes.

14. *Sex offenses* (except rape and prostitution and commercialized vice).—Includes offenses against chastity, common decency, morals, and the like. Includes attempts.

15. *Offenses against the family and children.*—Includes offenses of nonsupport, neglect, desertion, or abuse of family and children.

16. *Narcotic drug laws.*—Includes offenses relating to narcotic drugs, such as unlawful possession, sale, or use. Excludes Federal offenses.

17. *Liquor laws.*—With the exception of "drunkenness" (class 18) and "driving while intoxicated" (class 22), liquor law violations, State or local, are placed in this class. Excludes Federal violations.

18. *Drunkenness.*—Includes all offenses of drunkenness or intoxication.

19. *Disorderly conduct.*—Includes all charges of committing a breach of the peace.

20. *Vagrancy.*—Includes such offenses as vagabondage, begging, loitering, etc.

21. *Gambling.*—Includes offenses of promoting, permitting, or engaging in gambling.

22. *Driving while intoxicated.*—Includes driving or operating any motor vehicle while drunk or under the influence of liquor or narcotics.

23. *Violation of road and driving laws.*—Includes violations of regulations with respect to the proper handling of a motor vehicle to prevent accidents.

24. *Parking violations.*—Includes violations of parking ordinances.

25. *Other violations of traffic and motor vehicle laws.*—Includes violations of State laws and municipal ordinances with regard to traffic and motor vehicles not otherwise provided for in classes 22–24.

26. *All other offenses.*—Includes all violations of State or local laws for which no provision has been made above in classes 1–25.

27. *Suspicion.*—This classification includes all persons arrested as suspicious characters, but not in connection with any specific offense, who are released without formal charges being placed against them.[12]

It should be noted that the classifications used in the *Uniform Crime Reports* are divided into two parts. *Part I Offenses* comprise those crimes which are most generally and completely reported to the police.

[12] *Uniform Crime Reports*, 24, No. 2 (1953), pp. 117–118.

When the police authorities of the various cities and localities receive a complaint or otherwise learn of the occurrence of a Part I offense, they are expected to file a report of it whether an arrest has been made or not. It is then possible to use these reports as a basis for computing crime rates. With respect to the offenses listed in Part II, however, the *only* available information is derived from police arrests. Since there is no reliable way of determining how many separate offenses are represented by these arrests, it is not possible to calculate reliable crime rates for the violations included in Part II. For this reason, statistics of crime rates in the *Uniform Crime Reports* are confined to the offenses listed in Part I. Table II, based on the combined nation-wide urban and rural rates for Part I offenses, indicates the percentage contributed by each category in 1953.[13]

TABLE II

PERCENTAGE DISTRIBUTION OF MAJOR CRIMES (PART I OFFENSES) IN 1953

Offense	Per cent
Criminal homicide	0.5
Rape	0.8
Robbery	2.9
Aggravated assault	4.3
Burglary—breaking or entering	22.9
Larceny—theft (except auto theft)	58.1
Auto theft	10.5
TOTAL	100.0

Estimates of the Cost of Conventional Crime

Reliable estimates of the over-all cost of crime are virtually impossible to make; those who have most thoroughly investigated the problem have concluded that even approximate figures would be inaccurate. In 1949 the Special Crime Study Commissions of California published a pamphlet[14] that included a survey of previous estimates; these varied from 900 million to 18 billion dollars annually. (One of the estimates, made in 1924 and titled "The Economic Waste of Sin," was worked out to the last dollar and came to $3,329,813,788!)

[13] The percentages cited in Table II were derived by dividing the total number of Part I offenses by the number reported in each offense category (*Uniform Crime Reports*, 24, No. 2, 1953, pp. 117–118).
[14] Special Crime Study Commissions of California, *Sources for the Study of the Administration of Justice* (Sacramento, Calif.: State Board of Corrections, 1949).

The 1931 Wickersham Commission[15] listed the items that would require inclusion in any aggregate estimate of crime costs; a study of these items makes clear the insoluble problems involved. Aside from the direct losses resulting from the crimes themselves, the estimate would include: (1) The cost of the administration of justice and law enforcement, including the expenditures required for maintaining all police and court agencies. (2) The expenditures required for all correctional institutions and agencies, including probation and parole departments. (3) The expenditures made by private citizens for protection and insurance against theft. (4) The losses resulting from commercialized crime and racketeering. (5) The indirect losses resulting from the removal of law-enforcement officers and prisoners from the labor force.

REPORTED PROPERTY LOSSES. The *Uniform Crime Reports* annually publishes figures for reported losses and recoveries in the various property crimes recorded during the year. These figures are limited to direct losses and do not, of course, include the indirect costs cited above. Table III lists the property losses reported by 429 cities in 1956.

TABLE III

VALUE OF PROPERTY STOLEN, BY TYPE OF CRIME, 1956

(429 cities over 25,000. Total 1950 population 57,218,447. Values rounded off.)

Classification	Number of offenses	Value of property stolen	Average value per offense
TOTAL	1,217,247	$239,588,177	$197
Robbery	42,522	9,277,770	218
Burglary	283,594	48,574,319	171
Larceny-theft	740,489	50,177,483	68
Auto theft	150,642	131,558,605	873

Source: *Uniform Crime Reports*, 27, No. 2 (1956), p. 106.

RECOVERIES OF STOLEN GOODS. Approximately 56.9 cents out of each dollar-value reported stolen was recovered by the police in 1956. This *mean* figure is misleadingly high as a measure of the average recovery, however, since it is inflated by the customarily high percentage of recoveries of stolen automobiles. The recovery figures for currency, furs, jewelry, and clothing are considerably lower (see Table IV).

[15] National Commission on Law Observance and Enforcement, *Report No. 12: The Cost of Crimes* (Washington, D. C.: 1931). For a brief summary of this 657-page document, see "Real and Intangible Costs; Wickersham Report," *Commonweal*, 13:562–563, March 25, 1931.

TABLE IV

VALUE OF PROPERTY STOLEN AND VALUE OF PROPERTY RECOVERED,
BY TYPE OF PROPERTY, 1956

(419 cities over 25,000. Total 1950 population 54,484,808. Values rounded off.)

Type of property	Value of property		Per cent recovered
	Stolen	Recovered	
Total	$229,590,279	$130,601,794	56.9
Currency, notes, etc.	25,484,319	2,741,144	10.8
Jewelry and precious metals	18,925,693	1,616,563	8.5
Furs	7,778,764	280,946	3.6
Clothing	10,530,255	1,279,019	12.1
Locally stolen automobiles	124,111,093	114,900,047	92.6
Miscellaneous	42,760,155	9,784,075	22.9

Source: *Uniform Crime Reports*, 27, No. 2 (1956), p. 106.

The Geography of Crime in the United States

REGIONAL CRIME RATES. Rates of reported crime vary widely from one region to another. Table V shows the crime rates of nine major geographical divisions in the United States in 1955. For each of the six classes of major crime, the New England region ranks lowest. Its murder and negligent manslaughter rate is one fourth of the national rate for these crimes. Its rates for the crimes of aggravated assault and robbery are approximately one fifth and one third of the national average. The East South Central region, comprising the states of Alabama, Kentucky, Mississippi, and Tennessee, has the highest murder rates—more than twice the national average and over 10 times the New England rate. This region also ranks second in aggravated assault (after the South Atlantic region). The South Atlantic region ranks very high in this offense—its rate is more than twice the national average—and it takes second place for murder. The Pacific region shows wide variation, ranking first in robbery, burglary, larceny and auto theft but near the middle in murder. Larceny is highest in the Pacific region, next highest in the Mountain region, lowest in New England and the Middle Atlantic region—which, after New England, ranks lowest in the combined crime rate.

There are occasional yearly variations in the rank order of the different regions for the various crimes. Between January and June of 1954 the East North Central region ranked fourth lowest for murder and negligent manslaughter; one year later it ranked fourth highest. In

TABLE V

URBAN CRIME RATES, 1955, BY GEOGRAPHIC DIVISIONS AND STATES

(Offenses known per 100,000 inhabitants. Population based on
1950 decennial census.)

Division and state	Murder, nonnegligent manslaughter	Robbery	Aggravated assault	Burglary—breaking or entering	Larceny—theft	Auto theft
TOTAL	4.7	60.6	84.3	423.0	1,047.7	194.9
NEW ENGLAND	1.2	18.7	18.0	280.5	660.7	139.3
Connecticut	1.2	18.0	32.4	292.4	603.2	132.0
Maine	1.8	9.3	8.4	243.8	652.7	98.6
Massachusetts	1.2	21.4	14.4	276.7	654.1	158.5
New Hampshire	.7	6.6	7.0	146.9	538.3	52.1
Rhode Island	1.4	15.6	23.1	376.4	900.3	111.7
Vermont		7.2	.9	146.6	472.2	59.4
MIDDLE ATLANTIC	3.0	55.9	70.2	372.7	705.3	145.0
New Jersey	2.1	32.8	49.2	366.9	671.3	149.4
New York	3.1	65.3	80.2	401.8	789.2	144.8
Pennsylvania	3.2	51.1	63.1	318.7	560.3	142.7
EAST NORTH CENTRAL	4.4	77.1	69.9	338.6	987.6	165.1
Illinois	5.7	124.1	77.8	335.3	619.4	123.3
Indiana	4.4	37.1	36.8	431.0	1,077.7	221.9
Michigan	4.6	90.9	134.8	427.8	1,479.7	270.6
Ohio	3.7	51.2	41.6	297.6	1,015.4	133.3
Wisconsin	1.2	8.1	16.9	167.0	952.7	99.5
WEST NORTH CENTRAL	3.4	49.2	53.6	357.4	1,060.2	179.0
Iowa	1.1	12.4	9.7	227.9	912.3	81.6
Kansas	2.8	35.3	59.5	407.9	1,225.8	131.7
Minnesota	1.1	34.5	9.9	348.9	954.9	152.4
Missouri	7.2	100.7	123.3	467.4	1,158.7	298.1
Nebraska	2.0	22.9	30.0	258.5	1,038.2	147.8
North Dakota	1.8	9.1	4.2	228.1	1,209.2	102.5
South Dakota	2.2	6.0	4.4	170.2	904.3	61.9
SOUTH ATLANTIC*	9.4	59.7	206.6	528.5	1,197.2	246.1
Delaware	3.9	48.8	28.3	547.4	1,399.1	198.2
Florida	12.3	77.0	103.6	881.7	1,659.1	234.3
Georgia	13.6	36.6	193.3	462.4	989.2	208.3
Maryland	7.6	80.6	191.8	459.4	1,088.1	461.5
North Carolina	9.9	25.8	306.2	346.8	919.1	151.7
South Carolina	10.0	31.5	109.8	488.7	1,157.8	170.3
Virginia	8.4	66.0	239.3	548.7	1,506.0	272.8
West Virginia	2.6	28.1	43.2	274.7	519.8	100.9
EAST SOUTH CENTRAL	12.1	51.2	120.3	487.9	805.1	239.5
Alabama	17.1	41.6	155.4	511.0	810.2	161.2
Kentucky	9.4	96.1	143.5	600.4	1,157.8	441.5
Mississippi	9.4	14.2	53.0	324.5	618.8	103.3
Tennessee	10.8	41.3	100.9	452.2	618.7	212.6
WEST SOUTH CENTRAL	8.9	44.0	103.4	535.5	1,314.4	240.0
Arkansas	7.4	39.9	90.7	338.7	715.8	93.5
Louisiana	8.6	66.4	98.3	369.1	919.2	332.2
Oklahoma	5.2	33.0	55.8	497.8	1,295.2	194.0
Texas	9.9	41.3	117.2	606.3	1,479.3	242.6
MOUNTAIN	4.3	60.7	48.6	578.5	1,883.4	288.8
Arizona	6.7	91.5	158.3	955.2	3,304.8	538.3
Colorado	4.1	96.1	42.9	653.1	1,728.8	309.0
Idaho	3.0	6.9	11.4	324.8	1,880.8	148.0
Montana	2.8	22.7	29.0	365.6	1,708.8	170.9
Nevada	20.2	147.9	56.0	1,049.0	2,813.1	430.4
New Mexico	4.5	44.9	54.3	650.6	1,695.3	346.3
Utah	2.4	28.1	20.0	411.4	1,445.0	204.6
Wyoming	3.8	28.6	19.6	284.2	1,512.2	149.3
PACIFIC	3.5	93.7	95.4	661.1	1,903.8	324.8
California	3.7	105.7	109.8	714.2	1,959.1	358.5
Oregon	3.1	39.9	29.6	412.5	1,521.8	130.8
Washington	2.1	29.6	18.8	386.0	1,737.3	185.8

* Includes the report of the District of Columbia
Source: *Uniform Crime Reports*, 26, No. 2 (1955), p. 93.

1954 the Middle Atlantic region ranked third highest for robbery; it ranked fifth for this offense one year later.

Various explanations have been offered for these wide variations in the regional distribution of crime. In 1938 Lottier explained the higher concentration of murder and assault in the East South Central region in terms of a still vivid tradition of feuding and feeble law enforcement.[16] Other explanations have stressed differences in racial composition, differences in the extent of industrialization, and differences in the spatial concentration of the population. None of these explanations has been able to account for all of the variations found.

URBAN-RURAL VARIATIONS

Urban Crime Rates. With the occasional exception of murder, larceny, and rape, crime rates tend consistently to increase with increasing density of population. Table VI shows the 1955 rates for eight major offenses in cities of decreasing size. The differences between the most densely populated and the least densely populated communities are extremely large. In cities under 10,000, the rates for burglary are only half as great as those in the largest urban centers; the rates for murder, manslaughter, and rape, one third as large; the rates for aggravated assault, one fourth as large; and the rate for robbery, one eighth as large. The declining rate is least apparent in the case of larceny, where the discrepancy between the largest and the smallest cities is in the approximate ratio of 10 to 7. In this offense there is also a sharp reversal of the general trend: the highest rate for larceny is found in the Group II cities, while the cities of Groups III and IV have a higher rate than Group I cities.

The distribution of the different classes of offenses *within* each urban population category varies. In cities with more than 250,000 inhabitants, the crimes of burglary and larceny outnumber all other major offenses by a margin of 3 to 1: in the smallest cities the preponderance of these offenses over all others is much greater: 6 to 1. The crime of robbery is highly associated with the metropolis. In 1956 forty-one major cities accounting for approximately 35 million inhabitants reported three times the total number of robberies reported by 2,599 cities accounting for more than 56 million inhabitants. Two of these major cities, New York and Chicago, accounted for close to a third

[16] Stuart Lottier, "Distribution of Criminal Offenses in Sectional Regions," *Journal of Criminal Law and Criminology,* 29:329–334, September–October 1938.

of all the metropolitan robberies reported; between them they almost equaled the combined number of robberies reported in all other cities of less than metropolitan size accounting for five times their number of total inhabitants.[17]

TABLE VI

URBAN CRIME RATES, 1955, BY POPULATION GROUPS

(Offenses known to the police and rate per 100,000 inhabitants. Population figures based on 1950 decennial census.)

Population group	Criminal homicide		Rape	Rob-bery	Aggra-vated as-sault	Bur-glary-break-ing or enter-ing	Lar-ceny—theft	Auto theft
	Murder, nonneg-ligent man-slaugh-ter	Man slaugh-ter by negli-gence						
TOTAL GROUPS I-VI								
2,643 cities; total population, 80,350,125:								
Number of offenses known	3,780	2,702	10,634	48,732	67,736	339,846	841,864	156,631
Rate per 100,000	4.7	3.4	13.2	60.6	84.3	423.0	1,047.7	194.9
GROUP I								
40 cities over 250,000; total population, 34,465,364:								
Number of offenses known	2,147	1,472	7,066	35,865	43,066	175,876	368,392	90,215
Rate per 100,000	6.2	4.3	20.5	104.1	125.0	510.3	1,068.9	261.8
GROUP II								
64 cities, 100,000 to 250,000; total population, 9,432,863:								
Number of offenses known	552	400	1,014	4,936	8,238	47,909	114,199	21,024
Rate per 100,000	5.9	4.2	10.7	52.3	87.3	507.9	1,210.7	222.9
GROUP III								
128 cities, 50,000 to 100,000; total population, 9,052,062:								
Number of offenses known	349	279	720	2,797	6,369	34,177	101,483	15,026
Rate per 100,000	3.9	3.1	8.0	30.9	70.4	377.6	1,121.1	166.0
GROUP IV								
255 cities, 25,000 to 50,000; total population, 8,977,456:								
Number of offenses known	292	304	629	2,147	4,135	31,039	100,616	12,406
Rate per 100,000	3.3	3.4	7.0	23.9	46.1	345.7	1,120.8	138.2
GROUP V								
680 cities, 10,000 to 25,000; total population, 10,470,202:								
Number of offenses known	253	144	676	1,876	3,721	31,402	101,068	11,406
Rate per 100,000	2.4	1.4	6.5	17.9	35.5	299.9	965.3	108.9
GROUP VI								
1,476 cities under 10,000; total population, 7,952,178:								
Number of offenses known	187	103	529	1,111	2,207	19,443	56,106	6,554
Rate per 100,000	2.4	1.3	6.7	14.0	27.8	244.5	705.5	82.4

Source: *Uniform Crime Reports*, 26, No. 2 (1955), pp. 91–92.

[17] *Uniform Crime Reports*, 27, No. 2 (1956), p. 88.

Rural Crime Rates. For reporting purposes, the *Uniform Crime Reports* classify areas other than incorporated places having at least 2,500 inhabitants as "rural." Rural crime rates for 1955 appear in Table VII. Partly because of their incompleteness and lesser degree of uniformity, reports from rural areas probably reveal a lower percentage of actual crimes than do the reports from urban centers. Even when this is taken into consideration, however, the differences between rural and urban crime trends are striking. In rural areas the most serious of the major crimes occur with greater frequency than in the smallest cities. Combined rural rates for criminal homicide and rape are higher than those in the second-largest cities and double those in the smallest urban category.

TABLE VII

RURAL CRIME RATES, 1955

(Offenses known and rate per 100,000 inhabitants, as reported by 1,577 sheriffs, 161 rural village officers, and 13 State police; total rural population 41,889,165, based on 1950 decennial census.)

Offense	Offenses known	
	Number	Rate
Murder and nonnegligent manslaughter	2,075	5.0
Manslaughter by negligence	2,324	5.5
Rape	5,528	13.2
Robbery	7,308	17.4
Aggravated assault	15,296	36.5
Burglary—breaking or entering	96,485	230.3
Larceny—theft	137,660	328.6
Auto theft	26,307	62.8

Source: *Uniform Crime Reports*, 26, No. 2 (1955), p. 96.

In evaluating these figures, it should be recalled that the cumulative rural crime rate is still lower than the cumulative urban rate, largely because of the higher rate of property offenses in the larger cities. This difference in the ratio of property to personal crimes is great. In urban areas the ratio of property to personal crimes is about 18 to 1; in rural areas it drops to approximately 11 to 1. Consequently, the relatively greater percentage of personal crimes in rural areas must, to a considerable extent, be accounted for by the disproportionate swelling of the urban figures for nonpersonal crimes. Thus, *it is not so much that city criminals kill and maim less but that they steal and burglarize more.* This fact somewhat reduces the apparently glaring contrast between the seriousness of rural and urban crime—but it does not eradicate it. The cumulative rural rates for homicide and rape are still higher than the cumulative urban rates for these offenses, and when the two largest urban classes are excluded, they are strikingly higher.

Interpreting the Rural-Urban Crime Distribution. With the exception of larceny and certain types of rural crime, the apparently consistent relationships between population density and crime seem to invite a ready explanation: the higher the population concentration, the higher the crime rate. When the total number of urban centers is grouped in descending order of size, the rate of almost every category of crime is seen to decrease. (See Table VI.) There are three difficulties with this general explanation:

1. *Urban centers of similar size but in different regions of the country show great variation in their crime rates.* Thus, for example, the homicide rate for Group I cities in the Middle Atlantic region is less than a third of the homicide rate for cities of equal size in the West South Central region (see Table VIII). If this were the only source of discrepancy, it would be possible to retain the population density-crime hypothesis by adding the qualification, "within the same region of the country."

2. At this point the second difficulty becomes apparent. Even within the *same* geographical region, *the rates for the same and for different crimes do not always decline according to declining size of population groups.* In the South Atlantic region, for example, the smallest cities have a larger criminal homicide rate than the largest. Group III cities in New England have higher larceny-theft rates than do the larger cities of Group II, and close examination of Table VIII will reveal several similar reversals of the trend.

3. There is, finally, a third difficulty: *Among the cities of the same size and within the same region, there are often variations in crime rates too large to account for except in terms of factors specific to the particular city.*

This last difficulty may bring us close to the core of the problem. In the preceding pages the discussion of crime rates focused on progressively smaller units of analysis. We examine the distribution of crime at different distances and with different lenses. But the patterns and regularities seen at a telescopic distance tend to dissolve when one looks closer; likewise, the patterns seen at a binocular distance may not be appropriate to the picture viewed by the naked eye. Imagine, for example, a distant observer viewing a huge herd of African antelopes moving

TABLE VIII

URBAN CRIME RATES, 1956, BY GEOGRAPHIC DIVISIONS AND POPULATION GROUPS

(Offenses known per 100,000 inhabitants. Population based on 1950 decennial census.)

Division and group	Murder, nonnegligent manslaughter	Robbery	Aggravated assault	Burglary—breaking or entering	Larceny—theft	Auto theft
TOTAL	5.0	60.0	87.4	449.3	1,228.4	233.5
NEW ENGLAND	1.6	18.3	22.3	318.3	797.5	169.5
Group I	3.6	58.6	55.4	373.5	1,003.9	466.4
Group II	1.8	19.7	39.3	418.3	874.6	195.8
Group III	1.5	14.1	11.4	303.1	887.7	145.0
Group IV	1.1	7.3	10.5	246.3	715.8	97.4
Group V	.6	9.6	5.0	258.8	599.0	71.2
Group VI	1.3	5.8	7.0	245.9	583.8	53.3
MIDDLE ATLANTIC	3.0	50.1	75.6	360.4	786.0	167.4
Group I	4.3	74.3	113.7	446.7	858.5	206.6
Group II	1.7	31.9	43.5	316.9	749.4	178.3
Group III	1.3	19.3	34.1	294.9	717.2	138.1
Group IV	1.7	14.6	20.1	241.4	748.8	112.4
Group V	.9	10.7	12.5	197.1	668.1	85.2
Group VI	1.1	11.0	12.7	185.2	569.0	71.7
EAST NORTH CENTRAL	4.8	77.5	74.0	361.8	1,154.7	189.1
Group I	7.2	129.6	116.5	384.7	1,036.0	226.8
Group II	5.1	55.2	88.0	479.5	1,511.9	224.4
Group III	3.7	42.0	54.3	350.0	1,340.3	194.5
Group IV	2.3	26.7	22.0	336.4	1,332.3	158.9
Group V	1.7	24.2	19.6	339.0	1,345.0	132.9
Group VI	1.4	11.8	11.4	231.2	788.6	79.6
WEST NORTH CENTRAL	3.8	51.3	48.3	380.5	1,312.9	212.6
Group I	6.5	107.4	95.4	547.7	1,511.3	385.6
Group II	4.7	52.2	67.6	542.3	1,859.2	209.2
Group III	3.0	16.8	25.0	303.0	1,439.6	118.5
Group IV	.9	12.0	10.8	205.7	1,262.1	98.5
Group V	1.8	10.6	10.0	243.7	1,114.9	90.2
Group VI	1.2	9.8	6.4	201.5	684.5	71.7
SOUTH ATLANTIC*	10.0	56.0	201.3	539.6	1,370.8	285.6
Group I	9.9	77.1	251.9	458.1	1,196.0	417.1
Group II	12.0	99.1	202.6	839.4	1,938.2	404.2
Group III	9.5	38.5	196.7	486.1	1,342.8	206.0
Group IV	8.8	38.4	170.9	594.3	1,565.1	210.3
Group V	8.6	14.9	170.2	425.5	1,150.8	147.0
Group VI	10.4	23.3	142.4	385.5	873.5	114.1
EAST SOUTH CENTRAL	12.0	47.9	115.1	475.0	948.6	275.1
Group I	11.3	74.8	124.1	542.0	1,144.6	466.4
Group II	20.3	56.8	88.3	656.2	1,021.6	273.7
Group III	9.1	31.8	144.9	490.9	1,077.8	190.9
Group IV	9.5	23.2	153.1	343.4	841.9	140.7
Group V	9.8	22.6	102.6	368.3	771.4	123.8
Group VI	6.8	18.4	74.3	196.7	420.8	80.8
WEST SOUTH CENTRAL	9.4	46.6	101.3	608.7	1,501.6	297.9
Group I	14.8	78.0	97.7	832.1	1,599.1	497.8
Group II	6.1	40.2	114.6	647.9	1,819.7	264.5
Group III	6.6	39.0	178.5	611.9	1,933.0	222.9
Group IV	9.8	26.7	92.8	432.7	1,529.1	175.3
Group V	4.5	11.4	76.7	296.6	962.9	85.1
Group VI	5.1	14.1	47.3	266.2	786.3	83.7
MOUNTAIN	3.8	65.9	52.3	624.2	2,320.2	364.5
Group I	4.8	150.3	74.1	868.7	2,085.0	546.4
Group II	9.4	109.5	202.2	1,105.6	4,065.8	809.8
Group III	3.2	43.2	27.6	546.4	2,538.0	532.1
Group IV	4.0	63.4	59.4	661.3	2,971.2	370.7
Group V	2.6	29.1	36.3	524.3	2,313.2	217.9
Group VI	2.7	28.0	19.8	398.5	1,523.7	156.3
PACIFIC	4.0	99.9	109.2	757.2	2,242.1	413.6
Group I	4.8	143.8	169.6	871.5	2,016.8	512.6
Group II	4.2	73.5	33.0	555.2	2,176.2	293.3
Group III	2.7	63.6	50.0	672.6	2,381.4	381.4
Group IV	2.2	57.4	51.1	722.5	2,839.6	334.7
Group V	3.3	48.1	51.4	655.7	2,555.3	279.3
Group VI	2.9	27.5	35.9	531.8	2,329.4	254.3

* Includes the report of the District of Columbia.
Source: *Uniform Crime Reports*, 27, No. 2 (1956), p. 90.

through an arid region. Through his lens, the observer can see the entire herd, can estimate the barren character of the terrain, and can dimly discern a green area surrounding a remote water hole. At his present distance the observer is in an excellent position to explain the movement and the direction of the herd. Suddenly he sees a large segment of the herd veer off and run in an *opposite* direction—away from the water hole. Then this segment too breaks up, with isolated groups running in different directions. This he cannot explain: He is not close enough to have seen a section of the herd being attacked by a pair of lions. On the other hand, another observer, closer at hand, may be unable to explain the general movement of the herd but can quickly grasp the reason for the movements of the specific portion within his limited view. Something of an analogous situation is involved in the question of an appropriate geographical focus.

General Characteristics of Conventional Offenders

The "typical" criminal does not exist—except, perhaps, as a very vague abstraction built up out of a loose cluster of statistical frequencies. Nevertheless, these statistical frequencies are useful. They narrow the field considerably and tell us, in many cases, where *not* to look, what *not* to expect.

1. *Most Known Criminals Are Males.* Approximately 90 per cent of all persons arrested are males. The only arrest category in which women outnumber men is prostitution and commercialized vice; even here the ratio is less than 3 to 1. In most other categories of conventional crime, the 9 to 1 ratio holds or increases. The outstanding exception is murder and non-negligent manslaughter, for which females in 1956 contributed 25 per cent of the arrests. In the categories of aggravated assault and forgery and counterfeiting, the female contribution was somewhat smaller—approximately 18 per cent. However, only 4 out of every hundred arrested robbers and only 2 out of every hundred arrested burglars were females.[18]

2. *Most Criminals Are Young.* United States statistics generally indicate the age range of 20 to 24 as the period of "maximum criminality" but this figure is artificially raised because of our specialized

[18] *Uniform Crime Reports,* 27, No. 2 (1956), p. 112.

protective procedures for juveniles. When the offenses committed by juveniles are included, the peak period is found between early and middle adolescence. More than half of all persons arrested for property crimes are under twenty-one. In 1956, youths under eighteen accounted for over 66 per cent of all arrests for car theft and for 50 per cent of all arrests for burglary.[19]

Peak age periods for different offense categories vary widely. The offenses of the very young tend more toward property than toward personal crimes; persons under twenty-one usually account for less than 15 per cent of the arrests for crimes against the person. The peak periods for criminal homicide and assault occur after the age of twenty-five. Those for fraud and embezzlement are reached later in life, as are those for gambling and drunkenness. In general, however, the largest percentage of all crimes is committed during the second and third decades of life.

3. *Most Criminals Are Native-Born and Members of the White Race.* More than 70 per cent of all persons arrested for crimes in this country are members of the white race. However, Negroes, who contribute almost 30 per cent of the total arrests, comprise only one tenth of the total population.

The overwhelming majority of persons convicted of crimes is native-born. This number may be expected to increase as the number of foreign-born diminishes.

4. *Most Criminals Are Recidivists.* One of the first things the police do after apprehending a suspect is to investigate his legal biography. Between 50 and 60 per cent of all persons in prisons and reformatories have been imprisoned before. A larger percentage has previously been arrested. Offenders who relapse are known technically as *recidivists*.

The analysis of recidivism rates is an extremely important function of the criminologist. They provide the most objective over-all basis for evaluating the effectiveness of law-enforcement programs. They focus attention on the social areas and groups most in need of preventive work; in a sense, they are to the criminologist what the Geiger counter is to the geologist. Moreover, they furnish an important basis for differentiating the characteristics of different offenses. What crimes are more likely to be repeated? Which crimes usually go together, and which are rarely associated? Which crimes tend to be associated with criminal careers?

The data on recidivism are very fragmentary, but enough has been learned to provide law-enforcement authorities with several useful rules-

[19] *Ibid.,* p. 110.

of-thumb. Many policemen and institutional officials—and, above all, many intelligent prisoners—can predict with astonishing accuracy who will and who will not be "back." The systematic exploitation of these shrewd insights for predictive purposes is one of the major tasks of criminology.

5. *Most Criminals Are Members of the Lower Socioeconomic Classes.* The differentiation of the population into social and economic classes is necessarily arbitrary; social stratification is largely a matter of definition. Nevertheless, by virtually any definition, the large majority of known offenders derives from the more unspecialized occupational groups and from that portion of the population whose living standards, economically measured, are low. To a considerable—but unknown and probably very variable—extent, however, the criminality of this population segment is exaggerated by its greater vulnerability to involvement with the law. Walter Reckless has analyzed the differential liability of people to involvement with the law by means of actuarial devices called "categorical risks." His findings have led him to believe that the upper social classes, though the least represented in crime statistics, are relatively high in actual lawbreaking. He represents the probable class picture of actual lawbreaking in America as having "a high mountain peak for . . . the lower class, a low valley for . . . the middle class, and a high peak for . . . the upper class. . . ."[20]

The Relation between Facts and the Understanding of Facts

The preceding pages have been devoted to a broad and sketchy outline of some of the "hard facts" of crime and criminals in contemporary United States society. The question arises: What do these facts *mean?* Perhaps it is first necessary to clarify what we mean when we raise the question. How do the data on crime and criminals aid us in understanding criminal behavior, and the relation of this behavior to other phenomena? By "understanding" something, we usually mean comprehending the relation of this happening to other known events and conditions. Thus, *understanding* is more than a description of what can be

[20] Walter C. Reckless, *The Crime Problem* (New York: Appleton-Century-Crofts, 1950), p. 60.

seen and measured—it involves ideas about processes. To illustrate this distinction, we might contrast the sciences of anatomy and physiology. The structure of the human body was known for centuries before a correct account of physical functioning was available. The prescientific physiologists and physicians would illustrate the most fanciful theories of human physiology with the most accurate drawings of human anatomy. The gross anatomical and topographical details of crime are similarly available. They too have provided the "facts" used to support theories of proved invalidity.

There are many examples of the suggestiveness of raw facts, and of their susceptibility to explanatory double-talk. Some years ago *heredity* was considered the explanation of many forms of behavior—among these, drunkenness. Numerous investigators examined the family situations and hereditary backgrounds of drunkards. In a very large number of instances, father, mother, and children were found to be alcoholic. To those already persuaded by the genetic theory, this was sufficient proof of its validity. Some time later, when the theory of genetics had been more generally clarified, it was realized that drunkenness could not possibly be transmitted in the germ-plasm. At this point, the identical facts (the familial association with drunkenness) were used in support of the completely opposite explanation—namely, that patterns of drunkenness are *socially* transmitted. Environment rather than heredity was responsible.

The significant point of this illustration is that no new facts about the distribution of drunkenness, no new data about the "anatomy" or "topography" of drunkenness, had anything to do with this new explanation. The descriptive data about drunkenness were unchanged—they were the same facts that had been used to support the hereditary hypothesis. The element that had produced the change was a different *theory* of the relationship of the facts. The more valid theory made the same data sing a different tune.

This brings us squarely up against the problem of finding a way to make the facts talk, without saying more than they actually say, without saying what we unconsciously want them to say. This problem, in brief, is the problem of *method*, discussed in the following chapter.

Toward a Scientific Criminology

Fact, Frame of Reference, and Theory in the Social Sciences

LET US IMAGINE TWO PROFESSIONAL CRIMINOLOGISTS VISITING A maximum-security prison with the intention of making a report on institutional conditions. Both are equally intelligent and conscientious, differing only in background one of them, Criminologist X, has had some experience in penal administration; the other, Criminologist Y, has visited many institutions but has never worked in one.

They enter a prison cell block. It is shortly after five in the afternoon; the inmates have returned from their jobs and are awaiting the dinner bell. They are engaged in a wide variety of activities. Some are washing clothes; others are taking showers; still others are playing checkers and dominoes. On the upper tiers a few may be seen leaving and entering cells. In one corner of the ground floor of the large cell block a guard is talking to an inmate, who is holding what looks like a piece of paper and is gesturing animatedly.

The two criminologists approach the guard, make their presence known, and then step back to permit him to continue his conversation. Apparently the inmate, a rather excitable young man, has just received a disturbing letter from home. Discreetly listening in on the conversation, Criminologist Y notes that the guard is taking a friendly, almost fatherly interest in the inmate, patiently hearing him out and trying to "steady him down."

The inmate finally moves off and Y immediately takes up the subject with the guard. The officer, not at all averse to talking with a criminologist, presents a brief but comprehensive review of the prisoner's case. The inmate, a product of a broken home, had been in and out of institutions continually. While in these institutions, he had been in constant trouble, feeling himself mistreated and misunderstood. Even here, the guard concludes, he had been a bad disciplinary problem until his recent transfer to his present location. Since then he had settled down and was beginning to find himself.

Criminologist Y is deeply impressed, not only by the officer's sympathetic attitude and his knowledge of current penological theory but also by his modest omission of an obvious fact: the inmate apparently started to "find himself" only after meeting his new guard. But a lingering doubt remains. This, after all, is only the officer's story. What would the inmate say? And how would the record bear out his testimony?

Criminologist Y seeks out the inmate and, after some carefully casual remarks aimed at defining himself as an unbiased observer, gets down to the subject at hand. How is the inmate making out these days? How does he like his present location? And how is he getting along with the prison officials? Like the officer, the inmate is not in the least reticent—a fact that Y notes as a favorable diagnostic sign.

It requires only a few words for the inmate to substantiate the guard's picture of him. He is bitter—bitter about his parents, his sentence, the prison, its officials—bitter about everything and everyone, in fact, except his new guard. At the mention of the guard's name, his face brightens for the first time:

"Mr. Smith? You mean Jim! A great guy. Really interested in rehabilitation. There should be more like him."

But Criminologist Y still does not permit himself to be convinced. What about the possibility of some improper relationship between this officer and inmate? He questions other inmates; to a man, and in spite of different opinions on other subjects, they agree that Officer Smith— "Jim"—is a fine, friendly, and helpful person, a man who "really understands."

There is one more source to check: the Administration.

Criminologist Y completes his tour of the cell block, taking in the easy and informal atmosphere, and then hurries to the Classification

Files. Again the picture jibes. The inmate, rejected from childhood, responded to a pattern of frustration with a pattern of aggression. This pattern continued until very recently even in the present institution; the criminologist reads one disciplinary charge after another describing the inmate as hostile, crafty, and dangerous. Only after his transfer to his present cell block do the bad reports cease.

Leaving the Classification Room, Y stops at the office of the Captain of the Guards, intending to put in a good word about Officer Smith. The Captain, a rather gloomy man, hears him out in silence; then, without further preamble, he reaches for a file marked "Officers' Efficiency Reports." Criminologist Y listens with mounting surprise as the words "slack, careless, deficient in maintaining discipline, overdependent on inmates," fall from the Captain's lips.

"But what about his relations with the inmates? They seem to think well of him."

"Obviously," replies the Captain. "They can get away with anything on his shift."

Y is appalled. "But what about his work with Jones? He was one of your worst troublemakers. Yet, ever since he's been with Officer Smith, he hasn't gotten a charge."

"Of course not. Officer Smith doesn't ever give charges; that's one of the reasons his cell block is one of the worst here. Another reason is that inmate you mentioned. Ever since he's been there, we've been receiving very bad information about that place. Not from Officer Smith, I might add. That's why we're moving Smith out of there as soon as we can replace him."

Criminologist Y is dismayed as he leaves the Captain's office. The picture now falls completely into place. It was the old story. The new, forward-looking, treatment-conscious men come in, only to meet the flinty opposition of the old-style disciplinarians. The criminologist speculates on the inmate's future. His relationship with Officer Smith was the one clear spot in his otherwise distorted picture of people. Of all the officials in the prison, the guard alone had been sympathetic. Now the guard was to be removed. With a heavy heart, Y goes to meet his colleague.

And what of Criminologist X? As he entered the cell block, his impression of the scene before him was distinctly different from his colleague's. Observing the inmates in their varied activities, he made a quick calculation. Only about half of them were in view. What were the rest of them doing? Where was the cell block officer? Startled to find the guard engrossed in a lengthy conversation with an inmate, he was even more surprised to hear the subject of the discussion. Why did the inmate pick a time and place like this to discuss personal problems when he could have had much more privacy when fewer inmates were about?

Leaving his colleague to discuss rehabilitation with the officer, X ascended the tiers to find answers to these questions. Within a few steps his nose supplied part of the answer: inmates cooking in their cells, contrary to prison rules. Several yards further on he brushed into an inmate who was having trouble keeping his footing. As he staggered by, X's sense of smell ruled out the possibility of locomotor ataxia; the inmate had just been enjoying some "home-brew hooch." As X rounded a corner of the tier farthest away from the surveillance of the preoccupied guard, he bumped into something more serious. An inmate, heavily laden with cartons of cigarettes and other small items, was just leaving a cell. Unexpectedly catching sight of the civilian, he started in an unmistakably guilty manner, then hurried on. X noted the number of the cell and checked it on the location board. The occupant of the cell was listed as being in the prison hospital: apparently X had interrupted the visit of an uninvited caller. Unobtrusively he noted the cell to which the inmate went with his stolen goods, then rejoined his colleague, who was still talking to the guard. X interrupted to ask the officer one question: "That inmate you were talking to—the one with the home problem —what cell does he lock in?" The officer's answer confirmed X's suspicion: the thief and the inmate with the "problem" occupied the same cell. Later they would divide the spoils.

But Criminologist X must be sure. He consults the inmate's record, reading the same reports seen by his colleague. One fact does not immediately fit in: the reports of violations stop at the point where the inmate was transferred to his present location. Recalling the prisoner's long, friendly conversation with the officer, X also visits the Captain of the Guards, who reads for him the same efficiency report heard by his colleague a few minutes earlier. The picture jibes completely now: the inmate, playing on the guard's need to be liked, had diverted his attention while his buddy "pulled off the heist."

Little imagination is required to predict the reports made by these two criminologists. Each had visited the same place, yet each had undergone a different experience. Many of the same visual stimuli had been presented to the eyes of both, yet each had seen different things—and each will report different, and conflicting, facts. Both will leave the prison with a different theory to account for these facts, a different version of what was wrong, and different recommendations to correct what was wrong. How may we account for these differences? What methodological implications may be drawn from them?

The Selective Function of the Frame of Reference

As the two criminologists stood at the entrance of the cell block, a vast aggregate of visual and auditory stimuli impinged upon their consciousness. It would have been psychologically impossible for them to take in all of these; their first problem was to differentiate a few for selective attention, submerging the remainder, at least temporarily, below the level of awareness. What determined this selection? To what extent was it deliberate and intellectual?

Their candid report would acknowledge that their first impression was a mixture of thoughts and feelings. As Criminologist Y observed the informal scene, he experienced a good feeling. Asked to verbalize this feeling, he might have put it in the following terms:

> It is good for men to go about freely, to pursue their individual interests in their own individual ways—to play checkers or dominoes, or take showers, as they choose, without surveillance. It is also good for guards to be friendly and sympathetic toward inmates, and for inmates to bring their problems to guards. I recall how different it was in the old days—and I feel good that it has changed.

Criminologist X had a distinctly different feeling as he surveyed the scene. If his colleague had spoken his thoughts to him, he might have replied:

> Well, it is all very good, as a general principle, for men to be free and friendly—and *not* under surveillance. But I am also aware that most of these men have led lives based on a principle of *taking advantage of poor surveillance in order to exploit others.* I am not at all convinced that their new location has changed the pattern. The fact that the guard is preoccupied while the cells are open suggests to me the possibility that certain inmates may be stealing from other inmates, intimidating them, or otherwise breaking prison regulations.

These possibilities did not occur to Criminologist Y. Lacking his colleague's experience, he was forced to structure the situation in much more *general terms.* Nor could he subject his general ideas to the qualifications that grow out of personal familiarity with prison life. Criminologist Y had a wide knowledge of the activities of criminals *on the street;* he knew how they operated, how they exploited their victims. But his knowledge of criminals in prison was not at all in terms of what they did in prison *but rather in terms of what had been done in prisons to them.* Since most of the literature of penology has been concerned with *things done to inmates,* it was understandable for him to view the behavior of inmates almost exclusively as an outcome of their prison treatment. Consequently, what he saw before him was not a collection of dangerous criminals but a group of relatively helpless captives who have, historically, been subjected to the most shameful abuses. Viewing the scene before him, he felt good that, in this particular instance at least, those historical abuses were not being inflicted.

This aspect of his frame of reference—*the unverbalized assumption that the behavior of men in prison is a direct response to the behavior of prison officials*—determined the whole course of his investigation. It enabled him to reduce the difficult question, "What happens to men in prison?" to the much simpler question, "What are the officials doing to them?" If the officials are treating the inmates with fairness and understanding, it follows that the inmates will be well behaved; if the inmates are chronically getting into difficulty, it follows that they are being mistreated by the officials.

Criminologist Y never questioned these basic assumptions of his; he was probably unaware of them. Nevertheless, they crippled his investigation and biased his findings even before he began. For, when confronted with negative clues—the testimony of the Captain, the inmate's previous prison behavior—he quickly dismissed this evidence by explaining it away in terms of stereotypes: "the mistreated prisoner," "the old-style custodian." Thus, his frame of reference had actually stopped his investigation at the very point it should have started: the point at which serious negative evidence arose.

Criminologist X saw the same situation differently. His prison experiences had made it impossible for him to define what he saw in the uncomplicated terms used by his colleague. If these experiences had taught him anything, they had taught him how slight the impact of officials was on the world of the inmates. He was well aware that the inmates of most modern prisons lead a life of their own, in a tight society of their own, unimaginably remote from official scrutiny or effective interference. Consequently, in order to answer the question, "What is happening in this prison?" Criminologist X knew that he had to find some way of observing inmate behavior directly. What he found on the tiers of the cell block refuted the assumptions his colleague had adopted so unquestioningly.

The Dependence of Data on Theory

The fact that the two criminologists "saw" different things even though presented with the same visual stimuli raises important questions about the nature of fact itself. There is general agreement that the *interpretation* of experience is dependent on factors within the observer. Cantril and his colleagues have stated the position in the following terms:

> Man's only contact with this environment is through his senses. And the impressions man's senses give him are cryptograms in the sense that they have no meaning unless and until they become functionally related to man's purposive activities. The world man creates for himself through what Einstein has called the "rabble of senses" is one that takes on a degree of order, system, and meaning as man builds up through tested experience a pattern of assumptions and expectancies on which he can base action.[1]

The hypothetical case of the two criminologists illustrates the domination exercised over man's perception of external objects by concepts, ideas, and preconceptions inside his head. In the face of this dominance of the inner world of ideas over the world of experience, the assertion that *events in the external world somewhat suggest the true relations between them* becomes untenable.

People are continually organizing their assumptions into related systems or theories. Occasionally these assumptions, though useful in the past, lead men astray when applied to a new event. Cantril and his colleagues go on to say:

> Since the environment through which man carries out his life transactions is constantly changing, any person is constantly running into hitches and trying to do away with them. The assumptive world a person brings to the "now" of a concrete situation cannot disclose to him the undetermined significances continually emerging. And so we run into hitches in everyday life because of our inadequate understanding of the conditions giving rise to a phenomenon, and our ability to act effectively for a purpose becomes inadequate.[2]

Returning now to Criminologist Y: Though his conclusions were

[1] Hadley Cantril, Adelbert Ames, Jr., Albert H. Hastorf, and William H. Ittelson, "Psychology and Scientific Research," *Science,* 110:461, November 4, 1949.
[2] *Ibid.,* p. 462.

incorrect, his error did not create a difficulty for him—it did not create a "hitch" in his everyday life. Unaware that he was in error, he felt no need to investigate further. In this we see another effect of the frame of reference: the prevention of awareness of error which could lead to correction of that error.

Contrast this state of mind with that of the scientist who is able, in some way, to become aware of his conceptual inadequacies, and who tries to get to the bottom of them. This behavior is not haphazard. The scientist usually does not begin to investigate until his expectations break down in some way, creating "hitches" and doubts. It would appear that some feeling of doubt, intellectual inadequacy, or confusion—some psychological experience leading to the feeling "I do not know"—is an essential prerequisite of investigatory behavior. Few of us realize how infrequently this feeling crosses our minds in the course of daily life.

It certainly did not cross Criminologist Y's mind—even after the negative testimony of the Captain gave him a clear opportunity to test the adequacy of his conclusions. Why did he not grasp this opportunity? More specifically, *why did not the Captain's information create a problem for further investigation?*

The Emotional Aspect of the Frame of Reference

It will be recalled that Criminologist Y had a distinctly good feeling when he spoke to Officer Smith. The friendly, outgoing guard was more than a prison officer—he was the symbol of a better hope in penology. This feeling was reinforced by the inmate, whose apparent affection for the officer seemed to be a living vindication of the superiority of kindliness as a method of treatment. Whether or not he was aware of it, Criminologist Y had a lot invested in this view of the situation. Together with many other enlightened men of his time, he felt an inner revulsion whenever he saw his fellow human beings caged in cells. He could not help thinking of them as the victims of an unpardonable social ineptitude. This feeling of guilt had an important influence on his theory; because of it, kindliness was not merely a method of treatment but a way of atoning.

Criminologist Y's revulsions were, therefore, a compound of two strong elements. In part he identified with the prisoners, and felt something of their misery—and, in part, he felt anger and shame for those who inflicted this misery on them. He could not identify with them. At the distance he stood from the prison, he could distinguish only two groups: those who tried to understand and help prisoners, and those who did not. Officer Smith was clearly in the camp of those who help; the Captain, by obstructing Smith, had as clearly placed himself in the camp opposed. Taking *his* view of the situation would not only violate Y's deepest convictions but his strongest feelings as well.

Problem-Solving and the Frame of Reference

We are now in a position to examine the relationship among frames of reference, problems, facts, and theories. A frame of reference may be defined as *a complex of partly conscious, largely unquestioned assumptions, values, and feelings which prestructure the observer's orientation to a situation.* It has several functions and effects: (1) It brings the otherwise overwhelming universe of impressions within intellectually graspable limits by discriminating that which is significant from that which is not. (2) It directs inquiry by a further reduction of the situation into that which is known and that which is unknown (i.e., that which is to be questioned and that which is unquestionable). And in so doing, it provides a basis for the investigator's expectations. These expectations, linked logically together in a cause-effect relationship, may be called hypotheses. In effect, the investigator says: On the basis of what I know, I may expect events C and D to happen as a result of events A and B.

At this point the investigator is at the crossroads between science and nonscience. He has a pattern of expectations—a hypothesis—but he does not yet have a problem for investigation. *A problem is the awareness of a difference between an expectation and what may conceivably occur.* Now, unless the investigator defines his expectations in such a way that he can anticipate their nonoccurrence, he does not have a scientific problem. He merely has a hypothesis that is self-confirming and irrefutable.

This process may be illustrated by the following case. A habitual criminal in a maximum-security institution embarked on a successful campaign to get treatment at a diagnostic facility several miles from the institution. The therapist subsequently reported that the prisoner was making excellent progress and recommended that treatment be continued. One day the psychiatrist was unexpectedly called out of his office during a treatment session. The inmate seized this opportunity to escape.

On the day of the inmate's escape, the psychiatrist had given an enthusiastic report of progress and had spoken of certain deep insights his patient had achieved. Informed of the escape, he attributed it to the effectiveness of his probing.

Put in the form of a hypothesis, the psychiatrist's optimism about the effectiveness of his analytic work might be stated as follows: "The hypothesis that psychiatric treatment is effective will be confirmed if: (a) the patient remains in the treatment situation; (b) The patient leaves the treatment situation and escapes."

A scientific hypothesis is one that can be subjected to empirical test. No meaningful test is possible without a statement of the specific events that would invalidate it. Clearly, a hypothesis so framed that it can be confirmed by opposite occurrences in the world of events cannot be subjected to test. Moreover, a hypothesis—or any statement—framed in terms so general that it is impossible to determine the specific events predicted by it is also untestable.

Effective scientific investigation, as contrasted with other methods of problem-solving, involves a unique relationship between experience and the frame of reference. Scientific method is, at bottom, *an attempt to liberate the gathering and interpretation of data* from the domination of fixed assumptions. By requiring the scientist to deal only with hypotheses that predict specific events, it subjects those otherwise impregnable and self-confirming assumptions to a challenging test. In his deliberate and continual search for data critical of his concepts, the scientist rejects formulations permitting ambiguous, vague, or contradictory expectations about the world. He summarily rejects any formulation incapable of indicating the data that will invalidate it.

The Problem of Communication

In our previous discussion we defined scientific statements as having, among other characteristics, the property of *testability*. By this we meant, simply, that ways were available for determining whether the objects or relations asserted by the statement actually existed. At first glance, it might not appear that this requirement would be difficult to achieve. Nevertheless, the reader is frequently confronted with statements which, while purporting to say definite things about actual events —often with a ring of conviction—really do not do this at all. Once the reader is able to brush aside the suggestive *impression* made by these statements, he makes the discovery that they cannot be pinned down to any reference in the world of events. On closer inspection, they turn out to be not really descriptions of events at all but rather descriptions of words.

In order to refine his working concepts to the point where they are empirically testable, the scientist must critically evaluate the relation between his concepts and the *linguistic symbols* representing them. Certain discontinuities between the realms of language and experience must be realized. Aware that the logic of language is intrinsically different from the logic of operations, the scientist must simultaneously work in both realms without confusing the one with the other. For the criminologist, who, like his brother social scientists, has not yet evolved an impersonal mathematical language, the problem of communication is distressingly acute. Lacking this kind of speech, he is forced to communicate in the language of the forum and the market place, where a thousand linguistic traps await the unwary. One of the dangers of these traps is their subtlety; they usually anesthetize not only the speaker but his hearers as well, largely because both are well drugged in advance by the illusion of communication in everyday speech.

Statements about Things and Statements about Words

Consider the following statement: "Criminals are rebels against authority." Frequently this kind of statement is "proved" by the personal history of criminals. It is pointed out that the offenders in question were rebelling at an early age, disobeying their parents and school authorities. Eventually, they broke the law. Pursuing this track may seem to lead to the discovery: "People become criminals *because* of their rebellion against authority." These and similar statements are only pseudofactual. The concept *criminal* implies a deliberate flouting of legal authority. It is illogical to conceive of a criminal who is not "rebelling" against authority, since a criminal is defined as one who breaks a legal rule.

The philosopher and logician Carnap has suggested a simple test to distinguish *statements about words* from *statements about objects* and the relations between them. In a statement that is really about terms, it is always possible to substitute the word *means* for the word *is*.[3] Using Carnap's test, it is possible to say: "To be a criminal *means* to rebel against authority." At this point the "factual discovery" dissolves into a mere truism derived from an analysis of words. Consider now the statement: "John Smith commits assaults because of his unresolved aggressions." In other words, the unfortunate Smith is assaultive because he is assaultive.

This type of explanation, which arises out of the linguistic confusion of an effect with a process, is still highly contemporary despite its ancient history. The otherwise astute Aristotle explained the fact that fire rises by postulating an innate tendency of fire to rise; and certain modern psychological theorists have converted descriptions of behavior into traits, which are then looked on as forces that "cause" the behavior they were derived from. Thus, we hate "because" we are driven by hostilities. The circularity of these explanations reveals their purely verbal character. Evidence for the existence of the trait or drive is derived from the behavior to be explained. The behavior is then accounted for by means of the trait or drive. The process is reminiscent of the story about the two strangers applying for credit at a bank. John is a good credit risk because he is recommended highly by Jim. Jim's trustworthiness is beyond question because he has been recommended by John.

The Requirements of Testable Statements

We are now in a position to suggest the following requirements for truly empirical statements:

1. The associated concepts must be logically independent. This requirement is fulfilled only when
   a. They can be independently verified and
   b. They are not verbally or logically derived from each other.
2. It must be possible to state the conditions under which the relations described would *not exist*. If this cannot be done, there is no way of testing the statement.
3. The terms used must refer to identifiable things and must distinguish those objects from other things. The writer must be able to say: "By this term I mean to indicate *this* object or event or relation and *not* any other event or object or relation.

[3] Rudolph Carnap, *Meaning and Necessity* (Chicago: The University of Chicago Press, 1947).

The Problem of Specificity

This last requirement of specificity is extremely important; ignoring it can result in a host of linked pseudo explanations that lead, in the end, merely to the feeling of conviction without factual basis. Consider the following statement: "John and Mary are eating because they are hungry." This is a truly empirical statement because it is possible to verify the fact they are eating by observation and the fact that their stomachs are empty by fluoroscopic examination. This statement is, furthermore, adequate for anyone whose problem it is to determine why these people are engaged in the activity of *eating* rather than that of walking, flying kites, or robbing a bank. Note, also, that the term *eating* is roughly on the same level of generality as the term *hungry*. *Eating* describes one general form of activity as distinguished from other forms and *hunger* differentiates one physiological need-state from others. But let us now suppose that we are called on to explain why John is eating pork chops while Mary is eating a salad. It may still be true that Mary is eating a salad "because she is hungry" and that John is eating pork chops because he too is hungry. Nevertheless, this explanation fails to explain why Mary is eating a salad while John is eating pork chops. But this is precisely the question we want to answer.

Clearly, the unsatisfactory character of this explanation has little to do with its possible truth or falsity, and everything to do with its inability to differentiate. It now becomes apparent that verbal manipulation can make any question relatively "easy" to answer by lumping a variety of distinctions under one general term, thereby making them verbally identical. The more general we make the events to be explained, the more general we can make our explanation. Furthermore, no question of truth or falsity need be involved.

Let us take an example closer to home. After leaving the restaurant, John went out and stole a car, while Mary shoplifted a handbag. One way to "explain" these behaviors is to lump them together into a more general category: lawbreaking. It would seem now that all we need to do to "account" for this "single" activity is to hypothesize a single cause or motive. We might say: "They broke the law because they were frustrated" or "because of their unresolved hostilities against authority" (or a virtually innumerable variety of general explanations). Let us further suppose that we can independently verify the fact that these individuals were actually highly frustrated and hostile persons. We still have not accounted for the *manner in which* they expressed these feelings. Unless we can show that hostility and frustration are invariably (or in the great majority of instances) followed by lawbreaking, we shall have to confess that we are operating on the basis of a personal conviction or agreement we have made with ourselves. (Even then, we shall not have accounted for *why they stole* and why they stole *those particular objects*.)

Our first hypothesis—that lawbreaking results from frustration and aggression—would be difficult to substantiate on this general plane. This difficulty can be demonstrated by even a very generalized listing of all the possible activities engaged in by aggressive and frustrated individuals. Taking the concept *aggression* alone, we can list the following three general ways in which people express hostility: overt physical action, verbal activity, and various physiological reactions. Under each of these categories there are several more specific subgroupings:

SUGGESTED CLASSIFICATION OF WAYS IN WHICH AGGRESSION MAY BE EXPRESSED

Overt Physical Action	Verbal Action	Physiological Reaction
Assault	Slander	Increased heart rate
Bullying	Direct Insult	Increased breathing
Refusal to cooperate	Sarcasm	rate
Depriving of property	Innuendo	Suspension of digestion
or rights	Condescension	(etc.)
Overcompetitiveness	(etc.)	
(etc.)		

Under each of these subheadings of aggressive behavior, there are many more specific instances, a great many of which do not involve lawbreaking at all. Consequently, the highly general explanation "aggression" does not at all differentiate the myriad forms of noncriminal aggressive behavior from the specific criminal example in which we are interested. Many criminological explanations commit this error, which might be called the *fallacy of transgressing the level of generality*. They *seem* to explain, but their plausibility is merely a deceptive artifact of the generalizing power of language—a deception made all the more convincing when the language is technical and carries with it an aura of authority.

Evaluating the Descriptive Adequacy of Language

It thus appears that descriptions and explanations, while quite empirical and apparently plausible, can still be virtually useless for our

needs—as ineffectual as an ordinary twelve-inch ruler for making measurements scaled in thousandths of an inch. How can we determine the
adequacy of descriptive language in criminology? Is there any way of
measuring or evaluating it? A little reflection will reveal that the adequacy of any descriptive term is relative to two main considerations:
the needs of the describer and the existence of critical distinctions in the
things to be described.

Let us imagine a fairly common case. A detective is searching for a
certain forger in a large city. All he knows about the forger is that he is
redheaded; he has no other clues. Clearly, the adequacy of the description "redheaded forger" is directly related to the number of redheaded
forgers in the city. If there is only one in the entire metropolis, the
description is wholly adequate; if there are two, the description is only
half as adequate. Thus the adequacy of the description is directly determined by how *specifically it prepares us for what we will encounter in
experience.*

The task of finding concepts and words to symbolize our findings is
not an easy one. The condition of criminological theory is a reflection
of the fact that our present symbol systems are inadequate to describe
the situations we encounter, and the present state of correctional practice is a further indication of how inadequately our knowledge has
prepared us to cope with what we find. The individuals who work in
the fields of crime control and prevention are dealing with highly specific
persons in particular situations. In the penological literature there are
literally thousands of statements citing general principles of dealing with
offenders; eventually, however, the individual probation officer, correctional counselor, and prison guard must deal concretely with specific cases.

The widely deplored state of correctional affairs suggests that something unfortunate has happened between principle and practice. Does
this mean that the principles are wrong? There is no lack of critics to
volunteer this diagnosis. Nevertheless, it would probably be more nearly
correct to say that there is no way to determine whether many principles
are right or wrong because *the principles themselves are not communicated in terms that suggest specific operations.* The modern correctional
student is in many ways like a person who was taught to drive a car by
a series of lectures on the history and theory of combustion engines.
After all his study, he is still without instruction and practice in how to
proceed in a concrete operational situation. This condition suggests what
is probably the major problem of correctional theory today.

Though it by no means provides one, the problem also suggests the remedy. It suggests that criminologists rigorously re-evaluate their concepts, principles, and symbol-systems in the light of something like the following questions:

1. To what extent do descriptions enable us to recognize what we actually encounter in experience? Any descriptive category that leads to ambiguous expectations or fails to recognize critical distinctions found in experience should either be refined or rejected.

2. To what extent do operational principles suggest specific practices in specific eventualities? Any operational principle or value that does not eventually imply specific actions in concrete situations should be refined or rejected.

The Definition of Crime and Criminals

In the preceding pages we have actually been discussing certain similarities and differences between the language of science and the language of everyday speech. In both modes of communication one common intention is the use of symbols to stand for distinct and isolated things; we might call this the *differentiating* function of words. This function, which strives to express the differences between things, is contrasted with another function of language: the use of words to express qualities that different things have in common. This purpose has been called the abstractive or *generalizing* function of language. Both of these functions are necessary. Without words that differentiate, we would not be prepared for the enormous complexity of existence; without general terms, we would be overwhelmed by that complexity.

With the exception of proper names, virtually every word that stands for objects, qualities, and actions can be used either in its differentiating or generalizing function. Frequently these functions are combined in the use of the same word. The resulting confusion may be illustrated in the various meanings that have grown around the words *crime* and *criminal*.

Used in its differentiating sense, the word *criminal* separates one group of persons from another. This separation is made on the basis of one or more factors shared in common by the criminal group and not found in the larger noncriminal group. Opinion about what these factors are is divided, but there is general agreement that, whatever else they share, criminals by definition share the common characteristic of having committed, or having been convicted of, a crime. Note, now, that this common characteristic or fate is shared by a large number of otherwise heterogeneous people, individuals who are otherwise different from one another and may have many similarities with persons who are not criminals. All that the term *criminal* signifies, up to this point, is that one single factor has been isolated to provide a convenient way of identifying a number of people that society has chosen to distinguish and to deal with in terms of the fact that each has violated the law.

The Criminal as a Stereotype

So much for the meaning of the word in its restrictive and semantically correct sense; we must now deal with what is produced when psychological and sociological influences play upon the peculiar vulnerabilities of language. The word *criminal* is properly called a *conceptual abstraction*. It isolates a number of very different people on the basis of one single nonphysical characteristic. Yet there are no people in the world with only one characteristic in their make-up. All known people —all known organisms and objects—have many characteristics; consequently, in learning about them and thinking about them, we spontaneously conjure up a composite image based on these characteristics.

The peculiar thing about conceptual abstractions—especially one-factor abstractions—is that they do *not* have many characteristics, and they refer to no material qualities. Strictly spreaking, they do not even exist except as mental products. They are, moreover, a kind of mental product that stands in sharp contrast to the concrete images of daily experience. In contrast to *material abstractions*—such as the words *house, fox,* or *person* which are general terms for things that can be seen or touched—conceptual abstractions can only be *thought*. The confusion arises when these conceptual abstractions or constructs are applied to actual things and people. We never see, touch, or hear the factor called criminality, but we do encounter people who are called criminals, just as we encounter people called infants or men or women.

The man on the street, dealing as he does with the concrete and the actual, is accustomed to symbols that refer to recognizable things. The term *infant,* for example, conjures up a picture with definite characteristics rooted in the known attributes of small children. The fact that there is an important difference between words like *infant* and words like *criminal* is not indicated by anything in the structure or use of the terms. Thus we are unconsciously led to believe that *criminal* refers to a definite type of person. Misled by this assumption, we take the abstraction and flesh it out with additional characteristics that make it meaningful and recognizable in our everyday world.

In the case of the criminal, the added characteristics are largely the product of the public's emotional response to the danger of crime; taken together, this reaction and the vivid but artificial image it creates is called a *stereotype*. A stereotype arises when one or a few real or imaginary characteristics create an emotional response that colors and unifies the group's entire thinking about a subject. In the face of the vivid and fixed image, real differences are not recognized. Stereotypes tend to persist as long as the associated emotions persist. A few centuries ago, when Europe was torn by religious wars, most Catholics "knew" what Protestants were like, and most Protestants had a vivid image of Catholics. Today the single factor, religious denomination, has much less power to determine one's total image of a person. Thus an individual requesting information about Mr. Smith would not feel particularly informed if he were told that Mr. Smith was a Protestant. He would probably reply: "That's all very well—but now tell me what he's like. What kind of person is he?" In the case of the criminal, the traditional fear and hostility aroused have not been significantly diminished; consequently, the stereotype persists.

One of the consequences of the stereotype is that it removes the image of the criminal from any similarity with the layman and his friends. In this, the criminal himself is the sole beneficiary, since, as a matter of fact, the majority of crimes are committed by individuals indistinguishable in appearance and manner from the law-abiding. Thus, while the layman is looking over his shoulder for the comic-strip version of the desperado, he may be having his pocket picked by the respectable-looking gentleman standing beside him.

The Criminal as a Legal and Social Status

The recognition that the term *criminal* refers to a conceptual abstraction has important consequences for its definition. It requires that the question, "What are the characteristics of the criminal type?" be replaced by an entirely different kind of question. This question would ask:

"What operations lead to the assigning of the classification?" (Note, now, that we are not attempting to "explain" crime or the acts that lead to the assigning of the classification. We are merely attempting to list all the conditions leading to the affixing of a label.) Looking about, we note that a person may be a free man one day, a criminal the next day, and—as it has actually happened—the mayor of a city not long after. Looking closer—perhaps no further than the nearest mirror—we recognize that a person may frequently violate the law in small or large ways and never be called a criminal. Apparently the assigning of the classification need not have anything to do with what the person himself does— but it has very much to do with what others do.

Definition of the Criminal

These observations suggest that *to be a criminal* is to enjoy a certain *status* conferred by others. It is not a state of mind (which of us has not had larcenous thoughts?). It is not necessarily a guilty act (who is wholly guiltless?). Invariably, however, it requires certain acts on the part of others—acts that are social and judicial in character. These considerations suggest that the concept *criminal* would most usefully be defined in the following terms:

A person is assigned the status of a criminal when he is adjudged to be punishable by the authorities in continuous political control over the territory in which he is.

This definition deliberately omits any reference to laws, in recognition of the fact that political authorities have often adjudicated and punished in the absence of laws or under laws that were not appropriate. It also omits any reference to the actual breaking of laws. This is in recognition of the facts that (1) the innocent are occasionally punished and (2) the guilty are frequently not detected. This latter category of actual but undetected violators may be called offenders-in-fact and ought not to be confused with the class of *criminals-by-adjudication*. The requirement that adjudication and punishment be rendered by authorities in *political* control of a territory is included in order to exclude the case where a group seizes temporary actual power. A band of vigilantes may judge and punish an individual, but the status of criminal is not conferred by this process. The requirement of territoriality is included as a necessary aspect of political control. Finally, the requirement of punishment is included to differentiate judgments that do not result in the fixing of the criminal status (e.g., civil adjudications).

Definition of Crime

The definition of crime follows from the definition of criminal:

A crime is an act or omission ascribed to a person when he is punished by the authorities in continuous political control over the territory in which he is.

This definition makes no mention of laws and seems to carry the disquieting suggestion that, irrespective of laws, an act is not a crime until the offender is caught, tried, and punished. This is literally true, and may be demonstrated by the following illustrations: (1) There are certain classes of persons who are exempt from conviction and punishment even though they commit acts that would be punished if committed by others. These include children under the statutory age and persons judged legally insane. (2) Persons convicted of crimes have been released after appealing on purely procedural grounds. This release removes the status of criminal. (3) There are many unrepealed laws which are never enforced. (4) It is not always possible to predict the circumstances under which an apparent violation of the law will lead to conviction and punishment. The noted jurist Jerome Frank has pointed out that "legal rights are dependent on human guesses about the facts of cases."[4] Sutherland recognized this situation in his definition of crime as "Behavior which would raise a reasonable expectancy of conviction if tried in a criminal court or substitute agency."[5]

At this point some questions may arise. We may ask, How are those who actually break the law—but go undetected—to be differentiated from those who are detected and punished? Are not those in the former category equally criminal? Strange as it may seem, the only objective answer to this question is that at this point, *we simply don't know.* Take, for example, the hypothetical case of Jones, who, in point of fact, killed Smith. Concerning Jones' actual behavior there is no doubt. Nevertheless, concerning the further question, *Does Jones' act of homicide constitute a crime?* there may be considerable doubt.

If we asked Jones himself, he might well insist that his act was not a crime at all; on the contrary, he might assert, "I killed justifiably, in self-defense." If we put the same question to the policeman who

---

[4] Jerome Frank, *Courts on Trial* (Princeton, N. J.: Princeton University Press, 1950), p. 14.

[5] Edwin H. Sutherland, "White Collar Criminality," *American Sociological Review*, 5:6, February 1940.

arrested Jones and to the district attorney who indicted him for murder, they would insist that Jones' act was undoubtedly criminal. None of these assertions is as yet more than a prediction of an interpretation that has not yet been made. The assumptions underlying these predictions are quickly stated. The policeman who arrested Jones and the prosecutor who sought the indictment against him assumed that a judge and jury would later declare Jones' act to have been criminal. For his part, Jones' decision to plead not guilty was based on the contrary assumption that the same judge and jury would find him innocent—not of the act itself, which no one has denied—but of the criminal intent that would render the act criminal. The critical point is this: Though acts themselves may be indisputable, their *criminality* is always an interpretation—an interpretation that can only be conjectured about in advance. It is this socio-legal interpretation alone which confers the status of crime upon the act, and the status of criminal upon the actor.

Thus, the indispensable element in the definition of *crime* and *criminality* is the determination by the authorities that an individual be found guilty and punished. In modern societies that determination is usually related to the indignation aroused when certain social rules are violated. Nevertheless, in the absence of a determination to prosecute and punish, the offender-in-fact does not become a criminal.

One purpose of the foregoing discussion was to differentiate between persons actually committing acts likely to be defined as crimes, and those occupying the socio-legal status of criminals. With respect to the first category, the participation of the State is limited to the making of the law defining the offensive behavior as deserving of punishment. All persons engaging in this behavior may be considered offenders-in-fact and, presumably, should be caught and punished. However, both within and outside this large category of offenders-in-fact is the smaller category of offenders-by-adjudication, persons who have endured the elaborate social process of identification, conviction, and punishment as *criminals*. We may now distinguish four categories of actual or convicted offenders:

1. Those actually committing offenses without being known, either because:
   a. The offense was not discovered;
   b. The offense was not reported;
   c. The offender was not identified.
2. Those known to have committed actual offenses but unpunished either because of:

    a. Failure of the State to indict;

    b. Failure of the State to convict;

    c. Failure of the State to sustain its conviction on appeal.

3. Those actually committing offenses for which they are convicted and punished.

4. Those convicted and punished for offenses they did not actually commit.

Implications of a Status Definition of Criminality

The view that criminality is most usefully viewed as a status that can be conferred and removed has important consequences for criminological theory. In the first place, it requires a rejection of the simple question: "What are the causes of crime?" This question is now seen as involving two distinct problems: (1) What are the causes leading to the commission of the act? (2) What are the causes leading to the assigning of the status? The separation of these frequently confused issues is required not merely by logic but by fact. Even the law—which assigns the status—recognizes the necessity of removing it under certain conditions. Vengeance is not to be exacted forever; the stigma need not be eternal. Most, if not all, jurisdictions provide that the civil rights forfeited by the felon may be entirely restored after a period of good behavior.

The use of the term *criminal* to identify persons occupying a potential and removable status is in sharp contrast to the view that criminality is a sickness, a biological condition, or a type. The failure to distinguish between the ideas of status and type has led to costly errors and lost directions in criminology. It has led many to mistake the fact of a fairly clear legal category for the existence of an equally identifiable category of persons with similar characteristics. It has led brilliant investigators into life-long searches for common biological, social, or psychological traits. Despite the failure of these investigations to isolate within the offender a single characteristic not found in the law-abiding, the search for common factors continues to preoccupy those who are still unaware that the object of their quest is the product of a semantic confusion.

3

Crime Statistics:
Sources and Problems

IT WAS THE GREAT BELGIAN SCIENTIST QUÉTELET (1796–1874) WHO WAS responsible for the earliest application of statistics to crime and criminals. In 1831 he published a study in which crimes at various age levels were related to education, sex, climate, and season. His findings moved him to comment on the consistency of the yearly crime rate:

> Thus we pass from one year to another with the sad perspective of seeing the same crimes reproduced in the same order and calling down the same punishments in the same proportions. Sad condition of Humanity! . . . We might enumerate in advance how many individuals will stain their hands in the blood of their fellows, how many will be poisoners; almost we can enumerate in advance the births and deaths that should occur. There is a budget which we pay with frightful regularity; it is that of prisons, chains and the scaffold.[1]

In this country the first decennial census was taken in 1790. However, it was not until 1850 that the federal government systematically included data on criminals. The method of collection was crude. Assistant United States marshals were instructed to ask the free inhabitants whether they were—or had been—"deaf and dumb, blind, insane,

---

[1] Quoted in John G. Peatman, *Descriptive and Sampling Statistics* (New York: Harper and Brothers, 1947), pp. 5–6.

idiotic, pauper or convict." These questions were supplemented by a separate schedule, seeking information on the number of persons convicted, the number in prisons, their nativity, and, in the case of the native-born, their color. In preparation for the census of 1880 the method of collecting criminal statistics was rigorously revised under the direction of the noted penologist Frederick Wines. His plan called for the taking of information from prisons, court dockets, judges' reports, and reports from police departments. These were supplemented by additional schedules given to the regular enumerator, who received extra pay for filling them out. Unfortunately, the temporary shutdown of the census office prevented the complete realization of Wines' plan. Despite this setback, improvements in the collection of crime statistics were made in subsequent census years. Due to the ten-year gap between one census and the next, however, the data suffered from a lack of continuity. The only other nation-wide sources of crime statistics were the yearly reports of the Attorney General, which first appeared on a regular basis in 1872. It soon became apparent that additional sources of information, not connected with the census, were required.

Between 1900 and 1930 an increasing number of uncoordinated federal and state agencies published data on crimes and prisoners. Much of this information, poorly standardized and consequently useless for purposes of comparison, complicated rather than clarified the total picture. In 1927 the International Association of Chiefs of Police organized a committee to work out a nation-wide system of uniform crime reporting. Under the technical direction of Bruce Smith and with the assistance of a grant from the Rockefeller Foundation, the committee was able, within less than three years, to conduct its first monthly survey.

The Uniform Crime Reports

Issued continuously since 1930, the *Uniform Crime Reports* now constitute the most reliable source for estimating the nation-wide frequency of most types of conventional crime reported in the United States.[2] In addition to publishing biannual reports on twenty-seven major and minor crimes, the *Uniform Crime Reports* present data on

[2] Copies of the *Uniform Crime Reports* are issued by the Federal Bureau of Investigation, United States Department of Justice, Washington 25, D. C., and may be obtained free on request.

arrests and convictions; hence they provide the most reliable basis for evaluating the relative efficiency of law-enforcement agencies. To a great extent, this reputation for reliability has been earned by the caution and conservatism used by the F. B. I. in the collection and interpretation of the data, which are supplied voluntarily by local authorities in thousands of cities, towns, and rural areas in the various states.

In cooperating with these local authorities, the F. B. I. has had to combine caution and thoroughness with quiet diplomacy. Since all data are collected by the individual reporting localities (according to standard recording procedures), the F. B. I. has no authority to supervise the collection or to correct obvious errors in compilation. When an obviously incorrect report is received, the F. B. I. initiates correspondence with the reporting agency, offering, if necessary, to send its own experts to assist the local authorities. If the errors are not corrected, the F. B. I. merely exercises its right not to publish them.

In attempting to gain wide acceptance of its recording standards, the F. B. I. has carried on a campaign for police efficiency that has increasingly borne fruit. A quarter century of experience has provided F. B. I. statisticians with yardsticks for estimating the average crime rates for localities of all sizes in different areas. It has similarly established relatively consistent ratios between different types of offenses and the "arrest clearances" for these crimes. Any report that deviates markedly from these expectations—especially in the direction of low reported crime rates and high rates of arrest—becomes a matter of polite but searching inquiry.

In its publication, *Ten Years of Uniform Crime Reporting*, the F. B. I. cites several instances of improved reporting methods resulting from these procedures. Table IX indicates the difference this improvement made in the figures reported by one locality, identified by the F. B. I. as "City D."

TABLE IX

HIGHER CRIME FIGURES RESULTING FROM IMPROVED
REPORTING METHODS

Year	Offenses per 100,000		
	Robbery	Burglary	Larceny
1934	7.3	98.1	230.2
1936	40.5	372.9	593.4

Source: *Ten Years of Uniform Crime Reporting*, p. 89.

From 1930 to 1935 the figures had been improperly compiled from a record of arrests. During 1936 the local records were improved and expanded to make possible the compilation of data concerning the number of offenses committed.

"City E" was less cooperative. The comparison of its burglary and larceny figures with the national average of cities of comparable size in 1938 is shown in Table X.

TABLE X

MISLEADING CRIME AND ARREST RATES AS AN INDICATION OF
INADEQUATE REPORTING METHODS

Offense	City E		National average for cities over 250,000	
	Offenses per 100,000	Percentage cleared by arrest	Offenses per 100,000	Percentage cleared by arrest
Burglary	139.0	71	374.1	37.9
Larceny	454.7	75	927.9	22.6

Source: *Ten Years of Uniform Crime Reporting*, p. 90.

The F. B. I. comments with restraint on these figures for "City E":

The data are not entirely unreasonable. . . . However, they are such as to warrant a suspicion of the possibility that minor larcenies and burglaries for which no arrests were made are for some reason not represented in the statistical reports, thus causing a low rate and a high proportion of cleared cases.[3]

As a result of local improvements in reporting practices, the *Uniform Crime Reports* have been able to increase their total coverage markedly. In 1955 the estimated total crime reports included actual counts for about 90 per cent of the urban population and 68 per cent of the rural population.

Other Sources of Crime Statistics

Except for statistical studies made by individual investigators—and these are usually limited to small samples of criminals—the gathering of

[3] *Ten Years of Uniform Crime Reporting, 1930–1939* (Washington, D. C.: U. S. Department of Justice, 1939), p. 90.

statistical data on a large scale is necessarily a task of government. At present there are at least fifty separate and independent criminal jurisdictions in the United States—the federal government, the District of Columbia, and the various states. Each of these units of government has its own police agencies, its own criminal laws and procedures, its own correctional facilities—and its own statistical methods. Statistical information is at least potentially available from the following:

1. *The Police:* Officials involved in the investigation of reported crimes and the apprehension of criminals include municipal and state police forces, federal agents of various kinds, and a wide variety of sheriffs, constables, district attorney agents, and special peace officers.

2. *Judicial Agencies:* Reports on the prosecution and disposition of suspected offenders are made by municipal and police magistrates, trial courts, grand juries, and prosecutors.

3. *Correctional Agencies:* Statistics on the treatment of convicted offenders are compiled by institutional staffs and by probation and parole authorities.

4. *Crime Commissions:* The information routinely available through regular government channels is, on occasion, supplemented by temporary groups set up to investigate special problems of crime and law enforcement. Of these, the peculiarly American institution of the *crime commission* is perhaps the most interesting. Composed largely of private citizens and civic leaders, the crime commission has been a recurrent response to official apathy or corruption. Related in spirit to the vigilante tradition of the frontier, they have occasionally shed dramatic light—and heat—on the local and national crime picture. They have also produced volumes of statistics on critical but little-explored problems of crime control—for example, the extracurricular activities, acquaintances, and incomes of law-enforcement officials who have become unaccountably rich in the service of the people.[4]

5. *Legislative Committees:* In recent times, the Congress has made increasing use of its broad investigatory powers in the exploration of problems of crime control. In 1950 the Special Committee to Investigate Organized Crime in Interstate Commerce (under its chairman, Senator Kefauver) gained national publicity in televised hearings held across

---

[4] See Virgil Peterson, *Crime Commissions in the United States* (Chicago: Chicago Crime Commission, 1945). The author lists twelve local or state and three national crime commissions in operation between the years 1918 and 1945. In addition to gathering data on local and national problems of crime control, these bodies have stimulated considerable remedial legislation.

the nation. Congressional subcommittees have the power to subpoena witnesses and records, and, depending on their budget, they may employ statisticians and other experts to analyze and interpret their data.

Federal Sources

In addition to the *Uniform Crime Reports,* the federal government publishes data on offenders committed to state and federal correctional institutions. One of the most comprehensive of these was a series titled *Prisoners in State and Federal Prisons and Reformatories,* published annually by the Bureau of the Census and discontinued in 1948. An indication of the scope of these reports is given by the contents of the final issue, which covered the year 1946.

The 104-page report presented a total of 67 separate statistical tables. In the first part, dealing with the composition and movement of the nation-wide prison population, statistical information was broken down by sex, type of institution, region, and method of discharge. The second part, which dealt with felony prisoners newly received from court, presented what may be the most incisive analysis of law enforcement yet compiled in statistical form. The information was broken down and cross-referenced by sex, race, offense, age, region and state, nativity, marital status, type of sentence, length of sentence, and type of institution. By means of a brief glance through these tables, it is possible to determine who was committing what kind of offense where, and who was receiving what kind of punishment, and where. The third part furnished similar information on felony prisoners released, and objective indices of the factors related to the longer or shorter retention of offenders in various parts of the country. Part IV presented a survey of the institutional personnel employed in penal institutions—information indispensable for an evaluation of correctional treatment in the United States. The final section dealt with military offenders. Taken together, these reports formed an unparalleled resource for the researcher; their discontinuance must be regarded as a major loss to criminology.

After 1948 the responsibility for publishing nation-wide prisoner statistics was assigned to the Federal Bureau of Prisons, which circulates a brief annual report under the title *National Prisoner Statistics.* The 1954 report consisted of eight pages and provided six tables.[5] The Fed-

[5] In 1955 the Federal Bureau of Prisons also published a comprehensive 83-page survey of prisoners released from state and federal institutions in 1951.

eral Bureau of Prisons also publishes an annual report titled *Federal Prisons;* its statistical information is limited to federal offenders.

The National Bureau of Vital Statistics, in its annual report, *Vital Statistics in the United States,* includes nation-wide rates of the major forms of crime. Mimeographed reports on juvenile delinquency are published sporadically by the Children's Bureau, a section of the U. S. Department of Health, Education, and Welfare. These reports are based on information voluntarily supplied by juvenile agencies throughout the country. The issue covering the year 1953 included full reports from only 666 courts out of a nation-wide total of over 3,000 and cannot be considered representative of the national picture.

State Sources

According to Sutherland and Cressey,[6] only ten states (California, Louisiana, Massachusetts, Michigan, Minnesota, New York, Pennsylvania, Rhode Island, South Dakota, and Texas) and the Territory of Hawaii have central statistical bureaus that publish crime statistics. The statistical information published by the individual states is, in general, more sporadic, less carefully gathered, and considerably less standardized than the federal reports.

Problems of Statistical Analysis

An early statistician coined a phrase that has since been repeated to generations of students: "It's not that the figures lie—it's that the liars figure." Although dishonest figures are by no means unknown in crime statistics, it is probable that the largest number of statistical studies is compiled by those desiring to inform rather than misinform. Nevertheless, a statistic that misleads through an honest error can be just as confusing as one that is deliberately constructed to misrepresent. In the following paragraphs we will discuss several sources of error found in crime statistics; these may be divided into the following groups: sources of error in *collection,* in *presentation,* and in *evaluation.*

[6] Edwin H. Sutherland and Donald R. Cressey, *Principles of Criminology,* 5th ed. (Philadelphia: J. B. Lippincott Company, 1955), p. 36.

Sources of Error in the Collection of Crime Statistics

DELIBERATE SUPPRESSION. In 1949 the New York City Police Department reported that a total of 2,520 burglaries had been committed in the city and that 77.4 per cent had been cleared by arrest. In 1952 the same police department, under a different commissioner, reported a total 42,149 burglaries, with only 12.9 per cent cleared by arrest. Comparing these figures, the unsophisticated reader might have come to a variety of conclusions. He might have concluded that New York had been struck by a calamitous crime wave. While this disaster was developing, another had apparently overtaken the police: arrests had dropped from better than 3 out of 4 to little more than 1 out of 10.

Fortunately, these conclusions would not merely be incorrect but almost the reverse of the truth. In 1952 the F. B. I. accepted New York City's crime data for the first time. Prior to 1952, the city's crime-reporting methods had been well below standard as the result of a system that "canned" (failed to record) many complaints for unsolved cases. The 1949 figures had been based on a fraction of the burglaries actually committed. Commenting on the improved methods of reporting, a metropolitan newspaper pointed out that the new figures:

> ...for the first time disclose the extent to which the public was misled in previous administrations when the police simply failed to record most property crime complaints.
>
> By junking or "canning" so many of the complaints the police could not be held responsible for clearing them.
>
> Thus, in 1949 . . . the department reported only 1,472 robberies. By 1952, under honest crime reporting the figure had spiraled to 8,757. Hence in 1949 police were able to boast an astronomical robbery clearance rate of 74.2 percent as against 24 percent three years later.
>
> ...So obvious was the fraud that the F.B.I. finally refused to accept New York's police reports until its system was completely overhauled.[7]

Other cities have employed similar methods of biased crime reporting. Citing Virgil Peterson, Sutherland and Cressey have pointed out that:

> Police departments in some cities certainly conceal crimes known to them in order to protect the reputation of their city or department. Politicians up for re-election are likely to be accused of neglect of duty if the crime rate has gone up during their administration, and they are likely to be praised if the crime rate has declined. In 1928 the official police reports indicated that only 879 burglaries and 1,263 robberies

[7] *New York World-Telegram and Sun*, December 14, 1953.

were committed in Chicago; for the year 1931, after a report by the Chicago Crime Commission . . . the official reports revealed that 18,689 burglaries and 14,544 robberies had been committed in the city. Certainly this great difference is not due to a correspondingly great change in the number of crimes committed.[8]

There are other forms of suppression of crime data by the police; one of the most common seems to be related more to administrative inertia than to any darker motives. One of the perennial jobs of police officers is to keep their precinct clear of vagrants, loiterers, and other persons who *may* be up to no good. Frequently these people are merely "run out of the precinct"; very often, however, they are "run in" to the station house to be given a sound scare. In many cases, the arrest is made without any charge and without any pretense that the "offender" is charged with a known crime. If the police want to protect themselves they may prefer a charge of loitering. As often as not, however, they make neither a charge nor an entry in the blotter.

The distortions introduced into crime statistics deliberately or negligently form only a small source of the errors in collection. The large majority of these errors are either partly or totally unavoidable because of certain problems peculiar to data-gathering in this area. The following sources of error are highly difficult or impossible to eradicate:

FAILURE TO COMPLAIN. Since a crime cannot become "known to the police" until someone reports it, any statistic that purports to represent the total number of any type of crime committed is necessarily an informed guess based on the addition of an estimated number of additional *unreported* crimes of the same category. Experience has shown that certain types of crime tend to be reported with much greater frequency than others. This factor is so important for crime statistics that the F. B. I. has based its entire system of crime reporting on its recognition.[9] The *Uniform Crime Reports* tabulate all crime data in either one of two categories, depending on assumptions about the reliability and adequacy of this coverage. Offenses listed in the *Part I* category (homicide, rape, robbery, aggravated assault, burglary, larceny, and auto-theft) are, for the most part, those "in which it would be exceptional when the victim or his friends or acquaintances would not report the crime after it had occurred." Part II offenses—for which the total reports are only an unknown percentage of the actual incidence—comprise the following:

Other assaults

[8] Virgil Petersen, "An Examination of Chicago's Law Enforcement Agencies," *Criminal Justice*, 1950, pp. 3–6; cited in Sutherland and Cressey, *op. cit.*, p. 28.
[9] See *Ten Years of Uniform Crime Reporting*, p. 90.

Embezzlement and fraud
Stolen property—buying, receiving, etc.
Arson
Forgery and counterfeiting
Prostitution and commercialized vice
Other sex offenses
Narcotic drug laws
Weapons—carrying; possessing, etc.
Drunkenness, disorderly conduct, vagrancy
Gambling
Traffic and motor vehicle laws
Driving while intoxicated
All other offenses

A comparison of the Part I and Part II offenses reveals some of the difficulties inherent in any attempt to estimate actual crime rates on the basis of reported crimes. Every Part I crime has a definite victim. This is not true for more than half of the offenses in Part II. In a strict sense, the gambler, the drug addict, the vagrant, the drunkard, and certain types of sexual deviates are their own victims. The customers of commercialized vice rarely think of themselves as victims; moreover, the making of a complaint may expose the complainant to unwelcome notice. To a certain extent this qualification also applies to the rape cases of Part I—and this fact (among others) detracts from the accuracy of the reported total.

The victims of many types of crime either do not know the offender or consider the offense too trifling, troublesome, or embarrassing to report—this is especially true of minor thefts and simple assaults. A number of victims may seek other means of dealing with the offender. In numerous cases fulfilling all legal requirements of a criminal prosecution for fraud or embezzlement, businessmen attempt to recoup their losses either by informal agreement, the *threat* of criminal action, or a civil suit. Often the victims feel it is futile to complain.

Confidence men can usually rely on the embarrassment of their dupes as an effective shield against complaints. Similarly, many serious assaults between close relations and "friends" are never reported by victims because of strong feelings of humiliation.

There is another vast category of offenses in which the victim is the state treasury, the community at large, or public morality generally. The amount of unreported and otherwise undetected collusion between lawyers, clients, minor and major state officials is unknown—as is the resulting loss to the public. Even when the accomplices eventually defraud each other, the "victim" often finds it difficult to complain about his accomplices without damaging admissions concerning himself.

GEOGRAPHICAL VARIATIONS IN THE DEFINITION OF CERTAIN CRIMES. There is one obstacle to a uniform and general system of crime reporting that cannot be overcome until all jurisdictions employ similar definitions of crimes. Despite many movements for a "standard criminal code," the constitutional provision that the separate states shall govern their own internal affairs has remained an effective barrier to the general accept-ance of common definitions of many offenses. Thus, for example, dif-ferent jurisdictions may give the same *name* to an offense but actually apply it to different behaviors. Or the same behavior may be classified under different offenses in different criminal codes. Since nation-wide crime reporting is dependent on comparable units of measurement, these differences severely complicate the elementary process of adding up certain types of offenses.[10]

DIFFERENCES IN THE APPLICATION OF LEGAL PROCESSES WITHIN THE SAME JURISDICTION. There is one problem that no degree of uniformity in law can of itself eradicate. Police officials are usually the first on the scene after an offense has been committed; they are the first to be called, the first to investigate, and they usually have the first official contact with both the victim and the offender. Their interpretations, their biases and omissions are critical to all subsequent phases of the administration of justice. Undoubtedly their most important decision is *whether or not to make an arrest.*

A thorough analysis of the "arresting customs" of policemen would probably reveal many systematic variations (most of them entirely honest and well-intentioned), which introduce marked errors into criminal statistics. For example, a visitor from Saturn who examined daily arrest records for drunk and disorderly conduct would probably conclude that New Year's Eve is the soberest night of the year. Nevertheless, there is probably more drinking and carousing on New Year's Eve than at any other time. Yet the police of most jurisdictions, no more immune to the general good spirits of the occasion than anyone else, simply do not make many arrests during this period. In ancient Rome, during the Saturnalia, or festival of Saturn, many laws were formally suspended; in modern

---

[10] The criminologist Thorsten Sellin has repeatedly pointed out the need for a uniform, nation-wide system of recording crime data. The requirements of such a system are described in Thorsten Sellin, "The Uniform Criminal Statistics Act," *Journal of Criminal Law and Criminology,* 40:679–700, March-April 1950.

communities a similar "holiday from the law" is informally in force during great public festivals.

There are certain classes of persons whose "holiday from the law" amounts to a virtual year-round immunity. Minor and major public officials enjoy a high degree of informal immunity from arrest, and the policeman himself probably stands highest on the list. He rarely violates the camaraderie of the force by voluntarily becoming his brother's keeper.

A full description of the statistical distortions introduced by informal deviations from established procedure would involve nothing less than a survey of every aspect of law enforcement; it is sufficient here to point out that these distortions are present at every level at which statistics are collected, from arrest to final disposition.

LACK OF UNIFORMITY IN COLLECTING AND RECORDING TECHNIQUES. An indispensable requirement for a reliable system of crime statistics is a clear and uniform definition of the *unit for counting*. Tallying the number of known crimes and criminals is considerably more complicated than would appear on the surface because the definition of the same criminal behavior may undergo several transformations in the course of the enforcement process. For example, a victim may complain of a robbery within his home; in "crimes known to the police," the complaint is recorded as a robbery. The offender is captured and an entry is made in the column headed "crimes cleared by arrest." Now the prosecutor enters the picture. Perhaps the criminal is a multiple offender and the prosecutor decides he should be "put away for good." The prosecutor decides to prepare an indictment squeezing the last drop of criminal liability out of the robber's offense: he is charged with breaking and entering, with carrying a dangerous weapon, with armed robbery—and with whatever else seems applicable. At this phase, too, statistics may be taken. But now a new complication arises. The robber has considerable information about a notorious group of unapprehended criminals. With a little bargaining, he might be persuaded to "sing." Negotiations are opened. The offender's price is high, but the value of his commodity is higher. A conference is held with the victim. The higher virtues of charity are extolled; with a little persuasion, the victim discovers that he is interested more in rehabilitation than in vengeance. In the end the robber is allowed to plead to a charge of illegal entry by night. He is found guilty, but sentence is suspended. As a result of his information, several criminals are apprehended and convicted. Whatever other questions may be raised concerning these proceedings, there can be no question that the statistics of the case have become hopelessly confused.

The F. B. I., which has had to struggle with these problems in collecting statistics for its *Uniform Crime Reports,* has devised the following tallying rules for contributing agencies:

1. If the person is charged with more than one offense (several counts), he is carried as one "person charged" and classified according to the charge which comes first in the classification.
2. If the same person is apprehended and charged on separate occasions (days) for different offenses, each occasion is carried as one "person charged."
3. If two or more persons are charged with committing one offense, each is carried as a separate "person charged."
4. If a person fails to respond to a summons... and in consequence is arrested, only one charge is counted (one arrest)....[11]

In the tallying of *offenses* (as contrasted with offenders) the F. B. I. uses two methods, one for *crimes against the person,* the other for *crimes against property:*

For offenses against the person (criminal homicide, rape and aggravated assault) the general rule is to count one offense for each person against whom an offense is committed. In other words, the number of offenses reported and scored should be equal to the number of persons unlawfully killed, raped, maimed, wounded or assaulted, plus the number of attempts, with the exception that attempted homicides are scored as aggravated assaults. A typical offense is murder; if one person murders three persons, then three offenses must be entered under felonious homicide; on the other hand, if three persons murder one person, only one offense would be listed.

For offenses against property, the method of counting these does not depend so much upon the number of victims as it does upon the number of separate and distinct operations which have been undertaken. [Thus, in the case of a person who broke and entered and *then* robbed, two offenses would be scored.][12]

Sources of Error in the Presentation of Crime Statistics

In statistics there is probably no assertion more misleading than the frequently heard statement: "The figures speak for themselves." Because long columns of figures convey an impression of factuality, it is essential to discuss some of the more common misunderstandings that arise out of the faulty presentation of data.

[11] *Ten Years of Uniform Crime Reporting,* p. 11.
[12] *Ibid.,* pp. 12–13.

MISLEADING USE OF SIMPLE SUMS RATHER THAN RATES. The fact that Town A records 5,000 major crimes as compared with 10,000 reported by Town B does not necessarily mean that Town B is twice as crime-ridden as Town A. The reverse may be true. If Town B has four times the population of Town A, the reverse *is* true. Total crime figures do not become meaningful indications of the extent of crime until they are transformed into *rates* (ratios or percentages) based on the total population under consideration. This principle applies similarly to changes in the incidence of crime. Town C, in 1956, may have twice as many crimes as it had in 1920—yet its population may have doubled during this period. If this is true, the rate of crime remains the same.

MISLEADING USE OF AVERAGES AND PERCENTAGES. The elementary precaution of translating simple sums into averages and percentages does not assure the proper presentation of data; these measures can be as misleading as the raw totals. Consider the following statement: "The average family income on Sugarloaf Hill is $25,000 a year." This statement gives the unmistakable impression that the families living on Sugarloaf Hill make approximately—a little more or a little less—the stated mean figure. But this assumption may not be correct at all. A count reveals four families living on the hill. Three of these earn $4,000, $5,000, and $6,000 respectively, while the fourth earns $85,000 a year. Thus the "average" figure obtained by adding all earnings and dividing by 4 is arithmetically accurate but misleading.

As the illustration demonstrates, an *average* is meaningless in the absence of information about the *variation among the measures composing it.* The importance of this principle may be seen in an actual example taken from a recent statistical survey of juvenile delinquency. A 1953 Youth Board survey[13] of juveniles arrested between the ages of five and fifteen years of age in New York City revealed the following rates for each borough:

Delinquency Rates per 1,000 Youths (1950 Census)	
All boroughs	27.3
Bronx	30.4
Brooklyn	24.0
Manhattan	39.6
Queens	18.9
Richmond	25.1

[13] Research Department of the New York City Youth Board, *Juvenile Delinquency Rates: 1953.*

On the basis of these figures we might simply assert that the chances of becoming a delinquent between the ages of five and fifteen varied from 18.9 in a thousand if the child lived in Queens to 39.6 in a thousand if the child lived in Manhattan. However, a closer look at the area rates *within* the individual boroughs would raise serious questions about this statement. In one Manhattan neighborhood the rate was as high as 96.7 in a thousand. In a nearby neighborhood, not more than a mile away, the rate was as low as 3.4 in a thousand. In the borough of Queens the neighborhood-to-neighborhood rates varied from a low of 5.9 to a high of 54.5 in a thousand.

Any reader familiar with studies of juvenile delinquency would immediately question whether these rates reflect *actual delinquency* in the neighborhoods cited. Putting this question aside for a moment and limiting consideration exclusively to *arrests for delinquency*, we discover that the statistical chances of delinquency within one borough may vary as much as 30 to 1, depending on whether the child lives in one neighborhood or in another close by. In the face of this variation, any total rate for the entire borough must be carefully qualified.

Statisticians have evolved techniques for evaluating the significance of differences between averages; descriptions of these techniques are available in most statistical manuals. For our more general purposes it is sufficient to state the general rule that the significance of differences *between* averages declines sharply as variations *within* the compared populations increase.

PITFALLS OF GRAPHIC PRESENTATION. Long columns of figures are frequently more than impressive; to some readers they are downright intimidating. For this reason, statisticians and publicists often present their findings in graphic or pictorial form. This method relies on quick, easy-to-comprehend techniques, which are potentially highly misleading. Consider, as an example, the following hypothetical—but by no means fanciful—presentation of the "same" data by two rival newspapers.

Election time is near, and neither of these competing journals will be outdone in its objective presentation of the law-enforcement achievements of the current administration. *The Daily Hue and Cry* takes a dim view of the administration's crime-fighting record, and supports its criticism with the graph shown in the figure on page 65. The pro-administration newspaper, *The Daily Whitewash*, presents a quite different interpretation of the same statistics.

Each of the other common techniques of graphic presentation—the bar graph, the belt graph, the pie diagram, and the pictorial chart—is susceptible to analogous forms of distortion. In effect, a picture is not always worth a thousand words.

Sources of Error in the Interpretation of Crime Statistics

THE "SELF-EVIDENT" CONCLUSION. A statistical study that has somehow survived the pitfalls of collection and presentation may well founder on the reefs of erroneous interpretation. It should be recalled that statistics are merely presentations of data in numerical form. Like other kinds of data, they cannot be trusted to speak for themselves—or to suggest hypotheses, however "self-evident" on the surface. A valid statistic is merely a statement that certain measurable events have occurred; it is never an explanation of *how* or *why* these events came about. An immediate inference from the *what* to the *how* or *why* of a statistic is an unwarranted leap from the known to the unknown. Consider the following examples:

According to the *Uniform Crime Reports* of September, 1955,[14] 93 per cent of all reported murders were cleared by arrest in 1954. The percentages of arrest clearance for negligent manslaughter, rape, and aggravated assault were 88.0 per cent, 75.8 per cent, and 76.6 per cent respectively. During the same year in which these high percentages of clearance were recorded, the following low percentages of arrest clearance were reported for property offenses: robbery, 40.6 per cent; burglary, 29.6 per cent; larceny, 20.9 per cent; auto-theft, 27.5 per cent.

Moving from *offenses cleared by arrest* to *persons found guilty* of these types of offenses, we encounter a striking reversal: 67 per cent of all persons charged with murder, 42.5 per cent of persons charged with negligent manslaughter, 66.7 per cent of those charged with rape, and 49.5 per cent of those charged with aggravated assault were found guilty. Property offenders, on the other hand, fared considerably worse in court. Eighty per cent, 78.1 per cent and 65.0 per cent of all persons charged respectively with robbery, burglary, and larceny were found guilty. A comparison of the arrest and conviction figures for property and personal offenses indicates that the police arrested a larger proportion of personal offenders than they did property offenders. The courts, however, convicted a relatively larger proportion of arrested property offenders and a relatively smaller proportion of arrested personal offenders.

[14] *Uniform Crime Reports*, 26, No. 1 (1955), p. 2.

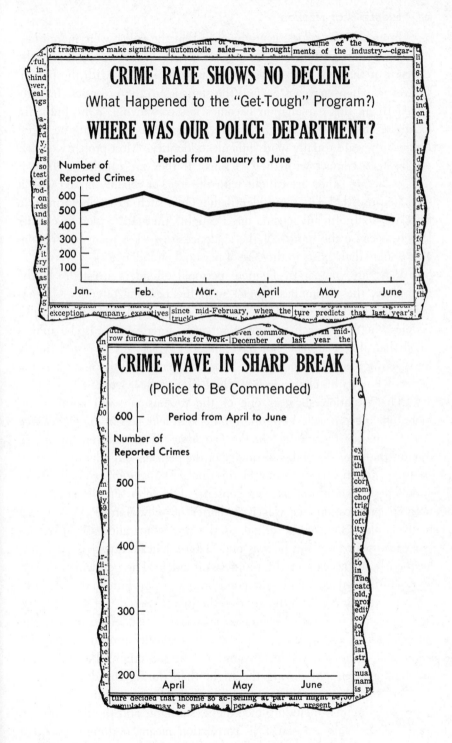

CRIME RATE SHOWS NO DECLINE

(What Happened to the "Get-Tough" Program?)

WHERE WAS OUR POLICE DEPARTMENT?

Number of Reported Crimes

Period from January to June

600
500
400
300
200
100

Jan.   Feb.   Mar.   April   May   June

CRIME WAVE IN SHARP BREAK

(Police to Be Commended)

600   Period from April to June

Number of Reported Crimes

500

400

300

200

April   May   June

From these statistics, it might seem that the police were more interested in protecting life than they were in protecting property, while the concern of the courts was more with property and less with the person. However, when one goes beyond the statistics to the processes that produced them, this explanation becomes less convincing. One finds, for example, that property offenders are generally more difficult to arrest because they are usually more difficult to identify. Most property offenders have no contact with their victims. If they are caught at all, it is usually because they are caught with the loot, or reliably linked with it —or because they left some identifiable clue, such as a fingerprint or a burglar's tool. In any event, once caught, they are easier to convict largely because the nature of the evidence leaves less room for "reasonable doubt" than exists in the case of personal offenders.

Why are comparatively more personal offenders arrested? In the first place, the victim has contact with the personal offender—he has *seen* him. In the second place, many offenses against the person involve people who knew each other beforehand. Finally, it must be understood that almost anyone can have almost anybody else arrested simply by swearing out a charge against him. In many assault cases, it is the person who gets his charge in first who becomes the "victim."

This situation suggests one of the reasons personal offenses are more difficult to prove. *Very often the person who gets in the first charge is the same person who got in the first blow.* The requirement of reasonable doubt works to the advantage of the personal offender much more frequently than it does to that of the thief. Was the girl actually raped —or did she tacitly indicate her consent? Did John actually attack Jim without provocation—or was it a matter of self-defense? Was Frank really at the scene of the crime, as the prosecutor alleges? There are ten witnesses who claim he was not. These delicate questions arise less frequently in the case of the property offender. The gentleman discovered with a mink coat and a diamond bracelet in his bureau drawer finds it difficult to stir doubt in the mind of the jury.

THE CONFUSION OF CORRELATION WITH CAUSE. One of the subspecies of the self-evident truth is the "statistically proved" cause. Innumerable factors have been found to vary together. Burglaries are much more frequent during the night than during the day. For this very reason, they are also statistically related to anything else that happens at night—including moonlight, starlight, and the dews of evening. Taken alone, a statistical correlation means nothing more than the coincidence of two or more events in a given space or time. It signifies nothing about causes and effects; the answers to these questions must be induced or inferred from a knowledge of processes.

There is little danger of a new explanation of night-burglary in terms of moon-madness; the hypothesis is much too implausible. On the other hand, many correlations in criminological research have led to the incorrect assumption of causality simply because of their plausibility. The attribution of criminality to low intelligence was accepted for a long time largely because the low test scores of most offenders suited a contemporary bias about the stupidity of lawbreaking. Similarly, theories accounting for criminality in terms of physical disease, left-handedness, and even hair color have been advanced on the basis of statistical correlations.

The Problem of Biased Sampling

The unwarranted assumption of causality is frequently supported by another source of error: biased sampling. Since it is impossible to compile exhaustive data on all offenders, it is necessary to deal with relatively small numbers—*samples*. But it is unsafe to generalize from a sample to a larger population unless the sample is truly representative of that population. There are two general ways of obtaining unbiased samples: selecting them entirely at random or choosing them with the utmost care to assure their representativeness.

Many criminological studies have been based on biased samples— on groups in which some factors of uncontrolled selectivity were at work. In a larger sense, nearly all crime statistics have a built-in bias, since they are based exclusively on offenders who have been convicted— a sample amounting to probably no more than 5 to 10 per cent of the total number of those breaking the law. Nevertheless, within this population of convicted offenders, valid research is possible provided careful sampling methods are used. Much criminological research is concerned with discovering what personal or situational factors distinguish people who become criminals—or, more correctly, *prisoners*—from persons who do not. If these comparisons are to be valid—if they are to compare what they are purporting to compare—it is essential that the members of both groups be reasonably typical of the groups as a whole. When this precaution is not taken, the results are bound to be misleading.

The technical procedures used to assure proper sampling cannot be discussed in this text. Nevertheless, even without a knowledge of these procedures, it is possible to make broad evaluations of statistical data provided one caution is kept in mind. A statistic is merely the presentation of an observation in numerical terms. It is neither more nor less reliable or valid than the operations that determined how the observation was carried out. Until the reader can satisfy himself of the soundness of the methods that produced the statistic, the wisest approach is a reasoned skepticism.

CRIME, LAW, AND SOCIAL CONTROL

Ways of Social Control

IN THE BROADEST SENSE, THE PROBLEMS OF CRIMINOLOGY FALL WITHIN the larger problem of social control. Criminologists and penologists deal with the behavior of those who attempt to assert and those who attempt to evade social rules. Since social rules, in a myriad of subtle ways, pervade virtually every aspect of individual and group life, it is difficult to represent their variety and complexity within the limits of a single definition. For this reason the concept *social control* is almost impossible to define in a way that distinguishes it from other concepts. Consider the following definition and discussion of social control taken from a modern text on the subject:

> *Social control is a collective term for those processes, planned or un-planned, by which individuals are taught, persuaded, or compelled to conform to the usages and life-values of groups.* Social control occurs when one group determines the behavior of another group, when the group controls the conduct of its own members, or when individuals influence the responses of others.[1]

Given this definition, the question naturally arises, What is there in social life that is *not* related to social control? Manners, morals, art,

[1] Joseph S. Roucek, *Social Control* (New York: D. Van Nostrand Company, 1947), p. 3.

fashion, religion, philosophy, social change, social stagnation, history itself—all may be viewed as clashes between those trying to assert old ways against new ways, dogmas against novel ideas, old patterns of power against new patterns.[2]

The issue is, in fact, more fundamental. To ask why anyone behaves as he does is, in one sense, to inquire why the person either conforms or fails to conform to a certain standard, a certain *accepted way* with which the questioner is acquainted. Thus, to be bad is to violate a standard definition of what is good, proper, or socially demanded. Those who set up these standards are asserting a kind of social control by the act of definition alone.

Because of the broad scope of social control, it is necessary to specify those aspects which are relevant to our subject. Since the primary focus of criminology is on violations of a special kind of social control—criminal laws—our first task is to isolate law as a specific type of social control and to compare it with other types.

Law as a Form of Social Control

There is a vast literature devoted to the history, philosophy, sociology, and anthropology of law, much of it concerned with distinguishing law from other forms of social control from which it may have evolved. In their book, *The Cheyenne Way*,[3] the legal scholar Karl Llewellyn and the anthropologist E. Adamson Hoebel single out four

[2] The discussion of law, crime, and social control in this chapter will confine itself largely to the processes relating law and custom to each other and to the individual. The broader study of the subject extends beyond these questions, examining the various media of communication and influence, and investigating how these media affect the general atmosphere from which conformity and deviation arise. Included in this broader study would be a discussion of the press, radio, television and the movies, and the advertising industry, among many others. The specific effect of these agents of influence on individuals may be difficult to demonstrate, but their importance in vividly suggesting patterns of emulation and avoidance cannot be doubted. The attitudes emphasized throughout these media are both stimuli and responses to the climate of public opinion. The study of the selective sensitivity of certain age and class groups to their influence is an important part of the broader study of crime in contemporary society.

[3] Karl N. Llewellyn and Adamson E. Hoebel, *The Cheyenne Way* (Norman: The University of Oklahoma Press, 1941).

distinguishing characteristics of law as contrasted with other social processes:

1. Laws are a part of the normative structure of a society; they define what is commanded and what is forbidden. In defining what is commanded, they identify obligations and duties which the social order insists on being followed despite any obstacles or contrary reasons. In defining what is forbidden and offensive, they identify those values and interests which the society insists on defending at all costs.

2. This aspect of insistence is revealed by the fact that laws involve sanctions—punishments—if they are not obeyed. They have teeth; they impose "musts" and "must not's" which are to be followed "or else"....

3. In cases of conflict or confusion with other social interests or norms, the legal rule must "win out" if it is to be considered truly lawful in the sense of actually influencing the course of affairs.

4. Laws form a part of a manifold legal system having an underlying philosophy—which may be more or less clearly articulated—a more or less consistent system of procedures, and a more or less organized and recognized body of officials to administer them.

Each of these four characteristics is essential for the differentiation of *the legal* from the other normative aspects of a social order. The first two characteristics are relatively obvious, since they may be discovered in the wording of any law; the second pair is less obvious and cannot be verified except by examining the conditions under which given laws are administered. The requirement that laws must "win out" when challenged helps to distinguish law-in-action from statutes that are merely "on the books" but are either unused or evaded with impunity. In every polity of any historical duration, there are unrepealed laws that represent the efforts of earlier inhabitants to defend customs long superseded by newer, more liberal usages. Because they are rarely, if ever, enforced, these laws may be considered purely "formal" and obsolete. On the other hand, in certain specific localities, laws that were recently enforced with vigor may suddenly lose their vital force as a result of political corruption.

The assertion that *the legal* reflects an underlying philosophy and represents a systematic application of established procedures distinguishes binding laws and legal decisions from those that may later be overturned. A law that violates a more basic legal or political value may be discarded as unconstitutional. Similarly, a decision that violates the rights of the accused or is based on false or improperly admitted evidence may be reversed by a higher legal authority. In either case what was formerly legal is no longer so; it has not "won out."

Law in the Broader Fabric of Social Control

Despite their great number, the part played by laws in the over-all drama of social control and in the enforcement of conformity may be surprisingly small. This probability is underscored when one attempts to answer the question: In what aspects of living is there most conformity? More specifically, what are the kinds of social rules that are almost never violated? It is significant that most of the examples that come to mind are in realms of behavior regulated largely by convention, propriety, and manners.

In every society there are scores of rules and usages that virtually no one violates. Though many of these usages apply to the incidental details of day-to-day existence, others govern the most basic processes of personal and social life—yet the great majority are not enforced by law. Rules of personal cleanliness, especially in the area of toilet training; rules defining certain forms of behavior as appropriate only to one sex and not to the other; rules defining the clothing appropriate to the different sexes—few of these are violated, and most of them are not even formally set down. Nevertheless, they are not only binding but highly coercive, in that their violation brings quick and peculiarly painful consequences. These consequences, though nowhere formulated in a book of rules, may be more punitive and distressing than many legal punishments.

Imagine a reckless and ruthless criminal—a man who would not hesitate to risk his own life or the lives of others in the pursuit of some criminal purpose. How would he react if he were sentenced to walk along Main Street clad in a pair of children's knee pants—or wearing a pair of earrings? Neither of these activities would entail any particular physical suffering; nevertheless, in all probability, this man, who would confront the ultimate terrors of the State, would cringe at such an exposure to public amusement. Take another case: Which of these two rumors is more terrifying—the rumor that one has stolen property, or the gossip that one's sexual preferences are dubious? The chances are that most people would consider the public suspicion of homosexuality more terrifying. These examples suggest that the dread of humiliation or embarrassment, the fear of being "talked about" or "made a laughing stock" may, in many instances, be a more potent deterrent to action than the fear of the organized, more remote and impersonal power of the state.

Significantly, many of the rules enforced by these nonlegal sanctions govern behavior not only in public but in private as well. There are certain things we cannot do—or allow to happen—even when we are totally alone: an accidental violation of toilet training, for example. As in the case of toilet training, many of these personally intolerable behaviors were tabooed in childhood, and their occurrence brings feelings of horror, nausea, and self-loathing. Many crimes fail to inspire such reactions, either in the criminal or in the public at large. The gangster may spread fear and indignation, but few people would think of belittling him. On the contrary, there are probably some who secretly envy his audacity—and his success, if he evades punishment and is able to enjoy the fruits of his labors. Here, then is another important difference between the consequences of violating many laws and many social conventions. Unlike the successful criminal, the person who "successfully" commits bad manners in public can hope for no particular reward.[4] The best he can hope for is to avoid derogatory public notice. The violation of criminal laws, on the other hand, can be quite rewarding—if the criminal is successful. By contrast, there may be no particular reward in merely being law-abiding. "You don't get rich by not stealing," says the thief, pointing to his poor but honest neighbor, "and nobody gives you a medal just for being good."

This last point—the possible reward of criminal violations as opposed to the nonrewarding character of other violations—may shed some light on the question, Why do certain social rules require teeth? We have already discussed the fact that the consequences of noncriminal deviations may be painful in ways that are often intimately distasteful and disturbing. Accordingly, most of the prohibitions defined by custom and convention are restraints people tend to impose on themselves. By contrast, the things forbidden by law are not necessarily things we would not want to do under any circumstances. It is not difficult to imagine situations in which we might desire someone else's property, might want to relieve our temper by assaulting someone, might want to deceive or take advantage of another. Putting the matter bluntly—and, perhaps, too simply: *If a breach of convention is something I would not want to*

---

[4] Oscar Wilde once underscored this point by suggesting that crime would become unpopular only when it came to be looked on as vulgar.

do to myself, a crime is something I might want to do to you, but would never want YOU to do to me. The possibility that YOU might want to do any of these things to ME arouses fear and indignation, and in order to prevent or punish you, I am prepared to call on physical force.

Law as a Response to the Breakdown of Other Social Controls

The readiness to use force, a distinguishing aspect of legal norms, need not disguise the fact that this extreme form of social control is necessary because the usually more effective nonforceful means have failed. Viewed in these terms, law stands out less as an optimal exercise than as a last resort of social control. The legalization of custom—the putting of "teeth" into previously nonforceful norms—identifies areas of strain rather than strength in the social structure. In effect, to know the social values that require legal forcefulness is to locate those values that are under attack or subversion; the law is needed to defend what is too weak to defend itself.

The view that interprets the emergence of new laws out of old customs as symptomatic of the weakening of social control is supported by many anthropological studies of societies striving to preserve their cultural autonomy against pressures of assimilation. In a study titled *"Controlled Acculturation: A Survival Technique of the Hutterites,"*[5] Joseph Eaton has described the attempts of a minority group to maintain its traditional ways under the impact of modern out-group influences. The Hutterites are descendants of an old Anabaptist sect which settled in various unpopulated sections of North America in the 1880's in the hope of practicing their distinctive religious and social customs in the security of an isolated, neighborless land. The core of their doctrine was simplicity, austerity, and strict communal ownership. As the neighboring areas became inhabited, the Hutterite community was forced into a series of battles and strategic accommodations with influences threatening to subvert its traditional austerity. Between the early 1900's and 1930's the community resisted but finally succumbed to such innovations as color in dress, buttons (instead of hooks) on clothing, motorized vehicles, and factory-made mattresses. In 1933 the elders

[5] Joseph W. Eaton, "Controlled Acculturation: A Survival Technique of the Hutterites," *American Sociological Review,* 17:331–340, June 1952.

staged a desperate rear-guard action against sweaters and other clinging garments which reveal the human form, asserting that "they do not belong to our world and only lead to improper dealings," and adding the threat: "He who does not obey shall have his [offending garments] taken away and burned."[6]

A significant feature of this resistance was that the elders felt the need to respond to each new threat by translating previously unwritten but well-observed customs into formal rules with definite punishments for violators. As Eaton has pointed out:

> New rules... are usually proposed at an intercolony meeting of elected lay preachers, and are intended to combat a specific innovation... which some of the preachers regard as a violation of the unwritten mores. The new practice must be more than an isolated deviation of the sort which is controlled effectively through the normal processes of community discipline—punishment of the offender by admonition, standing up in church, and temporary ritual excommunication. Only when a deviation becomes widespread in one or more colonies are the leaders likely to appeal for a formal statement of the unwritten community code.[7]

The emergence of law from custom-in-decay finds illustration not only in historical examples of the type described above but in the minute-by-minute transactions of people in crowds. During the subway rush hours in New York City, large numbers of subway riders collect in front of the change booths provided for customers who lack the special coins ("tokens") required for the turnstiles leading to the trains. Courtesy requires that each newcomer go to the end of the line formed in front of the change booth to wait his turn. No one enforces this custom; the subway employee making change from behind an iron grille is intent on speed and accuracy and will usually respond to any coin thrust into his window by any hand. Consequently, in order for the custom of "lining up for change" to operate smoothly, it must be enforced voluntarily by each person. Occasionally, however, a newcomer, more impatient or less considerate than the rest, ignores the line and goes directly to the booth.

At this point a variety of things may happen. *a*) No one protests or takes any action—in this case the custom, violated and undefended, becomes inoperative. *b*) Someone in the line may protest, putting into words the previously unvoiced rule about waiting in line. At this point the rule has undergone a kind of legalistic reformulation but is not yet

---

[6] *Ibid.*, p. 337.
[7] *Ibid.*, p. 334.

"law" because it still lacks an enforcer. The offender may or may not respond to this protest; if he responds by going to the end of the line, the custom has survived both the threat and the need for translation into "law." However, if the violator refuses to respond, the custom must become law or perish. c) It becomes "law" when a member of the crowd challenges the violator and forces him to withdraw.

The critical point in this example is the fact that external coercion was required for the enforcement of a rule which the troublemaker had not enforced upon himself—and which the group was unable to enforce by customary means. Something had to be done in order to resolve the trouble; since the troublemaker did not do it himself, someone else was needed. In primitive societies, where nothing approaching organized government exists, this "enforcer" may be virtually anyone acting with the support or tacit approval of the group. Hoebel cites an example in which the "enforcer" was the offender's own mother. The widow Kullabak, a Greenland Eskimo, had a boy who was chronically getting into trouble by lying, insulting people, and stealing:

> ... So she [the mother] asked Maryak [a neighbor] to get rid of the boy, and Maryak took the boy and pushed him down in a crevasse.... Kullabak went into traditional mourning, but her mourning was pretty effectively interrupted when the boy came walking into the house. By some miracle he had escaped death in the fall and had followed the crevasse to its portal near the sea.
>
> After that, no one dared to touch him and the boy played all manner of tricks to revenge himself.... His mother was at her wit's end, and finally decided that if she wanted to save the honor of her house she must do something desperate. One night while he was asleep... she made a sealskin-line noose, slipped it over his head and pulled it tight.
>
> Thus ended the criminal pranks of one young man, and his mother was highly honored for her good deed. Now she was remarried, and her great, booming voice was always an asset at parties.[8]

The Place of Punishment: A Theoretical Dilemma

One of the more thought-provoking implications of the incident related above was that the motive for the execution was not revenge or

[8] Peter Freuchen, *Arctic Adventure: My Life in the Frozen North* (New York: Rinehart and Company, 1935). Cited in Adamson E. Hoebel, *The Law of Primitive Man* (Cambridge: Harvard University Press, 1954), p. 91. © 1954 by the President and Fellows of Harvard University.

punishment. The child had repeatedly engaged in behavior which, as Hoebel has pointed out, "raised him to the status of the not-to-be-borne-any-longer." Since he did not change, something had to be done to get rid of him. In effect, he was tolerated—apparently without much interference—until he became intolerable, when he was permanently removed. The relative absence of intervening punitive alternatives between passive toleration and outright expulsion or execution seems to be typical of many primitive societies. In 1914 the sociologist Ellsworth Faris wrote:

> There is abundant reason for questioning whether any one inside the primitive group was ever punished, at least by those within his own tribe.... Present-day people of some uncivilized tribes do not punish their children. The writer, during a residence of several years among the Bantus of the upper Congo river... failed to observe a single case of the punishment of a child.... The child in a small community that is homogeneous and in a situation where outside influences do not penetrate, will find himself fitting in to the social situation where he grows up and is without the stimulus to commit acts of an anti-social character.
>
> And when, by any chance, such an act is committed, it is highly improbable that it will arouse any resentment whatsoever; in the event that it does there is no remedy, and the tribe simply does nothing save where the offense is so serious as to break all bounds. The situation is analogous to that in which one breaks or damages his own property by accident; it is regrettable, but there is no remedy save an imprecation.
>
> ... Those who have assigned the dominant part in early group control to force, physically understood,... have failed to understand that the sneer and scorn of those within their own group are infinitely more powerful forces....[9]

The observations of Faris have since been repeated by many anthropologists. Wissler, for example, has stated:

> Chastising the young seems to have been practiced in the centres of higher culture, but outside of these limits was practically unknown.... In fact, the whole control of the local group in aboriginal days seems to have been exercised by admonition and mild ridicule instead of by force and punishment.[10]

And Ruth Benedict has remarked:

> Punishment is very commonly regarded as quite outside the realm of possibility, and natives in many parts of the world have drawn the con-

[9] Ellsworth Faris, "The Origin of Punishment," *International Journal of Ethics*, 25:54–67, 1914–15.
[10] Clark Wissler, *The American Indian* (New York: Oxford University Press, 1922), p. 189.

clusion from our usual disciplinary methods that white parents do not love their children.[11]

Parents in many of these societies not only refrain from physically chastising their children but, apparently, are willing to tolerate a good deal of aggression by them. In this connection, Benedict cites an anecdote told her by the noted Indian scholar, George Devereux, about the present-day Mohave. A child had been disobedient and had struck his father:

> The child's mother was white and protested to its father that he must take action.... "But why?" the father said, "he is little. He cannot possibly injure me." He [the father] did not know of any dichotomy according to which an adult expects obedience and a child must accord it. If his child had been docile he would simply have judged that it would become a docile adult—an eventuality of which he would not have approved.[12]

These attitudes and procedures are in striking contrast to the orientation current in complex modern societies, where punishment—the deliberate infliction of suffering—is traditionally defended as a valuable or necessary device for ensuring conformity. Nevertheless, despite the general contrast, there are significant, though isolated, parallels. In his pioneer article Faris pointed out that "there are groups organized within civilized society which are so thoroughly social that there is no thought of punishment within the circle, as for example, a college faculty or a social club."[13] The social controls functioning to maintain conformity in these homogeneous groups are similar to those found in primitive societies. To most faculty members it would be intolerable to punish one of their own group and then permit him to remain. Once again, as in the primitive group, there appear to be few alternatives between passive toleration and expulsion.

Nevertheless, in the faculty group and the social club, as in the primitive society, individual members do mistreat and offend each other, creating crises that must be resolved. It is at this point that the differences between the machinery of informal group control and the machinery of punitive justice stand out most strikingly. In the political community, when one individual injures or offends another, the state—representing the group—combines with the victim in visiting punish-

---

[11] Ruth Benedict, "Continuities and Discontinuities in Cultural Conditioning," *Psychiatry*, 1:164, May 1938.
[12] *Ibid.*
[13] Faris, *op. cit.*, p. 165.

ment on the offender, or in forcing restitution from him. In the homogeneous group the victim and the other group members combine to induce the offender to feel shame and guilt—i.e., *to punish himself.* This act of penitence makes it unnecessary for anyone in the group to take the role of punitive agent. Moreover, provided that the degree of self-punishment and guilt is somehow commensurate with the resentment of the victim, it has the further effect of resolving the victim's hostility and sense of hurt entirely. In fact, should the offender go too far in his self-punishment *the roles of victim and offender may reverse themselves, with the erstwhile victim feeling guilt for having caused excessive suffering.*

The psychological validity of these processes is well within the experience of anyone who has quarreled and then become reconciled with a friend who had mistreated him. When the offender becomes penitent and self-punitive, the anger of the offended one instantly dissolves. Nothing less than this will do; no amount of formal restitution, apology, or group condemnation will have this effect, and until it happens the offended one is likely to remain cold and bitter. When it does happen, the transformation is almost magical: *It is as if the offender, in punishing himself, is actually discharging the hostility felt toward him by his friend.*[14]

These events are the commonplaces of human experience everywhere, and in primitive societies they tend to find a more direct and spontaneous expression in social institutions. Even in modern communities philosophers and religious thinkers have continued to stress the superior effectiveness of personal penance over punishment inflicted from without. The term *penitentiary* itself symbolizes this persisting

[14] The universality of this experience may account for the difficulty in grasping the full thrust of its implications. What is involved seems to go beyond such processes as "identification," "empathy," and "taking the role of the other." Although these and similar concepts attempt to deal with the subtle flow of feelings and the apparent blurring of the boundaries of the self between intimates, they fail to cope with an even more remarkable phenomenon. Why is it that the offending one, in punishing himself, seems able to effect the discharge of certain feelings in the other—feelings that the offended one would not have been able to discharge even if he had personally retaliated against the offender? Friends do retaliate, but the result is neither satisfactory nor similar. The question remains: *Why is it that no amount of counter-hostility can ease the feeling of hurt which is instantly eased when the offender becomes hostile toward himself?* And why is it that the only person who can accomplish this is the offender himself—rather than an external punitive agent? These events suggest processes operating at the most nuclear level of human experience—processes as yet unexplained by any current theory of personality.

insight that reformation is necessarily a personal and interior experience, involving some kind of conquest by the individual over himself—a conquest making his subjugation by others both irrelevant and unnecessary.

Implications for the Evaluation of Punitive Techniques of Social Control

It may be useful, at this point, to summarize some of the implications that have emerged from the discussion so far. There are two general ways in which the social order maintains conformity and copes with the problems arising when individuals deviate in ways that injure or offend others. One way relies largely on the individual's enforcing social rules upon himself. The person is, in effect, his own policeman, and if he violates, he becomes his own punisher. The second way, which appears to have arisen in response to a breakdown of the first, relies on the threat of punishment to prevent violations, and on the application of suffering or restraint to incapacitate the offender or to deter him in the future.

Each of these methods of control relies on different psychological and sociological processes to achieve its purposes, and each has characteristic effects. The first way relies on a high degree of emotional responsiveness between the member and the group, which renders the person peculiarly vulnerable to a wide range of subtle control processes having the effect of making his own feelings of security and self-worth dependent on the evaluation of others. Psychologists have used the term *identification, ego-involvement,* and *internalization* to label the processes by which the individual incorporates the group's values, attitudes, and prohibitions into his own mind, and they have used the terms *empathy* and *introjection* to refer to the universal but still mysterious ways in which he spontaneously mirrors the reactions of other group members in his own feelings toward himself.

The second method of control aims at impressing the person with the power of the group and with its capacity to hurt him. The principal psychological processes relied on are awe and fear rather than shame and guilt. There is no attempt to maintain the continuity of mutual responsiveness; on the contrary, the group tends to isolate the individual both in a psychological and a social sense, creating a polarity of feeling in which the group expresses indignation and rejection and the offender feels powerless and unsupported.

This polarization is in sharp contrast to the feelings produced among the members of the homogeneous group. When they learn that one of their number has committed an offense, they are likely to feel shame and humiliation—*the same feelings experienced by the offender.* It is almost as if they too are somewhat to blame, and they tend to view the event more as a mutual calamity than as an individual outrage. In this sense, the identification works both ways, and unless the offense is shocking beyond bounds—i.e. *beyond the limits of what they might imagine themselves doing under similar stress*—the solidarity of the individual and the group is preserved.

The different techniques used by the two methods of social control are appropriate to their different objectives. The main objective of the first way is to restore the group solidarity existing before the offense, and this necessarily includes a restoration of good feeling between the offender and the offended. Care is exercised to prevent the alienation created by the offense from being increased by a counter-offensive act against the offender. Thus, the major emphasis is not on justice—the equalization of suffering—but on the discharge of the feelings of guilt and resentment, which stand in the way of restoring the mutual responsiveness that existed before. This discharge of alienating feelings is accomplished in that remarkable and mysterious process by which the offender, in spontaneously and sincerely showing penitence (i.e., punishing himself), is able, simultaneously, to discharge his own guilt and to dissolve the hurt and resentment of the offended. The use of graded punishments, by which the offender is progressively alienated from the group and by means of which the victim discharges only his hostility but not his feelings of hurt, is avoided; the idea of "making the punishment fit the crime" is rejected. It is recognized, on the contrary, that all efforts must be bent toward preserving the offender's accessibility to group influence and toward the prevention of any further alienation. If these efforts fail, there is no further dallying with him; once he is considered to have "hardened his heart," he is physically expelled.

By way of contrast, it is the effect, if not the intention, of punishment in modern political communities to produce psychological alienation in the offender *while still keeping him physically within the group.* Hence, though physically permitted to remain, he has no psychological recourse but to seek another group membership. In most cases the only available group is the collective of other outcasts: the criminal group.

The point to be made is this: expulsion, whether it takes the form of physical exile or psychological rejection, is an ultimate sanction. Once it has been applied, the person is no longer a member of the group even though he remains physically within it. It is no longer a medium through which he can realize personal fulfillment.

Moreover, once the person is psychologically expelled, the group is no longer a medium of effective, nonforceful social control. The fine network of psychological interconnection is broken. The person is no longer responsive to the subtle pressures of inducement and inhibition that play on the others; a hide toughened by the ultimate blow of rejection loses its sensitivity. Consequently, he is more immune to those control processes that translate the group's reactions into the individual's own response to himself.

And this is precisely the problem. For, in releasing the prisoner to the community, in liberating him from forceful restraint, society is taking the gamble that he will now respond to less forceful measures of social control—i.e., to the pressures against which he has already acquired a relative immunity. This, in fine, is the theoretical and practical dilemma of formal punishment.[15]

Law as a Direct Contributor to Crime

The foregoing pages of this chapter have been concerned chiefly with what might be called the *positive relations* between social control, law, and the repression of crime. These relations may be described as "positive" because they represent attempts to translate public opinion into effective measures for the prevention and punishment of lawbreaking. Some of the dilemmas that tend to frustrate these attempts

[15] This position is not in accord with the view that considers punishment to be the cause of crime. As has been suggested in the foregoing discussion, punishment is too complex a concept to be related to any behavior in a direct or simple manner. The more significant distinction seems to be between punishment or pain inflicted from without and punishment inflicted by the offender upon himself in the form of guilt and penitence. As Faris and others have pointed out, the disapproval of the group—even when it does not reject the member—can be more painful than formal punishment in the sense that it "gets through" to the offender more intimately. By contrast, the rejected or alienated member—who may not otherwise be punished—may become relatively immune to the group's reactions. In this sense he is less punished by group disapproval.

have been discussed. Nevertheless, the discussion, if concluded at this point, might leave the implication that the forces of social control and the factors making for crime are still, somehow, either inherently or necessarily opposed.

This implication would not be correct—or, at best, would present merely a reassuring half-truth. While it is certainly at least the overt intention of public opinion to repress crime, it is not always the effect. Since the realities of crime and social control deal with consequences as well as objectives, it is necessary clearly to distinguish between the two, especially when there is some suspicion that public intentions may, on occasion, not only fail of realization but themselves produce undesirable results.

The checkered history of crime control offers more than one instance of precisely such an effect—the attempt to repress a certain type of offense going beyond mere failure and contributing directly to an increase in the kind of crime it was intended to attack. The outstanding modern example of this "boomerang effect" was the attempt to limit the consumption of alcohol during the more than ten years of aggravated lawlessness known as the Prohibition Era.

It would be unthinkable to credit the early Prohibitionists with any foreknowledge that their success would inflict upon law enforcement an injury from which it has never recovered. The entire purpose of prohibition was to protect public morality, not to corrupt it. Nevertheless, it is almost universally acknowledged that the adoption of national prohibition gave organized crime an impetus whose effect has persisted even though a quarter of a century has passed since the experiment was abandoned. The attempt to forbid the sale and consumption of alcoholic beverages succeeded in bringing about a degree of intimacy and mutual tolerance and cooperation between the criminal, the ordinary citizen and the public official which has never been paralleled.[16] Within a little more than ten years the good intentions of reformers had produced a situation which one hundred and fifty years of ordinary political corruption and civic cynicism had been unable to create: in effect, the angels had succeeded where the devils had failed.

The point of present theoretical interest is this: The Prohibition

---

[16] Cf. C. E. Merriam and H. F. Gosnell, *The American Party System* (New York: The Macmillan Company, 1950), pp. 273–274: ". . . the repeal of the Prohibition Amendment turned the energy of the ex-bootlegger into business racketeering. The step from political protection of illegal liquor rackets to other forms of criminal racketeering was an easy one."

Amendment was never directed against the evils it helped create. Though moonshining and bootlegging had existed in this country since colonial times, it had always been profitable to sell fermented waters legally, despite duties. The purpose of the amendment was not to stop the illegal traffic in liquor but to destroy what had been its *legal* sale. Unfortunately, the attempt to penalize the supply merely increased the demand, and the problem of supplying this demand was solved by organized crime. In the course of this process, a society with relatively strong moral feelings against alcohol (strong enough, at least, to carry the amendment) became a nation of determined tipplers almost overnight.

As this example suggests, certain types of new legislation may substantially contribute to situations out of which new crimes arise. The processes by which these effects are brought about may be summarized in the following general terms:

1. Whenever new legislation prohibits any previously legitimate activity or stops the distribution of formerly demanded goods or services without creating new legitimate channels of distribution, the former consumers have no alternative but to give up their demand or cooperate with illegal suppliers.

2. The more effective the new legislation in drying up previous legitimate sources (by enforcing the compliance of legitimate suppliers) the greater the scarcity and, therefore, the higher the market price of the prohibited goods or services.

3. The artificial inflation of the prices of these goods or services to levels far above their actual costs of production and distribution creates huge potential profits to be shared by those cooperating in evading the law. These profits are then available for the further expansion of illegal operations and for the corruption of those responsible for enforcing the law.

The self-defeating character of these laws now becomes apparent. The more rigorously they are enforced, the greater the risk to the suppliers; hence, the greater the scarcity. But the scarcity, in the face of undiminished or only slightly diminished demand, artificially inflates prices to the point where the profits potentially available create incentives outweighing the risks—especially when a portion of the profits is available for corrupting law-enforcement agencies and thereby reducing the risks. At this point, more efficient law enforcement merely increases the possibilities for corruption already inherent in the situation.

Candid police administrators often deliberately avoid rigorous enforcement of this type of law for the specific purpose of protecting their officers from corruption. A police official has put it this way:

> Sure, we know the places that book numbers—and they know we know them. What do you think would happen if we closed them up? The big operators would move in; we wouldn't know who they were until they ruined three quarters of the force. And by then we'd have a mob of big-time racketeers on our hands.[17]

As pointed out earlier in this chapter, many of the more potent forms of social control do not require the additional implementation of law. The criminal law, by definition, identifies those areas of social activity in which the informal processes of group control have required the added force of political power. The procedures by which the group mobilizes its political power to bolster its control inevitably influence the character and success of these attempts. Consequently, a study of the ways in which the group seeks to enforce its values by law becomes an essential concern of criminology.

---

[17] The ultimate in irony is reached when corrupt police officials assist their own criminal "clients" by cracking down on other illicit suppliers in competition with them. This maneuver has a threefold advantage: It improves the police reputation for law enforcement; it increases the scarcity of the illicit goods—thereby further inflating the prices; and, finally, it improves the bargaining position of the police, who can pose the vivid threat of a similar crackdown on the surviving racketeers—thereby forcing them to increase their payments for police protection.

Principles and Implications of the Criminal Law

DISCUSSIONS OF THE CRIMINAL LAW WILL APPEAR IN SEVERAL PLACES IN this text and will be presented from three different points of view: (1) the law as a self-contained system of principles, doctrines, and rules; (2) the law as a cultural and historical product; and (3) the law as a design for community action. In the course of these discussions, the differences between the law-in-principle and the law-in-action will frequently be pointed out. Nevertheless, the purpose of dividing the presentation is not to dramatize the distance between the ideal and the real. Failure to go beyond this observation would be to miss an even more significant one.

Basic Assumptions of the Criminal Law

One of the distinguishing peculiarities of Anglo-American jurisprudence is that it makes certain deliberately and obstinately unreal assumptions about human behavior. These assumptions include the following:

1. That most people are reasonable, rational, and prudent in the pursuit of their own self-interest. To the drunken driver who explains his behavior by saying: "I didn't know what I was doing," the law answers: "That may well be, but we insist that you *should have known.* A prudent man would not have driven so fast after drinking." To the man who bases his excuse on personal stupidity and can call on his neighbors to prove it, the law answers: "You have no right to make another suffer for your stupidity." The fact that a person has been imprudent all his life, that he has always neglected his own self-interest and conscientiously pursued his own destruction, is no extenuation. The law answers: "Unless you can prove you were legally mad, we shall assume you thought you were acting for your own good."

2. That justice—i.e., judges' decisions—may be objective, impartial, and beyond social influence or pressure. This assumption deliberately ignores the fact that laws are, in the first place, responses to group pressures and represent the consensus of social opinion. It involves the further assumption that the same fallible and opinionated mortal who quarrelled unreasonably with his wife in the morning and will be grossly unfair to his best friend later that night will somehow put all these foibles off when he puts on his judicial robes at ten o'clock, and remain perfect until the court adjourns.

3. That there are certain basic and permanent moral imperatives which are ultimate, invariant, and properly superior to human intervention.

4. That it is possible to apply rules in a consistent and precise manner—and that there is only one correct application of any rule to any situation. The fact that a court may reverse itself from one year to the next in an identical situation is not assumed to refute this assumption.

5. That it is possible to establish the facts in each case. This assumption is probably the most important and the least demonstrable in all of the law. It involves, in the case of jury trials, the assumption that twelve men who have no prior acquaintance with the events of the case and were neither present nor nearby when they occurred are, nevertheless, in a better position to discover what actually happened than the participants and observers who were on the scene. The noted jurist Jerome Frank has asserted that "facts are guesses."[1] Nevertheless, the law clearly prefers a carefully considered and disinterested guess to a biased eye-witness report, since it assumes that the parties involved may

[1] Jerome Frank: *Courts on Trial: Myth and Reality in American Justice* (Princeton: Princeton University Press, 1950), p. 14.

be more interested in establishing what the facts should have been than what they actually were.

These assumptions, taken together, add up to the implication that something approaching absolute justice is attainable in this world. It is essential to note that their truth or falsity is irrelevant to the fact that judges insist on behaving *as if they were true*. Although the social utility of these assumptions has been questioned, few doubt that the attitude exists or that it is central—if not essential—to our system of justice.

Before going on to an analysis of the law as a self-contained logical system, we might examine a viewpoint held by certain legal theorists, who have argued that it is fruitless to study the "law that is in the books" because the law *in action* is merely "what the judge says it is." These theorists would replace the rational study of legal principles and doctrines with psychological and sociological studies of *how judges and juries make up their minds*.[2]

There need be little dispute that the behavior of judges and juries is an essential field for study. But to justify this study by the statement that "the law is, after all, only what the judge says it is," is to be both inaccurate and illogical. In the first place, despite all that is validly reported of "judicial legislating," it is the legislature itself which originates laws; this fact places certain limits on judicial interpretation. Should these restraints fail, there is a further recourse: the right of Congress and the states to amend the Constitution. Second, in addition to these checks from *outside* the judiciary, there are internal judicial adjustments that weaken the factual weight of the "realist" position.

As a matter of plain fact, the law in any given case may *not* be what a given judge says it is at all, since his judgment may be at any time overruled by a superior judge on appeal. And this fact forms the basis for a criticism of the "realist" position on logical grounds. The statement that "the law is what the judge says it is" is logically similar to the well-known assertion that "all generalizations are false—including this one." Both involve the fallacy of paradox—i.e., in both, the negative is "true" without contradicting the positive. In the case of the statement about the law and the judges, the fallacy is more interesting because it is based on the very evidence used to support it. Thus: "The law is what

[2] Jerome Frank cites Professor Oliphant of the Columbia Law School as advising his students to view judicial decisions as responses "to the stimuli of the facts." A study of these responses, it is suggested, would enable lawyers to predict the future behavior—i.e., decisions—of judges. (*Ibid.*, p. 159.)

a judge says it is because Judge X, in a given case, said that thus-and-so was the law." However, on appeal, Judge Y *overturned* the decision of Judge X and stated that the law was *not* thus-and-so. Since it is granted that Judge X is, in fact, a judge and that he did, in fact, state what the law was, we are left with the paradox: the law *is* and simultaneously *is not* what a judge said it was.

The solution of this paradox may, by now, be obvious. The statement, "the law is what the judge says it is," should be replaced by the logically and factually more correct statement: "The judge says what the law is." (It should be clear now that these two statements are not at all equivalent, in the same way that the statement, "All dogs are animals," is *not* equivalent to the statement, "All animals are dogs.")

We will now attempt, briefly, first to explore the substantive and adjective (procedural) criminal law as a system of social goals and aspirations; secondly, to consider its historical and cultural origins; and finally, to understand how it creates a certain climate of possibility surrounding and partly defining what is actual and significant in human affairs.

The Inherent Conflict between the Substantive and the Procedural Law

One of the beliefs held by laymen about the criminal law is that its overriding objective is the protection of the community from malefactors. The layman's tendency to think in these terms is reinforced by the fact that when thinking of criminals, one naturally sees himself as a potential victim of criminals. In this frame of mind, one views the huge body of substantive law as an avalanche of social wrath poised to engulf the offender.

Nevertheless, when one turns from the *substantive* law—in which the forbidden acts and their punishments are described—to the *procedural* law, which describes how the community will deal with violators, one cannot help being struck by the fact that an equally important objective is the protection of the offender. Whereas one great division of the law seems designed to entrap and punish the criminal, another is fashioned to help him avoid entrapment and evade punishment. This apparent paradox can be neither resolved nor understood without an understanding of the basic conflict that has always existed between the individuals of a society and their organs of social control. The manner in which any given society resolves this conflict determines its political character.

To the extent that they acknowledge the necessity or advantage of doing so, individuals create and submit to authorities to which they surrender a portion of their personal initiative and power. Since one of the most urgent and continuous needs of individuals is protection against other individuals, they have more or less universally recognized that this authority must be stronger than any single person or combination of persons. The character and extent of the police powers of any governmental authority represents the extent of this surrender of individual power.

Once created, however, the authority seeks almost invariably to expand itself. This tendency toward expanded powers and functions occurs not only in administrations that are tyrannical and irresponsible but also among those that are conscientious and ambitious for the public good. An efficient administrator is typically more interested in getting a job done than in observing the letter of procedure. He is impatient of limitations; he wants to cut red tape. He feels constantly impeded by combinations of private individuals with selfish private interests—and he often comes to see himself as a preserver of the public welfare against these individuals. If he is, himself, an exponent of the ideals of personal freedom, it rarely occurs to him that his own behavior may be a threat to these ideals in practice; he rarely pays attention to the fact that every increase in the power of the State means a corresponding decrease in the power of the individual.

The tendency is universal. Efficient police officers, intent on apprehending criminals, are always pressing for expanded police powers. The more honest they are, the more they resent the implication that these increased powers might jeopardize the innocent. And they correctly point out that corrupt or lazy police officers are quite content to take refuge in their own powerlessness. Conscientious prosecutors are constantly demanding greater leeway and fewer limitations in their dealings with the accused; their business is obtaining convictions against the guilty. Public-spirited legislators are constantly passing new laws aimed at the greater protection of the many against the few, and their ardor is continually stimulated by new crises, with which their constituents as isolated citizens seem unable to cope.

Against this tendency toward ever-increasing State authority, individuals and combinations have always waged war. The peculiar character of the Anglo-American political system is due to the fact that these struggles were, at critical times, effective, and that the victories were somehow preserved—even, at times, against the wishes of the victors when they themselves gained power. It is significant that every individual right and safeguard against arbitrary political power was won by groups in conflict with constituted authority. The right to trial by jury, the right to counsel, the prohibition of ex post facto laws, the ban against cruel and unusual punishments—every right enumerated in the Bill of Rights—originated as a demand by persons outside the government and among groups who considered themselves oppressed. In the strictest sense, the offender of today is the beneficiary of the patriot of yesterday.[3]

The results of this successful struggle are clearly seen in the differences which exist between the substantive and the procedural criminal law. As a result of the special way the conflict was resolved in our own history, the body of the criminal law has grown side by side with increasing limitations and conditions imposed on its application. During times when the reigning power was most secure, the substantive criminal law enjoyed its greatest expansion; during periods when it was weak or under attack, the procedural safeguards won their securest foothold.

Historical Antecedents of the Conflict

The history of Anglo-American procedural law is, therefore, a history of how these anti-authoritarian victories were won, how they got to be preserved—and how they continue to exist. More important, it is a history of how the rationalizations of the victors came to be idealized as basic principles of justice. At all times those at war with arbitrary governmental authority have sought for moral and spiritual values with which to inspire themselves in the struggle against the weightier temporal power of the State.

The rationalizations have varied with the sophistication of the times. During the struggle against the Star Chamber and other courts, dominated by the king, the Supreme Being was invoked as a value superior to royal authority. There has been preserved a vignette from

[3] The layman's impression that trial procedure seems often to favor the accused criminal is made plausible by the fact that most of these procedural safeguards were forced from the State by groups which, at the time, stood practically in the status of outlaws and rebels.

this struggle, which eventually established the principle of an independent judiciary in England; it is given in the picturesque language of its prime mover, the celebrated Edward Coke:

> A controversy of land between parties was heard by the King, and sentence given, which was repealed for this, that it did belong to the common law; then the King said, that he thought the law was founded upon reason, and that he and others had reason, as well as the Judges: to which it was answered by me, that true it was, that God had endowed His Majesty with excellent science, and great endowments of nature; but His Majesty was not learned in the laws of his realm of England, and causes which concern the life, or inheritance, or goods, or fortunes of his subjects, are not to be decided by natural reason but by the artificial reason and judgment of law, which law is an act which requires long study and experience, before that a man can attain to the cognizance of it: and that the law was the golden metwand and measure to try the causes of the subjects; and which protected His Majesty in safety and peace: with which the King was greatly offended, and said, that then he should be under the law, which was treason to affirm, as he said; to which I said, that *Bracton saith, quod Rex non debet esse sub homine, sed sub Deo et lege.*[4]

In later times more sophisticated rationalizations were used; every student of history is familiar with the concepts of natural law and the social contract, which figured so large in the ideological preparation for our own struggle for political independence. These values had, as a common core, the idea that there were certain rights so inherent and essential to the condition of man that no man and no State authority could properly abridge them—since they had not been created by man but rather bequeathed to him as "inalienable rights" by his Creator.

Criminal Procedure and Political Liberties

That the special character of this principle has contributed to the supremacy of law and due process in this country is a matter for historical verification; whether the rights deriving from it will endure is a matter for each generation to determine—certain nations, during our own period, have spent their inheritance recklessly. There is no clearer

---

[4] "The king ought not to be under any man, but under God and the law." Roscoe Pound, *The Spirit of the Common Law* (Boston: Marshall Jones Company, 1921) pp. 60-61.

way to demonstrate the political significance of the safeguards embodied in the criminal law than to examine the social consequences to those countries which have abandoned them. In this connection, Judge Jerome Hall has stressed the supreme importance of the principle of legality—the doctrine requiring every crime and every punishment to be defined by law. Regarding this principle and its supporting corollaries of specific description and strict construction, Hall writes:

> In democratic countries the political significance of criminal law had been almost forgotten when the impact of dictatorship, with its unvaried first move to seize control of the coercive legal apparatus, revived a startled realization of the dependence of civil liberty on criminal law. By a sure and unconscious instinct, the forces of repression struck straight to the heart of the opposing institution—the principle of legality.[5]

In the developing dictatorship of Nazi Germany the attack on civil liberties was made in the form of a substitution of the "principle of analogy" for the principle of strict construction. Hall writes:

> The German Act of June 28, 1935 provided: "Any person who commits an act which the Law declares to be punishable or which is deserving of penalty according to the fundamental conceptions of penal law and sound popular feeling, shall be punished. If there is no penal law directly covering an act, it shall be punished under the law of which the fundamental conception applies most nearly to the said act."[6]

The Russian dictatorship early adopted the same principles. The Russian Penal Code of 1926 stated:

> A crime is any socially dangerous act or omission which threatens the foundations of the Soviet political structure and that system of law which has been established by the Workers' and Peasants' Government for the period of transition to a Communist structure.
>
> In cases where the Criminal Code makes no direct reference to particular forms of crime, punishment or other measures of social protection are applied in accordance with those Articles of the Criminal Code which deal with crimes most closely approximating, in gravity and in kind, to the crimes actually committed...."[7]

Summarizing the case for the preservation of our present structure of criminal law, Judge Jerome Hall has written:

[5] Jerome Hall, *General Principles of Criminal Law* (Indianapolis: The Bobbs-Merrill Company, 1947), p. 54.

[6] *Ibid.*, p. 42.

[7] *Ibid.*

Several common traits characterize...revolutionary authoritarian movements....Special police are exempt from legal constraint; they arrest, try, execute and exile without legal restraint. Appeal is limited or non-existent. Special tribunals for the trial of political offenders may be depended upon to effectuate the will of the government. There is sweeping abrogation of constitutional guarantees. All of this is rationalized and sustained by controlled philosophic thought, as interpreted by the leaders to implement their political aims. The salient feature of authoritarian political theory in its attack on *nulla poena* consisted in stressing the paramount importance of the Community. The subordination of the individual was the obvious corollary. Thus, during revolution, law, especially criminal law, is used as a party weapon.

The ultimate rationale of the principle of legality is the preservation of cherished ideals. Thus if one asks, why, at bottom, retroactivity of penal laws is objectionable, why innocent persons should be protected by law from the abuse of official power even though the immediate consequences might be good, why even convicted offenders should be legally protected from judicial as well as popular excesses, and so on, the answers must inevitably take the form of certain "first principles." Those lying at the basis of democracy affirm the ineffable value of the individual human being. No person is regarded as good enough or wise enough to dominate any normal human being or to dispose of his person or property arbitrarily. Even the all-powerful State, indeed especially the State, must use the legal channels of due process before any individual can be declared a criminal and punished.[8]

The views just cited represent the convictions of the large majority of those who make and those who interpret the laws in most free nations today. It would, nevertheless, be misleading to imply that these views have not been seriously challenged by responsible legal theorists.

As we have already indicated, many honest and responsible officials are impatient with procedural safeguards that limit the activities of law-enforcement agents.[9] These critics argue that, since the innocent rarely

---

[8] *Ibid.,* pp. 57–59.

[9] Among persons other than law-enforcement officials active in attempts to broaden State authority at some expense to procedural safeguard may be listed various groups interested in specific issues dealing with the protection of public safety and morality. Individuals and groups advocating censorship of books have consistently argued that the principle of a free press provides unwarranted protection for the obscene and salacious. Laws and ordinances dealing with sex offenders sometimes empower the State to detain persons who have not violated any law. For a comprehensive analysis of this type of procedure see *The Habitual Sex Offender, Report and Recommendations of the Commission on the Habitual Sex Offender,* Paul W. Tappan, Technical Consultant (Trenton, N. J.: Department of Institutions and Agencies, 1950).

come in contact with the criminal law, the safeguards do not, in fact, protect the innocent but rather those who prey on the innocent. They hold, moreover, that, in practice, these safeguards actually decrease the safety of innocent men by enabling clever and well-advised criminals to commit crimes with impunity.

One of the most thoroughgoing and forthright criticisms of our present criminal procedure may be found in a book titled *Law, the Science of Inefficiency*, by William Seagle, a legal scholar whose contributions to historical jurisprudence are drawn on elsewhere in this text. The immediate interest of Seagle's work lies in the fact that it gives articulate voice to the convictions of many whose silence was more in deference than in assent to the majority view.

Seagle does not hesitate to locate the source of the dilemma in the Constitution itself:

> In the United States the essentials of the criminal law are guaranteed in a judicially enforced bill of rights, and the justices of the Supreme Court of the United States, who are nothing if not articulate, constantly expound the philosophy that efficiency in the administration of the criminal law is irreconcilable with decency and liberty.... The frankest exposition of the philosophy of criminal law enforcement from a constitutional standpoint is to be found, perhaps, in Justice Jackson's statement that "the forefathers, after consulting the lessons of history, designed our Constitution to place obstacles in the way of a too permeating police surveillance, which they seemed to think was a greater danger to a free people than the escape of some criminals from punishment."... The inefficiency of the criminal law is indeed the pride of democracy.[10]

According to Seagle, the issue is seen as clearly drawn between liberty and efficiency:

> Power can be curbed only by making the law inefficient. Indeed the establishment of every limitation upon political power has been a tacit recognition of the undesirability of legal efficiency. Humanity has constantly drawn back from legal efficiency as from the brink of an abyss. When threatened by efficient law enforcement, it has loudly demanded Twelve Tables, codes, bills of rights, declarations of the rights of man, and full-fledged written constitutions—all for the purpose of protecting the weak against the strong, and the individual against the state. In short, it has always demanded inefficiency as an inalienable right of man.

[10] William Seagle, *Law, the Science of Inefficiency* (New York: The Macmillan Company, 1952), p. 102.

Of course, nobody literally demands "inefficiency," which as an ideal, has always been in bad odor. Everyone actually demands "liberty." Liberty, however, is only inefficiency in false face.[11]

It would be difficult to exaggerate the conflict between Hall's doctrine of constitutional restraint and Seagle's doctrine of executive latitude. For the question, "How far may the State go in enforcing social values?", has implications extending beyond issues of crime and punishment. Of relevance here is the long-standing controversy about the relation between means and ends. To press for unlimited enforcement efficiency is, in effect, to assert that the ends justify the means. To set limits on the reaches of law is, in effect, to assert that the individual is himself a social end.

[11] *Ibid.*, p. 9.

Criminal Law and Procedure

Sources of the Criminal Law

ALL MODERN CRIMINAL LAW, BOTH SUBSTANTIVE AND PROCEDURAL, derives from four general sources: (1) *Statutory law*—penal statutes enacted by legislatures; (2) *the common law*—a body of principles and practices gradually developed from the precedents of previous judicial decisions and otherwise referred to as "case law"; (3) *constitutional law* —a body of basic and chiefly procedural principles established in written form and viewed as controlling or limiting subsequent legislation, which must either conform to it or avoid conflict with it; and (4) *administrative law*—regulations made directly by administrative agencies given broad authority by the legislature to enforce policies for which they are responsible. This last-named source represents a relatively recent and highly controversial innovation in criminal law, and has occasioned much criticism by those who regard it as an encroachment by the executive on the powers of the legislature and the judiciary.[1]

[1] The rising tide of administrative law occasionally meets a constitutional obstacle. In 1933 the New York State Legislature passed a statute giving an Alcoholic Control Board power to make regulations supervising the manufacture and sale of beer throughout the state. The act provided that "violation of any rule of the state board shall be a misdemeanor, if such rule so provides . . ." In overruling a conviction obtained under this statute, the Appellate Court declared: "The legislative discretion to declare a crime has . . . been attempted to be delegated to the board. . . . We hold this attempt to be a violation of the legislative article of the Constitution. The legislative power to create an offense may not be so delegated."

Of the four general sources of criminal law, statutory law, as enacted by legislatures, has become, in recent times, the major source of expansion. It is now generally accepted that statutory law, when constitutional (more specifically, unless it is found to be *unconstitutional*), takes precedence over the common law. This relationship is not as direct and simple as superficial description might make it appear, since many of the doctrines originating in the common law have been established in the Constitution. It is, therefore, not unusual to find that a new statute which is in conflict with common-law doctrine is also in conflict with the supreme law of the land. Judges aware of a conflict, but reluctant to assert the outright unconstitutionality of a new statute, will frequently "interpret the ambiguities" of the enactment in the direction of greater conformity to legal precedent (i.e., the common law.)

A learned judge has illustrated this relationship between statutory and common law with the following simile:

> The Common Law is like the ancient Kingdom of China, which many invaders have attempted to conquer—in the end, the conquerors have been absorbed. Occasionally a vigorous new statute arises and invades the ancient provinces; at first the courts give way, asserting the oriental virtue of judicial passivity and statutory supremacy; actually they are merely retreating in order to surround it and absorb it. Gradually they find qualifications, analogies and "explanatory precedents." They may pretend that certain clauses are not clear and rather than attempt to infer the legislator's intention from his obvious objectives, they seek interpretations from precedents established in past centuries. ...In effect, they say that what the legislature *really* meant is discoverable only in the language of decisions made years before the legislators were born. Eventually the statute takes its place as a captive pillar in the eternal, unchanging edifice of the common law. Once again, China has absorbed its conquerors.[2]

The Substantive Criminal Law

Definitions

In his book, *Criminal Law and Procedure,* Professor Jerome Hall cites a representative legal definition of crime:

(Quoted in Jerome Hall, *Criminal Law and Procedure,* Indianapolis: Bobbs-Merrill Company, 1949, p. 12.)

[2] Private communication to the authors.

A "crime" is an act or omission forbidden by law and punishable upon conviction by: 1. Death; or 2. Imprisonment; or, 3. Fine; or, 4. Removal from office; or, 5. Disqualification to hold any office of trust, honor or profit under the state; or, 6. Other penal discipline.

Except that the acts defined as traffic infractions by the vehicle and traffic laws ... are not crimes.

Division of Crime. A crime is: 1. A felony; or, 2. A misdemeanor.

Felony: A "felony" is a crime which is or may be punishable by: 1. Death, or, 2. Imprisonment in a state prison.

Misdemeanor: Any other crime is a "misdemeanor." [3]

Distinctions between the Criminal Law and the Civil Law

The body of the criminal laws of any jurisdiction consists of acts or omissions viewed as offenses *against the community* rather than offenses against the person or groups harmed by them. This distinction is important, since it forms the clearest basis differentiating between violations of the civil and of the criminal codes. In criminal cases the prosecution is always initiated by the State as the plaintiff or injured party, and the punishment (execution, fine, or imprisonment) is always exacted by and on behalf of the State. In civil cases, the action is initiated and carried through by the person alleging harm, and the judgment against the defendant is always rendered on behalf of the injured party. Thus, a defendant found liable under a civil prosecution may be ordered to pay a fine or to undertake or desist from some behavior, or to compensate or relieve the injured party. Judgment against the defendant does not involve imprisonment *unless* it is demonstrated that he has committed the *criminal* offense of willfully refusing to comply with the court's decision. Thus, a person ordered to pay a certain amount of alimony in a divorce action (civil) may be indicted by the State for failure to comply with the court order.

There are other distinctions between the civil and the criminal law, and there are numerous parallels that make distinction difficult. In that branch of civil law known as *torts*, which deals with intentional but not specifically criminal injuries against individuals, the distinction is less clear-cut. In the most general terms, the law of torts fixes the liability of persons who intentionally engage in behavior which *in fact* injures another, usually through negligence. The crucial distinction is the absence of morally culpable motive and conduct.

[3] McKinney's *Consolidated Laws of New York* (1944). Quoted in Hall, *op. cit.*, p. 94.

Thus, for example, a circus knife-thrower who arrives for the performance in an intoxicated state and, through this negligence, kills his partner, is liable to a tort action by the victim's heirs, but is *not* liable to criminal prosecution. This same knife-thrower who, drunk or sober, merely threatens maliciously to stab his partner may be criminally liable for assault, though his attempt never reaches the stage of actually touching his partner. The crucial distinction is malicious intention, revealed by some form of conduct which, in itself, may never reach the stage of actual physical damage to the intended victim. In both civil and criminal law, accident (without negligence), self-defense, and unavoidable necessity are completely exonerating. Thus, an individual who has armed himself with a pistol with the deliberate and malicious intent of murdering another person and who actually kills his victim may be found guiltless of homicide if it can be proved that the intended victim shot at him first, forcing him to kill in self-defense.

Parallel Liability

In the majority of cases, persons convicted of criminal offenses involving actual harm to others are liable to civil prosecution in addition to criminal prosecution. The two actions are, however, entirely separate. If a person is convicted of assault and battery and sentenced to fine and imprisonment by the State, the fine is never paid to the victim. In order to collect damages for his injuries, the victim must himself, at his own expense, initiate suit against his assailant.

It is one of the idiosyncrasies of our present legal system that the criminal law makes no provision whatever for the welfare or compensation of the victim. In actual practice, the imprisonment of the offender usually renders him unable to pay any damages that might be levied against him and, in effect, renders him civilly immune. (In most instances, a civil suit is not even initiated.) Thus, a person who accidentally kills another in an automobile accident may not go to prison, but may be impoverished for the rest of his life because of the damages he is ordered to pay to the heirs of the deceased. On the other hand, a robber who in the course of his crime murders a police officer and happens to escape with a life sentence will most probably never be brought to trial for damages in a civil court. Though the family of the police officer may be impoverished, his children cut off from educational and vocational opportunities, the offender, if he is fortunate enough to be granted parole, has no legal or financial obligation to his victim's heirs. Unlike the noncriminal automobile driver, who may spend his life in poverty paying for the accidental death of his victim, the paroled murderer, in the absence of a civil conviction, has no further debt.

The Basic Elements of the Criminal Offense

THE PRINCIPLE OF LEGALITY. In the course of many centuries there has evolved a relatively stable body of fundamental principles defining the necessary elements of any criminal offense. As has been pointed out in the previous chapter, in Anglo-American law these principles represent a fusion of two basic—and, to a considerable extent, opposing—values: (1) the protection of the community from the offender and (2) the protection of the offender, as a community member, from the indiscriminate power of the State. At the highest level of generality, these objectives are harmonized in the *principle of legality*.

The principle of legality, sometimes summarized in two Latin phrases meaning "there is no crime without a (specific) law" and "there is no punishment without a (specific) law," is central to Anglo-American law. As Hall has pointed out:

> There is no logical reason why any law must be specific. From that viewpoint, a principle of legality would be implied if there was only one all-inclusive law, e.g., "punish socially dangerous conduct by any measures which the judge deems proper."
>
> But it is perfectly clear that the actual principle of legality means a great deal more than any such abstraction. Its meaning can be ascertained only by reference to its operation as a definite idea in legal history. The essence of this meaning of the principle of legality is limitation on penalization by officials, effected by the required prescription and application of *specific rules.* That is the historical, the actual meaning of the principle of legality so far as the criminal law is concerned. It is that meaning which is relevant to the present discussion. On the Continent this aspect of the principle of legality has been formulated with definite reference to the criminal law: *Nulla poena sine lege.*[4]

Around this basic principle of legality there have grown several defining doctrines that serve to guide its application in specific instances. Two of the most important of these doctrines are the ban on ex post facto laws and the requirement that penal statutes be narrowly con-

[4] Jerome Hall, *Principles of Criminal Law* (Indianapolis: Bobbs-Merrill Company, 1947), pp. 19–20.

strued. Pointing out that "strict construction has long been a corollary of the principle of legality applied to criminal law," Hall cites a relevant example:

> Suppose, e.g., that a larceny statute forbids the taking of "property," etc. The defendant is charged with taking (a) the use of machinery (b) an airplane.... Reference to the relevant decisions shows that "property" has always been limited to corporeal personal property. Accordingly, use of machinery is excluded despite the fact that an intelligent legislator might include it in his draft.... On the other hand, an airplane is corporeal personal property. Accordingly, even though an airplane had never been held a subject of larceny, a liberal interpretation would include it within the meaning of "corporeal personal property"— there is enough similarity, e.g., to automobiles to support that. But the principle of legality requires strict interpretation of penal statutes.... The question then becomes: is there "sufficient" difference between an airplane and, e.g., an automobile so that it (the airplane) may be excluded. Whatever opinion may presently be held on this matter, it is probable that at the time of McBoyle vs. United States, people generally regarded the airplane as distinctive in many ways. This raised reasonable doubt as to its inclusion; hence its exclusion from the scope of "vehicle" strictly interpreted.[5]

In the example just cited, the defendant, McBoyle, convicted of larceny under the statute, appealed to a higher court and had his conviction set aside even though the statute specifically contained the words, "or any other self-propelled vehicle." The reasons cited by the higher court in setting aside the verdict illuminate judicial thinking on the subject:

> Although it is not likely that a criminal will carefully consider the text of the law before he murders or steals, it is reasonable that a fair warning should be given to the world in language that the common world will understand, of what the law intends to do if a certain line is passed. To make the warning fair, so far as possible the line should be clear. When a rule of conduct is laid down in words that evoke in the common mind only the picture of vehicles moving on land, the [application of] statute should not be extended to aircraft simply because it may seem to us that a similar policy applies, or upon speculation that, if the legislature had thought of it, very likely broader words would have been used.[6]

What the Justice is, in effect, saying is that even though it *might*

---

[5] *Ibid.,* pp. 37–38.

[6] Justice Holmes in McBoyle *v.* United States. Cited in Hall, *Principles of Criminal Law,* p. 38.

seem reasonable to him—as it did to the prosecutor, the jury, and the trial judge—that an airplane should be included in the category of "self-propelled vehicles," the legislature had not taken care to include this relatively recent invention specifically in the statute. As a jurist, he refused to take it upon himself to improve legislation, and this refusal to assume the legislative function is bolstered by the doctrine of strict construction.

In addition to the *principle of legality,* Hall cites six other elements essentially present in a watertight case.

THE HARM. In his discussion of this principle, Hall has pointed out that "there must be an external injury . . . represented in each specific offense, i.e., a man dies, a house burns, property is taken from its owner . . . ."[7]

The doctrine stating that an ascertainable harm must have been caused has been modified where *attempts* to cause harm and *conspiring* with others or *soliciting* others to do harm have in themselves been made offenses by statute. Only in these specific instances is it possible to dispense with the requirement of a verified harm to the victim.

CONDUCT. In its broadest sense, this principle requires it to be shown that the harm occurring to the victim is in some way related to an act—or inaction—of the offender. This principle is narrowly qualified by the principles immediately to follow; nevertheless, whatever other elements are present, the elementary demonstration that the accused has *acted* must be made.

MENS REA (Literally, "Evil Mind"). A harmful action is not sufficient to warrant a criminal prosecution; it may be that the act was unintentional or the result of a nonculpable negligence. There must be demonstrated an *intention* on the part of the actor to injure the victim. This intent, moreover, must be highly specific to the act itself, as is required by the next principle.

FUSION OR CONCURRENCE OF MENS REA AND CONDUCT. It is not enough for the accused to have hated the victim, or wished him dead, or even plotted and schemed to injure him, *unless* the scheme or plot or bad intent was demonstrably related to the harmful act that eventually took place. Precedents have sharpened this condition to a razor's keenness; and many a resourceful defense counsel has used it to cut the noose from the neck of his client in a seemingly hopeless case.

Let us imagine that *A* plans to lure *B* to the top of a cliff with the

[7] *Ibid.,* p. 14.

intention of pushing him off. Halfway up the cliff, B becomes aware of A's intent and attempts to flee. In his panic B loses his footing, tumbles off the cliff, and is killed. Despite the fact that A planned to kill him, despite the fact that he lost his life as a result of falling from the cliff, despite the fact that he might still be alive if A had not lured him there, A is still not legally guilty of B's death. A had not counted on his ability to *scare* B off the cliff, nor had he deliberately planned that B should become careless and lose his footing, though he had every intention of *explaining* the "accident" in this way. *The act by which B lost his life was not the act that A had intended; consequently, there was no fusion of mens rea with conduct, and A is technically innocent.*

As the reader might have predicted from his own reaction to this example, legislators have not always taken kindly to this common-law principle and have, in certain cases, modified it drastically by statute. In most jurisdictions today, a death or injury unintentionally inflicted in the course of another felony is made punishable as if it were deliberate. Thus, a robber who accidentally kills a bystander with a wild shot is held guilty of murder even though he clearly lacked any intention to shoot that person.

A CAUSAL RELATIONSHIP BETWEEN THE HARM AND THE INTENTIONAL MISCONDUCT. It must be demonstrated that the injury was actually caused by the intended wrongful act *and no other*. At first glance this principle may seem identical with the requirement that some overt behavior be demonstrated; actually, there is an important distinction. A may have poisoned B with every intent to kill him. B, taken to the hospital, recovers from the poison but dies from the antidote. A's proved overt act had much to do with what happened, since it was the indispensable first link in the chain of events that brought B to his death. But between that first link and the final result another event intervened: the administration of the fatal antidote. This principle has been the basis of numerous successful appeals in homicide cases; as a result, the courts are chronically flooded with petitions from indignant appellants seeking to show that the victim did *not* die from the bullet but from the negligent medical care to which he was subjected.

LEGALLY PRESCRIBED PUNISHMENT. The principle of legally prescribed punishment has an important historical significance as a reaction against the sovereign's power to inflict unending suffering upon those who offended him. Perhaps the best-known example of the exercise of this power was the infamous *lettre de cachet,* by which a person was seized and confined "at the king's pleasure" for whatever period it pleased the king to confine him, and for whatever reason. The principle is double-edged: On the one hand, it asserts that an act cannot be considered legally criminal unless some form of punishment is provided for it; on the other, it strictly limits punishment to those measures provided in the statute defining the crime. The intention is to "make the punishment fit the crime."

This principle has come under attack in recent years by those who argue that the punishment—or treatment—should fit the *criminal* rather than the crime. In accordance with this new principle, certain states have adopted the "indeterminate sentence," the purest form of which is a prison term running from one year to life. Many other states have adopted partially indeterminate sentences—e.g., five to ten years, twenty to thirty years. When challenged in the courts, the indeterminate sentence has usually been sustained on the ground that it was, after all, legally prescribed in the statute defining the offense. With this issue decided, the indeterminate sentence has now become widely established, despite the objections of those who point out that "making the punishment fit the criminal" was precisely what King Louis had in mind when he sent people to the Bastille.

Criminal Procedure

The following outline of criminal procedure presents only the minimum of information essential to a general understanding of the sequence of events in a typical criminal case. Let us imagine that John Smith did, on a certain murky evening in December, willfully and maliciously assault James Jones against the peace and dignity of the State of New Jersey. Let us further assume that Smith, after assaulting his victim, disappeared into the white anonymity of the winter's night, leaving Jones to contemplate his bruises and the precarious state of man. By what processes will Smith be brought to justice?

The Complaint, the Warrant, and the Arrest

Every criminal action has its beginning in someone's sworn statement that a crime has been committed. The person making the complaint may be the victim, a bystander, or anyone who has learned of the offense. The complaint itself may be made to a police officer, to a prosecutor, or directly to a magistrate. The essence of the complaint is someone's willingness to swear, on his best knowledge or belief, that someone else has committed an act which the law defines as criminal.

When the complaint is brought before a magistrate—or before one delegated by him to evaluate complaints (an official called a "warrant officer" in most urban jurisdictions)—an attempt is made to see whether the facts as *alleged* add up to an actual offense. (Note that no attempt need be made to establish the *truth* of the allegations.) If the sworn allegations fit the description of a known crime, the magistrate issues a *warrant* for the arrest of the offender. If the name of the offender is unknown, the warrant details the best available description of the suspect, who in this instance is usually given the temporary name of "John Doe." The arrest warrant is an authorization for any police official in the jurisdiction to "bring in the body" (meaning the person) of the accused before a magistrate.

It is not always practical or necessary to obtain a warrant before an arrest is made. Any citizen has the right to arrest a person whom he reasonably suspects of having committed a felony, provided that felony has actually been committed. A peace officer has the additional privilege of arrest on reasonable suspicion alone, regardless of whether the offense was actually committed. In the case under discussion, no immediate arrest was possible. By the time the police arrived, Smith had already made good his escape into the night.

The warrant was issued, and the police broadened the search for Smith. If Smith had fled to another state, it would have been illegal for the New Jersey police to pursue him there, and the lengthy and involved process called *extradition* would have been necessary. Fortunately, however, Smith remained in New Jersey and was duly arrested and brought before a magistrate.

The Preliminary Hearing

The preliminary hearing (sometimes called the *preliminary examination*) is not in itself a trial of the case, though it may lead to an immediate trial in the same courtroom if it is decided that the offense charged is not actually a felony but a petty offense within the jurisdiction of the magistrate. The modern preliminary hearing has a fourfold purpose: (1) To determine whether the facts alleged in the complaint indicate a petty offense (misdemeanor), which can be tried summarily.

(2) To protect the accused if the evidence does not suggest "probable cause" for believing he is guilty of the offense charged; in this event the accused is *discharged* (set free). (3) To determine whether the accused is entitled to bail if the case is held for trial. (4) To preserve a written record of the testimony of witnesses.

As it has evolved in modern Anglo-American law, a prompt preliminary hearing is considered one of the most important rights of the accused. He is entitled to a full hearing of the charges against him; he is permitted to hear the testimony of all witnesses called against him and to cross-examine them; he has the privilege of requesting counsel. Though he may himself be cross-examined if he chooses to take the stand, he is under no obligation to testify; and the magistrate may not compel him to answer questions. He is not required to enter a plea to the charges nor in any way reveal his defense. Moreover the preliminary hearing may be properly waived only with his consent.

In the hypothetical case under discussion, the accused, Smith, requested counsel and, on his advice, chose to say nothing. The magistrate heard the evidence of the plaintiff and found probable cause to believe that an assault had been committed and that Smith had committed it. Accordingly, bail was set and the case was held over for trial in a felony court. But Smith did not at this point walk freely from the courtroom. Though his right to bail was protected by the Constitution, it was left for the magistrate to determine (within limits) how *high* it was to be. In this case the magistrate employed his discretion to set a bail higher than Smith could afford; consequently he was committed to the custody of the county jail to await trial.

The Accusation

The role of dominant actor in this judicial drama now passed to the public prosecutor. It was his duty to determine whether the evidence that gave the magistrate "probable cause" to believe the accused guilty actually added up to an accusation that could be proved *beyond reasonable doubt*. Between these two states of mind—"probable cause to believe" and "proof beyond reasonable doubt"—there is a world of difference; within this difference lies a vast area of discretion. If the prosecutor believes the evidence insufficient, he may not proceed further; in this event the case dies. If he considers the evidence sufficient to warrant a conviction, he prepares a detailed accusation.

In the United States there are two main ways by which the judicial process proceeds from this point. The first of these is the *grand jury indictment*; the second, the *criminal information*. The federal Constitution requires that "no [civilian] person shall be held to answer for a capital or otherwise infamous crime unless on presentment or indictment of a grand jury." A grand jury is a panel of private citizens drawn up to pass on accusations recommended by the public prosecutor for trial. In contrast to the trial jury (sometimes called the "petit jury"), the grand jury does not try cases; it merely evaluates or, in effect, "tries" accusations. If it approves the prosecutor's proposal for a trial, it returns what is called a "true bill" or indictment. If it fails to approve the accusation, the case ends then and there. Even when an indictment is returned by the grand jury, the decision to go ahead with a trial remains in the hands of the prosecutor; he may still elect not to press it. In this event the indictment is "nolle prossed."

Grand jury proceedings are private, with all members, witnesses, participants, and court reporters sworn to secrecy. The accused may be present but may not question witnesses; theoretically it is not yet the accused but the state's accusation which is under scrutiny. (On occasion, the grand jury may initiate its own investigations and make its own accusations, which are called *presentments*.)

Though the Constitution requires a grand jury to return indictments for "infamous crimes," certain states, by means of a re-interpretation of the word "infamous," have by-passed the grand-jury requirement and provided the *criminal information* as an alternative or substitute in all but capital or certain other extremely serious crimes. The criminal information is prepared by the public prosecutor, who is enabled to conduct investigations and subpoena witnesses—in effect, to act as his own grand jury.

The indictment (or information) must clearly name the offense charged and state all material facts concerning the time, place, and manner of the crime. On receipt of the indictment, the judge of the court at which the trial is sought schedules an *arraignment* of the accused to plead to the charge.

The Arraignment

Up to this point the defendant, who may have been confined and interrogated a score of times, has not yet been *formally* asked whether he is guilty or not guilty. The *arraignment* is a procedure in which the defendant is produced at the court that will try him, informed of the charges against him, and requested to state how he will plead. There are roughly three things the defendant can do at this point. (1) He can seek for delay (in order to obtain counsel, or to consult further with counsel, or for any other reasonable purpose); (2) he can *plead*; (3) he can, without pleading (i.e., without saying whether he is guilty or innocent), attempt to have the entire case thrown out by a variety of objections made in the form of *motions*.

THE PLEAS. The two most obvious and common pleas are *guilty* and *not guilty*. Certain states permit other pleas. One of these is called *nolo contendere* or *non vult*, and signifies that the defendant, without committing himself directly on his guilt or innocence, will not oppose the government's case. Since this plea has the effect of dispensing with the need for a trial, it has the same effect as a plea of guilty and is generally so understood. Although most states accept the plea of *not guilty by reason of insanity*, certain jurisdictions require that insanity be, of itself, a special and separate plea. Finally, the defendant may plead *former jeopardy*, stating that he has been previously tried for the same offense and cannot be tried again because of the constitutional prohibition against *double jeopardy*. One further recourse is open: the defendant may elect to say nothing—to "stand mute"—in which case the judge will enter a plea of not guilty.

MOTIONS BEFORE TRIAL. In former times the defendant could challenge the indictment by a wide variety of separate technical or procedural objections. Modern courts have tended to group these under the category of general motions to *quash, dismiss,* or *set aside* the indictment. These motions, which must be made before the defendant makes known his plea, rarely result in an immediate dismissal of the case. Nevertheless, they are very important, for unless the defendant registers his objections *before* he pleads to the indictment, it is assumed that he has waived them. Thus, if the defendant later plans to appeal on certain procedural grounds, he must state these objections in advance. In many criminal cases the *motion to quash* is made virtually as a matter of course, in order to safeguard the right to certain types of appeal.

In our particular case the defense, after making a series of motions to quash, registered a plea of not guilty.

The Trial

The Constitution has guaranteed the right of a jury trial "in all criminal prosecutions." The defendant may waive this right, however, and elect to be tried only by the judge, who then functions simultaneously as judge and jury. The function of the jury is to determine the *facts* of the case; the judge rules on matters of *law*.

SELECTION OF THE JURY. The Constitution has guaranteed the accused the right to a "fair and impartial trial by a jury of his *peers* [equals]." (The interpretation of the term *peers* has been in dispute, and appeals showing discrimination in the making of juror lists have lately been successful in federal courts.) Both the State and the defendant are allowed to take part in the selection of the jury. Both parties may argue for the dismissal of individual jurors on grounds of their personal interest, prejudice, or various legal reasons. In addition, both sides are entitled to a certain number of *peremptory challenges,* which enable them to have a limited number of jurors removed without any stated reason. Once the jury has been selected and sworn, the trial itself may begin.

Before discussing the trial proper, a few preliminary remarks are in order concerning the rights and immunities of the accused. Throughout the trial the accused has the right to confront his accusers and the witnesses against him face to face, and to cross-examine them. In effect, this insures that the prosecution will not use secret witnesses or testimony unknown to the defendant and immune to his attack. The defendant also has the related right to be present at every stage of the proceedings; nothing can be said or done behind his back. He has the right to examine and cross-examine witnesses, yet he is under no obligation to take the stand himself and he cannot be compelled to testify. He may, in fact, elect to say nothing and to have nothing said on his behalf, since he is not required to prove his innocence. The burden of proof is borne by the State; it must prove *beyond a reasonable doubt* every factual element essential to the crime. In practice, this means that the prosecution must be able to rebut alibis or alternative explanations presented by the defense. If the judge is not satisfied that the prosecution has sufficiently proved its case, he may *direct* the jury to find the defendant not guilty.

SEQUENCE OF EVENTS. The State has the first and the last word in the trial. The prosecution makes the opening statement, outlining its case. The opening statement by the defense follows; then the State submits its evidence and calls its witnesses. The defense then presents its witnesses and contrary evidence; thereupon defense and prosecution may take turns in offering rebuttals, in cross-examining opposing witnesses, and in re-examining its own witnesses. At the end of this rebuttal period, the State summarizes its case and is answered by the *closing argument* of the defense. The State then presents its closing arguments. (Note that this typical order of events normally gives the State three opportunities to address the jury compared with two provided for the defense.)

After the State's closing argument, the court is recessed to enable the judge to prepare the *instructions to the jury*. Both the defense and the prosecution are permitted to contribute suggestions to be included in the judge's instructions, or *charge,* to the jury; he may accept or exclude any or all of these suggestions at his discretion. The purpose of the charge is to relate the evidence offered by both sides to the points of law relevant to acquittal or conviction. Except in the federal courts, where the judge is given greater latitude in discussing the evidence, the charge is often little more than an additional opportunity for each side to summarize its case in the judge's words. His manner in making the charge, however, and his decisions about including or excluding the points offered by both sides, can have a considerable influence on the outcome.

THE VERDICT. At the conclusion of the charge, the jury retires to consider its verdict. In most states unanimity is required; in some jurisdictions, however, a majority (eight or ten out of twelve) is sufficient for lesser felonies or misdemeanors. Failure of the jury to reach a verdict results in a *mistrial.* Evidence of any form of misconduct by a juryman may also result in a mistrial.

A legally acceptable verdict must supply a "Yes" or "No" answer to the question: "Is the defendant guilty of the particular offense charged?" The verdict, in other words, must be "responsive" only to the crime being tried and not to any other. Thus, for example, a jury cannot return a verdict of "guilty of murder" to a charge of manslaughter—nor can it acquit a defendant of a charge of robbery and find him guilty of burglary (unless a charge of burglary was included in the indictment). Neither can the jury find the defendant guilty of any offense revealed during the course of the trial but not included in the indictment. In some cases it is possible for the jury to return a verdict of guilty to a lesser charge or a lesser degree of the offense, but only so long as the lesser offense is "comprised" in the larger. In the case of indictments carrying several counts or charges, the jury must clearly specify its verdict on each count and charge.

In some states the jury is permitted to recommend or participate in the determination of the sentence. In capital cases a recommendation of mercy is usually (but not invariably) effective in preventing a sentence of death. For certain offenses, the law permits the jury to determine the manner of punishment (e.g., fine *or* imprisonment *or* both). Occasionally, the judge may specifically invite the jury to make recommendations within the limits of his discretionary powers and the statute.

After receiving the verdict, the court is recessed while the judge considers the sentence. At this point both the defense and the prosecution may submit recommendations concerning the sentence and the judge may consult probation reports or other appropriate sources of information about the accused.

MOTIONS MADE AFTER THE VERDICT BUT BEFORE THE SENTENCE. After the verdict is in, either side may make a variety of motions presenting reasons for setting it aside. Most frequently these objections are summarized in a *motion for a new trial*. This motion may cite grounds asserting unfairness, errors, or the discovery of evidence previously unavailable. In most jurisdictions the denial of a motion for a new trial is a prerequisite for a later appeal; consequently the motion is often made as a matter of course.

Either side or the judge himself may make a *motion in arrest of judgment*. This motion is usually grounded on technical or procedural errors appearing on the face of the trial record—e.g., an ambiguous verdict, lack of proper jurisdiction, etc. Motions for a new trial and motions in arrest of judgment must be made within a time limit varying from three to five days after the verdict in most jurisdictions.

THE SENTENCE. Having heard the recommendations of both sides concerning the sentence, the judge is ready to announce his decision. The extent to which statutes permit the judge discretion in sentencing varies widely. The most common practice is to allow the judge a range within certain minimum and maximum time limits (e.g., "not less than one and not more than three years"). A similar discretion is usually permitted in the case of fines.

After passing sentence, the judge may elect to *stay its execution* for a limited time (either to permit the defendant a period of liberty pending an appeal or for other reasons), or he may suspend the sentence. The power of the judge to suspend sentence entirely on his own initiative (where statutes are silent) has been a matter of dispute; in most jurisdictions the dispute has been resolved by statutory provisions for agencies of probation. An individual may continue to be free on probation during the length of his sentence provided that he observes the special conditions of his probation, which may be decided jointly by the judge and the statute. During this period the sentence literally hangs over his head and may be put into effect at any time up to the expiration of the sentence, at which time the probationer must be *discharged* from his probation.

Appellate Review

After the sentence is pronounced and within various time limits during the period of its execution, the convicted offender is entitled to several forms of judicial review. The grounds and conditions of appeal are far too complex to be discussed here; in general, they are based on objections that certain trial or pretrial procedures infringed the defendant's rights. Appeals must be brought on the initiative of the party claiming the errors; in a limited number of rarely exercised privileges, the State may also appeal against a verdict of acquittal.

In general, reviews are restricted to matters of law and procedure and are conducted entirely by written arguments or *briefs*. Certain statutes in some places permit broader appeals, in which matters of fact as well as matters of law are re-argued; this type of appeal is virtually a retrial of the case.

Executive Clemency

The rejection of appeals ends the judicial consideration of the case; from this point the only recourse of the convicted offender is through executive *clemency* or mercy. In federal cases, clemency is given by the President; in the state jurisdictions, by the Governor. Clemency generally takes one of two forms: a *remission* of all or a part of the remaining sentence or fine or a full *executive pardon*, with complete restoration of civil rights.

We now return to our defendant, whom we left at the point where he made his plea of *not guilty* to an indictment charging *aggravated assault*. In view of the fact that he was without funds to employ an attorney, the court directed that counsel be provided and a date was set for the selection of a jury and for trial of the case. No objections were made to the selection of jurors by either side.

In its *opening statement*, the prosecution stated it was prepared to show how the defendant, Smith, after a barroom altercation with Jones, the victim, followed Jones stealthily out of the tavern, stabbed him, and left him lying in the snow while he made good his escape into the night. The defense indicated the direction of its case in its opening argument by acknowledging certain of the facts asserted by the prosecution but drastically re-interpreting them. Smith and Jones had argued in the tavern and had left together to continue their dispute in the street. There, the defense argued, Jones had attacked Smith physically, at which point the defendant, Smith, exercised his human and legal right to defend himself by any means at his disposal. After the fracas Smith, in a confused and agitated frame of mind, fled the scene, unaware that he had behaved in an entirely defensible manner and was not guilty of any crime.

The prosecution then began *presenting its evidence* and calling its witnesses. The first prosecution witness was the victim, Jones. Jones testified that he had entered the tavern for his usual "after-dinner beer," had not been there "long enough to have more than two" when Smith, whom he had never seen before, approached him and tried to start a conversation. Noticing that Smith appeared to be drunk and unusually quarrelsome, Jones testified that he had attempted to break off the conversation. At this, Smith appeared to be offended and became abusive, casting certain unrepeatable aspersions on Jones' paternity. At this point Jones decided it would be best to leave in order to avoid a fight. He testified that he had not walked five blocks when he heard someone running quickly behind him. "The next thing I felt was a burning pain in my back. I tried to grab whoever it was but I couldn't hold him. I did get a good look at him. It was Smith." Asked by the prosecution whether or not he had engaged in any speech with Smith outside the tavern, Jones insisted that his last words with Smith occurred inside the tavern. "The next time I saw him was when he stabbed me in the back, and I didn't have a chance to talk to him after that." Jones was then excused from the stand.

The knife was introduced as a *prosecution exhibit* and its ownership linked to Smith by the testimony of the hardware-store owner from whom he had purchased it. Several witnesses present at the tavern were called and testified that Smith had remained in the tavern for a few minutes after Jones had left and had appeared to be "brooding" and muttering to himself. The bartender testified, over the objections of the defense, that Smith had appeared to be intoxicated. The intern who had attended Jones testified that the victim had been wounded in the back and that the wound could have been made by an implement similar to the prosecution exhibit. A police officer testified that he had found the knife a few feet from where Jones had been lying. The policemen who apprehended Smith testified that he had tried to evade capture and had acted in a guilty manner—"as if he damn well knew he had committed a crime." The prosecution then moved to introduce police records showing several previous arrests for disorderly conduct. On the objection of the defense that "mere evidence of an arrest does not indicate conviction," the judge refused to accept these records, whereupon the prosecution moved to introduce F. B. I. records indicating that Smith had twice been convicted of minor assault charges. This evidence was accepted, over defense objections.

The prosecution concluded its *direct examination* and the defense called its own witnesses. Smith's employer testified that Smith had been a good worker, that he could recall no reports that Smith was quarrelsome or assaultive and that he "wished he had more like him." The defendant's landlord testified that Smith had always paid his rent promptly and that in the course of several disputes about usual landlord-tenant problems, Smith had always behaved like a gentleman and had never raised his voice or his hand. The defense did not elect to put Smith on the stand. Two witnesses present at the tavern were called and testified that they had heard Smith and Jones arguing. It was their "impression" that the two had left the tavern together. The defense concluded its direct examination of witnesses and the prosecution commenced its *cross-examination.*

The two witnesses who had testified about their impression that both parties had left the tavern together were intensively questioned. Under this questioning their recollection of the events appeared to become increasingly vague and they finally admitted that they "could not be absolutely sure" of their impression. Smith's employer was then called and, under questioning, acknowledged that Smith had not returned to work after the date of the alleged incident.

It was now the turn of the defense to cross-examine the State's witnesses. The victim, Jones, was called to the stand and closely questioned. He persisted in his earlier version of the event and could not be shaken in any detail. The witnesses who had testified that Jones had left earlier than Smith were next questioned and each one "stuck" to his story, insisting on the vividness of their recollection because the argument "stood out" and had drawn their attention. The defense then concluded its cross-examination.

The prosecution waived its opportunity to speak at this time, reserving its remarks for its *closing argument*. The defense was then called on to make a closing argument. In a brief address the defense counsel pointed out that it was necessary for the State to prove its case and that no witnesses of the actual fight outside the tavern had been presented. How then could the State prove that the two men had *not* argued outside the tavern—and that Jones had *not* attacked Smith?

The prosecution objected at this point, emphasizing that the story about an argument outside the tavern had been presented by the defense. "The prosecution cannot be held responsible for any fabrication . . ." ("Objection!") "made by the defense; it is up to defense to prove its own fairy tales. You might as well ask us to prove that Jones was not carrying a machine-gun or that Jones didn't attack Smith with an ax." All the State had to prove was the fact of the attack, "which we have done and which the defense has admitted took place. *If they claim self-defense, they have to prove it.*"

After this interchange, the defense continued. The State, it contended, must prove a motive. "How can we be expected to believe that a reasonably sane man would attack a person he never saw before over a little barroom argument?" At this point the prosecutor leaped to his feet and scored a telling objection: "But that's exactly what you're trying to have us believe Jones did! You're raising a point that destroys your own argument. We have had testimony that showed Smith was drunk. That and the knifing indicates motive enough—and you have *not* shown anything of the like about Jones." The judge intervened at this point and reminded the prosecutor that he would have an opportunity to give his own closing argument and admonished him to "let the defense have its say." The defense concluded that it would be inconceivable to believe that a person of Smith's character would commit an unprovoked attack without the strongest reason of self-defense, and it again emphasized that the State must carry the burden of proof.

The prosecution opened its final argument by summarizing the evidence. It dwelt on the fact that Jones had been stabbed in the back, in a way that indicated an attack from behind. It pointed out that the parties had not left together and that Smith, in his drunken condition, had sufficient time to conceive the "motive so plainly indicated by his behavior." It concluded with a statement of Smith's previous criminal record, "which the defense has not denied," and pointed out that any comparison of character would be most unfavorable to the defendant.

At this point the prosecution rested and the court was recessed until such time as the judge would *instruct the jury.*

When the court reconvened, the judge instructed the jury, which then retired to consider its *verdict.* After approximately two hours the jury returned with a verdict of "guilty to atrocious assault in the first degree." The defense immediately moved for a new trial. The motion was denied and the court recessed, to be reconvened at the time of *sentencing.*

In considering his sentence, the judge referred to a report prepared by the Department of Probation. This report stated that the defendant had had a poor work record, had been considered unreliable and "a troublemaker" by several previous employers, and had a generally poor reputation in his neighborhood. The details of the previous offenses were given. After determining the sentence he would impose, the judge reconvened the court and sentenced Smith to "not less than 3 and not more than 5 years in the State Prison." A motion for *stay of execution* pending appeal was made and denied, and the convicted offender was turned over to the sheriff to be delivered to the correctional authorities.

The brief summary of criminal procedure presented in this chapter was not intended, and cannot be used, as more than the most general introduction to a topic that should be of greater importance to the criminologist. The criminal law, with all its imperfections, remains one of the most important social defenses against the criminal. In cases where prevention has failed and correctional treatment is ineffective, it is virtually the only defense. The sophisticated criminal is aware of this fact and takes great pains to study the law in order to discover its weaknesses. It might be argued that the criminologist ought to know at least as much as the criminal.

There is another reason a study of the law should commend itself to the criminologist. The possibilities of improvement in correctional procedure are closely related to and highly dependent on the views of lawmakers, who, in turn, are highly responsive to the attitudes of judges. Any thoroughgoing reform in correctional procedure will require changes in statutes. Arguments for these changes will have a considerably greater chance of convincing lawmakers (who are usually lawyers) if they evince a recognition of the practical problems of law enforcement.

CRIME IN
CONTEMPORARY SOCIETY

Crime and the Social Structure

BECAUSE CRIME INVOLVES INTERACTIONS BETWEEN PERSONS IN AN organized community, it is related to the social structure at innumerable points and in innumerable ways. The criminal himself must be socialized to a considerable extent in order to be effective. He must learn the language, he must master complex social usages of dress and manner. His needs to avoid detection require him to behave in ways that make him indistinguishable from others; the criminal who "stood out" would arouse attention and be easily identified. Many criminal pursuits require the simulation of a high order of respectability and "regularity." The confidence man must truly inspire confidence; the successful embezzler must be a more careful and scrupulous accountant than his honest fellow-workers. The corrupt politician needs more friends and well-wishers than the honest politician, who, having less to lose, can afford to make more enemies. The efficient criminal must master many of the technical aspects of his culture. Crime as a craft and technology can survive only by successful competition with the skills and techniques of law enforcement. The modern safe-cracker must be something of a practical engineer; the efficient burglar must be half a locksmith. For these and many other reasons, a wholly "unsocialized" criminal would be an impossibility.

But there are many other interrelations between crime and the social structure. The community provides the criminal with his victims and his opportunities. In a very broad sense, it fashions his personality and shapes his motivations. And despite the fact that organized society is formally mobilized against his activities, crime continues to flourish.

The evidence for these interrelationships suggests at the very least the necessity of re-examining the commonplace doctrine of crime as an attack on society. That crime and other uncontrolled deviations are hostile to social institutions cannot be doubted; the mutuality of this hostility is posited in the definition of crime. Nevertheless, the conventional interpretation of this concept implies that the attack is mounted from some point outside the social structure and ignores the manifest possibility of internal origins. This chapter, therefore, will focus on four aspects of the social contribution to crime: (1) motives and incentives available for criminal exploitation; (2) means available for successfully carrying out these motives in criminal behavior; (3) factors contributing to the availability and vulnerability of victims and targets; (4) factors contributing to the neutralization of agencies of law enforcement.

Motives and Incentives Available for Criminal Exploitation

The social structure of any group may be viewed as essentially an organization of roles for the purpose of solving two general problems: (1) problems of living, as defined by the traditions of the group; and (2) problems arising out of tensions in the social structure itself. In the course of these attempts of the social group to adjust to the environment and to itself, there evolve patterned ways of thinking and acting that impose certain rights, responsibilities, and limits on individual members. Thus, in addition to the more obvious biological and psychological responsibilities of each individual to himself as a living, problem-solving organism, each person has certain obligations, immunities, privileges, and limitations arising out of his membership in the group.

Certain of these imposed conditions are general to all group members; others are specific to individuals. The process by which a person acquires these "conditions," which define (both to himself and to others) how he may live, are not very well understood. We can do no more, at this point, than describe the more apparent results. As a result of these complicated processes the individual acquires a specific pattern of *roles* which define what he may do with others, what others may do with him, and, vaguely (since he senses it vaguely), what his impressions and expectations are of himself and of people generally.

Thus, viewed abstractly, the social structure of any group is a continuing process which organizes roles into established patterns by involving all members of the group in certain status relationships with one another. In this way social life becomes a kind of perennial drama, in which each new generation of actors competes for essentially the same desirable parts, acts out essentially the same situations, and pursues essentially the same goals. Roles, status, and goals are so closely interrelated that they may be viewed as functions of each other, since certain goals are considered legitimate only for persons occupying the appropriate roles and status and employing the correct institutions—approved ways—for attaining them. Thus two young people who aspire toward the goal of living with each other must wait until they fulfill the role requirements defining marriageable persons, when they may properly attain their objective through the institution of marriage.

But the question arises—must they? Surely at this point in the discussion it will be pointed out that they can also break into the family kitty, leave town, and live in sin. It is at this critical point that reality-as-it-should-be and reality-as-it-can-be clash, and one is reminded that social institutions define merely the acceptable ways of attaining goals; they do not define the totality of realistically possible ways of reaching these goals. Of course, the young people who choose elopement as a solution will find themselves in great difficulties—and it is at this point that they encounter another aspect of the social structure—namely, its *normative* and *coercive* character. The social order attempts to create situations in which roles, status, institutions, and goals are maintained in a certain equilibrium by rewarding those actors who conform and punishing those who deviate. Thus—returning to the analogy of the drama—it is intolerable that the villain should walk off with the heroine (wrong role for winning the goal). It is also inconceivable that the hero should win the heroine by kidnaping and abusing her—right role, but wrong institution. Finally, it is totally improper for the hero who does treat the heroine properly to find out that he has acquired a Lucretia Borgia in disguise—right role, right institution, wrong result.

Status Mobility

Ways of determining individual roles and status vary greatly in different societies; in any given society they represent some characteristic combination of individual initiative, biological determination, social compulsion, and chance. Thus, in societies where the major roles are tied to hereditary status, it is virtually impossible for a person born to the slave status to become a king, despite his abilities and initiative. Again, no combination of high status, individual initiative, social compulsion, or chance can aid a person born to the biological status of a woman to achieve the role of father.

In all societies there exist ways of changing certain roles and statuses in both *horizontal* and *vertical* directions; sociologists describe this process of change as *mobility,* and they differentiate societies in terms of the ease or difficulty of mobility and the ways by which it is accomplished. Again, personal mobility depends on some combination of individual behavior, social action, and chance; almost invariably, however, the rate and extent of mobility is partly determined by the point in the scale of status from which the person starts out.

The degree of mobility possible (or statistically probable) for occupants of any given status is one of the most important characteristics of that status and, to a considerable extent, may come to define its value. This is especially true of societies that lay great stress on "getting ahead" i.e., on encouraging upward mobility; it is less true of societies that encourage their members to be content with their lot by distributing rewards on the basis of acceptable performance in any role rather than on the basis of high status. Societies that distribute their material and psychological rewards on the basis of position rather than performance must find ways of coping with the discontent of their socially immobilized masses. Such societies are able to preserve their structure by one or the other of two general types of coercion: *external coercion,* of which the most obvious example is political repression; and *internal coercion,* of which the most effective is some form of religious belief enabling the deprived members to cope with their discontent by some ethic of resignation. Thus the low-caste Hindu achieves resignation and avoids resentment by means of a religious philosophy which tells him (1) that his present miserable status is the result of misdeeds in a past incarnation *and that, therefore, he has no one to blame but himself;* (2) that it is both impious and fruitless to attempt to avoid his punishment; and, finally (3) that virtue and patience and resignation will result in an improved fate in his next incarnation. In the sense that they tend, simultaneously, to preserve the social structure and the peace of mind of its members, the values of the Hindu society facilitate a workable adjustment to social realities.

The Attainability of Major Social Goals

The relationship between *aspiration* and *attainability* forms a valid basis for the comparison of different societies and for the analysis of changes within the same society. The questions to be raised are:

1. To what extent are the means provided for the attainment of the major social goals available to the members of the society?
2. To what extent is there a correspondence between what people at different status levels want and what they may realistically attain?
3. To what extent have those who are unable to attain their goals through the medium of available institutions attempted to attain them by methods outside of, or in violation of, the institutional patterns?

Answers to the first two questions will reveal the extent and character of the frustrations with which the social structure must cope. Answers to the third question will reveal the extent to which the frustrations have led to innovations that tend to change or disrupt the pattern of social institutions and the social structure dependent on it.

It is improbable that there is any society in which the means evolved for the attainment of goals are available to all status levels. By its very nature, the institutionalization process is conducive to a certain degree of frustration because it selects from the totality of all possible ways of doing things only a limited number that is "acceptable." It will be recalled, however, that frustration has two aspects: actual deprivation (the objective lack of things) and subjective frustration (the feeling of deprivation). This distinction is crucial, since many findings indicate that either of these conditions may exist and vary without relation to the other. Anthropologists have described societies that have been able to preserve a relatively tension-free and stable social structure in the face of grave inequality and widespread want. They have also described societies in which frustration and social tension are severe in the midst of relative plenty. Occasionally it is found that frustration is most acute among those who are relatively well-to-do; in our own society, apparently, it is rather evenly distributed throughout all socioeconomic levels. Thus Merton has written:

> In the American Dream there is no final stopping place. The measure of "monetary success" is conveniently indefinite and relative. At each income level, as H. F. Clark has found, Americans want just about 25 per cent more (but of course this "just a bit more" continues to operate once it is obtained). In this flux of shifting standards, there is no stable resting point, or rather, it is the point which manages always to be "just ahead." An observer of a community in which annual salaries in six figures are not uncommon reports the anguished words of one victim of the American Dream: "In this town, I'm snubbed socially because I only get a thousand a week. That hurts." [1]

These findings suggest that the kind of frustration which is most significant socially must be measured in terms of the gap *between aspirations and achievable goals.*

The distinction between objective and subjective frustration may hold true for specific forms of deprivation, such as *poverty,* and it may in part account for the confused picture that emerges when one attempts to correlate poverty and theft. When poverty is defined in material terms, the poverty of the one-time offender who steals in order to feed his family cannot be compared with the poverty of the affluent bank president who embezzles in order to buy his young mistress a sable to match her Cadillac. Yet, in the psychological sense, both are suffering acutely from a poverty defined by an institutionally unbridgeable gap between aspiration and goal. The jobless thief is being coerced by the extortion of hunger; the affluent banker, by the extortion of unpurchasable love.

Crime as a Way of Achieving Social Goals

There is a view—well established in public opinion—which holds that society and the criminal are everywhere at odds. This view seems warranted when one considers certain types of conventional criminals. The homeless, friendless drifter who lives by petty theft as he moves in an endless round from rooming house to the county jail and "skid row"

---

[1] Robert K. Merton, *Social Theory and Social Structure* (Glencoe, Ill.: The Free Press, 1949), pp. 129–130.

certainly fits the picture of the social parasite who contributes nothing to the social order that nurtured him. He lives for himself, steals for himself, and gives nothing in return for what he takes. He is the eternal outsider—the shabby drifter pointed out by mothers to their small children, who must learn their necessary lessons of fear and coldness toward the stranger. Looking at him and his nondescript fellows as they crowd the police courts, it may seem plausible to assert: "He is a criminal *because* he has no friends, *because* he is so isolated with nothing to bind him, and no one to hold him back from doing wrong."

But what of the criminal who walks, invited, through the front door—who pets the dogs and numbers among his friends not only the policemen on the beat but "some of the best people in town"? Take, for example, the typical "big-time" racketeer who sends his children to college, who contributes handsomely to his church and favorite charity (and also, but somewhat less publicly, to certain other public institutions—such as the police force and the city council). Imagine him stripped of all these "social bonds"—stripped as bare as the drifter in skid row. What and where would he be then? Certainly not the successful racketeer.

The histories of many successful criminals, especially of those moving into the more serious and costly forms of crime, show increasing rather than decreasing respectability. The pattern is fairly consistent. They tend to marry respectable women; they bring up well-educated, nondelinquent children; they achieve good relations with neighbors; they participate in politics. Even their criminal behavior becomes more respectable, taking on more and more the character of "legitimate business." Violence is replaced by subtler forms of persuasion; the brutal threat is often replaced by the legal contract—and the contract is usually honored. They maintain good relations with many noncriminal enterprises; they pay their debts. Frequently, they own legitimate businesses and large tracts of real estate, administered by honest employees using efficient methods and sound bookkeeping. Thus, they are far better assimilated into "respectable" society than many honest persons living on the socioeconomic fringe.

These and many other examples that might be cited create an insoluble paradox for any theory attempting to correlate *crime as a whole* with social conflict and disattachment. A part of this dilemma springs from the fact that the term *criminal* itself is so broad as to be virtually useless for a meaningful description of all types of law violators. Adequate—or, at least, plausible—in the case of the obvious psychological deviate and the social outcast, a theory of disattachment breaks down completely when it is required to cope with the instance of the socially integrated offender. Moreover, it fails to allow for the possibility that many forms of criminal behavior have a positive rather than negative relation to the values and usages of the society in which they occur. This possibility has been explored with compelling suggestiveness by the sociologist Robert Merton in use of the essays in his book *Social Theory and Social Structure.*

In this work, Merton outlines the theoretical basis for investigating *"how some social structures exert a definite pressure upon certain persons . . . to engage in non-conformist rather than conformist conduct."* [2] One source of these pressures is found in a disequilibrium between two fundamental elements of the social structure: goals and the institutional means available for their achievement. Citing evidence that these two elements may vary independently of each other, Merton describes how "there may develop . . . a virtually exclusive stress upon the value of given goals, involving comparatively little concern with the institutionally prescribed means of striving for these goals." The extreme form of this process is reached when "the range of alternative procedures is governed only by technical rather than institutional norms." Among individuals this point is reached when these cease to control their behavior on any basis other than expediency—a state of mind expressed in the wisecrack, "Anything goes." According to Merton, "American culture appears to approximate the . . . type in which great emphasis upon certain success-goals occurs without equivalent emphasis upon institutional means." [3]

This end-result is due to the operation of many factors, among them the inadequate distribution of institutional avenues. Serious as this problem is, it is complicated by the fact that the constantly diminishing *possibilities* for success have not been paralleled by any decline in the *cult* of success. The encouragement of undiminished aspiration in the face of diminishing rewards creates a situation in which the objective and subjective frustration combine to make life increasingly intolerable to growing numbers of people who find themselves trapped between the desert and the mirage. It also leads to a type of individual adaptation which Merton calls "innovation"—a response which occurs "when the individual has assimilated the cultural emphasis upon the goal without

[2] *Ibid.,* pp. 125–126.
[3] *Ibid.,* p. 129.

equally internalizing the institutional norms governing ways and means for its attainment."[4]

Innovation is seen as a mode of adaptation characterizing the behavior not only of criminals but of many others in the white-collar occupations who would be classed as criminals if it were not for what Sutherland has called the "relatively unorganized resentment of the public against white collar criminals."[5] In this connection, Merton cites a study (see Chapter 1, page 5) of some seventeen hundred prevalently middle-class individuals, whose off-the-record admissions indicated that 99 per cent of them had committed one or more offenses under the penal laws of the state of New York. These "law-abiding lawbreakers" were successfully engaging in certain innovations which, though illegal, were tolerated so long as they were not publicly pointed out. In effect, they were operating as silent architects of a kind of social change—the subversion of certain ethical values by certain efficiency values. The question arises: Would this behavior have been permissible and effective without a certain kind of silent cooperation on the part of society itself? Putting the question more generally: Is it possible that society, while laying down certain rules of right and wrong, and indicating which avenues are closed and which are open, simultaneously provides ways to circumvent those same rules—and indicates certain trails and pathways by which the silent traveler can safely negotiate the forbidden routes?

Crime as a Response to Recognized Social Needs

Systematic Social Cooperation in the Violation of Social Rules

In his monograph *Crime and Custom in Savage Society* the anthropologist Bronislaw Malinowski describes his accidental discovery of a principle that drastically altered his former ideas about the one-way relation between public opinion and social rules:

> One day an outbreak of wailing...told me that a death had occurred

[4] *Ibid.*, pp. 134–146. *Innovation* is described as one among five general ways in which an individual may adjust to the frustrations arising out of his status in the social structure. The other four are: (1) *conformity*—acceptance both of social goals and institutional means; (2) *ritualism*—emphasis on means with neglect of goals; (3) *retreatism*—rejection of both goals and means; and (4) *rebellion*—ambivalence toward both goals and means.

[5] Edwin H. Sutherland, "White Collar Crime," *American Sociological Review*, 5:1–12, February 1940.

somewhere in the neighborhood. I was informed that Kima'l, a young lad of my acquaintance ... had fallen from a coco-nut palm and killed himself. ...

Only much later was I able to discover the real meaning of these events: the boy had committed suicide. The truth was that he had broken the rules of exogamy, the partner in his crime being his maternal cousin, the daughter of his mother's sister. This rival (of Kima'l) threatened first to use black magic against the guilty youth, but this had not much effect. Then one evening he insulted the culprit in public—accusing him in the hearing of the whole community of incest. ... For this there was only one remedy.... Next morning he put on festive attire and ornamentation, climbed a coco-nut palm and addressed the community ... bidding them farewell. He explained the reasons for his desperate deed and also launched forth a veiled accusation against the man who had driven him to his death, upon which it became the duty of his clansmen to avenge him. Then he wailed aloud, as is the custom, jumped from a palm some sixty feet high and was killed on the spot.[6]

Aware of the incest taboo, Malinowski was not, at the outset, surprised by this drastic outcome. Looking further, however, he was astonished to find that the young man's activities had been common knowledge for some time *before* his rival had publicly denounced him. Nevertheless, up until this time, writes Malinowski:

Public opinion was neither outraged by the knowledge of the crime to any extent, nor did it react directly—it had to be mobilized by a public statement of the crime and by insults being hurled at the culprit by an interested party. Even then he had to carry out the punishment himself. The "group-reaction" and the "supernatural sanction" were not therefore the active principles. Probing further into the matter and collecting concrete information, I found that the breach of exogamy —as regards intercourse and not marriage—is by no means a rare occurrence, and public opinion is lenient, though decidedly hypocritical. If the affair is carried on *sub rosa* with a certain amount of decorum, and if no one in particular stirs up trouble—"public opinion" will gossip, but not demand harsh punishment. If, on the contrary, scandal breaks out—every one turns against the guilty pair and by ostracism and insults one or the other may be driven to suicide.[7]

The anecdote related by Malinowski illuminates several relationships between social control, social change, and crime. The practice of

---

[6] Bronislav Malinowski, *Crime and Custom in Savage Society* (New York: Humanities Press, 1926), pp. 77–78.

[7] *Ibid.*, pp. 79–80.

13

0

CRIME IN CONTEMPORARY SOCIETY

clan incest represented an attempt to fulfill needs that could not be satisfied through legitimate channels. A way had to be found to re-open an avenue blocked by customary prohibitions. But the prohibitions also served a vital community need: the regularizing and legitimizing of marriage and kinship patterns and rights. If incest became *legitimate,* these arrangements would be jeopardized. For this reason, it was essential that incest remain an official crime. However, if it could simultaneously remain illegitimate and *yet be permitted,* no essential conflict would exist.[8] Young persons who did violate the taboo in either secret or at least informal ways would marry permissible mates later on. Thus, no efficiency value was really being violated, despite the violation of the moral taboo. Among other conclusions, this analysis suggests a rejection of the view that crime is, at all times, a destructive assault on society without any functional value whatsoever.

The Functional Value of Certain Forms of Crime

The situation described by Malinowski has many parallels in our own society. In a brilliant analysis of the functions of the political boss, Merton brings the point closer to home. The corrupt political boss, with his retinue of wardheelers and his almost inevitable connections with crime, has long been both a fixture and a symbol of the American political scene. The fact that he has *remained* a fixture, despite his opprobrium as a symbol, suggests that he is not without certain functions tacitly accepted as valuable by certain groups. Merton sees him serving the needs of at least three distinct subgroups.

He is, in the first place, the traditional friend of the underprivileged man-in-trouble:

> In our prevailing impersonal society, the machine, through its local agents, fulfills the important social *function of humanizing and per-*

[8] A penetrating analysis of the conflict between social ideals and social needs is given by Thurman Arnold in *The Folklore of Capitalism* (New Haven: Yale University Press, 1937), pp. 365–367:

> A conflict often arises between an ideal and a social need not accepted as legitimate or moral. This creates a situation in which an immoral and undercover organization will arise. The ideal will be represented by the moral organization ... the social need ... by an immoral organization, which will be accepted as a necessary evil. ...
>
> The respectable organization will satisfy the ideal by trying to abolish the nonrespectable one. The nonrespectable institution will survive because the struggle will compel it to maintain an efficient disciplined organization. A curious paradox will result. The reform organization will owe its existence to the vice which it attacks, while the vice ... will be tolerated because of the belief that it is the fault of no one, since all respectable people are in favor of reform.

sonalizing all manner of assistance, to those in need. Food-baskets and jobs, legal and extra-legal advice, setting to rights minor scrapes with the law ... the whole range of crises when a feller needs a friend, and, above all, a friend who knows the score and who can do something about it.[9]

Second, he is the friend of the businessman struggling in the toils of government regulations—many of which are designed to protect him by preventing his competitors from using the same "influence" he is seeking. In this regard, Merton cites a speech made by Lincoln Steffens to a group of businessmen in support of the view that the boss and his machine are an "integral part of the organization of the economy":

> You cannot build or operate a railroad, or a street railway, gas, water, or power company, develop and operate a mine ... or run any privi-leged business without corrupting or joining in the corruption of the government. You (the businessmen) tell me privately that you must, and here I am telling you semi-publicly that you must. And that is so all over the country.[10]

A third function of the boss and his machine is that of aiding those born low on the social ladder to advance themselves. In this connection, Merton cites William F. Whyte:

> The sociologist who dismisses racket and political organizations as deviations from desirable standards thereby neglects some of the major elements of slum life.... *He does not discover the functions they per-form for the members* [of the groupings in the slum]. The ... immi-grant ... people have had the greatest difficulty in finding places for themselves in our urban social and economic structure. Does anyone believe that the immigrants and their children could have achieved their present degree of social mobility without gaining control of the political organization of some of our largest cities? The same is true of the racket organization. *Politics and rackets have furnished an important means of social mobility for individuals, who, because of ethnic background and low class position,* are blocked from advancement in the respectable channels.[11] (Italics supplied.)

Finally, the political machine performs many of the same services for the criminal enterprises of vice, gambling, and other rackets that it performs for "legitimate" businesses:

> In this light it at once appears that the sub-group of the professional criminal, racketeer, gambler, has basic similarities of organization, de-

[9] Merton, *op. cit.,* p. 73.
[10] Lincoln Steffens, quoted in Merton, *op. cit.,* pp. 73–74.
[11] William F. Whyte, "Social Organization in the Slums," *American Socio-logical Review,* 8:34–39, February 1943. Quoted in Merton, *op. cit.,* p. 77.

mands and operations to the sub-group of the industrialist, man of business, speculator. If there is a Lumber King or an Oil King, there is also a Vice King or a Racket King.... If legitimate business regards the proliferation of small business enterprises as wasteful and inefficient, substituting, for example, the giant chain stores for the hundreds of corner groceries, so illegitimate business adopts the same business-like attitude, and syndicates crime and vice.[12]

Merton points out that, moral considerations aside, there are few, if any, basic differences between these legitimate and illegitimate enterprises. Did the illegal liquor traffic (he asks) cease to perform an economic service between 1920 and 1933—the years Prohibition was in force?

Can it be held that in European countries, with registered and legalized prostitution, the prostitute contributes an economic service, whereas in this country, lacking legal sanction, the prostitute performs no such service? Or that the professional abortionist is in the economic market where he has approved legal status and that he is out of the economic market where he is legally taboo? Or that gambling satisfies a specific demand for entertainment in Nevada, where it is one of the largest business enterprises of the largest city in the state, but that it differs essentially in this respect from movie houses in the neighboring state of California?[13]

The close economic parallels between many legal and illegal enterprises suggest that the observation, "Every society gets the crime it deserves," might be reconstrued in a more limited and technical sense: "Frequently, society gets the crimes it demands." In this light, the conventional picture of the noncriminal world as a pool of passive victims from which the criminal filches his wealth becomes highly distorted.

Consider the question: What makes it profitable for a thief to steal a car, a fur piece, a diamond bracelet? These thefts are profitable only if the objects can be sold. The thief sells his stolen goods to a fence or a pawnshop or a dealer in "used goods." Why is it profitable for the dealer to buy these things? Eventually, they will be sold to a person who will buy them to use them: a noncriminal out for a bargain.

The continued flourishing of property crimes demonstrates the existence of a large pool of economic demand continually unsatisfied by conventional economic channels. Without this noncriminal ultimate consumer, most forms of property crime would be unprofitable. Viewed entirely in economic terms, many property thefts are essentially transfers of goods from the noncriminal victim to the noncriminal consumer, with

[12] Merton, op. cit., p. 77.
[13] Ibid., pp. 78–79.

the thief acting as a kind of middleman or distributor. The economic advantage of this arrangement is obvious. Because he does not pay for the stolen goods, the thief saves the costs of production—a saving he is then able to pass on to the noncriminal consumer. Thus, to the conventional relationship of the thief and his victim, there must be added the relationship between the thief and his economic beneficiary. Without the latter relationship, the former would be meaningless.

The implications of the foregoing analysis for the problem of remedial social change seem apparent. Merton has stated them in the form of a "basic social theorem":

> Any attempt to eliminate an existing social structure without providing adequate alternative structures for fulfilling the functions previously fulfilled by the abolished organization is doomed to failure.... When "political reform" confines itself to the manifest task of "turning the rascals out," it is engaging in little more than sociological magic.[14]

Factors Contributing to the Availability and Vulnerability of Victims

There are very few studies of crime as a function of the criminal's relationship with the victim; the entire problem must be considered one of the silent areas of criminology. The noted European criminologist, Von Hentig, has pointed out that "nothing is known statistically of those who are victimized by larceny, burglary, robbery, or even the confidence game . . ."[15] Nevertheless, a crime without a victim or target would

[14] *Ibid.*, pp. 79–80.

[15] The fullest exploration of this subject available in English is found in Hans von Hentig's *The Criminal and His Victim* (New Haven: Yale University Press, 1948). Anything approaching a full rendering of this author's original and provocative thesis is impossible in this text. Von Hentig has attempted to describe various types of victims (the young, the old, the female, the immigrant, etc.) and to suggest certain aspects of the psychological relations linking the criminal with his victim in what he has called the "duet frame of crime." The following excerpt (p. 385) is illustrative of the tendency and flavor of his analysis:

> In a sense the victim shapes and molds the criminal. The poor and ignorant immigrant has bred a peculiar type of fraud. Depressions and wars are responsible for new forms of crime because new types of potential victims are brought into being. It would not be correct or complete to speak of a carnivorous animal, its habits and characteristics, without looking at the prey on which it lives. In a certain sense, the animals which devour and those that are devoured complement each other. Although it looks one-sided as far as the final outcome goes, it is not a totally unilateral form of relationship. They work upon each other profoundly and continually, even before the moment of disaster. To know one, we must be acquainted with the complementary partner.

be impossible—and, in this sense, the possibility of crime varies directly with the availability and vulnerability of victims.

The neglect of the victim by criminologists is not shared by criminals themselves; the victim is, in fact, an object of constant study. The search for susceptible victims, for ways to exploit their vulnerability with the greatest possible immunity from detection or prosecution, is the perennial concern of the professional criminal; his success in this search is what distinguishes him from the amateurs and the bunglers who populate prisons.

The Increased Vulnerability of the Individual in Modern Society

One of the paradoxes of the modern age is the increasing power of man-in-general over his environment and the decreasing control by men-in-particular over their own destinies. Individuals today live in closer physical proximity and compression than ever before—yet we are constantly reminded of the loneliness and isolation of the modern city-dweller. The improved physical health and security of modern man has almost doubled his life expectancy within the last hundred years—yet the proliferation of personal insecurity has suggested a description of the present period as an "Age of Anxiety." Man's knowledge, control, and exploitation of physical resources has increased fantastically—yet the average man knows so little about the technical details of his specialized and mechanized civilization that he is daily more dependent on experts.

The burgeoning dependencies and decreasing self-determination of modern man have produced characteristic psychological effects. In their provocative work, *The Lonely Crowd—A Study of the Changing American Character*, Riesman, Glazer, and Denney posit the emergence of a "new" characterological type: the *other-directed man*, who governs his behavior by means of a heightened sensitivity and conformity to the wishes and values of those on whom he feels dependent.

Factors Contributing to the Vulnerability of the Modern Urban-Dweller

ISOLATION. Disasters isolate: to fall victim to a disease, to a toothache, or to an armed robber is to experience an isolation-within-pain into which no one who does not share the discomfort can enter. The isolating consequences of misfortune tend to fall more frequently on those who are isolated already from closely supporting friends or relations. The person alone, the person whom no one expects to hear from and whom no one will miss, the person without friends to protect or avenge him—this person is particularly vulnerable to exploitation.

DEPENDENCY. To survive in relative isolation in an interdependent society is to be dependent on impersonal, uninterested third parties—on an impersonal boss for a job, on an impersonal police force for protection, and on strangers for friendship, recreation, and rapport. In the increasing complexity of modern life, the modern urban-dweller—and, to a lesser extent, the inhabitant of rural areas as well—has less and less control over the processes producing the goods and services essential for living. The multitudinous figures on whom he must depend are interested in him largely as an impersonal, paying consumer; and their interest is defined and limited by his ability to pay. There are clear differences between the businessman's interest in the customer and the criminal's attitude toward his victim, but there are also situations in which these differences shrink. The Better Business Bureau has described over eight hundred different gyps, dodges, and frauds in which the differences between the businessman and the criminal have, in fact, shrunk to the vanishing point.[16] In all of these situations the basic process was similar: The victim-consumer needed or wanted something he could not produce himself; he was dependent on an impersonal third party—the vendor—over whom he had no control; he was ignorant of the technical details and dangers of the transaction and had to trust in the vendor's good faith; this trust was abused—in most cases, with impunity.

What is true of the isolated, dependent individual is also true of the individual small producer and distributor. The increasing complexity and specialization of modern production has rendered the modern entrepreneur increasingly vulnerable to coercion and extortion by groups who are strategically placed to interrupt the flow of essential goods and services. This general situation suggests a working principle: The greater the complexity and interdependence of an aspect of production, distribution, or any related function, the greater the vulnerability to exploitive manipulation. Every exposed point in the intricate network is, in a sense, a point open to attack; every link in the complicated chain, a link that can be broken. A corollary of the principle applies to the susceptibility of any form of activity to corruption. The more indispensable, the more irreplaceable the service or commodity, the greater

[16] Better Business Bureau publications may be obtained either from local offices in various large cities or from BNA Incorporated, a division of the Bureau of National Affairs, Inc., Washington 7, D. C.

the opportunity and temptation to exploit. The growth of extortionate rackets in various segments of the transport industry is one of many instances of the operation of this principle.

The Neutralization of Law-Enforcement Agencies

Whatever increases the vulnerability of the victim automatically increases the power of his exploiter. In this sense, the greater resources and increased immunity of the criminal are a direct reflection of the diminished defenses of his potential victim. Many aspects of modern social life contribute to this relationship.

Protective Anonymity

The isolation that tends to make the modern city-dweller a stranger to his next-door neighbor tends to confer a protective anonymity on the criminal. In a community of strangers, there is less interest in and curiosity about the newcomer; and where there is less interest, there is less likely to be suspicion. In the small community one's private business tends to become everybody's business and everyone, in a sense, is more or less his neighbor's keeper. This aspect of the small-town atmosphere can be somewhat stifling, but it is also protective. The stranger in town is regarded with the closest scrutiny; and he is either not a stranger for very long or not in town for very long. In the city, however, the rules tend to be reversed: one "minds one's own business," and a studied, almost deliberate indifference replaces the small-town curiosity about the newcomer. In the city, in fact, this indifference becomes elevated to a rule of courtesy, and its violation may be regarded as a breach of good manners. All of this works to the advantage of the criminal stranger.

Increased Mobility

Speed, time, and distance are functions of each other: the faster one travels, the more distance one can cover. Mobility may be either spatial or social; in both senses, the mobility of the modern criminal has increased. The increase is related not only to the faster tempo of modern living but to the other factors already discussed: the increased anonymity, isolation, impersonality, and complexity of many aspects of contemporary social relations.

The increased *spatial* mobility of the modern criminal in a mechanized age needs no illustration. Surprise, speed of execution, and getaway, and the ability to confound pursuit by rapid changes of location, are the traditional techniques of the professional criminal; modern advances have only improved them. (There is an anecdote about a letter sent by John Dillinger to Henry Ford, praising the getaway qualities of the Ford car.)

The increased *social* mobility of the modern professional criminal is as important as his ability to move rapidly in space. In a community where people expect to know only superficially many of those with whom they deal, one's apparent social level is frequently a matter of dress and manner. Within the limits of their ingenuity—and the credulity of their victims—skillful criminals have taken advantage of this situation by simulating virtually any social role and status they chose. The polished confidence man may become a banker, a prosperous businessman, or even a diplomat by a simple change of dress. The jewel thief who puts on his tuxedo and crashes the big society ball is relying on his social graces rather than his social antecedents; his "rise" in the social scale need last only the few minutes or hours required to carry out his thefts.

The use of disguises and simulated roles for offensive and defensive criminal purposes is not confined to the less violent type of criminal. One of the most able bank robbers of modern times, Willie Sutton (known, significantly, as "Willie the Actor"), frequently used false roles to gain entry into banks before opening time. On one occasion, he posed as a Western Union messenger; on another, as a special bank guard. The most notorious gangland assassination—the St. Valentine's Day Massacre—was carried out by killers wearing the uniforms of policemen. Their victims, knowing they had less to fear from the police than from their criminal rivals, apparently submitted to the "officers" and turned their backs to be searched—a fatal mistake. Each of these instances involved an effective assumption of a false role by criminals who knew they would be accepted in that role despite the fact that they were personally not known to their victims.

Immunity-Conferring Relationships: The Criminal and the Scoundrel

The preceding discussion dealt with the criminal advantages of simulating certain roles that enable the offender to lull or deceive his victim before the offense. This role-playing has one great disadvantage, however: after the crime, the performance is over and the angry victim is left with his loss and a desire for revenge. At this point, he usually goes to the police—and the criminal goes into hiding. The resentment of the victim is decisive at this juncture. Unless he goes to the police, the crime will not become known. Moreover, even after the arrest, the continued cooperation of the victim is essential in order to obtain a conviction. If he suddenly changes his mind—or has it changed for him— the case will fall to the ground.

At this point the question arises: What if the offender, instead of merely *simulating* a relationship with the victim, *actually occupies it,* and continues to occupy it even after the offense? What are the possible and probable effects of this situation on the subsequent behavior of the victim? Are there relationships that, while making one or the other party vulnerable to criminal exploitation, simultaneously tend to neutralize the victim's resentment or revenge—thereby granting the other a virtual immunity?

"It's criminal the way that man beats his wife," say the neighbors. True; and should anyone else abuse her in that manner, the police would probably hear about it. Nevertheless, probably only a fraction of wife-beatings are ever reported to the police; and when they are, by the time both parties have realized the possible consequences to each, both the victim and the offender have usually become firmly reunited against the common threat of the law. It is a very angry wife who will punish herself and her children by having the family breadwinner sent to jail.

The contrast between the immune wife-beater and the stranger who assaults an unknown or casually known victim on the street suggests a series of critical distinctions between people who behave "criminally" but go unpunished and those who violate laws and are punished as lawbreakers. This distinction is between the *scoundrel* and the *criminal,* and the decisive and frequently the only difference is the reaction of the victim. *The scoundrel is a relation or acquaintance who behaves criminally toward us. The criminal is frequently the scoundrel whom we do not personally know.*

The scoundrel is favored over the criminal-stranger at every point leading up to and following the criminal act. Even the law favors him over the stranger. The scoundrel walks invited through the front door; when he takes the jewels or the bonds out with him in his pocket, he has committed only the crime of *larceny.* But the criminal stranger must either rob the victim on the street or force his way in through a jimmied window or door; when he leaves with the jewels or bonds, he has committed the graver crimes of *robbery* or *burglary*. In either case, the criminal is forced, by his absence of a relationship with the victim, to take a course of action more drastically punished by the law.

Of greater significance, however, is the scoundrel's better chance of avoiding criminal prosecution in the first place. Apart from subjective consideration springing out of a personal attachment, it is frequently advantageous for the victim to refrain from criminal prosecution. Almost any criminal harm may be dealt with as a tort (civil) case rather than a criminal case. At the outset the choice lies exclusively with the victim; he can either call the police or call his lawyer. Should he use the civil remedy, his chances for restitution are probably better; the offender is not jailed and his earning power is not curtailed.

The distinction between the scoundrel and the criminal makes it possible to resolve the paradoxes arising when criminality is uncritically related to factors of social attachment or disattachment. The fact that most conventional criminals are strangers to their victims made it appear that crime and social disattachment were positively related. The example of the successful racketeer, who may be on friendly terms with local authorities—and even on cordial, businesslike terms with his victims—confused the picture considerably. Here social attachment, in the sense of continuous links and contacts with cooperative supporters and unresisting victims, seemed decidedly favorable to crime. Finally, the case of the immune scoundrel suggests a further distinction that may help to clarify the problem.

This distinction is actually a refinement of the distinction between *criminality as an act* and *criminality as a status*. Criminality as a pattern of *behavior* is favored when the criminal can avoid the threat of criminality as a *status*; the lawbreaker behind bars is out of business. The scoundrel—and the successful racketeer—is better able to avoid the status of criminal because his hold on the victim is strong enough to resist the estranging consequences of the crime. The conventional criminal, on the other hand, is less efficient as a criminal actor—partly because he is forced to more drastic action and partly because he is less immune to retaliation by the victim, who is usually a stranger on whom he has no personal claim. Thus, social attachment becomes a factor favorable to the effective committing of anti-social acts but unfavorable to the status of criminality. Conversely, social disattachment becomes a factor more favorable to criminal conviction and, for that and other reasons, less favorable to the most efficient forms of criminal activity. In this added sense, the conventional criminal, like his conventional target, is something of a victim of social circumstances.

We are now in a position to attempt a brief summary of the positive relations between crime and the social structure:

1. Every society seeks to establish certain material and non-material goals of life. In effect, it indoctrinates its members to pursue certain objectives as requirements of happiness.

2. It also provides the realistic material, technical, and situational means for attaining these goals.

3. However, for purposes related to its own organization, it defines certain of these *actual* ways of attaining goals as illegitimate and improper.

4. Thus, in every known society, the number of permissible ways of achieving desirable goals is less than the number of actual or possible ways of achieving them. Moreover, no society provides its members with all or even most of the legitimate means of goal-attainment.

5. Consequently, in every society, there exist gaps between *legitimate expectations* and *legitimate ways of fulfilling them*. In response to the frustrations created by these gaps, there arise attempts to circumvent prohibitions and to create new ways or "innovations" for reaching objectives unattainable by permissible means. Many forms of criminal behavior fall into this category of innovation. In many ways, *the career criminal, far from rejecting conventional social goals, has so deeply absorbed them that he is willing to improvise ruthlessly and daringly in order to attain them.*

6. Viewed in this perspective, the struggle between the criminal and society becomes one in which the conformers attempt to frustrate the intolerable innovations of the "improvisers" by mobilizing public indignation against them and punishing them, thereby making their innovations inefficient in the end. Thus the large majority of patient wage-earners band together against the criminal who can, in an hour, "make more money" than they can earn in years of work.

7. Unfortunately, however, the struggle against crime is complicated by the fact that large numbers of law-abiding citizens labor under certain frustrations and deprivations that, while not motivating them personally to crime, create in them a demand for goods and services not available through legitimate channels. In fulfilling certain of these demands, the criminal acts not in conflict but rather in collaboration with the noncriminal elements of society, which, in effect, create an economic demand for his services.

8. Thus, simultaneously with attempts to suppress criminal innovations, there arise techniques of cooperation and collaboration with them. In the most general terms, this collaboration takes the form of a mutual search for ways of redefining the criminal behavior in a manner that does not stimulate resentment and enmesh the offender in the rituals of public indignation.

Classifications of Crime and Criminals

IF IT WERE POSSIBLE TO ANTICIPATE WHAT TYPE OF PERSON WOULD commit what type of crime, the task of law enforcement would be greatly simplified. Knowledge of persons and groups likely to become involved in crime—as perpetrators, collaborators, and victims—would permit the most strategic concentration of preventive efforts before offenses occurred and maximal efficiency in detection after they had taken place. Police departments maintain extensive files dealing with the operational techniques used by different known criminals: the skilled safe-cracker, like the skilled painter, frequently leaves the personal marks of his craft on his work. But this information is available only after the crimes have taken place. The search for reliable correlates of criminal behavior continues to occupy criminologists, penologists, and law-enforcement officials at all levels, theoretical and practical.

The classification of criminal behavior in terms of criminal types, criminal life organization, and criminal careers represents an attempt to organize the data of crime in meaningful patterns. Essentially, this task involves the construction of *models*, through which the shape and workings of the originals can be grasped. There are two general types of models: those that help us to recognize the originals, and those conveying an understanding of their working processes. We require different

142

things from each. A model that illustrates how something works need not be pictorially realistic; the principle of filtration by which the kidneys function may be illustrated by an artificial membrane. In the case of models for recognition, however, the expectation is different. These models do not purport to be explanatory but descriptive. The conceptual models of crime and criminals discussed in the following pages are largely of this second type. The question arises: How well do they enable us to recognize the actual individuals and activities involved?

At this point we encounter one of the paradoxes of model-making. The more definite a model, the more clearly we can grasp it. But models, however clear and sharply drawn, are realistic only if the originals they represent are equally clear and sharply demarcated. What if the originals are, instead, shifting and capable of transformation? Here the act of model-building may become self-defeating, for in rendering the model sharp enough to be clearly grasped, we may allow the original to escape.

The use of static word-symbols to create models thus runs the risk of increasing clarity of conceptualization at the expense of reality. Where the reality is dynamic rather than static, fluid rather than concrete, the only alternative is to use terms suggesting these variable and elusive qualities. But this procedure is directly opposed to the requirements of clear, sharp model-building. These difficulties become apparent when one tries to fit the recognition models described below to the actual data of crime and criminals.

Classification by Legal Category

The earliest and still the most common way of classifying criminals is in terms of the legal title identifying the criminal act. Thus, a felon is one accused or convicted of a felony; a murderer, one accused or convicted of murder. This method suffers from a variety of disadvantages. (1) It creates a false impression of homogeneity by suggesting that individuals committing the same act are similar in other respects. (2) It tells nothing about the person, or about his personal characteristics or circumstances. (3) It creates a false impression of specialization by implying that criminals confine themselves to the one particular kind of crime for which they happen to be caught or convicted at a particular time. (4) Finally, though it purports to define the actor in terms of his act, its precision in describing the act itself is frequently questionable.

Legal definitions of criminal acts vary in different places. Since the crime of statutory rape, for example, is dependent on the statutory definition of the age of consent, it is entirely possible for a person committing the same act under the same circumstances to be condemned, in one state, as a "rapist," and, in another, to be without any criminal liability. Thus, legal definitions of criminal acts do not necessarily provide direct descriptions of the behaviors themselves, but may serve rather as declarations of public policy toward them.[1] This characteristic is inherent in all legal definitions and applies equally to broader classifications, such as the "property" offender, the "political" criminal, and similar categories specifying the type of victim or the kind of social interest violated.

Classification by Type of Person

The legalistic classification, which ignores individual differences and defines the criminal in terms of his act, is frequently contrasted with the *personalistic approach,* which bases itself on a study of the criminal actor. Advocates of the personalistic approach point out that society cannot cope with the criminal deed without dealing with the criminal doer; in order to deal with the doer one must understand him, and this is impossible in terms of arbitrary legal distinctions analyzing his act but ignoring his state of mind. To illustrate this point, the psychiatrist Benjamin Karpman has contrasted the legalistic concept of the murderer with the psychological concept:

> Let us take the instance of John A, who fires several shots at William B, with the obvious intention of killing him. He only succeeded, however, in injuring him, and he is charged with aggravated assault, for which he gets a sentence, say, of five years. Had he succeeded in his original aim, he would have been charged with first degree murder and punished accordingly. In either situation, however, his full intent was to kill; he was a murderer in every sense of the word; it was by sheer accident that he failed of his purpose. Yet the punishment is neatly differentiated on the basis of results rather than intent.[2]

[1] This is especially true of the legal definition of certain sex offenses; in some jurisdictions a variety of deviant sex practices may be lumped under the category of "crimes against nature" (see Chapter 9).

[2] Benjamin Karpman, "An Attempt at Revaluation of Some Concepts of Law and Psychiatry," *Journal of Criminal Law and Criminology,* 38:206–217, September–October 1947.

Classifications based on the study of the criminal actor have differentiated offenders in the following general ways:

1. *By hereditary physical type.* Lombroso's *born criminal* and Hooton's *constitutional defective* are illustrations of this type of classification.

2. *By psychological type or condition or disease.* Psychologists and psychiatrists have attempted to distinguish different criminal types in terms of different motivational patterns arising out of personality structure and various psychological states or disabilities. The various forms of crime are viewed as the symptomatic products of these underlying mental conditions. The individual's criminality is defined in terms of his underlying motivational pattern rather than his overt act. On this basis, a person arrested for a petty misdemeanor may frequently have stronger criminal tendencies than one apprehended for a major felony—and should be classified and treated accordingly.

Though they are often viewed as diametrically opposed, both the legalistic and the personalistic approaches to criminal classification may employ the same underlying method. The legalistic approach suggests that a certain type of crime defines or implies a certain kind of person. The personalistic approach inverts the same reasoning by suggesting that a certain type of person commits a certain type of crime. Each employs the criminal act as the basic point of reference, the difference being that the personalistic approach arrives at the act as a final destination while the legalistic approach starts out from it as a point of departure.

For this reason, the difficulties involved in the personalistic approach frequently mirror those of the legalistic. (1) Where the legalistic approach ignores psychological differences, the personalistic approach tends to ignore situational factors as causal elements. (2) While appearing to reject arbitrary legal categories, it may produce equally rigid diagnostic categories to match them. (3) The false impression of homogeneity may merely be transferred from the behavioral level to the diagnostic level, with the persisting implication that similar personality types commit similar offenses. In summary, where psychological and psychiatric theories have produced exclusive diagnostic categories, the result has often been the construction of a diagnostic nomenclature that parallels the legal nomenclature it purports to reject. The limitations of these orientations suggest the need for classifications dealing with the behaviorial and situational context on a level which is maximally descriptive and minimally theoretical.

Classification by Life Organization

For some offenders, crime is a career and a livelihood; for others, a single, never-to-be-repeated outburst; for still others, a recurring alternative. In recognition of these distinctions, Mayhew and Moreau, two European criminologists of the last century, proposed a system of classification based on the way in which crime is related to other life activities.[3] Mayhew distinguished two major types of criminal: *professionals*, who earned their living at crime, and *accidental offenders*, who turned to crime under pressure of unanticipated circumstances. Since the professional offender earns his living at crime, he usually concentrates on theft and property offenses and commits these crimes repeatedly. The accidental offender, on the other hand, has usually made his living by honest means and, when given the opportunity, will probably return to his earlier trade without offending again.

Moreau adopted Mayhew's classification but recognized that it failed to deal with a third class of offenders, who are responsible for most crimes against the person. These offenders are deficient in intelligence and self-control rather than dishonest; under pressure of temptation or circumstance they yield to their impulses and eventually form the habit of yielding. For this reason Moreau called them "habitual criminals" and cited as examples the person who repeatedly loses his temper and becomes assaultive and the individual who recurrently commits crime under the influence of alcohol. Because of their superior skill and caution, professional criminals are hard to catch and convict, whereas offenders of the other two classes are caught and convicted with relative ease and frequency.

When compared with the two systems previously described, the advantages of the third are readily apparent. (1) Although uncommitted to a theory of personality or to literal adherence to legal definitions, it consistently links recognizable groups of individuals to broad types of crime. (2) Thus it is more descriptive, relying neither on legal formalism nor on diagnostic intuitions. (3) It seeks to make the individual's criminal behavior intelligible in terms of his total life organization. (4) It avoids a rigid separation of the criminal from the noncriminal, but suggests how individuals engage and *disengage* in crime under the influence of personal and environmental factors. Thus, criminality is no

[3] Cited by Alfred R. Lindesmith and Warren H. Dunham, "Some Principles of Criminal Typology," *Social Forces*, 19:307–314, March, 1941.

longer something entirely outside of normal social life. The personalistic approach, on the other hand, is silent on the question of disengagement, since crime is viewed as a condition that is either inherited or fixed in the personality. (5) It includes both personal and situational factors but recognizes that their relative influence varies in the different classes of crime, personal factors being dominant in the accidental type. (6) It neither identifies the actor with the act (as the legalistic system does) nor separates him from it (as the personalistic system purports to do) but integrates the act, the actor and his character, and circumstances in systematically different ways to describe recognizably different criminal patterns. (7) Finally, it relates criminal typology and behavior to the efficiency of law enforcement. In summary, the Mayhew-Moreau classification is objective, integrative, and suggestive, and, for these reasons, available for further development.

Lindesmith and Dunham, who called the Mayhew-Moreau classification to the attention of modern criminologists, have suggested a refinement of it. They point out that individuals are not considered legally liable for their criminal acts if it can be shown that they are not mentally responsible. The insane, or those considered too young to have developed a sense of responsibility, are legally immune from criminal prosecution. But Lindesmith and Dunham point out that legal responsibility is actually another definition of socialization: to know right from wrong is, at bottom, to know what society considers right and wrong. In these terms, both sanity and the sense of responsibility become equated with socialization.

Lindesmith and Dunham then range all criminals along a single continuum of socialization. At one pole of this continuum is the completely *socialized criminal,* typified by the professional offender who uses illegitimate means to pursue the same ends—wealth and security—accepted by the culture at large. This type of criminal is social in another sense as well: He works in concert with criminal groups whose values and sanctions he must accept. At the opposite end is the completely *individualized* offender, typified by the criminal insane, who lives in no social world at all, who is beyond group influence, and whose behavior is considered irrational because its ends are incomprehensible in terms of common social goals. The crimes of the psychotic cannot be understood in terms of group values; they are meaningful only as symptoms of mental disease. "In this sense," writes Lindesmith and Dunham, "the insane person is incapable of crime, sometimes probably because the sense of right and wrong which depends on the mores of the group is not there by reason of the fact that [he] is, in large part, isolated from other men . . . ."[4]

Taking the completely individualized and the completely socialized criminal as two extremes of a single conceptual continuum of criminality, Lindesmith and Dunham suggest that all other criminals may be ranged somewhere between. Crimes of passion and crimes committed under the stress of unanticipated circumstances are more typical of the individualized criminal; many white-collar crimes, certain forms of companionate delinquency, and political crimes "lean in the direction of the opposite pole."[5]

The system proposed by Lindesmith and Dunham is essentially a condensation of the classifications of Mayhew and Moreau. The condensation is drastic, and is achieved first by equating sanity with socialization and responsibility and linking these factors with gainful crime, and, secondly, by equating individuality with mental malfunctioning and legal irresponsibility and linking these with nongainful crime. By means of this condensation, all types of offenders, from the homicidal maniac to the corrupt financeer, can be comprehended within a single bi-polar framework.

Although this system gains greatly in generalizing power over the previous systems, it does so at a price. The equating of sanity with socialization overtaxes the elasticity of both concepts. Both terms cover a wide variety of different phenomena; to equate and then contrast them with their dictionary antonyms is to create an impression of homogeneity that fails to persist when the data are examined at closer range. Thus, the gain in generalizing power is achieved through the sacrifice of other descriptive dimensions which are implicitly dismissed, on theoretical grounds, as irrelevant. In this sense, the system is more of a theory of crime causation than a method of classification.

Classification by Criminal Career

The American criminologist Walter Reckless has suggested a classification based on descriptions of specific criminal career patterns.

[4] *Ibid.*, p. 310.
[5] *Ibid.*, p. 311.

Although he rejects the view that all criminal behavior can be ranged along a single continuum—as has been proposed by Lindesmith and Dunham—Reckless recognizes a "continuum within the separate spheres of ordinary and professional criminal careers." His classification is essentially tripartite, with ordinary criminal careers seen as developing in "one world of crime," professional criminal careers in another, and organized crime—which may or may not recruit from these two lower orders—developing and operating in still another.[6]

Ordinary Criminal Careers

Those comprising Reckless' category of ordinary criminal careers include most of the offenders who make their living by means of the "conventional" property crimes listed in the *Uniform Crime Reports*—the burglars, forgers, robbers, embezzlers, and thieves who make up the lower working classes of crime. Members of this criminal proletariat usually come from poor, disorganized homes in deteriorated neighborhoods, serve a delinquent apprenticeship in street gangs and juvenile institutions, and emerge as "socially processed" journeymen in one or more of the lower criminal crafts.

Reckless cites four criteria that distinguish ordinary criminal careers both from the still lower classes of occasional petty thieves, habitual drunkards, sex offenders, drug addicts, and unspecialized lawbreakers, who cannot be considered careerists, and from the professional criminals who occupy the higher social strata of crime:

1. Since the ordinary criminal pursues crime as a livelihood, his offenses are usually limited to crimes of gain—chiefly offenses against property. Though he frequently carries a weapon and uses the cruder forms of intimidation, he generally prefers to avoid violence or any unnecessary injury to the victim—acts that would lengthen his sentences if he is caught.

2. The ordinary criminal career is a way of life, a milieu, and a life organization. The ordinary criminal must choose his friends, his associates, and even his recreation with care. He is, in a sense, always "on the lam," and it is safest and most comfortable to consort with those who share his situation or are more or less sympathetic to it. There is a certain continuous tension in his life, a deliberation and caution that becomes habitual even when he is not on the job. Unlike the ordinary worker or businessman, the ordinary criminal cannot "leave his job in

[6] Walter Reckless, *The Crime Problem*, 2d ed. (New York: Appleton-Century-Crofts, 1955).

the office"; he must always be more or less on the lookout for those who are looking for him. The "underworld" he inhabits is more a state of mind than an organized subcommunity; it is a different underworld from that of the professional and the organized criminal. In a sense, it is more a way of behaving, or being inconspicuous, of being constantly self-aware—of *avoiding*. His social world is segregated as much out of apprehension as out of choice.

3. The ordinary criminal careerist is a craftsman of sorts—a specialist with certain skills, a certain distinguishing jargon, and a pattern of attitudes embodying his identification with and pride in his chosen line. These attitudes are supportive, generally self-justifying, and usually rationalized on the basis of a belief that everyone is more or less dishonest. Apart from these attitudes, which are more or less specifically tied to his criminal pattern, his general social, moral, and political views are likely to be little different—if perhaps slightly more cynical—from those of noncriminals with a similar background.

4. According to Reckless, criminal careers of any type—ordinary, professional, or organized—are not usually chosen because of underlying psychological problems. They represent patterns of skills and lifeways rather than patterns of mental disease, and, as in the case of any skill, a more or less healthy psychological adjustment is required to carry them out efficiently. Thus, in terms of Jenkins' psychiatric distinction between adaptive and maladaptive offenders, they would clearly represent the former type.[7]

Professional Criminal Careers

Reckless differentiates the professional from the ordinary criminal on several grounds: (1) a different, more intelligent and "polished" type of person; (2) more efficient and intricate techniques; (3) different criminal activities; and (4) generally higher stakes. The professional has "class"—and class-consciousness:

> Professionals recognize their own artistry and, by contrast, the crude work of amateurs. Professionals identify professionals. They look down upon amateurs . . . and avoid association and identification with them.[8]

In the sense that the term *professional* may describe any activity carried out with more than ordinary or pedestrian skill and sophistication

---

[7] For a discussion of Jenkins' diagnostic categories, see Chapter 12.
[8] Reckless, *op. cit.*, p. 160.

—and with better results—almost any kind of crime becomes professional in the hands of a master. Thus, though burglars are usually included among ordinary criminals, a master second-story man may be considered a "professional" if his skill keeps him in the money—and out of jail. In general, however, the professional confines himself to one of several less violent and more "brainy" kinds of activity; Reckless lists eight: (1) picking pockets; (2) sneak-thieving from stores, banks, and offices; (3) shoplifting; (4) stealing from jewelry stores by substitution; (5) stealing from hotel rooms; (6) confidence games; (7) passing of illegal checks, money orders, and other papers; (8) the shakedown of, or extortion from, persons engaged in or about to engage in illegal acts.[9] Other criminal activities sometimes included in the professional class are blackmail, the counterfeiting of currency or other valuable objects (paintings, historical signatures, etc.), and circus "grifting" (dishonest or rigged games of chance).

Reckless holds that professionals and ordinary criminals come from different social strata. In this connection he cites the views of Sutherland's "professional thief," Chic Conwell, who writes:

> The members of the profession generally started their occupational life in legitimate employment, although some of them entered other illegal occupations before becoming professional thieves. Few of them came from the amateur thieves who are reared in the slums, for these youngsters seldom have the social abilities or front required of professional thieves.[10]

Though Reckless appears to concur with this point of view, Sutherland is skeptical of it. In a footnote to Chic Conwell's remark about the social origins of the professional thief, he writes:

> There is a good deal of evidence that many pickpockets did have their origins in the slums. . . . On the other hand, there is little evidence available which either supports or contradicts the description of the origin of other types of thieves.[11]

The validity of the social stratification and division of criminal labor suggested by Reckless is open to some question. It may well be that, in stressing his superior origins, the professional is merely expressing the same snobbery that inspires other class-conscious groups to boast about their ancestry. Perhaps the less arbitrary position is to view the profes-

[9] Reckless cites these categories from Edwin H. Sutherland, *The Professional Thief* (Chicago: The University of Chicago Press, 1937).
[10] Sutherland, *op. cit.*, p. 21.
[11] *Ibid.*

sional criminal as a member of the more democratic aristocracy of talent —rather than birth—which arises no less out of the slums than out of the higher social classes.

The view that most professional criminals confine themselves to one or a few related specialties of theft is based largely on the writings of the professionals themselves—con-men writing about con-men, pickpockets about pickpockets. Large-scale analysis of criminal records would be required in order to verify this impression; a few observers have questioned it. Sutherland cites one writer who asserts that "confidence men, who, a generation ago, would have been ashamed to engage in any theft outside of their own specialty, are now engaging in banditry, kidnaping and other crimes." [12]

There is little question, however, that the more intricate techniques of the criminal specialties imply training—and, hence, at least an informal system of selection, testing, and tutelage. This guidance is available only from other criminals—and to the extent that they provide it, specialized crime may be viewed as *organized* in the sense that it is cooperative and self-perpetuating. The degree and character of its organization is different from that distinguishing the more complex, almost bureaucratic, structure found in the type of crime next discussed.

Professional thieves have been described as having many of the characteristics of a distinctive social group, including distinctive codes, status systems, traditions, consensus, organization, esprit-de-corps, and conventions of mutual aid. As a group they are certainly the most articulate of all criminals, and the list of their autobiographical impressions is long. Most, if not all, of these were produced while their authors were temporarily out of circulation, and the suspicion arises that the memoirs written in these circumstances may be influenced somewhat by motives of psychological compensation. The caught thief, like the defeated general, may have a need to regain in print a little of the glory lost in the field.

Organized Criminal Careers

The ordinary criminal typically works alone or with a partner or two, or as part of a larger group temporarily assembled for a specific job. The professional often works alone but is frequently a member of a more or less cohesive team or "troupe"—many confidence men, and most pick-

[12] *Ibid.*, p. 199.

pockets, work in highly organized, quasi-permanent gangs. Most of these groups, however, represent the association of independent criminals on equal terms, on a share-and-share-alike basis. The organized criminal, by contrast, is usually the temporary hireling, the steady employee, or the administrator of a criminal bureaucracy.

Organized crime is not only "more" organized than ordinary or professional crime, but differently organized. The combinations used by ordinary and professional criminals tend to be voluntary, cooperative, and nonhierarchical. Although there may be joint planning, in which everyone participates, there is a minimum of direction and supervision. According to Sutherland's professional thief:

> There is not much distinction between members of a mob as far as leadership is concerned except in *cannon* mobs and not always there. The cannon mob is generally designated by the name of the *hook,* and it will be said, for instance, that Brown is now on the coast in Manny Gloob's mob. The hook is recognized as leader because he controls the *fall-dough,* when there is fall-dough, since he is the one most likely to be arrested; also, because he is the one who generally has the right *grift,* when there is right grift. . . . At the same time it is recognized that every one of the mob knows as much about the racket as he does, where to grift and where not, when to grift and when to *pack in.* Therefore the hook cannot get away with anything out of line. . . . There is no leadership in the *boosting mobs.* It is a general rule that one thief actually takes the merchandise, while the other protects. But both parts are regarded as of the same importance, and neither one is boss, either sarcastically or otherwise. In the con rackets there is no approach to the boss idea except that there is a boss in the *pay-off joints.* In a particular city one may have police protection for the pay-off joints, and he is the boss of the pay-off joints, just as someone else is the gambling boss or vice lord. When a *steerer* arrives in a city, he approaches the boss of the pay-off joints and asks permission to steer his prospects against one of these joints. This boss is boss of the whole pay-off end of the racket but not of the mob.[13] (Italics supplied.)

HIERARCHY AND ADMINISTRATION. The free-and-easy individualism typical of the professional troupe contrasts with the tight, centralized

___

[13] *Ibid.,* pp. 33–34. Sutherland has provided the following definitions of the italicized terms in the quotation: *cannon:* pickpocket; *hook:* the member of the pickpocket mob who extracts the pocketbook from the pocket of the victim; *fall-dough:* money to be used in case of an arrest; *grift:* stealing technique; *pack in:* cease, desist, abandon; *boosting mob:* gang of shoplifters; *pay-off joint:* an elaborate confidence game establishment; *steerer:* the member of the confidence mob who guides the victim to the "inside man," (i.e., the man inside the establishment). *Ibid.,* pp. 235–243.

hierarchy of the criminal syndicate. These differences in organization reflect the need for administrative controls in the face of problems having a greater similarity to those of the businessman than to those of the conventional criminal.

"Ordinary" and "professional" criminals are organized to deal efficiently with their victims. The criminal combinations controlling gambling or prostitution in a given area are dealing with people who would be more appropriately described as *customers* than as victims. These individuals are not usually coerced; most of them come voluntarily and pay for what they consider value received. The coercion, intimidation, extortion, and bloodshed that have become identified with organized crime are rarely evident in the organized criminal's relations with his client. They are significantly related, however, to the organized criminal's problem of gaining and maintaining monopolistic control over his service or product. This control is usually gained by eliminating or intimidating the competition. Thus, the syndicated criminal must organize to control other criminals. Most of the bloodshed and brutality of organized crime—including that efficient administrative expedient known as "Murder Incorporated"—have involved other criminals as victims. As an employer, the organized criminal has a particularly delicate problem with respect to workers who become inefficient or dissatisfied. The safest way to eliminate personnel problems is to eliminate the particular personnel involved. The American gangster—when he is not an anachronistic survival of the free-wheeling outlaw of frontier times—is often a paid employee of an organized criminal combination.

Criminal businesses are rackets that must be organized with reference to the problem of neutralizing or gaining immunity from law-enforcement authorities. The individual "fixer" used by the professional criminal is largely inadequate for this purpose. Organized crime usually involves a large number of operators and operations—and depends typically on a large clientele. The sheer scope of its operations often makes secrecy impossible. For this reason, the large-scale rackets cannot survive without the bought cooperation or tolerance of law-enforcement authorities. The neutralization of law enforcement is achieved in various ways and at various levels of efficiency. The most efficient technique involves the secret corruption—or, at best, the outright control—of the elected public officials in charge of the over-all administration of local government. Organized crime diverts a portion of its huge profits for the maintenance of campaign contributions to candidates who will cooperate if elected. The theory behind these operations is simple and sound. Feeding the watchdog is more efficient than trying to sneak past him.

ORGANIZED CRIMINAL ENTERPRISES. Organized crime has traditionally functioned in the supply and distribution of goods and services forbidden by law and closed to legitimate business. Its persistence is related to the fact that the demand for these goods and services has persisted. In a sense, organized crime is a mechanism through which society assures the uninterrupted continuation of the activities which it publicly condemns as vices. In its mood of self-denial, the community outlaws these activities, forcing them underground, where they can exist without visibly offending public policy. In its mood of self-indulgence, it patronizes the underground enterprises and tolerates their protection. In the most general terms, the appearance or disappearance of illegal gambling, prostitution, and bootlegging at any time and place may reflect the vacillation of the community between its moods of self-denial and self-indulgence.

Since the repeal of Prohibition, the principal enterprises of organized crime have been built around gambling, bookmaking, narcotics, prostitution, and smuggling. In recent years there has been an expansion into areas of legitimate business. Organized crime has invaded areas of industry, labor, and the distributional services. The Senate Crime Commission for the Study of Interstate Crime (the Kefauver Committee) has cited evidence of infiltration into at least fifty areas of business.[14]

Despite their diversity, the offenders discussed in this chapter are all dealt with according to the conventional criminal procedures described in Chapter 6 of this text. There is another large and heterogeneous grouping of offenders for which special procedures of adjudication and disposition are frequently provided. The relation between these broad categories of law-violators can be stated only in the most general terms. The offenders subject to special criminal proceedings tend to fall into Lindesmith and Dunham's category of the "individualized," as contrasted with the "socialized," criminal. By and large, they are not engaged in gainful crime; very frequently they are manifestly disturbed—and in most cases they are their own victims.

Nevertheless, the distinction between the *special* and the *conventional* offender categories ought not to be stretched too far. An examination of a large number of criminal histories would reveal many offenders

[14] U. S. Senate, *Third Interim Report of the Special Committee to Investigate Crime in Interstate Commerce*, 82d Congress, Report No. 307 (Washington, D. C.: Government Printing Office, 1951), p. 171.

whose records include convictions for both categories of crime. It is not unusual to find criminal records in which drug convictions alternate with convictions for larceny, burglary, forgery, and various other gainful crimes. Very frequently the criminal records of adult offenders are prefaced by relatively long histories of juvenile offenses, a fact which gives point to the observation that "today's delinquent is tomorrow's criminal." In view of the absence of hard-and-fast distinctions, the discussion of the special offender categories in Chapter 9 will concentrate largely on specialized legal definitions and matters of procedure.

Special Offender Categories

IN ALL JURISDICTIONS CERTAIN KINDS OF OFFENSES ARE DEALT WITH BY special judicial and administrative procedures. These procedures reflect the insistence by the public that certain classes of crime be handled in specially preferential or punitive ways. This public insistence is based, in part, on the belief that those committing these crimes represent distinct types of human beings and, in part, on the related belief that their crimes represent either special forms of depravity and menace justifying extraordinary severity or special types of disability meriting unusual leniency. On occasion both of these contradictory attitudes may be expressed toward the same kinds of crime, with the result that legislation dealing with them may mix motives of indignation and sympathy. Moreover, since the laws created in response to these conflicting attitudes tend to be less bound by legal precedent than other laws, the traditional safeguards of criminal procedure may often be superseded by measures reflecting a variety of unverified theories of treatment. The offender categories usually set apart for special handling include sex offenders, drug offenders, military offenders, and juvenile delinquents.[1]

[1] The purview of this chapter is limited to those offenses entailing special judicial or administrative procedures for the disposition of the offender. Because of its broader significance for the general problem of legal disposition, the question of the *insane offender* is discussed in Chapter 18.

Sex Offenders

Legal Definitions

The laws relating to sex offenses usually deal with two broad types of definition: (1) Descriptions of the particular behaviors to be defined as "sex offenses"; and (2) definitions of the legal or medico-legal status usually known as *sexual psychopath*. This legal status, and its special consequences, *may or may not* be affixed to a person convicted of committing a given sex offense. Judge Ploscowe has pointed out:

> The basic task of the sex-psychopath laws is to differentiate dangerous sex offenders from minor criminals who commit sex crimes and who should be handled by the ordinary procedures of the criminal law, either because they are not mentally abnormal or because they are not inherently dangerous to the community.[2]

DEFINITIONS OF THE ILLEGAL ACTS. It is one of the fundamentals of criminal procedure that the defendant be informed of the specific details of the crime charged against him, so that he can prepare an adequate defense. In practice, this means that the charge must spell out the particulars of *what* he did and *how* he did it. Ordinarily, if the charge is not sufficiently specific, the defendant has the right to demand a "bill of particulars." Furthermore, in order to sustain its charge, the prosecution must prove these specific allegations in detail. In many instances, definitions of illegal sexual acts fail to meet this traditional requirement of specificity.

Though the technical terms and descriptions identifying different forms of sexual behavior are well established in medical terminology, the descriptions used in different laws vary greatly. In some statutes it is necessary merely to charge that the accused committed an act other than ordinary sexual intercourse, all other variations being lumped in the single broad category of "crime against nature." This procedure has the effect of preventing the accused from being informed of the particular "perversion" charged against him. Thus, in jurisdictions where this broad form of definition is used, it may merely be necessary for the prosecution witnesses to testify that the accused committed an act "against nature," with the defense being prevented from cross-examination for specific details. In this connection, Ploscowe cites a ruling made by a judge during a trial when this question arose:

[2] Morris Ploscowe, *Sex and the Law* (New York: Prentice-Hall, Inc., 1951), p. 227.

It was never the practice to describe the particular manner or the details of the commission of the crime, but the offense was treated in the indictment as the abominable crime not fit to be named among Christians. The existence of such an offense is a disgrace to human nature. The legislature has not seen fit to define it further than by the general term [i.e., crime against nature], and the records of the courts need not be defiled with the details of the different acts which may go to constitute it. A statement of the offense in the language of the statute is all that is required.[3]

The use of a single broad category, such as "crime against nature," for all prohibited sexual behavior represents legal definition at its vaguest; the sex-crime laws of most states range from this extreme of generality to different degrees of specificity. In only a few states do the legal definitions approximate the precision found in medical terminology.

DEFINITIONS OF THE SEXUAL PSYCHOPATH. In addition to legislation punishing specific sexual acts with fixed or indefinite prison sentences, several states have adopted laws designed to deal with habitual or especially dangerous sex offenders. This is usually done through the medium of special procedures, by which an individual is legally certified as a *sexual psychopath* or *habitual sex offender* (the terms vary) and then incarcerated for an indefinite period. From a legal and practical point of view, the sexual psychopath, though not considered legally insane, occupies an analogous status. He is usually confined indefinitely and may not be released until he is certified to be either "cured" or no longer dangerous.

The purpose of the sexual-psychopath laws is to distinguish especially dangerous or habitual sex offenders from others violating sex laws and to isolate them from the community. Since, in some states, they may not be released until they are certified to be no longer dangerous, the confinement may be permanent. Some sexual-psychopath laws in effect impose sentences of life imprisonment, which may be remitted only by legally appointed medical or psychiatric authorities.

Judge Ploscowe has raised four questions with respect to the operation of the sexual-psychopath laws:

(1) How do the laws distinguish the dangerous, mentally abnormal sex offender from the great mass of individuals who commit sex crimes, who may or may not be mentally abnormal, but who are definitely not dangerous? (2) Since a man can be incarcerated for life on a judgment that he is a sexual psychopath, what procedural safeguards surround this judgment? (3) Are release procedures adequate so that individuals

[3] *Ibid.*, p. 197.

adjudged sexual psychopaths will not be kept in custody any longer than necessary? (4) What treatment facilities are provided in the various states to deal with the mentally abnormal individuals who are committed under the sex-psychopath laws? [4]

In an attempt to evaluate whether consistent criteria were available for the precise definition of *sexual psychopath,* the New Jersey Commission on the Habitual Sex Offender circulated a questionnaire among sixty-six psychiatrists in order to discover "what measure of agreement there might be as to the types of individuals covered by the term." Of the sixty-six psychiatrists returning the questionnaire, sixty-five "expressed the belief that there was insufficient accord in the field to justify legislation specifically for the 'sexual psychopath.'" [5] In its report, the New Jersey Commission cites a statement by a group of psychiatrists warning against the use of a concept "so variously defined as is the psychopath":

> The Committee cautions against the use of the appellation, psychopath, in the law on several grounds. There is still little agreement on the part of psychiatrists as to the precise meaning of the term. Furthermore, the term has no dynamic significance. The Committee believes that in statutes the use of technical psychiatric terms should be avoided whenever possible. Psychiatric knowledge and terminology are in a state of flux. Once having become a part of the public law such a term attains a fixity unresponsive to newer scientific knowledge and application. [6]

Trial and Disposition

Prior to the passage of special sex-psychopath legislation, offenses of a sexual nature were everywhere a regular part of the criminal code, and violators were subject to the conventional criminal proceedings described in Chapter 6 of this text. That is to say, a person suspected of an offense had to be formally charged, arraigned, indicted, tried, and convicted according to established rules of evidence and procedure before he could be subject to penal treatment. In a majority of the jurisdictions adopting the special sex-psychopath laws, the older statutes are still in force, with the result that the state may exercise its own discretion in

[4] *Ibid.,* p. 226.
[5] *The Habitual Sex Offender,* Report and Recommendations of the Commission on the Habitual Sex Offender, as formulated by Paul W. Tappan, Technical Consultant (Trenton, N. J.: Department of Institutions and Agencies, 1950), p. 37.
[6] *Ibid.*

deciding to prosecute by means of conventional criminal proceedings or by means of the special powers granted it by the new legislation.

The special sex-psychopath statutes embody a variety of departures from traditional criminal procedure. The characteristic vagueness of the definitions of illegal acts has already been discussed; its practical effect has been to magnify the powers of the prosecutor by greatly widening the range of behavior he may construe as violating the statute. In consequence, when confronted with a case in which the evidence is insufficiently persuasive to pass the rigorous standards of an ordinary criminal trial, the prosecutor may elect to mobilize the wider powers of the special proceedings.

Thus, for example, in five of the thirteen jurisdictions studied by Tappan in 1949, it was not necessary for the state to bring or to prove a charge of crime. Acting on the petition or affidavit of the complainant or, in some jurisdictions, on information furnished by some private person, the prosecutor was empowered to bring the suspect before a tribunal that would adjudicate his mental status. If adjudged a sex-psychopath, the subject could be committed to mental hospital or correctional institution for an indefinite period of treatment. In making this disposition, the tribunal was not required to determine whether the suspect had, in fact violated the law; evidence or opinion suggesting a *mental predisposition* was considered sufficient. In the words of the California statute: "Marked departures from normal mentality—in a form predisposing to the commission of sexual offenses" constituted grounds for commitment.[7]

In most jurisdictions the accused may demand a jury. In the states of Ohio, Minnesota, New Hampshire, Vermont, and Indiana, however, the right to trial by jury is not granted; in Massachusetts the use of a jury is at the discretion of the court. All jurisdictions using sex-psychopath statutes provide for the medical or psychiatric examination of the suspect; depending on the provisions of the statute, the decision of the court may or may not follow the medical findings. In most cases, however, the decision to release the committed sex offender is conditional on a psychiatric finding that he has been cured or is sufficiently recovered to pose no threat to society.

The psychiatric status of the sexual psychopath is as ambiguous as his legal status. When committed to a mental hospital, he is rarely permitted the off-grounds privileges or periodic home visits usually granted other psychiatric patients. When committed to a penal institu-

[7] *Ibid.,* p. 69.

tion, his major—and frequently his only—distinction from the other inmates is his ineligibility, or restricted eligibility, for parole. In effect, as a mental patient he is treated as a prisoner—and as a prisoner, he is treated as a person too disturbed for privileges granted to other prisoners. Thus his status, which combines the aspects of prisoner and mental patient, tends to assure him the disadvantages of both and the benefits of neither.

The stringent provisions governing the disposition of sex offenders reflect widespread public anxiety. Whether this anxiety is based on reliable evidence of the actual social danger of sex deviants is highly doubtful. What seems more likely is that the public is reacting to a vivid stereotype derived from a small number of sensational and unrepresentative atrocities. In any event, neither the present consensus of psychiatric opinion nor the evidence derived from commitment records can be cited in support of the view that the average or typical sex offender represents a menace to society.

Fallacies Concerning the Sex Offender

In the absence of agreement concerning the diagnosis of sexual psychopaths and sex offenders generally, it is necessary to rely on pragmatic statistical findings. From the community's point of view, the most important diagnostic question concerning sex offenses is the likelihood of their repetition rather than their underlying etiology. The statistical evidence dealing with the recidivism of sex offenders reveals that, contrary to public opinion, the rates of repetition are low compared with other categories of criminals. The general and false impression of the high recidivism of sex offenders is related to a variety of other fallacies. The New Jersey Commission on the Habitual Sex Offender has discussed ten major errors current in public opinion on this subject. Taken together, these fallacies and the evidence refuting them constitute a comprehensive and practical survey of the objective knowledge available.

1. *That there are tens of thousands of homicidal sex fiends abroad in the land.* In fact the vast majority of the sex deviates are minor offenders, most of whom never come to official attention (e.g., there are sixty million homo-sexual acts performed in the United States for every twenty convictions in our courts). It has been carefully estimated by Dr. Kinsey that not more than 5 per cent of our convicted sex offenders are of a dangerous variety, exercising force or injury upon a victim.

Crime reports support this finding. Homicide associated with sex crimes is unusual. A recent study by the criminologist, Dr. Sutherland, shows that the "danger of murder by relative or other intimate associate is very much greater than the danger of murder by an unknown sex fiend." Nearly 90 per cent of the murders of females he studied were committed by relatives or suitors, and 25 per cent of those who murdered females committed suicide. The sex fiend as portrayed by D. Wittels, *et al*, is a rare phenomenon in the criminal history of any state; the tens of thousands that he hypothecates are the much publicized creatures of his well-stirred imagination. Most of those who do occasionally appear are insane, not merely sexual deviates.

2. *That sex offenders are usually recidivists.* Sex offenders have one of the lowest rates as "repeaters" of all types of crime. Among serious crimes homicide alone has a lower rate of recidivism. Careful studies of large samples of sex criminals show that most of them get in trouble only once Of those who do repeat, a majority commit some crime other than sex. Only 7 per cent of those convicted of serious crimes are arrested again for a sex crime. Those who recidivate are characteristically minor offenders—such as peepers, exhibitionists, homosexuals— rather than criminals of serious menace.

3. *That the sex offender progresses to more serious types of sex crime.* It is the consensus of opinion among psychiatrists, confirmed by crime statistics, that sex deviates persist in the type of behavior in which they have discovered satisfaction. Any thoroughly frustrated, rigidly repressed personality may conceivably explode into violence it is true. There is no evidence, however, that this occurs more frequently among sex offenders than others; indeed there is good psychological ground to believe that individuals who experience some outlet of sexual tensions are less likely to need release of rage and aggression. Progression from minor to major sex crimes is exceptional, though an individual may engage at any given time in a variety of forms of sex outlets.

4. *That it is possible to predict the danger of serious crimes being committed by sex deviates.* Reports from 75 prominent psychiatrists reveal a consensus that it is impossible to predict the occurrence of serious crime with any accuracy. That the behavior sciences have not attained this level of prognostication is attested in these statements by authorities:

Dr. J. B. Gordon, Medical Director, New Jersey State Hospital: "This would require superhuman intelligence and the gift of prophecy."

Dr. Hilding Bengs, Commissioner of Mental Health, Pennsylvania: "It is impossible to predict accurately commissions of serious crimes in a person of certain tendencies. There are the unpredictable facts of circumstances, opportunity, and the timely reaction of the person."

Dr. Philip Q. Roche, Chairman, Committee on Forensic Psychiatry, Group for the Advancement of Psychiatry: "The expedience of the law would call upon unqualified physicians to make guesses or to express prejudices. There are very few psychiatrists who have sufficient training and experience with offenders."

Dr. Edwin H. Sutherland, Professor of Criminology, Indiana University: "Accurate prediction could not be made in any case or percentage of cases."

This inability to predict is of special importance in relation to recent laws that are designed to constrain individuals who have committed no law violations as well as minor sex deviates and even juveniles.

5. *That "sex psychopathy" or sex deviation is a clinical entity.* Two-thirds of the psychiatric authorities consulted by the writer pointed to the wide disagreement among psychiatrists as to the meaning of the term, sex psychopath. More than half of them maintained that this condition is not a sufficiently clear diagnostic entity to justify legislation concerning the type. Hospital authorities handling cases of "sex psychopaths" committed by the courts find, in fact, a wide variety of psychological types: neurotics, psychotics, schizoids, feebleminded, epileptics, constitutional homosexuals, alcoholics, and many who are normal. In different states the authorities look for different qualities as evidence of dangerous sexual psychopathy; the cases they adjudicate as such display varied forms of sex deviation and assorted types of personality organization.

6. *That these individuals are over-sexed.* From the point of view of their treatment and their dangerousness, it is important to realize that most of the sex deviates treated under the laws are under-sexed rather than hypergonadal types. A majority are passive or non-aggressive. The problem is very rarely one of drives too strong to control, as commonly recommended programs of castration, sterilization and close correctional custody would imply.

7. *That effective treatment methods to cure deviated sex offenders are already known and employed.* As compared with other types of psychological and constitutional abnormality, we are peculiarly at a loss in the handling of abnormal sex offenders. Methods of effective treatment have not yet been worked out. The states that have passed special laws on the sex deviate do not attempt treatment! The "patients" are kept in bare custodial confinement. This point is central to the atrocious policy of those jurisdictions that commit non-criminals and minor deviates for indefinite periods to mental hospitals where no therapy is offered. Most psychiatrists indicate that pyschotherapy of some sort should be given to sex offenders, but they are in agreement that professional staffing is not available to perform this work and that an unknown but undoubtedly very high percentage of deviates would not respond to such treatment. In private practice the treatment applied to the sex deviate

by many psychiatrists is designed to help him accept his peculiarity without guilt feelings and to be more discreet in its expression. The point should be stressed that commitment of a sex deviate to a state mental hospital *does not imply clinical treatment*. These institutions lack the space, the personnel, the treatment methods, or even the desire to handle deviated sex offenders who are non-psychotic.

8. *That the laws passed recently in one-fourth of the states are getting at the brutal and vicious sex criminal*. Data secured from the several jurisdictions reveals that, although the laws have been passed in response to public fears about the dangerous and aggressive offenders, in fact these are the types least frequently brought under the statutes in actual administration. Most of the persons adjudicated are minor deviates, rarely if ever "sex fiends."

9. *That civil adjudication of the sex deviate and/or indeterminate commitment to a mental hospital is similar to our handling of the insane and, therefore, human liberties and due process are not involved*. This type of thinking has been used in several states to support long-term custody of minor deviates, many of them without a criminal charge. Under these laws the insane and mentally defective are specifically excluded. Those covered are in fact a variety of psychological types that have never before been exempted from criminal responsibility nor commitable to mental hospitals. No sound reason has ever been advanced for committing a "peeper" to a mental hospital for an indeterminate period (or any period) of time where he will be segregated from his community and family in an unproductive existence at state expense. Nevertheless this has become common practice today under the recent legislation throughout the country. Regardless of the type of court employed to attain this result, it is in effect a serious punishment in which liberty and due process are vitally involved. Reasoning to the contrary is founded in a technical legalism of the most vicious sort.

10. *That the sex problem can be solved merely by passing a new law on it*. Common sense must indicate to the contrary. Certainly experience with these laws reveals the futility of ineffectual legislation. In general the statutes appear to have served only the purpose of satisfying the public temporarily that "something is being done." In fact, and fortunately, very little is being done under the sex psychopath laws, but that little is worse in effect than leaving the offender to the operation of the traditional criminal law would have been. Thus far no problems have been resolved by the new sex laws that have been enacted. On the contrary, some extremely dangerous precedents have been established 1) for adjudicating individuals without ordinary due process—even in five states without a criminal charge, 2) for indeterminate commitments to mental hospitals of individuals who are not insane and who

deviate little or not at all from normal psychologically, and 3) for providing hospital custody to a growing body of minor sex deviates who are to be held until "cured" though without treatment, at great cost to the taxpayer and with serious diminution of the facilities available for those mental patients who are seriously disturbed.[8]

The Extent of Sex Offenses

Discussion of the incidence of sex offenses must differentiate between two very different questions: (1) How much illegal sexual behavior is actually taking place? (2) How much illegal sexual behavior is being defined and prosecuted as criminal?

ESTIMATES OF THE EXTENT OF ILLEGAL SEXUAL BEHAVIOR. Estimating the incidence of deviant sexual behavior is complicated by the fact that most people are reticent about even their "normal" sexual activities. The most thoroughgoing and comprehensive survey of sexual behavior of all types appeared in the volumes by Kinsey, Pomeroy, and Martin.[9] Though these studies have been subjected to a variety of criticisms based on the sampling and interviewing techniques used, they represent the only objective source of nation-wide data.

Perhaps the main and least challenged finding was that former opinions about the incidence of all types of sexual behavior were markedly erroneous. One of the most widely held popular misconceptions concerned the extent of premarital intercourse among young men and women. On the basis of his samples, Kinsey concluded that more that 73 per cent of American males and almost 50 per cent of the females sampled had had sexual intercourse before marriage.

The findings concerning deviant sexual behavior were perhaps even more startling. On the basis of his findings, Kinsey and his associates estimated that 37 per cent of the males had had some overt homosexual experience,[10] that 59 per cent had participated in oral-genital contacts,[11] and that 17 per cent of boys raised on farms had participated in some form of bestiality—sexual contact with animals.[12]

[8] *Ibid.*, pp. 13–16.
[9] Alfred C. Kinsey, Wardell B. Pomeroy, and Clyde E. Martin, *Sexual Behavior in the Human Male* (Philadelphia: W. B. Saunders Company, 1948), and *Sexual Behavior in the Human Female* (Philadelphia: W. B. Saunders Company, 1953).
[10] Kinsey et al., *Sexual Behavior in the Human Male*, p. 650.
[11] *Ibid.*, p. 371.
[12] *Ibid.*, p. 671.

Though the studies did not investigate the less active forms of sexual deviance, such as indecent exposure and peeping, the other findings leave no alternative to the conclusion that abnormal sexual behavior is extremely widespread. Even were the estimates cut in half, deviant sexual behavior, if prosecuted to the extent that other reported crimes were prosecuted, would constitute the largest single group of offenses in the country.

THE INCIDENCE OF PROSECUTED SEX DEVIATIONS. The *Uniform Crime Reports* publish separate data on rape, prostitution, and commercialized vice combined (as a unit) and "sex offenses except rape and prostitution." This last category, which partly reflects specialized legal treatment, includes the deviant sex offenses. The number and rate of persons charged with these offenses in 1956 are shown in Table XI.

TABLE XI

NUMBER AND RATE OF PERSONS CHARGED WITH SEX OFFENSES IN 1956

	Rape	Prostitution and commercialized vice	Other sex offenses
Number of persons charged	6,557	26,388	29,115
Rate per 100,000	9.9	40.0	44.1

Source: *Uniform Crime Reports*, 27, No. 1 (1956), p. 54.

Some indication of the wide extent of deviant sexual behavior is provided by the relatively high number and rate of persons charged with sex offenses other than rape and commercialized vice.[13] The available data concerning the age of offenders in each of these three categories are also of interest. Of those arrested for rape—a crime rather than a "perversion"—62.9 per cent were under twenty-five years of age. By contrast, only 28.2 per cent of those arrested for prostitution and vice were younger than twenty-five. Of those arrested for other sex offenses, more than 60 per cent were older than twenty-five, a fact that gives some support to the impression that the majority of known sex deviates are beyond the average age of maximal sexual activity.[14]

[13] The figures for *persons charged* with these offenses are drawn from a larger population than are the figures for *persons arrested* for the same crimes. For this reason they more reliably represent the total incidence than do the arrest figures. Age data, however, are available only in connection with arrest figures.

[14] *Uniform Crime Reports*, 27, No. 2 (1956), p. 110.

Drug Offenders

Narcotic addiction was a medically recognized condition and the sale of drugs a legitimate business long before either became criminal. Under legal regulation, the production and distribution of narcotics are still legitimate, and individuals under medical care may still obtain and use narcotic drugs by prescription. The drug *offender*—the criminal seller and user of narcotics—came into being as a result of a series of progressively more stringent laws limiting the legitimate use and distribution of narcotics and defining unauthorized sellers and users as criminals or misdemeanants. In some jurisdictions it is now illegal to be in unauthorized possession of a hypodermic syringe or needle. Possession of either implement, even in the absence of discovered narcotics, is a violation of narcotic laws in many states. Persons convicted of drug violations are, in some jurisdictions, required to register in each locality they enter for more than a brief period of time—in some cases, over twenty-four hours—and to report each change of address. Failure to comply with registration provisions is a separate violation.

Federal and state legislation dealing with narcotics usually differentiates between two broad categories of drug offenders: users and sellers. The laws dealing with unauthorized sellers, producers, and distributors are considerably more severe than those dealing with users. Nevertheless, the problem of legal differentiation and disposition is complicated by the fact that sellers (peddlers or "pushers") frequently are users as well.

The Physiology of Drug Addiction

In terms of their action on the nervous system, drugs may be divided into two general categories: *depressants* and *stimulants*. The depressants include the following: (1) the opiates—derivatives of opium —of which the narcotics in major use are heroin and morphine; (2) the synthetic analgesics, including demerol and methadone; (3) the hypnotics and sedatives, including chloral, paraldehyde, various bromides and barbiturates, and marijuana. The *stimulants* include (1) derivatives of the coca leaf, especially cocaine; (2) benzedrine; and (3) mescaline, a derivative of the peyote plant.

Though each drug produces a more or less specific physiological reaction, the general effect of the depressant drugs is to produce feelings of lassitude, a decrease in tension, and a sense of liberation from anxiety.

The opiates are distinctive in that they tend to produce these effects without such side-effects as mental confusion and disturbance of muscular coordination—disadvantages found in alcohol and the barbiturates. Where the depressants "cool" the person down, the stimulants "hot" him up. Under the influence of cocaine and the other stimulants, the individual experiences a combined physical and emotional activation; he feels stronger, keener, and generally "keyed up."

The different effects of the various drugs provide some general clues to the relation of choice of drug to the addict's problems. On the individual whose inadequacies are related to irritability, excessive tension, and worry, the depressants confer a feeling of well-being by temporarily dulling his capacity to feel. In effect, since what he was feeling was largely unpleasant, he feels better by feeling *less*. For the individual who feels chronically dull, unresponsive, and generally unable to summon the energy to cope with his problems, the stimulants produce a temporary sensation of power and sharpened reactivity; he feels better, in effect, because he feels *more*.[15]

The effectiveness of narcotics in producing these reactions tends to decline increasingly with increasing use. This diminishing effectiveness is a consequence of one or more of three related aspects of the organism's total adjustment to the drug. They are most characteristically seen in addiction to the opiates:

> The opiate addiction syndrome includes the separate but related phenomena of *tolerance, habituation,* and *physical dependence.* Tolerance is the decreasing effect on the user of repeating the same dose of a drug, or the need to keep increasing the dose as the drug is taken frequently over a long-time span. Habituation is the personality's emotional and psychological dependence on the drug in lieu of the more usual kinds of satisfactions. Physical dependence is the body's need to continue the drug in order to avoid the acute characteristics of the abstinence syndrome.
>
> In the abstinence syndrome, the addict who is deprived of the drug he has been taking will show an almost schematic pattern of behavior which is a function of the patient and the length, strength, and nature

[15] There are frequent individual variations, however. "Thus, morphine is a depressant, but in the widely-found 'cat' reaction, the drug produces an excitatory effect. And how a drug may serve different purposes for the same user is seen, for example, in the case of the prostitute starting her career who takes heroin to deaden her responses to her customers, but also uses it to enable her to enjoy sexual activity with her 'boy friend.'" Charles Winick, "Narcotics Addiction and its Treatment," *Law and Contemporary Problems,* 22:15, No. 1, 1957. Published by the Duke University School of Law, Durham, N. C. Copyright 1957 by Duke University and reprinted by permission.

of his addiction. Its intensity can be measured on a point scale. In an addict who has been taking morphine every day, a fairly predictable series of symptoms will set in if the drug is withdrawn. He will be restless about eight hours after his last "shot" and sleep restlessly in about twelve hours. After twenty-four hours, the patient will lacrimate, yawn, vomit, sneeze, sweat, develop gooseflesh (the origin of the phrase "cold turkey"), pupil dilation, running nose, and have involuntary movements of his limb muscles ("kicking" is the addict's argot for ceasing his "habit"). Diarrhea, aches, some fever, rapid respiration, slightly higher blood pressure, increase in the white cell count, and many other symptoms may appear as the abstinence syndrome unfolds. These symptoms are usually at their agonizing peak between forty-eight and seventy-two hours after the last "shot" has been taken. From five to ten days usually are necessary before these manifestations of the abstinence syndrome disappear. Some lesser abstinence characteristics may continue for several months.

Heroin abstinence symptoms are likely to be analogous to, although more accelerated and more intense than, those for morphine. N-allylnor-morphine (nalorphine) helps produce short abstinence syndromes within a quarter hour after being administered to opiate addicts. When given to nonaddicts, its effects are like those of a small dose of morphine. Nalorphine, thus, shows the presence of addiction within a half hour, by producing typical symptoms of withdrawal, although it is not a legally binding test of addiction. There is no adequate laboratory test to confirm that a person is or is not an addict unless he exhibits withdrawal symptoms, which are then presumed to show that he had been taking drugs which have been abruptly withdrawn.

The administration of methadone prevents the appearance of symptoms of abstinence from most known analgesic drugs, and abstinence symptoms from methadone are milder than abstinence symptoms from the other drugs, which is why it is widely used in systematic withdrawal treatment of addicts.

Abstinence from barbiturates produces its own very severe withdrawal symptoms, including insomnia and anorexia, within one day after the last dose of drugs. Most barbiturate addicts undergoing the abstinence syndrome have had at least one convulsion by the second or third day after their last dose, and some sixty per cent undergo a psychotic period during the fourth to seventh days of abstinence. These symptoms usually disappear within a week. Abstinence symptoms are *not* found in users of cocaine, marijuana, peyote, or benzedrine, because these drugs do not cause physical dependence.[16]

Despite the more or less specific physiological reactions produced by the various drugs, differences in their use and their effects are so great that any generalization is likely to be misleading. For the individual, addiction is simultaneously a physiological, psychological, and social experience; in each of these dimensions the variation from person to person may be extreme. To the community, depending on the culture, the drug user may be a criminal, a sick person or a divinely inspired visionary. Community attitudes are important, since they largely determine the availability of the drugs and the range of operations necessary for obtaining them. In England, for example, where addiction is viewed as a medical problem, the addict may legally obtain drugs at low cost and is less likely to experience the severe physical and emotional stresses of deprivation. In the United States, where most addicts must of necessity deal with criminal suppliers, addiction is more likely to be a matter of feast or famine, and the extreme symptoms of intoxication and abstinence are more widespread. Thus the total physical and social picture of addiction for any particular person represents a fusion of many elements, each of which must be evaluated in order to understand the significance of the problem for that individual.

Drug Addiction and Crime

There are sharp differences of opinion concerning the relationship of drug addiction to other forms of crime. The issue has tended to become complicated by conflicting public attitudes, one viewing the addict as a sick person, the other as a menace to society. The attempt to accommodate these attitudes occasionally leads to inconsistencies.

Law-enforcement officials have generally been represented as believing that addiction in itself is a potent cause of crime. One of the most emphatic and sweeping presentations of this position appears in a statement of the Senate committee investigating the illicit narcotics traffic:

> Drug addiction is responsible for approximately 50 per cent of all crimes committed in the larger metropolitan areas and 25 per cent of all reported crimes in the nation. . . . In addition to direct narcotic law violations, drug addicts are responsible for a large majority of the burglaries, thefts, prostitution, and other offenses committed to support their drug habits costing from $10 to $100 a day. Addicts also have been associated with crimes of violence, such as murder, armed robbery, safecracking, and rape.

The subcommittee is convinced that crime in the United States would be substantially reduced if drug addicts were taken off the streets and placed in appropriate institutions for treatment or detention.[17]

The clear implication of this point of view is that the addict tends to commit his crimes after he has become addicted—and as a result of his addiction. Nevertheless, in another installment of the Subcommittee's Proceedings, the opposite position is presented:

It is the general public belief that a drug addict becomes addicted first, and then resorts to crime in desperation to feed his habit. This study reveals that such an assumption is only partly true; a majority of the 85 [drug addicts with criminal records] showed criminal tendencies prior to their addiction.

The FBI Bureau of Criminal Identification fingerprint record was compared to the stories given by the addicts on when they became addicted: 62 or 75 per cent of the total had records prior to their current Federal arrest; 53 or 64 per cent had records prior to their confessed date of addiction. This must be regarded as a conservative figure when it is considered that the FBI report does not show early evidences of criminality which might have taken the subject into children's court, truancy hearings, the police department juvenile aid bureau and so on. In all probability more than 64 per cent showed early signs of criminality which went unrecorded.

Of the group studied, a large number had been arrested many times after being addicted, and more than half of them had received treatment either through private or public hospitals or through serving jail sentences. Some had undergone withdrawal at least 10 times before appearing in Federal court on the cases herein noted.[18]

The relation of these inconsistencies to the moral dilemma presented by the drug addict seems obvious. In order to rationalize a punitive approach to the problem of addiction in general, it seems necessary to demonstrate that the menace of the drug habit is largely criminal in character. The criminalistic aspect of addiction thus justifies a stern anti-criminal program. Furthermore, when dealing directly with the punishment of the specific addict, his status as a sick person creates a moral difficulty. The punishment of the physically or mentally ill is contrary to public feeling. Consequently, at this point it is more convenient

[17] U. S. Senate, *The Illicit Narcotics Traffic: Summary of Preliminary Findings and Recommendations*, 84th Congress, Report No. 1440 (Washington, D. C.: Government Printing Office, 1956), pp. 2–3.
[18] U. S. Senate, Committee on the Judiciary, *Hearings before the Subcommittee on Improvements in the Federal Criminal Code*, Part 3, June 24–25, 1955 (Washington, D. C.: Government Printing Office, 1956), p. 784.

to view the addict primarily as a criminal and as a sick person more or less incidentally.

The moral dilemma is brought into sharpest focus by the problem of the drug peddler who is also an addict. Like many other addicts, the addict-peddler is occupied more or less full time in the supplying of his own drug needs. The peddling of narcotics is his particular method of meeting the demands of his addiction. Because of his obvious role in the spread of the drug habit, however, it is necessary to curb his operations drastically by penalizing them stringently. (The recent federal law imposes a possible sentence of death for the sale of heroin to juveniles.) This necessity creates something of a moral pressure to conceive of the addict-peddler largely in terms of his peddling rather than in terms of his addiction.

In the Third Report of the New Jersey Commission on Narcotic Control the point is made that, in more than 90 per cent of the cases of addict-peddlers, "addiction is a part of their criminal pattern rather than a cause." On the other hand, the Report asserts, relatively few addicts become peddlers. In a study of the case histories of narcotic offenders in New Jersey it was found that barely 6 per cent had also been convicted for the sale of drugs. Nevertheless, in another section of the Report, the statement is made that "more than 90 per cent of all drug addicts have habitually participated in delinquent or criminal behavior."[19]

The larger body of representative medical opinion is critical of any direct cause-effect relationship between drug addiction and criminality. Although acknowledging that present legislation forces the addict to deal with criminal sources—and that the high cost of drugs functions as a powerful incentive toward certain forms of theft and pilfering—medical authorities tend to be skeptical about the involvement of addicts generally in more serious forms of crime. Their arguments are based chiefly on the effects of the drugs themselves. Dr. Lawrence Kolb of the United States Public Health Service wrote in 1925:

> Insofar as its influence on crime is concerned, addiction to opium or any of its preparations creates two tendencies directly opposed to each other. The immediate effect of excessive indulgence in all forms of the drug is to soothe abnormal impulses, while the ultimate effect is to create a state of idleness and dependency which naturally enhances the desire to live at the expense of others and by antisocial means. The

[19] New Jersey Commission on Narcotic Control, *Third Report of Study and Recommendations* (Trenton, N. J.: The Commission, 1957), pp. 34–37.

effect of addiction on the psychopathic murderer is to inhibit his impulse to violent crime. At the same time it saps his vitality and reduces the ambition and courage that prompt him to convert his abnormal impulse into action. He, therefore, becomes less a murderer and more a thief. In other cases, where the degree of abnormality is not so great, the indirect effect is to increase the impulse to lie and steal. The factor most important in this is the desire to secure the drug in order to avoid the discomfort caused by the lack of it.[20]

The comparison of the crime rates of addicts with those of the general population generally reveals a higher ratio of property to personal offenses. In a survey conducted by the Chicago Police Department and the Narcotic Bureau in 1951 it was reported that the larceny and robbery rates of addicts were considerably higher than those of the general population, that the burglary rate was about equal and that the rates for sex offenses, auto theft, weapons carrying, and assault were very markedly lower. In the category of aggravated and other assaults, for example, the rate for addicts was 1.3, compared with 19.7 in the general population.[21]

The increase in crime among drug addicts is partly related to the recent increase in addiction among groups which are disproportionately vulnerable to crime in the first place. In Chicago, between 1938 and 1951, the arrest rates for narcotics violations of persons in the 16–20 age group rose from 0.43 to 13.64. In the 21–30 age group the rates more than quadrupled. In the age groups over 31, the rates rose by less than 0.3 per cent.[22]

The Extent and Distribution of Drug Addiction

The percentage of drug addicts in the general population has greatly declined since the passage of the first national control act in 1914 (The Harrison Act). In 1924 Kolb and DuMez estimated the total number of addicts in the country to be somewhere between a maximum of 150,000 and a minimum of 110,000.[23] Present official nation-wide

[20] Lawrence Kolb, "Drug Addiction in Its Relation to Crime," *Mental Hygiene,* 9:74–89, January 1925. (Also cited in "Illicit Narcotics Traffic," Part 6 of the *Hearings before the Subcommittee on Improvements in the Federal Criminal Code of the Committee on the Judiciary, United States Senate,* 84th Congress, p. 2337.)

[21] Harold Finestone, "Narcotics and Criminality," *Law and Contemporary Problems,* 22:71, Winter 1957.

[22] *Ibid.,* p. 70.

[23] Lawrence Kolb and A. G. DuMez, "The Prevalence and Trend of Drug Addiction in the United States and Factors Influencing It," *Public Health Reports,* 39:1202, May 1924.

estimates cut the 1923 minimum almost in half. The following report summarizes a recent official estimate of the trend and distribution of narcotics addiction in the country at this time:

Before the passage of national control legislation there was 1 addict in every 400 persons in the United States. By World War I this incidence had been reduced to about 1 in every 1,500 persons, and by World War II the incidence was found to be roughly 1 in 10,000 rejected for military service because of addiction. At this time the narcotic traffic in the United States was probably at the lowest ebb since the enactment of Federal legislation to control narcotics.

The total number of addicts in the United States today is estimated at between 50,000 and 60,000, or an incidence of about 1 in 3,000 of the population. An interim report on the survey of drug addiction begun by the Bureau of Narcotics in January 1953 shows 28,514 addicts counted to date. It is believed that this count, consolidated monthly from reports received from Federal, State, and local authorities throughout the United States, will approach the above estimate in 2 to 3 years.

Among the addicts reported in the survey, 77.83 per cent used heroin, 9.81 per cent used morphine, 1.47 per cent used opium, 6.3 per cent used synthetic drugs and 4.52 per cent and 0.07 per cent were reported as using marihuana and cocaine respectively.

Males accounted for 79.01 per cent of the total; age groups of both sexes were as follows:

Years	Per cent
Under 21	13.1
21 to 30	50.3
31 to 40	19.4
Over 40	17.2

A further study of the group under 21 years of age revealed that 87.61 per cent of this group were 18 years old or over.

Reports relating to the United States Public Health Service hospital at Lexington show that the majority of persons addicted to opiates come from cities of 1 million or more population.

Addiction statistics maintained by the Bureau of Narcotics show the greatest concentration of addicts in the areas of New York City, Chicago, and Los Angeles, with these areas showing 7,937, 6,975, and 1,896, respectively for the 2-year period 1953–54. The strength of the Bureau of Narcotics is concentrated in these areas of the most illicit activity, and here is also found a pooling of equipment with other agencies and the police departments.

Drug addiction among adolescents took on major proportions after

World War II, and reached its peak about 1951. Since then it has shown signs of abating except in several areas.[24]

The Military Offender

Military personnel comprise a special-offender category for two reasons: (1) they are subject to a separate body of laws, trial procedures, and dispositions; and (2) many of the behaviors defined as military offenses would not be punishable if the offenders were under civilian criminal jurisdiction. In this last sense, military law, by creating special offense categories, creates a special type of offender much as do the extra-criminal provisions of juvenile laws; in both cases the status of offender is made possible because the individual occupies a social status involving special liabilities or responsibilities.

Offenders and Offenses Punishable under Military Law

The behaviors defined as punishable under the Uniform Military Code[25] may be divided into two broad categories: acts that would be crimes or misdemeanors under civilian criminal law (larceny, rape, homicide, etc.) and offenses of a largely or purely military nature. Military personnel committing crimes of the first category within the United States may be prosecuted by civilian as well as military authorities. In cases involving serious felonies of this type, the military services frequently elect to discharge the offenders dishonorably and send them directly to federal prisons.

Persons defined as subject to military law include all members of the armed services and certain classes of persons employed by or accompanying them. Jurisdiction does not extend to cases or suits that would ordinarily be considered civil—e.g., suits for civil damages, breach of contract, etc.

[24] "Illicit Narcotics Traffic," Part 1 of *Hearings before the Subcommittee on Improvements in the Federal Criminal Code of the Committee on the Judiciary, United States Senate, 84th Congress,* pp. 9–10.

[25] The Uniform Military Code, with its accompanying *Manual for Courts-Martial* (effective May 31, 1951) represents a modernization, liberalization, and consolidation of the separate military codes of the different military services into one unified body of laws and procedures for all members of the armed forces.

Until 1955, federal law provided that offenses committed while in military service but discovered after discharge to civilian status were still punishable under military jurisdiction. A 1955 Supreme Court decision declared this law unconstitutional. On the basis of this decision, military jurisdiction over military personnel is terminated following their resumption of civilian status.

The strictly military offenses—those which, with a few exceptions, would not be prosecuted under civilian criminal law[26]—fall into three broad categories.

BREACHES OF DISCIPLINE AND MILITARY COURTESY. There is a wide variety of minor and major offenses, some of them broadly defined, which may be classed as violations of military discipline, courtesy, or custom. Disrespect to superiors, behavior unbecoming an officer and gentleman, deliberate unwillingness, neglect, or refusal to carry out orders, riotous or disorderly behavior of varying degrees of seriousness, and a variety of loosely and specifically defined infractions are included in this general class. Many of these offenses, if committed by civilians, would entail no more than loss of job; in the military services they are regarded with much greater seriousness.

DERELICTION OF DUTY. This broad category includes various minor and several major offenses, certain of which are punishable by death. The most serious crimes include misbehavior before the enemy, neglect or destruction of government property, falling asleep while on guard duty, and various infractions risking the safety, security, or morale of the military service or bringing discredit to it. Abuses of authority and mistreatment of subordinates also fall in this category.

There are serious offenses that may be committed by military personnel while prisoners of war in enemy hands. According to international agreements relating to the treatment of prisoners of war, captured military personnel are not to be forced to aid the capturing power. According to American military law, an American prisoner is forbidden to reveal any information beyond his name, rank, and serial number. The giving of any other information, especially of potential or actual military benefit to the enemy, is a serious offense and may be defined as giving aid and comfort to the enemy. During the Korean War the Chinese and North Koreans frequently applied coercion and offered

[26] The exceptions include treason, espionage, destruction of government property, and certain others.

inducements to influence American prisoners to give information, to make themselves available for propaganda purposes, or to inform on and coerce other prisoners. Though physical force was occasionally used, many of the coercive techniques were of the psychological or "brainwashing" variety familiar in the Communist treatment of political prisoners but never before experienced—and therefore not anticipated—by American soldiers. After the war a number of prisoners who had been coerced or induced to cooperate with their captors were prosecuted, and a serious moral and legal controversy arose over what differentiated irresistible coercion from treasonable cooperation. Though military policy on this question has been somewhat clarified by directives, the controversy continues.

ABSENCE WITHOUT LEAVE AND DESERTION. By far the most frequent of the more serious offenses committed by military personnel are *absence without leave* (AWOL) and desertion. One is absent without leave when one "fails to repair at the fixed time to the properly appointed place of duty, or goes from the same without proper leave, or has absented himself from his command, guard, quarters, stations or camp without proper leave."[27]

Although desertion is defined as an unauthorized departure without intention to return, or during a period of critical need, the distinction between it and AWOL is sometimes difficult to make and remains a matter of interpretation in the individual case. Leaving one's unit even temporarily under fire may be defined as AWOL, desertion, or misbehavior before the enemy. The distinction between AWOL and desertion while in garrison depends on a variety of factors going to the interpretation of the intention to return or remain absent. These include the length of time away, the manner in which the departure was made, and the way the return took place. Absentees who return voluntarily, even after relatively long periods, are generally given the benefit of the doubt. Similarly, absentees who are apprehended and forcibly returned after a brief period are often presumed to have merely been absent without leave. On the other hand, a soldier who destroys or discards his uniform and makes arrangements to leave the country may be considered a deserter even after an absence of only several hours. Though AWOL and desertion are considered especially serious in wartime and in combat, there was only one occasion during World War II when the death penalty was applied.

[27] Articles of War, Article 61, 1948 amended.

Military Trial

There are three types of court-martial: summary, special, and general. The jurisdiction of each is determined by the maximum punishment authorized for the offense involved and by the rank of the offender. The *summary court* consists of one officer and is empowered to try enlisted personnel for minor offenses for which the maximum punishment does not exceed one month's confinement, or hard labor without confinement for forty-five days, or restriction to a limited area for up to two months, or forfeiture of two thirds of one month's pay. In many cases the sentences of summary courts are less than these maxima, and may be limited to a few days' restriction to quarters or a reprimand.

Special court-martial may be convened to try cases in which the maximum punishment does not exceed six months' confinement, hard labor without confinement for three months, or forefeiture of two thirds of the monthly pay for six months. A special court-martial may order a bad-conduct discharge (as distinguished from a dishonorable discharge) from the service. The court must consist of three members and is empowered to try enlisted personnel.

The *general court-martial* may try any military person for any offense in the code, and may apply any punishment not forbidden in the code. It is the only court that may impose the death penalty and the dishonorable discharge. The court must consist of at least five members and a law officer who advises on legal questions but does not otherwise participate in determining the verdict or sentence.

The right to counsel without expense to the accused is provided in all courts-martial above the summary-court level. Should the accused prefer defense counsel other than that provided by the court, he may request another of his own choice, and the request must be complied with unless due cause can be shown for rejecting the request. Theoretically—and, frequently, in practice—an accused enlisted man can obtain an officer of any rank to represent him. There is one limitation on his choice, however, and this is for his own benefit. If the counsel for the prosecution (called the "trial counsel") is a lawyer, the defense counsel must also be a lawyer. If the accused wishes to be represented by a civilian rather than a military defense counsel he may obtain one, but at his own expense.

The members of the court-martial are selected by the commanding officer authorized to convene the court. However, both the defense and the prosecution can challenge any members of the court for cause.[28] In addition, both have the right to one *peremptory challenge*—a demand for the withdrawal of a member without cause. Under the provisions of the Uniform Military Code, accused enlisted men may request that qualified enlisted men be included among the members of the court. If the request is made, the number of enlisted members must comprise at least one third of the total membership of the court.

The accused cannot be compelled to testify himself and he may elect to stand mute. As in civilian criminal trials, the burden of proof is on the prosecution, which must prove its case beyond reasonable doubt. The accused may not waive the right to counsel—as is permitted in civilian trials—and the trial may not begin until he has obtained a counsel of his choice or has accepted the appointed counsel, and has had time to prepare his defense. He is permitted to plead guilty or not guilty, except in capital cases, where a plea of not guilty is automatically entered for him. Prior to the trial he must be informed that any statement made by him may be used against him; unless this statement is made, evidence obtained against him during pre-trial investigations is not admissible. He may directly, or through his counsel, examine and cross-examine witnesses. He is not compelled to take the stand himself, and his election not to do so may not be alluded to by the prosecution and creates no presumption against him.

Punishments

The Uniform Military Code specifically forbids the use of corporal punishment and repeats the constitutional provision against cruel and unusual punishments. The use of irons or other forms of physical restraint is authorized only for purposes of secure custody; these restraints must be removed immediately when the prisoner is once again in a secure situation.

The range of military punishments includes death, confinement at hard labor, hard labor without confinement, forfeiture of pay, and dishonorable or bad-conduct discharge. Death is mandatory in the event of a conviction for spying. In convictions of premeditated murder or

---

[28] The number of challenges for cause is unlimited and may be made by other members of the court to each other. Members may also disqualify themselves. The purpose of the challenge is to ensure that the court is constituted to the satisfaction of both sides. This is especially important in military trials, where members of the court function both as judges and as jury.

murder while engaged in another felony, the sentence must be death or life imprisonment. The death penalty is discretionary in cases of desertion, absence without leave, misbehavior before the enemy, rape, and certain other military offenses. In this connection, it is significant that of 102 American soldiers executed during World War II, only one was executed for a purely military offense. The remaining 101 executions were for murder or rape under circumstances that would be capital in many civilian criminal jurisdictions.[29] The dishonorable discharge is usually ordered for those convicted of crimes that would be considered serious felonies under civilian law, and for grave military offenses; in sentences involving death or life imprisonment it is mandatory. Under certain conditions, however, the dishonorable discharge may be suspended for a period during which the offender is given an opportunity for restoration.

The Treatment of Military Offenders

The governing purposes of military punishment are the preservation of discipline and the restoration of reformable offenders to duty status. These motives are deterrent and rehabilitative. Apart from humanitarian purposes, the rehabilitative interest of military punishment is closely related to practical military needs. During the Second World War, one out of every three draftees was rejected for military service. Preventing the permanent loss of any large number of trained military personnel because of military offenses was considered urgent, and within a short time after the beginning of the war the military authorities sought for ways of effecting the maximum number of possible restorations to duty.

In line with this objective, a number of installations known as "Rehabilitation Centers" were set up for the treatment and retraining of military offenders convicted of violations serious enough to entail dishonorable discharges and long prison sentences. Increasing numbers of these prisoners, who would otherwise have been permanently lost to military service, were sent to the Centers for periods varying from six months to a year.

Because of the urgency of the problem and the absence of validated techniques of intensive, large-scale correctional treatment, the latitude of the treatment authorities was wide and the approach frankly oppor-

[29] Arnold Rose, "The Social Psychology of Desertion from Combat," *American Sociological Review*, 16:614, October 1951.

tunistic and experimental. Early in 1943 an intensive group-therapy program was organized at the pioneer Rehabilitation Center at Fort Knox; within a year the program was able to accommodate from five hundred to seven hundred prisoners with a turnover of fifty to one hundred ten per month. Though an adequate evaluation of the results was prevented by the fact that most of the restored men left for service in combat areas, the available data indicated impressive results. Approximately 47 per cent of the prisoners in the program were restored to duty, and the rate of recidivism was low—from 6 to 10 per cent.[30] The group-therapy techniques worked out at the rehabilitation centers have been used by an increasing number of civilian correctional institutions.

The Extent of Military Offenses

The number of military offenders varies with the number of personnel in the armed forces. In the peak year of 1945, military courts dealt with approximately 730,000 cases, more than three times the total number of cases in the federal courts and in the State of New York combined.[31] Should the present level of mobilization persist, the military services will continue to cope with the largest number of offenders handled under a single system of law and a single complex of correctional procedures. As such, this system merits the attention of researchers interested in the emergence and treatment of unlawful behavior under special conditions of stress and opportunity.

The Juvenile Offender

Discussions of the meaning, extent, and treatment of delinquency are limited by definitions of what delinquency is. As the following discussion will indicate, the question, What is delinquency? is itself a highly loaded one because it seems to suggest that a direct factual answer is possible. Because of the multitude of legal, clinical, administrative,

[30] Joseph Abrahams and Lloyd W. McCorkle, "Group Psychotherapy of Military Offenders," *American Journal of Sociology*, 51:455, March 1946. See also Abrahams and McCorkle, "Group Therapy at an Army Rehabilitation Center," *Diseases of the Nervous System*, 8:3-15, February 1947.

[31] Delmar Karlen and Louis H. Pepper, "The Scope of Military Justice," *Journal of Criminal Law and Criminology*, 43:296, September–October 1952.

and behavioral definitions in existence, the assumption that any directly factual or consistent answers are possible is itself one of the principle sources of confusion. Consequently, one of the first requirements of a discussion of delinquency is a rejection of the question, What is delinquency? and the substitution of the question, What is meant when the term *delinquency* is used?

Approaches to the Definition of Delinquency

THE LEGAL APPROACH. As a legal concept, delinquency is considerably broader and vaguer than the legal concept of crime, for two reasons: (1) It covers many behaviors that would not be considered criminal if committed by adults; and (2) the juridical definition of these behaviors (e.g., "incorrigibility") is frequently much more general than would be constitutionally tolerated in criminal statutes, which require precise descriptions of the activities labeled as illegal. The New Jersey Juvenile Statute provides a representative modern illustration:

NEW JERSEY STATUTE 2A:4–14

Juvenile delinquency is hereby defined as the commission by a child under 18 years of age of (1) any act which when committed by a person of the age of 18 or over would constitute:
a. A felony, high misdemeanor, misdemeanor, or other offense, or
b. The violation of any penal law or municipal ordinance, or
c. Any act or offense for which he could be prosecuted in the method partaking of the nature of a criminal action or proceeding, or
d. Being a disorderly person, or (2) the following acts:
e. Habitual vagrancy, or
f. Incorrigibility, or
g. Immorality, or
h. Knowingly associating with thieves or vicious or immoral persons.
i. Growing up in idleness or delinquency, or
j. Knowingly visiting gambling places, or patronizing other places or establishments, his (or her) admission to which constitutes a violation of law, or
k. Idly roaming the streets at night, or
l. Habitual truancy from school, or
m. Deportment endangering the morals, health or general welfare of said child.[32]

Evaluations of these and similar juvenile statutes sometimes reveal

[32] *Helping Youth in Trouble*, Report and Recommendations of the State of New Jersey Youth Study Commission, 1957, pp. 131–132.

ambivalent attitudes on the part of officials called on to administer them. In 1957 the State of New Jersey Youth Commission issued a report based on an extended study of its judicial and treatment provisions for juveniles. In the course of its study the Commission took testimony from a wide range of legal, clinical, and administrative experts. Critically commenting on the juvenile statute just quoted, the Commission states, on page 3 of its report:

> Certain categories of acts defined as delinquent are extremely broad and can be interpreted to include almost any type of deviant behavior by those under 18.[33]

On page 132 of the same report, the Commission states:

> While there are both advantages and disadvantages to an ambiguous statute, it certainly cannot be said that police in New Jersey are unduly limited....[34]

THE PERSONALISTIC APPROACH. One of the functions of law is to define the status of individuals whose behavior brings them within the jurisdiction and control of judicial tribunals. In this sense the terms *criminal* and *delinquent* define a status conferred on individuals as a result of their being brought under the control of law-enforcement authorities. Though the actual differences between these individuals may be great, public opinion tends to conceptualize them in a more or less stereotyped way. Thus the term *delinquent*, like the word *criminal* (of which it is a kind of semantic step-child) rarely fails to conjure up a distinct mental image with strong emotional coloring. As has been pointed out in Chapter 2, the existence of this stereotype is made possible by a confusion between the ideas of *status* and *type*. In effect, the existence of a fairly clear and distinguishable *legal status* has led many to assume that a similarly distinguishable *type of person* exists, and that individuals of this type share essentially similar personal characteristics or are suffering from the same kind of pathological condition. In a recent article the psychiatrist Richard Jenkins has stated:

> Much of the confusion relating to current discussions of delinquency relates to a tendency to treat delinquency as though it were an entity resident within the personality of the delinquent. This is related to a failure to recognize that the patterns of behavior which the law lumps together under the title of delinquency have little universally in common except their illegality.[35]

[33] *Ibid.*, pp. 2–3.
[34] *Ibid.*, p. 132.
[35] Richard Jenkins, "Adaptive and Maladaptive Delinquency," *The Nervous Child*, 2:9, October 1955.

THE BEHAVIORAL APPROACH. A definition of delinquency in behavioral terms would have many advantages. If it were possible to point to certain distinct activities as delinquent it would be possible to say, "Delinquents are children who engage in these activities; children not engaging in these activities are not delinquent." Two characteristics of delinquency statutes militate against this method of distinguishing delinquents from nondelinquents: (1) either the delinquent behavior is described in highly general terms, covering a wide variety of possible activities; or (2) the delinquent acts, when they are specifically indicated, are frequently no different from those engaged in, at one time or another, by all children. This impression is confirmed by a review of juvenile statutes, where such generally described concepts as incorrigibility and disobedience to parents may alternate with activities as specific as smoking in a public place. In effect, delinquent behavior may be virtually any behavior that distresses the adults concerned to the point where they feel it necessary to turn to the juvenile authorities.

Problems in Estimating the Extent of Juvenile Delinquency

INDICES OF DELINQUENCY. Estimates of the extent of delinquency vary according to the index of delinquency used. If *commitment* by a juvenile court is used, one figure will result; if *court appearance* is used, the figure will be different; if *police complaints* are used, a third figure for the number of delinquents will result. In a study investigating the estimates of delinquency based on different indices of delinquency, Kobrin found the following:

> During the seven-year period 1927–1933 the rate of commitment per 100 boys of juvenile court age residing in Chicago in the ten square mile areas with highest rates was 6.1. In the highest rate square mile area this rate was 9.2. During the same period the rate of official court delinquents in the ten square mile areas of highest rates was 14.6, with a rate of 18.9 in the top square mile area.
>
> In contrast to both commitment and juvenile court appearances, police complaint cases, as may be anticipated, include in the delinquent classification a considerably larger proportion of boys residing in urban delinquency areas. Thus, the Chicago data show that the average rate of delinquents based on police complaints for the ten square mile areas of the highest rates for the year 1926 was 20.6.[36]

Thus, when the police complaints were used as an index of delin-

[36] Solomon Kobrin, "The Conflict of Values in Delinquency Areas," *American Sociological Review*, 16:654, October 1951.

quency, one out of every five children between the ages of ten and seventeen in the area could be considered delinquent in 1926. But these rates, being based on only one year, do not provide an estimate of the incidence of delinquency during the seven-year period of eligibility (ages ten to seventeen).

On the basis of a survey of police complaints, it was found that 65.9 per cent of the children in the area had engaged in behavior "serious enough to warrant recorded police attention" between the ages of ten and seventeen.

> "Thus," writes Kobrin, "... when the most inclusive measure based on police records is used, not one-fifth but almost two-thirds of the boys in delinquency areas may be regarded as official delinquents.[37]

Commenting on the problems of definition raised by these figures, George Vold has raised these questions:

> How delinquent does a boy need to be before he is found delinquent? Is a boy delinquent whenever a social worker, or a neighbor, or some other citizen so reports him? If that criterion is accepted, it seems clear that the proportion of the total number of delinquents in any area called delinquent would be greatly increased. It might even be true that the majority of all juveniles in all areas would be found to be delinquent—in which case one would be confronted with the awkward conclusion that all areas are delinquency areas![38]

STATISTICAL ESTIMATES OF THE INCIDENCE OF DELINQUENCY. The most comprehensive survey of the nation-wide incidence of delinquency is published in *Juvenile Court Statistics,* issued by the Children's Bureau of the United States Department of Health, Education and Welfare. This survey, which is based on the most conservative index of delinquency—juvenile court proceedings and dispositions—is dependent on the voluntary contribution of information from state agencies, and its coverage is inadequate. In 1950, for example, the coverage extended to no more than 29 per cent of the total child population of the United States. Twenty states—including New York—did not report at all; most of the reporting states sent information covering less than two thirds of their child population.[39] (By 1953 the coverage had risen to 36 per cent of the total population of children between the ages of ten and seven-

[37] *Ibid.,* p. 655.

[38] George Vold, "Discussion of Kobrin's Findings," *American Sociological Review,* 16:661, October 1951.

[39] U. S. Department of Health, Education, and Welfare, *Juvenile Court Statistics 1950–52,* Children's Bureau Statistical Series No. 18, 1954, p. 1.

teen.[40]) In spite of these inadequacies, *Juvenile Court Statistics* provides valuable information about the functioning of the juvenile court system and further insights into problems of definition and disposition.

ESTIMATES OF THE TREND OF DELINQUENCY. According to every index, rates of juvenile delinquency are rising. At least two definitely known factors decrease the reliability of trend estimates, however. The increased number of juvenile court cases is in part related to the increased number of juvenile courts. On the other hand, the increased activity of private agencies dealing with behavior problems without court intervention works to mask the number of known delinquencies. The effect of the activities of these private agencies—many of whom receive referrals directly from the police or the complaining adult—is to deal with the children in a manner that avoids imposing the status of delinquent and its consequences.

The Juvenile Court

The closing years of the last century saw a rising demand for the creation of separate judicial facilities for younger offenders. Though special proceedings in behalf of minors had long been know to the law, the first court for youthful offenders was created in 1899 in Cook County, Illinois. By 1945 juvenile courts had been established in every state of the Union.

PHILOSOPHY OF THE JUVENILE COURT. From the outset the proponents of the juvenile court possessed an articulate philosophy, which they recognized and defended as radically different from basic canons of conventional criminal procedure. The foundation principles of this philosophy are the concepts of *individualized justice* and *treatment,* as contrasted with impartial adjudication and punishment. A third working principle, designed to facilitate the implementation of the others, is the replacement of conventional courtroom formalities and rules by more informal procedures calculated to create a less threatening atmosphere for the young.

The noted juvenile court judge, Paul W. Alexander, has vividly contrasted the principle of individualized justice with the older doctrine of equality before the law. Illustrating his analysis with an allusion to the conventional symbol of justice—the blindfolded woman with the scales—Judge Alexander writes:

[40] *Juvenile Court Statistics 1953,* No. 28, p. 1.

You have seen her hundreds of times, a statuesque female figure with arm extended, holding in her hand a balance. Into one scale goes the crime, into the other the punishment. When the two balance evenly then even-handed justice is done. And just so the lady won't be subjected to temptation, or be influenced by the wealth or poverty or other attributes of the individual affected, she is kept blindfolded. She is blind to the individual.

A new concept of justice has been rapidly gaining acceptance in recent decades. It is sometimes called "individualized justice." It strips the blindfold from the lady. It not only permits her to see the individual, it bids her scrutinize him. It transfers much of the emphasis from *what* has he done to *why* has he done it; from what should we do *to* him to what should we do *for* him.[41]

Judge Alexander discusses the court's second guiding principle— treatment rather than punishment—by means of an analogy. "The court," he writes, "is more like a hospital or clinic than like anything else":

If a person's bodily functions deviate so far from the normal that he cannot be properly treated in his home, he is ordered to a hospital. If a child's conduct deviates so far from the normal that it cannot be successfully corrected in the home, he is ordered to juvenile court.

The hospital gets the patient after he is sick. The court gets the child after he is delinquent. The hospital's function is to cure the patient and prevent him from becoming a chronic invalid; the court's, to correct the child and prevent him from becoming a chronic criminal.

The hospital's primary concern is the individual patient; it serves society, first by curing the patient and restoring him to society as an able-bodied citizen; second, through research, developing techniques, disseminating knowledge, preventive medicine, and by quarantining the occasional dangerous patient. The court's primary concern is the individual child; it serves society, first by reclaiming the future citizen; second, through research, developing techniques, disseminating knowledge, leadership in preventing delinquency and crime, and by quarantining the occasional dangerous child.[42]

In conventional criminal proceedings the major purpose of the trial is to determine whether the accused actually committed the act of which he is accused. The juvenile court, by contrast, is less insistently concerned with the objective facts of the case. Continuing with his analogy of the hospital, Judge Alexander writes:

[41] Paul W. Alexander, "Of Juvenile Court Justice and Judges," *1947 Yearbook of the National Probation and Parole Association* (New York: The Association, 1948), p. 189.
[42] *Ibid.*, pp. 191–192.

Generally speaking, the hospital doesn't have to find out whether the patient is sick, but why. Just so, *the court doesn't have to find out whether the child is delinquent, but why.* To digress a moment, this usually comes as something of a shock to laymen, lawyers, and most trial and appellate judges, and even to a new juvenile judge. What is either unknown or overlooked is the thoroughly established fact that children, unlike adults, almost always confess their offenses before they appear before the judge finally. In my own experience with over 12,000 delinquency cases, barely one in a thousand children has failed or refused to confess the offense charged. Even in the larger cities where some of the youngsters come from the heart of gangland and might be expected to have been schooled not to "talk," I am assured that confessions are received in 99 out of 100 cases. This is the experience of juvenile court judges throughout the country. Usually the arresting officer has a confession before we meet the child. If not, the probation officer or psychologist in the course of his efforts to win the child's confidence is nearly always presented with a confession, often covering offenses police or teacher or parent never dreamed of.[43] (Italics supplied.)

Subsequent commentators have become increasingly restive about this assumption of virtually certain guilt, and they have raised questions about the adequacy of a confession as proof of the facts of the case. Acknowledging that the great bulk of cases coming before the court are not contested, Bloch and Flynn concede that nine out of ten delinquents brought before the court freely admit to behavior they actually committed. Even so, they continue:

> ...the one child in ten who does not belong in court or who denies the alleged act needs protection. Some writers have contended that the child is "protected" because the probation officer acts as "counsel" for the child. This position is open to serious question. The probation officer, like the judge, ultimately may impose his own bias or his standards of culture and morals upon children who stand before the court.[44]

Certain observers have suggested that the juvenile court, in protecting the child from the rigors of courtroom formality, may be "protecting" him from basic rights as well. Professor Paul Tappan has sharply criticized attempts to justify:

> ...the abandonment, partial or complete, of even the most basic conceptions of due process of law: a specific charge; confrontation by one's adverse witnesses; right to counsel or appeal; rejection of prejudicial,

---

[43] *Ibid.*, pp. 192–193.
[44] Herbert A. Bloch and Frank T. Flynn, *Delinquency* (New York: Random House, 1956), p. 325.

irrelevant, and hearsay testimony; adjudication only upon proof or upon a plea of guilt.[45]

Dean Roscoe Pound, an early advocate and continuing historian of the juvenile court movement, has recently expressed his concern in similar terms:

> The powers of the Star Chamber were a trifle in comparison with those of our juvenile courts and courts of domestic relations.... It is well known that too often the placing of a child in a home or even in an institution is done casually or perfunctorily, or even arbitrarily.... Even with the most superior personnel, these tribunals call for legal checks.[46]

In a purely procedural sense, at least, the allusion to the Star Chamber seems appropriate. There is no jury. The community's case is typically presented by the probation officer, an official of the court—the same person, presumably, who examined the child and obtained his confession. The child may not necessarily be permitted to confront the complainants or to hear all of the evidence against him; frequently he is excused in order to protect him from humiliating or disillusioning disclosures by— or concerning—important figures in the case. In most instances there is no provision for an appeal to a higher court. Since the court's action is viewed as an order for treatment rather than a directive for punishment, appellate procedures are considered inappropriate. To carry the hospital analogy further, the patients in the children's ward are not to be allowed to appeal against their medicine.

JURISDICTION AND POWERS OF THE JUVENILE COURT. The powers of the juvenile court are very broad, both in scope and in forcefulness.[47]

[45] Paul Tappan, *Juvenile Delinquency* (New York: McGraw-Hill Book Company, Inc., 1947), pp. 204–205.

[46] Roscoe Pound, *Foreword* in Pauline V. Young, *Social Treatment in Probation and Delinquency* (New York: McGraw-Hill Book Company, Inc., 1952), p. xv.

[47] That the wide discretion of the court opens the door to a variety of abuses is beyond question. In 1944 Austin Porterfield reported the results of a study in which he investigated court dispositions of delinquency petitions brought by parents against their own children ("Parents and Other Complainants in the Juvenile Court," *1944 Yearbook of the National Probation Association,* New York: The Association, 1945). Characterizing a large number of these complaints, Porterfield writes:

> Many ... are proper, but sweet reason and the stark facts are far from supporting them all. Parents frequently complain . . . about a child's disobedience, even though the data may make it very clear that the parental personality merits no respect.... Frequently a parent says, "Since Jill won't mind me you must send her to the training school." And the courts do not always resist. They actually do it.
> ... One mother, on hearing that her son had been detained, wrote, "Keep him

In addition to intervening in cases of juvenile misconduct, the court has jurisdiction over complaints of neglect or mistreatment by parents. In cases of alleged neglect or mistreatment, the authority of the court extends to the adult parents or guardians as well, and the judge may order those concerned either to cease or to undertake such action as he deems appropriate. Their failure to comply may subject them to penalties, usually without a separate criminal proceeding. The court, in addition, may be empowered to suspend or to terminate parental rights over the child, to appoint guardians for the child's person, and to rule on issues of legal adoption.

SUGGESTED IMPROVEMENTS AND LIMITATIONS. In 1953 the Children's Bureau of the United States Department of Health, Education, and Welfare convened a panel of experts for the purpose of developing a comprehensive statement of the appropriate standards for juvenile courts. The following description of proposed improvements and safeguards is cited from the document prepared by the panel:

1. The conditions under which the State is empowered to intervene in the upbringing of a child should be specifically and clearly delineated in the statutes. Whenever the State seeks to intervene, it should be required to show that those conditions do in fact exist with respect to a child and that its intervention is necessary to protect the child or the community, or both. The State should not be able to interfere with the rights of the parents with respect to their child and assume jurisdiction over such child on the generalized assumption that the child is in need of the care or protection of the State or merely because it disagrees with the parent as to the "best course to pursue in rearing a child." Nor should it be authorized to take children from their parents "merely because, in the estimation of probation officers and courts, the children can be better provided for and more wisely trained as wards of the State."

2. Both the child and his parents are entitled to know the bases on which the State seeks to intervene and on which it predicates its plan for the care and treatment of the child. They are equally entitled to rebut these bases either directly by questioning witnesses, or indirectly by presenting facts to the contrary. This means that rules of evidence calculated to assure proceedings in accordance with due process of law should be applicable to children's cases. However, it is essential that these rules of evidence be especially designed. They should protect the informality of the hearing and avoid the needless legalisms of the rules

in jail awhile, it might do him good." ... One gets the impression after reading many hundreds of children's cases that the popular theory of the tenacity of a mother's love has been overdone. More often than not, it is the mother who complains. (pp. 58-60) of evidence customarily applicable to other judicial hearings. But at the same time they must assure that there will be an orderly presentation of credible facts in a manner calculated to protect the rights of all concerned.... This principle also entails written findings, some form of record of the hearing, and the right to appeal. The court should give clear reasons for its decision as to the finding with respect to allegations made and any order affecting the rights of the parents or the rights and status of the child. Any order for treatment, care or protection does, in fact, affect these rights.

3. The statute should authorize the court to take specific actions in relation to certain causes rather than allow it unlimited discretion to make any disposition or to order any treatment that it may think advisable. It must, however, have wide discretion within the range of specific actions authorized.

4. There should be certain procedural safeguards established for the protection of the rights of parents and children. Although parties in these proceedings may seldom make use of such safeguards, their existence is none the less important. They are important not only for the protection of rights but also to help insure that the decisions affecting the social planning for children are based on sound legal procedure and will not be disturbed at a later date on the basis that rights were denied.

Where these principles are observed, individualized justice is not hampered but rather strengthened by being placed within the traditional framework of American constitutional rights and judicial practice.[48]

DISPOSITION OF JUVENILE COURT CASES. Between 1950 and 1952, 75 per cent of the cases reported dealt with delinquency, 19 per cent with dependency and neglect (cases in which parents were reported for neglect, cruelty, etc.), and 6 per cent with special proceedings concerning adoption, commitment of mentally defective children, and determination of custody. Thus, in addition to their judicial function, many juvenile courts serve as the agency to which various kinds of child-welfare problems are referred for disposition to community child-care facilities. Many cases referred to the court are handled unofficially—without a formal judgment or mandatory disposition. Between 1950 and 1952, 53 per cent of all cases reported and 57 per cent of all delinquencies reported were dealt with unofficially.[49]

The statistics concerning the handling and disposition of cases reveal

[48] Children's Bureau, Department of Health, Education, and Welfare, *Standards for Specialized Courts Dealing with Children* (Washington, D. C.: Government Printing Office, 1954), pp. 7–8.
[49] *Juvenile Court Statistics 1950–52*, p. 2.

widespread variations in procedure and in the quality of facilities available. One third of the delinquent children were held overnight or longer; of these, 75 per cent were detained in juvenile detention homes and 25 per cent in jails or police stations. Although the most frequent disposition of neglected and dependent children who required shelter care pending the court hearing was placement in boarding homes or homes of relatives and friends, 40 per cent of these children were placed in detention homes or jails or police stations with delinquents.[50]

This last-named method of disposition raises significant questions about the relation of juridical definitions to administrative procedures and resources. In 40 per cent of the cases involving no problems of delinquency or misbehavior, the status of *nondelinquent* resulted in the same treatment provided for delinquents. Though not defined juridically as delinquents, they were subjected to the same procedures, underwent the same experiences and contacts. For these children, the administrative disposition rather than the legal status defined the most meaningful aspect of the events leading up to the court appearance.

Of the 385,000 children dealt with in delinquency cases reported by the juvenile courts in 1952, the ratio of boys to girls was 5 to 1. The median age of the boys was 16.1, that of the girls, 15.6. Dismissals or adjustments were higher for the boys; institutional placements, higher for the girls—a fact partly reflecting the higher incidence of more seriously considered sexual misconduct among the girls. Of the total number of official dispositions for both sexes, commitment to an institution or referral to an agency accounted for 21 per cent of the cases, probation for 39 per cent. Twenty-one per cent of these officially handled cases were dismissed, adjusted, or held open. Of the unofficially handled cases, 68 per cent were dismissed, adjusted, or held open; 18 per cent resulted in probation; 6 per cent in referral or commitment to an agency or institution.[51]

The Question Reframed: What Is Meant by Delinquency?

The frustration of attempts to find a substantive definition of what a delinquent "is" leads ultimately back to a re-examination of the procedures by which the label was affixed. Viewed in these terms, a delinquent is a person who has been assigned a certain legal status as the result of a certain kind of contact with a specialized legal agency having

[50] *Ibid.*, p. 5.
[51] *Ibid.*, p. 6.

a specialized jurisdiction over individuals within a certain age range. The grounds for assigning this status vary greatly. A person may "become" a delinquent for reasons as diverse as committing an armed robbery or distressing his parents or teachers or neighbors to the point where they feel unable to control him without mobilizing official agencies of coercion or guidance. The decision to call on these official agencies is dependent on factors extending beyond the behavior or character of the child. What is unbearable to one parent may be tolerated by another; a youngster who rebels under one domestic regime might well have been tractable under another. Finally, such diverse variables as ethnic background, socioeconomic status, community attitudes, and community facilities may determine whether the parents or adults concerned turn to the court, the psychiatrist, or the social worker—provided, always, that the authorities permit this range of alternatives in the individual case.

Does this administrative definition go any further than the redundant statement that delinquency is merely what the law and the juvenile court says it is? Does it provide a basis or setting for the discovery of other significant variables? In its avoidance of preconceptions about the individual delinquents themselves, it provides what is perhaps the broadest basis. Furthermore, it directs attention to a range of questions that might not have arisen if the inquiry had been limited at the outset. Are there, for example, any distinguishing uniformities in the situations leading to the affixing of the legal status? To what extent do these factors, if any, differentiate delinquents from others in similar community situations? Once this status is assigned, are there any uniformities in the consequences? What happens when large numbers of children differing in personality and background are funneled into the same socio-legal process? Does becoming a delinquent in this sense expose these young people to experiences not undergone by others? If being adjudged a delinquent in Township X results in being sent to a certain juvenile institution, the objective bases for distinguishing delinquents from nondelinquents in Township X are increased. However else the delinquents and nondelinquents were different from or similar to one another previously, they are now sharply dissimilar with respect to one outstanding experience: being sent to the juvenile institution. Moreover, the uniformity of events taking place in this situation may have effects transcending the widest individual differences. The response of the children in this situation would then be open to analysis in terms relevant to their common situation and common status as inmates—and irrelevant to their differences as individuals.

In concluding this survey of the special offender categories, it might be useful to restate certain of the basic orientations that have guided the discussion thus far. Earlier in this text it was pointed out that the term *criminal* frequently conjures up an image whose vividness is disproportionate to the indefiniteness of the concept. This is particularly likely to be true of the special offense categories. Partly because they are more specific and partly because they suggest activities that seem more bizarre, the terms *sex offender* and *drug addict* may suggest distinct types of human beings rather than specific types of violations. Moreover—and in the case of the sex offender especially—this semantic error tends to be powerfully bolstered by an understandable bias. In view of the wide public aversion to many forms of sexual deviation, it is definitely reassuring to consider the "deviates" as somehow distinct in kind or nature from the rest of us.

We are thus provided with at least two alternative ways in which to regard the special offender categories. On the one hand, we can conceive of these violators as individuals, essentially similar in their basic human nature to the rest of us, who, because of a variety of somewhat unusual personal and situational factors, have come to engage in activities somewhat more unusual and repugnant than those engaged in by most. On the other hand, we can view them as freaks who are committing acts unimaginable for us but quite normal and expectable in them. It should be granted that the second viewpoint greatly simplifies what would otherwise be a difficult task of research. Once it is possible to view these individuals as distinct from the rest of humanity, it is no longer necessary to account for how they came to their odd behavior; the question itself has disappeared. All one has to do is prove that they exist—i.e., that they are present. As for why they behave that way, they do so because they "are" that way.

The first viewpoint offers no similarly facile solutions. It requires us to discover how persons apparently exposed to most of the same cultural and physical conditions to which most of the rest of us are subject —and similar in many other personal respects—have come to modes of life and behavior that seem so remote from what the rest of us would do. So difficult and discouraging is this task that it has little to recommend it except to those seriously interested in a science of human behavior.

SECTION IV

THEORIES OF CAUSATION

....

Genetic, Glandular, and Constitutional Theories of Crime

BIOLOGICAL THEORIES OF CRIME SHARE, AT BOTTOM, THE ASSUMPTION that criminal behavior is determined or decisively influenced by the genetic inheritance of the offender. Whether the inherited factors are viewed as common to all members of a group, or merely confined to its genetically defective members, the underlying assumption is identical: The determinants are transmitted from the germ plasm of a genetically defective family stock. This point of view has important corollaries. If the factors determining criminality are present, by inheritance, in the newly conceived embryo, then the influence of subsequent environmental factors must be negligible. Put another way, the genetically defective individuals are fated to be criminals in spite of any advantages or disadvantages in their later experiences.

This logical corollary of hereditary determinism has a further implication, critical for any valid resolution of the question. In order to demonstrate hereditary criminality in individuals with similar genetic backgrounds, it is essential to show that environmental conditions were different. Unless this is proved, it is still possible to conclude that the outcomes are the result of similar environmental experiences rather than similar genetic factors. On the other hand, where genetic backgrounds are different and environmental conditions similar, findings of similar outcomes would cast doubt on the theory.

198

The theory of hereditary determinism carries one final implication, infrequently cited in discussions of the heredity-environment controversy. If criminality is inherited, then noncriminality—or resistance to criminality—must similarly be inherited. Any appreciable finding of criminal behavior in persons with "uncontaminated" genetic backgrounds would render the heredity position untenable.

Though theories locating the causes of criminality in specific physical dysfunctions are not subject to the special requirements of a genetic explanation, they are conditioned by logically analogous considerations. Thus, for example, a glandular explanation of criminality must be supported by evidence that similar glandular dysfunctions in persons in different psychological and social situations resulted in similar criminal symptoms. Conversely, the presence of glandular dysfunctions in appreciable numbers of noncriminals or of adequate glandular functioning in large numbers of offenders would tend to refute the theory.

Heredity and Crime

In recent times investigators have sought for hereditary factors in crime by means of comparisons of identical (one-egg) and fraternal (two-egg) twins. Theoretically, the advantages of this method are great. One-egg or *monozygotic* twins are genetically identical; they are literally mirror-images of each other. This fact permits the investigator to assume an absolutely similar heredity. Two-egg or *dizygotic* twins, on the other hand, are merely siblings who happen to be born at the same time because of the presence of two ova in the mother's womb at the time of conception. Consequently, except for similarity in age, they are generally no more or less alike than other brothers and sisters. Since the genetic background of the one-egg twins is identical, the hereditary theory would predict that the subsequent career of each would be similar to that of the other—or, employing the terminology of the investigators, "concordant."

Ashley Montagu[1] has summarized the findings of several studies of criminality and heredity. These findings are shown in Table XII.

[1] M. F. Ashley Montagu, "The Biologist Looks at Crime," *Annals of the American Academy of Social and Political Science*, 217:53, September 1941.

TABLE XII

CRIMINAL BEHAVIOR OF TWINS

Author	One-egg twins (monozygotic)		Two-egg twins (dizygotic)	
	Concordant	Discordant	Concordant	Discordant
Lange (1929)	10	3	2	15
Legras (1932)	4	0	0	5
Kranz (1936)	20	12	23	20
Stumpfl (1936)	11	7	7	12
Rosanoff (1934)	25	12	5	23
Total	70	34	37	75
Per cent	67.3	32.7	33.0	67.0

On first examination, the data are impressive, even after allowance is made for different techniques and varying standards of precision. More than two thirds of the one-egg twins had concordant criminal careers. Among the two-egg twins, the figures are almost exactly reversed, with only a third showing concordance. Thus, on their face, these findings appear to indicate the decisive influence of genetic factors.

Nevertheless, the majority of criminologists who have discussed these findings has failed to consider them conclusive, subjecting them to one or more of the following criticisms:

1. The size of the samples used in each study is small. In the Stumpfl study, for example, a shift of two twin-sets would make the figures for the one-egg and two-egg twins virtually identical (9–9 for the monozygotics, 9–10 for the dizygotics). This criticism holds, to a lesser but still serious degree, for the other studies.

2. The differentiation of one-egg from two-egg twins is a matter of external observation. It is not possible to determine with sufficient assurance that twins of similar appearance were actually derived from a single fertilized egg. This criticism is serious, because it introduces a source of error highly favorable to the hereditary position and biased against the opposing view. For, though it is difficult to prove that a given pair of twins is identical, it is relatively easy to recognize twins that are *not* identical.

3. It has been held that identical twins are more likely to receive similar treatment (i.e., to have a similar environment) than fraternal twins. If this is in fact the case, the greater similarity of environment for the one-egg twins could account for the discrepancy in results.

4. The studies are all deficient in the extent to which environ-

mental factors were controlled—admittedly, a difficult and, possibly, an unattainable requirement with human subjects.

5. There is a further widely cited criticism by Reckless, which attaches directly to the data. If we are to accept the hereditary position, says Reckless, then a *discordant* one-egg set would be impossible.[2] (It should be noted, however, that there were no discordant one-egg sets in the study by Legras.) Though Reckless' criticism is theoretically sound, it seems to require a perfection not generally demanded of similar studies with human subjects.

In summation, the twin studies, which represent the most rigorous attempt to settle the question of hereditary determinism in crime, have failed to achieve conclusiveness. Nevertheless, the suspicion that "there's something to heredity" in criminals persists. Animal breeders have been producing specific physical and psychological characteristics in higher domestic animals for centuries; it would be difficult to convince a breeder of English pit bulldogs that the courage, tenacity, and gentleness which characterize this national symbol could be produced in a chow merely by rearing it with a litter of bulldogs. Moving from bulldogs to people, there is little doubt that hereditary factors are at least partly involved in the determination of psychological traits, abilities, and limitations. If the issue is to be clarified, a more careful analysis is needed of the differences between the concepts of inherited traits and criminality.

This analysis would pose questions concerning *what* is inherited, how the inherited factors are related to what is learned and experienced, and how the interactions between these broad determinants—heredity and experience—are mutually limiting in their power to change structure and function. Should it be possible to clarify these biological issues, it would then be possible to relate the results to the separate problem of criminality. What are the current views of biologists on these issues?

1. Most modern biologists have come to regard the heredity-versus-environment controversy as without reference to known biological facts. From the moment of fertilization of the ovum, the new organism is dependent upon environmental stimulation for its growth. Certain alterations in the internal environment of the womb—critical changes in the acid-alkali balance, for example—will produce characteristic structural defects in the embryo. Deliberate or accidental intervention in the living conditions of the embryonic organism produces monsters. Even after birth the infant, who is structurally still an "unfinished" organism, is

[2] Walter Reckless, *Criminal Behavior* (New York: McGraw-Hill Book Company, Inc., 1940), p. 186.

dependent on proper environmental conditions for the emergence of sound structures. A child born with structurally perfect eyes will become blind if denied the stimulation of light; without this (purely environmental) stimulation, the neurological tissues responsible for vision fail to develop and rapidly deteriorate. Children denied contact with human speech between certain critical ages cannot later learn to understand or to speak words. The significant point here is that the environmental stimulus must not only be appropriate but must occur at an appropriate time in the developmental sequence; in the case of certain functions, delays of a few weeks or months may be irremediably late.

The general principle is quickly stated: Environment is a continuous, active, and decisive factor in the development of hereditary growth potentials.[3] This interaction, moreover, is not one-sided; it is not a question of the hereditary structures and functions lying ready and waiting to emerge intact when the environment pushes the right buttons. Hereditary factors set *upper* limits on the capacities that can be called forth by the best environmental conditions. It also appears that hereditary factors are involved in determining how much stress different structures and functions can tolerate under different adverse environmental conditions. In summation: Heredity appears to determine and set limits on what *might* emerge under different environmental conditions of facilitation and stress; the environment seems to determine *whether* they will emerge, *how* they will emerge, and *how* they will be expressed in behavior.

2. If correct, these conclusions are directly relevant to the question of the relation of hereditary factors to criminality. The concept of criminality is inseparable from the concept of behavior; there can be no crime —hence, no criminality—unless the person *does something*. The hereditary determinists view behavior as the more or less inevitable outcome of structure, just as they view structure as the inevitable outcome of heredity. If it is acknowledged—as the data appear to require—that the environment participates in determining *structure* during the first stages of life, then the argument for pure hereditary determinism is undermined at the outset. Even if it is asserted that *a point is quickly reached where no amount of subsequent environmental variation can change the results*, the hereditary-environment controversy now dissolves into a dispute over when and how this point is reached.

3. There are additional, more specific implications of modern bio-

[3] For a brilliant brief discussion of the problem see T. Dobzhansky, "Heredity, Environment and Evolution," *Science*, 111:161–166, February 17, 1950.

logical thought. The available information about genetically determined traits suggests that they are specific. The individual inherits eyes and hair of a specific color; presumably he also inherits certain specific psychological potentialities as well. But "criminality" is not at all specific; there are almost as many kinds of crime as there are different kinds of behavior. If criminality is inherited, the genetic factor should be similarly specific; one should inherit tendencies to be a pickpocket rather than an embezzler, a housebreaker rather than a forger. Unfortunately, the twin studies merely compare "criminality" with "noncriminality," without indicating whether or not the genetically determined crime patterns were, in fact, specific, as required by Mendelian mechanics.

4. It is conceivable, of course, that an individual may be biologically fated to be *both* a pickpocket and an embezzler—having inherited the "genetic factors" for each of these behavior patterns. However, if genetic patterns determine the specific vocations of criminals, they must also determine the occupation of noncriminals. Accordingly, we would have to conclude that heredity rather than environment determines all vocational choices, and that a man is as "fated" to become an electrical engineer as he is to have blue eyes.

5. It is possible to counter this objection by holding that the *genetic factor for criminality works by motivating the individual to break laws generally, no matter what they are.* Although this position fails to satisfy the Mendelian requirement for genetic specificity, it seems to evade the difficulty posed by the fact that laws vary greatly in different times and places. But the difficulty is evaded only for the moment. As a matter of fact, most criminals *obey* most laws. The typical forger usually confines himself to forgery; the typical pickpocket, to picking pockets. Actually, most career criminals are more than normally scrupulous in their observance of most laws, if for no other reason than to avoid unnecessary and irrelevant danger. Thus, the postulate of an *inherited general tendency to break laws* again runs aground on the issue of specificity (though, in this instance, in a different way), since it cannot explain why criminals violate some laws and observe others.

6. When confronted with these objections, the proponents of hereditary determinism in crime may fall back on various hereditary predispositions to behave in devious, exploitive, aggressive, or rebellious ways. But to do this is to concede the whole position, since one can behave aggressively, be rebellious, and exploit others deviously without running afoul of the law.

This last point underscores a fact neglected by all biological theories of crime—namely, that criminality, whatever else it is, is also a status conferred by society. There is nothing inevitable about the processes by which this status is conferred; many people who, in fact, break laws, avoid the status, and there has been no attempt to explain the vagaries of law enforcement in biological terms. To assert, in rebuttal, that the biologist is interested only in *real criminals, in criminals-in-fact rather than in criminals-by-status* is to become involved in yet another difficulty. For the biologist himself uses legal criteria in his selection of cases. Short of searching the criminal records, he has no other objective way of differentiating his criminal group from his noncriminal group.

The enormous labor expended in the search for hereditary causes of crime illustrates the extent to which research may be diverted into blind alleys by careless definition of terms and by a failure to examine the implications of an underlying point of view. In the case of the biological determinists, this result seems to be related to two basic confusions, the first semantic, the second (for want of a readier term), professionally biased. The semantic confusion arises out of a failure to distinguish between criminality-as-behavior and criminality-as-status. The second error relates to the identification of this already blurred conception of criminality with disease or inferiority. These errors are not singular to biological theories of crime; they will appear in various forms in subsequent chapters of this text.

Glandular Theories of Crime

The belief that physical substances may be directly responsible for behavior is probably as old as the doctrine that spiritual agents are similarly responsible, and both ideas have flourished continuously in the same minds with little sense of contradiction. The faith invested by primitive peoples in invisible spirits was paralleled by an equally firm reliance on magical potions; this faith is undiminished in many parts of the world today. In every large city there are shops which sell potions guaranteed to make people love, hate, forget, reform, and grow young again. Nor is the search for the healing elixir confined to the ignorant and credulous. The noted endocrinologist Hoskins has pointed out that the science of endocrinology:

... stems from the primitive belief in organ magic—the belief that man can augment his powers by consuming appropriate portions of his fellow man or of animals taken in the chase. In the olden days the warrior thought to increase his courage by eating the heart of his enemy. Today the retarded child improves his intellect by eating the thyroid of a sheep.[4]

The importance of the endocrines in the regulation of growth, metabolism, reproduction, sexual development, and general physiological balance has been well established. A number of specific diseases have been traced to hormonal deficiency or overproduction. Abnormal pituitary function may result in a variety of developmental defects, including gigantism, dwarfism, and acromegaly, among others. Virilism, the condition responsible for the bearded ladies of the circus, has been traced to overactivity of the adrenal cortex.

The results of endocrine dysfunction are by no means confined to physical pathology. Disturbed hormonal function may have characteristic effects on behavior. Thyroid deficiency in early childhood produces the mentally and physically retarded child known as the *cretin;* a similar deficiency in later life produces the disease known as *myxedema,* in which the sufferer, for no apparent reason, becomes dull, forgetful, apathetic, and unable to concentrate on any sustained activity. In the absence of a correct diagnosis of this condition, the patient—who shows many of the symptoms of severe psychiatric disorder—will merely continue to deteriorate under the most intensive psychotherapy. Many of these sufferers, incorrectly diagnosed as mental patients, underwent years of unnecessary and fruitless treatment and hospitalization when a few milligrams of thyroid could have entirely restored them to health and normal functioning. The striking similarities between many symptoms of behavior pathology and endocrine insufficiency, and the equally dramatic results obtained by treatment with appropriate hormone extracts, have persuaded some that the cause and the cure for most behavior disorders may be found in the endocrines.

The Contributions of Schlapp, Berman, and Podolsky

As is typical of great scientific discoveries, there was an inevitable application of the new findings to unsolved problems in other fields. In 1924 M. G. Schlapp estimated that one third of all prison inmates were

[4] R. G. Hoskins, *Endocrinology* (New York: W. W. Norton and Company, 1941), p. 15.

victims of some form of toxic infection or glandular dysfunction.[5] Four years later the same author and a collaborator published a treatise on criminology, in which *all* criminality was attributed to glandular dysfunction.[6] In 1933 Louis Berman asserted that a "definite, detailed, systematic study of the condition of the different endocrine glands in juvenile delinquents and criminals" had led to the conclusion that:

1. Crime is due, in a Gestalt sense, to a perversion of the instinctive drives dependent upon a deficiency and imbalance of the endocrine glands.
2. Certain types of crimes are associated with certain types of endocrine malfunctioning.[7]

According to this theory, it merely remained for research to discover the specific glandular imbalances associated with specific crimes, and for penologists to supply the appropriate hormone extracts to correct these imbalances. Berman himself suggested the causal relations shown in Table XIII.[8]

TABLE XIII

CRIME AND HORMONE IMBALANCE

(The plus and minus signs stand for excessive and deficient hormone production.)

Crime	Hormone imbalance				
	Pituitary	Parathyroid	Thyroid	Adrenal	Thymus
Robbery and burglary	+	−			
Murder		− − −	+	++	++++
Arson	− −	− −			+++

Later investigators have broadened the list. Edward Podolsky, in a report entitled "The Chemical Brew of Criminal Behavior," has cited correlations reportedly found among inmates at Sing Sing. Certain of his findings are in conflict with those reported earlier by Berman. (Thus, for example, the robbers and burglars cited by Podolsky suffered from a *deficiency* rather than an excess of pituitrin.)

Podolsky cites other reports purporting to demonstrate that many

[5] M. G. Schlapp, "Behavior and Gland Disease," *Journal of Heredity,* 15:11, January 1924.

[6] M. G. Schlapp and E. H. Smith, *The New Criminology* (New York: Liveright Publishing Corporation, 1928).

[7] Louis Berman, "Crime and the Endocrine Glands," *American Journal of Psychiatry,* 12:226, September 1932.

[8] *Ibid.,* p. 226.

categories of offenses are associated with *hypoglycemia,* an endocrino-logically produced inability of the body to maintain an adequate level of blood sugar. Instances of "hypoglycemic crime" were said to include theft, violence, traffic violations, clashes with policemen, murder, cruelty to children and other domestic offenses. The causal pattern in these cases was seen as similar, the severity of the offense varying with the degree of "sugar starvation." The susceptibility to criminal behavior was also seen as a function of the blood-sugar level: "The lower the sugar level falls, the greater is the tendency to commit a criminal act."[9] Though convicts said to be suffering from hypoglycemia exhibited various psychological symptoms, including impairment of will-power, irritability, loss of associational power, and decreased moral sense, among others, these manifestations were viewed as effects rather than causes. Significantly, a universal finding among these prisoners was "an early loss of spontaneity"; this too Podolsky explained as caused by the physiological conditions unrelated to other psychological or situational factors.[10]

An Estimate of the Validity of Endocrinological Research on Crime Causation

In evaluating the validity of endocrinological and other biological theories of crime causation, sociologists and other nonmedical men are frequently at a disadvantage. Though they may criticize the characteristic neglect of situational and psychological variables, this criticism is usually of little effect except among those sharing their views in the first place; the biological theorists have dismissed these factors in advance. Evaluations based on analysis of research and statistical techniques are generally on sounder ground; critics can point to a typical neglect of control groups, the unrepresentativeness of samples, the use of arbitrary norms, and the naive assumption that legalistic rules framed by legislators define biologically meaningful distinctions in behavior. These approaches to evaluation are valid, appropriate, and necessary in the analysis of conclusions; nevertheless, they are still incomplete because they do not deal directly with the findings themselves. In effect, they take issue not with what the findings are but rather with what they are not. A theory must ultimately be evaluated on its own terms, and this is as true of a biological theory as it is of a sociological theory. To avoid

[9] Edward Podolsky, "The Chemical Brew of Criminal Behavior," *Journal of Criminal Law, Criminology, and Police Science,* 45:676, March–April, 1955.
[10] *Ibid.*

evaluating the biological theory on biological terms is merely to accuse the biologist of not being a psychologist or a sociologist—a charge he will not only accept but reciprocate. Accordingly, there appears to be no alternative but to examine the biological evidence directly and in biological terms.

In a paper dealing with the technical difficulties of endocrinological research, Hemphill and Reiss urge "great caution in interpreting abnormalities of total metabolism or of the endocrine system . . . ." Pointing out that "normal levels may be found on one day and not on another . . . ," the authors conclude that "until it can be demonstrated that the physiological pattern is constant, the figures given by any single investigation are meaningless." Their estimate of broad conclusions is not reassuring: "It is our experience, borne out by the literature, that limited biochemical investigations give disappointing results, and special claims often turn out to be invalid if the investigations are repeated on a larger series of patients."[11]

THE EXTENT OF ENDOCRINE AND METABOLIC ABNORMALITIES AMONG CRIMINALS. Since the only part of the criminal population available for large-scale research is that percentage confined in institutions, the conclusions drawn from this limited and selective group can be applied to "criminals" generally only with the appropriate qualification. It may be significant that the large majority of investigations reporting a high incidence of physical and physiological abnormalities occurred at a time when both medical research and penal conditions were considerably less advanced. The vast improvements, both in medical research and in health and sanitary conditions in correctional institutions, today make it possible to evaluate the physical condition of prisoners with considerably less fear of distortion by such special factors as poor diet, restricted physical activity, and unsanitary conditions. These environmental improvements, together with much more painstaking and comprehensive systems of medical record-keeping, now provide a much clearer picture of the general physical health of the modern prison inmate. By comparing this picture with that presented by a representative sample of the noncriminal population, it is possible to obtain an estimate of the relative incidence of endocrine and metabolic disturbances in each group. The following conclusions emerge from this comparison:

1. There is no medical evidence that the rate of endocrine and

[11] R. E. Hemphill and M. Reiss, "Perspectives in the Endocrinology and Pathophysiology of Mental Disturbances," in D. Richter, ed., *Perspectives in Neuropsychiatry* (London: H. K. Lewis & Co., Ltd., 1950), p. 119.

metabolic disturbances among confined criminals is significantly different from that among noncriminals.

2. There is no medical evidence that the great majority of confined criminals suffer from any discovered endocrine or metabolic disturbance.[12]

ALTERNATIVE INTERPRETATIONS OF THE DATA. Those asserting that metabolic and endocrine imbalances are responsible for crime insist that the relationship is a one-way cause-and-effect process. The assumption is that the person becomes a criminal *because* of glandular imbalances, which pervert his motives and contaminate his behavior. The possibility that motivational and emotional factors may affect the endocrine system is ignored or denied. The neglect of the possibility of a reciprocal relationship is surprising, both in view of the early experimentation in endocrinology and in the light of many recent findings. The pioneer experiments in this field were concerned with producing emotional reactions in experimental animals and then observing the subsequent effects on the endocrine system and on behavior. In this connection, the great experimental physiologist Cannon, whose name is closely associated with experimental endocrinology, had this to say:

> The bodily reactions attending great emotional excitement are elemental. In many respects they are common to man and to lower animals of the vertebrate series. They involve changes which may be regarded as instinctive adjustments to critical situations, and as directed toward self-preservation. They may dominate behavior. They may thoroughly disturb beneficent functions, such as secretion and digestion. A method which will permit the securing of further insight into emotional reactions is therefore important.[13]

As early as 1913 the evidence of the profound effects of emotional stimulation on bodily function was sufficiently persuasive to move the neurologist Cushing to assert:

> ...psychic conditions profoundly influence the discharges from the glands of internal secretion, but we are on a much less secure footing when we come to the reverse, namely, the effect on the psyche and nervous system of chronic states of glandular overactivity or underactivity.[14]

Commenting on this statement, Flanders Dunbar has pointed out:

[12] Montagu, *op. cit.*

[13] Walter B. Cannon *et al.*, "The Influence of Motion and Emotion on Medulliadrenal Secretion," *American Journal of Physiology*, 79:433–465, 1927.

[14] Harvey Cushing, "Psychic Disturbances Associated with Disorders of the Ductless Glands," *American Journal of Insanity*, 69:971, No. 5, 1913.

Since that time we have accumulated considerably more evidence on both sides, but the fallacy which he [Cushing] points out in our method of approach to the problem is still productive of confusion in the field.[15]

Recent Findings

Much of the present research concerning the effects of situational and emotional stress on the endocrine system is an outgrowth of the classical animal experiments of Cannon. These experiments were largely restricted to temporary emotional stress and their temporary physiological effects. The questions remained: What are the effects of chronic or prolonged stress on (1) the endocrines; (2) the physiological state of the organism; and (3) its behavior? In an attempt to answer these questions, Hans Selye conducted a series of experiments in which normal animals were exposed to continuous noxious (disturbing) stimuli. Long exposure to these stimuli resulted in a characteristic complex of structural changes and behavior symptoms, which Selye has called the "adaptation syndrome." Because of the direct relevance of this experimental work to analogous reactions in humans, the psychosomatic specialist Franz Alexander has summarized Selye's findings in his text on psychosomatic medicine:

> ...Selye's concept is that the organism responds to a great variety of stresses with physiological defense mechanisms which are essentially dependent upon the integrity of the adrenal cortex and that excessive activity of this gland is responsible for the diseases of adaptation. The organism is damaged by an excess of its own defensive measures.[16]

Many clinicians have reported that the metabolic and endocrine disturbances found in their patients were the direct result, rather than the cause, of their emotional difficulties. One of the most conclusively demonstrated examples of psychogenic disturbances of the metabolism is the condition known as *functional hypoglycemia,* a psychogenically produced inability of the body to maintain an adequate level of blood sugar. Numerous investigators have reported the onset of hypoglycemia *after* the onset of emotional difficulties, and the restoration of normal sugar metabolism after the patients had resolved their difficulties.[17]

[15] Flanders Dunbar, *Emotions and Bodily Changes* (New York: Columbia University Press, 1946), p. 137.
[16] Franz Alexander, *Psychosomatic Medicine* (New York: W. W. Norton and Company, 1950), p. 77.
[17] Several case reports are summarized by Alexander, *op. cit.*

In view of the fact that hypoglycemia has been cited as one of the prime chief physical causes of crime, these findings are of great importance. In reading Alexander's summary, the reader may recall that the data found by the endocrinological theorists of crime were gathered exclusively among prisoners, *persons chronically subjected to the situational frustrations, restrictions, and monotonies of prison life.* The individuals cited in Alexander's summary were, of course, noncriminals; nevertheless, the psychological reaction patterns are highly suggestive of attitudes and reactions widely reported among prisoners:

> Frustrated in their genuine desires and proclivities, being forced to engage in routine activities against their own inclinations, these patients developed their own form of protest. Often this emotional state is accompanied by regressive fantasies and daydreams in which these persons give up all effort and ambition; they indulge only in wishful imagery. The physiological counterpart of this emotional state is characterized by a flat sugar-tolerance curve: a slower and a lesser rise of the blood sugar half an hour after injection than in the normal cases and a lower blood-sugar level after two hours. Like Szondi and Lax, Alexander and Fortis found that the original blood-sugar level was not lower than normal. They assumed that there was a causal relationship between the psychological situation and the disturbance of the carbohydrate-regulating mechanisms—i.e., that the disturbance of the carbohydrate metabolism was the physiological counterpart or concomitant of the patient's emotional state.[18]

In his authoritative text, *Glandular Physiology and Therapy,* the physiologist William Young has summarized the conclusions emerging from half a century of speculation and research on the endocrines:

> The relationship between hormones and behavior in man long has been enigmatic. In the early years of endocrinologic diagnosis and treatment, clinicians were impressed by what was regarded as the higher incidence of deviations of behavior in persons with the endocrine disorders than in persons with no evidence of abnormality of endocrine function. During this period, many efforts were made to associate specific mental disorders, personality changes and deficiencies of intelligence with specific endocrine dysfunction. For the most part, claims of such relationships never were substantiated.... Many cases of endocrine dysfunction and metabolic derangement have been recorded in which there were no deviations in behavior. The incidence of gross endocrinopathies in institutionalized mental patients is not necessarily high. Many attempts with glandular therapy failed to change the mental con-

[18] *Ibid.,* pp. 188–189.

dition of patients. Most different psychopathologic states can develop under identical endocrinologic disturbances, and a variety of biochemical and endocrinologic changes are evident in psychiatric cases which up to now have been considered identical entities.[19]

Constitutional Theories of Crime

Phrenology

Throughout the centuries the belief in biological determinants of behavior has led to a recurring search for reliable clues and symptoms in the human physique. In an effort to bypass the difficult problems of determining human character by analyzing human actions, men have read palms and searched faces in order to discover the signs left by the soul on the body.

One of the most ambitious, systematic, and influential attempts to gauge character from physical conformation was *phrenology*. Founded in the early 1800's by the anatomist Gall, phrenology was based on the theory that character and behavior are determined by the balance among thirty-five faculties or "propensities" localized in the brain. Led by his observations to the mistaken notion that the shape of the skull conforms to the contours of the brain, Gall and his followers developed a system of character analysis based on the examination of the bony surface of the head. The degree of influence of any propensity was to be seen in the size and prominence of the associated skull area: there were bumps for destructiveness, hope, cautiousness, and a host of other emotional and intellectual powers.

Within a generation of its inception, phrenology became not only a household word but a design for the reconstruction of society. Despite early critics its influence continued throughout the 19th century with adherents among the most notable scientists of the age, including Comte and the otherwise skeptical William James. As late as 1899, Alfred Wallace, celebrated with Darwin as co-founders of the theory of evolution, wrote: "In the coming century phrenology will . . . prove itself to

[19] William C. Young, "Behavior and Intelligence," in *Glandular Physiology and Therapy*, 5th ed., prepared under the auspices of the Council on Pharmacy and Chemistry of The American Medical Association. (Philadelphia: J. B. Lippincott Company) 1954, p. 517.

be the true science of mind. Its practical uses in education, in self-discipline, in the reformatory treatment of criminals, and in the remedial treatment of the insane, will give it one of the highest places in the hierarchy of the sciences."[20]

The inevitable application of phrenology to penology was the work of the Scotch phrenologist and tireless prison-visitor, George Combe. Combe's argument that every prisoner should be phrenologically classified was embodied in the internationally influential penal code proposed by Edward Livingston. A few American prisons openly associated themselves with the new doctrine and in 1847 the American Phrenological Journal was able to hail Sing Sing as a "phrenologically conducted institution."[21] The phrenologists were among the first to maintain that crime was a disease as well as a sin; in general they favored more humanitarian treatment of criminals and opposed retributive justice. Like the later followers of eugenics, however, there was a sterner side to their program. Certain criminals were held to be incurably morally insane; these incorrigibles—who could be detected by phrenological examination —were not to be included in the general social reconstruction. Thus, as in the case of all earlier and later typologies, mankind was divided between the redeemable and the damned, with the typologists accepting the responsibility of distinguishing between the two.

Lombroso's Theories

By far the most influential constitutional theories of crime were those of Cesare Lombroso (1836–1909), an Italian military physician whose work started a new direction in criminology.[22] Despite the fact that Lombroso continued to develop and modify his position throughout his life, he is, today, identified with what is essentially one of the earlier versions of his theory: the notion that the criminal represents a physical and psychological atavism or "evolutionary throwback." Struck by the observation that many military offenders were tattooed, Lombroso began to suspect that anti-social behavior might have other physical signs. This

[20] John D. Davies, *Phrenology, Fad and Science* (New Haven: Yale University Press, 1955), p. ix.

[21] *Ibid.*, p. 102.

[22] Lombroso's more famous conceptions have tended to obscure his other achievements. A pioneer in the introduction of experimental methods in psychiatry, Lombroso consistently emphasized the importance of objective and measurable factors in the social sciences. His constitutional theory, though widely repudiated, provided criminology with one of its first opportunities to employ the methods of empirical science in a conclusive way.

suspicion was confirmed for him by the examination of civil prisoners and became the basis for a comprehensive biological hypothesis.

THE "BORN CRIMINAL." Lombroso's theories went through at least three phases, the outlines of which are more or less blurred, partly because of his attempt to synthesize earlier and later views. His earliest theory was based on little more than an analogy between the appearance and behavior of criminals and those of primitive men and lower animals. The shifty eyes of the thief reminded him of the beady, furtive eyes of the rat, and Lombroso thought it more than coincidental that both these predators depended on stealth, quickness, and cunning. Examinations of the skulls and brains of criminals seemed to reveal resemblances to those of prehistoric and primitive men; Lombroso concluded that these offenders were living remnants of an earlier type of humanity, "veritable savages in the midst of this brilliant European civilization." To these men crime represented a natural and inevitable way of life: they were "born criminals" because nature had designed them to live as their predatory ancestors had lived and had not equipped them for civilized ways.

THE INSANE CRIMINAL. As Lombroso broadened his investigations, he found it necessary to broaden his views and his categories—an adjustment some of his critics have failed to recognize. Disease and arrested development could produce the same constitutional changes brought about by heredity, and Lombroso cited the frequently violent behavior of the insane and the epileptic as examples in point.

CRIMINALS BY PASSION AND OCCASIONAL CRIMINALS. Toward the end of his career Lombroso recognized the existence of types of criminality that are without organic basis. His discussion of the *criminal by passion* anticipates many of the views of the psychological theorists of crime. Similarly, his description of the *occasional criminal* deals with several factors later of concern to the sociologists. His discussion of the *habitual criminal* (one of the three subtypes of the occasional criminal) is highly "sociological."

THE INVALIDATION OF LOMBROSO'S CONSTITUTIONAL THEORY. It was Lombroso's lot to be identified with the most vulnerable and least defensible of his theories. The most thorough and systematic test of his concept of the constitutional criminal was undertaken by the English physician Charles Goring, who followed a procedure suggested, interestingly enough, by Lombroso himself. In 1899 Lombroso had suggested that the question of the existence of a criminal type could be settled by a comparison of the physical measurements of criminals and noncriminals. Following this procedure and using the measurements considered critical by Lombroso, Goring compared thousands of prisoners (all recidivists) with a variety of noncriminal groups, including college students and sailors. No differentiating physical characteristics were found. Goring next proceeded to test Lombroso's contention that different types of criminals could be identified on the basis of physical "stigmata of degeneracy." Again the findings were negative, and Lombroso's constitutional theories were shown to be without basis. Goring's conclusions can be cited as an accurate summary of the position held by the great majority of criminologists today:

> We have exhaustively compared with regard to many physical characters, different kinds of criminals with each other, and criminals as a class with the law-abiding public. From these comparisons, no evidence has emerged confirming the existence of a physical criminal type, such as Lombroso and his disciples have described. Our data do show that physical differences exist between different kinds of criminals; precisely as they exist between different kinds of law-abiding people. But when allowance is made for a certain range of probable variation, and when they are reduced to a common standard of age, stature, intelligence and class, etc., these differences tend entirely to disappear. Our results nowhere confirm the evidence nor justify the allegations of criminal anthropologists. They challenge their evidence at almost every point. In fact, both with regard to measurements and the presence of physical anomalies in criminals, our statistics present a startling conformity with similar statistics of the law-abiding classes. The final conclusion we are bound to accept until further evidence in the train of long series of statistics may compel us to modify or reject an apparent certainty—our inevitable conclusion must be that there is no such thing as a physical criminal type.[23]

Hooton's Theories

Despite Goring's refutation, constitutional theories of crime continued to be presented, though to an increasingly skeptical audience. In 1939 the physical anthropologist Ernest Hooton published the results of a twelve-year study in which he compared over eleven thousand prisoners with a much smaller number of civilians on 107 anthropometric measurements. On the basis of his findings, Hooton asserted the following conclusions:

[23] Charles Goring *The English Convict* (London: His Majesty's Stationery Office, 1913), p. 173.

1. Criminal behavior is a direct result of *inherited biological inferiority:*

Criminal behavior is capable of considerable diversification ... but whatever the crime may be, it ordinarily arises from a deteriorated organism. ... The primary cause of crime is biological inferiority.[24]

2. Particular types of crime are caused by particular types of biological inferiority, as manifested by different patterns of defective anatomical traits:

Thieves and burglars tend to be sneaky little constitutional inferiors. ... Robbers lean to several variants of the wiry, narrow, hard bitten, tough, not notably undersized. ...[25]

It is a remarkable fact that tall, thin men tend to murder and rob, tall heavy men to kill and to commit forgery and fraud, undersized thin men to steal and to burglarize, short heavy men to assault, to rape and to commit other sex crimes, whereas men of mediocre body build tend to break the law without obvious discrimination or preference.[26]

3. Different racial stocks and different national groupings commit characteristic patterns of offenses.

According to Hooton, the role of the environment is negligible compared with inherited biological inferiority as the cause of crime. The environment merely brings out the latent biological predispositions:

Inherently inferior organisms are, for the most part, those which succumb to the adversities or temptations of their social environment and fall into antisocial behavior ... it is impossible to improve and correct environment to a point at which these flawed and degenerate human beings will be able to succeed in honest social competition.[27]

Hooton's conclusions have been widely rejected by a variety of observers who have questioned his methods, his statistical techniques, his reasoning, and, on occasion, his anthropological findings. The following summarizes these criticisms:

STATISTICAL INVALIDITY AND UNRELIABILITY. Some of Hooton's control groups were not only small but, actually, "controlled" in name only. A total of 1,976 "normals" drawn from two urban areas were contrasted with 10,953 prison and reformatory inmates, 743 criminally insane inmates, and 173 defective delinquents drawn from ten different

[24] Ernest A. Hooton, *Crime and the Man* (Cambridge: Harvard University Press, 1939), p. 130. © 1939 by the President and Fellows of Harvard University.
[25] *Ibid.*, p. 374.
[26] *Ibid.*, p. 376.
[27] *Ibid.*, p. 388.

states. Among the "normal" civilian controls were 146 municipal firemen from Nashville, Tennessee, and an assorted number of militiamen, bath-house patrons, and out-patients from Boston. Moreover, in a study explicitly rejecting environmental variables as causes of crime, no attempt was made to match the compared groups in terms of social, economic, or occupational levels. Hooton freely admits that his selection of controls was on a catch-as-catch-can basis, but he does not recognize his failure to use equated groups as fatal.

The size of the groups on which Hooton depends to carry the burden of his conclusions occasionally approaches the ludicrous. The number of Italian civilians with which the Italian criminal series is compared is 29. The number of French civilian controls is given, on one page, as 21, on another as 18. A total of 27 Irish criminals is held sufficient to establish the Irish crime pattern. In view of the size of his samples, it is not surprising that many of his assertions about the distribution of crimes among nationality groups have not been corroborated by other surveys. His finding that "Italian-Americans in general seem to go in for murder (and assault) more than do the native Italians"[28] is grossly inaccurate. Sutherland found that the murder and assault rate among Italians dropped from 192 per 100,000 for native-born Italians to 24 per 100,000 for the persons of pure Italian parentage born in America.[29] Hooton called his findings about Irish criminals "contradictory and somewhat unreliable"—his sample of Irish criminals, it will be recalled, numbered 27. Nevertheless, the admitted unreliability of his sample did not prevent him from asserting that "our transplanted sons of Erin are much higher in offenses against the person than are those born in the mother country."[30] Again, reliable information about crime trends among native and American-born Irishmen tends to refute Hooton.

A more serious factual and statistical defect vitiates Hooton's findings. Setting aside all other questions and criticisms, the one indispensable requirement of Hooton's conclusions is that the criminal groups differ more from the control groups than the members of the control groups differ from one another. In the absence of this finding, the assertion of distinctive criminal types is undemonstrable. Nevertheless, Hooton's own data reveal greater differences between his Tennessee "normals" and his Boston "normals" than were found between either of these samples and the prisoners.

[28] *Ibid.*, p. 158.
[29] See Table XIV, Chapter 11.
[30] Hooton, *op. cit.*, p. 146.

THE LACK OF A CRITERION OF "BIOLOGICAL INFERIORITY." No independent criterion of "biological inferiority" was given by Hooton, and no attempt was made to demonstrate how this condition leads to crime. Hooton merely assumed that the status of imprisonment indicated some form of inferiority and that this inferiority must be manifested by some constitutional signs. Thus he started out by assuming as self-evident the precise conclusion he was purporting to test. Moreover, he was as unfortunate in his selection of morphological signs as he was in his selection of samples.[31] The physical anthropologist Ashley Montagu has pointed out that a re-examination of Hooton's findings in terms of generally accepted biological standards defining advanced, primitive, and indifferent human characteristics reveals that his criminal series showed "only 4 per cent of primitive, 15.8 of indifferent and the astonishing amount of 49.5 per cent of *advanced* characters, more frequently than the non-criminal population. Therefore," he concludes, "we see that Hooton's findings actually make his criminal series a considerably more advanced group biologically than his non-criminal series."[32]

The remedies suggested by Hooton as solutions to the crime problem are offered as unhesitatingly as his research conclusions. Paroled delinquents and criminals should be permanently exiled in a self-governing reservation sealed off from the rest of the country. Married criminals would be allowed to bring their wives and children; Hooton did not quite make up his mind whether they should be allowed to have more children. "While optimum eugenic considerations would demand that none of these delinquents raise offspring, it seems probable that the processes of genetic selection . . . would produce . . . a good many useful and capable citizens, and even a few of outstanding ability."[33] (Hooton

[31] Even the layman, unsophisticated in anthropometric matters, may be struck by the arbitrariness of Hooton's evaluations of the human physique. He several times alludes to the tendency toward higher stature and narrower head, face, and body breadths found not only among native-born Americans but among the offspring of immigrants as well. But he says, "It may be doubted that these coltish physical trends are biological improvements." (*Ibid.*, p. 379.) At another point he states, "First of all, it should be understood that the increase in the tall and skinny does not signify a general improvement, but rather the contrary. . . . My own impression is that inferior organisms are likely to come in long thin packages, and that the net result of modern medicine and hygiene has been to preserve what is less and less fit to keep." (*Ibid.*, p. 170.) Here Hooton not only denies prevailing medical and actuarial findings but contradicts his own data as well. One of the metric indices of his criminal groups was their shorter height—1.02 cm. shorter than the noncriminal controls.

[32] Montagu, *op. cit.*, p. 51.

[33] Hooton, *op. cit.*, pp. 391–392.

was firm on one point: "It would, however, be quite essential to keep out extraneous politicians, criminologists and uplifters.") In the end Hooton seemed to incline toward permitting the less defective delinquents to reproduce. However, no such privilege should be allowed "habitual criminals." These "hopeless constitutional inferiors should be permanently incarcerated and, on no account, should be allowed to breed. Nevertheless, they should be treated humanely and *if they are to be kept alive*, should be allowed some opportunity for freedom and profitable occupation within their own severely restricted area." (Italics supplied.)[34]

Sheldon's "Constitutional Psychiatry"

In 1949 the psychiatrist William Sheldon published the results of an application of his theory of "constitutional psychiatry" to the study of two hundred "more or less delinquent" young adults referred to the Hayden Goodwill Inn in Boston.[35] In a previous work Sheldon, building largely on the earlier theories of Kretschmer, had sought to demonstrate that individual differences in behavior and personality are basically determined by differences in physiological functioning. This general orientation was neither new nor startling, but what Sheldon added was not merely new but unparalleled in its diagnostic potentialities. Sheldon held that the different forms of behavioral functioning—and, hence, different forms of criminality—could be identified by *visual inspection of the individual's physique*. If Sheldon's assumptions were correct, he had discovered a diagnostic device that fulfilled the most ambitious dreams of the phrenologists—a device that would, in fact, render all other forms of diagnosis obsolete and replace both the psychologist and the sociologist with the anthropometrist and his camera.

Proceeding from his foundation principle that behavior is a function of structure, Sheldon proposed a threefold classification of "somatotypes" (types of body build) to describe three basic components of temperament and personality. Though the make-up of everyone represents some combination of the three components, their distribution in any individual is usually unequal, with one component tending to predominate slightly or markedly over the others. The person's predominant component indi-

---

[34] *Ibid.*, p. 393.
[35] William H. Sheldon *et al., Varieties of Delinquent Youth* (New York: Harper and Brothers, 1949).

cates his predominating psychological tendencies. Sheldon has described the structural and mental characteristics of each of the three types.

The *viscerotonic* person is identified physically by a relative predominance of smooth muscle, a general roundness, and a tendency to fat. Viscerotonic individuals are called *endomorphs,* and Sheldon states that their personalities are characterized by "relaxation, conviviality and gluttony for food, for affection, for company or social support."[36] (Thus when Shakespeare's Julius Caesar said, "Let me have men about me that are fat," he was really expressing a desire for the company of complacent convivial endomorphs.) The primarily *cerebrotonic* person, by contrast, is nervous, overexcitable, and unpredictable because of a relative predominance of nerve tissues derived embryonically from the skin or ectoderm. *Ectomorphs* are characteristically thin, linear, and fragile, and their extreme sensitivity, says Sheldon, creates in them "a love of concealment and avoidance of attracting attention."[37] (Again, Julius Caesar was using excellent constitutional logic when he suspected the conspirator Cassius because of his "lean and hungry look"—and because he "thinks too much.") Finally, the *somatotonic* person, who is identified by a relative predominance of striped muscle, bone, and connective tissue and a generally athletic appearance, is characterized by a general assertiveness and a desire for muscular activity. These people are called *mesomorphs,* and Sheldon says that their "primary motive in life seems to be the vigorous utilization and expenditure of energy."[38]

Sheldon proposed a seven-point scale to indicate the extent of each component in the individual. A person somatotyped as 1–7–1 would be an extreme mesomorph. (The first figure is the index of endomorphy; the second, of mesomorphy; the third, of ectomorphy.) By means of this three-figure index, the individual's body type can be read off at a glance.

In order to test the relation between physical type and delinquency, Sheldon set up a seven-factor index of "disappointingness"—an over-all diagnostic impression combining the individual's delinquent history with various medical, psychological, and psychiatric aspects. The individual's total "D" ("disappointingness") was then correlated with his somatotype. The average somatotype of the two hundred delinquents was found to be 3.5–4.6–2.7: somewhat on the mesomorphic side. The mean reading for a selected group of sixteen seriously delinquent boys was 3.4–5.4–1.8: more decidedly mesomorphic. With the exception of these findings,

[36] *Ibid.,* p. 25.
[37] *Ibid.,* p. 28.
[38] *Ibid.,* p. 27.

however, the results of the correlation of body type with the traits summarized by the index of "disappointingness" were either inconclusive or inconsistent.

Sheldon's findings and conclusions have been criticized on a number of points. His basic assumption—that body type determines personality type and delinquency—was not demonstrated. Though he was critical of the "unscientific" measures used by psychologists, psychiatrists, and sociologists—at one point he referred to the "Babel of psychiatry"—his own work is filled with impressionistic and offhand diagnostic evaluations. An illustration in point is the "DAMP RAT Syndrome," a deliberately humorous acrostic in which each letter stands for a different "personality" trait: Dilettante, Arty, Monotophobic, Perverse, Restive, Affected, Theatrical.[39] His physiological explanations are often equally speculative and impressionistic. In discussing one case he comments: "The fire of somatotonia is best extinguished with a blanket of fat. Nothing seems to take the edge off misbehavior like an expansion of the waistline."[40]

This comment itself suggests a criticism of Sheldon's basic thesis that the personality is fixed by the individual's inherent body type. Overeating can obviously make one fat; undereating makes one thin. A regimen of exercise develops the muscles. Any of these activities can change the body type, as defined by Sheldon, markedly. Finally, it is a well-observed phenomenon that the bodily configuration may change as a function of growth and senescence. Adolescents frequently undergo striking changes from fat to lean and vice versa in their course of development; later in life the pattern may alter. From which point in the individual's life cycle is the "true" body type to be selected? These unresolved questions, together with the inconclusiveness of Sheldon's findings, render his theory highly inconclusive.

In a recent study the Gluecks[41] attempted to test Sheldon's somatotype theory. Their use of a control group to some extent remedied this methodological deficiency in the earlier study. Like Sheldon, they found that delinquent boys were significantly more mesomorphic—i.e., muscular—than the nondelinquent controls, and, on this basis, they included mesomorphy as a factor in the causation of delinquency.

The findings and conclusions of the Gluecks have also been sub-

[39] *Ibid.*, p. 29.
[40] *Ibid.*, p. 673.
[41] Sheldon and Eleanor Glueck, *Physique and Delinquency* (New York: Harper and Brothers, 1956).

jected to a series of criticisms, of which one of the more searching is their neglect of sociological factors. In the competitive social world of the adolescent, physical strength is a highly significant factor in the assignment of roles. In the delinquent milieu this factor is of obvious social and practical advantage. It is therefore at least plausible that the same factor which, in other areas, is important in the recruitment of adolescents for sports activities might, in a highly delinquent area, lead to participation in the active, physically competitive society of delinquents. Since the importance of role in channeling and sharpening personality characteristics is widely acknowledged, this possibility would provide an alternative hypothesis for interpreting the data.

In concluding this survey of genetic, glandular, and constitutional theories of crime we might consider precisely what has and what has not been accomplished. The major conclusion is quickly stated: Research in the relationship between crime and physical factors has not only failed to reveal any causal link but has failed to produce evidence of any association whatever. The barren character of this conclusion becomes evident when it is understood what this result does *not* mean. It does not imply that physical factors have no relationship with criminal behavior. It does not prove the correctness of psychological or sociological views of criminal behavior. Finally, it does not even prove that the main theses of the physical theorists are wrong.

This indecisive state of affairs is ironic, since it is precisely the unsatisfactory methodology of the physical theorists that still protects their views from the risk of conclusive test and possible refutation. For while inadequate research techniques cannot prove a doubtful hypothesis, neither can they refute it. This point is crucial. The failure to *prove* a theory—in criminology or in any other field—cannot in itself be taken as justifying the rejection of the theory. The most that can be said is that, to date, the researchers have functioned as poor lawyers for their client, with the result that the issue has virtually been thrown out of court. The possibility still exists that future investigators, working with similar hypotheses, may employ methods that satisfy the conditions of a rigorous test. The anthropologist Ashley Montagu has set down the minimal conditions of such a test:

> In order to make any biological test of differential behavior, it is necessary that both the criminal series and the check noncriminal series be in every respect similar except in the one condition of behavior. The two series must be drawn from the same population or populations, from

the same areas, and must come from the same social, economic and occupational levels. When these requirements have been satisfied, and a significantly higher frequency of certain physical characters is found among the criminals than among the non-criminals, it may be legitimately inferred that there is some significant *association* between criminal behavior and the presence of a high frequency of such characters in an individual or in a group. But to infer from this that such characters reflect the cause of criminal behavior is to misunderstand the nature of causation.[42]

In the end, then, we would be left with a demonstrated but still unexplained association. The causal question would still be open; it would still be necessary to explore the possibility that *both* crime and physiological defect are the products of other factors, and that the same conditions which produce a defective physical organism produce a socially objectionable human being as well.

[42] M. F. Ashley Montagu, *The Biosocial Nature of Man* (New York: The Grove Press, 1956), p. 93.

Ethnic and Racial Theories of Crime

Nativity and Crime

DURING THE LATTER HALF OF THE NINETEENTH CENTURY, A PERIOD OF intense nationalism in Europe, there developed a peculiar brand of racial anthropology on the basis of which the white race was divided into four or more categories or "racial stocks," with purportedly different virtues and deficiencies. Despite the dubious anthropological validity of these classifications, the claims made for and against different "stocks" intensely stimulated national pride and prejudice; and there ensued a kind of pseudo-scientific struggle for "racial" supremacy, which in many ways paralleled the political conflicts then taking place. This struggle, conducted by book and pamphlet, rapidly developed into a contest for national superiority in world public opinion. By 1900 the scientific public relations contest had been decisively won by the Nordics, closely followed by the Alpines, with the Mediterraneans third and a heterogeneous collection of "Eastern Europeans" (Slavs, Balkan peoples, and Jews) following far in the rear.

The political consequences of these doctrines of "racial" superiority and inferiority were not fully felt in Europe until the second decade of the twentieth century; in America, which had traditionally had an open immigration policy, they created something of a minor hysteria in certain intellectual and political circles. Stimulated by the writings of Gobineau and other racial theorists,[1] an influential group in the United States became alerted to the necessity of preserving the purity of the "Anglo-Saxon" stock against the incursions of Eastern European and Irish immigration. The year 1894 saw the foundation of the Immigration Restriction League of Boston, an organization dedicated to reversing the traditional American policy of open immigration. Later joined by the influential Senator Henry Cabot Lodge and endorsed by President Lowell of Harvard University, this organization served as the nucleus of a joint intellectual and political movement which culminated in the restrictive legislation of 1917, 1921, and 1924. The purpose of this legislation was to preserve the ethnic composition of the country as it stood in 1890; its practical effect was to favor immigration from northern Europe at the expense of other European immigration. Recent immigration legislation continues this policy.

During the height of the agitation to restrict immigration to this country, a number of theories were advanced to justify the exclusion of the "inferior races." Certain of these concerned the higher involvement of the foreign-born in crime. It was argued that certain countries of southern and southeastern Europe were highly criminalistic. It was held that immigrants in general come from poor "racial stock," and could not adjust in their own countries—why else did they emigrate? It was suggested that immigrants were so different culturally from native Americans that they could never adjust themselves to the higher standards of native morality. In view of the traditional association of crime and poverty, the poverty of most immigrants was also used as an argument against them.

The intense public interest in the issue of immigration stimulated many amateur and some few professional studies of crime among the foreign-born. Most of the studies found a higher rate of crime and vice among immigrants than among native-born Americans. A few did not. The report of the United States Immigration Commission in 1910 found "no satisfactory evidence . . . to show that immigration has resulted in an increase in crime disproportionate to the increase in the adult population."[2]

---

[1] Joseph A. Gobineau, *Essai sur L'inégalité des Races Humaines* (Paris: Firmin-Didot et Cie, 1854). Translated into English as *The Inequality of the Human Races* (New York: G. P. Putnam's Sons, 1915).

[2] *Reports of the Immigration Commission*, Vol. 36, "Immigration and Crime," Senate Document 750, 61st Congress, p. 1.

In any event, according to every recent statistical index, the crime rates of the foreign-born have fallen markedly below those of native-born Americans. In 1939 the over-all arrest rate of native-born Americans was three times as high as the over-all rate for the foreign-born. In 1946 the foreign-born population of state and federal prisons was 3.2 per cent of the total prisoner population[3]—less than half the percentage of the foreign-born in the country as a whole.

It should be recalled, however, that present-day statistics on the foreign-born are based on a virtually disappearing segment of the population. The large majority of foreign-born in this country today are well beyond the age levels during which crime is high in any group. For this reason any gross comparison of this group with the native-born population (which includes the younger age groups) is misleading. In a study that corrected the comparison for the age disparity, Van Vechten found the ratio of foreign-born to native-born white prisoners admitted to state and federal penal institutions to be 10 to 9.[4] In view of the differential legal treatment of the foreign-born, this ratio may be considered at least equal.

Patterns of crime have varied widely among different immigrant groups. These variations usually reflect the crime distributions in the country of origin. For example, rates of homicide and assault among Italian immigrants tend to be significantly higher than those for German immigrants, while the Italian burglary rates tend to be much lower.

The crime patterns of the children of immigrants, however, rapidly conform to native American patterns. In a study comparing crimes of first- and second-generation immigrants with those of native-born Americans, Sutherland found unmistakable evidence of the assimilation of American crime patterns in the children of immigrants. His findings, summarized in Tables XIV and XV, effectively refute the "racial" explanation of national crime patterns.

The rate of delinquency among the children of immigrants tends to remain low where the immigrant community is relatively isolated, spatially or socially, from contact with native communities. It tends to rise rapidly when contact with native influences increases, especially in deteriorated urban areas. On the other hand, when immigrant families move away from deteriorated areas, their delinquency rates fall.

[3] *Prisoners in State and Federal Prisons and Reformatories, 1946* (Washington, D. C.: U. S. Bureau of the Census, 1948), p. 27.

[4] Carl Van Vechten, "The Criminality of the Foreign-Born," *Journal of Criminal Law and Criminology*, 32:139–147, July–August 1941.

TABLE XIV

RATE OF CONVICTION OF SPECIFIED GROUPS

Offense	Irish		Native white of native parentage
	Immigrants	2d Generation	
Homicide	2.3	1.0	0.5
Rape	0.0	0.3	0.7
Gaming	1.2	2.7	3.6

Source: Edwin H. Sutherland and Donald R. Cressey, *Principals of Criminology*, 5th ed. (Philadelphia: J. B. Lippincott Company, 1955), p. 146.

TABLE XV

FREQUENCY OF COMMITMENTS TO STATE PRISON AND STATE REFORMA-
TORY OF MASSACHUSETTS FOR MURDER, MANSLAUGHTER, AND ASSAULT,
IN SPECIFIED GROUPS, 1914-1922, PER 100,000 IN EACH GROUP IN 1915

Nativity and parentage	Number committed for specified offenses
Born in Italy	192
Native-born, one or both parents born in Italy	24
Native-born, of native parentage	24
Native-born, one or both parents born in any foreign country	22

Source: Sutherland and Cressey, *op. cit.*, p. 147.

These findings strongly suggest that the assimilation of native American crime patterns is a much more valid explanation of immigrant crime than the "importation of foreign criminal elements." Crime rates among the children of immigrants tend to increase in proportion to their *loss* of identification with the foreign ways of their parents. In effect, crime among the second-generation is a function of Americanization, rather than the absence of it.

Race and Crime

Theories of racial determinism in crime share the same core of basic assumptions underlying the genetic theories already discussed. Each of these orientations employs heredity as the basic determinant in crime; each denies significance to cultural, experiential, and other environmental factors. The only major variation introduced by the racial theorists is that the genetic patterns are assumed to work selectively through the different races—a point vehemently disputed by certain genetic theorists, who insist that patterns of genetic criminality appear among certain family stocks in *all* races. Since the objections raised against hereditary determinism apply also to racial theories of crime, their repetition would be redundant. Instead, the present discussion will deal first with the concept of race, then with the data relating race to crime, finally with some of the alternative explanations that have been proposed.

The Concept of Race: Problems of Definition and Differentiation

Despite the fact that most individuals can be "racially" classified by visual inspection, the problem of defining race objectively has remained a matter of scientific convention. To say this is to acknowledge that the problem of racial differentiation is still a matter in dispute. In 1950, UNESCO (The United Nations Educational, Scientific, and Cultural Organization) issued a statement by an international panel of experts convened for the purpose of obtaining at least a minimal consensus of informed current opinion. When measured against the vast literature on race, this report, consisting of twenty-one brief paragraphs filling seven pages of a small pamphlet, illustrates the meagerness of sound opinion which may be distilled from a field rife with misconceptions. As a kind of platform on which most anthropologists can agree to stand, it is directly pertinent to any discussion of race and cultural phenomena.

The report opens by asserting the general agreement of scientists that all men are probably derived from the same common stock and belong to the same species, and that the differences between them are due to "evolutionary factors of differentiation," such as isolation, hybridization, and natural selection. From a biological point of view, the differences between the races are not due to certain genes exclusive to one racial group but rather to the relative frequency and concentration of the same genetic factors in different population groups which developed in relative isolation from one another. Accordingly, the term *race* designates "a group or population characterized by some concentrations, relative as to frequency and distribution, of hereditary particles (genes) or physical characters, which appear, fluctuate, and often disappear in the course of time by reason of geographic and/or cultural isolation." [5]

[5] *Unesco Statement on the Nature of Race and Race Differences by Physical Anthropologists and Geneticists,* 1950, p. 76.

It should be noted that this conception of race is relative and quantitative rather than qualitative and absolute. It does not describe different species of men but merely recognizably different concentrations of the same genetic factors found among all. Should these differences in concentration diminish—as they have in many groups of individuals—the description would become meaningless. At the present time most scientists agree in recognizing three broad classifications: the Mongoloid, the Negroid, and the Causasoid. But these classifications are neither static nor, necessarily, permanent. "These divisions," asserts the report, "were not the same in the past as they are at present, and there is every reason to believe that they will change in the future."[6]

PHYSICAL DIFFERENTIAE. From an anthropological point of view, the statement, "Race is only skin deep," is almost literally true. A few micrometers beneath the epidermal layer of the skin, race entirely disappears. Anatomically, race consists of color and texture of skin and hair, a certain general (but unreliable) conformity of skull and bone structure, a certain variation in eyelids, lips, and noses, and little or nothing else. There is no way of distinguishing any of the internal organs of the different races. No hypothesis that neural tissue or organization is different has yet been proved—a point of considerable relevance to discussions of racial differences in intelligence. For many years it was claimed that the cranial volume of whites was somewhat greater than that of other races; after the discovery that Eskimos have larger skulls than whites, the comparison was quietly dropped. Analysis of the blood types found among different races has revealed certain gross variations in the relative *concentration* of the various blood groups. Among the Chinese, for example, there are relatively more individuals with Blood Type A_1 and relatively fewer with Type A_2.[7] But the blood of a Chinese with Blood Type A_1 is indistinguishable from that of a Negro or a white with the same blood type; the blood of each can be exchanged in transfusion with that of the others.

None of the races as a unit reveals any consistent or reliable differences in size, weight, strength, sensory acuity, or longevity. There are tribes of Negro pygmies whose average height is under four feet, and there are other Negro tribes where a six-foot adult is considered short. Because of their modern advantages in medicine, nutrition, and sanitation, certain large population groups of Caucasoids tend to live longer

---

[6] *Ibid.*, p. 77.

[7] William C. Boyd, *Genetics and the Races of Men* (Boston: Little, Brown and Company, 1950), p. 268.

than population groups of Mongoloids and Negroids, but this development is recent and unrelated to any known genetic factors. In view of these facts, the statement has frequently been made that there are greater differences between members of the same race than between those of the different races.

RACIAL MIXTURES. The problem of racial differentiation is complicated by the fact that all members of the human species can mate and produce offspring of all varieties of blending. Recognition of this fact alone would require one to speak of race in quantitative rather than qualitative terms. Since race is a matter of degree, one should not say "Negro," "Chinese," or "White," but *how much* Negro, *how much* Chinese, etc. Pursuing the implications of this fact could lead to some startling conclusions about race and criminality. For example: The probability that Negroids commit a proportionately larger percentage of crimes than do whites in this country has led some to assume the existence of a racially selective trait for Negro criminality. But the overwhelming majority of Negroes in this country have at least some white parentage in their background. It has been estimated that not more than 25 per cent of the persons called Negroes in this country are of unmixed Negro extraction.[8] Consequently, in order to assess the operation of the genetic Negro crime factor, it is necessary to observe the crime rates among the "racially pure" Negroes of primitive Africa, where, according to the theory, we would expect the criminality to be highest because the racial factor is least diluted. But every index reveals that the extent of criminality among the few still primitive Negroes of Africa is negligible —and very much less than that of the racially mixed Negroes of America. Apparently, then—and contrary to expectation—the Negro crime rate *"rises"* when pure Negro racial characters are mixed with white racial factors.

The "conclusion" just cited illustrates the results that emerge when the racial hypothesis is measured against actual evidence and then pushed impartially to its logical conclusions. Needless to say, the idea of a "white genetic factor for crime" has never been considered in racial crime theories—despite the fact that, from a purely biological viewpoint, it makes as much sense as a "Negro factor" or any other racial factor. The fact that this possibility has been ignored despite evidence that crime is most highly concentrated in modern, urbanized nations with predominantly Caucasoid populations suggests a more significant con-

[8] M. J. Herskovits, *The American Negro: A Study in Racial Crossing* (New York: Alfred A. Knopf, Inc., 1928).

clusion—namely, that differences in racial attitudes have been more critical than actual differences between the races in determining these theories and their supporting data.

The Genetic Validity of Negro Crime Statistics

In the discussion of the genetic conception of race and racial mixture, reference was made to the fact that race is quantitative and relative rather than qualitative and absolute. In the United States racial mixtures include the almost totally white octoroon (seven-eighths white ancestry), the predominantly white quadroon (three-quarters white ancestry), and the mulatto (one-half white ancestry). Since, from a genetic viewpoint, octoroons and quadroons are predominantly white and mulattoes at least half white, any valid racial study of criminality should apportion the criminality of these groups under both white and Negro categories. Thus, in figuring the totals of white and Negro offenders, unmixed whites and unmixed Negroes would count as one (1.0) for each racial category; every octoroon would add 0.875 to the white and 0.125 to the Negro categories; each quadroon would add 0.75 to the white and 0.25 to the Negro categories; the equally mixed mulattoes, 0.5 to each category, etc.

Unfortunately, the methods of race reporting employed in census records do not attempt to reflect the actual extent of racial mixture but follow, instead, the popular conception whereby *any* degree of known Negro ancestry or apparent Negroid characteristics classifies the individual as a Negro. This procedure weakens the genetic validity of Negro crime studies at the very outset.

This objection would not be serious if the percentage of mixed white–Negro individuals were small. The most careful studies, however, indicate the reverse. In his study, *The Anthropometry of the American Negro,* Herskovits estimated that of the total of all persons classified as Negro, almost 15 per cent were more white than Negro, approximately 25 per cent were equally white and Negro, approximately 32 per cent were more Negro than white, and approximately 6 per cent were Negro mixed with Indian. This leaves a total of 22 per cent unmixed Negroes.[9] Since there is no evidence to suggest that Negro criminals are more or less mixed than Negroes in the general population, there is no alternative to the conclusion—assuming the correctness of the percentages—

[9] M. J. Herskovits, *The Anthropometry of the American Negro* (New York: Columbia University Press, 1930), p. 177.

that almost 40 per cent of the offenders contributing to the total of "Negro" crime are either half or more than half white. Any correction of the totals of Negro offenders toward greater conformity with this genetic distribution would have the effect of redistributing a very considerable number of criminals from the Negro to the white side of the ledger. The percentage "transferred" by this procedure would be large enough to reduce the presently "unfavorable" picture of Negro crime drastically.

We come now to a critical distinction: though the doctrine of Negro uniqueness and racial inferiority is an illusion, the reality of the Negro's unique social treatment is undisputed. The fact that Negroes do not form a unique and biologically pure population is now beside the point; in isolating them as a group, the statistician is reflecting a social reality at the expense of a socially irrelevant genetic error.[10] Put another way, the validity of isolating Negroes in a separate statistical category depends on the validity of conceptualizing them as a distinct, relatively isolated minority group with common values, attitudes, and problems.

The Statistics of Crime among Negroes

Estimates of the crime rate of any group must be based on the number contributed by the group to the total population. At the last census (1950) there were 15,042,286 persons classified as Negroes in the United States.[11] Negroes thus constitute 10 per cent of the total population of the country. It is against this basic figure of 10 per cent that the arrest, offense, and prison rates of Negroes must be calculated for comparative purposes. The following discussion examines the available statistics of crime among Negroes and interprets them with reference to the various hypotheses that have been advanced to explain them.

ARRESTS. Between the years 1950 and 1956, arrests of Negroes varied from 26 per cent to 34 per cent of the total of all arrests reported to the F. B. I. by its contributing police sources.[12] This over-all Negro arrest rate is approximately three times as high as the percentage of Negroes in the population. Negro arrest rates vary greatly from one part

[10] The Census Bureau has frankly described the basis of its racial classifications:

> The concept of race, as it has been used by the Bureau of the Census, is derived from that which is commonly accepted by the general public. It does not, therefore, reflect clear-cut definitions of biological stock, and several categories obviously refer to nationalities. (*Census of Population: 1950*, Vol. II, Part 1, p. 35.)

[11] *Ibid.*

[12] *Uniform Crime Reports*, 1950–1956.

of the country to another, from rural to urban areas, and from one specific locality to another. They are highest in certain western states, where there are comparatively few Negroes, but they are disproportionately concentrated among younger male groups living in urban localities. Negro arrest rates in large urban areas are very high compared with city-wide arrest rates for whites. However, in most of these cities the white arrest rate varies greatly from one neighborhood to another, whereas the Negroes are usually concentrated in one neighborhood. Consequently, the comparison of urban Negro arrest rates with over-all white urban arrest rates oversimplifies a complex problem. When urban Negro arrest rates are compared with those of whites living in equally deteriorated neighborhoods, the discrepancy is invariably reduced, and sometimes reversed.

Distribution of Arrests According to Offense. The distribution of arrests by type of crime is markedly different for whites and Negroes. Like all statistics of arrest, it must be interpreted with extreme caution; nevertheless, the higher rate of Negro arrests for crimes against the person (compared with crimes against property) is clearly indicated by statistics that break down the total number of arrests *between* the two groups. Table XVI divides the percentage of arrests for each crime category between whites and Negroes and, in addition, indicates the *rate* of arrest per 100,000 of the population in 1946. Though the over-all contribution of Negro arrests was 24.7 per cent of the total, the proportion contributed to crimes against the person was consistently higher: 44.3 per cent in the case of criminal homicide; 42.2 per cent in the case of assault.

Time Trends. Though the rate and number of arrests for whites and Negroes have regularly increased during the last twenty-five years, the Negro arrest rate has increased at a faster pace. The acceleration has been disproportionately greater for the more serious crimes. Between 1940 and 1946 the over-all arrest rate for whites rose from 391.6 to 578.6 per 100,000—a net increase of approximately 45 per cent. During the same period the total Negro rate for all arrests rose from 1,078.4 to 1,938.7 per 100,000—an increase of 80 per cent. During this period, however, the white arrest rate for murder rose by only 25 per cent—considerably less than the over-all increase in white arrests. In the same six-year period the Negro arrest rate for murder almost doubled, rising from 19.8 to 35.0, and the robbery arrest rate almost tripled.[13] Thus,

---

[13] Derived from a comparison of arrest rates for 1946 (Table XVI) with arrest rates for 1940, as given in the *Uniform Crime Reports.*

TABLE XVI

DISTRIBUTION OF ARRESTS ACCORDING TO RACE AND TYPE OF OFFENSE
(EXCLUDING THOSE UNDER FIFTEEN YEARS OF AGE): 1946

	Per cent Negro of total in each offense	Rate per 100,000 population*	
		Negro	White ††
Criminal homicide	44.3	35.0	4.3
Robbery	38.5	89.1	13.9
Assault	42.2	263.8	35.3
Burglary—breaking or entering	28.0	119.3	30.2
Larceny-theft	31.5	217.6	46.5
Auto theft	14.9	37.1	20.8
Embezzlement and fraud	13.5	21.1	13.3
Stolen property: buying, receiving, etc.	32.0	12.5	2.6
Arson	23.0	2.0	0.6
Forgery and counterfeiting	14.9	11.6	6.5
Rape	27.8	28.2	7.1
Prostitution and commercialized vice	36.3	46.4	7.7
Other sex offenses	17.2	34.1	16.1
Narcotic drug laws	32.2	11.0	2.4
Weapons: carrying, possessing, etc.	49.8	73.3	7.2
Offenses against family and children	15.1	20.9	11.6
Liquor laws	38.1	33.0	5.2
Driving while intoxicated	8.5	32.0	33.9
Road and driving laws	19.5	15.6	6.3
Parking violations	22.0	†	†
Other traffic and motor vehicle laws	25.4	17.8	5.1
Disorderly conduct	26.5	43.1	38.9
Drunkenness	14.2	261.5	152.6
Vagrancy	21.8	100.0	34.1
Gambling	51.2	81.1	7.3
Suspicion	28.3	148.4	36.9
Not stated	22.7	12.7	4.2
All other offenses	20.2	72.6	28.1
TOTAL	24.7	1,938.7	578.6

* Poulation bases taken as of 1940.
† Less than one-tenth of one per cent.
†† White includes both foreign-born and native-born.

Source: *Encyclopedia of Criminology*, edited by Dr. Vernon C. Branham and Dr. Samuel B. Kutash (New York: Philosophical Library, 1949), p. 269. Compiled from *Uniform Crime Reports*, Annual Bulletin, 17; No. 2 (1946), p. 124, and *Sixteenth Census of the United States: 1940, Population*.

with isolated exceptions, the Negro increases for the more serious crimes had exceeded the over-all Negro increases by a wide margin.

By 1956 the absolute number of Negro arrests for certain crimes had come to exceed the absolute number of white arrests for these offenses. In 1956 Negroes contributed more than half of the total arrests for murder and non-negligent manslaughter—more than twice the figure for whites. Ten years previously they had contributed less than one half of the total. By 1956 the crimes for which Negro arrests were in absolute excess of white arrests included murder, robbery, aggravated assault (by a ratio of more than 2 to 1), narcotics violations, weapons carrying, and gambling (by a ratio of 3 to 1).[14]

Arrest Statistics as Indices of Crime. These figures would be more impressive if it were not for the fact that statistics of arrest are poor indices of crime generally, and extremely unreliable for Negro crime in particular. For purposes of comparing the volume and distribution of crimes committed by whites and Negroes, they are especially untrust-worthy.

They are generally unreliable for a variety of reasons. In the first place, arrest figures cannot be taken as indices of criminality because they do not indicate whether the persons arrested were later charged and convicted. If a considerable percentage of arrests failed to result in later official action—if large numbers of people were merely arrested and then merely released—the arrest records would greatly overstate the case against these individuals. To complicate this difficulty there is another, equally systematic source of error that understates the actual crime rate. Crimes against property consistently make up over 90 per cent of all crimes reported to the police every year. However, the percentage of these crimes which are *cleared by arrest* in any year has never risen beyond 27 per cent. In other words, for more than seven out of every ten property crimes reported, there is no arrest to begin with.

In contrast to crimes against property, the proportion of crimes against the person which are cleared by arrest is high. (In 1956 the police cleared 78.5 per cent of reported personal crimes against 25.4 per cent of property crimes.) Arrest clearances for murder were particularly high: 92.7 per cent. However, since personal crimes constituted *less than 6 per cent of all crimes reported*, the *over-all* arrest record was not high. (In 1956 only two out of every seven crimes were cleared by an arrest.[15])

As has already been pointed out, a disproportionately high percentage of Negro arrests is concentrated in the personal crime categories. But it is in these categories—which make up less than 6 per cent of reported crime—that the highest arrest clearances occur. In larceny and theft—for which the white arrest figures are higher than the Negro—the total clearance rate was only 21 per cent in 1955.[16] The question arises: What of the unsolved crimes, the uncaught offenders? And how

---

[14] *Uniform Crime Reports*, 27, No. 2 (1956), p. 113.
[15] *Uniform Crime Reports*, 27, No. 1 (1956), p. 46.
[16] *Uniform Crime Reports*, 27, No. 1 (1956), p. 49.

reliable are the available arrest figures as clues to their racial classification?

PRISON COMMITMENT. Nation-wide statistics on the racial composition of prison populations and on the distribution of prisoners according to offense have been available from two sources: *Prisoners in State and Federal Prisons and Reformatories,* published by the Bureau of the Census and discontinued in 1946, and *National Prisoner Statistics,* an abbreviated and less informative version of the former publication, issued by the Federal Bureau of Prisons of the Department of Justice. Statistics on federal prisoners are currently available in *Federal Prisons,* also issued annually by the Federal Bureau of Prisons.

More than 30 per cent of all adult inmates of state and federal prisons are Negroes (see Table XVII). This figure is over three times as high as the percentage of Negroes in the general population. The Negro population in federal prisons has consistently been slightly lower than that in state prisons, varying from 24 to 27 per cent of the total. In 1939 the comparative rates for prison commitment per 100,000 of the population were 137.7 for Negroes against 42.4 for native-born and 23.6 for foreign-born whites.[17]

Statistically, arrests and prison commitments represent the two most "visible" points in the law-enforcement chain. Of course, the largest number of cases is eliminated in the many intermediate processes *between* arrest and imprisonment, and only a small fraction of all those arrested for crimes ever reach prison. Since statistics on these intermediate steps are either deficient or lacking, statements about what happens between arrest and imprisonment are necessarily conjectural; we can only speculate about what happens in between on the basis of the two visible ends of the chain. Nevertheless, a comparison of these two polar points of contact with legal processes is valid. Though it may not be possible to ascertain precisely what happened to each group, it is possible to determine whether the over-all outcomes were similar.

In 1946 arrests of Negroes constituted about 44 per cent of the total arrests for criminal homicide (see Table XVI). However, Negro prisoners contributed more than 57 per cent to the total of all prisoners received from the courts for criminal homicide in 1946. Negro arrests for assault comprised 42 per cent of the total arrests, but 57 per cent of the prisoners committed for assault were Negroes. Forty-seven per cent of the prisoners received for robbery were Negroes, though Negroes had

[17] Gunnar Myrdal, *An American Dilemma* (New York: Harper and Brothers, 1944), p. 554.

TABLE XVII

FELONY PRISONERS RECEIVED FROM COURT IN FEDERAL AND STATE INSTITUTIONS, BY RACE AND NATIVITY, FOR THE UNITED STATES: 1942 TO 1946

Race and nativity	Number					Per cent distribution				
	1946	1945	1944	1943	1942	1946	1945	1944	1943	1942
All Classes	56,432	43,281	41,058	40,273	47,761	100.0	100.0*	100.0*	100.0	100.0
White	37,146	29,539	28,280	27,616	32,482	65.8	68.2	68.9	68.6	68.0
Native	35,333	27,825	26,584	25,888	30,179	62.6	64.3	64.7	64.3	63.2
Foreign-born	1,813	1,714	1,696	1,728	2,303	3.2	4.0	4.1	4.3	4.8
Negro	18,655	13,207	12,165	12,131	14,660	33.1	30.5	29.6	30.1	30.7
Other races	631	535	613	526	619	1.1	1.2	1.5	1.3	1.3

Excludes statistics for state institutions as follows: Mississippi all years; and Michigan and Georgia, 1942 to 1945. Includes statistics covering year ending May 31 for state institutions in Pennsylvania; and for those in Georgia, statistics for year ending March 31, 1947, adjusted to a calendar year basis.
* Apparent discrepancies in percentage totals are due to the rounding off of decimals to tenths of a percentage point.
Source: *Prisoners in the State and Federal Prisons and Reformatories, 1946* (Washington, D. C.: U. S. Bureau of the Census, 1948), p. 27.

contributed only 38.5 per cent of the total arrests for robbery. Of the prisoners received for the carrying or possession of weapons, 57 per cent were Negroes, though Negroes had been involved in less than half of the arrests for this offense.[18] These discrepancies suggest that the processes of judicial elimination work less favorably for the Negro than they do for the white offender. The resulting disproportionate representation of Negroes in prisons suggests that the Negro's involvement in crime increases at each stage of the law-enforcement process.

Time Trends in Prison Commitments. There has been a consistent increase in the Negro population of American prisons and reformatories. This increase has occurred during a period of over-all decline in the nation-wide prison population. In 1939 there were approximately 179,000 adult offenders in state and federal institutions—about 137 prisoners for every 100,000 in the general population. By 1953, after a marked rise in the general population and in the rate of crime, the total institutional population had fallen to 173,000—approximately 110 prisoners for every 100,000 members of the general population.

Between 1931 and 1940 the Negro population of adult federal institutions more than doubled, while that of whites declined by a little more than 3 per cent. The increase has been nation-wide, though greatest in those areas which have received the greatest influx of migration from the South. In New Jersey, Negroes constituted 25.1 per cent of the adult males received from the courts between 1930 and 1934; between 1940 and 1944 the percentage rose to 34.1 per cent; between 1950 and 1954 it reached 41.3 per cent.[19]

Prison Commitments as Indices of Crime. The thesis that crime statistics are actually statistics of law enforcement is nowhere more clearly illustrated than in the analysis of prison commitments. The disproportionately high representation of Negroes in the prison population seems to be related to a combination of the following factors:

A relatively smaller percentage of Negro offenders receive probation. The use of probation as an alternative to imprisonment is widespread, especially for first offenders and for less serious felonies. Practices vary considerably from state to state; nevertheless, probation is granted to approximately one third of all convicted defendants. Though statistics

[18] Prison commitment statistics taken from *Prisoners in State and Federal Prisons and Reformatories, 1946* (Washington, D. C.: U. S. Bureau of the Census, 1948), p. 48.

[19] *Recent Statistics on Certain Aspects of the Crime Situation in New Jersey* (Trenton, N. J.: Bureau of Social Research, Departments of Institutions and Agencies, 1955), p. 4.

providing a breakdown of probationers by race are unavailable, there is reason to believe that Negroes, as a group, tend to receive this alternative to prison less frequently, for the following reasons: (1) Eligibility for probation is usually based on requirements that Negroes, as a group, tend to fulfill less often than white offenders. (2) Probation is less frequently granted to repeated offenders; the higher rate of recidivism among Negroes would automatically lower their eligibility. (3) A relatively greater number of Negroes tends to be involved in the more serious crimes, for which probation is infrequently granted.

The crimes for which Negroes are sentenced tend to include a higher proportion of those felonies for which prison sentences are ordinarily longer.

In addition, Negroes tend to receive longer sentences than whites for the same crimes. Though direct evidence of this fact is not available, it may be inferred from statistics on *time served before first release,* published in *National Prisoner Statistics.* The amount of time served by prisoners is partly influenced by their behavior in prison, but it is to the largest extent determined by the length of their original sentence. Table XVIII provides a breakdown of time served by white and Negro felony prisoners for the same crimes in different states and national regions.[20]

A comparatively smaller percentage of Negroes receives parole. Moreover, those who are paroled probably receive their parole after spending a longer period of their sentence in prison. Table XIX breaks down the total number of persons released from state and federal institutions by race and method of release. In 1946—the last year for which figures are available—71.7 per cent of the white prisoners were released conditionally (i.e., granted some form of parole) against 57.8 per cent of the Negro prisoners, an average difference of about 14 per cent. Since inmates released on parole can no longer be counted among the prison population, this discrepancy lends serious distortions to any estimate of criminality that bases itself on the number of men in prison.

[20] Examination of Table XVIII reveals that for most offenses in most areas, Negroes served more time than whites. There is one striking exception: the crime of murder. In all sections except the South, Negroes served considerably less time for murder than did whites—in the nation as a whole, a median of twenty-five months less. Von Hentig's data on the racial status of murderers and their victims supports the impression that the great majority of the victims of Negro murderers are also Negroes. In view of this probability, the lower sentences meted out to Negro murderers may reflect relatively less concern for their victims. (See Von Hentig, *op. cit.,* p. 180.)

TABLE XVIII

TIME SERVED BY WHITE AND NEGRO FELONY PRISONERS BEFORE FIRST RELEASE FROM STATE INSTITUTIONS, BY REGION AND OFFENSE: 1951

| Region and offense | Number | | Time served in months | | | |
| | | | Median | | Range of middle 80% | |
	White	Negro	White	Negro	White	Negro
All States	30,225	14,469	20	25	9–54	9–72
Murder	594	841	111	86	35–242	33–189
Manslaughter	585	950	27	33	9–78	11–74
Robbery	2,837	1,678	31	36	13–89	15–89
Aggravated assault	1,317	1,723	23	21	8–59	8–57
Burglary	7,385	3,883	20	25	9–48	11–60
Theft, except auto *	5,375	2,597	16	19	8–38	8–44
Auto theft	1,704	451	21	20	9–43	9–42
Embezzlement and fraud	1,061	136	15	19	8–36	8–45
Forgery	4,351	603	18	18	9–38	10–40
Rape	1,208	436	32	42	11–86	12–113
Other sex offenses *	1,012	185	26	28	9–72	9–78
Drug laws	182	159	18	15	9–38	6–30
Weapons	156	108	18	23	8–62	8–53
Escape	448	74	15	15	8–33	6–28
Other *	2,010	645	12	13	6–36	5–34
Northeast	5,141	2,202	24	30	11–68	14–77
Murder	62	51	188	145	96–281	64–245
Manslaughter	73	110	40	45	18–120	18–92
Robbery	754	399	30	35	15–116	17–99
Aggravated assault	323	372	26	30	9–67	13–60
Burglary	1,389	484	23	30	11–60	15–72
Theft, except auto *	893	414	22	28	12–51	14–55
Auto theft	209	44	19	18	11–41	11–33
Embezzlement and fraud	84	14	16	19	10–29	–
Forgery	237	23	20	30	10–48	–
Rape	316	82	36	38	14–86	16–95
Other sex offenses *	315	51	30	36	9–71	13–85
Drug laws	16	15	24	20	–	–
Weapons	51	55	26	29	12–67	12–58
Escape	57	11	20	21	10–48	–
Other *	362	77	18	18	9–53	9–36
North Central	8,279	2,448	21	26	11–56	12–75
Murder	111	99	185	142	93–279	91–302
Manslaughter	141	147	36	36	12–95	14–75
Robbery	727	457	36	38	12–115	16–91
Aggravated assault	264	187	25	24	10–61	10–60
Burglary	1,792	651	24	24	12–49	13–54
Theft, except auto *	1,297	383	17	20	10–39	11–45
Auto theft	772	144	22	23	12–48	12–48
Embezzlement and fraud	374	38	17	30	9–40	12–48
Forgery	1,379	123	18	19	10–39	12–40
Rape	346	90	32	45	11–81	13–115
Other sex offenses *	276	28	24	30	11–95	15–77
Drug laws	5	11	16	18	–	–
Weapons	38	13	15	24	11–62	–
Escape	152	16	16	16	9–32	–
Other *	605	61	12	12	9–34	9–33

The releases of 477 prisoners who were members of other races are excluded. Range of middle 80 per cent not shown where number of cases is less than 25.
* Offenses previously shown separately have been combined as follows: "stolen property" with "theft, except auto"; "commercialized vice" with "other sex offenses"; and "nonsupport or neglect," "liquor laws," and "traffic laws" with "other."
Source: *National Prisoner Statistics:* "Prisoners Released from State and Federal Institutions, 1951" (Washington, D. C.: Federal Bureau of Prisons, 1955), p. 29.

TABLE XVIII (Continued)

TIME SERVED BY WHITE AND NEGRO FELONY PRISONERS BEFORE FIRST RELEASE FROM STATE INSTITUTIONS, BY REGION AND OFFENSE: 1951

| Region and offense | Number | | Time served in months | | | |
| | | | Median | | Range of middle 80% | |
	White	Negro	White	Negro	White	Negro
South	10,627	8,981	17	21	8–48	8–72
Murder	304	658	77	81	24–168	28–162
Manslaughter	283	657	21	29	6–72	11–72
Robbery	774	650	32	35	12–83	13–92
Aggravated assault	491	1,090	18	19	6–49	6–50
Burglary	2,895	2,569	18	24	9–44	10–59
Theft, except auto *	2,200	1,674	15	17	7–33	7–40
Auto theft	442	234	20	17	9–42	7–42
Embezzlement and fraud	355	82	13	17	6–32	6–38
Forgery	1,411	386	16	18	8–36	10–40
Rape	295	247	28	42	8–80	11–120
Other sex offenses *	201	86	18	19	8–55	7–43
Drug laws	80	91	15	10	7–30	5–23
Weapons	43	35	12	10	6–27	5–43
Escape	83	31	9	9	3–20	4–20
Other *	770	491	10	13	5–27	5–28
West	6,178	838	19	30	8–47	12–60
Murder	117	33	120	80	50–239	48–138
Manslaughter	88	36	29	34	10–47	22–48
Robbery	582	172	30	36	12–54	22–62
Aggravated assault	239	74	22	24	9–54	9–60
Burglary	1,309	179	18	27	8–40	12–51
Theft, except auto *	985	126	16	21	7–35	8–36
Auto theft	281	29	18	20	7–33	11–40
Embezzlement and fraud	248	2	13	12	8–36	–
Forgery	1,324	71	18	20	8–36	12–36
Rape	251	17	30	59	12–96	–
Other sex offenses *	220	20	33	41	9–72	–
Drug laws	81	42	24	24	13–36	16–30
Weapons	24	5	24	66	–	–
Escape	156	16	18	15	12–36	–
Other *	273	16	15	24	6–84	–

The releases of 477 prisoners who were members of other races are excluded. Range of middle 80 per cent not shown where number of cases is less than 25.
* Offenses previously shown separately have been combined as fcllows: "stolen property" with "theft, except auto"; "commercialized vice" with "other sex offenses"; and "nonsupport or neglect," "liquor laws," and "traffic laws" with "other."
Source: *National Prisoner Statistics:* "Prisoners Released from State and Federal Institutions, 1951" (Washington, D. C.: Federal Bureau of Prisons, 1955), p. 29.

To illustrate this clearly, let us assume that in a certain newly built prison 1,000 white and 1,000 Negro prisoners are received in 1965. Every one of these prisoners received the same sentence—five to ten years—for identical crimes. At the end of the fifth year and at any time thereafter, all of the prisoners, white and Negro, are technically eligible for parole. But now let us assume that the number of Negroes paroled in any year is always less than the number of whites paroled during that same year by 10 per cent. Thus, during the first year of eligibility, if 200 whites were paroled, only 180 Negroes would be released on parole. If, during the second year, 300 whites were paroled, only 270 negroes

TABLE XIX

MALE FELONY PRISONERS RELEASED, BY TYPE OF INSTITUTION, METHOD OF RELEASE, AND RACE, FOR THE UNITED STATES: 1946

Type of institution and race	Number					Per cent of all releases			
	All releases	Unconditional release			Conditional release	Unconditional release			Conditional release
		Total	Expiration of sentence	Executive clemency		Total	Expiration of sentence	Executive clemency	
All institutions	47,312	15,262	14,658	604	32,050	32.3	31.0	1.3	67.7
White	33,380	9,456	8,995	461	23,924	28.3	26.9	1.4	71.7
Negro	13,298	5,611	5,480	131	7,687	42.2	41.2	1.0	57.8
Other races	634	195	183	12	439	30.8	28.9	1.9	69.2
Federal institutions	12,668	3,040	2,919	121	9,628	24.0	23.0	1.0	76.0
White	10,009	2,278	2,186	92	7,731	22.8	21.8	0.9	77.2
Negro	2,321	687	662	25	1,634	29.6	28.5	1.1	70.4
Other races	338	75	71	4	263	22.2	21.0	1.2	77.8
State institutions*	34,644	12,222	11,739	483	22,422	35.3	33.9	1.4	64.7
White	22,371	7,178	6,809	369	16,193	30.7	29.1	1.6	69.3
Negro	10,977	4,924	4,818	106	6,053	44.9	43.9	1.0	55.1
Other races	296	120	112	8	176	40.5	37.8	2.7	59.5

* Includes statistics covering year ending May 31 for Pennsylvania, and for Georgia, statistics for year ending March 31, 1947, adjusted to a calendar year basis; excludes statistics for Michigan and Mississippi.
Source: *Prisoners in State and Federal Prisons and Reformatories, 1946* (Washington, D. C.: U. S. Bureau of the Census, 1948), p. 65.

would be paroled. During the third year, the parole of an additional 400 whites would reduce the Negro population by an additional 360. At this rate, the yearly changes in the original population would be as follows:

	1965	1970	1971	1972
Whites	1,000	800	500	100
Negroes	1,000	820	550	190

By 1972, using the 1965 prison population as a base, the number of Negroes in the prison would be almost twice the number of whites. Anyone reading the 1972 population figures as direct indices of the comparative criminality of whites and Negroes would be seriously misled.

CONCLUSIONS EMERGING FROM THE FOREGOING ANALYSIS: 1. *Statistics available at present do not permit a reliable determination of the actual distribution of crime among whites and Negroes.* All statistics concerning criminals stem originally from arrests. But arrests, in any year, never represent more than 30 per cent of the total number of crimes reported. Consequently, any conclusions drawn from the available sample must remain tentative until some valid method is found for distributing the remaining 70 per cent.

2. On the basis of the available sample, however, it can definitely be stated that *the status "Negro" carries with it a significantly greater statistical risk of involvement with law-enforcement processes than does the status "white." This risk, or statistical probability, increases at each stage of the law-enforcement process from arrest to imprisonment.*

3. *A large but unknown portion of this higher rate of involvement with law enforcement must be attributed to distortions introduced into the statistics by differential legal and penal treatment of whites and Negroes. Until the extent of these distortions is known, there is no way of determining whether the higher Negro rate represents a higher rate of actual crime or a greater liability to involvement with law-enforcement agencies.*

4. *If the distortions introduced by differential liability and penal treatment are considered extensive enough to account for the discrepancies, then it cannot be held that Negroes have a higher crime rate than whites.* The apparently higher rates could then be considered statistical artifacts, and the factual basis of the question would dissolve. If, on the other hand, as many people believe, they are not considered large enough to account for the discrepancies (an over-all ratio of 3 to 1) there is no

alternative to the conclusion that Negroes commit a relatively greater number of crimes. Since this belief is widespread, we should do well to consider it briefly.

Opinions and Hypotheses Concerning the Higher Rate of Negro Crime

Though acknowledging inadequacies and distortions in the data, many contemporary students of Negro crime believe that the trends indicated in them reflect the actual crime distribution, though in an exaggerated form. Two general types of explanation have been offered to account for the purportedly higher rate of Negro crime: the genetic (racial) hypothesis, and various environmental hypotheses. Unless and until the environment of whites and Negroes can be at least roughly equated, the racial hypothesis remains untestable. In view of the generally inferior environment of Negroes, the theory of genetic Negro inferiority continues to be little more than a self-fulfilling prophecy.

ENVIRONMENTAL EXPLANATIONS OF NEGRO CRIME. The proponents of the environmental hypothesis generally believe crime among Negroes to be related to the same factors responsible for crime among whites. The higher rate of crime among Negroes is explained in terms of a relatively greater exposure to these factors. The explanation usually proceeds by citing the factors known to be associated with crime among whites and then estimating the extent to which Negroes are exposed to them.

Socioeconomic Status. The statistical association of low socioeconomic status with the more "visible" forms of crime has been demonstrated repeatedly. The great majority of arrests and convictions among whites is concentrated among those wage and occupational groups making up approximately one third of the employed white population. But more than three quarters of the employed Negroes are concentrated in these groups. *Thus, the overwhelming majority of all employed Negroes is concentrated in those occupational groups from which the majority of employed white offenders derive* (see Table XX). Certain white occupational groups are practically free of known crime. These groups, which include professional and technical workers (scientists), managers, proprietors, and officials constituted over 20 per cent of the white employed population but only 5 per cent of the employed Negro population in 1956.

Most white offenders change their employment frequently and spend less time on given jobs than do law-abiding whites. A comparison

TABLE XX

PERCENTAGE DISTRIBUTION OF EMPLOYED PERSONS, BY COLOR AND MAJOR OCCUPATION GROUP: 1948–1956

Major occupation group	White					Nonwhite				
	1948	1951	1954	1955	1956	1948	1951	1954	1955	1956
Professional, technical, and kindred workers	7.2	8.4	9.8	9.8	10.1	2.4	3.2	3.7	3.5	3.3
Farmers and farm operators	7.8	6.6	6.4	6.0	5.7	8.5	6.9	5.8	5.0	4.6
Managers, officials, and proprietors, except farm	11.6	11.1	11.1	11.1	11.0	2.3	2.1	2.1	2.3	2.1
Clerical and kindred workers	13.6	13.6	14.3	14.2	14.6	3.3	3.5	5.0	4.9	5.0
Sales workers	6.7	6.7	7.0	6.9	6.9	1.1	0.9	1.5	1.3	1.1
Craftsmen, foremen, and kindred workers	14.6	14.8	14.6	14.1	14.3	5.3	4.8	5.0	5.2	5.5
Operatives and kindred workers	21.0	20.9	20.0	20.2	19.5	20.1	19.3	20.5	20.9	21.5
Private household workers	1.5	1.7	1.6	1.8	2.0	15.6	15.9	14.3	14.8	14.8
Service workers, except private household	6.4	6.8	7.1	7.2	7.4	14.7	15.4	17.0	16.8	17.4
Farm laborers and foremen	4.6	4.0	3.5	3.9	3.8	12.5	11.2	9.3	9.5	9.9
Laborers, except farm and mine	4.9	5.4	4.8	4.7	4.6	14.3	16.7	15.7	15.8	14.6
TOTALS*	100.0	100.0	100.0	100.0	100.0	100.0	100.0	100.0	100.0	100.0

Annual averages based on data for four quarterly months: January, April, July, and October. Occupation data not tabulated in other months.
* Apparent discrepancies in percentage totals are due to the rounding off of decimals to tenths of a percentage point.
Source: U.S. Bureau of the Census, *Current Population Reports*, Series P–50, No. 66.

of the duration of employment on current jobs in 1951 reveals that Negro workers had been on their current jobs an average of 2.4 years compared with an average of 3.5 years among white workers. These figures reflect a comparatively higher rate of layoffs and a generally lower level of job security among Negroes.[21]

Income. In 1950 the Negro wage and salary worker earned an average of about $1,300—approximately 52 per cent of the average for white workers. The average income of Negro families in 1950 was $1,869, compared with $3,445 for white families.[22]

Unemployment. A disproportionately higher number of white offenders was unemployed at the time of their arrest. Between 1947 and 1951 the unemployment rates of the Negro civilian labor force were more than 50 per cent higher than those of the white civilian labor force.

Educational Status. Inferior educational achievement—one of the concomitants of low socioeconomic status—is highly correlated with crime. Though recent over-all statistics on the educational level of pris-

[21] *Negroes in the United States*, U. S. Department of Labor Bulletin 1119 (Washington, D. C.: Government Printing Office, 1952), p. 21.
[22] *Ibid.*, p. 11.

oners are lacking, individual studies indicate that prisoners have generally completed fewer years of schooling than nonprisoners. Price Chenault has estimated that between 10 and 30 per cent of all prisoners admitted to correctional institutions of all types throughout the country are illiterate.[23] In 1940 the median grade of school completed by prisoners was 7.4, compared with 8.3 for civilians at large.[24] In 1950 it was estimated that Negroes over twenty-five had completed an average of 7 years of school—3 years less than the average for whites.[25]

Nevertheless, the relationship between education and crime among Negroes is far from clear. The educational level of Negroes has risen rapidly since 1930, but so has the over-all rate of Negro crime. The educational level of Negroes is highest in the northern urban centers, where the Negro crime rates are high. In the South, where illiteracy rates are highest, crimes rates are lowest.

Urbanization. The highest rates of crime among whites occur in urban centers, especially in the deteriorated sections of these centers. At the present time a roughly equal proportion (60 per cent) of the Negro and the white population lives in urban areas. However, over-all comparison is not valid, since Negroes, unlike whites, are not evenly distributed throughout the cities. Of the Negroes in the North, more than 90 per cent live in cities—and in their most deteriorated neighborhoods. Thus the concentration of the Negro urban population is greatest in those areas whose contribution to the white crime totals has always been highest.

Family Disorganization. A significantly higher proportion of white offenders derives from families in which one or the other parent was absent through death, divorce, or desertion. Estimates of the percentage of delinquents coming from broken homes have varied from 30 to 60 percent.

The extent of family disorganization among Negroes is high. Of the total of white husbands in 1950, 2.9 per cent reported their wives absent through separation or causes other than death or divorce, compared with 9.5 per cent of Negro husbands reporting their wives absent for the same reasons. The percentage of wives reporting husbands

[23] Price Chenault, "Education," in Paul Tappan, ed., *Contemporary Correction* (New York: McGraw-Hill Book Company, Inc., 1951), p. 224.

[24] Joseph D. Lohman *et al.*, "Description of Convicted Felons as a Manpower Resource in a National Emergency." Cited in Edwin H. Sutherland and Donald R. Cressey, *Principles of Criminology*, 5th ed. (Philadelphia: J. B. Lippincott Company, 1955), p. 204.

[25] *Negroes in the United States, op. cit.*, p. 9.

absent for similar reasons was 2.6 for the whites and 11.1 for the Negroes.[26] Desertion and illegitimacy are higher among Negroes. In 1940 slightly more than one out of every five Negro births in the District of Columbia was illegitimate. In the same year the number of Negro families with female heads in cities of over 100,000 population ranged from 21 to 34 per cent.[27] When linked with the factor of segregation in highly deteriorated neighborhoods, the factor of family disorganization among Negroes undoubtedly assumes greater weight in delinquency.

THE "CULTURAL" EXPLANATION OF NEGRO CRIME. Another non-racial explanation of the higher rate of Negro crime bases itself on the belief that Negroes, as a group, have a significantly different "culture" than whites do. These cultural differences according to the theory, are to be traced to the Negro's origins in Africa and, later, to the special social and family traditions created by the institution of slavery. The total result of these influences is said to render Negroes, as a group, more emotional, impulsive, somewhat more violent, less provident, generally less restrained in their sexual relationships than whites. In effect, this explanation suggests psychological rather than environmental causes for Negro crime and differs from the racial explanation only by referring these differences to cultural rather than genetic causes.

The concept of a distinct Negro culture has been seriously questioned by white and Negro scholars, who do not deny the Negro's status as a distinct minority. Thus, Frazier, while acknowledging the impact of slavery on certain usages among Negroes, denies that these influences add up to a separate subculture in American life:

> Having completely lost his ancestral culture, he [the Negro] speaks the same language, practices the same religion, and accepts the same values and political ideals as the dominant group. Consequently, when one speaks of Negro culture in the United States, one can only refer to the folk culture of the rural Southern Negro or the traditional forms of behavior and values which have grown out of the Negro's social and mental isolation.... It is seldom that one finds Negroes who think of themselves as possessing a different culture from whites and that their peculiar culture should be preserved.... The Negro minority is striving for assimilation into American life. The Negro has striven as far as possible to efface or tone down the physical differences between himself

[26] U. S. Bureau of the Census, *Seventeenth Census of the United States, 1950, Population*, Vol. II, Part I (Washington, D. C.: Government Printing Office, 1953, pp. 1–325 through 1–330.
[27] E. F. Frazier, *The Negro in the United States* (New York: The Macmillan Company, 1957), pp. 631–632.

and the white majority. In his individual behavior as well as in his organized forms of social life he attempts to approximate as closely as possible the dominant American pattern.[28]

The cultural theory of Negro crime resolves itself either into a special trait-psychology of the Negro or into a statement of the Negro's specialized reactions to his specialized environmental difficulties. In its latter sense, it is merely a restatement of the environmental position already outlined. In its former sense, it suffers from the same difficulties dogging any purely psychological theory of crime. Assuming that Negroes *are* "impulsive, irresponsible, lazy, etc.," it is still necessary to explain how these traits lead some to murder, robbery, and assault and others to law-abiding lives. None of these traits can account for the increasing emergence and distinction of Negroes in the fields of science, industry, and social service. In a word, they do little more than define the Negro in terms of Uncle Remus without explaining how some of his children become rich men, poor men, beggarmen, or thieves.

Crime among Other Racial Groups in the United States

Since Negroes comprise over 95 per cent of the total nonwhite population of the United States, the proportion of other nonwhite races in the population is negligible. At the last census there were 343,410 Indians, 117,629 Chinese, 141,768 Japanese, and 110,240 individuals of other nonwhite "races" (Asiatic Indians, Koreans, Indonesians) in this country. Though these groups form no more than 0.5 per cent of the total population, they comprise approximately 1.1 per cent of the populations of state and federal prisons—somewhat more than twice their population rate in the country at large.

The largest number of these prison commitments is accounted for by Indians, whose arrest rates are extremely high. (In 1956 one out of every 85 Indians in the country was arrested.) However, most Indian arrests are for drunkenness; in 1956 this offense accounted for no less than 80 per cent of the Indian totals. Disorderly conduct and driving while intoxicated were the next most numerous offenses among Indians. Serious felonies are rare among this group: in 1956 there were a total of 5 arrests for criminal homicide, 52 for aggravated assault, and 43 for robbery.[29]

[28] *Ibid.*, p. 680.
[29] *Uniform Crime Reports*, 27, No. 2 (1956), p. 113.

Up to a few years ago, the arrest rates of Chinese were higher than those of whites, while those of Japanese were approximately half those of whites. By 1956 the Chinese arrest rates had fallen appreciably below those of whites—a fact probably reflecting the cessation of Chinese immigration. Crime among American-born Chinese is negligible. The Japanese arrest rate has remained consistently low.

Psychological Theories of Crime

PSYCHOLOGICAL THEORIES OF CRIME DERIVE FROM THREE MAIN SOURCES: law, psychiatry, and psychology. The earliest students of criminal psychology were the jurists, lawyers, and legislators who created the criminal law. Many centuries before the founding of medical psychology, legal theorists had defined crime in psychological terms; their doctrines of motivation, criminal responsibility, and insanity are interwoven in criminal law and procedure.[1] During the early part of the nineteenth century a number of psychiatrists interested themselves in criminals and, at the invitation of the court, began to participate in trials and medical examinations. The last to enter the field were the psychologists, who, around the turn of the century, began applying their new experimental and statistical techniques to the study of offenders.

The Contributions of Psychiatry

Dictionaries define *psychiatry* as "the medical specialty that deals with mental disorders." When this definition is compared with the

[1] The legal contribution to criminal psychology is discussed in Chapter 18.

range of the nonmedical contributions of psychiatry, its incompleteness becomes apparent. Psychiatrists have contributed to the study of anthropology, history, comparative religion and mythology, and philosophy. They have analyzed the lives and works of great artists and major historical figures, and they have added new dimensions to the art of biography. Their contributions to the practical problems of social living are no less varied and intensive. Psychiatric writers have interested themselves in virtually every critical aspect of individual and group life. They are particularly concerned with the relationship of social and political agencies to the individual, and they have been conspicuous in many fields of social reform. Their theoretical and practical contributions to criminology and penology are instances of this general concern.

Turning from the interests of psychiatrists to psychiatric theories, concepts, and techniques, one encounters an almost equal scope and diversity. There are many schools of psychiatric theory, and a wide range of diagnostic and therapeutic techniques. Since the field, as a whole, is in a continuous state of development and experimentation, it is necessary for psychiatrists to engage in critical evaluations of their own work and the work of their colleagues. To the outside observer, this condition of growth sometimes gives a disturbing impression of conflict. This is especially likely to be true of those who turn to psychiatry for authoritative solutions to questions for which the field itself is still attempting to find answers. In a sense, the high promise of psychiatry and the high hopes it inspires have tended also to inspire demands upon it which, in its present stage of exploration and discovery, it cannot always meet.

The diversity of psychiatric theory and application also makes it inappropriate to speak of psychiatry as a "single" discipline or to talk in terms of *the* psychiatric approach to this or that issue or problem. One can speak only of *this or that* psychiatric approach to a given problem area, adding the caution that the view presented does not necessarily reflect the views of the field as a whole.

In criminology and penology, many of the most active and articulate writers have come from a group identified as the *psychoanalytic* school. For this reason, when speaking of the contributions of psychiatry to criminology, it is convenient to present the discussion under two main headings: the psychoanalytic contribution and the contributions of psychiatrists not related to this school. The latter group—a large and heterogeneous one—includes many psychiatrists, neuropsychiatrists, and clinicians whose theories are relatively more eclectic and less systematized than those of the psychoanalysts. Their contribution to the study of offenders has largely consisted in relating criminal behavior to various specific mental disorders.

Theories Relating Crime to Specific Mental Disorders

There are virtually no psychiatric or neurological disorders that have not been linked, in one way or another, with crime. Organic brain disease, epilepsy, alcoholism, drug addiction, psychoses, and neuroses have been viewed as causally significant in criminal behavior generally or in specific types of crime.

In general, studies relating crime to various mental disorders share certain limitations: (1) They are usually based on small or selective groups of offenders. (2) They rarely employ control groups. (3) Their findings are rarely, if ever, duplicated when larger samples of offenders are used. (4) The findings usually consist of either statistical correlations without a causal hypothesis or causal hypotheses illustrated by one or a few cases. (5) Comparative studies of the incidence of mental disease among criminal and noncriminal groups have failed to show significant differences.[2]

Until it is established that the rate of mental disorders is significantly higher among offenders, discussions about causal relations are premature. The noted British psychiatrists Henderson and Gillespie have summarized the consensus of present informed opinion on this subject:

> It must be clearly understood that the criminal suffers from exactly the same forms of mental illness as the average member of the community.... Theories and hypotheses which have not been generally accepted by the medical profession are constantly put forward as an explanation for crime. This has been particularly the case where the crime has been the first indication of mental abnormality. Mental disorder does not start suddenly without warning; usually there is a history extending over a period of weeks, months or years.... Therefore when a crime is committed by someone who up to the moment of the crime was looked upon by the majority of his fellow-men as an ordinary individual, it is fair to assume in the first place, at least, that the criminal act was that of a sane and responsible individual.[3]

[2] For a review of the literature on this question see Warren H. Dunham, "The Schizophrene and Criminal Behavior," *American Sociological Review*, 4:352–361, June 1939.

[3] D. K. Henderson and R. D. Gillespie, *A Text-Book of Psychiatry*, 6th ed. (London: Oxford University Press, 1948), p. 688.

Psychoanalytic Theories of Crime

The adjective *psychoanalytic* identifies any concept or technique derived from the theories of Sigmund Freud (1856–1939) and his followers. Though there are many branches and outgrowths of psychoanalytic theory and several more or less distinct schools, the term *psychoanalytic* may be used to designate any psychiatrist, psychotherapist, or psychologist to the extent that he uses or subscribes to the following fundamental doctrines: (1) the principle that behavior is determined largely by unconscious psychological forces or drives; (2) the corollary principle that functional behavior disorders arise primarily because of conflicts related to these drives (or to their repression, or to their inadequate socialization), which interfere with the normal or required activities of the individual; (3) the *therapeutic* principle that the most appropriate treatment of these disorders is to help the patient to gain insight into unconscious drives and, consequently, better control over them, by means of a technique called *psychoanalysis*.

CRIMINALITY AS AN EXPRESSION OF UNCONTROLLED INSTINCTUAL FORCES. Psychoanalytic theory divides the human personality into three basic components or levels: The lowest and most fundamental is the *Id*, a deep, instinctual reservoir, the source of the basic biological drives, present in undifferentiated form at birth. Soon after birth, the self-absorbed infant, originally unconscious of anything outside it, begins to develop an awareness of the world—including the human world—and the beginnings of an awareness of itself as a thing distinct from and reacted to by the environment. Out of the interactions with the environment, the originally undifferentiated Id begins to develop another component, the *Ego* (self). This component becomes the tool through which the Id attempts to satisfy its needs by manipulating the environment. At this point the personality—consisting of the Id and its obedient tool, the Ego—is still unsocialized; the child wants what it wants when it wants it. The child in its selfish pursuit of pleasure is essentially no different from the criminal: its relations with the human world are exploitive; it takes but feels no particular need or duty to give. This behavior is tolerated for a while, but eventually the child finds its pursuit of pleasure being blocked by the wishes of others. It experiences punishment and learns from punishment what is "bad" (not allowed); it experiences reward and learns what is "good" (allowed). Thus the Ego has now to contend not only with objective reality but also with social reality—with the demands of others. Many of these demands are in conflict with the drives of the Id, and the Ego—once the faithful servant of the Id—is now between two fires.

The personality now stands at a critical point. It must either learn to accept the rules of its human environment and chart its course through the circuitous channels and shoals of social tolerance—or it must reject them and chart its own course. If the ego accepts these rules, it normally does so by incorporating them into its consciousness—thereby developing a third component, the *Super-ego*. The Super-ego is a device for coping with social rules. By internalizing these rules, the Ego can respond to them as from within, as from itself. This is not only more efficient but more tolerable, because it fosters the illusion that the Ego is responding to its own rules. Sometimes, however, the Ego learns its moral lessons too well, with the result that it tends to forsake its old master, the Id, and becomes the slave of a new master, the Super-ego. In order to accomplish this thoroughgoing transfer of allegiance, the Ego must shut its consciousness off from the demands of the Id, which, being frustrated, shouts all the louder. The mechanism by which the Ego shuts off the voices of the Id is called *repression*. But this mechanism is rarely, if ever, totally efficient; the thwarted Id, seeking ways to gratify its needs, strains to throw off or elude the controls.

At this point, a variety of things may happen. The Ego, under assault from its partly restrained prisoner, may become even more vigilant, more repressive—and more anxious as the Id struggles to express itself. Occasionally, in spite of all the Ego's *defenses* against it, the Id manages to break out nonetheless—sometimes in patterns of uncontrollable behavior, sometimes in covert, chronic infiltrations of which the Ego is hardly aware. Individuals subject to uncontrolled behavioral patterns are called *compulsive*. Certain types of criminal behavior— kleptomania, for example—are clearly compulsive.

The theoretical framework outlined above provides a basis for hypotheses about the motivation of criminal behavior. Individuals who fail to develop an adequate Super-ego may become criminal because of a deficiency of control over their instinctual drives. Other individuals may become criminal because of the effects of over-control—as a result of the starved Id's overpowering demands for satisfactions that were denied or not provided with legitimate outlets. Criminals of the first kind are said to be deficient in character (another word for Super-ego) and are sometimes called *psychopathic*. Offenders of the other type are called *neurotic* and *compulsive*.

LIMITATIONS OF PSYCHOANALYTIC THEORIES OF CRIME. Any brief

outline of a comprehensive theory invariably omits many important details. The psychoanalytic literature dealing with personality formation is especially rich and detailed, consisting of thousands of volumes and papers; the cursory summary provided above cannot possibly do it justice. For this reason, a detailed critique based on such a summary would be unfair. With this qualification in mind, the following general observations may be made.

Psychoanalytic theory views the basic motivational forces as instinctual and biological. "They represent," writes Freud, "the somatic demands upon mental life . . . they are the ultimate cause of all activity."[4] Psychoanalytic theory tends to minimize the importance of social and cultural forces in determining behavior; since man is biologically more or less the same in every culture, it is assumed that his basic motivations, being biological, are also relatively constant. For this reason, when most psychoanalytic writers speak of "society," they usually mean *any* society and *all* societies. Society is often viewed as a threatening, ordering, and frustrating agent—with different societies merely providing local variations in the ways of threatening, ordering, and frustrating. Viewed in these terms, society is something the individual reacts *against,* and the cultural content of the given society is largely irrelevant to the fact of this response. Different cultures merely provide the external stimuli and the outward forms for this antagonistic behavior—so that in Melanesia, for example, the frustrated offender expresses his aggression with a spear; in New York, with a revolver.

This universal definition of instinct and of the function of society leads to a universal definition of crime. It also leads to serious complications when one attempts to account for the different types of crime. But there is a further and more fundamental difficulty. The forces and mechanisms held responsible for criminality are essentially no different from those leading to neurosis. The difficulty with the theory is that it fails to explain why certain people merely become neurotic while other neurotic people become criminalistic as well. Though psychoanalytic writers on crime have occasionally admitted this difficulty, they do not generally appear to realize its seriousness. Thus, in his book, *The Psychology of the Criminal Act and Its Punishment,* Gregory Zilboorg writes:

> The mysterious thing about the whole matter is that there seems to be as yet no satisfactory explanation of why certain individuals start

[4] Sigmund Freud, quoted in N. Fodor and F. Gaynor, *Freud: Dictionary of Psychoanalysis* (New York: The Philosophical Library, 1950), p. 98.

acting out their fantasy life either in the form of annoying neurotic behavior, or in the form of criminal acts. Psychoanalysis has discovered a wealth of clinical data enriching our understanding of the deeper psychology of the normal, the neurotic, and the psychotic, whether he be criminal or not. But it has no answer as to what it is that makes man succumb or give in to his fantasies so that they become criminal acts.[5]

Few critics of psychoanalytic crime theory would disagree with this statement. Zilboorg's criticism is, in fact, their own. For to acknowledge that a theory of crime causation cannot account for the different behavior of criminals and noncriminals is to acknowledge that the theory does not explain crime. Nevertheless, in the same work, Zilboorg writes of the psychoanalyst's ability to solve the mystery and "fit the pieces together":

> The medical psychologist is a clinician who deals with a special kind of material which is called psychological; his work can be likened to that of putting together a jigsaw puzzle. If all the pieces... fit and make a picture, the right solution has been found.... All this is not in the manner of traditional science; but it is accurate, true in its results, and there is no arbitrariness about it.[6]

In these statements Zilboorg comes close to suggesting that facts which fit into a theoretical framework are sufficient to confirm a theory, while facts which do not are merely "mysterious" and do not seriously challenge the theory. It is significant that Freud, the founder of psychoanalysis, viewed this difficulty as much more critical:

> So long as we trace the development from its final stage backwards, the connection appears continuous....But if we proceed the reverse way, if we start from the premises inferred from the analysis and try to follow these up to the final result, then we no longer get the impression of an inevitable sequence of events which could not be otherwise determined. We notice at once that there might have been another result.[7]

Critics of psychoanalytic crime theory have frequently contrasted the acknowledged inadequacy of the theory with the frequently authoritative diagnostic pronouncements which various psychoanalysts derive from it. This criticism tends to become especially severe when psycho-

---

[5] Gregory Zilboorg, *The Psychology of the Criminal Act and Its Punishment* (New York: Harcourt, Brace and Company, 1954), p. 51.

[6] *Ibid.*, pp. 53–54.

[7] Sigmund Freud, cited in Ronald Dalbiez, *Psychoanalytic Method and the Doctrine of Freud* (New York: Longmans, Green and Company, 1941), Vol. II, pp. 299–300.

analysts appear to insist that their theories and techniques are refined enough to solve the major problems of criminology and penology.

Crime and Mental Disorder Contrasted Rather than Equated

Despite its continuing persistence in modern psychiatric thought, the identification of criminality and mental illness no longer goes unchallenged by individual psychiatrists. The sharpest skepticism is expressed by those in daily working contact with offenders. Thus, Dr. Richard Jenkins:

> ...The assertion that all or a major fraction of delinquency can be accounted for as neurotic behavior neither rings true nor makes sense.
>
> Inner conflict and neuroticism are typically associated with a high level of inhibition, sense of duty, introjected standards and super-ego controls. The typical delinquent, on the other hand is characterized by a personality and way of life relatively free from the dominance, let alone the tyranny, of such inner tendencies. In this regard he is quite likely to be freer than the rest of us. Usually he has a certain earthy realism and is less, rather than more, inclined to be neurotic than is the non-delinquent.[8]

Jenkins' critique raises serious questions about the classical psychoanalytic orientation. To view criminality as a direct outcome of neurotic disease is analogous to thinking of it as one conceives of the skin rash in measles. This way of thinking completely ignores the fact that certain forms of delinquency and crime—whatever else they may be—are also skilled and directed activities. Some forms of crime are correctly called *professional*, and merit this denomination because of the high skills they require. If it is to be believed that success in the carrying out of skilled noncriminal tasks usually requires a fair degree of personal adjustment, there seems little reason to exclude the skilled crafts of the criminal from this general rule. Seen in this light, the relationship between good psychological adjustment and criminal behavior may often be complementary rather than reciprocal, and is so viewed by law-enforcement authorities and the offenders themselves. The police tend to regard the ruthless and calculating professional criminal with considerably more apprehension than they do the neurotic and bungling amateur; the discriminating bank robber will have nothing to do with a get-away man upset by neurotic feelings about theft.

[8] Richard L. Jenkins, "Adaptive and Maladaptive Delinquency," *The Nervous Child*, 2:9–11, October 1955.

258 · THEORIES OF CAUSATION

Sociologists have long held the view that many forms of crime and delinquency may be well within the range of normal behavior. Merton, for one, has pointed out that certain areas of crime and vice "constitute a 'normal' response to a situation where the cultural emphasis upon . . . success has been absorbed, but where there is little access to conventional and legitimate means for becoming successful."[9] This opinion is shared by Jenkins, who views a major portion of delinquency as the product of "the same motivation our culture sanctions as the force which keeps our competitive economy ticking . . ."[10] Jenkins has called this type of delinquency "adaptive." Adaptive delinquents are distinguished from those whose clearly disturbed adjustment and poorly integrated behavior indicate an etiology based on compulsive response to frustration rather than on discriminative and adaptive goal-seeking.

This critical distinction in etiology would clearly call for an appropriate discrimination in the methods and directions of treatment. According to Jenkins, the primary emphasis in the treatment of *adaptive* delinquents must be upon thwarting the delinquent activities. (Presumably this method would entail a frustration of the needs the delinquent is attempting to satisfy by unacceptable means—at least until newer and more acceptable techniques for satisfying them are learned.) By contrast, the first emphasis in the treatment of maladaptive delinquents should be the reduction of the frustration responsible for the adaptation. If this formulation is even approximately correct, it would logically predict the failure of any standard therapeutic approach applied indiscriminately to all delinquents.

Psychological Approaches to the Study of Criminals

Though many psychologists have engaged in the specific study of criminals, a considerable number have studied criminals chiefly in connection with a more general objective; the development of scientific techniques for the measurement of individual differences. This independent interest in problems of method is of profound significance for a self-critical, self-correcting science of criminology. Though not directly related to criminology, it brought to the study of criminals

[9] Robert K. Merton, *Social Theory and Social Structure* (Glencoe, Ill.: The Free Press, 1949), p. 136.
[10] Jenkins, *op. cit.*, p. 11.

increasingly refined statistical and experimental techniques. It laid stress on the critical use of control (comparison) groups in the testing of assumptions about the characteristics of criminals. Furthermore, it was concerned not only with immediate fact-finding and theory construction but with the development of more reliable methods of fact-finding and theory construction for future use. The following discussion will deal with the two areas in which the psychological study of criminals has been concentrated: (1) the testing of intelligence; and (2) the evaluation of personality factors.

Psychological Studies of Intelligence among Criminals

There are few aspects of criminological research more instructive from a methodological point of view than the history of intelligence-testing among criminals. By the first decade of the twentieth century psychologists had developed relatively objective and reliable techniques for measuring, describing, and comparing the test responses of large numbers of people. The standardization of a test battery that purported to measure intelligence was achieved in 1905. For criminology this achievement seemed especially timely, since it occurred during a period of intense controversy about the characteristics of criminals. The new technique offered great promise, and it was eagerly seized on in the hope that it would provide a reliable and objective basis for differentiating criminals from noncriminals. In view of the popularly held theory that crime was a product of mental deficiency, the intelligence test seemed ideally suited for purposes of differentiation, and large numbers of offenders were tested in an attempt to validate the theory. The chronicle of this attempt—its early promise and its ultimate failure—forms one of the most instructive chapters in the history of criminology.

THE MEANING OF INTELLIGENCE AS MEASURED BY THE TESTS. The scientific era of intelligence-testing may be dated from the publication in 1905 of the Binet-Simon scale for measuring the intelligence of children. The Binet-Simon test, as later developed and adapted by Terman and others, possessed several advantages over all earlier methods. Perhaps the most important of these was that it avoided the necessity of a theoretical definition of intelligence.

Binet and Simon selected a graded series of questions that could be answered by representative samples of children at each age level. This method enabled them to establish statistical norms, or typical *mental ages*, for each age level from one to fourteen. Thus, the average child of 12 years could answer all the questions up through those for the "mental age" of 12. In this case, chronological age and mental age were the same. A mentally defective child of twelve might be unable to answer any questions beyond the typical six-year level. In this case, the mental age was exactly half the chronological age. *It thus became possible to express intelligence in terms of a number relating an individual's test performance to the test performance of the average individual at his age.* Intelligence, so defined, was a measure of the extent to which an individual's ability to answer questions fell below or rose above the ability of others at his age level.[11] The *nature* of the questions, the kind of abilities or performances tested, was no longer the central issue, since norms—mental ages—could be determined for any type of performance. This fact assured the complete comparability of all scores of the same test. Moreover, by relating performance to age level, the intelligence quotient (I. Q.) was rendered *independent* of the age factor. Thus, for example, an I. Q. of 200 at age seven is directly equivalent to the same I. Q. at age three; in both cases it indicates that the individual's performance (expressed in terms of his mental age) was double the average performance for his chronological age. The three-year-old was able to answer the questions of the average six-year level; the seven-year-old was able to answer those of the fourteen-year level. It thereby became possible to compare the I. Q.'s of persons of *all* ages. Furthermore, since research had indicated that the I. Q., under ordinary conditions, tends to remain relatively constant throughout life, the person's score might be considered more or less typical of his particular performance level.

The advantages of the I. Q., as well as those of measures similarly derived, may be summed up as follows: (1) it was entirely objective and independent of any particular theory or subjective definition of intelligence. (2) It was quantitative, permitting intelligence to be expressed in terms of a single number. (3) It was independent of age and relatively constant, indicating the individual's typical performance level. (4) It made possible the distribution of entire populations along a single mathematical continuum ranging from idiocy (minimum performance) to genius (maximum performance). (5) It thereby made possible the definition of broad gradations of intelligence ("average," "feeble-minded,"

[11] The intelligence quotient (I. Q.) is obtained by dividing the individual's test score—which gives his mental age—by the number standing for his chronological age, and then multiplying the quotient by 100, according to the following formula:

$$\text{I. Q.} = \frac{\text{M. A.}}{\text{C. A.}} \times 100$$

"superior," etc.) in statistical terms. (6) It made possible a calculation of the distribution of intelligence (i.e., the number of people with inferior, average, and superior ability) in the general population. (7) Consequently, it became possible to compare the distribution of intelligency in any specific group—including the prisoner group—with that found in the general population. The way now seemed open for an objective comparison of the intelligence of criminals with that of the general population, thereby providing a decisive test of the relation between crime and mental ability.

THE CRITICAL PROBLEM OF THE AVERAGE ADULT MENTAL AGE. One important technical problem remained to be solved. The Binet-Simon Scale provided norms up to the age of fourteen years. How would it be possible to test adults without establishing mental-age norms for each age level of adult life? Fortunately, research proved this lengthy procedure unnecessary. The testing of samples of adults at different age levels indicated that the performance abilities tested did not increase beyond a certain age in adolescence. This age lay somewhere between fourteen and sixteen or seventeen. Since a further narrowing down would have required extensive experimentation, *the decision was made to establish the average adult mental age at sixteen years.* This decision, as will be seen, was of the greatest importance for the subsequent findings. It meant that adults, in order to attain an I. Q. of 100—the theoretical average—would have to answer the questions of the sixteen-year level.

APPLICATION TO PRISONER GROUPS. Armed with adapted versions of the original Binet-Simon scale, psychologists tested delinquent and adult prisoners all over the country. The results did not fail to confirm expectations. Findings of mental deficiency rose as high as 90 per cent in certain populations. In a study of sixteen early reports, Pintner found a median of 64 per cent feeble-minded as against 2 to 9 per cent to be expected in the general population.[12] In a similar study of reports made between 1910 and 1914, Sutherland found an average of 50 per cent diagnosed as feeble-minded.[13] Similar findings were reported among various adult prisoner populations. The evidence seemed to provide conclusive corroboration of a relationship between crime and low intelligence, and in 1921 Goddard, the author of the famous Kallikack study,

[12] R. Pintner, *Intelligence Testing: Method and Results* (New York: Henry Holt and Company, 1923).

[13] Edwin H. Sutherland, "Mental Deficiency and Crime," in *Social Attitudes,* ed. by Kimball Young (New York: Henry Holt and Company, 1931), p. 358.

asserted: "It can no longer be denied that the greatest single cause of delinquency and crime is low-grade mentality, much of it within the limits of feeble-mindedness."[14]

These conclusions were not seriously challenged until after the First World War, when the analysis of the military testing program provided the first large-scale adult comparison group. On the basis of army tests using the *mental-age* method, it was found that the true average adult mental age was 13.08—almost three years lower than the sixteen-year norms previously used.[15] Wechsler has pointed out that an application of the sixteen-year norm to the army population would have resulted in a diagnosis of 34 per cent feeble-mindedness (I. Q. below 75) for English-speaking whites. Among nonwhites and southern whites, the percentage of mental deficiency would have been almost double.[16]

The publication of the Army data stimulated a critical re-evaluation of the earlier findings. In 1925 Adler and Worthington found that the average of scores of Illinois prisoners was *higher* than those of selected samples of officers and enlisted men at the end of World War I.[17] In a similar comparison of Illinois prisoners and Illinois Army draftees, Tulchin found the distribution of intelligence scores roughly equal for matched groups of native white, foreign-born white, and Negro inmates and draftees. His findings, reproduced in Table XXI, reveal a slight but consistent difference in favor of the prisoners.

LATER FINDINGS. After the First World War the estimates of mental deficiency among intimates dropped remarkably. In a comparison of 16 prewar with 16 postwar reports, Pintner found the average estimates of feeble-mindedness to have shifted from 64 per cent to 26 per cent.[18] In his study of 350 pre- and postwar reports, Sutherland found a similar drop in estimates: from 50 per cent to 20 per cent.[19] After carefully equating the methods of various testers, Zeleny concluded that the ratio of feeble-mindedness among delinquents to feeble-mindedness in the general population was approximately 1.3 to 1.[20]

[14] Henry Goddard, *Juvenile Delinquency* (New York: Dodd, Mead and Company, 1921), p. 22.
[15] David Wechsler, *The Measurement of Adult Intelligence*, 3d ed. (Baltimore: The Williams and Wilkins Company, 1944), p. 14.
[16] *Ibid.*, p. 16.
[17] Herman M. Adler and Myrtle R. Worthington, "The Scope of the Problem of Delinquency and Crime as Related to Mental Deficiency," *Journal of Psycho-Asthenics*, 30:47–57, 1925.
[18] Pintner, *op. cit.*
[19] Sutherland, *op. cit.*, p. 358.
[20] L. D. Zeleny, "Feeble-mindedness and Criminal Conduct," *American Journal of Sociology*, 38:574, January 1933.

TABLE XXI

SCORES ON THE ARMY ALPHA INTELLIGENCE TESTS FOR PENITENTIARY
AND REFORMATORY INMATES AND MEMBERS OF THE DRAFT
FOR THE FIRST WORLD WAR (ILLINOIS, 1920–26)

	% Inferior scores (0–25)	% Average scores (26–104)	% Superior scores (105–212)	Number of cases
Native-born whites				
Illinois State Penitentiary	9.2	73.9	16.9	3,199
Illinois State Reformatory	9.5	75.2	15.3	3,646
Illinois Army Draftees	10.3	73.6	16.1	2,102
Foreign-born whites				
Illinois State Penitentiary	44.6	47.6	7.8	1,011
Illinois State Reformatory	25.3	64.6	10.1	336
Illinois Army Draftees	44.2	50.3	5.5	728
Negroes				
Illinois State Penitentiary	41.6	56.2	2.2	1,302
Illinois State Reformatory	36.8	59.9	3.3	766
Illinois Army Draftees	43.1	53.1	3.8	1,139

Source: Simon H. Tulchin, *Intelligence and Crime* (Chicago: The Chicago University Press, 1939) pp. 19–20, 24.

As the postwar evidence accumulated, an increasing number of researchers took the position that the distribution of intelligence among prisoners groups was roughly similar to that in the general population. Goddard amended his earlier genetic view and acknowledged that everyone is a potential delinquent. In a study made in 1926, Healy and Bronner had reported that feeble-mindedness occurs from five to ten times more frequently among delinquents than among the general population.[21] Ten years later, in another study, they reported:

> Reckoning it all up, it appears that the great amount of carefully conducted and intensive psychological testing resulted, quite unexpectedly, in establishing no signs of differentiation between the mental equipment of the delinquents and the controls in our series.[22]

Nevertheless, a good many studies continue to report a relatively higher distribution of dull-normal and defective intelligence among offenders, and a relatively lower distribution of above-average and superior scores. Many of these findings are based on revised versions of the

[21] William Healy and Augusta F. Bronner, *Delinquents and Criminals, Their Making and Unmaking* (New York: The Macmillan Company, 1926).
[22] William Healy and Augusta F. Bronner, *New Light on Delinquency and Its Treatment* (New Haven: Yale University Press, 1936), p. 61.

earlier tests,[23] and with respect to this, Wechsler has a significant comment:

> In view of the fact that the army data were derived from a much better statistical sample of adult population than that of the original Stanford-Binet standardization, one might have supposed that the new norms made available by them would have replaced the old ones; but this was not the case.... Such has been the wide acceptance of the Stanford-Binet norms, that in spite of the cumulative evidence as regards their inaccuracy when applied to the measurement of adult intelligence, their use for this purpose has continued without much abatement.[24]

It is also significant that reports of large-scale testing of inmates with the better-standardized Army tests continue to reveal average mental ages equal or superior to the 13.08 level found among World War I draftees. In a study of 13,454 adult male admissions to Illinois penal institutions between 1930 and 1936, Brown and Hartman found an average mental age of 13 years and 11 months.[25] In addition to their superior standardization for adults, the Army tests differed from the adaptations of the original Binet-Simon scale in a lesser emphasis on material related to education.

FACTORS AFFECTING THE DISTRIBUTION OF INTELLIGENCE SCORES AMONG PRISONERS. It is conceivable that nonintellectual factors may affect the scores received on intelligence tests. If these factors operate systematically in favor of one of the groups being compared, an accurate comparison of the two groups on the basis of intelligence alone is impossible. There is reason to believe that several of these special factors operate systematically in favor of noncriminal groups.

Motivation. It is widely acknowledged that test performance is affected by the subject's motivation and the degree of rapport with the examiner. Most offenders are tested during a period of court appearance or shortly after institutional commitment. Neither of these situations can be expected to stimulate good rapport or strong motivation.

Variations in Commitment and Admission Policies. The sample of offenders available for testing is influenced by a variety of uncontrolled selective factors. The most commonly used criteria of delinquency, for example, are court appearance and institutional commitment.

[23] Chiefly based on the Binet scale.
[24] Wechsler, *op. cit.*, p. 15.
[25] A. W. Brown and A. A. Hartman, "A Survey of the Intelligence of Illinois Prisoners," *Journal of Criminal Law and Criminology*, 28:707–719, 1938.

With respect to the former, Williams has pointed out that delinquency, so defined, "is subject to the caprice of anyone who wishes to file an information."[26] Institutional commitment policies, by administratively including or excluding certain categories of offenders, directly affect the distribution of scores in any inmate population. In this connection, Williams has cited a study in which the percentage of feeble-minded in a juvenile institution was reduced, by a changed admissions policy, from 29.9 per cent in 1918 to 2.2 per cent in 1926.[27] Localities without sufficient resources to maintain separate institutions for nondelinquent mental defectives frequently care for them in juvenile correctional institutions—a situation that automatically skews the distribution of intelligence scores.

Type of Test Materials Used. The materials used in different tests vary considerably. Test questions are of two general types: those requiring *verbal* answers, and those requiring solution by means of nonverbal *performance.* Questions requiring verbal responses depend in part on a knowledge of vocabulary—which, in turn, is dependent partly on education. Such questions are completely inappropriate for testing the intelligence of the foreign-born, and of variable appropriateness for those who are deficient in education. For this reason, the use of verbal test materials to compare the intelligence of delinquents and nondelinquents is inappropriate unless educational levels are equated.

THE RELATION OF INTELLIGENCE TO CRIME AND CONDUCT GENERALLY. The variation of anti-social behavior with intelligence would in itself, be insufficient to demonstrate a cause-and-effect relationship between the two since it could not exclude the possibility that *both* are due to the operation of other factors. Consequently, even had the early investigators succeeded in substantiating their view that crime and low intelligence are *statistically* related, it would have been necessary to demonstrate that they are *causally* related. Shulman has listed seven hypotheses that seek to explain the relation: (1) The mental defective is a "born criminal"—a "moral idiot" (Lombroso's view). (2) Feeble-mindedness is a Mendelian unit-character linked to criminality. (3) The feeble-minded are prone to crimes of violence and sex offenses—either because they lack the intelligence to satisfy their needs by more indirect means or because they cannot control their impulses. (4) The feeble-

---

[26] Harold M. Williams, "Intelligence and Delinquency," National Society for the Study of Education, Thirty-ninth Yearbook, Part I (Bloomington, Ill.: Public School Publishing Company, 1940), p. 293.

[27] *Ibid.,* pp. 292–293.

minded are unable to grasp the social values of their culture, including its definitions of right and wrong conduct. (5) The feeble-minded cannot foresee the consequences of their behavior. (6) The feeble-minded are easily led into crime and cannot be deterred by the threat of punishment. (7) Feeble-mindedness in neighborhoods where delinquent examples are common leads to delinquency (an elaboration of the preceding hypothesis).[28]

Certain of these hypotheses are variants of each other; others ascribe both criminality and mental deficiency to heredity, suggesting no other relation. The hypothesis that mental defectives are unable to control their impulses does not explain why the impulses are anti-social, unless it is to be assumed that any impulse, if uninhibited, leads to anti-social behavior. In effect, these suggested explanations boil down to two hypotheses directly related to crime: the poorer ethical discrimination of the feeble-minded and their greater susceptibility to the influence of behavioral models—including delinquent models.

Experimental efforts to test these hypotheses have generally produced negative results. Weber compared the responses of 138 female delinquents and university women on the Brogan test of moral perception and found only slight differences.[29] In a similar comparison of the responses of 517 reformatory boys and 1,000 high-school students to a conduct rating scale, Hill found negative results.[30] In an extensive survey of the research into the relationship between intellect and morality, Chassell found correlations that usually varied between 0.10 and 0.39.[31]

The methodology of these and similar verbal tests of attitudes is open to some question, however. A stated preference for certain moral values, though indicating an awareness of social expectations—and, more specifically, of the expectations of the tester—may not indicate the respondent's actual attitudes.

Offenders frequently tend to rationalize their behavior in terms of the misdeeds of others, and they often relate to correctional workers on a high level of verbal platitude. Since the need to rationalize is strengthened by the realization that other explanations and excuses are

[28] Harry M. Shulman, "Intelligence and Delinquency," *Journal of Criminal Law and Criminology*, 41:763–764, March–April, 1951.

[29] C. O. Weber, "Moral Judgment in Female Delinquents," *Journal of Applied Psychology*, 10:89–91, March, 1926.

[30] G. E. Hill, "The Ethical Knowledge of Delinquent and Non-Delinquent Boys," *Journal of Social Psychology*, 6:107–114, February, 1935.

[31] C. F. Chassell, *The Relation between Morality and Intellect* (New York: Bureau of Publications, Teachers College, Columbia University, 1935), p. 133.

unconvincing, the tendency to take strong moral positions may often be positively rather than negatively related to delinquency. In this connection, the finding that delinquent boys helped by group therapy tend to be *less* moralistic after their treatment seems suggestive.[32]

AN ALTERNATIVE HYPOTHESIS. In view of the growing doubt that offenders and nonoffenders differ appreciably in intelligence, the search for a unique relationship between criminal behavior and mental ability becomes somewhat academic. It may be that intelligence is related to illegal activities in many of the same ways it is related to lawful activities. Thus Hiller, after reviewing the evidence, writes:

> Such findings indicate that the attempts to base explanations of misconduct on intelligence levels (as measured by present methods) is futile; for although abilities affect the proficiency with which conduct of a given kind is pursued, other factors are involved in determining the way...this equipment is employed....A boy may devote first-rate abilities to leading a vicious gang, just as an adult may apply more than average capacities to a career of swindling, confidence games, forgery, or counterfeiting.[33]

The view that intelligence affects the *how* rather than the *why* of criminal behavior is more in line with modern conceptions of intelligence and motivation. To hold that intellectual factors cause crime is, in a sense, either to confuse intelligence with motivation or to suggest that criminals make up their minds to engage in crime because of very poor but nonetheless rational (i.e., intellectual) reasons. Viewed in this light, the criminal is merely a very foolish or a very careless thinker. But most modern psychologists and psychiatrists have rejected this rationalistic view of behavior; they differentiate between ability and motivation, and they consider motivation to be primarily related to emotional factors—many of which may not even be conscious. Thus, on conceptual as well as empirical grounds, the intellectual theory of criminality appears inadequate.

Crime and Personality Characteristics

Investigations into the personality characteristics of offenders necessarily reflect the difficulties and problems inherent in personality research

[32] Lloyd W. McCorkle, Albert Elias, and F. L. Bixby, *The Highfields Story* (New York: Henry Holt and Company, 1958), p. 125.

[33] E. T. Hiller, *Principles of Sociology* (New York: Harper and Brothers, 1933), p. 589.

generally. Psychologists have devoted much effort to the search for objective ways of defining, describing, and measuring personality. At each successive phase of this effort—definition, description, and measurement —the difficulties increase because of unresolved problems in the preceding phase. Thus, for example, a study that attempts to measure the trait or factor "honesty" yields a collection of responses to a series of questions. These responses are scored by means of a numerical scale, which assigns a higher rating to the more "honest" responses and a lower —or negative—rating to the "dishonest" answers. The final result is an *honesty score*. At this point the question arises: What does this score represent—other than a numerical description of the responses? If the answer to this question is that the score describes the trait called honesty, or its weight in the personality, several other questions arise: How is a trait defined? Is it a structure? Is it a force? Or is it merely a social evaluation of behavior by an onlooker? And how can it be related consistently to concrete activities?

The difficulties involved in trying to find objective behavior correlates of traits is illustrated in *Studies in Deceit*, by Hartshorne and May.[34] These investigators sought to discover whether or not *trait descriptions* such as honesty were appropriate to the behavior of school children. If honesty—or deceitfulness—were relatively stable structures or forces within the personality, their presence should be indicated by relatively consistent behavior in appropriate situations. But this was not generally the finding. It might be found, for example, that a child who cheated in one classroom would cheat in another; but this same child might be scrupulously honest in athletics, games at parties, and other situations. A child who stole, they found, might be unwilling to cheat on examinations. In view of these behavioral inconsistencies, Hartshorne and May concluded that trait descriptions were inappropriate to these responses and that "the secret of (the child's) performance lies in the specific experiences which have brought satisfaction and disappointment to him in the course of his short career."[35] However the inconsistencies may be explained, the evidence clearly indicated the inadequacy of the trait concept for dealing with the variability of human behavior.

The theoretical problems raised by this and many other representa-

[34] H. Hartshorne and M. A. May, *Studies in Deceit* (New York: The Macmillan Company, 1929).

[35] H. Hartshorne, M. A. May, and F. K. Shuttleworth, *Studies in the Organization of Character* (New York: The Macmillan Company, 1930), p. 374.

tive examples of variation in behavior have not been solved by trait psychologies or by any diagnostic approach that purports to account for this variability by means of a relatively few fixed "dynamisms," "mechanisms of adjustment," "drives," etc. Nevertheless, most personality studies of offenders have used one or more of these approaches.

THE PROBLEM OF DEFINITION. One of the difficulties with the concept *personality* is that it is unmanageably vague unless defined. However, when it is more specifically defined, there are apparently equally pertinent definitions that differ from each other. Personality may be defined as a response, but it may also be defined as a stimulus—as the effect a person has on another. Many trait names—Allport has counted over 4,000—are actually adjectival descriptions of the perceptions of others. Thus John is "uncooperative" with Mary—but quite "cooperative" with Jane. Which is John's *real* trait—which is the mask and which the substance? After an intensive survey of various definitions of personality, Allport proposed the following: *"Personality is the dynamic organization within the individual of those psychophysical systems which determine his unique adjustments to his environment."* [36] Boiled down to its communicative essentials, this definition asserts that personality is something inside the individual that makes him—and his behavior—recognizably individual. This serves only to define the problem, not the concept. In another definition, Cattell moves further away from a substantive description and closer toward the methodological dilemma. For Cattell, *"Personality is that which permits a prediction of what a person will do in a given situation."* [37] At this point Cattell, going one step further than Allport, is defining the psychologist's problem of definition.

PROBLEMS OF DESCRIPTION AND MEASUREMENT. The problems involved in describing and measuring traits or personality factors derive from the difficulties of relating these factors to behavior. The difficulties of description are apparent in the attempt to answer the question: What do you point to when you are indicating a trait? As Cattell implies, this question should be referred back to the questioner. Personality is something that helps one make predictions; it is not necessarily a thing that can be directly seen or touched, but a *symbolic construct,* an organization of concepts about processes.

Personality, in this sense, is something that enables individuals to

---

[36] Gordon W. Allport, *Personality, A Psychological Interpretation* (New York: Henry Holt and Company, 1937), p. 48.

[37] Raymond B. Cattell, *Personality* (New York: McGraw-Hill Book Company, 1950), p. 2.

recognize and describe the uniqueness of others—and to predict their more or less characteristic behavior. Accordingly, those concepts or symbolic constructs which enable people to do this more efficiently are the more desirable; those which do not, should be rejected. A principal contribution of Cattell's definition is its implication that all personality concepts should be measured against the harsh, objective criterion of efficiency and adequacy. When trait descriptions of personality are evaluated against this criterion, their inadequacy becomes apparent.

The objective of the trait approach to personality is to obtain a more or less consistent and relatively stable and constant picture of the inner structure or internal mental functioning of the individual in order to explain and predict his behavior. But behavior varies markedly from situation to situation, from problem to problem, from role to role. Moreover, this ability to vary behavior appropriately is one of the principal resources of the human animal and one of the universal symptoms of a healthy adjustment. An individual who could not adjust to a changing reality could not survive. The major difficulty with the trait approach to behavior is the powerlessness of static constructs to anticipate the necessary and complex variability of human response.

The problem may be clarified by reference to readily available examples. The behavior of criminals both before and after they are imprisoned readily lends itself to such adjectival descriptions as *dishonest, conniving, anti-social.* To the ordinary citizen—the victim of the criminal—these descriptions may seem appropriate not only to the behavior but to the "essential" personality or character of the criminal—and the reasonable suspicion arises that he is "like this" in everything he does. There may conceivably be people who are wholly dishonest, conniving, and anti-social, but it is doubtful whether they would long survive in any world—including the criminal world. A criminal who invariably cheated his partners, constantly maneuvered them to their disadvantage, and in addition, was constantly hostile to them would not be likely to create problems for the courts. He would be much more likely to create a problem for the harbor police when—and if—his body floated ashore.

Shuessler and Cressey have exhaustively surveyed the researches in personality-testing of criminals conducted since 1925. Apart from their criticisms of the methods employed by these studies, they reached the following conclusions concerning the relevance of the data for problems of crime causation and criminal typology:

3. The results of this method do not indicate whether criminal

behavior is the result of a certain personality trait or whether the trait is the result of criminal experiences....

*   *   *

5. The results of these studies cannot be grouped together for the purpose of establishing generalizations about criminal behavior and personality, because they are not equally valid. Few experiments were designed in such a way that comparisons could be drawn between criminals and non-criminals similar in regard to age, intelligence and cultural background. In many studies control groups were not used at all, but, rather, the average score for the experimental group [i.e., the criminal group] was compared with a test norm....

6. Most studies proceeded as if the criminal population is homogeneous, since they grouped all types of offenders together. Future studies of this type should at least classify individuals by type of offense in order to determine whether differences between different classes of offenders exist.[38]

The Social-Psychological Approach to Crime

The behavior of the criminal, baffling when subjected to trait analysis, becomes intelligible when it is related to his *roles* vis-à-vis the ordinary citizen (his victim), the prison officials (his confiners), and the total situation in which the three are integrated. With respect to his victim, it is essential for the criminal to behave in a dishonest and conniving way—and to have attitudes appropriate to this behavior. With respect to the prison officials, similar behavior and attitudes may be appropriate, because of a basic similarity in roles. With respect to his criminal associates, however, a different set of roles and objectives and a different situation defines and mediates a different range of responses. Carrying the analysis further, a particular criminal may be involved in a variety of other primary relationships: he may be married or have a sweetheart; he may have parents. Toward each of these figures he will behave in ways related to his—and to their definition of mutual roles.

A theoretical framework for the analysis of personality and behavior in terms of self-other definitions and roles was developed over fifty years ago by the social psychologists. The concepts developed by these theorists, which are considered particularly valuable for purposes of theoretical integration, are discussed in Chapter 14.

[38] Karl F. Schuessler and Donald R. Cressey, "Personality Characteristics of Criminals," *American Journal of Sociology*, 55:483–484, March 1950. Copyright 1950 by the University of Chicago.

The attempt of psychological theorists was to relate crime to personality traits or types of psychological problems. In each theory the explanation proceeded more or less directly from a type of person or problem to criminality or a form of crime. To date, however, these attempts have failed to isolate a single psychological factor not found among noncriminals as well.

This negative evidence suggests a different explanation of the relation between psychological variables and criminality. It may well be that psychological factors do not ordinarily determine *whether* a person becomes a criminal but rather *how he functions* as a criminal. Consider, for example, a collection of barbers and shoemakers. Some are pleasant, and prudent; others are aggressive and stupid; still others, passive and dependent—but all are barbers and shoemakers. Similarly, there are skillful thieves, foolish thieves, amiable thieves, etc.

Attempts to relate crime directly to various kinds of psychological motives suggest a similar conclusion. Just as the evidence fails to warrant a restriction of criminality to a limited number of personality types, so also does it fail to justify a limitation of the kinds of motives associated with criminal acts. Reasons for committing crimes may be almost infinitely variable. Just as there are sick criminals, healthy criminals, intelligent and moronic criminals, so also there are sick reasons, healthy reasons, and stupid reasons for engaging in crimes—and sick, healthy, intelligent, and stupid ways of carrying out criminal acts. Thus, for example, a psychotic person may rob a bank in order to raise money for a paranoid objective. However, he may *execute* the robbery with the smoothest efficiency, turning out a thoroughly workmanlike job. On the other hand, a highly intelligent and well-adjusted person may decide to rob a bank for the purpose of obtaining funds to support a worthy political cause. (During the Nazi occupation of Europe there were many bank robberies carried out by members of the Resistance.) In carrying out the task, however, the otherwise well-adjusted but inexperienced bank robber may be nervous and careless, and bungle the job. In one case, a madman turned out a well-executed piece of work; his efficiency was not impaired by his madness. In the other case, a healthy individual worked himself up into a bad state of nerves and turned out a poor job; his performance was not salvaged by his general mental soundness. Clearly, the blanket descriptions "healthy" and "unhealthy" have no relevance here.

Sociological Theories of Crime

SOCIOLOGISTS HAVE APPROACHED THE PROBLEM OF CRIME FROM TWO distinct vantage points. The first approach viewed crime as a social phenomenon related to other social phenomena. Sociologists inquired: How is crime, viewed broadly, related to social structures and institutions? What is its place in the social system? More fundamentally, how does crime arise in the first place—and what does its existence imply about the functioning of the social order?

The second approach attempted to explain how individuals acquired criminal behavior patterns. How are these patterns learned, how are they transmitted—and why do they vary? Thus, where the first approach raised the question: *How does crime come about—how does society acquire crime?* the second approach asked: *How does the individual acquire criminality—how does the person become a criminal?*

Though it was possible to deal with the first order of questions in more or less traditional sociological terms, the second raised serious difficulties. It involved sociologists in the task of translating broad, relatively abstract concepts into variables that could be meaningful on the level of individual motivation. How do factors such as "culture conflict" and "social disorganization" get into the heads of people and determine their behavior? Furthermore, how can sociologists describe these processes without dealing with variables traditionally in the domain of psychology?

The contributions of sociologists to the clarification of these questions have been so rich and so diverse that it is difficult to present them in any systematic fashion. Accordingly, for purposes of greater clarity, the discussion has been divided into two broad sections: the first presenting theories relating crime to the social structure; the second, theories concerning the criminalization of individuals. In following this outline, it has been necessary to present the various theories in their logical rather than chronological relation to one another.

Theories Relating Crime to the Social Structure

How does crime arise in any given society? What does its existence signify? Does crime indicate that the society is to some extent sick or malfunctioning? How are the goals and activities of criminals related to those of noncriminals—are they essentially parallel or different? Are criminals and their actions relatively "normal" or relatively "abnormal" in relation to their culture of origin? It is with these and with related questions that the following contributions deal.

The Contribution of Emile Durkheim (1858–1917)

In the brief treatise in which he attempted to formulate the "basic rules" of sociological method, Durkheim found occasion for several highly pertinent references to crime and the social order. These references, made chiefly as asides or illustrations of a point, were little more than sparks from an anvil on which Durkheim was forging something else; nevertheless, they touch on a surprisingly wide range of issues critical to modern criminological theory.

Durkheim wrote at a time when criminological theory was absorbing the new doctrines of the positivists. The positivists had defined the criminal as an anthropological deviant, and in so doing had suggested answers for some of the most fundamental sociological problems of crime by the direct expedient of doing away with the questions. If the criminal is the product of a defective biological organization, he cannot simultaneously be a product of his culture—except insofar as the culture tolerates the reproduction of misfits. In causal terms, however, the question of the criminal's relation to society does not arise; and the explanation of the existence of crime can be viewed as contained within any theory that explains the existence of the criminal. In effect, the positivists were asserting that crime exists because criminals exist—an assertion carrying with it the corollary that crime will be abolished when criminals are no more. It was against these views and their implications that Durkheim leveled his critical fire.

DURKHEIM'S DEFINITION OF CRIME AND THE FIELD OF CRIMINOLOGY. Durkheim's explicit definition of crime occurs, significantly, as an illustration of a point he is making about the importance of clear definitions ("since a theory . . . can be checked only if we know how to recognize the facts of which it is intended to give an account.") A social fact is to be defined in terms of its essential external characteristics ("our only clue to reality"), and not according to an intellectual ideal. The essential external characteristic of those acts called *crimes* is that they evoke punishment; "hence we call every punished act a crime, and crime thus defined becomes the object of a special science, criminology."[1]

In subsequent passages Durkheim sharpens his definition by contrasting it with others. He takes Garofalo (a leading positivist) to task for restricting the definition of crime to acts that violate "universal moral feelings," and insists that Garofalo's elimination of other punished acts is entirely subjective.[2] Pointing out that the moral feelings that are universal today may not have been universal yesterday—and may not be tomorrow—Durkheim hews to punishment as the sole reliable external characteristic of crime. By this he does not mean that punishment is the "essence" of crime; it is not the function of definitions to get at the essence of reality; their "sole function . . . is to establish contact with things; and since the latter can be grasped . . . only from its exterior qualities, the definition expresses them in terms of their external qualities."[3]

At another point Durkheim makes it clear that it is the *social reaction to the act*, rather than the act itself, which determines its character as criminal. Thus: "What confers this [criminal] character . . . is not the intrinsic quality of a given act but rather *that definition which the collective conscience lends it*."[4]

[1] Emile Durkheim, *The Rules of Sociological Method* (Glencoe, Ill.: The Free Press, 1938), pp. 34–36.
[2] *Ibid.*, p. 39.
[3] *Ibid.*, p. 42.
[4] *Ibid.*, p. 70.

THE MEANING AND FUNCTION OF CRIME IN THE SOCIAL ORDER. Having defined crime, Durkheim next considers its significance for the social order. He is concerned, at one point, with distinguishing what is normal in society from what is pathological. Rejecting any absolute definition, he asserts that normality is always relative to a given social organization. Normality defines what is ordinary and typical in a given social framework—what is "normal" for one may well be pathological for another. Moreover, certain social conditions may be quite "morbid" and undesirable without being abnormal. Pain, the infirmity of age, death itself—these are "morbid" but nevertheless quite normal. Certain of these conditions—pain, for example—are not only normal but have a definite function. Others do not; Durkheim shows how conditions that are maladaptive may still persist as normal in a culture long after their usefulness has passed; he points out that there are more "relics" in society than in biology. How does crime stand in this contest?

Durkheim acknowledges that all criminologists view crime as pathological. But he doubts the correctness of this view:

> Crime is present... in all societies of all types. Its form changes; the acts thus characterized are not the same everywhere; but, everywhere and always, there have been men who have behaved in such a way as to draw upon themselves penal repression. If, in proportion as societies pass from the lower to the higher types, the rate of criminality... tended to decline, it might be believed that crime, while still normal, is tending to lose this character of normality. [Actually] it has everywhere increased.... There is, then, no phenomenon that presents more indisputably all the symptoms of normality, since it appears closely connected with the conditions of all collective life.[5]

Crime is not only normal but inevitable; without it, society as we know it would be inconceivable—and not quite desirable. Unless social norms become rigid and so all-pervading that personal individuality is lost, there will be violations of norms. *Crime is an inevitable consequence of social complexity and individual freedom; it is one of the prices paid for freedom.* More than this, it is one of the ways in which individuality expresses itself. If the collective sentiments at the basis of morality were too strong, there could be no change—and, hence, no progress or moral evolution. "Nothing," writes Durkheim, "is good indefinitely":[6]

[5] *Ibid.*, pp. 65–66.
[6] Cf. Tennyson:

> The old order changeth, yielding place to new,
> And God fulfills Himself in many ways
> Lest one good custom should corrupt the world.
> —*Morte d'Arthur*

... To make progress, individual originality must be able to express itself. In order that the originality of the idealist whose dreams transcend his century may find expression, it is necessary that the originality of the criminal, who is below the level of his time, shall also be possible. One does not occur without the other.[7]

Crime, then, is one expression—usually an undesirable expression—of a tendency that is supremely desirable in society. It is not only the price of freedom but the price of social changes which freedom makes possible and which new conditions make absolutely essential. Moreover, while acknowledging the importance of combating crime, Durkheim suspects that even in its most noxious forms, crime serves some useful social function. Its very persistence suggests aspects of personal and collective utility hitherto unsuspected. In terms that anticipate very recent conceptions of individual delinquency as a possible alternative to neurosis, Durkheim raises the question: How could these processes have maintained themselves "if they had not enabled the individual better to resist the elements of destruction?"[8]

> Contrary to current ideas, the criminal no longer seems a totally unsociable human being, a sort of parasitic element, a strange and unassimilable body introduced into the midst of society.[9]

Nevertheless, with characteristic precision, Durkheim is careful not to deny the possibility of abnormal individuals committing essentially normal criminal acts. He recognizes that the issues of crime and personal pathology involve two different questions—a distinction missed by many modern writers, who unhesitatingly infer the abnormality of the act from the abnormality of the actor. Actually, neither condition necessarily implies the other. In occupations where cheating and misrepresentation have become routine, the neurotic cheater is functioning in no less a normal manner because he happens to be neurotic. The pathological criminal is a criminal still—there are many other ways to express the symptoms of disease than in crime. And there are many forms of crime, some of which are undoubtedly pathological—but this must be shown through analysis of the act as well as the actor. In order to understand the various kinds of crime, one must first clearly describe the different situations under which they arise:

> In order to classify the different kinds of crimes, one has to try to reconstruct the ways of living and the occupational customs that are practiced

[7] Durkheim, *op. cit.*, p. 71.
[8] *Ibid.*, p. 58.
[9] *Ibid.*, p. 72.

in the different worlds of crime. One will then recognize as many criminological types as there are different forms of this organization.[10]

The conception of crime as normal and functional is unique with Durkheim. It may be counted among the outstanding—and perhaps the most significant—contributions of sociology to the study of crime. Nevertheless, as the following discussion will demonstrate, it is a concept that has fallen considerably short of wide acceptance among modern criminologists concerned with the problem of crime.

Theories of Crime as Social Pathology

Durkheim's conception of crime as a normal product of social standards and values must be contrasted with more recent conceptions of crime as an expression of social disorganization. According to this view, the criminal is responding to values that are outside the major norm systems of his society, or in conflict with them.

In order to explain how it is possible for a person brought up within a single culture to be responding to values external or extrinsic to it, it is first necessary to explain where these values originated and how they became critical parts of the individual's social awareness. To account for this, sociologists have cited the commonly observed phenomenon that in all complex societies there arise value systems that are mutually contradictory or inconsistent. This phenomenon is sometimes viewed as a product of social disorganization; sometimes the terms are used synonymously. This phenomenon, which might also be called "norm-conflict," has been of considerable interest to criminologists.

CRIME AS A RESULT OF CULTURE CONFLICT. The sociologist Thorsten Sellin has presented a systematic exposition of the culture-conflict theory of crime. Rejecting a legalistic definition of the criminal, Sellin argues that the major difference between the criminal and the non-criminal is that they are responding to different conduct-norms. Sellin defines the conduct-norm in the following terms:

> For every person...there is from the point of view of a given group of which he is a member; a normal (right) and an abnormal (wrong) way of reacting, the norm depending upon the social values of the group which formulated it.[11]

* * *

[10] *Ibid.*, p. 46.
[11] Thorsten Sellin, *Culture Conflict and Crime* (New York: The Social Science Research Council, Bulletin No. 41, 1938), p. 30.

A conduct-norm in its irreducible form ... is a rule which prohibits, and conversely enjoins, a specific type of person, as defined by his status in (or with reference to) the normative group, from acting in a certain specified way in certain circumstances.[12]

Conflict between conduct-norms, says Sellin, results from a more fundamental process, which may be called *culture conflict*. Sellin identifies two forms of culture conflict: primary and secondary. *Primary culture conflict* results when the norms and value systems of different cultures clash—as in the case of immigrants who, in their new country, continue to observe the customs of their country of origin. In this connection, Sellin cites the case of a Sicilian father who killed the sixteen-year-old seducer of his daughter in New Jersey and was shocked to learn that he had committed a crime.[13] *Secondary culture conflicts*, on the other hand, "grow out of the process of social differentiation which characterize the evolution of our own culture."[14]

Since the great majority of crimes are committed by the native-born, it is the secondary type of culture conflict which must be viewed as the dominant social cause of crime. Sellin's account of the origin of secondary culture conflict is central to his explanation of crime:

> ... Culture conflicts are the natural outgrowth of processes of social differentiation, which produce an infinity of social groupings, each with its own definitions of life situations, its own interpretations of social relations, its own ignorance or misunderstanding of the social values of other groups. The transformation of a culture from a homogeneous and well-integrated type to a heterogeneous and disintegrated type is therefore accompanied by an increase of conflict situations.[15]

The fundamental differences between Durkheim's position and the culture-conflict theory are clearly indicated in the foregoing quotation from Sellin. The heart of these differences lies in two related assumptions made by proponents of the culture-conflict theory:

1. The assumption that criminals are responding to norms and values at variance with those of the general culture.

2. The assumption that criminals derive from groups who are more or less culturally isolated.

Taken together, these assumptions add up to the conclusion that crime is the product of value systems fundamentally at odds with those of culture at large.

[12] *Ibid.*, pp. 32–33.
[13] *Ibid.*, p. 68.
[14] *Ibid.*, p. 105.
[15] *Ibid.*, p. 66.

Despite its internal consistency, the culture-conflict theory labors under two difficulties. The first of these derives from a failure to distinguish between the idea of values as means or techniques and the idea of values as goals or ends. Are criminals and other deviant groups actually pursuing different goals by means of different techniques? When Sellin speaks of *norms* as defining right and wrong ways of doing things, he seems to be referring to differences in means or techniques, and to leave the question of goals or ends open. At another point he speaks of a norm as "dependent on the social values of the group which formulated it." This definition carries the implication that differences in means derive from differences in ends.[16] This interpretation is strengthened when he speaks of "an infinity of social groupings, each with its own definitions of social situations . . . its own ignorance or misunderstanding of the social values of other groups."

A second major difficulty of the culture-conflict position derives from the first. The assumption that the conflict between criminals and noncriminals arises from different values and goals neglects the possibility that conflict may arise between individuals and groups who are pursuing the same goals—and who may even be using essentially similar techniques. When ten individuals are engaged in running a race which only one can win, there is an obvious conflict among them though each is pursuing an identical goal with identical means. What is involved in the competition between the runners is not a conflict of ends or techniques but a *conflict of interests,* arising from the fact that the number of goals is less than the number of contestants.

Many similar conflicts of interest may arise in a society where large numbers of people compete to achieve the same goals. Moreover, it is precisely because the values and goals are similar that the conflict arises in the first place. If the different competitors were each pursuing a different goal, there would be no danger that some would deprive others —and no conflict would arise.

[16] In *Social Theory and Social Structure* (Glencoe, Ill.: The Free Press, 1949), the sociologist Robert Merton has stressed the importance of differentiating cultural goals from institutional norms:

> To say . . . that cultural goals and institutional norms operate jointly to shape prevailing practices is not to say that they bear a constant relationship to each other. The cultural emphasis placed upon certain goals varies independently of the degree of emphasis placed upon institutionalized means. . . . [In a society] with such differential emphases upon goals and institutionalized procedures, the latter may be so vitiated by the stress on goals as to have the behavior of many individuals limited only by considerations of technical expediency. In this context, the sole significant question becomes: Which of the available procedures is most efficient in netting the culturally approved value? (pp. 127–128).

This analysis may also be applied to the conflict between the criminal and the noncriminal. Both the thief and the merchant are engaged in the pursuit of money—an object which both value for similar reasons. The conflict between them arises from the fact that the thief, in pursuing his occupation, threatens to deprive the merchant—not of a *different* goal, but of an *identical* one. To test this analysis we may raise the question: What if all thieves were engaged in stealing objects of no value? Would any conflict arise? This question is critical because it poses the further question: In objecting to the activities of thieves, is society merely objecting to a certain technique of obtaining objects— or is it objecting because this technique deprives others of objects of value?

These considerations and the unanswered questions they raise point up the major difficulties of the culture-conflict theory of crime. They suggest that, in construing the conflict between the criminal and the noncriminal as lying in the realm of ultimate cultural values, the proponents of the culture-conflict theory may have mistaken a conflict of interests for a conflict of basic principles. The fact that society at large rationalizes its opposition to crime in terms of moral principles tends to foster this confusion. Nevertheless, the widespread existence of white-collar crime and other forms of deception and corruption in the general culture serves to weaken the validity of these rationalizations as a true basis of differentiation. In the end, the actual differences between the shrewd business operator and the thief may have less to do with actual differences in procedure and more with differential patterns of social tolerance and indignation—patterns that enable the shrewd manipulator to move through the mine fields of social defense without setting off explosions. These considerations give point to Durkheim's refusal to define crime in any way substantially differentiating it from other forms of behavior; and they underscore his insistence that the essential characteristic of crimes is that they evoke punishment.

The contemporary sociologist Donald Taft has presented a systematic restatement of Durkheim's original position; two brief quotations from Taft will serve to summarize it in a manner that emphasizes the contrast between the two schools of thought:

> The criminal underworld gang is dependent upon the normal upperworld, and some of its values reflect those approved in normal social groups.... Our argument has thus repeatedly suggested that unusual criminal behavior is not unrelated to typical characteristics of the American scene generally. We find crime to be one form of human exploita-

tion, largely resulting from other forms of exploitation not defined as crime.[17]

*　　*　　*

Given a culture dynamic, complex, materialistic, admiring the successful in competitive struggles but permitting many to fall short of success, relative failures will collect in its slums and there develop patterns of behavior hostile to the interests of the general community, but in harmony with the community's basic ideals.[18]

The Contribution of the Ecologists

We turn now to a group of sociologists whose innovations in the field of method have tended to obscure the magnitude of their contribution to theory.[19] In a discussion that distinguishes between theories relating crime to society and theories of the criminalization process, their contribution is difficult to classify—for the significant reason that they were able to relate these two theoretical problems in a logically consistent manner, without obscuring the distinction between them.

The ecologists viewed crime as a more or less normal and inevitable by-product of social change. In the course of social change there occur sharp discontinuities in the physical and interpersonal modes of life— discontinuities unevenly operating in space and, for this reason, unevenly and unequally affecting people at different times and places. Having

[17] Donald R. Taft, *Criminology* (New York: The Macmillan Company, 1950), p. 266.

[18] *Ibid.*, p. 239.

[19] The contributions of the ecologists to sociology in general and to criminology in particular have been far-reaching. Though originally interested chiefly in the distribution of groups, artifacts, and institutions in space, they subsequently became concerned with the processes which relate structure to function and to the dynamics of social change. Their descriptions of the operations underlying human interactions were among the earliest specifications of the idea of process in social theory, and they provided the field with such distinctively sociological concepts as mobility, segregation, centralization, accommodation, and competition. Their contributions to criminology included significant innovations of theory, method, and treatment. The area studies of crime discussed in this chapter represent probably the earliest objective and quantified research in the diffusion of behavior patterns as a function of social milieu. Burgess' suggestion that the delinquent peer group provides a natural basis for the understanding and the treatment of individual delinquents antedates the use of group therapy by two decades (see Ernest W. Burgess, "The Individual Delinquent as a Person," *American Journal of Sociology*, 28:657–680, May 1923). The genesis of modern attempts to modify delinquent patterns by dealing directly with juvenile groups in their natural ecological setting may be traced to similar early researches of the ecologists.

established this fact by means of an impressive array of empirical evidence, the ecologists then went on to investigate how people learned ways of behavior that were appropriate to their immediate milieu but inappropriate to a set of sociological norms that were fixed as standards for the society as a whole. In their theory of criminalization, which was largely implicit because of a marked empirical bent, they attempted to explain how individuals, in the normal process of appropriately responding to their environment, revealed on an interpersonal level the strains of discontinuity affecting the community at large.

VARYING CONCEPTS OF ECOLOGY. The sociologist R. D. McKenzie has defined human ecology as the study which deals

> ... with the spatial aspects of the symbiotic [i.e., mutually dependent] relations of human beings and institutions. It aims to discover the principles and factors involved in the changing patterns of spatial arrangements of populations and institutions resulting from the interplay of human beings in a continuously changing culture.[20]

In their survey of theories of human ecology, Llewellyn and Hawthorne point out that certain writers regard ecological factors as distinct from cultural factors, while others speak of ecology in terms of the spatial distribution of cultural phenomena. Once made, this distinction can be crucial. In the former sense the concept suggests that ecological factors determine cultural relations and behavior; in the latter sense it is suggested that cultural factors determine the ecological framework within which behavior occurs. None of the writers of the first school deny the importance of the cultural factor within society, but, as Llewellyn and Hawthorne point out, "they generally assume that human society is organized on two levels, the biotic [read "ecologic"] and the cultural, with the cultural resting upon the biotic, which is basic."[21]

Occasionally the same writers use the concept in both senses. Thrasher (citing Robert Park), for example, compares the physical living arrangements of a pueblo in New Mexico with those of a neighborhood gang of delinquents in order to show how "the size, the character of membership and even the solidarity are sometimes determined for a group by the nature of its physical surroundings."[22] In the Indian village each

---

[20] R. D. McKenzie, cited by Emma Llewellyn and Audrey Hawthorne in George Gurvitch and Wilbert E. Moore, *Twentieth Century Sociology* (New York: The Philosophical Library, 1945), p. 468.

[21] *Ibid.*, p. 469.

[22] Frederick Thrasher, *The Gang*, 2d ed. (Chicago: The University of Chicago Press, 1936), p. 325.

family compartment faced the common meeting place. "This form of living," writes Thrasher, "was enough to insure solidarity and loyalty to traditional ways of doing. (However) when the young men got their separate shacks on the prairie, the old communal unity was broken up." [23] Thrasher sees similar factors operating to influence the organization of delinquent groups, where "boys living in a restricted or cut off area tend to form a play-group or a gang set off from their neighbors." [24] Nevertheless, at an earlier point in his discussion Thrasher speaks of "two-and-three boy relationships," "intimacy," and "palships," and asserts: "It is relations of this sort, existing before the gang develops, that serve as primary structures when the group is first formed and that shape the growth of its future organization." [25]

The ecological concept is similarly used in both senses by Shaw, in dealing with the same problem of neighborhood gangs. At one point he seems to view delinquency as the more or less inevitable result of certain consequences of city growth and expansion. Such factors as poor housing, overcrowding, low living standards, and social and racial conflict are viewed as symptoms that "reflect a type of community life" rather than as direct contributors. Shaw writes: "Even the disorganized family and the delinquent gang, which are often thought of as the main factors in delinquency, probably reflect community situations." [26] But at another point Shaw writes: "Behavior of a delinquent may be in part a reflection of family conflict which drives him into a gang.... The delinquent gang may reflect a disorganized community life or a community whose life is organized around delinquent patterns.... The point is," continues Shaw, "that . . . behavior of persons becomes intelligible when studied in terms of the social situation in which it has occurred." [27]

MILIEU STUDIES OF CRIME. Except for certain general purposes, a person does not *live* in a geographical or a national region—or even in a large city. The area in which he functions—in which he does things, in which things happen to him—may be much smaller: it may be limited to his neighborhood; for certain withdrawn, seclusive individuals, it

---

[23] *Ibid.*, p. 326.

[24] *Ibid.*

[25] *Ibid.*, p. 322.

[26] Clifford R. Shaw, Frederick M. Zorbaugh, Henry D. McKay, and Leonard S. Cottrell, *Delinquency Areas* (Chicago: The University of Chicago Press, 1929), pp. 204–205.

[27] *Ibid.*, p. 9.

may be no larger than a single house or apartment. For all practical purposes, an individual's effective environment—*his milieu*—may be defined as the area within which significant things happen to him. Conditions within this area which *do not* affect him, or do not make any particular difference in his behavior, can, for all practical purposes, be considered outside his milieu, even though they may be close by—as close, say, as the neighborhood recreation center is to a gang of delinquents who never go inside it. Conversely, conditions or events entering this area from without and decisively affecting him can be considered *within* his milieu, even though they may have originated at distant points.

The development of the complex idea of milieu from an essentially geographical concept of ecology was the achievement of a group of sociologists known collectively as the "Chicago School," which included such pioneers as Park, Burgess, and McKenzie. This process of theoretical refinement occurred in progressive stages, starting with a relatively literal analogy between plant and human communities and eventually coming to include complex psychological and sociological variables.

Taking his basic premises from Darwin, Park noted that humans, like plants and animals, are continuously involved in a competitive struggle for the necessities of life. This struggle is expressed—and reflected—in a competition for space and ecological advantages. If this is the case, the signs of this human struggle should be evident in man's living areas—much in the same way that a struggle between competing species of plants leaves signs in patterns of vegetation on the earth. The most intensive concentration of human competitors is the city. By a careful examination of urban communities it might be possible to read the telltale marks of the human struggle in the different zones and neighborhoods in which people live.

This examination was undertaken by Burgess, and resulted in his theory of the "radial expansion" of cities. Burgess found that the city of Chicago—built in a rough semicircle along the shores of Lake Michigan—exhibited five relatively clearly demarcated zones radially distributed around the Loop; (1) a central business district, "at once the retail, financial, recreational, civic and political center," (2) an interstitial zone-in-transition, "in the throes of the change from residence to business and industry"; (3) a zone of workingmen's homes, whose inhabitants "are constantly being recruited from those making their escape from the zone of transition, but at the same time . . . being depleted by those . . . seeking more desirable residence in the zone beyond"; (4) a better residential zone, "inhabited chiefly by . . . persons engaged in professional and clerical pursuits, and who have had high school if not college education"; and (5) a commuters' zone, inhabited by the more well-to-do.[28] As the city grows, those residential neighborhoods around the expanding industrial and business center undergo a destructive invasion and progressively deteriorate. Burgess found that the decline of neighborhoods occurred in stages:

> First, the stage of residential home ownership, with a high degree of community spirit; second, the stage of tenancy, with a decline of neighborhood loyalty; third, the invasion of business; fourth, rooming-house stage; fifth, entrance of a racial or nationality group of imputed inferior cultural status; sixth, the intrusion of crime and vice; seventh, the stage of social chaos; and eighth, the final stage, when business or industry takes full possession of the area. This is the general cycle of the life-history of the neighborhood. There are, of course, certain variations in this pattern, as when a residential area of single homes is transformed into an apartment house or residential hotel area.[29]

In his theoretical description of the natural growth pattern of the city, Burgess had pinpointed the zone in transition, the *interstitial area*, as the casualty of the dynamic growth process; it was here that those who had been defeated and displaced in the competitive struggle would find themselves segregated and trapped; it was here, accordingly, that vice and crime might be expected to abound.

This expectation was confirmed by a brilliant series of investigations undertaken by Burgess' students. Between 1921 and 1929 Clifford Shaw, joined later by Frederick Zorbaugh, Henry McKay, and Leonard Cottrell, analyzed the distribution of truancy, juvenile delinquency, and adult crime in the city of Chicago. Their findings, published in 1929, revealed a gradient of crime and delinquency radiating outward from the center of the city according to the pattern predicted by Burgess.[30]

Shaw and his collaborators drew six major conclusions from their findings: (1) There were marked variations in the rate of truancy,

[28] Ernest W. Burgess, "Social Forces in the Community Making for Mobility," *Proceedings of the Minnesota State Conference and Institute of Social Work,* 1927, pp. 116–118.

[29] Ernest W. Burgess, "The Natural Area as the Unit for Social Work in the Large City," *Proceedings of the National Conference of Social Work,* 1926, p. 509.

[30] Shaw et al., *op. cit.*

delinquency, and adult crime in different areas. (2) These rates tended to vary inversely according to distance from the center of the city: those nearest the center had the highest rates; those furthest from the center, the lowest. (3) Areas with high rates of truancy tended to show similarly high rates for delinquency and adult crime. (4) The highest rates were found in areas characterized by physical deterioration and declining population—a finding directly supporting the hypothesis of Burgess. (5) The areas in which the higher rates were found had been characterized by high rates for a long period—at least thirty years—despite marked changes in the composition of the population. (6) Rates of recidivism and rates of repeated court appearance varied directly with delinquency rates—a fact indicating that delinquents from high-rate areas were more likely to become recidivists than those from areas with less delinquency.[31] Since the appearance of *Delinquency Areas* in 1929, the conclusions reached by Shaw and his collaborators have been confirmed by similar investigations in at least fifteen cities.

From a theoretical point of view, one of the most provocative of these findings was that "high-rate" neighborhoods tended to retain their delinquent character despite wholesale changes in the national and racial composition of their inhabitants over the years. Apparently it made little difference whether the neighborhood was occupied primarily by Italians, Syrians, Poles, Negroes, or Puerto Ricans—after a roughly equivalent period of exposure, a roughly equivalent toll was taken of each. Other investigators have reported similar findings. In her study of Moloccan settlement in Los Angeles, Pauline Young found that the original juvenile delinquency rate of 5 per cent had risen to 46 per cent within five years; within another ten years no less than 83 per cent of the Moloccan children had accumulated records in the juvenile courts.[32] This evidence suggests that delinquency is related directly to the neighborhood rather than to the ethnic or racial background of the groups composing it.

Shaw and his co-workers recognized from the outset that their conclusions were descriptive rather than explanatory; they were prepared to offer only tentative interpretations. They assumed that delinquent behavior was "closely related to certain situations which arise in the process of city growth." The specific relations between these situations and individual delinquency were felt to be matters for future research.

[31] *Ibid.*, pp. 198–204.
[32] Pauline V. Young, "Urbanization as a Factor in Juvenile Delinquency," *Publications of the American Sociological Society*, 24:162–166, 1930.

They suspected that a critical factor in the deteriorated neighborhood was the weakening of social controls:

> Under the pressure of the disintegrative forces which act when business and industry invade a community, the community thus invaded ceases to function effectively as a means of social control. Traditional norms and standards of the conventional community weaken and disappear. Resistance on the part of the community to delinquent and criminal behavior is low, and such behavior is tolerated and may even become accepted and approved.[33]

As study after study confirmed the predictions of Burgess and Shaw, enthusiasm for the ecological approach mounted. It seemed that a factor had been found which transcended all biological, psychological, and even sociological considerations. This factor, moreover, was entirely *physical.* There seemed no further need to grope in the shadowland of "personality," "mental deficiency," and "Mendelian degeneracy." Urban deterioration was a physical fact, just as neighborhoods, houses, and factories were physical facts. Here, then, was a description that was entirely objective. It was not only confirmable but it had actually been confirmed—with a weight and unanimity of proof almost unique in criminological research.

But gradually the negative evidence began to come in. Cities were found that did not conform to the pattern. Deterioration sometimes jumped whole neighborhoods; in other places it appeared spottily and according to no rational pattern—more like isolated patches of infection than like a gradually, constantly spreading plague. More critical still, the inhabitants of these ecological plague areas did not always succumb. Here and there were found population groups that showed an unaccountable resistance. In an investigation of delinquency in the Puget Sound area, Hayner discovered that the children of Japanese families living in the most deteriorated areas were relatively free from delinquency.[34] By the end of the 1930's, enough negative evidence had been accumulated to cast doubt on the adequacy of the ecological account.

LATER CRITICISMS AND RE-EVALUATIONS. Later investigators have found the "delinquency area" concept open to the following objections:

1. *Neglect of the possibility of selective migration.* Implicit in the earlier formulations of the "delinquency area" concept was the idea that

---

[33] Shaw *et al., op. cit.,* p. 205.
[34] Norman S. Hayner, "Delinquency Areas in the Puget Sound Region," *American Journal of Sociology,* 39:314–328, November 1933.

people moving into deteriorated neighborhoods were contaminated at some point *after* they had entered and settled down. This implication neglected the possibility that many of the settlers might have been seriously delinquent before they arrived. In other words, instead of functioning as the primary corrupting factor, the deteriorated area, with its cheap rooming houses, its low rentals, its poolrooms and saloons, might merely be a kind of passive receptacle for those who had fought and lost their status struggles elsewhere. The high concentration of bums, migrants, and other unattached drifters moving through the slums suggests an ecological wastebasket rather than a baited trap. Though the factor of selective migration cannot apply to the delinquent children studied by Shaw and his colleagues, it could conceivably apply to their fathers and mothers; those who had failed in other aspects of social adjustment might have been parental failures as well. Thus, selective migration becomes an alternative explanation of the data.

2. *Neglect of the possibility of selective law enforcement.* The crime and delinquency rates compiled by Shaw and his colleagues represent hundreds of individual actions by official agencies. Shaw's findings have been criticized on the ground that these high rates might reflect unusually intense activity by law-enforcement authorities. Persons of low socioeconomic status are peculiarly vulnerable to the action of official agencies. Similarly, the misbehavior of their children is more susceptible to official definition as delinquent though this factor would not necessarily refute the high delinquency rate in the poorer neighborhoods, it might well operate to mask high rates of actual delinquency elsewhere—a critical possibility, since Shaw's findings are all comparative. Though Shaw and his co-workers were aware of this possibility, they doubted that selective law enforcement could account for the magnitude of the differences they found.

In addition to the objections cited above, the finding that delinquency rates were unaffected by changes in the racial or national composition of the population has been seriously questioned. The neighborhoods investigated by Shaw and other ecologists usually had long and continuous histories of delinquency and social disorganization. As such, they were more likely to provide a corroboration than a refutation of the ecological hypothesis. The critical test of the nonsignificance of population types would be supplied by a neighborhood that was *not* markedly delinquent when a new population group settled in it. What happens when a depressed minority group previously segregated in a deteriorated section breaks its barriers and spills over into adjacent areas? In New

York City the Negro population, after generations of confinement in Harlem—a four-square-mile neighborhood in upper Manhattan—has been expanding very rapidly into adjoining neighborhoods on the upper East and West Side. This expansion has generally been accompanied by rising rates of delinquency in the new areas of settlement. The recent migration of Puerto Ricans to New York City has been accompanied by similar findings in the neighborhoods of concentration. These changes in the composition of the population were not preceded by significant *structural* changes in the areas of settlement; the traditional expansion of industrial and factory zones at the expense of residential zones never took place. If anything, the physical character of these neighborhoods had *improved* because of an intensive slum-clearance program.

FURTHER REFINEMENT AND DEVELOPMENT OF THE MILIEU CONCEPT. Underlying each of these criticisms is the implication that the milieu is something more than the physical structure of an environment. It should be pointed out that the ecologists themselves were among the first to grasp this implication; their successive publications shown an increasing emphasis on psychological and interpersonal factors. The contrast between earlier and later conceptions of milieu is evident in Thrasher's *The Gang*, a classic work of the ecological school, published in 1936. In his Preface to this book, the pioneer ecologist Robert Park states the more or less orthodox ecological position:

> It is not only true that the habitat makes gangs, but what is of more practical importance, it is the habitat which determines whether or not their activities shall assume those perverse forms in which they become a menace to the community. Village gangs, because they are less hemmed about by physical structures and social inhibitions of an urban environment, ordinarily do not become a social problem....[35]

Turning from the Preface to the text of the work, one finds the original physical conception in various phases of transformation. Occasionally the transition is made with some strain—as when Thrasher attempts to give the topographical concept, *interstitial area,* a sociological flavor:

> Probably the most significant concept of the study is the term *interstitial*—that is, pertaining to spaces that intervene between one thing and another. In nature foreign matter tends to collect and cake in every crack, crevice and cranny—interstices. There are also fissures and breaks in the structure of social organization. The gang may be regarded

[35] Robert E. Park, Preface to Thrasher, *op. cit.,* p. xi.

as an interstitial element in the framework of society, and gangland as an interstitial region in the layout of the city.[36]

In later sections of the book, however, Thrasher deals directly with the psychological implications of gang behavior. The increasingly personal character of the original "delinquency area" concept is apparent in his discussion of "personality and areas of intimacy":

> The area of individual orientation may be defined both geographically and emotionally. For the gang boy there is an area of geographical range including home and familiar territory, beyond which lies enemy territory and the external world.
>
> In addition to this there is an area of intimacy in which he has relations of close emotional dependence.... The member of the gang ...becomes absorbed in these emotional contacts. Rapport based on sympathy is set up.... This is the area of greatest familiarity.[37]

The progressive liberation of the milieu concept from its earlier topographical limitations is apparent in later studies by members of the Chicago School of ecologists. In 1930 Shaw published *The Jack-roller: A Delinquent Boy's Own Story*,[38] and in the following year Shaw and Moore brought out a case study of delinquency: *The Natural History of a Delinquent Career*.[39] In each of these studies extensive reference is made to the social psychology of Mead and Cooley as the authors attempt to explore the subjective meanings of delinquency and the impact of social forces on personality.

The ecological studies of delinquency began by relating behavior to certain topographical conditions conceived as a delinquent milieu. The effects of this milieu on individual activities were described in very general and largely negative terms: the disintegration of conventional traditions, the breakdown of neighborhood institutions, etc. But as the investigators came closer to the individual delinquents, it became necessary to understand why certain children succumbed to these influences while others did not. It became necessary, in other words, to find processes through which the delinquent influences "got into the heads" of individuals and conditioned their behavior.

[36] Thrasher, *op. cit.*, p. 22.

[37] *Ibid.*, p. 298.

[38] Clifford R. Shaw, *The Jack-roller: A Delinquent Boy's Own Story* (Chicago: The University of Chicago Press, 1930).

[39] Clifford R. Shaw and Maurice E. Moore, *The Natural History of a Delinquent Career* (Chicago: The University of Chicago Press, 1931). See also Shaw and McDonald, *Brothers in Crime* (Chicago: The University of Chicago Press, 1938) and, by the same authors, *Juvenile Delinquency and Urban Areas* (Chicago: The University of Chicago Press, 1942).

From this point on the focus of attention began to shift from the relation of the delinquent with his physical environment to his relationship with other delinquents and other neighborhood groups. In this altered frame of reference, the milieu came to be defined as a certain continuity of interpersonal relationships rather than a continuity of physical conditions—and it became possible to understand why the delinquency of the slums continues to flourish in the physically altered but socially unchanged atmosphere of the housing project.

In recent years the milieu concept has become a point of convergence for the various disciplines at work on common problems of individual and group behavior. It has served to bring the psychologist closer to study of the environment and the sociologist closer to study of the individual. In this process of theoretical integration, the conflict between the "individual" and the "group" orientation has become increasingly obsolete. In consequence, a large number of social scientists would probably concur with Gardner Murphy's statement:

> We cannot define the situation operationally except in reference to the specific organism which is involved; we cannot define the organism operationally, in such a way as to obtain predictive power for behavior, except in reference to the situation. Each serves to define the other; they are definable operationally while in the organism-situation field.[40]

The relevance of the milieu concept to crime and delinquency is discussed further in Chapter 14.

Sociological Theories of the Criminalization Process

The recognition that *criminalization, as a process,* is distinct from the question of criminal types on the one hand and criminal motivations on the other, is one of the major contributions of sociology. Though these distinctions may be obvious when pointed out, they are nonetheless crucial. What is involved is the recognition that the problem of explaining *what* a person does *and how he does it* is not solved by understanding *why* he does it or *what kind of a person* he is.

Sociologists were led to these distinctions partly by their suspicion

[40] Gardner Murphy, *Personality: A Biosocial Interpretation* (New York: Harper and Brothers, 1947), p. 891.

that criminal behavior might be actuated by the same motives that move other people to other responses. If the same motives underlie different forms of behavior, it becomes necessary to understand how different people come to pursue similar ends through different means. This distinction, grasped by the sociologists, was largely missed by the biological and psychiatric theorists, who, on the whole, felt that criminal behavior was explained once its motives were accounted for. Since the criminal was assumed to be sick or otherwise different from other people, it was assumed that his motivations must be different. Consequently, there was no particular point in stressing the varied characteristics of the criminal's external behavior. Having missed the distinction between behavior and motivation by merging them, the psychiatric and biological theorists missed or dismissed the critical distinction between means and ends. For them, criminality was not a process but a *condition*; its different symptoms—robbery, arson, assault—were of lesser interest. Accordingly, the problem of understanding how a relatively small number of basic criminal motives or pathological conditions produced so wide a variety of different criminal activities and skills did not arise.

Nevertheless, the community as a whole, perhaps because it suffers different consequences from them, continues to be interested in the distinctions between murder, embezzlement, arson, and the other crimes, and it continues to ask how different criminals made the decisions, learned the skills, and manipulated the circumstances enabling them to carry out these different activities. The sociologist's concern with criminalization as a process lead him directly to the consideration of these questions.

The Contribution of Gabriel Tarde (1843–1904)

Largely because of his ability to make sociology sound like obvious common sense, Tarde's novel ideas carry with them no atmosphere of discovery; one is often persuaded that Tarde is merely giving words to what he, the reader, knew all along. Nevertheless, there are few concepts in social psychology which Tarde failed to anticipate in the course of one casual paragraph or another—including the modern theory of criminalization shortly to be discussed.

Tarde was humorously critical of the current Lombrosian doctrine of the criminal as a biological atavism; he compared Lombroso's search for the "born criminal" with the search for the reborn Grand Lama among Tibetan infants, and he cited a colleague's comment that Lombroso's pictures of prisoners reminded him of photograph albums of his friends. In a more serious vein, he pointed out the circular reasoning in Lombroso's argument that the antisocial behavior of criminals is proof of their subhuman character. Having defined cooperation and "sympathy," as the essence of the human, Lombroso used the uncooperative, heartless behavior of the offender to "prove" what he had assumed in the first place.

Tarde uses the example of the Borgias and other notables of their period to demonstrate that bloodthirstiness and lack of scruples may not in the least violate current social usages. "Were the tyrants, were the artists of the Italian Renaissance, who were as lavish with their assassinations as with their achievements and masterpieces, monsters?" he asks.[41]

Just as he denied that they were physically unique, Tarde doubted that the basic psychology of criminals was different from that of every man; he saw too many similarities:

> The psychology of the murderer is, in the last analysis, the psychology of everybody; and in order to go down into his heart it will be sufficient if we analyze our own. One could without any very great difficulty write a treatise upon the art of becoming an assassin.[42]

Moreover, Tarde grasped the essential distinction between a state of mind and criminality. Even if one's mind were warped from birth, this condition alone could not make him a criminal. Thus: "Perhaps one is born vicious, but it is quite certain one *becomes* a criminal."[43]

CRIMINALIZATION AS A LEARNING PROCESS. How, then, does a person become a criminal? He *learns* crime, just as others learn a trade —through training and association with others. Usually his apprenticeship begins early, in "schools" found in the city streets:

> The majority of murderers and notorious thieves began as children... and the true seminary of crime must be sought for upon each public square or each crossroad of our towns... in those flocks of pillaging street urchins who, like bands of sparrows, associate together, at first for marauding and then for theft.... Without any natural predisposition on their part, their fate is often decided by the influence of their comrades.[44]

Now Tarde poses a crucial question. How is it to be explained that these children follow the lead "of a small minority of rascals over the

---

[41] Gabriel Tarde, *Penal Philosophy,* tr. by Rapelje Howell (Boston: Little, Brown and Company, 1912), p. 221.
[42] *Ibid.,* p. 256.
[43] *Ibid.*
[44] *Ibid.,* p. 252.

example of the immense majority who are laborious ... ?" Tarde takes note of the argument that this preference denotes some "anomaly of nature in them," but he finds a readier explanation closer at hand. It is their relationship with one another that isolates these children from contact with those who might furnish better models for imitation:

> Thus it would be permissible for the child who was the most normally constituted to be more influenced by half a score of perverse friends by whom he is surrounded than by millions of unknown fellow citizens.[45]

CRIME AS A PROFESSION. What are the characteristics of the criminal when he emerges from his training period on the streets? They are, says Tarde, basically those of a tradesman plying his trade. Crime is a profession, fundamentally, no different from other professions—except that it renders a disservice rather than a service. It has its schools, its special idiom, its special techniques—even its own professional relationships, no different from those to be observed "between people carrying on the same trades or trades of a similar character." There are even syndicates of crime, formed by those who have merged their careers in a common enterprise.[46]

Thus, in less than a dozen paragraphs of his *Penal Philosophy*, Tarde summarizes several of the major sociological concepts of crime and the criminalization process. Crime is not a disease or a physical or mental state of being, but an activity, an activity that is learned—a profession. Moreover, the social processes that produce the criminal are no different in kind from those that produce members of other professions; the only difference is *what is learned*. Thus, criminals are not born, but made—through association with others, usually in childhood, usually in the streets. Here Tarde anticipates not only the ecological school of crime but the theory of differential association as well.

The Contribution of William Adrian Bonger (1876–1940)

Bonger's reputation as a socialist has tended to eclipse his achievements as a criminologist, a consequence at least partly brought about by his own confusion between the roles of social scientist and social reformer. Nevertheless, these two influences of Bonger's thought are readily distinguishable.

BONGER'S DEFINITION OF THE THEORETICAL TASKS OF CRIMINOLOGY. Bonger set himself three theoretical problems, which he carefully

[45] *Ibid.*
[46] *Ibid.*, p. 251.

distinguished: (1) the task of accounting for criminal motivations; (2) the task of defining the situations through which criminal motivations are executed; and (3) the task of defining the forces enabling man to prevent both criminal motivations and their execution.

In making this analysis of the theoretical problem of crime, Bonger, like Tarde and Durkheim, was careful to distinguish the motivational factor from the behavioral. Thus: "It is possible for the environment to create a great egotist" (for Bonger, criminal motivation was subsumed in the concept of *egotism*) "but this does not imply that the egotist will necessarily become criminal."[47] Then Bonger went further than Tarde and Durkheim by pointing out that neither the motive nor the behavior itself is sufficient to account for the *execution* of criminal acts; in order for crimes to be committed, there must exist *facilitating environmental conditions*. A thief without victims, a bank robber without banks, cannot commit crimes, notwithstanding their criminal motives and techniques. Though Bonger's isolation of the facilitating "occasions" of crime represents a major theoretical contribution, he himself was largely content with pointing it out; his main interest was concentrated in the areas of motivation and prevention.

Bonger's main contribution was theoretical, and in this, it was substantial. Tarde and Durkheim had held that criminals were neither psychologically nor physically different from other men. Tarde, going further, had sought to account for the transmission of criminal behavior and had found its explanation in the processes of learning and acculturation. But neither of these sociological theorists had dealt except in a very general way with the problem of *motivation*. Had Tarde been asked, "Why does a person wish to become a thief?" he might well have replied, "Why does a person wish to become a tailor?"—and then given his answer in terms of imitation.

But imitation does not answer the question *why*; it merely deals with the question, *how*. True, men learn from each other—especially when they associate together, especially when they experience fellow-feeling. But is this all there is to it? Do they merely imitate whatever happens to be going on—or is there some relation between what they imitate and their needs and problems? In a word, does what they imitate *do* something for them? This, in brief, is the question of motivation—an area of criminology occupied almost exclusively by the psychologists and the physiologists until the time of Bonger.

[47] William A. Bonger, *Criminality and Economic Conditions* (Boston: Little, Brown and Company, 1916), p. 402.

It was Bonger who showed how a social institution—for him, the economic institution in a capitalist society—could create a general climate of incentive which motivated its members to similar behavior. He showed, moreover, how social stratification functioned to define this behavior, in superficially different ways, sometimes as "crime" and sometimes as "business." In this, he anticipated Sutherland's later parallels between ordinary crime, white-collar crime, and economic royalism.

What Bonger tried to demonstrate was that a *pervading social institution* could impose upon different individuals, with different personalities and in different walks of life, a *prevailing climate of motivation,* which, cutting across individual differences, involves them in conflict with one another by encouraging them to unrestrained self-centered effort. This *climate of motivation* Bonger called "egoism"; it has also been called "rugged individualism" and many other names. The emphasis on the individual ego is apt, since the criminal, by any definition, is one who violates the common interest in favor of a personal interest. Moreover, this climate of motivation, by encouraging unrestrained self-interest, represents an attack on the social organization itself, inspiring violation of the norms that hold the group together. In a sense, it is the active agent which produces that situation of "normlessness," that dissolving of values, which Durkheim had called *anomie.*[48]

Bonger attempted to show how society produces this destructive agent out of its own institutions, creating out of itself a kind of motivational and situational solvent tending toward its own dissolution. He attempted to show how individuals, under temptation or pressure, incorporate this socially destructive motive in their own behavior, thus becoming the active instruments of their own destruction. He next attempted to show that crime, though operating in disguise and under a cloud of ineffectual social disapproval, is merely one manifestation of this pervasive process. Finally, he tried to show that crime, as a symptomatic manifestation of the general destructive process, cannot be cured merely by symptomatic treatment.

The Contribution of Edwin H. Sutherland (1883-1950)

Sutherland is associated with two significant contributions to criminology: his description of *white-collar crime* and his theory of *differential association*—an account of the criminalization process. Though

[48] See Merton's discussion of "anomie" in Merton, *op. cit.,* pp. 125–149.

Sutherland subjected his theory to persistent revision, it is perhaps most clearly stated in its original formulation:

1. The processes which result in systematic criminal behavior are fundamentally the same in form as the processes which result in systematic lawful behavior.

2. Systematic criminal behavior is determined in a process of association with those who commit crimes, just as systematic lawful behavior is determined in a process of association with those who are law-abiding.

3. Differential association is the specific causal process in the development of systematic criminal behavior.

4. The chance that a person will participate in systematic criminal behavior is determined roughly by the frequency and consistency of his contacts with patterns of criminal behavior.

5. Individual differences among people in respect to personal characteristics or social situations cause crime only as they affect differential association or frequency and consistency of contacts with criminal patterns.

6. Cultural conflict is the underlying cause of differential association and therefore of systematic criminal behavior.

7. Social disorganization is the basic cause of systematic criminal behavior.[49] [Sutherland states that social disorganization and culture conflict are "smaller and larger aspects of the same thing."]

As first formulated, differential association was essentially a theory of contamination-by-exposure. The processes by which the exposure produces the criminal behavior are not described; Sutherland merely states that the behavior is "determined in a process of association," and then goes on, in his final postulates, to account for the existence of these contacts or associations in terms of culture conflict. The only other reference to the possible mechanisms of transmission occurs in the fourth postulate, in which Sutherland suggests that criminal behavior is determined by the *quantity* of the contacts with criminal patterns: the greater the number, the greater the possibility of contamination. A further implication that contamination is largely a matter of exposure is contained in the fifth postulate, where it is explicitly stated that individual or social differences are influential only as they affect the frequency and consistency of the contacts with criminal patterns. In other words, there are no personal or social differences in *resistance* or *immunity* to contamination; all are equally vulnerable, and whether one escapes or

[49] Edwin H. Sutherland, *Principles of Criminology*, 3d ed. (Philadelphia: J. B. Lippincott Company, 1939), pp. 4–8.

succumbs depends entirely on the degree of exposure. Thus differential association is analogous to a disease, against which the only defense is distance or isolation.

Sutherland's later formulations of the theory suggest that he realized the necessity of dealing more directly with the problem of process. In the 1947 edition of his text, he introduced *learning* as the psychological mechanism through which criminal patterns are transmitted to individuals. Once again, however, the process is somewhat passive and quantitative. Thus:

> A person becomes delinquent because in his association with others he learns an excess of definitions favorable to violation of law over definitions unfavorable to violation of law, and thus differential association is the cause of criminal behavior.[50]

Sutherland's theory of learning seems to derive from a once widely held psychological theory which accounted for the retention of learned material solely in terms of the frequency, recency, and intensity of associations. This learning theory ignored problems of personality, motivation and individual differences, and did not deal with questions of individual meanings and interpretations. Current learning theory in psychology, on the other hand, lays stress on questions of meaning, need, motivation, and individual differences. In the light of these newer conceptions, Sutherland's theory of learning is inadequate. Nevertheless, it is entirely consistent with his conviction that personality variables are not of primary importance.

It is a curious fact that some of the most critical evidence against the differential association theory derives from another major contribution of Sutherland—his analysis of *white-collar crime*. Many individual cases of embezzling and trust violation cannot be accounted for in terms of contacts with other embezzlers or white-collar offenders. Some of these violators work entirely alone and in secret, have lived law-abiding lives up to the time of their crime, and rarely number criminalistic persons among their associates. Often the violation of trust seems to be related to a personal crisis arising in the life of an otherwise conscientious individual, whose reputation for trustworthiness earned him his strategic position in the first place. In contrast to the typical delinquent, whose career is marked by progressively more frequent and more serious delinquencies—as predicted by the differential association theory—the

[50] Edwin H. Sutherland, *Principles of Criminology*, 4th ed. (Philadelphia: J. B. Lippincott Company, 1947), pp. 3–9.

careers of many white-collar offenders, up to the time of their crimes, reveal no previous criminal involvements or activities.

Not all forms of white-collar crime, especially those approximating the organized racketeering of criminal syndicates, fit this pattern. Sutherland's description of the diffusion of illegal practices among businessmen in certain fields seems entirely consistent with the theory of differential association.[51] In these situations, however, the illegalities have become institutionalized as sound business practices; in effect, some business concerns have evolved criminal practices in the course of competitive survival. But the bank teller who juggles his deposits and withdrawals is not engaging in the ordinary practices of bank tellers; banks do not survive and expand through these methods. Similarly, the corporation treasurer who pockets the fictitious payments to fictitious creditors is not engaging in an ordinary corporate violation. His particular corporation may, itself, be engaged in a variety of accounting swindles and tax dodges, but his own form of white-collar crime is entirely different in intent and consequence. In a sense, he is operating like an ordinary felon in the midst of respectable manipulators; he is picking the pockets of his own gang.

The inadequacy of the differential association theory to account for many crimes of financial trust violation has been candidly admitted by Sutherland's collaborator, Donald Cressey, who prepared the 1955 revision of *Criminology* after Sutherland's untimely death. In a report of a study of one hundred convicted trust-violators, Cressey concluded: "It is doubtful that it can be shown empirically that the differential association theory applies or does not apply to crimes of financial trust violation or even to other kinds of criminal behavior."[52] Caldwell, who cites this comment in his own text, points to the untestability of the theory as a revealing and damaging weakness:

> If the claim is now made that this theory explains all criminal behavior, then the claim is made with Cressey's admission that it is doubtful whether the theory can be proved. But if the theory merely

[51] See the following publications by Sutherland: "White Collar Criminality," *American Sociological Review*, 1:1–12, February 1940; "Crime and Business," *Annals of the American Academy of Political Science*, 217:112–118, September 1941; "Is 'White Collar Crime' Crime?" *American Sociological Review*, 10:132–137, April 1945; *White Collar Crime* (New York: The Dryden Press, Inc., 1949).

[52] Donald R. Cressey, "Application and Verification of the Differential Association Theory," *Journal of Criminal Law and Criminology*, 43:51–52, May–June 1952.

means that many persons learn to be criminals through association with others who do not...respect...the law, then it has been reduced to a polysyllabic elaboration of the obvious—a fate that has befallen many other oversimplifications of human behavior.[53]

When all this is granted, Sutherland's theory remains a most important and timely contribution to the sociology of crime. During a period when sociologists had largely abandoned the attempt to encompass the data of crime in a systematic and integrative theory, it re-asserted the significance of social and environmental factors against the otherwise predominant claims of the biological and psychological schools.

Limitations of Sociological Theories of Crime

Theories accounting for the existence of crime in general cannot, by their nature, explain the appearance of criminal behavior in particular persons. The brilliant hypotheses of Durkheim and Merton may suggest general motives and even general social functions of crime, but they cannot explain why John Jones steals and his brother does not.

The inability of general social theories of crime, however profound and "true," to accomplish this is itself of interest. The heart of the difficulty seems to be this: A social condition, or series of circumstances, however universal within the community—or within a segment of the community—does not fall with equal effect on all members of the community. In other words, a universal social condition does not imply a universal adjustment or a universal motivation. The failure of general theories must be traced to their inability to account for this differential impact—and this failure has nothing to do with their adequacy as general theories. It will be recalled that one of the central dilemmas of any psychological theory of crime is to account for the manner in which personality "results" in criminal behavior. Similarly, one of the major problems of any sociological theory of crime is to explain why the "'social factors" that "lead" certain individuals into crime do not have the same effect on other individuals exposed to them. These theoretical dilemmas are actually identical.

[53] Robert G. Caldwell, *Criminology* (New York: The Ronald Press Company, 1956), p. 185.

Thus, where a sociological theory may seem to account adequately for the emergence of a relatively uniform group response to similar social conditions—for example, the emergence of widespread delinquency in a deteriorated neighborhood—it fails to account for the fact that a sizable number of children, exposed to similar conditions, does not become delinquent, and for the fact that some children, exposed to different conditions, also become delinquent. Similarly, a psychological theory apparently able to explain certain criminal acts as the "result" of certain personality traits fails to account for the fact that persons with similar traits do not all commit crimes, or commit similar crimes—and that the same criminal behavior may be found among persons with different psychological characteristics.

14

Toward the Clarification of Criminological Theory

General Introduction and Overview

IN ANY FIELD OF STUDY THERE MAY BE SOME HAPPY MEDIUM BETWEEN not knowing where one is going, and knowing too well. Those who do not know at all where they are going tend to wander anywhere, arriving nowhere. Those who know too well, arrive inevitably; like guided missiles, they move from the preconceived notion to the foregone conclusion with little interest in the irrelevant scenery between. A good deal of the subject matter of criminology derives from orientations of one or the other of these types: data-gathering with limited reference to theory, and theorizing with limited reference to data.

Comparison of these two orientations—unguided empiricism and unsupported theorizing—reveals a consistent, though antagonistic, relationship between the two. The conclusions of the "guided missile" research method are typically based on a minimum of harmonious data which, in one way or another, exclude the negative cases that would challenge the theory. This exclusion of critical evidence is usually achieved in one or both of two general ways: selective sampling, calculated to discover only instances confirming the theory; or a technique of theory construction that is internally insulated against testing. In this latter technique, the possibility of a negative case may be prevented in advance by an act of definition that renders hypotheses self-confirming and, thereby, untestable.[1]

In contrast to the self-confirming methods that in one way or another preclude the negative case, the typical empirical approach—in its various experimental, observational, and clinical varieties—deliberately seeks out the negative case. For example, a study seeking to determine the incidence of broken homes among a population of delinquents would be subjected to severe and valid criticism if it did not survey the home situations of *all*—or of at least a representative sample —of the delinquents under study. And if, by some chance, it were found that all the delinquents studied came from broken homes, the probable reaction of the investigator would be to widen his sample of delinquents. Implicit in this activity is the search for the negative case, for the *nonoccurrence* of the factor without an estimate of which it is scientifically impossible to test the presence or absence of a relationship with the other factor studied.

We have said that the relationship between this rigorous kind of data-gathering and theories based on small samples of positive cases is *antagonistic*. This antagonism is especially evident when the theories are subjected to the more rigorous test of wider, less selective sampling. Thus, for example, in any large population of offenders there are enough diseased, neurotic, and underprivileged individuals to provide impressive positive evidence for theories of criminality based on disease, neurosis, or poverty—provided, of course, that the sample is restricted to positive cases. In every study in which these theories have been rigorously tested by unbiased sampling enough negative cases have been found to refute them.

The total result has been that criminology is without parallel in the behavioral sciences for the sheer prevalence of invalidated ideas over positive knowledge. In virtually every instance, the application of rigorous methods has produced a Pyrrhic victory; with the result that the scientific criminologist, in contrast to the layman, may be defined as one who knows what is *not* true, what is *not* to be believed about crime and criminals. It is almost as if criminology, in trying to become a science, had threatened to destroy itself as a body of knowledge.

[1] As indicated in Chapter 2, such hypotheses are usually statements about words rather than statements about events, which can be confirmed or refuted. Thus, for example, the hypothesis, "Crime is a manifestation of disease" can be "proved" by a definition of disease broad enough and vague enough to include any conceivable type of crime. Or the hypotheses may be statements capable of "proof" by both positive and negative evidence—as, for example, the psychiatrist's hypothesis about the success of his treatment, also referred to in Chapter 2.

The Functions of Theory

In the foregoing chapters we have attempted to describe the major orientations to the data of criminology. We must now deal with the problem of evaluating these attempts to understand crime and criminals, together with the theories they produced. Before turning to this delicate and difficult task, it might be well to clarify, as precisely as possible, what we mean by *evaluation* and how we propose to go about it. One way to approach the task is to raise the question, *What may we reasonably expect a theory to do for us?* Students of scientific method have repeatedly cited the following requirements of a theory: description, explanation, prediction and control.[2] In concrete terms, what do these requirements imply?

The Descriptive Function:
How Well Does the Theory Prepare Us to Anticipate
What We May Find Happening Outside?

Imagine for a moment that our only advance acquaintance with crime and criminals was to be provided by one or another of the theories that have been described. Imagine, further, that we were required, on the basis of the theory, to anticipate what was actually going on in the outside world of crime—specifically, what crimes were being committed, who was committing them, how they were being committed; finally, how society, through its social agencies, its courts and institutions, was dealing with them. How comprehensively, how accurately, would the theory prepare us to anticipate, to recognize what we might encounter in experience?

This question is supremely important because it is necessarily anterior to each of the further requirements of a theory. One can only explain what one has previously recognized. An explanation based on only a partial recognition of what is happening can be only a partial explanation. Moreover, since many events are likely to be interrelated, the correct understanding of any given event may well depend on an understanding of other events likely to affect it. Consequently, an explanation which is only *partial* is likely to be wrong as well. Explana-

---

[2] Since correctional authorities must necessarily respond to a wide variety of social, administrative, and political influences, it is unrealistic to expect treatment procedures to be governed by purely scientific considerations. For these reasons the scientific requirement of *control* will be omitted from the discussion.

tions based on inaccurate descriptions of what is happening will, in most cases, be similarly *inaccurate*. (If they happen to be correct, they will be correct only by chance—or because of unwarranted inferences from the wrong premises.) Finally, explanations based on hazy, undifferentiated or overgeneralized accounts are likely to be useless in arming us to cope with what we may encounter. On the street, in the prison, we do not meet the typical criminal who presents the general problem that can be solved by the over-all solution. Experience has a way of presenting specific people with concrete problems requiring particular choices between particular alternatives.

In order to evaluate the descriptive adequacy of a theory, it is first necessary to summarize whatever is reliably known about the complexity of the events likely to be encountered in experience and then, turning to the theory, to discover how much of this data the theory is dealing with, what it is ignoring, what it is emphasizing, *how cognizant it is of distinctions that seem important as we encounter them in the world outside.*

The Explanatory Function:
How Convincingly Does the Theory Demonstrate the Relations between Events?

What do we mean when we ask for an explanation of crime? The closer we look into this question, the more complicated it seems to become. If we were asked, for example, to "explain" an automobile, we might start talking about the internal combustion engine and describe how the vertical movement of the pistons is transformed into radial movement by the drive shaft and the wheels. In another sense, however, the question, Explain the automobile, means something entirely different. This question asks, How did the automobile come to exist? Clearly, there was a time when there were no automobiles; until they existed, they could not operate. This sense of the question is sometimes called "genetic," since it deals with the origin or *genesis* of the event or object being explained. It raises the question: *What had to exist and happen in order for the object to exist, or for the event to take place?* With respect to criminals, this sense of the question would ask: *What events account for the fact that a person, originally not a criminal, eventually became one?*

The foregoing questions dealt with issues of processes and origins, they posed the problems, *How, Whence?* When concerned with human beings, we may also find it necessary to raise questions asking *Why?* In this sense, the question, How did the crime come to happen? also means, Why, or for what purpose or reason, or because of what needs or desires, did the person commit the crime? How does it happen that, for certain individuals, the goal of possessing things of value is regularly pursued by theft—while, for others, a similar goal is pursued by work activities? Note, here, that we are not merely asking, Why did the person steal? but rather the more complex question, Why did he steal instead of doing something else—such as buy the object, or save up to buy it, or give up the idea of having it altogether? This more complicated form of the question is also more realistic, because it recognizes the fact that other alternatives exist.

This fact of "other alternatives" is significantly related to the plausibility of explanations. To explain why certain individuals steal for a living is, in a strict sense, to explain why they do not *earn* a living, or depend on others for a living—alternatives pursued by many other people in the same and in different circumstances, *alternatives which the criminals themselves may at one time have pursued.* Thus, an explanation is "convincing" to the extent that it disposes of alternate possibilities. *A thoroughly convincing explanation is one capable of rejecting the widest range of conceivable or plausible alternatives.* This accounts, in part, for the disturbing effect that new knowledge has on old explanations. New facts pose new alternatives. For this reason, theory must remain continuously responsive to the new alternatives presented by a wider or more sensitive awareness of the complexity of events. It is in this sense, again, that *description* and *explanation* are inextricably related.

The Predictive Function:
How Accurately Will the Theory Anticipate Findings Not Yet Known?

As we have already pointed out, one of the tests of a theory is its ability to account for facts already known. There are at least two reasons that make this test inadequate for the purposes of the scientist. In the first place, the scientist is not content with an explanation which is capable merely of accounting for the limited sample of data he has investigated; he is also concerned with the extent to which his conclusions are applicable to a wider sample of similar data—ultimately, to the entire universe of the data he is studying. Thus, criminologists study the conditions under which a few crimes have already taken place in order to understand the conditions under which a great many crimes are likely to take place in the future. But even apart from this interest in the widest possible range of future cases, there is another reason why the investigator must seek to test his conclusions on wider samples. This reason has little to do with his curiosity about the future, and everything to do with his curiosity about the past. *For unless the investigator can extend his conclusions beyond his original confirming sample, he can have no confidence that he was right about that original sample in the first place.* Let us try to see why.

Let us imagine that Investigator A wished to account for the fact that, out of a hundred children in a certain neighborhood, fifty have become delinquent and fifty have remained law-abiding. On studying the hundred children, he is fortunate enough to discover that each of the fifty delinquent children was exposed to factors X and Y, while every one of the nondelinquent children escaped this exposure. On the basis of this evidence he feels able to assert, "Factors X and Y account for the fact that the fifty children became delinquent."

But imagine now that Investigator B appears on the scene with an entirely different hypothesis to account for the delinquency of the fifty children. He might say, "I acknowledge that each of the fifty delinquents was exposed to factors X and Y, but I also suggest that these factors were irrelevant to what happened. My hypothesis is that factors P and Q were actually responsible."

The first investigator is now confronted with a dilemma. A doubt has been cast on his explanation: another alternative has been proposed. He has now no way of demonstrating that the fifty children in his sample became delinquent because of factors X and Y, *for the obvious and irremediable reason that they are already delinquent, and he cannot turn back the clock to the time when they were not.* He has one recourse: In order to test his conclusion concerning his original sample, he must find another sample of children who share factors X and Y but not factors P and Q. (If he wishes, in addition, to challenge Investigator B's hypothesis, he must find a sample of children exposed to factors P and Q but not to factors X and Y.) If his original hypothesis was correct, he should be able to predict that the new group of children exposed to factors X and Y will be found delinquent, while the group exposed only to P and Q will not. Thus, the function of the findings in the new cases is to test the hypothesis advanced to account for the original findings.

These considerations are directly relevant to research in criminology. Criminologists have completed observations on the intelligence, personal traits, body type, genetic and social backgrounds of known offenders, and they have offered explanations accounting for the criminality of these offenders in terms of these factors. However, until it becomes possible to test these explanations by projecting them as *expectations in future cases,* there is no way of knowing whether the conclusions are relevant beyond the small samples which were observed. More important still, *unless it is possible to predict from the original sample to other samples, there is no way of testing the significance of their findings even in the original cases.* And there is nothing to prevent others from offering any number of different interpretations of these particular cases, since, in the absence of future observations, there is no further evidence to prove these interpretations wrong.

In the past few pages we have discussed some of the requirements of a scientific theory. To what extent does the present state of criminological theory fulfill these requirements?

The Present Situation of Criminological Theory

The present scene of criminological theory conveys an impression of divergence unique in the social sciences. This situation has sometimes moved commentators to strong language. In 1919 the British prison psychiatrist Mercier wrote:

> With the exception of logic, there is no subject on which so much nonsense has been written as this of criminality and the criminal. The books are extremely numerous and of vast bulk, but we arise from their perusal dazed and stunned by the clamor of assertations of the wildest and most improbable character, advanced without proof and with scarcely any evidence worthy of the name. If I have made little reference to the writings of my predecessors it is not because I am unacquainted with them . . . it is partly because I have derived so little assistance from them.[3]

The divergences extend not only to disagreements in point of view and to methods of observation and analysis, but to data as well. Thus,

[3] Charles Mercier, *Crime and Criminals* (New York: Henry Holt and Company, 1919), p. ix.

for example, should the student consult a recent work by the psychiatrist David Abrahamsen, he would read as follows:

> In all my experience I have never been able to find one single offender who did not show some mental pathology, in his emotions or in his character or in his intelligence. The "normal" offender is a myth. . . . There is little doubt that if we had sufficiently refined methods of examining delinquent persons, we would find that all of them suffer from some form of mental disorder.[4]

Taken as it stands, the statement is as concise and straightforward a summary of the psychological condition of criminals as may be found in print. A psychiatric specialist in crime has been able, on the basis of personal observation, to verify a certain fact beyond question. He has, moreover, verified this fact in 100 percent of the cases observed—a percentage confirming his conclusion at a level of statistical confidence virtually without parallel in any field of human research. At this point the student need have no doubt concerning the mental status of criminals.

No doubt, that is, unless he happens to read a review of Dr. Abrahamsen's book by the sociologist George Vold. Commenting Dr. Abrahamsen's conclusions, Vold writes:

> If this is to be accepted at face value, one can only marvel at the ability of this psychiatrist to maintain contact for many years with groups of prisoners and not to have encountered the businessman in crime, the "operator" who functions in crime in a manner similar to that of his counterpart in legitimate business activity. The author seems unaware of the well-established fact that about 90 percent of the offenses known to the police are those not directed against persons but against property in the understandable quest of getting a maximum return for a minimum of effort.
>
> If the phenomenon of crooked and dishonest dealing, of which crimes against property represent a small fraction, is interpreted as mental abnormality, this is in effect saying that the entire population is sick and abnormal, except, perhaps, for the few misunderstood psychiatrists so valiantly struggling to stem the tide of all-pervasive misconduct.[5]

Set side by side, these quotations reveal the following:

1. A failure to agree on what is to be included in and excluded from definitions of *crime* and *criminal*.

2. A rejection by one observer of the data reported by another.

[4] David Abrahamsen, *Who Are the Guilty?* (New York: Rhinehart and Company, 1952), p. 125.

[5] George Vold, Review of "Who Are the Guilty?" in the *American Journal of Sociology*, 43:614, May, 1953. Copyright 1953 by the University of Chicago.

3. An implied rejection of one investigator's rationale of research.

4. An unequivocal rejection of his interpretation and conclusions. This instance of total disagreement between two authorities on crime is not an isolated case of conflict between two professional biases. It exists within as well as between the various disciplines contributing to criminology,[6] and its cumulative effect is to surround virtually every research finding with an aura of doubt and controversy. It is the classic story of the doctors disagreeing:

> When the Masters all fall out,
> What can the Student do but doubt?

Arguments are generally of two kinds. In one, the disputants agree on the facts and issues in controversy, but disagree on how the issues are to be resolved. In the other, the facts and issues themselves are in dispute. Arguments of this type tend to become interminable. There can be no resolution of issues unless the issues are agreed on. In the absence of this agreement, discussion dissolves into a confusion of tongues in which the same terms are used to express unshared meanings. When matters have reached this pass, there can be no further progress until the disputants have achieved agreement concerning the referents of their terms.

Toward Consensus

Most of us are familiar with one or another version of the story of the blind men and the elephant. In this ancient parable about dogmatism and the disunity of knowledge, the audience is encouraged to smile at the predicament of the blind men arguing with each other, one claiming that the object is a tree, the other that it is a snake. The parable usually ends at this point, leaving the blind men in their plight and the audience laughing at them.

Nevertheless, the story might have had another message if it had not ended at this point, with the audience in so favored and flattering a position. The audience could afford to laugh at the blind men because it knew that the object of their confusion was, in fact, an elephant. It

---

[6] See Frederick Wertham, "Psychoauthoritarianism and the Law," *University of Chicago Law Review*, 22:336–338, Winter, 1955 and Review of *The Psychology of the Criminal Act and Punishment* by Gregory Zilboorg, *loc. cit.*, pp. 569–581.

was this awareness on their part that made the mistakes of the blind men seem so ridiculous. But suppose the audience did not know—what then?

Suppose, in fact, that they were as much in the dark as the blind men. At this point the more realistic question might arise: How might they all move from a state of ignorance to a state of knowledge? Perhaps a first step would be to stimulate the blind men to some doubts about the validity of their hypotheses. Someone might suggest that the object cannot, after all, be both a snake and a tree; at the very least it would have to be either one or the other. This suggestion might result in the two blind men sitting down to a conference with each other. The chances are, however, that little would come of this, and the conference would probably end up with each side restating its own evidence and rejecting the views of the other on procedural, theoretical, factual, or patriotic grounds.

A wiser suggestion might be that each of the blind men return to the object and gather more information about it by means of direct examination. After all (it could be argued) neither of them had run his hands over the *whole* "snake" or the *whole* "tree." This procedure would have the advantage of returning both investigators to the original scene of the data, removing the dispute from the realm of dialectics to the realm of reality.

Accordingly, we might imagine the blind men returning to the elephant, the one to obtain more accurate measurements of the "snake," the other to get a more precise description of the "tree."

In order to pass his hands over the whole "snake," the first blind man has to shinny up the elephant's trunk. He does this and finds, to his amazement, that the "snake" does not end as a proper snake should but is, on the contrary, attached without a break to something else. This finding is momentous. In his empirical pursuit of the logical conclusion of his hypothesis, the investigator has encountered the famous *negative case*. Though shocking, the experience is enormously liberating. The snake hypothesis goes out the window, and the investigator is intellectually free to work his way over the rest of the elephant—and toward new and better hypotheses.

In the meantime, the author of the tree-hypothesis has climbed up the elephant's leg, has encountered the elephant's body—and has undergone a similar experience. He too moves on. Somewhere on the back of the elephant they meet, exchange admissions, and compare notes.

Another decisive stage has now been reached. Prior to this meeting over the unified body of the data, each investigator had been acquainted only with facts known to one or the other, but not to both. This privacy and limitation of experience had prevented communication and consensus. Now both have encountered similar problems, both have undergone a similar disillusionment—and both have had contact with the same data. And both are aware of the necessity for agreeing on a description that will deal adequately with the findings of each. What had previously been an irreconcilable dispute between two theories based on mutually exclusive findings has dissolved into a natural—and curable—misunderstanding based on a limited knowledge of the facts. The two blind men had been wrong, not because their findings had been wrong, but because they had built a complete theory out of a small segment of the total data.

Assuming that the situation of specialists and students in the field of criminology is somewhat analogous to that of the characters and the audience in the fable, how might the story proceed from this point? Presumably, a certain consensus has been reached—but what does this fact imply? A consensus, at bottom, is merely a sharing of meanings. It exists when A's idea of what A is talking about is fully understood by B, and vice-versa. It is not an agreement to view matters in the same way; it is not an accord about what ideas are right or wrong. *In the fable it is actually no more than a mutual acknowledgment of the hitherto unsuspected variability of the data.* A has agreed that B has come across something which is very snake-like, but is no snake; B has agreed that A has found something which is very tree-like, but is no tree. In effect, the consensus was an agreement about how *not* to describe the animal, since its characteristics were still unknown.

Though it ought not be overestimated, this agreement about what *not* to call the unknown object is significant and productive. It is *significant*, in the first instance, of an awareness that *the working definition of the object must not assign it characteristics which have not yet been proved.* It is *productive* because it *leads to a search for a working definition which is objectively and theoretically neutral; which defines not what the thing is—since this is not known—but rather, what is being referred to when the term is used.*

Consensus on a Working Definition of Crimes and Criminals

We have now come to the point of agreeing that, since *verifiable descriptions* of crimes and criminals must be an end result rather than a starting-point of theory, we are in need of a *working definition* that is absolutely neutral.

The reader may recall that a definition of this type was proposed in Chapter 2 of this text. A criminal was defined as *any* person judged (or likely to be judged) punishable by the authorities of a polity. A crime was defined as an act—any act—ascribed to a person as a reason for calling him a criminal. Each of these definitions leaves the nature of the act and the actor entirely open; neither indicates anything factual or theoretical—each is, in fact, little more than an agreement to refrain from doing just that.

One thing has been accomplished, however. A distinct, identifiable and distinguishable class of persons has been set up, a class whose members can fairly readily be differentiated from all nonmembers. True, this class shares only one attribute—and a highly general one at that. Nevertheless, it enables us to identify all members of the category in a way that clearly differentiates them from all others. This is indispensable. One cannot describe what one has not identified. Putting the matter bluntly, it is difficult to tell what is happening down on the race track unless you can tell the horses from the track.

Consensus on the Phenomena to be Described

Having agreed on an unobjectionable definition of *what to look at,* we can, presumably, start looking. But at this point the question arises: Look for *what?*

One of the parlor tricks of psychology is to ask a person to recall a street on which he walks every day of his life, and then describe various familiar objects on that street. A surprisingly large number of people do very poorly at this, for a reason which is readily apparent. One cannot ordinarily tell what is going on simply by "looking"; one must look for *something.* Putting it another way, one can begin to know what is happening only when he asks his experiences specific questions. It is only then that experience becomes intelligible, and it becomes intelligible in terms of these questions.

This is another way of saying that different people looking at the same phenomena will "see" different things if they look for different things. (We saw a hypothetical instance of this in Chapter 2, in the story of the two hypothetical criminologists visiting a prison, and an actual instance in the dispute between the two actual criminologists referred to several paragraphs ago.[7]) Granted, then, that we become aware of the details of experience only in terms of the questions we put to it, and granted, further, that the nature of our observations will vary with the character of these questions, the problem emerges: *How shall the questions be selected?*

This issue is critical, for it is obvious, at least in the field of criminology, that people can ask no end of questions. The various investigators who inquired into the body shape, the physical health, and the genetic, national, and social antecedents of criminals produced findings that were articulate on these questions—and silent on others. How were these questions chosen? Or, to put it another way, where did they get the notion to ask these kinds of questions in the first place?

This query leads directly to the issue of the conceptual context out of which questions arise. The investigators who raised the various questions referred to above asked them because they considered them important—important in terms of some over-all frame of reference, a theory of behavior which suggested in advance what was necessary—and unnecessary—to consider in the explanation of human actions.

A theory claiming to provide an adequate explanation of the events likely to be encountered in any field must be capable of demonstrating that it is, in fact, dealing with the totality of data that requires explaining. It is only on this basis that certain kinds of variables may justifiably be excluded from consideration in advance of investigation. In certain fields of study this exclusion of irrelevant data may be defended with relative assurance. For example, a physiologist embarking on a new study of protein metabolism finds it unnecessary to investigate the racial, social, economic, or political differences of his subjects. In effect he is saying: We have reason to believe that all people, regardless of differences in their backgrounds, tend to metabolize protein in ways irrelevant to these differences. Or, putting it more explicitly, whatever their racial, social, economic, or political variation, the phenomena of protein absorption and utilization can be described without reference to

---

[7] One of the criticisms directed by the sociologist at the psychiatrist in the review article just cited was that the psychiatrist had failed to take cognizance of a fact which the reviewer considered highly important—namely, that over 90 percent of all reported crimes are property offenses. (By contrast, nearly all of the cases presented by the psychiatrist were personal offenses—a category of crime which accounts for less than 10 percent of the reported total.) In view of the fact that the psychiatrist had extended his conclusions to *all* criminals, the reviewer was critical of what seemed an unwarranted bias in sampling.

these factors—and exclusively and entirely with reference to certain biochemical events. This conclusion is defended by two arguments. First, it can be demonstrated that all or most of the "encountered events" of protein metabolism can be dealt with in a framework more or less limited to biochemical factors. Second, it can be shown that variations in other kinds of factors normally have no demonstrable effect on the findings.

It is essential to emphasize that the validity of the second assumption is critically dependent on the validity of the first. In spite of the persuasiveness with which various theories have been advanced, criminological theory has not yet reached that state of conclusiveness capable of determining, in advance, what factors may be included or excluded by any given explanation of crime or criminals. For this reason, the search for critical variables must proceed without the guidance of conceptions that limit investigation at the outset.

Deriving the Questions with which a Theory Must Deal

In the discussion of the descriptive function of a theory it was suggested that a description is adequate to the extent that it anticipates what the observer is likely to encounter in experience. Conversely, the explanatory adequacy of a theory was posited on its ability to provide a convincing (i.e., testable) account of the relations between the events encountered. What are the events which a criminological theory must anticipate? And how do they suggest questions for which theory must seek answers?

Perhaps the most direct way to ensure that a description will adequately represent the complexity of actual events is to raise the question: In what ways do the phenomena to be described exhibit variation? With respect to criminals we would inquire, How are criminals distributed in the population? How do they differ from one another with respect to age, sex, location, activities, etc.? The extent of this inquiry into the differences exhibited by criminals need be limited by only two conditions: (1) the observer's sensitivity to the actual dimensions of variation; and (2) his access to objective and accurate data.

How does the analysis of descriptive data suggest the questions for which a theory must seek answers? Let us assume, for the moment, that the observer had no basis for a preliminary estimate of the distribution of criminals in the population. In the absence of information to the contrary, the most probable estimate is that criminals are *randomly* distributed—i.e., that the number of criminals in different elements of the population is roughly proportional to the percentage contributed by each of these elements to the total. This is the most probable guess because it is the one which calls for no special assumptions. It says, in effect: In the absence of contrary information, we have no reason to believe that special factors are operating to concentrate disproportionately large numbers of criminals among certain categories of persons— and to distribute disproportionately low numbers among others.

Let us now suppose that the investigator found this expectation to be incorrect. Suppose, in fact, that he found certain categories or classes of persons in which criminals were represented out of all proportion to the percentages contributed by these categories to the total population. This finding would demand explanation, since it would clearly reveal the presence of some factor or condition as a result of which certain categories of persons are more likely to be found involved in crime than others. It would then become the task of theory to account for this discrepancy.

We are now in a position to define more precisely what we require of a comprehensive and adequate theory of crime. A criminological theory is *comprehensive* to the extent that it deals simultaneously with the *full range of questions uncovered by unaccountable variations in the data.* It is *adequate* to the extent that it suggests *mutually consistent answers* to this broad range of questions—answers capable of a logical or experimental defense against alternative hypotheses.

Before summarizing the range of problematical data with which a criminological theory must deal, we might examine how available theories have coped with the need for identifying critical data and problems.

As we have seen in the four preceding chapters, there has been no general consensus on the data with which theory must deal. Biological, psychological, and sociological theorists have given independent accounts of criminological phenomena based exclusively on variables familiar to the disciplines of each. Each has proceeded on the tacit assumptions (1) that the observed variations can be accounted for exclusively in terms of certain limited kinds and numbers of variables; and (2) that other kinds of variations are irrelevant. Moreover, instead of dealing initially with the problem of *how criminals vary from one another,* each theory concerned itself from the outset with the very different—and premature—question of how *criminals differ from noncriminals.* The genetic theorists of crime looked at offenders and saw an otherwise homogeneous collection of genetic misfits. Psychological theorists, viewing or purporting to view the same population, usually saw either a group of mental defectives or a collective of the emotionally or characterologically maladjusted. And many social theorists, observing the same community, saw the consequences of a social world in conflict. In all or most instances, *it was tacitly assumed that criminals could be differentiated from noncriminals without the necessity of first inquiring how criminals differed from one another.*

This omission was crucial. In order to understand how critical it was, let us, for the moment, make a totally unwarranted assumption. Let us assume that each of these theories was entirely adequate for the limited range of data it dealt with and correct in the conclusions it produced. In disregard of the evidence, then, we will momentarily concede that all criminals are, simultaneously, genetically defective, mentally disturbed, and socially deprived.

The question then arises, *how would any of these theories, taken separately or together, account for the curious fact that over 90 percent of all known offenders are males? Or that a vastly disproportionate percentage is concentrated between the ages of fifteen and thirty? Or that a similarly disproportionate percentage is concentrated in large urban centers? Or that the huge majority of all reported offenses involve some form of theft?* Nothing in the structure of any of the theories could have predicted these findings.

Moreover, nothing that is reliably known about the incidence of hereditary defect or mental disease can account for these distributions. With certain statistically insignificant exceptions, recessive genetic defects strike males and females indiscriminately. Epidemeological surveys of mental disturbances reveal no over-all partiality for one sex over another. And there is no basis for assuming that the daughters of socially deprived parents are so much less deprived than the sons. Similar considerations apply to the other disproportions cited. In each instance, the theories were unable either to predict or to account for data and problems excluded in advance from their frame of reference.

A Partial Summary of the Problematical Data with which a Criminological Theory Must Deal

We may now attempt a brief and selective survey of the data which demand explanation in any theory of crime. Needless to say, though space limitations are a factor, the brevity of the summary will chiefly reflect limits imposed by inadequacies of knowledge.

I. Statistical Findings

PROBLEMATICAL DATA CONCERNING CRIMINALS

1. *Upwards of 90 percent of all known criminals are males.* In view of the fact that the number of males roughly equals the number of females in the population, this finding of a nonrandom distribution of criminals among the sexes must be accounted for.

2. *Disproportionately high percentages of known criminals are found among persons in adolescence or young adulthood.* The great majority of known offenders are in the age range between fifteen and thirty. The percentage of persons arrested for first or for new offenses declines sharply and disproportionately in the age ranges below fourteen and after thirty.

3. *Disproportionately high percentages of criminals are found in localities classified as urban.* Upwards of 65 percent of the present United States population now resides in localities classified by the Census Bureau as urban. Both the number and rate of crimes and criminals in urban areas disproportionately exceed the percentage of urban residents in the total population.

4. *Disproportionately high percentages of known criminals are found in the lower socioeconomic classes.*

5. *Highly disproportionate percentages of known criminals are found in certain racial or ethnic groups.* In the United States at present, more than 30 percent of all known criminals derive from a racial classification comprising only 10 percent of the total population. Among certain other racial and ethnic groups the percentage of criminals is disproportionately low.

PROBLEMATICAL DATA CONCERNING CRIMES

1. *Crimes involving some form of theft comprise more than 90 percent of the total of all crimes reported.*

2. *Rates of crime generally, and rates of different types of crime vary nonrandomly by region, by type of locality, and, within given localities, by type of neighborhoods.*

II. Problematical Data of a Nonstatistical Character

In addition to the data available in statistical form, other information derives from the direct examination of criminal behavior. Though consistent with universally accepted conceptions of human behavior, none of this data is dependent on a particular theory of behavior, and none involves assumptions going beyond the level of observation.

1. *Every criminal act represents a composite of responses requiring integration at a high level of the central nervous system.* In nontechnical language, all this observation asserts is that the physical acts required for even the most "primitive" criminal behavior require an organism capable of coordinating sensation, perception, and movement for the purpose of expending energy in some organized manner.

2. *The separate actions comprising any criminal act are in no case exclusive or specific to criminal behavior alone.* This observation merely asserts that the responses required for any criminal act are also appropriate to, and required by, a variable range of noncriminal behavior. The crime of rape, for example, involves certain responses which, under different circumstances, are legal. The crime of car-theft involves some of the same activities required for driving a car under legal conditions. Consequently, when viewed as patterns for the expenditure of muscular energy, there is nothing distinctive or inherently "criminal" about any criminal act.

3. *Most of the activities comprising criminal acts are learned.* (This observation follows as a necessary inference from those preceding.)

4. *The crimes committed by the same criminal may vary in type and in frequency.* The same offender may confine himself to one form of crime, to a few forms, or to several forms. The *frequency* with which he commits crimes may vary from a great number over a brief period, to a very few over a long period, to a temporary or permanent cessation.

5. *The activities carried out through the entire range of the offender's daily behavior are likely to include more legal than criminal actions.* This is another way of observing the fact that it is literally impossible to behave criminally twenty-four hours a day, seven days a week. All criminals engage in many forms of permissible activities. Most, if not all, offenders find it necessary to pay for many of the things

they need. There is no thief who steals everything he wants, no assaulter who attacks everyone he meets.

6. *The totality of the offender's contacts and relations with others is likely to include a number not related to illegal objectives.* Just as it is inconceivable for the offender to behave criminally in every situation and toward every person he meets, so it is also unlikely that his every relationship or contact with other human beings is linked to some criminal activity or purpose. Offenders have friends, sweethearts, and relatives—persons with whom they occupy roles involving conventional obligations and expectations.

7. *Most forms of crime require a victim.* With the exception of some few categories of forbidden acts, most crimes require a victim whose person or property is deliberately harmed or exploited without his consent. Thus, to behave criminally is, in most instances, to place oneself in a certain type of relation with another person, or with his property or interests, for a specific limited purpose and, usually, for a limited time—the time required to carry out the criminal objective. Accordingly, a comprehensive theory of crime must account not only for the differential likelihood that persons will engage in illegal acts but also for the differential availability and vulnerability of the victims required for the full consummation of those acts.

The Search for Variables Consistent with the Full Range of the Data

We now have a more definite idea of the range of variations for which a criminological theory must provide a consistent account. Taken together, these findings constitute the *dependent variables* which the theory must be capable, on the one hand, of predicting and, on the other, of relating to causally antecedent factors or *independent variables*. In their total context, the data posit certain criteria for the appropriateness of any independent variable which may be proposed. *The factors must be consistent not merely with one or a few of the findings but with all of them simultaneously.* Variables capable of accounting for the disproportionate distribution of offenders among males and females but incapable of anticipating the disproportionate age, social, and spatial distributions would be unacceptable. The requirement of *simultaneous and consistent relevance* to all of the conditions posed by the data makes it possible to test the "fit" of different causal factors.

Testing the "Fit" of Different Kinds of Independent Variables

Each of the following has been proposed as capable of accounting for criminal behavior. To what extent does each exhaust the range of variations found in the data?

CRIMINALITY AS A RESULT OF PHYSICAL DEFECT OR DYSFUNCTION. Of all theories of crime, those attributing criminality to various kinds of physical deficiencies or malfunction are the least capable of dealing with the full range of variability found among criminals. Among the inadequacies of these theories, the following may be noted: (1) Failure to anticipate the disproportionate distribution of criminals among the sexes. (2) Failure to anticipate disproportions in the age distribution of criminals. (3) Failure to anticipate disproportions in the urban-rural distribution of criminals. (4) Failure to anticipate the disproportionate distribution of criminals in certain racial and ethnic groups. (5) Failure to provide a physiological basis for differentiating between those physical acts which are criminal under certain circumstances but legitimate in others. (6) Failure to cope with the variable periodicity of criminal behavior in the same criminals.

In addition to their failure to suggest physiological processes capable of accounting for the nonrandom statistical distributions cited above, physical theories of crime labor under an inability to cope with the fact that many criminal activities require learned skills. Most, if not all, physical disabilities with known effects on behavior *impair* the organism's ability to learn or to perform. But many criminal acts involve performances requiring perceptual and manual skills of a high order. Theories equating criminal behavior with the symptomatology of physical defects are incapable of dealing with this aspect of criminality.

Many of the difficulties cited above would seem to disappear if the physical defects were viewed as predisposing factors rather than direct causes. Reformulated in these terms, a physical theory of crime would suggest that persons with certain physical defects were more likely to become involved in crime than those without these defects. This interpretation would, however, require the theory to differentiate between those of the physically defective who succumb and those who do not succumb to criminality. At this point the "physical" theory of crime would be forced to rely on nonphysical factors to account for the critical differentiation between offenders and the law-abiding.

CRIMINALITY AS A RESULT OF RACIAL INFERIORITY. Except insofar as it purports to deal with the disproportionate distribution of criminals in certain racial groups, the racial hypothesis of criminality suffers from each of the inadequacies cited above. It suffers, in addition, from a major inconsistency in the definition of race itself. The most persuasive evidence for a racial crime factor derives from the crime rates of certain socially disadvantaged racial groups—in this country, the Negro group. Nevertheless, as was pointed out in Chapter 11, the statistical evidence for Negro criminality is based on a definition which characterizes a person with *any* perceptible degree of Negro ancestry as "Negro." The effect of this definition, which is social rather than anthropological, is to include in the "Negro" category many persons who, from a strictly "racial" point of view, may be more white than Negro. Accordingly, the major evidence for the racial theory of crime derives from the invalid superimposition of a genetic hypothesis upon a cultural definition of race.

CRIMINALITY AS A RESULT OF PSYCHOLOGICAL MALADJUSTMENT OR DEFICIENCY. In common with the other theories discussed, psychological explanations of criminality generally tend to equate criminal behavior with some form of disturbed and maladaptive behavior. The maladjustment is viewed as deriving from one or a combination of two general kinds of factors: (1) original deficiencies in mental endowment and (2) exposure to experiences having a pathological effect on the mind.

Attempts to relate criminal behavior directly to psychological variables encounter some but not all of the difficulties confronting the theories already discussed. The disproportionate distribution of criminals among the sexes presents its usual problem. Though certain forms of mental disturbance have different rates of incidence among males and females, the over-all distribution of mental defects and diseases does not approach the 90 percent–10 percent division of known criminals among the sexes. With respect to the disproportions in age, class and geographic distributions, theories viewing criminality as a result of pathological experiences fare better. The onset of several forms of psychological disturbance has been associated with the stresses of adolescence and young adulthood. A higher incidence of most forms of mental disease is apparent among the underprivileged social classes—especially among those exposed to the heightened pressures of poverty in deteriorated urban settings.

Nevertheless, there are two kinds of difficulties which a psychological explanation of criminality seems incapable of resolving. Mental disabilities, like physical disabilities, tend to manifest themselves in behavioral deficits of various kinds. Perhaps the outstanding criterion of mental disturbance is the individual's inability to cope with the environmental problems of living. Though this conception is highly compatible with certain self-destructive forms of crime, it is largely incompatible with those forms which are clearly related to the pursuit of the same goals and problems pursued by the noncriminal. Most crimes involving theft represent goal-directed attempts to *solve* rather than avoid environmental problems. In many cases, the attempts are relatively successful. Crimes of this general category constitute about 90 percent of all reported offenses. A theory which fails adequately to cope with them is, in effect, unable to account for the huge preponderance of the data with which it must deal.

There is a further and more fundamental difficulty, shared by other crime theories but most apparent in psychological theories; for this reason we have reserved discussion of it to this point. The assumption underlying any psychological theory of crime is that *criminality is accounted for when the criminal motivation of the offender is accounted for*

But neither a motive by itself nor an act by itself can constitute a crime. A crime is always the conjunction of an act and a motive. The most malevolent hostility, the most insatiate greed, is not sufficient. Conversely, acts as realistically destructive as the taking of human life may not be criminal unless conjoined with a hostile intent or with a negligence suggesting a culpable indifference on the part of a person known to be aware of the possible hazards of his carelessness. Thus, neither the intent in the absence of the act, nor the act in the absence of the intent, satisfies the requirements of a crime. These joint requirements of the criminal act serve also to define the requirements of a criminological theory. Since motivation alone is insufficient for the criminal act, the attempt to explain the act solely by accounting for the offender's motives (or needs or personality) is an insufficient explanation of the crime. *The task of theory is to explain how the individual's psychological needs or problems lead to the choice of a criminal alternative.*

CRIMINALITY AS A RESPONSE TO VARIOUS SOCIAL CONDITIONS OR VALUES. Various theorists have attempted to relate crime to specific social factors such as social inequality, social conflict, and economic deprivation. Others have derived the motives for criminal behavior from such broad cultural values as materialism, individualism, competitiveness, and aggression. These attempts run afoul of the same difficulties just cited.

Though the available evidence strongly suggests that adverse social conditions are favorable to crime, the same evidence indicates that identical conditions are related to a host of other social evils. Similar considerations apply to the relation between criminality and certain cultural values. How are the aggressive, self-seeking values of the conniving business operator to be differentiated from the values of the self-seeking, aggressive criminal? It seems apparent that the differentiation cannot be made on the basis of broad social values alone. Once again, theory is confronted with the necessity of finding additional variables to differentiate criminal from legitimate alternatives.

The Question Reposed: Are General Criminological Theories Possible?

Our attempts to find variables capable of dealing simultaneously with all aspects of the data of crime and criminals have, so far, merely led us from one impasse to another. The problem is not unlike that which confronts the solution of a difficult jigsaw puzzle: whatever seems to fit one part of the puzzle throws the rest of the picture out of focus. Certain kinds of criminal behavior seem appropriate to the symptomatology of mental disturbance; other kinds seem disturbingly rational. Many criminals are socially deprived—but the concept of social deprivation cannot deal with the offender who is relatively well off. Sexual status seems to be a strong indicator—until we confront the female criminal. "The slums of today (runs the popular slogan) breed the criminals of tomorrow." But many of tomorrow's doctors, lawyers, policemen, and priests are growing up in the slums—and not a few of tomorrow's criminals are now breathing clean country air.

Perhaps it is not possible to deal with the complexities of all or of large segments of the data of crime and criminals by means of a limited number of concepts and variables. Perhaps, in the last analysis, there must be almost as many separate accounts as there are individual crimes or criminals. If this is so, the search for general theories of crime is illusory. Before coming to this conclusion, however, we might raise the question: Are there any other kinds of behavior which present similar problems of complexity and, therefore, similar problems of description and explanation?

Suppose, for a moment, that instead of seeking a general theory of criminality we were trying to find a general way of accounting for the behavior and characteristics of that large category of persons known as *traveling salesmen*. In what ways are these people similar? What determines the products they sell? Why is it that certain groups use a very aggressive approach—the "hard sell"—while others employ a casual, offhand, easy technique—the "soft sell"? What factors in their personalities, their backgrounds, their motives, determine these things? How does one become a salesman in the first place? And what population groups are likely to be found in this field?

As before, we might begin investigation by deriving problematical data from the range of variations exhibited by the subjects. We would probably find that the overwhelming majority are males. A disproportionate percentage—but by no means all—would probably be on the young side, men in their twenties and thirties. Their products would reveal an almost infinite variety; their techniques would show wide variation. Their histories as salesmen will vary. Some will have sold several different types of products; others will have confined themselves to one or a few. Their previous careers will vary. Many will have drifted in from other fields; very many will drift out again.

Nevertheless, many of the questions that bedevil criminological theory would fail to create difficulties in the case of the salesman. For some reason, it might not surprise us to find that most "drummers" are males, or that very many of them are rather young. Certain questions would probably not even arise. For example, we would be unlikely to inquire what different psychological factors impel certain salesmen to sell encyclopedias, others to sell brushes, still others to sell magazine subscriptions. Or why the vacuum cleaner salesman behaves so aggressively, with his foot always in the doorway, while the medical salesman (the "detailer" who represents the pharmaceutical houses to doctors) typically behaves in a very courteous, soft-spoken, almost scholarly manner? Similarly, those familiar with the beer business would be unlikely to ask what personal problems make the beer salesman drink so much.

The reason these questions would not be likely to arise is perhaps as interesting as the questions themselves. The different techniques and mannerisms of the different categories of salesman are readily understood as appropriate to their different occupational specialties. Conversely, certain general similarities in the behavior of *all* traveling salesmen are easily accounted for in terms of the over-all requirements of a general occupational role—a role requiring its occupants to travel from place to place persuading people they do not personally know to buy things they may or may not need. This task requires the carrying out of certain learned skills—which may or may not be congenial to those carrying them out. The hard-driving vacuum cleaner salesman may be a gentle, quiet fellow in his private life. The beer salesman may dislike beer. Nevertheless, the door-to-door vendor of vacuum cleaners is expected—in fact, required—to be aggressive on the job; and if the beer salesman refused to drink convivially with his customers he might not have many. Finally, if we asked the question, Why are these people doing these things instead of other things? we might not be surprised to learn that many would be very glad to be doing other things, if they had the chance.

What is particularly suggestive about the role of the salesman is the manner in which it clarifies the theoretically puzzling problem of the relation between individual activities and personality variables. The attempt to relate the person's activities directly to psychological factors inevitably foundered when confronted with the implications of two kinds of commonplace observations: (1) Large numbers of people with obviously different personalities may be found engaged in similar activities. (2) Many persons with similar psychological characteristics may be found involved in different activities.

The Critical Need for Intervening Variables in a Theory of Behavior

The obvious error in any attempt to relate an individual's personality directly to his overt activities is the failure to realize that certain other factors may intervene between his inner state of mind and his ultimate responses—factors which may change those responses radically. A factor intervening between a causal or *independent variable* and an end effect or *dependent variable* is technically known as an *intervening variable*. A theory which ignores these intervening factors is incapable of dealing with findings that different people behave similarly—and similar people behave differently.

The concept of *role* profoundly clarifies these universal but otherwise baffling findings. The similar activities of dissimilar personalities clearly seem related to the fact that these different personalities are involved in a similar role. Conversely, the dissimilar activities of relatively similar personalities may be accounted for by the fact that each is behaving with reference to a different role.

It is true that individual reasons for the same role involvement may vary widely. It is equally true that different people play the same roles in different ways, and with different consequences. Nevertheless, though individual differences color the manner and affect the consequences of role-playing, the uniformities imparted by the role itself may often transcend these idiosyncratic factors. Caruso and Peerce may sing *I Pagliacci* in different ways—but the role is still Canio.

Application of the Role Concept to the Problematical Data of Crimes and Criminals

Because *roles* simultaneously have subjective, interpersonal, and social-structural aspects, they are capable of definitions which relate to any one or a combination of these referents. For our purposes the most adequate definition is that which most comprehensively relates the psychological, interactional, and sociological components in a single formulation. Accordingly, a role may be defined as *a socially standardized and socially transmitted configuration of reciprocal attitudes and activities which organizes selective aspects of the actor's total behavior with reference to certain goals pursued by means of certain interactions with the occupants of other roles.* In order to evaluate the appropriateness of the role concept for criminological theory, we may test its "fit" against the requirements of the *problematical data* previously outlined. We will deal first with the nonstatistical and, second, with the statistical findings which the concept is required to anticipate.

The Descriptive Function of the Role Concept:
How Well Does the Concept Prepare Us to Anticipate What We May Find Happening Outside?

Perhaps the most direct way to test the appropriateness of the role concept to the nonstatistical criminological data is to substitute in each of the seven requirements listed on pages 320 to 321 the term *role* wherever the terms *crime* or *criminal act* appear. If the resulting statements still satisfy the conditions of the definition of *role* (cited above), the fitness of the concept is demonstrated *prima facie*. Examination of each of the seven statements confirms the essential interchangeability of the concepts.

Role behavior requires an integration of responses at a high level of the central nervous system.

The separate acts comprising any role are not exclusive to that role alone.

The acts comprising the role, together with the role itself, are learned.

Role behavior varies in type and frequency. (A person has different roles; the frequency with which he acts in any one of them may vary.)

The totality of activities carried out through the entire range of the offender's daily behavior is likely to include a greater total of acts related to different roles than acts related to any one given role.

The totality of the offender's contacts with others is likely to include a number not related to certain of his given roles.

Most roles require interaction with another person.

Testing the "fit" of the role concept to the statistical findings requires a somewhat analogous but necessarily more detailed procedure. In this instance we must substitute for the word *criminal* the terms *certain roles* or *certain role occupants,* and then provide relevant examples consistent with the definition and with the broad sociological data of role-taking in the community at large.

1. THE SELECTIVE DISTRIBUTION OF CRIMINAL ROLES AMONG THE SEXES. Two general findings must be anticipated and accounted for: (1) the disproportionate percentage of males involved in crime and delinquency; and (2) the wider range of crimes and delinquency encountered among males.

The Sex-Linked Character of Many Social Roles. Many legitimate social roles, activities and vocations are differentiated on the basis of sex. For many of these membership in one sex is a virtual requirement—and membership in the other a virtual disqualification. Even in an era which has seen the unprecedented appearance of the lady wrestler there are still certain activities from which the gentler sex is barred. (By the time this text is a few years old the number of these exclusively male activities will probably have decreased.) Most activities requiring heavy physical labor, physical danger, or violence are still restricted to males. (The policewoman is a recent exception to this general rule; the female mugger is still rare.)

Differences in the Role Aspirations and Role Preparations of Boys and Girls. The play activities of children are universally related to preparations and aspirations for the later assumption of socially defined adult roles. In this sense, play activities are themselves an essential aspect of preparation. Certain contrasts in the preparations and aspirations of boys and girls are relevant to the later development and division of various roles among the two sexes.

There is a greater degree of continuity in the role preparations of girls as contrasted with boys. In their play activities girls generally prepare for roles which will be realistically available to them as adults. They play at keeping house, at tending children, at cooking, etc. Their mothers and other female relatives provide models and examples for these roles. *Boys tend to play at roles which will be less realistically available to them as adults.* Margaret Mead has written: "In peacetime the small boy's heroes, whether his own father keeps a grocery store or is president of a bank, are policemen, firemen, flyers, cowboys, and baseball-players . . ."[8]

The role aspirations and preparations of girls are not only more conventional but *more limited and less variable than those of boys,* a condition anticipating their less variable role activities as adult females. Thus, girls learn early to restrict their aspirations within more realistic limits. In contrast, boys must face the frustration of giving up their earlier, more heroic images in exchange for less active, less exciting conventional pursuits structured around earning a living. They will be expected to be earners, fathers, husbands—roles that hardly preoccupied the fantasies of their youth.

Acceptable and unacceptable ways of deviation and rebellion vary for boys and girls. The culture which sets certain limits on role and activity alternatives for the two sexes tends also to surround these limits with a pale of acceptable and unacceptable deviation. There are highly significant differences in both of these areas for boys and girls. In the first place, even the rebellious activity of girls is largely related to their demands for the perquisites of conventional female roles at ages considered premature by society. The girls demand to be allowed to wear lipstick, to smoke, to stay out late on dates—rights which are the prerogatives of older females. Thus the girl frequently rebels by insisting on playing conventional roles earlier than she is permitted to, and her rebellion often takes the form of carrying out these roles in behavior considered intolerable not because of its content but because of its precocity. In contrast, *the rebellion of boys is frequently related to a rejection of*

[8] Margaret Mead, *Male and Female* (New York: The New American Library of World Literature, 1955), p. 230.

the activities of conventional adult males. Unlike the girl, who dreams of exchanging the uncertain life of waiting and dating for the security of the role of wife, the young man may be less willing to surrender his freedom as the unfettered lover for the role of steady husband and father. Unlike the little girl, who dreams of puttering around the kitchen and taking care of the baby, he is less likely to dream of a day in the office or the factory and an evening at home with the wife and kids.

To a considerable extent society recognizes the realities of the young male's greater frustrations by tolerating less deviation and rebellion by girls—and more by boys. These differences are mirrored in the peer-group traditions of each. Among the girls, successful conformity to adult conduct rules—good manners, neat dressing, etc.—are ways of obtaining status among peers. *Among the boys, a too-yielding conformity to adult conduct rules is cause for lowered status.* For the girl, the role of teacher's pet is a desirable goal; for the boys, the mere accusation may be a deadly insult. Thus the traits for which girls learn they will be liked are charm, prettiness, gentleness, cooperation, *compliance.* Boys, on the contrary, will be admired for being courageous, combative, competitive, and, within limits, *noncompliant.*

The Activity Alternatives Open to Boys and Girls. Boys are encouraged by their peers to engage in competitive activities, to master manipulative skills, to fight, to be independent, to remove obstacles by direct aggressive action. Girls are encouraged to be—or at least to behave as if they were—more dependent, to rely on the boys for help. A girl who is too independent, who defends herself too effectively, who competes, who wants to "show the boys up," is less likely to be popular among the boys. *Therefore she is also less likely to be popular among the girls, among whom status is highly related to the ability to attract and hold males.* The greater initiative, the greater aggressiveness, the greater insistence on abilities of self-help and self-defense among the boys serve as preparations for the presumably greater rigors of the male's destined part in life.

As it turns out, the actual performance for which these heroic rehearsals are presumably the preparation may fall short of the expectations of the aspiring actors. And herein lies a point that need not be labored at any greater length than the sentence required to state it: *For the modern boy growing up in a conventionalized, routinized, and increasingly immobile adult society, the more liberal tolerance of deviation may serve as an increasingly inadequate preparation for conventional adult roles—and as an increasingly efficient preparation for unconventional pursuits.* The endemic rise in juvenile delinquency and the increasing involvement of boys at all class levels may be related to this longer-term trend.

2. THE DISPROPORTIONATE INVOLVEMENT OF THE YOUNG IN DELINQUENCY AND CRIME. Many of the relevant relations of role selection and role behavior to the age distribution of offenders have already been anticipated in the previous discussion. The increase in nonproductive leisure, especially among urban youth, the longer postponement of adult responsibilities, the decreased contact with visible models of working adults, the greater dependency on peers for models, the wider range of activity alternatives open to the unemployed but money-hungry adolescent—each of these factors tends to increase the possibility of experimentation in unconventional activities. Although the organization of these experimental activities into delinquent role patterns may require the intervention of additional factors, the activities themselves provide raw material potentially available for criminal exploitation.

The proportionately greater criminal involvement of the young is, of course, a direct function of the comparatively lesser involvement of older adults. Patterns of role involvement typically change as a function of increasing age. This fact suggests a basis for understanding differential age-rates of criminality. Where the late teen-ager and the twenty-year-old is still likely to be single and not yet strongly tied to an occupational career, the man in his late twenties and early thirties is likely to be married, to be raising a family, and to be heavily engaged in earning the living necessary to fulfilling the responsibilities contingent on his roles of husband and father. These roles, and the increasingly conservative, security-conscious attitudes they engender, are less compatible with the occupational and social hazards of crime.

3. THE DISPROPORTIONATE INCIDENCE OF CRIME AND DELINQUENCY IN URBAN LOCALITIES. As before, the previous discussion has anticipated many of the ideas relevant to the present subject. Leisure is largely an urban invention. The prolonged childhood and unproductivity of the urban adolescent contrasts sharply with the earlier vocational maturity of his country cousin, at work with his father or his neighbors in the fields. In addition to his greater involvement in gainful activities, the rural child is confronted with far fewer activity alternatives and fewer opportunities for diversion. Living and working side by side with adult behavior models, he is less dependent and less involved with a peer

society which concentrates on personal consumption to the relative neglect of personal productivity.

Since various other characteristics of urban living have already been discussed elsewhere in this text, it is unnecessary to cite them here. In summary, it is evident that the urban, as contrasted with the rural, setting presents a wider range of both conventional and unconventional role alternatives and a greater possibility of role conflicts. This occurs, moreover, in a situation where the powerful influences of informal social control are vitiated and diluted by the impersonality and isolation characteristic of big-city life.

4. THE DISPROPORTIONATE INVOLVEMENT OF MEMBERS OF THE LOWER SOCIOECONOMIC CLASSES. Few sociological conclusions have been more convincingly confirmed than the conclusion which states that the distribution of social roles is largely a function of social class. Members of the lower socioeconomic strata have less access to the educational and vocational perquisites of the more desirable social roles. Beginning at a lower rung of the status ladder, the extent of their climb is highly conditioned by their original starting point. The lower-class child requires talent and perseverance to reach a point that, in many cases, is lower than the level from which the more privileged child will start as a matter of course. Moreover, many of the economic and social obstacles confronting the lower-class child will be unknown to middle- and upper-class children. The occupants of the less desirable vocational roles have gained less by their social conformity —and stand, consequently, to lose less if they cease to conform. To the sophisticated lower-class child who is able to contrast the lot of his hard-working parents with that of the neighborhood racket-men, the doctrine that honesty is its own reward may cease to be persuasive. In any case, the vivid contrast between legitimate and illegitimate alternatives presents the lower-class youth with role conflicts that are much less likely to confront the children of more privileged parents.

THE DIFFERENTIAL INVOLVEMENT OF CERTAIN RACIAL AND ETHNIC GROUPS IN CRIME. The situation of certain racial and ethnic groups may be considered as a special case of social deprivation, with resulting exposure to the same limited range of less desirable role alternatives confronting members of the lowest social classes. Among the findings supporting this conclusion is the evidence that the small percentage of minority-race members who, for one reason or another, have escaped entrapment in the lowest economic stratum contribute little to the statistics of crime. Like the middle-class members of the majority race, they tend to occupy roles antagonistic to involvement in criminal activities.

The Explanatory Function of the Role Concept in Criminology

THE ROLE AS AN INTERVENING VARIABLE BETWEEN THE PERSON AND THE ACT. One of the most significant contributions of the role concept is the way in which it resolves the dilemma of relating personal traits, needs, and problems to criminal behavior. As was previously pointed out, individual psychological factors were, by themselves, incapable of differentiating between the variety of legal and illegal ways these factors might express themselves in actual behavior. What was clearly called for was a factor intermediate between the personality and the response. The concept of *multiple roles* makes it possible to retain the idea of personality as a relatively stable and distinctive structure while at the same time accounting for the variability of responses under different conditions and in different relationships. Thus, the professional pickpocket, after a day devoted to the highly specialized activities and relationships called for in his occupation, may board the train with other commuters and return to his family to spend a highly conventional evening in his roles of husband, father—and, like as not, good neighbor.

THE ROLE AS AN INTERVENING VARIABLE BETWEEN THE SOCIAL GROUP AND THE PERSON. One of the dilemmas of a sociological account of criminality was the problem of explaining how similar cultural values or exposure to similar social conditions was related to a wide range of different legitimate and illegitimate activities. The role concept provides a plausible basis for dealing with this critical problem of different responses to the same social factors. Roles, on the one hand, are the media through which society distributes its functions—its major and minor chores—among different members. On the other hand, for the members themselves, roles provide alternate routes (of varying difficulty and desirability) to the attainment of similar social values and goals. Moreover, just as society creates roles to fulfill its acknowledge needs, so it creates others to satisfy its unacknowledged needs. (The roles of prostitute, racketeer, and gambler are examples of roles that fulfill unacknowledged social demands, just as the roles of physician, teacher, and businessman are examples of those through which the group carries out various acknowledged needs.)

Thus the role concept serves sociological theory as a *distributor* of different social functions. At the same time, it serves psychological theory as a *unifying* factor, channeling diverse individual trends into recognizable patterns of behavior. In this latter aspect, roles function as instruments of social control, bringing about the predictable uniformities essential for group living.

Linking the Individual to the Criminal Role

So far, in our attempt to build a negotiable bridge of intervening variables between the individual and his criminal act, we have suggested one structural concept that partly spans the gap: the idea of *role*. The sequence of concepts might now be ranged as follows: Instead of relating the person directly to the criminal act, we speak of the *person,* the *person's role,* and the *activity* which is attached to the role. In effect, the act has now been detached from its direct link with the individual and attached, instead, to a given role—one among many—which he might occupy. We must now deal with the question: What links the person to the role?

At this point it becomes apparent that the thorny question of individual motivation has merely been postponed. If the role concept relieves psychological theory of the task of finding a separate "personal" significance behind every single activity performed by the individual, it may have done no more than defer the identical problem to the next level of analysis. Even if it is granted that the individual's choice of activities is largely determined by his choice of roles, the question still remains, *What determines his choice of roles?*

Before proceeding further, it should be noted that this way of putting the question is not the only way the question can conceivably be put. On closer examination it becomes evident that this formulation begs a question—actually two questions. In the first place it assumes that individuals *choose* their roles—that role involvement is, in one way or another, a matter of personal motivation. The second unquestioned assumption derives from the first. It suggests that the individual's range of alternatives is unlimited.

Ignored by these assumptions is the possibility that a person's role alternatives may frequently be limited by factors beyond his control, that many of them may be imposed rather than chosen, that many may frustrate rather than satisfy his personal needs. Nevertheless, these possibilities are actualities in many areas of human experience. Consider the following commonplace situation.

Enforced Politeness toward a Relative One Dislikes

In a typical family gathering a group of the younger people, animatedly chatting, are suddenly broken in upon by a senile and garrulous relative whom each of the young people heartily dislikes. If the older man had approached any one of them individually, they would have quickly moved off, brushing him aside. But now they are trapped and condemned to listen to one more version of the old man's interminable stories.

What traps them? It is not the old man himself; he would not have been able to corner them had he found them alone. It is clearly not their own desires; every one of them would be glad to find a pretext to leave. What keeps them there is something entirely "social," as contrasted with anything "individual" or "personal." Each one of the young people is immobilized by a felt need to conform to a certain social expectation, which might be called *"the duty to act attentively toward an old relative no matter how bored you are."* This obligation is, of course, very weak, and could be evaded without guilt if it were not for the fact that the young people have been caught in a group. Thus, they are actually trapped and immobilized by each other.

In a theoretical sense this situation is highly interesting, for the following reasons. (1) The behavior of the young people is in conflict with the private desires of each. (2) Nevertheless, it can be accounted for entirely without reference to conditions in the personal field of the actors and with reference only to forces related to the interpersonal or social field. In other words, in order to understand this behavior, it is not necessary to know the personal characteristics or wishes of the actors—except insofar as they contribute to a forced commitment to a certain social value.

The significance of the interpersonal context of motivation is underscored by the next example to be cited. In his classic work, *The Gang,* Thrasher writes about a group of college students, who, one night, for reasons which none of them could explain, suddenly decided to rob a post-office. Thrasher presents the story in the form of a verbatim report by one of the participants.

The Reluctant Robbers

We three college students—Mac, Art, and Tom—were rooming together while attending V——— University, one of the oldest colleges in the South. On the day of our crime all three of us spent over three hours in the library—really working. That was on Sunday and our crime was committed at 1:30 that night (or rather Monday morning).

The conversation began with a remark about the numerous recent bank failures in the state, probably stimulated by one of us glancing at a map of the state. It then shifted to discussion of a local bank that had closed its doors the day before. Tom, who worked at the post-office occasionally as special mail clerk, happened to mention that a sack containing a large amount of money had been received at the post-office that afternoon, consigned to a local bank that feared a run.

The conversation then turned to the careless way in which the money was handled at the office—a plain canvas sack thrown into an open safe. We discussed the ease with which a thief could get into the building and steal the money. Tom drew a plan showing the desk at which the only clerk worked and the location of the only gun in the office. At first the conversation was entirely confined to how easily criminals might manage to steal the money. Somehow it shifted to a personal basis: as to how easily we might get the money. This shift came so naturally that even the next morning we were unable to decide when and by whom the first vital remark had been made.

A possible plan was discussed as to how we might steal the package. Tom could go to the office and gain admittance on the pretense of looking for an important letter. Then Art and I, masked and armed, could rush in, tie Tom and the clerk, and make off with the package. We had lost sight of the fact that the package contained money. We were simply discussing the possibility of playing an exciting prank with no thought of actually committing it. We had played many harmless pranks and had discussed them in much the same way before; but the knowledge that there was danger in this prank made it a subject to linger over.

After about an hour and a half of talk, I started to take off my shoes. As I unlaced them, I thought of how it looked as if I were the one to kill our interesting project. I foolishly said something to the effect that if Tom was going down town, I thought I would write a letter that was already overdue. Tom was anxiously awaiting a letter that should be in that night. He suggested that I go down also as it was a very decent night. I consented and Art decided to join us. I sat down and wrote the letter—meanwhile we continued our talk about the money package.

My letter finished, something seemed to change. We found further inaction impossible: we had either to rob the post-office or go to bed. Tom brought out his two guns; I hunted up a couple of regular plain handkerchiefs, and Art added some rope to the assortment. At the time we were still individually and collectively playing a game with ourselves. Each of us expected one of the other two to give the thing the horse laugh and suggest going to bed and letting the letters wait till morning. But it seemed that we forgot everything—our position in school, our families and friends, the danger to us and to our folks. Our only thought was to carry out that prank. We all made our preparations more or less mechanically. Our minds were in a daze.

Putting on our regular overcoats and caps, we left the rooms quietly. On the way down town we passed the night patrolman without any really serious qualms. Tom entered the post-office as was his usual custom, being a sub-clerk, and Art and I crept up to the rear door. Tom appeared at a window with his hat, a signal that there were no reasons why our plan would not be effective. At the door, in full illumination of a light, we arranged our handkerchiefs over our faces and took our guns out of our pockets. We were ready.

"Have you enough guts to go through with this thing?" I asked, turning to Art, who was behind me.

"If you have," he answered.

Frankly I felt that I had gone far enough, but for some unknown reason I did not throw out a remark that would have ended it all then and there. And Art didn't. He later said that he was just too scared to suggest anything. We were both, it seems, in a sort of daze.

Tom opened the door and we followed our plan out to the end. There was no active resistance by the regular night man.

Then after we left the office with thousands of dollars in our hands we did not realize all that it meant. Our first words were not about getting the money. They were about the fact that our prank (and it was still that to us) had been successful. When we reached our rooms, having hidden the money in an abandoned dredger, the seriousness of the thing began to penetrate our minds. For an hour or so we lay quietly and finally settled on a plan that seemed safe in returning the money without making our identity known. Then I went to sleep.[9]

This incident, reported by one of the participants, describes a cooperative group activity directed toward a criminal object. What is interesting about the incident is that none of the participants was a criminal, that each was secretly opposed to the undertaking, and that all were personally disinterested in the goal. Why, then, did they do it?

The narrative suggests several clues. In the first place, each was reluctant to occupy the humiliating role of the one who "backs out." Apparently, then, though each was afraid, the prospect of humiliation was more threatening. Moreover, in order to avoid the appearance of reluctance, each found it necessary to keep up the pretense of his own willingness—at the same time nourishing the secret hope that *somebody else* would realize that things were going too far and back out. At this point it is probable that each still felt that the others were merely testing him, and that nobody really intended to go through with it. Then, as

[9] Frederic M. Thrasher, *The Gang* (Chicago: The University of Chicago Press, 1936) pp. 300–303.

preparations advanced, the security of this belief began to wane and each boy began to believe that the others might not be fooling after all. This served to isolate each in the intolerable position of the only one who would be chicken-hearted. When the illusion of group daring reaches this level of mutual deception, there could be no turning back. In this manner, with the need to conceal their mounting anxiety forcing them to shows of increased bravado, the boys literally pushed each other over the threshold of fantasy into the criminal act.

Thus there arose a situation of group motivation, based on an illusion and contrary to the actual wishes of each participant. A condition of group motivation exists *when each member is behaving in accordance with the same interpretation of what is expected of him*— whether or not this is in accord with his own wishes and regardless of the correctness of the interpretation. Each of the unwilling bandits was behaving *as if* the others were expecting him to participate. (Actually, they were hoping he would back out.) The illusion went further: though each personally dreaded participating, each was eventually convinced that the others were willing. The curious thing was that none of the group, at any point, put any direct pressure on the others to go along. Each was coerced by a similar image of what the others expected and each dreaded an imagined group reaction.

What was it that committed each to conform to this imaginary expectation in violation of his own wishes? A tentative answer might be that conformity involved certain psychological rewards; nonconformity, certain penalties. Apparently, in the mutual roles in which they found themselves *the way each boy felt about himself was dependent on how he imagined the others were feeling about him.*

Here again, the group authority was exercised by each member over himself. The strength of this authority was related to the extent to which each one's self-evaluation was open to influence by the real or imagined attitudes of the others. Each was intent on fulfilling the expectations of his role, on conforming to its conceived requirements. The behavioral requirements of the role were, as it turned out, secondary, since none of the boys actually desired to engage in the activity itself. Thus the commitment was not to the *act* or to the *goal* of the act (the money), but rather to the *group expectations*—which, in the given situation, ordained that each take the role of a fearless, daring character. In another situation the usages of this group might have cast the members in different roles, ordaining different responses.

Conformity: The Need to Fulfill a Group Expectation

The companionate character of the overwhelming majority of delinquent activities underscores the significance of conformity as a transcendent motivation. *Conformity* may be defined as *a global motive on the part of an individual committed to a group to fulfill the expectations of the group regarding his attitudes and behavior.* The frequent salience of this motive over the most fundamental personal needs and wishes is a matter of universal experience. Soldiers going into battle with the clearest knowledge of the risks, and with strong personal desires to avoid danger, report that the thing that kept them going was the fear of "letting the other guys down." In studies of the behavior of front-line soldiers, the feeling of commitment to "other guys in the outfit" was found to be the strongest single factor in the maintenance of individual combat morale.[10] Apparently the same process works with equal effectiveness in the maintenance of anti-social morale.

A recently reported juvenile gang incident illustrates this point. A neighborhood boy was assaulted and killed by a juvenile gang. On examination it was discovered that the victim had been stabbed many times. The explanation for the multiple wounds was not apparent until, on questioning, it was found that each member of the gang had personally struck him. When individually questioned by the police, several of the boys were able to convince the police that they had actually not wanted to participate in this ritualistic wounding but had gone along because they were afraid of "being called chicken."

A reporter present throughout the trial of these delinquents has recorded his impressions of one of the defendants as the youth was called to the witness stand:

> As he mumbled his name, there was a sudden shock of recognition of how exactly alike these children are. Vincent Pardon was like every other ward of the Children's Court we have seen over the last seven days. He had, as an instance, the same hair, drawn back with some care with a wide-toothed comb, and then splattered at the forelock with concentrated devotion.
>
> These children even talk the same way. There is a voice of 152d St. and Broadway which is different from the voice further up on the Heights. It is a voice without reference to ethnic origin. Children

[10] See: S. A. Stouffer, *The American Soldier*, Studies in Social Psychology in World War II, Volumes I and II, (Princeton: Princeton University Press, 1949).

named Lago, O'Kelly and Pardon have the same precise inflection. They say "cluck" for "clock," and "Reeversyd" for "Riverside." It makes no difference whether their parents be Irish or Spanish; they do not talk like their parents. It is as though they did not learn to talk from parent or teacher, but from other children; as though they had no homes, but only streets called Amsterdam or Broadway.[11]

Commitment: The Process of Personal Involvement with a Group

In our search for concepts capable of dealing with the variability of criminal behavior, we have consistently proceeded in one direction: from the overt or "outward" activities backward or, rather, "inward" toward the person. Thus we found that the otherwise confusing multiplicity of individual activities could be organized meaningfully by the concept of *role*. Coming closer to the person, we found that many aspects of role-playing might be accounted for by a global, unifying, and transcending motive or need to *conform to the expectations of certain groups*. We must now deal with the question, What psychological processes link or "tie" the person to the groups to which he conforms? Why do certain individuals slavishly conform, others less rigorously or totally—others only up to a certain point, beyond which they will not go? Why do certain people conform to certain groups and not to others? How is membership in certain groups related to alienation toward (and by) other groups?

These questions raise issues central not only to criminological theory but to virtually every other field of interpersonal behavior. Needless to say, an adequate description of the subtle and complex processes determining individual involvements in groups has yet to be evolved. Nevertheless, there are at least three reasons a concept standing for the end-result of these processes can serve a useful theoretical function. In the first place, this end-result can be recognized and differentiated—even if only on a descriptive level. It is possible to compare two members of a group and to make the statement, *"A is more (or less) involved and differently involved than B."* Secondly, a comprehensive description of the range and character of the individual's total group involvements has meaningful implications for an understanding of many aspects of his

[11] Murray Kempton, the *New York Post*, February 21, 1958.

behavior. Finally, there is highly suggestive evidence that *the extent to which the individual conforms to the requirements of any given group is significantly related not merely to the character of his involvement in that specific group but to the character and range of the totality of his group relationships.* Putting it in terser terms, the manner in which A behaves as a member of Group X is meaningfully related to the character of his membership in Groups Y and Z. For a variety of reasons, including the lack of a more precisely adequate term, we have suggested the word *commitment* to identify certain global characteristics of the kind of personal involvement we have in mind.

A Working Definition of Commitment

For our purposes, a person may be said to be *committed* to the extent that his self-evaluation is critically dependent on the evaluations of a person or a group with which he is involved. Psychological commitments have at least two describable dimensions: *intensiveness* and *extensiveness.* A person is *intensively committed* when his feelings about himself and his behavior more or less precisely reflect the group's feelings about him. He is less *intensively* committed when his self-evaluation is less open to influence by the evaluations of the group. (Thus we may say: "The group strongly disapproved of John and Frank today. John was very upset, but Frank was merely irritated; he looked as if it didn't bother him very much.") An *extensive* commitment to a group refers to an involvement in which a large proportion of the individual's total activities are in some way dependent on his membership in that group. A vivid example of this subtle and manifold penetration of the influence of commitment is given by Whyte in his *Street Corner Society.*

> . . . One Saturday night I stumbled upon one of my most exciting research experiences in Cornerville. It was the night when the Nortons were to bowl for the prize money; the biggest bowling night of the whole season. I recall standing on the corner with the boys while they discussed the coming contest. I listened to Doc, Mike and Danny making their predictions as to the order in which the men would finish. At first, this made no particular impression upon me, as my own unexpressed predictions were exactly along the same lines. Then, as the men joked and argued, I suddenly began to question and take a new look at the whole situation. I was convinced that Doc, Mike and Danny were basically correct in their predictions, and yet why should the scores approximate the structure of the gang? Were these top men simply better natural athletes than the rest? . . . Then I remembered

the baseball game we had had a year earlier against the younger crowd on Norton Street. I could see the man who was by common consent the best baseball player of us all striking out with long, graceful swings and letting the grounders bounce through his legs. . . . I went down to the alleys that night fascinated and just a bit awed by what I was about to witness. Here was the social structure in action right on the bowling alleys. It held the individual members in their places—and I along with them. I did not stop to reason then that, as a close friend of Doc, Danny and Mike, I held a position close to the top of the gang and therefore should be expected to excel on this great occasion. I simply felt myself buoyed up by the situation. I felt my friends were for me, had confidence in me, wanted me to bowl well. As my turn came and I stepped up to bowl, I felt supremely confident that I was going to hit the pins that I was aiming at. I have never felt quite that way before— or since. Here at the bowling alley I was experiencing subjectively the impact of the group structure upon the individual. It was a strange feeling, as if something larger than myself was controlling the ball as I went through my swing and released it toward the pins.

When it was all over, I looked at the scores of all the other men. I was still somewhat bemused by my own experience, and now I was excited to discover that the men had actually finished in the predicted order with only two exceptions that could readily be explained in terms of the group structure.[12]

It seems likely that *intensiveness* and *extensiveness* are rather highly correlated. In the sense that the self may be said to be expressed in the totality and configuration of a person's roles, the *dispersion* or *concentration* of these roles among various group memberships provides some basis for estimating the person's dependency on each. An individual whose personally significant roles are concentrated within the confines of a single group is likely to be highly dependent on that group and, therefore, intensely committed to it. In a sense, he is carrying all his eggs in one basket. On the other hand, a person whose major roles are *dispersed* among a variety of groups is less likely to be dependent, less likely to be intensely committed to any one of them. In this sense, a person who has the significant roles of *father* in one group, *son* in another, *employer* in a third, and *clandestine lover* in still another relationship is less likely *and less able* to be committed to any one of these roles than the child-less, kinless, and jobless wife whose total life activities are concentrated in her marital relationship.

[12] William F. Whyte, *Street Corner Society*, 2d. ed. (Chicago: The University of Chicago Press, 1955), pp. 318–319.

The Constricting Effect of Delinquent versus Nondelinquent Commitments

Should the relationship between the *dispersion* of commitments and their *intensity* prove valid, it might offer a plausible basis for interpreting many aspects and variations of delinquent behavior. It seems obvious that membership in certain groups tends to increase or decrease the practical possibility of membership in other groups. Mr. X, who is already a member of the exclusive Country Club, will probably have an easier time becoming a member of the equally exclusive Yacht Club than Mr. Y, whose only other group affiliation is the Delancey Street Bowling and Billiard Association. Membership in a delinquent group is likely to have a constricting effect on the possibility of nondelinquent group memberships for the self-evident reason that delinquent groups are typically in conflict with more conventional groups. The persistent delinquent, who is also likely to be a persistent truant, may find himself thrown out of school, thrown out of the "better" neighborhood social clubs, kept away from the "nicer" girls—and not asked to join the choir. As the number of groups among which he might have distributed his activities shrinks, he is forced more and more to depend on his delinquent associations for his personally significant experiences. The vicious circle of *constricted commitment leading to intenser commitment* is thus set in motion. The earlier the age at which this process begins, the tighter the circle from the beginning.

Contrast, now, the situation of two children—one born in a deteriorated urban slum area, the other in highly integrated middle-class residential neighborhood. Awaiting the more privileged child are a variety of potential memberships, all or most of which serve as entrees to other groups. From the well-supervised nursery school he will proceed to the well-supervised kindergarten and elementary school. In the summers he will go to the country with his parents—or to the summer camp. At every stage his leisure and his associates will be evaluated, controlled—and, if necessary, changed by adult intervention. His earlier group commitments will constantly be pointed toward later commitments. As a member of the Cub Scouts he will look forward to the time when he can be a Boy Scout. As a new Boy Scout he will associate with his more recent acquaintances in the troop. He will tend to leave his Cub Scout friends—"those kids"—behind him. Thus, his newer commitments will frequently have the effect of terminating his dependency on earlier ones.

For the child emerging on the slum street the situation will be different, the range of alternatives narrower. Like his neighbor across the tracks, he will have play as the main business of his life. Unlike his neighbor, he will play the game with a different pack of cards—a pack with more deuces than aces.

Competition for Control of the Commitment Process

In most modern urban communities the child effectively emerges onto the street somewhere between the ages of four and seven. In the street he finds other children, doing a variety of things. If the street happens to be located in an exclusive section of New York or Boston or Paris, the activities of the other children will be different from the activities going on in a street located in a slum section of any of these cities. On both streets it is likely that the children are trying to have fun. In the better residential sections, this fun will be rather carefully watched and supervised. Unacceptable group activities will tend to be nipped in the bud; control by the adult world, sternly or benignly exercised, will be the rule.

The upper- or middle-class residential neighborhood is not the optimal locus of a juvenile gang. The children lack the extreme autonomy necessary for the existence of such a group. This contrast suggests a dimension of comparison. As the purveyors of activity-alternatives for the child, peer groups differ in the extent of their autonomy from adult control. The extent of the autonomy may be measured—as it is realistically measured—by the effective limits set upon its activities by adults. These limits become defined when the initiatives of the peer group encounter obstacles from adults; they emerge as a resolution of conflict over who will control the child in the given instance—the group or the adults.

THE JUVENILE GANG VERSUS PARENTS AND OTHER AUTHORITIES. The tyical gang forces the choice between who will control the individual child—the peer group or the parent—in a very decisive and dramatic manner, and virtually as a matter of course. In no other child group is the conflict-forcing situation so marked and so inevitable. It happens in the most natural manner. A new boy, recently moved into the neighborhood, has made friends with some of the gang, has tested and been tested by the other children, and is in a fair way toward acceptance and social success. He is invited to go along on a gang activity —an activity that may not in itself be delinquent but that may keep the boys out late and take them some distance away. More likely than not, a particular evening's program would not be approved by the new boy's parents. The issue is clearly drawn: *Will he go along with the rest, or show himself up as a Mama's boy?* If he refuses to go along, he is socially ruined. If he defies his parents, he will have to maintain this defiance until they "give in"—or "give up." *All the advantages are on the side of the gang.* By forcing the child to make a decision that emphasizes his independence of parental control, the gang is strongly encouraging a trend toward autonomy, which is one of the most necessary features of adolescent development. In effect, the gang is on the side of the maturation process. From a purely psychological point of view, anything that enables the child to achieve independence of the parents—within certain limits, and other things being equal—is fulfilling an increasingly felt need of the child.

Thus, again from a psychological point of view, the peer group becomes the device through which adolescents break out of their dependency and subservience to the parent. This is true regardless of the activities of the peer group. It may be a delinquent gang or a Boy Scout troop.

There is one extremely important distinction, however. The Boy Scout troop, as a new allegiance of the child, does not demand the sharp break with parental values and wishes that the gang demands. The transfer of allegiance is in this case peaceful, willing, and not in conflict with older allegiances. There is no war or revolution, no final break. Moreover, even though the locus of the child's important commitments is now transferred to a new source of control, there is mutual accommodation rather than conflict. In the gang, the reverse is true: the new boy is either "with us" and "against his old man"—or "with his old man," and "finished with us."

The familial rupture created by "going with the gang" is likely to be followed by other ruptures with other figures of authority. The gang may find it fashionable to play hooky often: again the conflict; again the more or less inevitable choice on the "with us or against us" pattern. The gang may want to cut a few capers among the "faggots" (sissies) in the playground or on the sand-lot. Some children may be roughed up. Complaints rain down on parents. Again the ultimatum: Stop going with the gang. And again defiance—and the tacit confession of parental helplessness in the face of the tidal attraction of the gang. Thus, one by one, the gang and its members test the limits posted by the adult world, and find that these limits are flimsy. Successful defiance becomes a sport, a mark of distinction—a competition. Instead of Who can hit more home runs?, it is Who can get away with more without getting stopped? Again, this works hand in hand with the maturational need for self-direction—which is operationally defined as freedom from adult direction, since the gang is actually almost tyrannical in its control.

Thus the activity-alternatives presented by the peer group have, in the natural course of events, produced at least two proto-delinquent results: incorrigibility and truancy. The next move is up to the adults. *Their* alternatives are either to yield or to call in official authority. Calling in the punitive authority of the State may entail a final break with the child—as well as a stigma.

Assuming that neither the parents nor the truant officers use their alternative—what next? The initiative then passes to the street. What else is going on? Gang fights? Petting parties? Promiscuity? Drinking? Drugs? Joy-riding in "borrowed" cars? Junking? Flunkying for older gangs? Shoplifting? Whatever is going on in the street, it is likely the gang will get into it. The initiative is now in the hands of the street.

THE PROGRESSIVE SHRINKING OF ALTERNATIVES. In the last several pages we have been concerned with the individual's access to alternate routes of personal and social development. Alternatives, like roads, are of two kinds: those that lead to wider vistas and those that lead to dead ends. The period between adolescence and young manhood is normally one of rapidly broadening alternatives; at each successive stage of his growth and education, the young person stands at a wider threshold of possibility. During the early years of adulthood the individual normally commits himself to one of the routes that his earlier preparation has opened up, and from this point on the alternatives tend to narrow. Somewhere in the thirties the possibilities tend to converge to a point where the person's future alternatives can often be predicted in advance, given his occupational status, his family status, and a few other actuarial data.

The early periods are critical. In a sense, the adolescent is taking roads that lead to other roads, while the adult is traveling roads that lead to destinations: places where the roads stop. In a highly competitive and relatively open society the period of wide-open alternatives is alarmingly brief. The riders on the merry-go-round have only a few chances to snatch for the brass rings; after a few turns have gone by, the supply for that particular group of riders is exhausted. The young men and women who fail to qualify in the marriage competition shortly find themselves alone, in the company of others left behind in the race. Those who fail in the job market may face a life-long struggle against poverty and the threat of being swept into the occupational sewers.

There is another difference that sharply distinguishes the free and easy era preceding adulthood from the period quickly to follow. During childhood and adolescence the individual is offered many helping hands. His parents must support him, his community will send him to school— he is cheered on and encouraged, if not lulled, by the prospect of the good future. He has time to loaf and experiment. But this period is brief, and when he is finally launched into the economic arena, the situation is drastically changed. Now he must compete, not only with the newcomers but with those who already occupy the desirable seats. And he has little room for experiment and less time for loafing. To drift now is to drift downward. Thus the society that brought him to the threshold of adult achievement may offer him little help in getting over it—and many opportunities to be moved aside and sifted down. Moreover, at each lower level the competition may become keener, the available jobs scarcer, the space at the bottom more crowded.

THE OCCUPATIONAL HOSPITALITY OF CRIME. We come now to a curious distinction between the occupational opportunities available in legitimate and illegitimate pursuits. The criminal world has always had room for the psychological and occupational misfits who failed in conventional pursuits, provided they were willing to trade risks for chances. The friendless, isolated teen-age bully who waited in ambush for the unaccompanied boy coming home from school has had scant psychological preparation for the social requirements of conventional living. The criminal syndicate, on the other hand, has good opportunities for those whose inability to form friendships can be relied on: the hired gunman must not permit sentimental attachments for other criminals to get in the way of his job.

Crime offers similar opportunities for the occupationally handicapped or retarded. In the legitimate world the field of the unskilled laborer is crowded, insecure, unrewarding. But the lower echelons of crime and vice require little in the way of occupational skill from their apprentices and hired hands. For the uneducated, unskilled, unemployed, or unemployable girl, prostitution may offer occupational solutions which the legitimate world is unwilling or unable to duplicate.

There is a further distinction. In the conventional world one's social status is often no more secure than one's job. The community of successful merchants, the fraternity of successful salesmen, may have no particular interest in the continued good fortune of any one of their number; under certain circumstances they may have a vested interest in his failure. In conventional pursuits, continuance in a given status tends to depend on continued performance; the man who "loses his grip" or has a run of bad luck may find himself deprived not only of his livelihood but of an essential inner prop of his self-image.

No similar threat surrounds the status of the criminal. Once "in the rackets," his role as a criminal is relatively secure—frequently so secure that even reformation cannot shake it. *In this specific sense, his social status is not dependent on his performance.* Not only his associates but those in the legitimate world will tend to regard him in a relatively fixed way no matter what he does. Once he is officially tagged as a lawbreaker, the legitimate alternatives tend to narrow to the vanishing point, and his chances to actualize himself in conventional roles virtually disappear while he maintains his known identity.

These considerations have a direct bearing on the questions of role fixation and the strength or intensity of personal commitments. When a young man flirts with the possibility of becoming an aviation engineer or a stockbroker, when he sees himself in these roles and "tries them on for size," the adult world may smile indulgently, may help him toward the threshold—and then leave him there to shoulder his own way through. When a young person flirts with delinquency, when he commits a few violations in the course of a similarly tentative trying-on of roles, the official and unofficial authorities in the community tend to take his experiments very seriously, especially if they result in damage to persons or property. Since the process of self-definition is intimately related to definition by others, the fact that delinquent experimentation tends to produce a relatively powerful and definite social definition may be decisive in resolving a personal commitment that is still tentative and ambiguous. In this sense, society may "help" the person become and remain a delinquent much more effectively than it helps other young people in their legitimate careers.

An Attempt at Summarizing and Concluding

As one approaches the end of a lenthy presentation of a highly problematic subject, there comes an inevitable moment when the introduction of new material ceases to clarify, ceases to inform, ceases to cultivate any other feeling than a desire for the presentation to be over. For the authors this moment has now arrived; for the reader it may have arrived some pages ago.

At this moment too, in addition to the need for an end, there is often a desire for a few pithy conclusions which the reader can lightly carry with him as a reminder that the long journey finally reached a destination. In a field where even the most restrained speculation quickly carries the thinker beyond the pale of reliable data, the search for satisfying conclusions is likely to be frustrating. Nevertheless, the criminologist in his social role of penologist cannot always indulge in the scientific luxury of looking before he leaps. He is called upon to do— and he must do what he can with what he has. Accordingly, the question arises: To what extent does the material suggest implications of possible significance for treatment and prevention? Though this issue is dealt with in some greater detail in the final chapter of this text, it may be useful to summarize certain aspects of the data that seem immediately relevant.

If Wordsworth's aphorism about the child being the father of the man has general validity, it would follow that the delinquent is the father of the adult criminal. Though there are many apparent exceptions to this general rule, there appears to be a sound statistical basis for the conclusion that the great majority of adult criminals—especially those involved in gainful crime—were originally involved in delinquent activities. It is partly in recognition of this fact, and partly a reflection of society's greater concern for its youth, that facilities for treatment and prevention tend to be concentrated in the field of juvenile offenders. What aspect of delinquency present the most critical implications for measures of treatment and prevention as they exist in contemporary practice?

Four things stand out about delinquent behavior generally. (1) *In the vast majority of instances delinquency is companionate behavior.* This observation has been repeatedly confirmed. In a study comparing 500 delinquents with 500 nondelinquents in the same area, the Gluecks found that 98.4 percent of the delinquents associated with other delinquents, while only 7.4 percent of the nondelinquents had delinquent associates. On the basis of these findings they concluded, "Delinquents almost without exception chummed largely with other delinquents while the nondelinquents, *despite the fact that they too lived in the slums,* had few intimates among delinquents."[13] In a study of 4,663 juvenile

[13] Sheldon and Eleanor Glueck, *Delinquents in the Making* (New York: Harper & Brothers, 1952), p. 89 (italics supplied).

court records Shaw and McKay found that 88.2 percent of the delinquents as a whole and 93.1 *percent of those engaged in theft* had at least two or more companions.[14] (2) *Delinquent behavior is highly conformist.* The deviant character of delinquent norms as compared with the norms assumed to be characteristic of the social group as a whole tends to mask the fact that delinquent children, like children generally, are almost ritualistic in their adherence to peer-group patterns. This conformity-in-rebellion is perhaps even more marked among delinquent children, and is probably related to their need to defend themselves against severer forms of social disapproval. Assertive, ostentatious display is one of the characteristic ways in which delinquent groups maintain their morale and unity in a hostile social world.

The conformist character of delinquent behavior takes on added theoretical significance when related to other characteristics typical of delinquent activities. (3) *Delinquent behavior is frequently non-utilitarian in object.* Unlike the offenses of older, more sophisticated delinquents and adult offenders generally, the gregarious antisocial activities of younger delinquents often seem lacking in guiding purposes or external goal objects. It is frequently difficult to distinguish them from unusually destructive or disruptive but otherwise childish forms of play.[15] (4) *Delinquent behavior is highly variable in content.* The nonutilitarian character of many delinquent activities is reflected in their typical variability. On one occasion the group may be involved in street fighting. On another, the members may go joy-riding in stolen cars.

[14] Clifford R. Shaw and Henry D. McKay, "Social Factors in Juvenile Delinquency," National Commission on Law Observance and Enforcement, *Report on the Causes of Crime* (Washington, D.C.: U.S. Government Printing Office, 1931) II, 195–196.

[15] One offender has described the evolutions of a career of gainful theft from earlier patterns of gregarious delinquent thievery:

> When we were shoplifting we always made a game of it. For example, we might gamble on who could steal the most caps in a day or who could steal in the presence of a detective and then get away. We were always daring each other that way and thinking up new schemes. This was the best part of the game. I would go into a store to steal a cap, by trying on one and when the clerk was not watching walk out of the store, leaving the old cap. With the new cap on my head I would go into another store, do the same thing as in the other store, getting a new hat and leave the one I had taken from the other place. I might do this all day and have one hat at night. It was fun I wanted, not the hat. I kept this up for months and then began to sell the things to a man on the west side. It was at this time that I began to steal for gain.

Chicago Area Project, *Juvenile Delinquency,* A Monograph Prepared by the Institute for Juvenile Research and the Chicago Area Project (revised edition; Chicago: 1953), p. 5.

A destructive raid on a school building may be followed by a shop-lifting raid on a department store.

Theoretical Implications for Treatment and Prevention

On any of these occasions of gregarious fighting, gregarious theft, or gregarious destruction, some of the gang members may be caught, taken into custody, tried, and ultimately sent away to be treated. At this point the question arises, *treated for what?* For stealing? For fighting? For a delinquent state of mind? For antisocial values generally?

If the orientation suggested in the foregoing pages is even approximately valid, any therapeutic approach which stresses the delinquent's psychological involvement in antisocial activities to the neglect of his involvement in a delinquent group may be seriously misguided. Nevertheless, the treatment procedures available in the majority of therapeutically oriented institutions and agencies typically stress an individual treatment orientation. According to this orientation, the treatment situation is defined as an exploration into the specific psychological difficulties which led the individual into his specific behavioral difficulties with the law. Moreover, since these behavioral difficulties reflect what seems to be a personal inability or refusal to conform to the expectations of adult authority, it is entirely consistent to understand the therapeutic process as one in which the patient re-achieves a healthy acceptance of authority through the medium of a therapeutic relationship with a benign, understanding adult.

Though logical in relation to its premises, this view neglects the possibility that the conflict with adult authority is largely a derivative of a more fundamental acceptance of another source of authority—the authority of the delinquent peer group. If this interpretation is correct, the basic problem of the delinquent is not his original difficulties with, and present rejection of, authority, but rather in his excessive conformity, *his excessive dependency on acceptance by certain others*—a dependency so extreme that it persists in the face of the threat of alienation from the community at large. Since this dependency requires the delinquent to follow the group in any and all of its activities—legitimate as well as illegitimate—the essential causal factors may lie not in any relation between the delinquent's personality and his activities, nor in the conflict with authority brought about by these activities, but rather in the factors determining his personal commitment to his group. For this reason, any therapeutic or preventive program which limits its purview exclusively to the relations between the delinquent and his activities or to his conflict with authority may be not only inappropriate but ineffectual as well.

Penology

PAST AND PRESENT MODES
OF PUNISHMENT

....

Variations in the Social Reaction

to Crime

DEVIANT BEHAVIOR HAS ALWAYS STIMULATED GROUP REACTION. WHERE the behavior is viewed as desirable, the responses have varied from admiration to envy; where the deviation is considered undesirable, the responses have varied from mild individual disapproval to general condemnation and punishment. Like other group responses, reactions to deviance also tend to become institutionalized. By means of these institutions, the group attempts to limit not only the deviations themselves but also the character and intensity of its own responses. These limits vary greatly with time and place. In the Puritan New England of the 1660's, a man overhearing his neighbor using the Lord's name in vain would have been justified in seizing him on the spot and arresting him for the crime of blasphemy. A person seizing his neighbor for the same offense today would either be prosecuted for false arrest or put away as a lunatic.

What has taken place? The group, in its greater tolerance of swearing, has abandoned organized community punishment of the practice. What was formerly considered a crime is now merely impolite. Instead of enduring public punishment, the "blasphemer" is turned over to the informal chastisement of his friends. Thus, by liberalizing its definition of what was formerly considered offensive, the group simultaneously narrowed the range of permissible retaliation by those who feel offended.[1]

Punishment as the Ultimate Form of Group Disapproval

The business of this chapter is to deal with those social reactions in which group intolerance goes beyond mere individual disapproval or even general ostracism and reaches the point of *systematic, organized community action against the deviant, who is now legally defined and punished as an offender.* More or less precise definitions of who—and what—is punishable may be found in the criminal statutes. When one asks, however, *What determines how individual offenders are punished?,* one is immediately involved in the second most complex problem in the field of criminology—a question almost as complicated as that which asks why people commit crimes. An indication of the complexity of the question is obtained when one tries to answer the deceptively simple inquiry: Why did John get ten years for burglary when Jack got probation for the same crime?

The first problem in approaching this question, which is constantly being asked by a wide variety of interested persons—including, notably, John and Jack—is to restate it in answerable terms. We may ask: As a function of what factors does the punitive reaction to the untolerated act vary? Examining the question more closely, we discover an unresolved ambiguity in the key phrase, "punitive reaction." Going back to the example of John and Jack, let us assume that it was the intention of the State (as represented by the prosecution) that both offenders be punished. Nevertheless, actual punishment was meted out to only *one* of the two. Clearly, a distinction must be made between the community's *punitive intentions,* as expressed in laws, and its *punitive acts,* as carried out in its prisons, jails, and reformatories. The original question is now

[1] This reciprocal relationship seems to be universal: the more intolerable the behavior, the more extreme the tolerated response; the more tolerated the behavior, the less permissible any extreme response. Thus, in ancient Rome, filial disrespect was held in such repugnance that the father was permitted to execute the disrespectful child on the spot. Within recent times the toleration of defiant behavior by children has increased to the point where a brisk spanking by parents may entail the risk of criminal prosecution.

divided into two large parts: (1) What factors determine the community's intentions to punish? (2) What factors determine how these intentions are carried out? The following outline suggests the range and complexity of the factors that must be explored before reliable answers can be expected.

Factors Influencing the Punishment of Offenders

I. Factors Producing Variation in the Community's Intentions

    A. *On the Level of Public Opinion*
1. Factors influencing the community's orientation to the offense, including religious, political, and economic values.
2. Immediate or recent events conditioning the community's toleration of or indignation at the offense (e.g., a crime wave).

    B. *On the Level of Legislation*
Factors influencing the decisions of lawmakers to enact legistion, including:
1. Public opinion (including all in section A, above).
2. Pressure groups.
3. Political and party considerations.
4. Personal motives of individual legislators.

II. Factors Determining How the Community's Intentions Are Carried Out

    A. *After the Offense but before the Charge*
1. Relationship between the offender and the victim. (Will the victim complain?)
2. Efficiency of the law-enforcement authorities. (Will the offender be detected?)
3. Attitude of the local law-enforcement authorities to the offender, the offense, and the victim. (How will the police define what occurred? How will they present the situation to the magistrate?)

B. *After the Charge but before the Indictment*

    1. Factors influencing the decision of the magistrate. (Will the charge be dismissed?)

        a. The nature of the offense.

        b. The character of the evidence.

        c. The presence or absence of extralegal pressures, including political dependency or obligation.

    2. Factors determining whether an indictment will be sought and what kind of an indictment will be sought, including:

        a. All of section B, immediately above.

        b. The offender's bargaining position with the prosecutor. (If other offenders are involved, will this particular offender cooperate by becoming a State witness? If the evidence is not airtight, will the offender plead guilty to a lesser charge?)

        c. Local factors rendering conviction unlikely. (Regardless of the quality of the evidence, can a jury be depended on to convict? In that case, is it likely that the accused will take an appeal and win?)

C. *Factors Determining the Outcome of the Trial*

(Is the accused guilty or not guilty?)

Factors influencing the attitudes, conduct, and decisions of the judge, the jury, the accused, the complainant, the witnesses, the attorneys for both sides. These include:

    1. The nature of the offense.

    2. The character of the evidence.

    3. The social standing of the complainant and the accused.

    4. The age, sex, and mental condition of the accused and the complainant.

    5. The impression made upon the judge and the jury by both sides.

    6. The effect of local public opinion on judge and jury.

D. *Factors Influencing the Sentence*

    1. Statutory limitations (minimum and maximum) on the length of sentence for the given offense.

    2. All of section C, immediately above.

    3. The previous criminal record of the accused.

    4. The prevailing climate of opinion concerning the handling of the given type of offender.

5. Orientation of the sentencing judge to the offender. (Does this offender require primarily treatment, re-education, or punitive custody?)

6. Various administrative and economic factors influencing the selection of a given type of punishment.[2]

E. *Factors Determining How Sentences Are Carried Out*

Let us imagine that the offender has been duly convicted and sentenced; he is now duly transported to his place of confinement. Are we now able to assume that the "intentions of the community" will be carried out? We might imagine that the judge, in sentencing John to ten years at hard labor, concluded his formal remarks with these words:

> In passing this sentence upon you, the court has taken into account your serious criminal history and the failure of numerous previous attempts to reform you. It is to be hoped that this present attempt will be more effective than those in the past, in that it will most strongly impress, not only upon you but upon others of a similar mind, that the laws of this state cannot be flouted with impunity.

Such, then, was the intention of the community as interpreted by its duly authorized officer. What is the probability that these intentions will be realized?

Barring a pardon by the governor, a successful appeal, an early parole, a successful escape attempt, or a change in penal policies, John will probably spend between five and seven years[3] in confinement. Whether or not he spends that time in the same place may depend on a variety of administrative considerations, including the construction of other institutions. Whether or not he will spend his time at hard labor—or at any kind of labor—and whether or not he and "others of a similar mind" will be impressed with the futility of crime, is another matter altogether. It is a matter that has received very little scientific investigation.[4]

[2] Extralegal, extrapunitive economic considerations are less important today than in former times. In colonial America the practice of contracting convict labor to private persons began as a response to a labor shortage. The chain-gang systems of the South were similarly related to economic interests. Administrative considerations are increasingly important, however. The opening of a new state reformatory frequently results in a larger number of reformatory sentences and a decrease in the number of commitments to "punitive" walled institutions.

[3] After deduction of time off for work and good behavior.

[4] Public interest in the criminal reaches a height after the offense, remains

A fuller exploration of the ramifications of the problem of carrying out the community's declared intentions concerning the offender will occupy many subsequent pages of this text; here it is merely necessary to cite the following general principle:

> *Although the activities undertaken to implement society's intention's toward its offenders may be significantly related to what happens to the offender and to how he subsequently reacts, the mere description of those intentions and activities, however accurate, cannot be taken as a reliable guide to the effects of those activities upon him.*

The foregoing outline, however incomplete, makes it apparent that the same punitive act has many more implications than may be exhausted by the most thoroughgoing analysis. This conclusion is suggested by the fact that changing any one of the thirty-odd factors listed while keeping all the others constant may lead to an entirely different outcome. It thus becomes apparent that a complete answer to the deceptively simple question, Why did John get ten years and Jack probation?, may include such discordant elements as the news of a crime wave in the next county, the presence in court of Jack's two young children, the fact that John's victim was a pathetic character who evoked much sympathy while Jack's victim created an unfavorable impression, the judge's decision to invoke the social intention of punishment in John's case and guidance in Jack's.

Teleological Explanations of Punishment

Penologists have attempted to order this chaos of factors in various ways. The most widely used method involves working from the sen-

---

at a high level during the trial, then drops off almost completely until the offender is released and commits a new offense. At this point there is usually a slight awakening of interest in the offender's recent penological career. Like most inquests, this inquiry, often conducted on the editorial pages of the public press, is chiefly concerned with fixing blame. If the offender committed his new crime after spending many years in a "tough" prison, there may be articles deploring the futility of "old-fashioned ideas of punishment." On the other hand, if the offender has recently emerged from a reformatory or training school, the same newspaper may decry the foolishness of new-fangled ideas of treatment and call for a return to the old, reliable rock pile. Frequently paralleling this kind of inquiry is a similar inquest on higher scholarly levels; this, too, is usually in the form of a debate rather than an investigation.

tencing decision backwards. In effect, this method makes the following assumption: Granted that there is a vast number of anterior factors, granted that these factors are subject to different causal cross-currents, in the end they all boil down to one thing: a decision to do or not to do something to the offender—to kill him, to inflict physical pain upon him, to inflict financial loss upon him, to imprison him, to humiliate him, or to treat him. This decision is not, of course, taken out of the air; it is usually viewed as based on one or more of a limited number of social objectives or purposes. These are: retaliation, disablement, deterrence, protection of society, and reformation.

Historians and anthropologists have compiled much material concerning hundreds of specific methods of punishment. Dealing with any one of these methods, the penologist is to ask the question: What is the intended effect of this punishment on the offender, and what is the estimated benefit to society? One or another of the five "purposes" then suggests itself. At this point the question is raised: How well does examination of the social, political, and legal traditions of this society support the hypothesis that this particular purpose (rather than others) was the main intent of the punishment? If the cultural data are seen to favor certain of these purposes over others, the hypothesis may be considered confirmed and the social reaction "explained."

Recast in this framework, the task of constructing a history of penology reduces itself to a demonstration of how the different purposes manifested themselves through changing social conditions, how they were influenced by contemporary religious and philosophical teachings, and how they were implemented by various technological means (e.g., the guillotine, the electric chair, etc.). As the account proceeds from the stage of history in general to an actual historical era, it merely seems necessary to show how they wove themselves into the social fabric and found local expression in the specific laws, customs, and practices of the time. These local manifestations are to be understood as effects rather than causes, which may be adequately explained by an analysis of their deeper motivation. Time and time again one encounters explanations that evoke a picture of the basic purposes hovering like the Fates over the scene of penological history, intervening from age to age in different forms and guises. Thus, one reads:

> In actuality, no other explanation of criminal codes than the retributive one is possible: they were and still are constructed in accordance with the idea of retributive punishments.

* * *

The very possibility of overcoming the retributive structure of punishment is doubtful...even the boldest reformers dare not break completely with the tradition based on retaliation.[5]

This kind of purposive analysis may retain its plausibility until the account nears the contemporary period. Then a change is apparent. Details are richer; outcomes are more complex and uncertain; and the generalizations that carried the reader easily through broad tracts of historical time have difficulty navigating the narrower channels of the present. A host of new factors, almost wholly neglected in the description of earlier periods, must now be taken into account; these usually crowd the older theoretical considerations off the page. For virtually the first time the reader learns that factors such as pressure groups, local public opinion, bureaucratic efficiency and inefficiency, favoritism, and corruption all play their part in the social reaction to crime. These modern details are usually presented with a specificity that contrasts sharply with the systematic theoretical reconstruction of the past—a procedure that raises the unanswered question: If these matters are so important now, why were they not equally important then? At this point the reader may well speculate about the usefulness of a conceptual framework that becomes less and less pertinent as the present is approached, finally dissolving entirely in a mass of unanalyzed contemporary data.

The gathering of data is a necessary task of any scientific field; nevertheless, a scientific penology must also produce concepts able to account for those data, past and present, with an equal impartiality. In the following pages we shall attempt to outline certain of the problems confronting this task.

Problems of Historical Reconstruction in Penology

The search for the historical origins of penal policies leads quickly back into that cloudland where history merges with myth. Surviving records of actual procedures are few; what has come down consists mainly of declarations of purposes, warnings against evildoers, and justifications of the acts of rulers. In evaluating these ancient materials for the purpose of discovering what actually took place, and why, certain cautions are necessary.

[5] N. S. Timasheff, "The Retributive Structure of Punishment," *Journal of Criminal Law and Criminology*, 28:400–401, September–October, 1937.

Credibility of Historical Sources

In the first place, many of the statements are in the nature of public pronouncements, intended for a wide audience. This, in part, accounts for their survival; many of them were found preserved on stone monuments designed to memorialize the achievements of the ruler for future generations. If there is any reasonable basis for skepticism in evaluating public declarations of present-day rulers, there seems little reason to relax that skepticism when dealing with the rulers of the past. In those days, as in these, authorities felt the need to satisfy certain expectations and to cope with basic problems of public relations. Then, as now, they were subjected to the vagaries of public opinion, to the inefficiency and corruption of subordinates, and to the myriad frustrations of administration. Then, too, it must often have seemed expedient to bridge the gap between hopes and achievements with words, and to appeal from the censure of an ungrateful present to the friendlier audience of the future.

Consistency of Historical Sources

There are further reasons for conservatism in evaluating these materials. Frequently they are not only vague, allegorical, and obviously self-glorifying but, even within the same limited period, highly contradictory. These qualities offer a wide latitude to liberal interpreters, especially to those seeking to show that there is nothing new under the sun. There are, for example, certain passages in the Mahabharata, an ancient Sanskrit text, which not only appear to condemn capital punishment but to favor the modern doctrine of reformation as opposed to vengeance. In a dialogue between King Dyumutsens and his son, Prince Satyaban, the son pleads against the execution of certain offenders:

> Without destroying the body of the offender the King should punish him as ordained by the Scripture. ... By killing the wicked, the King kills a large number of innocent men. Behold, by killing a single robber his wife, mother, father and children are all killed. When injured by wicked persons the King should, therefore, think seriously on the question of punishment. Sometimes *a wicked man is seen to imbibe good conduct from a pious person.* ... *The wicked, therefore, should not be uprooted.* ...[6]

[6] Quoted in Prosanto K. Sen, *From Punishment to Prevention* (London: Oxford University Press, 1932), p. 10.

This quotation is found in a body of literature that minutely details such forms of capital punishment as devouring by dogs and slow death by fine razors. Nevertheless, the passage is cited as giving "early glimpses of the problems of criminal sociology," which indicate that "the ancient Hindoo writers . . . were keenly alive to some of the greatest problems of sociology and penal philosophy that confront us today."[7]

Many similarly compassionate statements may be found in the ancient literatures, with no reliable evidence that they were translated into systematic working programs. On the other hand, there are several historical instances in which rulers whose cruelties and exactions were highly systematic performed acts of fatherly forbearance or permitted social reforms that were nothing short of visionary for the time. A closer look at the circumstances surrounding these concessions almost invariably shows that they were granted to recalcitrants who were quite powerful at the moment. The concern of these rulers for the betterment of mankind may not have been unmixed with considerations of personal safety.

Rationalized Explanations of Penological History

A considerable portion of penological literature has been devoted to constructing the universal evolution of principles and practices from ancient to modern times. One widely current version of this evolution has been summarized in a recent textbook:

> In the history of early criminal jurisprudence, the crimes that were considered a danger to the public and were punished by the local group were those that exposed the group to spiritual or human enemies, particularly the former. Crimes against persons were not controlled by the tribe or the family but by the clan under the principle of the blood feud. Under the unrestrained action of this principle, responsibility and retaliation for crimes were collective on both sides, and the intent of the offender was ignored. Worse than all else, the clan revenge failed to put an end to the affair and furnished the means of keeping up a perpetual feud between clans.
>
> *Owing to the disadvantages* of the principle of blood feud, agencies for mitigating and reforming it arose in the duel and in compensation or composition. *Growing out of these new principles* came the impartial third party that is now considered the essential element in adjudi-

[7] *Ibid.,* p. 9.

cation, namely, the court. This agency, at first, had peacemaking rather than judicial functions, but, with the establishment of a strong central authority, the powers and functions of the court expanded, and the principle of the blood feud and the agencies mitigating it correspondingly declined. Responsibility became individualized, and intent was considered. As the power of the king and the central authority grew, nearly all violations of the legal code were looked upon as public offenses. The old principle of vengeance was retained, but transformed from private into public revenge. To this principle was added the theory of deterrence, and there ensued a period of great severity in the determination of guilt and the punishment of the guilty. In time, increasing enlightenment disclosed the fallacy in this theory of punishment. Some of the barbarities have been gradually removed. The old idea of vengeance and the later one of deterrence are giving way to those of social protection and reformation.[8] (Italics supplied.)

This brief and comprehensive statement, which sums up the consensus of what might be called penal anthropology among certain modern penologists, has been cited in order to provide a closer look at its major premises and implications. These are:

1. The assumption that an orderly evolution has taken place, in which private and tribal justice have been superseded and replaced by public justice.

2. The implication that this process came about as a result of a rational enlightenment among those who perceived the disadvantage of the older methods.

3. The implication that methods of settling disputes by compensation and composition are now extinct because the grievances originally handled by these techniques have all been redefined as offenses against the State and are now prosecuted as crimes.

Each of these statements is debatable; one is highly questionable, and another is factually incorrect. We shall deal with each in turn.

1. One of the recent advances of modern anthropology involves the abandonment of attempts to demonstrate universal patterns of social evolution. Criticizing these attempts, the anthropologist Ruth Benedict has pointed out:

> Early anthropologists tried to arrange all traits of different cultures in an evolutionary sequence from the earliest forms to their final development in Western civilization. But there is no reason to suppose that by discussing Australian religion rather than our own we are uncover-

[8] Harry E. Barnes and Negley K. Teeters, *New Horizons in Criminology*, 2d ed. (New York: Prentice-Hall, Inc., 1951), pp. 342–343.

ing primordial religion, or that by discussing Iroquoian social organization we are returning to the mating habits of man's earliest ancestors.[9]

The construction of these universal evolutionary patterns is said to lead to synthetic creations without any realistic counterpart outside of the mind of the synthesist:

> ... Practices are illustrated by bits of behavior selected indiscriminately from the most different cultures, and the discussion builds up a kind of ... Frankenstein's monster with a right eye from Fiji, a left from Europe, one leg from Tierra del Fuego, and one from Tahiti. ... Such a figure corresponds to no reality in the past or present.[10]

The reconstruction, in penology, of a universal evolution from private vengeance to public justice has been accomplished by the same method and with similar materials. The more "primitive phase," for example, has been illustrated by examples of blood feuds from contemporary nonliterate societies; the Germanic practice of wergild has been used to illustrate a later, transitional stage during which the blood-feud principle of "an eye for an eye" was being mitigated by the practice of settlement by compensation. A still later stage, the emergence of a dominant national power subordinating the clans and tribes, has been illustrated by descriptions taken from such ancient civilizations as the Babylonian and the Egyptian. Most frequently these constructions are advanced without the caution that *logical continuity in the realm of ideas does not imply a parallel continuity in the world of events,* and that the origins of practices must be sought *for in demonstrated historical, social, and economic continuities* rather than in deductions from general premises.

2. The difficulty posed by the evolutionary concept is further compounded by the teleological implication that newer procedures were adopted because men were rationally persuaded that they were better. Thus, in the excerpt quoted, it is stated that the method of compensation arose "owing to the disadvantages of the blood feud." The question arises: disadvantages for whom?

Not, probably, for the *victorious clan,* which succeeded not only in avenging the injury but in wiping out or enslaving the defeated clan and, frequently, in appropriating their lands as well. As for the defeated clan, the difficulties must have been painfully apparent; but it is impossible to imagine this group in a position to change the system at that low

---

[9] Ruth Benedict, *Patterns of Culture* (New York: New American Library of World Literature, Inc., 1946), p. 16. (Published by arrangement with Houghton Mifflin Company, Boston, and quoted by permission.)

[10] *Ibid.,* p. 44.

ebb of the clan's fortunes. Furthermore, as Barnes and Teeters themselves point out, the blood feud was, by its very character, both irrational and interminable. Its abandonment in favor of another method
would therefore, almost necessarily, have been imposed by a superior
power.

The inadequacies of the teleological approach are most apparent
when the attempt is made to visualize its operation against the realistic
background of historical events. In this setting the idea of progress by
rational enlightenment quickly becomes overshadowed by the brutal
historical realities of power. What is perhaps more important, the traditional distinction between private, tribal, and public vengeance is overshadowed as well.

Use of the concept of *successful power struggle* lends, at the least,
a greater economy to the account of changes in patterns of social control.
Thus it may be hypothesized that, at different times and places and
under widely varying local conditions, certain clans, factions, or tribes
gained dominance through success in conflict. This dominance probably
was held through some method of maintaining a preponderance of armed
strength. Frequently it was reinforced by restricting the privilege of
bearing arms to members of the dominant group. Thus, during this
phase, while the right of private or clan vengeance remained intact as a
principle, its universal exercise became less and less practical.

With the emergence of dominant individuals within the controlling
group, the practical possibilities of private and clan retaliation were even
further restricted. This is not to say that they disappeared, but rather
that the power to exercise them safely became more and more restricted
to the leader and his followers and friends. Early or late during this
process it became expedient to find ways of legitimatizing these facts of
power by the use of symbols. The techniques and symbols for legitimatizing the realities of power varied from one group to another; their
intention and effect was to make authority less continuously dependent
on the show of force. By manipulation of the legitimatizing symbols,
the personal wishes of the ruler—including his private vengeance—
became increasingly redefined as public policy. Thus, the apparent
transition from a stage of private or clan vengeance to one of public
justice becomes not so much a matter of the group will finding expression through a responsive leader but rather the imposition upon the
group of the will of a dominant minority. At this point, though the
general right may have remained, indulging in private vengeance be-

came increasingly unsafe without the tacit consent or connivance of the ruler or his friends.

When private justice is stripped of its historical connotation and is viewed in an action-context of *immune private retaliation,* it becomes apparent that we are dealing more with a *process* than with an evolutionary stage. Defined in these terms, private justice exists wherever private individuals or groups, either in the absence of, in defiance of, or in connivance with established authority are able to *take punitive action with immunity.* It existed on our western frontier, in the *absence* of established authority. In parts of the country where racial inequality is institutionalized, it exists today, in *defiance* of established authority. Wherever government is corrupt, it exists in *connivance* with established authority. In a more general sense, it exists as a condition of government wherever governments exist—since those in whose hands the law is are in the ultimately favorable position to take the law into their own hands.[11]

The basic point of this discussion is that processes of private, clan, or public justice are not separate stages of political evolution but *permanent possibilities at any stage.* Wherever government is strong, responsible, and responsive to the public will, a condition of public justice may be said to exist. Where government is selectively responsive to a dominant minority group, a situation of clan justice exists. Where government is corruptly responsive to individuals, the generating conditions for private justice are present. This principle seems to hold whether the authority in question is an intimidated child-pharaoh, an imbecile Burgundian king, or the aged president of a tottering German republic.

3. The concept of progressive evolutionary stages has led to the impression that certain procedures predominant at one stage become extinct once the "stage" is passed. One of the more curious examples of this is the notion that settlement of disputes by means of compensation belongs to an extinct period of political development and that the major judicial business of the modern State is the trial of criminal violations (cf.: "As the power of the king and the central authority grew, nearly all violations of the legal code were looked upon as public offenses"— i.e., crimes).

---

[11] Despite changes in the symbols of legitimatization, the ability of the autocratic leader and his coterie to engage in personal initiatives forbidden to others has been a continuous historical reality. It does not matter whether the examples are drawn from ancient Babylonia or from the political machine of a modern American metropolis.

There is very little to say about this except that it is simply not so. It is not so today; it was even *less* so in the past, when the "power of the king" was at its height. What makes the notion curious is the fact that the vast majority of Anglo-American criminal laws were unwritten prior to the nineteenth century and *the criminal law,* as we know it, is almost exclusively a development of the last two hundred years. This is not to say that the men of two hundred years ago were not committing many of the same crimes that are committed by people today; it merely means that the victims, in most instances, had no other recourse than to apply to courts of civil jurisdiction. Putting it another way: A large part of the injuries or harms considered criminal today were, in the recent past, considered to be merely civil harms or tort actions. Up to the year 1700, in England, one might embezzle, engage in larceny by trick, indulge in virtually every variety of fraud and false pretenses without any other fear than that he might be haled into a civil court and ordered to pay a certain amount of damages.

The addition of scores of felonies to the lawbooks has changed this picture only slightly. Inspection of the calendars of the courts will reveal that only a fraction of the total number of adjudicated matters are criminal: the vast majority of cases are civil. *Thus, today, as in the past, the major business of the courts is the settlement of grievances by the award of some form of compensation to the aggrieved party.* The overwhelming majority of persons injured in life, limb, property, or reputation still seek redress and expiation through the payment of money. In these procedures the element of retaliation is by no means absent—as indicated, for example, by the phrase "punitive damages." Nevertheless, it is not the State but the injured party who is seeking retaliation in a judicial duel refereed by the State as an impartial third party. Thus, far from having declined as an agency mitigating the blood feud, the court maintains today the basic peacemaking procedures of organized society.

We turn now from a discussion of the difficulties of historical reconstruction to approach the rather more onerous task of presenting a historical chronicle of penal methods and rationales based on certain of the principles made explicit above. In the course of this chronicle the reader, like the authors, will have occasion to note that it is easier to declare principles than to follow them.

16

A Selective History of Penal Rationales
and Procedures

PENAL HISTORY IS THE STORY OF WHAT HAS HAPPENED TO PEOPLE WHO got into difficulty with the law. Strictly speaking, it is the more limited chronicle of what was done to them after they were convicted, after they were adjudged guilty and deserving of suffering. It is only after this stage that their "legal" punishment may be said to have begun. In a factual sense, however, this purview is too restricting, since their actual suffering may have begun much earlier in the process. It may have begun when they were first suspected or arrested. It may have continued long after they were acquitted. For several hundred years, torture was a common technique of interrogation on the Continent. If the accused survived the torture and satisfied his inquisitors, he might be acquitted and escape "legal" punishment. But he might well bear the scars of his acquittal to the grave. Legal procedure may thus be as punitive as formal punishment itself.

There are additional reasons for including a history of judicial pro cedure and penal administration in a penology that seeks to relate itself to some of the broader implications of social life. Only a fraction of the population is ever subjected to the formal punishments of the law. But a considerably greater portion is subject to profound influences emanating from the administration of criminal justice. At bottom, the procedures available to law-enforcement agents represent actual and potential powers to bring sudden disruption and disaster into the lives of almost everyone. The existence of these powers, together with rumors, traditions, and evidence about their use and misuse, creates a certain atmosphere—an indefinable but characteristic climate of personal security or insecurity permeating many areas of social life.

The traveler is often able to sense this atmosphere when visiting countries less free than his own. It can be sensed in the way people talk to each other and to strangers. It can be felt in the lowered voice, the anxious look, the attitude of strained listening as if for the hidden eavesdropper when certain subjects are discussed. It can be seen in the deferential slope of the shoulder when the individual passes a policeman or other public functionary. In fine, it helps determine whether people will stand up straight or will slouch or crawl through their human world. It is in this larger sense too that the study of penal techniques must extend beyond formal punishments and must deal with administrative and judicial procedures which may have become punitive for whole populations.

A chronicle of four thousand years of penal history is necessarily selective—which is by way of admitting that it is inevitably biased. The attempt has been made to deal in some detail with the major historical forces that have, directly or indirectly, affected the structure and spirit of penal policies in the modern western world. This restrictive principle has dictated certain omissions—most notably, that of the Greek juristic tradition, which was without demonstrable historical effect on later developments in the West. On the other hand, there are certain inclusions which cannot be justified on this basis—and which were retained largely because of their inherent fascination. Of these, perhaps the most unique is that with which this chronicle begins: the story of the laws of the great Babylonian King, Hammurabi.

The Code of Hammurabi, King of Babylon

One of the earliest written survivals of ancient penal practices is the Code of the Babylonian King, Hammurabi (circa 2130–2087 B.C.). Credited by many commentators as forming the basis of the later legislation of the western Semites, the Code is one of the earliest and most systematic attempts to achieve social and ideological objectives through *minutely detailed technical procedures.* It is, at once, a code of laws; a manual of instructions for judges, police officials, and witnesses; a handbook on the rights and duties of husbands, wives, and children; a set of regulations establishing wages and prices; and a code of ethics for government officials, merchants, and doctors—detailing throughout, clause by clause, the particular obligation to be met, the particular action that is forbidden, and the precise punishment to be meted out. As a historical landmark, the Code looks both backward and forward, embodying or reforming many features already ancient and anticipating others that would not be achieved elsewhere for many centuries—including one or two that would be considered utopian today.

Asserting his authority as the chief agent of Marduk (and thereby uniting the highest religious with the supreme secular authority), Hammurabi announces his mission "to cause justice to prevail in the land, to destroy the wicked and the evil, to *prevent the strong from oppressing the weak,* to go forth like the sun . . . , to enlighten the land and to further the welfare of the people."[1]

Objectives of the Code

REINFORCEMENT OF THE POWER OF THE STATE. The Code details a comprehensive intervention by the State into minute details of social and economic life. For enforcement of these regulations, the sole reliance is on a detailed system of *state-administered punishments:* personal redress of any kind is sternly ruled out. Not only are blood and clan revenge forbidden in matters of deliberate personal injury, but even forms of self-help in civil matters are severely penalized. Thus:

> If a man hold a [debt of] grain or money against a man, and if he takes grain without the owner's consent from a heap or the granary, they shall call that man to account [i.e., summon him to judgment] for taking grain without the consent of the owner . . . and he shall return as much grain as he took and *he shall forfeit all that he has lent,* whatever it be.[2]

In the passage just cited, the major, though not the explicit, purpose was to reinforce the authority of the State by forcing the creditor to bring suit in the courts in order to collect his debts. Many other passages,

---

[1] Robert H. Harper, *The Code of Hammurabi, King of Babylon,* 2d ed. (Chicago: The University of Chicago Press, 1904), p. 3.
[2] *Ibid.,* p. 39.

though explicitly dealing only with the specific moral issue at hand, simultaneously pursue other objectives which are only implied.

Many of these objectives are political and administrative, revealing a concurrent and pervading objective of strengthening the king's power. The ban on private justice was one expression of this objective: the punishment of corrupt judges, officials, and witnesses was another. The punishment of corruption was severe; a judge who changed his decision after pronouncing it was to be "expelled from his seat of judgement" and pay "twelve-fold the penalty" he had pronounced. A witness testifying falsely in a capital case was himself to be put to death, likewise a man falsely accusing another. The determination to defend the machinery of justice from private abuses went far beyond punishment of deliberate falsehoods. A man suing another for the recovery of property would be well advised to be sure of his case, for "if the owner . . . does not produce witnesses to identify his lost property, he has attempted fraud (has lied) he has stirred up strife (calumny), he shall be put to death."[3]

If the Code may be taken at face value, the king held his officials to a higher, severer degree of accountability than has ever been exacted before or since.[4] The higher an official's rank, the more rigorous the king's supervision. Lower officials were carefully protected from abuse and exploitation by their superiors.[5]

PROTECTION OF THE WEAKER FROM THE STRONGER. Again and again the Code re-emphasizes this dominant theme, announced first in the Prologue as the sacred duty of the king. The widow must be protected from those who would exploit her, the distant or captured husband from the betrayal of the wife he left behind, the aged, impoverished father from the sons who would disown him, the pregnant slave from the beatings of the impatient master, the lesser official from the higher official. Though differences in rank are acknowledged and even fortified

---

[3] *Ibid.*, p. 15.

[4] The safety of the stranger's person and property was the direct responsibility of the city and the governor through whose province the stranger was traveling. Thus, if the stranger were robbed, and "if the brigand not captured, the man who was robbed shall, in the presence of God, make an itemized statement of his loss, and the city and the governor in whose province and jurisdiction the robbery was committed, shall compensate him for whatever was lost." (*Ibid.*, p. 19.)

[5] Cf.: "If a governor or magistrate take the property of an officer, let an officer for hire, present an officer in a judgement to a man of influence, take the gift which the King has given to an officer, that governor or magistrate shall be put to death." (*Ibid.*, p. 23.)

by the Code, the guiding principle seems to be punishment of anyone taking any kind of advantage, either of rank or of temporary circumstances, in order to exploit another.

RESTORATION OF EQUITY BETWEEN OFFENDER AND VICTIM. The Babylonian wrath against the offender extended also to the offense; it too, was to be wiped out, and things were to be made as if it had never happened. Where this could not be done—where lives or limbs had been lost—the only alternative method of restoring equity was to force the offender to share, as precisely as possible, the loss and the suffering of his victim. Thus: "If a man destroy the eye of another man, they shall destroy his eye." [6]

Subsequent commentators, in deploring the savagery of the *lex talionis,* have tended to favor the hypothesis that revenge was the principle or major motive for the "bloody doctrine of an eye for an eye." There is little in Hammurabi's Code to suggest that this "pre-Mosaic Moses" would shrink either from blood or revenge; nevertheless, the weight of internal evidence clearly favors the hypothesis of equity over the hypothesis of revenge. Thus, in Clause 200: "If a man knock out the tooth of a man of his own rank, they shall knock out his tooth." [7] Note here that both teeth belong to gentlemen. Now, if a gentleman knock out the tooth of a freeman, he pays only one half mina of silver. Clearly, to the Babylonian way of evaluation, knocking the gentleman's tooth out in return for a freeman's would be a violation of the principle of equity. Similarly, if a gentleman brings about a miscarriage in another gentleman's daughter and she dies, the offender's daughter must also die. Why not execute the offending gentleman, instead of his innocent daughter? Because, while that would be good revenge, it would be bad equity.

All of the foregoing is not to deny that revenge was a dominant, perhaps the dominant, motive in the treatment of serious violations. If the offense violated a sensitive moral issue, if it threatened either the king's policies or their honest administration, the principle of equity could be subordinated to or even submerged by the most prompt and terrifying retaliation. It is in relation to these last two general objectives—*the punishment of deceit, deception, false pretenses, corruption, and malfeasance of office, and the punishment of offenses against family morality*

[6] *Ibid.,* p. 73.
[7] *Ibid.,* p. 75.

—that the Babylonian Code earned its reputation for remorseless savagery.[8]

Forms of Punishment

Exclusive of fines, four forms of punishment seem to have existed in the Babylon of Hammurabi: death, mutilation, branding, and banishment—the last, apparently only for paternal incest. Among the techniques of execution, death by burning, drowning, and impaling are mentioned specifically; in the majority of instances, the form of death is not specified. Approximately thirty-seven specific offenses were punishable by death; these include rape and kidnaping; the crime of murder is not specifically mentioned. Eight crimes are punishable by mutilation; these included disrespect by a slave to his master, disrespect by an adopted son, the fatal clumsiness of a physician, and the false branding of a slave. Though the branding of slaves for purposes of identification was practiced, there is only one mention of the directly punitive use of branding: slander. There is no mention of torture. In summary: a total of forty-six separate offenses were punished either by death or by some form of physical insult. The largest number of offenses was dealt with by fines, the remaining few by purgation. By contrast, in the England of 1780 there were approximately three hundred and fifty capital offenses alone.

The Mosaic Legal Tradition

Turning from the Babylonian to the chronologically later Mosaic tradition, we encounter a body of legal lore that represents a considerably less sophisticated, less professional approach to the perennial problems of social control. Despite their many real and apparent similarities, there was one significant and basic difference between the two systems: a drastically altered relationship between the religious and the secular power.

[8] Certain of these penalties seem obviously designed to make the punishment "fit" the crime as literally as possible. Thus, "If a woman bring about the death of her husband for the sake of another man, they shall impale her." (*Ibid.*, p. 55.) A wet nurse who substitutes another infant for the nursling of her employer shall have her breasts cut off. A son denying his mother or father must have his tongue cut out; should he strike his father, he must lose the offending fingers.

In the Babylon of Hammurabi, the secular power was clearly superior to the religious; actually, the secular authority had absorbed the religious. Purely religious offenses are rare in the Code; virtually every violation of religious interests is simultaneously a violation of a State or secular interest. Though the punishment is graver if a religious institution is the victim—as in the case of theft from a temple—it is impossible to say whether the added severity is in deference to piety or in defense of the king's secular authority. By contrast, the Mosaic codes fairly bristle with fatal sacerdotal crimes. Oppenheimer has listed the following capital offenses:

> Idolatry, especially the *cult of Moloch,* divination in the name of false gods, sorcery, blasphemy, *violation of the Sabbath; sodomy; bestiality,* the beast being killed too; *incest with mother, father's wife or daughter-in-law; marrying mother and daughter; adultery;* ravishing or seducing a "virgin betrothed unto an husband" and for such virgin to be a willing victim; for a damsel to enter matrimony without the tokens of virginity; for the daughter of a priest to prostitute herself; man-stealing; smiting or cursing father or mother, or being a stubborn and rebellious son and incorrigible withal. Apostasy of a city is punished with its utter destruction; the inhabitants and the cattle thereof are smitten with the edge of the sword; the city and all the spoil thereof is burnt with fire, to remain an heap for ever, and not to be built again.[9]

Certain of these offenses entailed the alternative punishment of the *kerith,* a special ancient Hebrew sanction combining certain elements of excommunication with a self-enforcing curse, by which the offender was doomed to an early end. The effect of this curse—pronounced by the religious authorities but executed only by the Almighty—was virtually a sentence to a living death in exile.

In addition to the death penalty and the kerith, mutilation and scourging are specifically mentioned. The Mosaic codes, in common with equally undeveloped systems of earlier and later periods, reserved the punishment of murder to the vengeance of the victim's clan. Nevertheless, despite the direct Biblical support for the doctrine of an eye for an eye, the issue of intent was considered, and provision was made to protect the man who slew by accident. Deuteronomy 19 makes mention of three "cities of refuge," in which the accidental slayer might find sanctuary "so that innocent blood be not shed in the midst of Thy land":

... who so killeth his neighbor unawares, and hateth him not ... shall

---

[9] Heinrich Oppenheimer, *The Rationale of Punishment* (London: University of London Press, 1913), p. 108.

flee into one of these cities and live, lest the avenger of blood...overtake him and smite him mortally.[10]

The graver offenses were crimes against God as well as against man; if not detected and punished, they were capable of exposing the entire community, innocent as well as guilty, to the wrath of the Lord. Many of the Mosaic punishments have the double objective of appeasing the victim and removing the pollution created by the offense. This dual purpose fortified the power of the religious authorities, especially in times of trouble, when public indignation would be diverted against individuals or policies obnoxious to the priests. The privileged status of the priestly class led to a continuing struggle between religious and secular authorities for political power.

The foregoing account of the Hebrew law has confined itself to the earlier Biblical myths and traditions and does not deal at all with the development of law in later Jewish communities. This emphasis is deliberate. Curiously enough, the historical importance of the Hebrew legal heritage has very little to do with historical fact and everything to do with myth; it was not the reality but the tradition that had the profoundest historical consequences.

This history was written in the moral and physical agonies of later generations dominated by authorities who found in the Bible a blueprint for social control. Centuries after the Jews had lost the last vestiges of their temporal authority, had been scattered in isolated ghettoes over the face of Europe, and had, in fact, succeeded in developing a legal system entirely dependent on moral suasion and informal social sanctions, their abandoned superstitions were being translated into precise manuals for the persecution of witches, sorcerers, and others who jeopardized the State by commerce with the devil. (The medieval *Directorium Inquisitorium* followed Deuteronomy word for word.) The influence of this transplanted theology, which was dominant in European jurisprudence well into the eighteenth century, has been summarized by Maestro in the following terms:

> The domination of theology manifested itself, first of all, in the very conception of justice. The Mosaic Law, which is based on the *talio* (an eye for an eye, and so forth) was regarded as a direct divine command. The principles of the Bible being often interpreted narrowly and most strictly applied contributed in a great measure toward making the criminal law extremely cruel, and the more so since the supposed divine origin of these principles precluded any compromise

[10] *Deuteronomy*, Chapter 19:4–6.

or mitigation. For example the dominant principles in the Swedish-Finnish penal codes at the beginning of the eighteenth century were still the following: (1) The "lex talionis" is the highest justice according to the Law of God, i.e., the Mosiac Law; (2) the legislator shall endeavor to restrain miscreants from criminal actions by the most severe penalties; (3) the legislator shall seek to soften the wrath of the Deity and save the realm from His vengeance by the most severe punishments.[11]

The Heritage of Rome

The historical fate of the Roman heritage has much in common with that of the Hebrew: what survived in later centuries had little to do with the Roman legal tradition at its height. Because of the maturity of this tradition, the loss is apparent even in the ruins that have survived. By the time of the Empire, the Roman State had developed a formal code of civil and criminal proceedings, a system of legal education with state-supported law schools, and a high tradition of legal scholarship.

The uninterrupted reign of Roman law was the longest and widest the world has yet known. Despite numerous lapses created by tyrants at home, it enjoyed a high reputation among its many subject peoples; it is no accident that the world *justice* is of Latin origin. The weight of historical evidence favors the view that the Roman criminal law was a later development of civil procedures. Urch has described a typical civil suit between private parties:

> The process opened with an oral pleading before the praetor. Then both disputants seized the object in dispute, or something which represented that object. At the same time each grasped a rod (the rod replaced the original spear, symbol of early trial by combat). This was done to symbolize a fight. Next, the praetor, acting for the state in the interests of peace and order, intervened in this dramatization of the primitive method of settling disputes. He gave temporary possession of the object in dispute to one of the parties, but at the same time required him to pledge sureties to his adversary that, should he lose the case, he would return to his adversary the object and whatever profits should accumulate ad interim from its possession. The praetor then

[11] Marcello Maestro, *Voltaire and Beccaria as Reformers of Criminal Law* (New York: Columbia University Press, 1942) pp. 2–3.

nominated an index (judge) with whom the parties arranged for a trial at the end of thirty days.[12]

During the life of the Republic and the early Empire, criminal trial procedure retained its quasi-private character. With both parties (and, later, their lawyers) pleading their own cases, there was no need for an official prosecutor, and the State could maintain a total impartiality.

The Shift from Accusatory to Inquisitorial Methods

Judicial procedures in which charges are brought and argued by one private party against another are called "accusatory" and "adversary." In this form of adjudication the role of the State is severely limited. The government merely supplies an impartial referee who decides the issue, awards the victorious "adversary," and determines the penalty or forfeit of the loser. This form of proceeding is in sharp contrast to that in which the State supplies not only a referee but a government prosecutor, who supplants the private accuser. The process in which the State initiates and presses the accusation is called "inquisitorial" (from the Latin word meaning "seek into"), and places enormously greater power in the hands of the political authorities.

The political and social consequences flowing from the use of one or the other of these basic methods are far-reaching. Historically, a shift from accusatory to inquisitorial proceedings has almost invariably paralleled—has, in fact, been one of the principal instruments of—a shift toward more autocratic systems of government.[13] This shift was apparent during the progressive growth of absolutism in imperial Rome, where criminal proceedings initiated by private persons and tried in public

[12] Erwin J. Urch, "The Origin of the Actio Formularum," *The Classical Weekly*, 26:169, No. 22, April 1933.

[13] The noted law historian Esmein speaks of:

...a ceaseless strife between the two tendencies which in these days [still] divides the domain of the criminal sciences. The *Classical School* is above all individualistic, demanding new safeguards in favor of the accused, a continual control over the criminal authorities, the diminution of arbitrariness, and the increase of liberty. The *Modern School,* which is above all collectivist, desires to strengthen the "social defense," to deprive the prisoner of those safeguards which are summed up in the "presumption of innocence," to substitute for a humanitarian procedure a scientific procedure, to transform the penal action into a clinical examination and the judges into expert specialists, who must have a very special education in matters of psychology, anthropology, and criminal sociology. (Adhemar Esmein, *A History of Continental Criminal Procedure,* Boston: Little Brown and Company, 1913, p. 41.)

gradually gave way to the system by which accusations were brought by the State and tried in secret.

The shift toward inquisitorial proceedings was confined, at first, to the provinces, which were under the absolute rule of appointed Roman governors. However, the advantages of the system were not lost on the Roman emperors, who were able to contrast their greater power abroad under the new method with their restricted authority at home under the old. Gradually, the application of the inquisitorial method was extended to cover not only the provincial foreigners but the Roman citizens as well.

Forms of Punishment

In their punishments as in other aspects of their culture, the cosmopolitan Romans were wide borrowers as well as ingenious inventors. There was virtually no form of punishment known to the ancient world that was not at one time or other meted out under Roman auspices. Every method of execution was practiced, including burial alive, impaling, crucifixion, drowning, enforced suicide, beheading, sawing in half, burning, and death by wild beasts in the arena. In earlier Roman times capital offenders were hurled from the Tarpeian Rock, but this practice declined under competition with more popular forms of execution. One uniquely Roman method, responsible for the death of many eminent citizens (including Cicero) was the *proscription*. This technique, mentioned in Shakespeare's *Julius Caesar*, involved the secret preparation of lists of citizens to be assassinated during a temporary suspension of the laws.

Many varieties of noncapital punishments were administered by the Romans. Numerous forms of temporary and permanent humiliation were inflicted, including degradation to slave status, branding on the forehead, and leading lesser offenders about by the ear while a crier proclaimed their misdeeds. Book-burning was probably of Roman invention. Mutilations were common. Fines and confiscations were frequent, especially during the Empire, when the rulers sought to enrich themselves at the expense of prominent men out of favor. Imprisonment at hard labor was practiced, especially during periods of labor shortage in the mines and galleys. Sentences of exile were occasionally pronounced against notables, frequently after they had already fled. At the height of the popularity of the Roman Games, sturdy young offenders were often sentenced to serve as gladiators.

As this list suggests, Roman punishments were highly discretionary, varying with administrative or economic considerations and, frequently, with political expediency.

Laws and Penal Methods of the Germanic Invaders of Rome

The law-ways of the Germanic conquerors, while somewhat similar to the private, accusatorial traditions of the earlier Roman Republic, were radically different from the inquisitorial system of the declining Empire. The barbarians were acutely aware of these differences and, from the first, were determined to preserve their own methods.

They were especially determined to preserve the private initiation of proceedings by the victim or his kinsman. This principle of private accusation survived through the feudal period, long after other aspects of Germanic procedure had succumbed to the general revival of Roman jurisprudence. From the outset, however, the cruder laws of the invaders, adapted to the less complex problems of nomadic life, were unequal to the ramifications of litigation in the decaying Roman society and required implementation by Roman procedures. The laws of the barbarians shortly became hybrid mixtures of Roman and Germanic procedure.

Of the Germanic groups within the borders of the old Empire, only the Franks and Lombards resisted the pressures making for legal assimilation. As late as the twelfth century the teaching of the revived Roman law was forbidden in schools under the control of the decendants of the Lombards. This resistance was a desperate and foredoomed rearguard action. In Italy, legal scholars had discovered the lost Law Digests of Justinian. Upon men increasingly impatient with the confusion of legal tongues, the discovery burst like a revelation that could rescue them from the Tower of Babel. Seagle has stated:

> The famous law school of Bologna...became the centre of the revival of Roman jurisprudence, and the fame of the Bolognese doctors spread far and wide. They contemptuously referred to the Lombard law as *ius asininum* (the law of asses) and adopted Justinian's law-books as their Bible. They regarded them as *ratio scripta*, or written reason,

and it has aptly been said that they reasoned "as if the Lord Justinian was still holding sway over Italy."[14]

Thus it was that the Roman law finally reconquered the barbarians where Roman arms had failed. The only Germanic tribes to evade its influence were those of northern Europe and Scandinavia: The Angles, Saxons, Jutes and the Northmen. Shortly after the Roman legions had been recalled to defend the heart of the Empire, these tribes invaded various parts of Britain, bringing a more primitive form of Germanic law with them. Within five hundred years, the Anglo-Saxon conquerors of England had developed a pattern of social life, a system of judicial procedures, and a tradition of local self-government strong enough to resist radical change under pressure of the inquisitorial influences imported by the Norman Conquest.

Early Germanic Legal Systems

Earliest records of Germanic law suggest a society where social control was in an early stage of transition from private vengeance to group arbitration. In a social organization based on clans loosely organized into tribes, both crime and punishment were largely private matters. Except for a few offenses against religion, morality, and military discipline, injuries inflicted on the person, property, or reputation of individuals merely established the right of retaliation by the victim. This right, which was hereditary, was strictly limited to the victim or his closest kin; if they took no action, no action was taken and the group remained uninvolved.

The transition from a system of private vengeance based on the blood feud to a system providing the alternative of group arbitration and, eventually, group adjudication appears to have resulted from increasing limitations imposed, *not on the principle of individual retaliation, but on the times and places where it could be exercised.* These limitations were imposed by a gradual extension of the *frede* or *peace.* At the times and places the peace was in force, all individual violence was strictly prohibited; and the offender was therefore at least temporarily immune from retaliation.

The earliest forms of the peace occurred during the sacred festivals. Later it became permanently attached to the sacred woods where these

---

[14] William Seagle, *The Quest for Law* (New York: Alfred A. Knopf, Inc., 1941), pp. 166–167.

ceremonies were held, affording the offender a more or less permanent place of sanctuary. The first arbitrations of disputes probably occurred at the great tribal assemblies (*all-things*) held during these sacred festivals.

During periods when the army was on the march the peace was in force. Gradually it was extended to include the sowing and harvesting seasons. The early Germanic tribes attached a particular religious sanctity to dwellings; in the Norse language the word *grid* signified both peace and house. Consequently the peace was in force within the owner's dwelling and not even the victim could rightfully exact vengeance on the malefactor within his own house. Probably as a result of early attempts by avengers to smoke offenders out, the peace of the house was extended to cover an area around it; from that point on, the offender was safe on his own ground. Historically, the most important form of the peace was that which surrounded the person of the king. Oppenheimer has described this as follows:

> The king's presence imparted peace, not only to his residence but to a considerable district around it. Three miles, three furlongs, and three acre-breadths, nine feet, nine palms, and three barley-corns, constituted the mystical radius of the verge which was reckoned from the town or mansion where the king held his court; and within this ambit the protection by royalty was to remain unviolated.[15]

The persons and vicinities of priests conferred a peace upon the area around them; a breach of this peace or any peace sanctioned by religion was an extremely grave sin and laid the violator open to sacrifice to the offended god. In time the peace was attached to any agreement made between the offender and his victim; thereafter any attempt to continue the feud was a breach punishable by death.

The burgeoning of the institution of the peace suggests a hypothesis for the origin of group arbitration. With the multiplication of so many times and places of immunity, it must have become increasingly difficult for the private avengers to execute their vengeance. The offender was immune during religious festivals, during military campaigns, in his home and on his ground, in the sacred woods, and in the neighborhood of the king. With some ingenuity in the timing and placing of his activities, he could avoid the retaliation of his victim indefinitely. In a community whose safety in a war-filled world depended on its unity, the existence of many unresolved hostilities would have

[15] Oppenheimer, *op. cit.*, p. 166.

created unbearable internal dangers. Some alternative method of resolution was therefore required. This method was found in a system of compensations developed to an astonishing degree of thoroughness in all Germanic societies.

Three kinds of payment were involved in this system of compensation: the *wergild* (man-money), payable to the next of kin if the victim died; the *bot,* a compensation for any injury other than death; and a *wite* or *fridesbot* (peace-price) payable to the State if the composition was made by an official decision of the group. The wergild varied with the rank of the dead man: the price of a thane was approximately six times that of a ceorl (freeman); that of a king, approximately six times the price of a thane. The fee paid by the offender to the group was not originally a punitive fine. If the parties reached agreement without group arbitration, it was not paid at all; if the offender's property could not cover both the bot and the wite, the victim was paid first. Commentators have suggested that the wite was a payment either for arbitration services or for a guarantee against any subsequent satisfaction demanded by the victim.

CRIMES IN THE GERMANIC CODES. Since all personal injuries were matters for personal retaliation or compensation, it follows that the only crimes known to the early Germanic tribes were offenses against religion or morality and the group. Oppenheimer has listed the following: Treason against the king or the tribe, desertion, sacrilege, murder *if by magic or poison,* killing in violation of a peace or a composition, killing hostages, murder of a husband by his wife (or vice versa), parricide, murder of close relatives or of a household intimate, murder by stealth or during sleep with concealment of the body, and secret theft. After the conversion of the barbarians to Christianity, the spoilation of a dead warrior was made capital; later this offense was extended to include the spoilation of dead bodies generally.[16]

FORMS OF PUNISHMENTS. Death and outlawry were the original punishments for religious and tribal crimes. For these offenses the priests were the judges and usually the executioners as well. Frequently the executions were sacrificial, serving to appease the gods and to remove a pollution from the group. In cases where the offense not only violated a sacred group value but injured an individual as well, the victim or his kindred were frequently permitted to execute the sentence. This provision, which harmonized group retaliation with private vengeance,

[16] *Ibid.,* p. 131.

appeared in many forms in the earlier Teutonic codes and persisted in derivative legal systems until much later periods.[17]

In many cases where the execution of the sentence was turned over to the plaintiff, he could refrain from exercising his prerogative—a fact clearly indicating that the accuser was not carrying out a public function but merely exercising the right of personal vengeance awarded by the court. At this stage the right of pardon belonged to the victim rather than the State. The placating of the victim (and the resulting reestablishment of peace) remained a dominant concern of penal legistion well into the modern period.[18] A vestige of this practice survives today in the publication of the names of prisoners scheduled for parole consideration. The feelings of the victim and the community are considered and may play no small part in the decision to grant parole.

Some form of exile or removal from group protection appears in many primitive societies. Among the early Germanic tribes, outlawry was a sentence of exile on pain of death; if the outlaw were found within the realm after a certain date, he might legally be slain by anyone.

The Later Evolution and Decline of Germanic Law on the Continent

Between the dissolution of the Roman Empire and the Revival of Learning the intervening darkness was briefly illumined by one period which, had it realized its promise, might have spared Europe that thousand years' retardation known as the Middle Ages. Within the borders of the old empire the sixth and seventh centuries merely continued the work of destruction that had shattered Rome in the fifth. The decendants of the original barbarian conquerors, with none to fight but each other, subsisted on the still fertile ruins of the old economy and squandered the material and cultural heritage of the West. Their unproductivity and the sense of superiority encouraged by their military power effectively prevented any reception of the Graeco-Roman culture. The

---

[17] Cf. Oppenheimer (op. cit., p. 21):
The Frisian common law, which was in force up to the ... sixteenth century, provides: "When a thief is caught, he is to be taken before the magistrate. If he is condemned to death, it is not for the magistrate to provide for his execution. The court beadle must bind him and lead him to the gallows. There the man whose property he has purloined must either himself hang the thief or hire another to do it for him."

[18] Cf. Oppenheimer (op. cit., p. 26):
In Antwerp, as late as the seventeenth century, it availed a murderer but little to receive his sovereign's pardon unless and until he had succeeded in reconciling the relations of the murdered man. ... In Spain, up to quite modern times, the ... royal ... pardon was dependent upon the consent of the victim.

skilled artisans and mechanics, mercilessly exploited, died off, and their arts and engineering died with them. Within two hundred years the barbarians had almost spent a treasure it had taken a thousand years to gather—and would taken another millenium to recover.

The process of cultural disintegration was temporarily arrested by the ascension of the Frankish king Charlemagne as "Holy Roman Emperor" in 800 A.D. For a brief time it seemed that the empire had, indeed, revived. The old Roman roads had not yet been reclaimed by the forests. Along these roads, on swift horses, ran Charlemagne's ministers, the famous *missi dominici* ("those sent by the king"), bringing justice and sound administration to all parts of his vast realm. These ministers were a stroke of genius by a master administrator. Traveling in pairs (a secular noble and a cleric) and on a fixed circuit, they carried the king's decrees (called *capitularies*) simultaneously to many distant points. Thus there occurred not only a cultural revival but a juristic renaissance as well. Historians of the criminal law have looked back on this period as a premature golden age.[19]

Criminal Justice During the Feudal Period

The collapse of the Carolingian Empire brought on the long night of feudalism and the Middle Ages. In the general darkness an even blacker night descended on law and order. Neither the plowman in his fields nor the nobleman at his board could be safe from the sudden onset of an iron-plated ruffian, who might at any moment snatch away field, wife, and life itself and then retire to his impregnable castle. The disintegration of kingdoms into innumerable feudal localities with their own armed forces, their own system of tolls and taxation—and frequently their own coinage—had created a power vacuum irresistibly inviting to the anarchy previously restrained by the Carolingian Empire.

Any discussion of criminal justice during this period must begin with the reminder that the feudal lords were simultaneously the sole

[19] It was too good to last. Royalty had not yet hit upon the idea of primogeniture as a way of preserving its realm from the consequence of its own fertility; when a king died, his territory was divided among his sons. Charlemagne had only one son, but he had far too many grandsons. Within seventy years of the great king's death, the squabbles of these grandchildren had dismembered the Empire, blasted the revival, and put off the best hopes of mankind for seven hundred years.

arbiters of law and order and the greatest disturbers of the peace. Many of the peculiarities of medieval criminal justice may be traced to this duality of roles. The complicated processes of *subinfeudation*—a system making it possible for one lord to be the vassal of another who, in turn, owed fealty to a third who held part of his lands under vassalage to the first—often made it uncertain whether a given noble would appear as judge, defendant, or accuser in given criminal action. Occasionally the same lord would occupy two or more of these roles within the same month.

The basic source of medieval justice was the Germanic law, which had been but briefly superseded by the reforms of the Carolingian revival. The searching inquest of the far-ranging *missi dominici* was a thing of the past; accusations were again restricted to the victim and his next of kin, and the man who lacked kinfolk lacked justice as well.

The early Teutonic assemblies, relying extensively on the testimony of the contesting parties and their witnesses, had reached their decision by majority vote, after individual deliberation over the evidence. With the exception of those cases in which it retained the old Germanic method of *compurgation* (acceptance of testimony on the basis of a solemn oath), medieval jurisprudence attempted to remove the evaluation of evidence from fallible human judgment altogether, placing the decision—and the responsibility for it—securely in divine hands. In order to accomplish this objective, two techniques were employed: the *ordeal*, which probably derived from an old Germanic custom originally used *after* the judgment had been reached, and the *trial or wager by battle*, a method unique to the feudal era. This latter method was ideally suited to the temperament of the medieval nobility, enabling them to combine the appeal to force with the appeal to God in one decisive maneuver.

In a further development of the trial by battle, litigants unable to fight for themselves were permitted to engage champions to fight for them. At first confined to women, to the young, to the aged and the infirm, this privilege was later extended to all who could afford it, and there developed a class of professional champions who rode about selling their services on trial days. It was thus possible for a malefactor who lacked compurgators and was reluctant to submit to the doubtful issue of the ordeal to remedy the deficiencies of his arms by the valor of his purse. The right to trial by battle persisted, with increasing restrictions, long after the extension of the king's peace had removed most criminal breaches from private to public jurisdiction. Long obsolete, it was not formally abolished in England until 1819.

Like the trial by battle, the *ordeal* was supposed to reveal the divine judgment on the guilt or innocence of the accused. Ordeals, which first appeared in Germanic Europe and became widespread during early medieval times, were unknown in Greece, Rome, China, Japan, or ancient America. In other parts of Asia, and especially in Africa, they were practiced among advanced primitive tribes until recent times. In Europe the judicial ordeal took many forms, varying widely from place to place.

One of the most common forms was the *ordeal by water*, in which the accused, bound, was thrown into a stream. If he remained afloat, this was taken as a sign of guilt, since the water which had originally accepted him during baptism was now "rejecting" him. (In other places, by a similar but reversed logic, guilt was evidenced if the accused *failed* to float.)

Many ordeals involved the infliction of specific injuries on the person of the accused. The wounds were sealed and the question of guilt was decided by an examination of the extent of healing after a number of days. Certain ordeals required feats of extreme agility. In the *ordeal by morsel*, for example, chunks of bread and cheese were stuffed in the mouth in a manner which impeded breathing, and the accused was considered innocent only if he was able to avoid swallowing. The ordeals were usually presided over by the clerics, who invoked the Lord's protection of the innocent at the start and declared His judgment at the conclusion of the proceedings.

Most modern commentators have accepted the medieval rationale that the ordeals were methods of determining guilt or innocence rather than devices for intimidating and punishing accused persons who refused to confess. This nonpunitive interpretation was, of course, the version insisted upon by those who administered the ordeals. Nevertheless, there is strong internal and external evidence that these procedures, far from being impartial tests of guilt, were actually disguised forms of coercion and punishment.

The more drastic ordeals were almost invariably inflicted on the accused and rarely, if ever, on the plaintiff. (In cases where both parties accused each other, the far less drastic and sanguinary method of drawing lots was frequently used.) Medieval justice placed the burden of proof on the accused; it was he who had to "bear the law." Unless and until he proved his innocence, he was considered guilty. Secondly, the nature of the ordeals themselves suggests their punitive intention. The most common form involved physical suffering or injury of some kind, and, as Seagle has pointed out, its advantage lay in the fact that "it could be not only a form of proof but an automatic means of punishment, for the guilty person might not survive the test."[20]

Ordeals were eventually abandoned in favor of a more efficient method for extracting confessions, and after the Fourth Lateran Council in 1215, the clergy were forbidden to take part in them. Latinist scholars had rediscovered the superior uses of Roman torture, and the Church, plagued by an endemic spread of heresy, was in no mood to take chances with miracles.

The Inquisition and the Transformation of Continental Criminal Procedure

Among the clerics who formed the only body of scholars in the Middle Ages, the eleventh and twelfth centuries were periods of intellectual ferment. A revival of learning in the ancient tongues had opened the pages of the Bible, and all over Europe men were comparing official dogma with original Scripture for the first time. The new sources were powerfully stimulating to scholars, for whom the scanty intellectual fare of the preceding centuries had become a repetitive and tasteless diet, and within a short period a variety of original doctrines arose.

The initial response of the papacy was mild, but as the new thinking persisted and grew, the official attitude slowly changed from fatherly chiding to hostility and estrangement. The gradual hardening of feeling can be seen in the treatment of the Waldenses, a sect which preached evangelical poverty and a return to gospel simplicity as the way of salvation. A large band of Waldenses arrived in Rome in 1179 and were personally blessed by Pope Alexander III but forbidden to preach. They disobeyed, and in 1184 all persons professing the Waldensian heresy were condemned.

The shift from official opposition to official persecution did not noticeably diminish the number of heresies or heretics. For many, the prospect of martyrdom merely created an additional incentive. The con-

[20] Seagle, op. cit., p. 89.

flict was sharpened when the dissenters broadened their criticism of dogma to an attack on papal practices, and by the turn of the thirteenth century the Church saw itself in a desperate struggle for survival.

In 1252 Pope Innocent IV issued his papal bull *Ad Extirpanda*, establishing an elaborate machinery for the persecution of heretics in every city and diocese in Christendom. Henry Charles Lea, an outstanding scholar of the Inquisition, has summarized the instructions contained in this fateful document:

> All rulers were ordered in public assembly to put heretics to the ban, as though they were sorcerers. Any one finding a heretic could seize him, and take possession of his goods. Each chief magistrate, within three days after assuming office, was to appoint, on the nomination of his bishop and of two friars of each of the Mendicant Orders, twelve good Catholics with two notaries and two or more servitors whose sole business was to arrest heretics, seize their goods, and deliver them to the bishop or his vicars.
>
> The ruler was bound when required to send his assessor or a knight to aid them, and every inhabitant when called upon was obliged to assist them, under a heavy penalty. When the inquisitors visited any portion of the jurisdiction they were accompanied by a deputy of the ruler elected by themselves or by the bishop. In each place visited, this official was to summon under oath three men of good repute, or even the whole vicinage, to reveal any heretics within their knowledge, or the property of such, or of any persons holding secret conventicles or differing in life or manners from the ordinary faithful. The State was bound to arrest all accused, to hold them in prison, to deliver them to the bishop or inquisitor under safe escort, and to execute within fifteen days all judgments pronounced against them. The ruler was further required, when called upon, to inflict torture on those who would not confess and betray all the heretics of their acquaintance.[21]

Procedures of the Inquisition

Inquisitorial proceedings were sudden, secret and virtually immune from successful defense by the accused. Lea has described them as follows:

> A man would be reported to the inquisitor as of ill-repute for heresy, or his name would occur in the confessions of other prisoners. A secret inquisition would be made and all accessible evidence against him

[21] Henry Charles Lea, *The Inquisition of the Middle Ages* (New York: The Citadel Press, 1954), pp. 34–35.

would be collected. He would then be secretly cited to appear at a given time, and bail taken to secure his obedience, or if he were suspected of flight, he would be suddenly arrested and confined until the tribunal was ready to give him a hearing.... When the mass of surmises and gossip, exaggerated and distorted by the natural fear of the witnesses, eager to save themselves from suspicion of favoring heretics, grew sufficient for action, the blow would fall. The accused was thus prejudged. He was assumed to be guilty, or he would not have been put on trial....[22]

The Revival of Torture

Except among the Visigoths, the use of torture had been unknown in the law-ways of the barbarian conquerors of Rome. The Church had always been opposed to it, and its use in the extracting of confessions was forbidden by canon law. The rediscovery of the Codes of Justinian, in which torture was sanctioned, gave the Inquisition an appropriate legal authority for a method toward which the logic of its processes was irresistibly drawn. Torture was explicitly authorized in the papal bull of 1252, and manuals detailing precise instructions for its administration were placed in the hands of the inquisitors.

The Use of Imprisonment as a Penance

Heretics who evaded the death penalty by means of confession were required to undergo various forms of penance. Of these, the most severe and the most common was imprisonment. Lea has described two kinds:

> There were two kinds of imprisonment, the milder or "murus largus," and the harsher, known as "murus strictus" or "durus" or "arctus." All were on bread and water, and the confinement, according to rule, was solitary, each penitent in a separate cell, with no access allowed to him....[23]

The rules against contact were difficult to enforce and, on occasion, were relaxed to permit visits by the clergy and, more rarely, by laymen. There was one extreme form of solitary confinement in which no human contact whatever was permitted. This was known as in pace—literally, "in peace"—and was tantamount to a living entombment.

[22] Ibid., p. 103.
[23] Ibid., p. 182.

Juridical Consequences of the Inquisition

The broader religious and social effects of the Inquisition remain matters for interpretation and dispute. Concerning its effects on the still plastic and impressionable legal structure of the period there is less room for argument. The force of its impact is demonstrated by the fact that its procedural grip on continental criminal law did not relax for five hundred years. Concerning this, Lea writes:

> Of all the curses which the Inquisition brought in its train this, perhaps, was the greatest—that until the closing years of the eighteenth century, throughout the greater part of Europe, the inquisitorial process, as developed for the destruction of heresy, became the customary method of dealing with all who were under accusation; that the accused was treated as one having no rights, whose guilt was assumed in advance, and from whom confession was to be extorted by guile or force.[24]

Medieval Punishments

With temporary and local exceptions, each succeeding century of the medieval period saw a worsening in the severity of all forms of punishment. By the dawn of the Renaissance the older, more lenient sanctions characteristic of the Germanic system of fines and compensations had been virtually swallowed up in a juridical blood bath.

Death

By the fourteenth century the most common penalty cited in continental records was death. As the number of crimes punishable by death increased, there was a corresponding increase in the ingenuity and variety of techniques of execution. Probably during no other period of western civilization was there so intensive a search for new ways of making men die. Death by burning, suffocation, drowning, poisoning, impalement, fracture (breaking at the wheel), and burial alive was refined to the point where execution had become a profession combining many characteristics of an art, a science, and a public spectacle.

Certain executioners achieved a wide reputation for a particular specialty and were numbered among the foremost public entertainers of

[24] *Ibid.*, p. 256.

the day. The city of Hanover developed a specialty in which death was inflicted by wasps. Later this method was refined to provide a slower death by ants and flies—an innovation that increased audience appeal by prolonging the length of the entertainment. The ingenuity and technical skill of the executioners is suggested by the complexity of the instructions they were required to follow. Sometimes the victim had to be kept conscious for a considerable period, during which a detailed sequence of tortures and mutilations was carried out. In order to follow these instructions, the executioners were required to master the art of preserving life even while they destroyed it. It was one of the age's ironies that the anatomical knowledge and sheer medical competence of the executioners often rivaled that of the doctors of the day.

Mutilation

Second in frequency to the death penalty was the punishment of mutilation. This penalty too was exacted for a wide range of offenses and with corresponding variety and ingenuity. Dismemberment, disfigurement, castration, and blinding were the main divisions of a catalog that ran to scores of subtitles. Here again medical skill played a critical role, the objective being to keep the victim alive after the surgery.

Humiliation

For lesser offenses, public humiliation was a frequent punishment. This included exposure in the pillory and the enforced wearing of badges, headgear, and other distinguishing symbols of degradation. The purposes of these forms of punishment were several: They identified the offender and his offense and they invited the abuse of any passerby who might be in need of venting his spleen without danger of retaliation. Often the wearing of these symbols of degradation involved considerable physical suffering. A common penance for religious misdemeanors was the wearing of heavy iron crosses, which were forged around the offender's neck or trunk. These weights were frequently to be carried for long periods; in many cases the offender bore his crosses to the grave.

Corporal Punishment

Exclusive of torture—which was looked on more as a method of interrogation than as a punishment—physical chastisement was a relatively infrequent punishment during the medieval period. Whipping and birching were chiefly restricted to children. Such devices as the ducking stool did not come into vogue until much later. The use of the knout and the cat-o-nine-tails and the development of whipping into a mathematically graded system of punishments were also reserved for later periods.

Banishment

The penalty of banishment was frequently pronounced against persistent minor offenders, beggars, and local nuisances. Because of the small size of most medieval communities, this punishment was not as severe as it later became, being somewhat analogous to being "run out of the precinct." Nevertheless, the banished offender suffered, as well, the confiscation of his property—which, in the case of the poor, who were the principal objects of this penalty, usually amounted to little. In any case, a punishment which spared life and limb during this period was to be looked on as a comparative act of clemency.

Fines and Confiscation

Vestiges of the old Germanic system of compensation survived, though in altered form and intent, in an elaborate system of fines. These levies—which were a major source of income for the local ruler—were occasionally shared by the offender's victim; in most cases, however, the lord was the principal beneficiary.

There was wide local variation in the offenses subject to fines. A frequent target of fines was the merchant who misrepresented his goods, the landholders who tampered with a deed—the intent being to punish the fraudulent where punishment might hurt most: in his pocketbook. In the highly formalized legal proceedings of the period, errors in pleading and violations of court decorum were a lucrative source of fines. These might be visited on anyone involved in the proceedings, including the lawyers and, on occasion, the judges themselves. Whenever the king or the local overlord was in financial straits he might send his legal specialist to the local court; this individual would listen with a predatory ear to whatever was said or done, from time to time halting the procedure with a triumphant cry of "Error!" The unfortunate speaker—who might have done no more than mangle a legal formula—would then be fined.

A much more serious form of fining was confiscation and destruction of property. Either or both of these penalties was the usual concurrent to capital punishment, the ruler receiving all removable valuables and destroying whatever could not be moved or converted into money. One curious form of property destruction was reserved to farm animals and, on occasion, even to nonliving physical objects that had in one way or another figured in an accident involving life or limb. The intent here was to punish the offending object rather than its owner; the effect, however, was to deprive the owner of his goods. Thus a bull that had gored someone might be ceremonially tried and destroyed; a tree under which someone had been struck by lightning might be cut down.

Imprisonment

Prior to the eighteenth century, except for certain categories of heretics, imprisonment was not generally viewed as a punishment and was used chiefly as a method of detention before trial. Prisoners of war and eminent personages held for ransom might be restrained for long or short periods—Richard I of England, for example, was kept in secret confinement until his ransom had been negotiated. As previously noted, members of the clergy and heretics were occasionally imprisoned. In general, however, the significant emergence of confinement as a punishment for ordinary crimes was the development of a later era.

Severe as they were, medieval punishments were singularly uncertain and capricious. In different—and, occasionally, in the same—localities, identical offenses would receive widely different treatment, the variation extending from incomprehensible cruelty to inappropriate leniency. A number of quaint traditions of clemency were available to save especially favored or fortunate culprits. One of the oldest and most curious of these was the provision that a felon might be saved from death and recommended for pardon if a maiden offered to marry him. In addition, special dispensations were sometimes granted to those whose services were considered essential. Because of the almost superstitious veneration of learning, students and others able to read and write were frequently granted these special dispensations. The famous *benefit of clergy* (originally confined to the clerics, who once formed the only body of educated men) was, at an early point, extended to anyone who could prove his literacy, and many a knowledgeable rogue read his way out of the hangman's noose by picking out a few halting phrases from the village Bible.

Standardization of Continental Criminal Procedure During the Renaissance

As the chronicle of penological history moves from the late medieval period into the Renaissance, the main focus of interest turns away from the punishments themselves and fixes on procedure. This focus will not significantly alter until the eighteenth century, since the next five centuries of penal history added very little that was new to the treatment of convicted criminals.[25] The major forms of punishment remained, though certain older techniques fell away and certain refinements were added. Many new crimes were added, but these were punishable by the same penalties. As before, death, mutilation, humiliation, banishment, and fines remained the basic responses of the political community toward its offenders.

Nevertheless, despite the lack of significant change in punishments, the emerging patterns of criminal procedure were to have the profoundest effect on unborn generations of men, criminal and law-abiding as well. For all its capriciousness and uncertainty, the juridical chaos of the feudal ages had left room for individual idiosyncrasy and local initiative. Despite the barbarity of the punishments, there were procedural chinks through which a man might crawl, and there were some quaint customs and legends he could cite against the bloodiest letter of the law. The bold, free, individualistic spirit of the ancient Teutonic law-ways had not wholly died out, and the vestiges that remained tended to mitigate some of the harshness of an otherwise iron age. All this was swept away in the irresistible historical movement that fused the innumerable political fragments of feudalism into a small number of national states.

The centralization of political power was accompanied and promoted by a widespread movement toward consolidation and standardization of judicial procedures compatible with the growing absolutism of the rulers. As has already been pointed out, this consolidation took its inspiration from the inquisitorial procedures of imperial Roman law, revived and perfected by the Church in its assault on heresy.

[25] There was perhaps one genuine innovation—forced penal labor—though even this had historical antecedents. Sentences to penal servitude in the galleys seem first to have appeared in France in the early sixteenth century. The practice spread rapidly throughout the maritime countries. Later, forced labor in the mines and the leasing of convicts to private contractors became popular.

Procedure as Punishment:
The Criminal Trial as an Instrument of Coercion

The meaning of trial procedures during the long continental reign of the inquisitorial jurisprudence becomes clear once it is understood that the State had already made up its mind about the guilt of the accused and was determined to exact a penalty. In secret meetings with witnesses and paid or voluntary informers, the prosecutor had prepared the accusation, had cleared it with influential or interested officials, and had readied all concerned for their roles in the predetermined judicial drama. From this point on, the trial itself was little more than a ceremony in which the foregoing conclusion of the offender's guilt was to be demonstrated to the public. Thus, from the time of his arrest, there could be little doubt in the mind of the accused that he had met with an almost inescapable calamity.

Nevertheless, in spite of the obviously staged character of these proceedings, there was a considerable effort to preserve the tradition of a fair trial. The length to which legal casuists went to justify their methods almost suggests a latent moral uneasiness about a system few dared to attack. Thus, apologists for the system argued that they were inspired by a search for a truly infallible justice—a true science of jurisprudence. Their discussions betray an almost aggressive self-righteousness, nowhere more evident than in the argument for the use of torture as a means of interrogation.

The argument ran as follows: In order to ensure absolute justice, it is necessary to prove beyond doubt that the accused actually committed the crime. Anything less than infallible proof is conjecture— and it is morally repugnant to punish a man on the basis of a mere leap in the dark. How may certainty be achieved? The testimony of witnesses is open to doubt, since the friends of the accused may be moved to lie in his favor while the friends of the victim may be moved to tell lies against him. Even the testimony of the victim cannot be uncritically relied on—he too may be moved by malice or, as in the case of attack at night or by an unseen assailant, misled by an honest error. There is only one person with an infallible knowledge of the identity of the offender, and that is the criminal himself. Only the criminal can conclusively implicate himself, and he must do this out of his own mouth, by his own confession.

The logic of this argument led to widespread adoption of the principle of requiring a confession before conviction for a serious crime. But (the argument continued) what if the accused does not confess? Is a person to be believed merely because he maintains his innocence? Some way must be found to test his sincerity, to establish the strength of his innocence. The test was torture—a method sanctified by religious practice and ancient usage. If the accused satisfactorily sustained the torture, maintaining his innocence in the face of this painful test of his integrity, he was to be declared acquitted.[26]

Though capable of using an attack on the credibility of testimony as the basis for a defense of torture, the legal casuists of the period were equally capable of justifying the use of rumor and other forms of hearsay when occasion demanded. Like the argument for confession, the defense of rumor, gossip, and common repute as forms of evidence was developed in highly rationalistic terms and surrounded with an almost scientific aura of precision. A curious outgrowth of this trend of reasoning was the development of a method of compounding items of hearsay in a cumulative way until they added up to a "mathematical" proof. Later this practice, known as the system of "demi-proofs," was bitingly characterized by Voltaire:

> The parliament of Thoulouse has a singular degree of accuracy in weighing the testimony of witnesses. In other places demi-proofs are admitted, which is at most admitting doubts, there being no such thing as demi-truth; but at Thoulouse they admit of quarters and eighths of a proof. We may, for example, look upon [one] hearsay as a quarter, upon another hearsay, more vague still, as an eighth; so that eight rumors, which are but the echo of unfounded report, may become a complete proof.[27]

Progress and Calamity

Relief from the excesses of the inquisitorial mode of criminal justice was slow and cautious in coming. It might have come sooner had not a frightful calamity befallen western Europe at the height of its greatest intellectual triumph. The consolidation of the national states had been followed, in the High Renaissance, by an unparalleled outburst of creative energy. In virtually every area of human activity, and on every level, there was a bursting through to new frontiers. The progress was con-

---

[26] Unless, of course, the authorities were determined to obtain a conviction, in which case the torture could be continued until the accused expired or confessed.

[27] Voltaire, "A Commentary on the Essay on Crimes and Punishments," in Cesare B. Beccaria, *An Essay on Crimes and Punishments* (Stanford, Calif.; Academic Reprints, 1953), p. 237.

tinuous and accelerating. Copernicus was followed by Kepler and Galileo, who looked ahead to Newton. Bacon and Montaigne were followed by Hobbes and Descartes, who dared to ground his whole philosophical system on universal doubt. In England the creative ferment had been paralleled by a political struggle which began by lifting men's eyes to new vistas of personal freedom and ended by securing British liberties once and for all. Bold ideas of freedom of conscience and toleration were in the air as the new critical spirit made inroads into long-sacrosanct areas of superstition and prejudice. Then, almost at the moment of fruition, there broke a storm which almost drowned reason out. Theology had searched the Scriptures and discovered that witches still walked among men. An orgy of witch-hunting and witch burning broke out. Against the tide, which spread from one end of Protestant Europe to the other, science was impotent and philosophy either covered its mouth or looked away.

The theological terror revived the worst excesses of the Inquisition and served to fetter the old procedures on the back of European jurisprudence for another hundred years. The human toll was frightful. Von Bar has cited figures suggesting that "whole areas were periodically decimated":

> In the bishopric of Bamberg...there were executed during the years 1627–1630, 285 persons. A witchcraft-judge in Fulda in 18 years brought his number of death sentences up to a total of 700.[28]

The Enlightenment and the Attack on the Inquisitorial Mode of Justice

For a century, resistance to the witchcraft trials and the procedures supporting them grew and smoldered in the minds of thinking men. Though a few isolated voices expressed their doubts and misgivings, by and large it was understood that protest would be both dangerous and futile until the revulsion became more general. Nevertheless, throughout the early decades of the eighteenth century, resistance increased, though still expressing itself indirectly, in the gradual reduction and, here and there, the quiet suppression of the trials themselves. No one had, as yet,

[28] Carl Ludwig Von Bar, *A History of Continental Criminal Law* (London: John Murray, 1916), p. 226.

frontally attacked the basic evil: the system of jurisprudence and the theory of punishment that made the witch trials and similar barbarities possible. When the attack finally came, it came with the suddenness and effect of two lightning bolts striking a forest in a state of tinder-box readiness.

In 1764, Cesare Bonesana Beccaria, a twenty-nine-year-old mathematician and economist, published in Italy a slim treatise entitled *An Essay on Crimes and Punishments*. This book, which has repeatedly been called the single most consequential work on criminal justice, created an immediate sensation. Within a short time it reached Voltaire, and two years later there appeared in France a translation of the Essay, to which was appended an unsigned commentary by Voltaire. Few failed to recognize the author, who had often before used his pen to aid individual victims of injustice, and the double-barreled assault on the old judicial order started an intellectual shock wave through educated Europe. Within a short time scores of scholarly pens were at work, advocating the new ideas. The learned academies set up contests offering prizes for the best essays on the subject. "Among the prizewinners in these competitions," writes Von Bar, "were men who later played an important role in the Revolution—and we note among these names, not without surprise, Robespierre and Marat."[29]

In those days it was once more fashionable for kings to be cultured and on good terms with philosophers; one by one, the absolute monarchs of Europe sought to demonstrate their humanity and learning, almost jostling each other in their haste to publish revisions of their criminal codes. Catherine II of Russia and Maria Theresa of Austria—shared the first honors, publishing their earliest revisions in 1768. Two years later Frederick II of Prussia came forward with a number of reforms, and in 1786 Leopold II of Tuscany became the first to follow Beccaria's proposal to abolish capital punishment. A year later the son of Maria Theresa, Joseph II of Austria, followed suit, abolishing the death penalty in a revision of the code adopted by his mother. Impressive as they were —especially from a public relations point of view—none of these efforts matched the sweeping scope of the reforms passed by the French revolutionary assemblies. In rapid-fire fashion the abuses of the inquisitorial jurisprudence were swept away. Toleration was declared, and all religious offenses were wiped off. The rights of the accused to a speedy and public trial were guaranteed, and the barbarous punishments of the

[29] *Ibid.*, p. 318.

ancient regime were abolished. Torture was anathematized. The powers of the state prosecutor were sharply curtailed; henceforth a jury of citizens would stand between the defendant and his hitherto omnipotent judges. And the accused was to have the advice of counsel to guide him through the mazes of the law.

Despite the revolutionary excesses, the absolutism of the Napoleonic interlude, and the otherwise stultifying reaction of the Bourbon restoration, the reforms, in the main, survived, spreading throughout the Continent. Even the wave of repression which visited new forms of oppression on political dissenters during the Holy Alliance left the ordinary criminal and the prisoner relatively undisturbed in their new safeguards. The clock might slow down but it would not be turned back.

The extraordinary vitality and staying power of the reforms proposed by Beccaria and seconded by the liberal scholarship of Europe may be traced to several causes. In the first place, the reforms were not merely negative. Beccaria and his supporters had a positive philosophy and a detailed practical program to replace the abuses they attacked. The core of this philosophy was a revolutionary new conception of the relation between man and the State, from which there followed a new conception of the role of law and the proper function of punishment.

The new view of the relation between the individual and the State was based on the theory of social contract. This theory, first elaborated by Hobbes Locke and then adapted by Rousseau and the other Encyclopedists, rejected the doctrine that man owed any absolute obedience to his government and insisted that the obligations between the two were both mutual and analogous to a contract voluntarily entered upon by free contractors. It was the obligation of the State to protect the safety and promote the happiness of its constituent members. In return for these services, it was the obligation of the individual to surrender a small portion of his natural liberty in obedience to the valid laws of the State. The purpose of these laws—which express the obligations of the State— *was to promote the greatest possible happiness for the greatest possible number*.[30] On the other hand, the purpose of punishment was to protect these laws and the social services they rendered from abuse by individual members. To best secure this end, the proper objective of punishment was not to exact vengeance but to deter the individual from committing crimes. This goal, in turn, could best be achieved by adjusting the degree of punishment to the crime in such a way that threat and

[30] This principle, frequently ascribed to the English philosopher Bentham, was actually derived by him from Beccaria.

unattractiveness of the penalty would slightly exceed the advantage and temptation of the offense in the mind of a rational and responsible human being.

Having promulgated his positive philosophy, Beccaria proposed a penal program to carry it out. The method was to be imprisonment for a stated period of time, this system offering the most benign and flexible possibilities for adjusting punishments to crimes. As for the means to carry out the program, they were already at hand, though as yet insufficiently used. The jails and houses of correction, familiar to Europe for over one hundred and fifty years but hitherto restricted to minor offenders, vagrants, and children, provided a sound—and, fortunately, an available—basis for developing the positive program.

The availability of an already known, presently existing means of carrying out his program was the keystone of Beccaria's success. At this point, then, it becomes necessary to turn to an account of the development of the early jails, workhouses and houses of refuge into the major instruments of the correctional process.

The Evolution of Contemporary Imprisonment

Any form of punishment requires that the offender be detained in some manner until the execution of his sentence. Where adjudication was swift and the sentence followed hard upon the judgment, this period of detention was short; where there were delays between the trial and the carrying out of the judgment, it was necessary to find some secure place to detain the offender. In this limited sense of detention, prisons existed long before the formal use of imprisonment as a punishment.

This distinction was not lost on the authorities of earlier times. During periods when offenders multiplied faster than judges could try or officials punish them, there was a recurring tendency to use imprisonment as an administrative expedient. In an obvious effort to stem the practice, Justinian cited a principle elaborated earlier by the Roman jurist Ulpian: "Prisons ought to be used for detention only, but not for punishment." Nevertheless, the conflict between legal principle and administrative expediency continued throughout the Middle Ages and well into the modern period.

Isolated instances of punitive incarceration appeared on the Continent in the early Middle Ages. As early as 1275 the English Statute of Westminster punished the crime of rape with two years' imprisonment. In Denmark, life imprisonment for manslaughter was decreed in 1294. Generally, however, prisons either retained their purely detentive aspect or were used to extort the payment of fines.

As usual, the strongest impetus for change in penal practices came from entirely external sources. By the end of the fifteenth century the impact of profound social and economic changes had drastically altered the older pattern of communal life, which had been based on self-sufficient localities. In England the rapid rise of the great towns and the dispossessing of large numbers of small landholders through the Enclosure Acts had stimulated an increasing migration toward the larger centers of population. Beggars and vagrants swarmed the roads, overflowed the common gaols and, in the absence of adequate provision for food and shelter, turned increasingly to illegal forms of self-help. The inadequacy of local police protection and the greater availability of small arms converted many of these "sturdy beggars" to crime; it is generally agreed that the appearance of the habitual, professional criminal dates from this time. The authorities were thus simultaneously presented with two pressing problems: the relief of the poor who were honest and relief from the poor who were not.

The Development of Workhouses and House of Correction

Two institutions were developed to cope with these problems: the *workhouse*, which provided jobs for those able and willing to work, together with training for the indigent or abandoned young; and the *house of correction* for those who appeared able to work but were unwilling. Though originally differentiated in purpose (the former intended for poor-relief, the latter chiefly penal), these institutions failed to maintain their differentiation in practice.

Under the initiative of two Protestant clerics, Thomas Lever and Bishop Ridley, the first house of correction was set up in 1552 at Bridewell in an abandoned royal palace. Its success led in 1576 to an enactment that "Bridewells" were to be provided by each county; in 1609 this provision was strengthened by the assessment of penalties against counties failing to comply. Max Grunhut has described the early operation of houses of correction as follows:

> ... Bridewells or Houses of Correction provided facilities for setting idle and disorderly people to work with the threefold purpose to make

them earn their keep, to reform them by compulsory work and discipline, and to deter others from vagrancy and idleness. In the London Bridewell inmates included habitual vagrants and poor boys who should be trained in craftsmanship. In the beginning, at least, work was fairly well organized. There were several departments under the supervision of governors. Some inmates were occupied with clothmaking, weaving and spinning; others worked as ironmongers. Raw materials were given by tradesmen who collected the manufactured goods and sold them at the market. The worst men were employed at the mill or in the bake-house—with the possibility of being removed to a better occupation. ... Later on wages were paid to the inmates in return for their work. The first social reaction was a strict differentiation between the poor and beggars. The former might be cared for, the latter had to undergo institutional treatment at the Bridewells. In 1557 Orders for the Government of the Hospitals stated this: "There is a great difference between a poor man and a beggar, as is between a true man and a thief." ... While the impotent poor were to be maintained by the parishes, those who refused to work or were punishable as rogues should be committed to the new institutions and set to work by coercive measures.[31]

Like many another penal experiment, the new hope began to languish not long after it was launched. Grunhut continues:

The first results...were highly satisfactory. The new industrial spirit and a resolute practice of committals to Bridewells seemed more effective in settling down or deterring the vagabond than the traditional criminal law with pillory, stocks and gallows. Coke stated that, unlike those suffering from the bad and even deteriorating effects of the common gaol, people committed to the House of Correction..."come out better." ... Later on, when the first enthusiasm of the public faded away, the funds at the disposal for the maintenance of the new institutions were shrinking. Conditions of labor deteriorated, until industrial work was finally abandoned. Coke stated that "the excellent work" was hampered by the lack of interest among justices of the peace: as long as they "were diligent and industrious, there was not a rogue to be seen in any part of England, but when Justices and other officers became *tepidi and trepidi* (i.e., luke-warm and fearful) rogues and so on swarmed again."[32]

The new institutions had a better career in parts of the Continent. In 1595 a house of correction was built in Amsterdam, to be followed a year later by a spinhouse exclusively for women. In addition to provid-

[31] Max Grunhut, *Penal Reform* (New York: The Clarendon Press, 1948), pp. 15–16.
[32] *Ibid.*, pp. 16–17.

ing segregate quarters for four categories of persons—vagrants, disorderly women, thieves, and neglected children—the Dutch system protected the institution's work program by making its products a State monopoly. By this device, any competition with free labor was avoided; thus the Dutch anticipated an objection that was to plague the advocates of prison labor centuries later.

The Dutch example was quickly followed elsewhere. Within thirty five years similar institutions had been established in Bremen, Nuremberg, Danzig, Lübeck, Hamburg, Berne, Basle and Fribourg. Wages were paid, different categories of inmates were segregated; a few institutions adopted the wise policy of refusing admittance to offenders who had previously undergone criminal punishment.

The new method had a slower progress in the Latin countries. It was not until 1656 that France built its first institution for beggars and vagrants. In 1703 Pope Clement XI advanced the method further by the construction, in the famous Hospice of St. Michael in Rome, of a special institution for incorrigible boys.

Deterioration of Houses of Correction

The early achievements of the new correctional approach were remarkable in the light of penological thinking at the time. As Grunhut has pointed out: "The whole tendency of the new foundation was fundamentally opposed to contemporary criminal law. It did not involve exclusion from society by death, mutilation and branding with permanent degradation. The ultimate aim was to lead back the prisoner into society." [33]

It was, perhaps, inevitable that a movement so advanced for its time should, in time, falter through lack of sustained support. The deterioration was rapid and complete. Grunhut has described it as follows:

> In England, at the end of the seventeeth century, Houses of Correction lost their avowed reformative character. The treatment of vagrants by enforced work was no longer the specific aim of the Bridewells. Rogues and vagrants were received for corporal punishment and discharged, or sent to private workhouses.... A statute of 1720 ... authorized Justices of the Peace ... "to commit such vagrants and other criminals ... either to the common gaol or House of Correction, as they in their judgement think proper." Thus far there was no practical difference between the two institutions. Vagrants were treated as

[33] Ibid., p. 18.

offenders and sent to the gaols, and criminals were committed to the Houses of Correction.[34]

Soon the houses of correction, subjected to the same public neglect and private exploitation that had made pestholes of the county gaols, became indistinguishable from them:

> General regulations were scarce, central control almost non-existent. ... No funds were set aside for necessary repairs. To keep the prisoners in irons was cheaper than to guarantee the safety of the prison by sufficient walls and proper locks. To avoid window tax, the keeper diminished the access of light and fresh air. Sometimes prisoners were hired out to private employers, or even sent out begging. Often a private contractor catered for the inmates, or the whole maintenance of the prison was a profit-making enterprise in private hands. The keeper, often relying on a private title and sometimes not even resident in the gaol, required and received fees—often illegally extended and arbitrarily multiplied—for every single stage of prison life from reception to release, for all accommodations from the bare necessities of feeding and bedding up to luxurious comfort in separate "sponging houses" for wealthy and collusive prisoners.... Many prisons were licensed for spirits, with the tap running endlessly for the keeper's private profit. Consequently, an endless incitement to drink, to revels, and to all sorts of vices was a favorite means of exploitation.[35]

The Beginning of Agitation for Jail Reform

The first report on gaol conditions was published in 1618 by an ex-inmate. Almost another century passed before the first English prison report was made by a committee specifically delegated to investigate jail conditions. Under the chairmanship of the noted physician Dr. Bray, a committee of the Society for Promoting Christian Knowledge visited several prisons and, in 1702, submitted a report entitled "An Essay towards the Reformation of Newgate and other Prisons in and about London." Grunhut has summarized the Committee's criticisms:

> The Essay makes six "vices and immoralities" responsible for the desperate state of contemporary prison conditions: personal lewdness of the keepers, their confederacy with prisoners, the unlimited use of spirits, swearing and gaming, corruption of new-comers by old criminals, neglect of all religious worship.[36]

[34] *Ibid.*, pp. 24–25.
[35] *Ibid.*, p. 28.
[36] *Ibid.*, p. 29.

Though not attacking the core of the problem—unsupervised private operation of the prisons—the committee made several significant suggestions for improvement: the institution of prison work, separate confinement, prohibition of liquor, and abolition of the vicious system of fee-taking by keepers. One additional recommendation seems somewhat similar to a provision used by some parole boards today: the requirement that habitual prisoners be required to furnish financial surety for good behavior and proof of immediate employment after release. Another recommendation, visionary even for present times, attempted to reduce the social stigma attached to imprisonment; it suggested publication of the names of well-behaved prisoners in the hope that sympathetic persons would aid them on release.

This and similar investigations and proposals were without effect while most serious offenders were still being dealt with by means of the older penal methods, lately supplemented by a new system: penal transportation to the Colonies. It was not until the eighteenth-century reformers had made their proposals that public interest was awakened to the broader possibilities of the improved and expanded jail. Even so, action to implement this interest was deferred until after the American Revolution had made penal transportation to North America impractical. Not until great numbers of convicts, crowded into shore-side hulks during the long suspension of transportation, had begun to overflow their quarters did the State commence to interest itself seriously in prison construction.

The Eve of the Nineteenth Century:
Penal Reform Merges with Law Reform

Thus, the same century which had seen a successful attack on the antiquated criminal law had also mounted a successful assault on the derivative evil: antiquated methods of punishment. By the end of the eighteenth century these two movements merged, derived force from each other, and became more and more synonymous.[37] Linked in effect

[37] While the English prison reformers were building up the case against domestic jail conditions, the French *philosophes* were becoming increasingly impressed with English criminal procedures and increasingly critical of judicial abuses at home. On the other hand, jail conditions on the Continent were generally superior to those in England and provided more than one model of emulation for the English prison reformer, John Howard. Howard (1726–1790), a towering figure in the history of penal reform, had undergone an experience of captivity as a prisoner of war in his youth. On his return to England he increasingly occupied himself with problems of social welfare, and in 1773 his con-

as well as cause, each tended to catch fire from the other. The reform of the criminal law, by reducing the number of capital crimes, restricting corporal punishment, and virtually abolishing mutilation, required a universal substitute. Imprisonment fulfilled this objective. At the same time, increasing concern for the welfare of prisoners, confined in hulks and noisome, overcrowded jails, sparked a demand for jail reform and new construction.

The union of the interests of law reform and penal reform was symbolized in the person of the utilitarian philosopher, Jeremy Bentham. This outstanding thinker, whose basic tenet was that the worth of any idea lay in its practical usefulness, proposed a penological program comprehending all legal, psychological, and physical aspects of correctional treatment. Though denied the experience of prison administration himself, he became the model for a new kind of administrator, typified by Obermaier in Bavaria, Montesinos in Spain, Aubanel in Switzerland, and Demetz in France. The underlying approach of each of these men was the same: the search for greater treatment effectiveness by means of carefully rationalized innovations. Together, they originated many of the procedures that characterize advanced prison administration today.

The Pennsylvania System of Prison Administration

From the outset, the concentration of numbers of prisoners in one restricted area had raised critical problems of prison discipline. At an earlier point in the history of jails and houses of corrections, these problems had crystallized around one outstanding question: the degree and kind of association to be permitted among prisoners. As long ago as the late 1600's, observers had complained of the pernicious effects of unrestricted contact between young and old, male and female in the overcrowded, haphazard English prisons. Certain institutions—such as Newgate—had become notorious centers of debauchery. Similar conditions existed in the colonial jails up to the outbreak of the Revolution.

---

scientiousness was recognized by an appointment as county sheriff—a position which included responsibility for the county's gaols. Appalled by the sanitary standards and demoralized living conditions in these institutions, he embarked on a series of inspections, the results of which he summarized in a report. In the following year he testified in Parliament on the subject of necessary penal reforms for the Kingdom. His fame as an expert on prison conditions spread rapidly, and he devoted the remainder of his career to prison inspections and reports. His recommendations set international standards of prison administration, becoming the basis of widespread remedial legislation.

The earliest opportunity for a drastic break with the congregate system came shortly after the end of the Revolution in the predominantly Quaker state of Pennsylvania. The Quakers were uniquely fitted to undertake the experiment. Over one hundred years before, William Penn and his followers had been granted a charter to found the Province of Pennsylvania. In the "Great Law" adopted by the Quaker Assembly in 1682, it was decreed that imprisonment should supplant all other punishments for major crimes—with the single exception of homicide, which alone remained capital. This major break with contemporary penal usages, with their many corporal punishments, mutilations, and humiliations, provided the first historical instance of an almost complete reliance on imprisonment. In place of the idle gaols of the home country, the Quakers provided workhouses with segregate quarters for male and female offenders. But, at Penn's death in 1718, the Great Law was abrogated, English criminal law re-introduced, and the penal reforms were swept away. Within a few years, conditions in the Pennsylvania workhouses had sunk to the level of the typical English county gaol.

By 1790 the Pennsylvania state legislature had re-enacted the essentials of the old Quaker charter and had established a new jail on Walnut Street in Philadelphia, to be operated according to an extension of Penn's original doctrines. All new prisoners were first quartered in solitary confinement, the more serious or dangerous offenders remaining isolated for the major part of their sentence. Minor offenders were permitted, after their initial period of isolation, to work together in silence during the day. The apparent success of the new system moved the Quakers to go further along the road toward complete isolation. In two new prisons—the Western Penitentiary, erected at Pittsburgh in 1818, and the Eastern Penitentiary, built at Cherry Hill in 1829—a completely solitary system prevailed. Each prisoner had his individual cell and exercise yard in which he lived and worked during the entire length of his sentence without once coming in contact with another inmate.

The solitary system—now generally known as the Pennsylvania system—was generally approved and emulated by European penologists. British visitors were largely unimpressed; one of them, Charles Dickens, wrote a frightening description of the possible psychological consequences of the isolation. Opinion in America was sharply divided, and only one other institution—the New Jersey State Prison, built in 1833—adopted the system.

The Auburn System of Prison Administration

Advocates of the Pennsylvania plan relied on the Quaker principles of prayer, meditation, and work to accomplish the task of reformation. Vigorously dissenting from this program, members of the Boston Prison Discipline Society, under the leadership of Louis Dwight, offered another solution to the problem of prisoner association. Dwight proposed that the inmates be permitted to work together in a strictly enforced silence, arguing that this system would avoid the horrors of isolation without the risk of mutual contamination.[38] An institution embodying these principles was built at Auburn, New York in 1823; henceforward the program was know variously as the Auburn system and the silent system.

In order to enforce the rule of silence, the first warden of Auburn imposed a rigid system of discipline and repression. Outside of their cells inmates were forbidden not only to speak to each other but to look at each other face to face: visual communication might lead to gesturing, gesturing to whispering. To ensure that the looks of prisoners would not meet, they were required to walk with downcast eyes, to remain in constant activity when outside of their cells, and, when traveling from location to location in groups, to march in a peculiarly shortened, heavy gait known as the *lock step*. Violation of any of these or a large number of other regulations could bring punishment by flogging.

In the polemical battle between the advocates of the two systems, the Auburn system rapidly became ascendant. The result of this ascendancy was to fasten the repressive discipline, the lock step and the downcast eyes of the Auburn system on several decades of American penology —a circumstance which gave penology a new field of prison reform— that, namely, of undoing the repressive discipline it had itself created. This objective was accomplished after several more decades, during which prisoners gradually were allowed to look at each other, to walk naturally, to whisper a little, and then, finally, to talk to one another. At the end of this great reform movement, which was generally complete in all but a few maximum-security prisons by the end of the second decade of the twentieth century, association between inmates had regained something of the easy familiarity and casualness it had known under the old colonial jail system. During the period in which these

[38] For a stimulating review of the triumph of the silent system and of the career of its prime mover, Louis Dwight, see Stewart H. Holbrook, *Dreamers of the American Dream* (New York: Doubleday and Company, 1957), pp. 240-244.

advances took place, mankind had discovered electricity, the radio, and the internal combustion engine; had learned to travel through the air and under the sea; had increased the life span of civilized humanity by more than a third; and had written thousands of books and pamphlets on the state of penology.

Except for a very considerable easing of its self-imposed restrictions and a vast increase in the physical decencies of living, the American prison system produced little of what was to become new in correction. The far-reaching innovations of probation, parole, and the indeterminate sentence came from sources outside and were imposed from without.[39] The great correctional fortresses had become conservative.

[39] These innovations are discussed in Chapters 18 and 26.

APPREHENSION, ADJUDICATION, AND DISPOSITION

The Police

Police Agencies

THE POLICEMAN OCCUPIES A STRATEGIC POSITION IN THE ADMINISTRATION of criminal justice. As he discharges his responsibility for conspicuous control, he is the overt symbol of "the law." As he discharges his responsibility to detect and apprehend lawbreakers, he makes decisions that determine whether or not the remainder of the machinery for the administration of justice will start to grind.

The frustration of the lawbreaker was originally the responsibility of the private citizen. In time this responsibility was delegated to public officials with police power. The modern United States policeman can trace his historic origins to the sheriff and constable of medieval England. In the United States these two police officers are traditionally elected by the people—the constables by townships, the sheriffs by counties. Although they still retain their formal powers of original jurisdiction in criminal matters, two historic developments have sharply curtailed their functions. The development of the city created a need for a municipal constabulary, and in 1844 New York City established the first publicly paid police force in the country. Sixteen years earlier Sir Robert Peel had created in London the famous metropolitan police force, which provided a day-and-night patrol. With the establishment of the municipal police forces, some of the powers of constables and sheriffs were delegated to the new agency. Later, an increasingly mobile population generated pressure for state-wide law enforcement agencies—a development that completed the eclipse of the sheriff and the constable as police officers in many parts of the United States. The sheriff, especially in the Middle and Far West, has retained many of his original duties, and has not relinquished his powers in criminal matters to municipal police agencies. The functions of sheriffs are varied and complex and include those of county administrator, jailer, court officer, and executioner. The constable, less able than the sheriff to withstand the pressures of change, is now primarily dependent on fees he receives as a minor functionary in the lower courts.

In addition to municipal, county, and state police, various departments of the federal government maintain police agencies with specialized functions. These agencies developed as part of the trend to assign increased responsibilities to the federal government. A more complex federal government, discharging increasing responsibilities in an era of more rapid communication and transportation, has resulted in a multiplication of federal police agencies. It has been estimated that there are over 50,000 federal police in no less than forty agencies of the government. The most famous of these are the "G Men" of the Federal Bureau of Investigation, Justice Department, and the "T Men" of the Treasury Department. The expansion and growth of federal police activity has been spurred by the passage of statutes making certain crimes federal offenses—for example, the famous Lindbergh kidnaping law. In addition, there are specialized public law-enforcement agencies with limited police powers—for example, state motor vehicle patrols; interstate agencies, such as the New York Port Authority; park police, etc. Finally, any list of police agencies must include the various private police forces, of which perhaps the best known are the railroad police. These specialized police agencies have developed in response to unsatisfied needs for additional or specialized police protection.

Although the number of separate police departments is not known with any certainty, Table XXII gives the number of police employees and the average number of police employees per 1,000 inhabitants in 3,732 cities accounting for approximately half the population of the United States on April 30, 1955.

TABLE XXII

POLICE DEPARTMENT EMPLOYEES, APRIL 30, 1955, NUMBER AND RATE PER 1,000 INHABITANTS, BY GEOGRAPHIC DIVISIONS AND POPULATION GROUPS

(3,704 cities, total population 87,066,845, based on 1950 decennial census)

Division	Total	Population group					
		Group I (Over 250,000)	Group II (100,000 to 250,000)	Group III (50,000 to 100,000)	Group IV (25,000 to 50,000)	Group V (10,000 to 25,000)	Group VI (Less than 10,000)
Total							
Number of police employees	167,862	84,731	16,570	15,040	15,528	18,531	17,462
Average number of employees per 1,000 inhabitants	1.9	2.4	1.8	1.7	1.6	1.5	1.4
New England							
Number of police employees	14,405	3,045	3,771	2,259	2,660	1,993	677
Average number of employees per 1,000 inhabitants	2.1	3.8	2.3	1.9	1.9	1.6	1.3
Middle Atlantic							
Number of police employees	51,642	34,206	3,138	3,209	3,230	4,209	3,650
Average number of employees per 1,000 inhabitants	2.3	2.8	2.0	1.9	1.9	1.6	1.5
East North Central							
Number of police employees	36,022	20,262	2,274	3,217	3,354	3,290	3,625
Average number of employees per 1,000 inhabitants	1.8	2.3	1.5	1.5	1.4	1.4	1.4
West North Central							
Number of police employees	10,020	4,501	782	872	759	1,404	1,702
Average number of employees per 1,000 inhabitants	1.5	1.9	1.3	1.3	1.2	1.2	1.2
South Atlantic *							
Number of police employees	17,675	6,006	2,648	2,457	1,876	2,146	2,542
Average number of employees per 1,000 inhabitants	2.0	2.8	1.8	1.7	1.9	1.8	1.8
East South Central							
Number of police employees	5,475	1,475	893	426	630	819	1,232
Average number of employees per 1,000 inhabitants	1.5	1.4	1.7	1.6	1.4	1.5	1.5
West South Central							
Number of police employees	9,991	3,823	1,490	816	824	1,588	1,450
Average number of employees per 1,000 inhabitants	1.4	1.7	1.5	1.3	1.3	1.2	1.1
Mountain							
Number of police employees	3,782	711	465	270	659	695	982
Average number of employees per 1,000 inhabitants	1.5	1.7	1.6	1.2	1.6	1.5	1.4
Pacific							
Number of police employees	18,850	10,702	1,109	1,514	1,536	2,387	1,602
Average number of employees per 1,000 inhabitants	2.1	2.3	1.7	1.8	1.8	1.8	1.9

* Includes the District of Columbia.
Source: *Uniform Crime Reports*, 27, No. 1 (1955), p. 23.

Police Power

The United States does not have a centralized police force. Decentralized law enforcement was written into the Constitution by the Founding Fathers, who had every reason to be skeptical of a strong, centralized police power. In discussing this aspect of American law enforcement, J. Edgar Hoover has written:

> I am unalterably opposed to a national police force. I have consistently opposed any plan leading to a consolidation of police power, regardless of the source from which it originated. I shall continue to do so, for the following reasons, which, in the same words, I have set forth on many earlier occasions:
>
> 1. Centralization of police power represents a distinct danger to democratic self-government.
>
> 2. Proposals to centralize law enforcement tend to assume that either the state or federal government can and should do for each community what the people of that city or county will not do for themselves.
>
> 3. The authority of every peace officer in every community would be reduced, if not eventually broken, in favor of a dominating figure or group on the distant state or national level. It is conceivable that such an official or group might be given the power by law to influence or dictate the selection of officers, the circumstances of their employment, and the decision they make in arresting and prosecuting those who violate the law.[1]

In their efforts to prevent crime or detect and punish criminals, the police must constantly deal with those sections of the law that are designed to protect the individual against the coercive power of the State. Critically commenting on these limitations, Seagle has stated:

> The visitor from another planet would be particularly puzzled by the difficulties put in the way of the police in their struggle with crime. While the police may ordinarily seize a person who commits a crime of a serious nature under their very eyes and noses, they cannot take a person into custody when they merely have good reason to suspect that he has committed or is about to commit a crime. They have to apply to a court for a warrant of arrest, which not infrequently acts as an announcement of their coming, or otherwise allows the criminal to escape. Even when they have a warrant of arrest, they do not always have a legal right to conduct a general search of the premises where they have seized the person named. Searches ordinarily require the

[1] J. Edgar Hoover, "The Basis of Sound Law Enforcement," *Annals of the American Academy of Political and Social Science*, 291:40, January 1954.

procurement of a search warrant from a judge, who must be convinced that the police are not merely acting on sound suspicion. Searches under general warrants are forbidden.[2]

Seagle believes that the restrictions placed on the police by the Constitution put them at a distinct disadvantage in securing the evidence and confessions necessary for convictions. He suggests that some of the lawlessness of the police can be traced to these restrictions:

> The requirements that a suspect be promptly arraigned, and be given a public trial, are often in themselves sufficient to prevent proof of his guilt. Secret and prolonged questioning by the police immediately after arrest is often the only way of getting a suspect to talk. He is then psychologically at a low ebb, and will make revelations which cannot be obtained once he is publicly arraigned, and provided with astute legal counsel. Moreover, once a suspect has been arraigned, his accomplices are warned of their danger. To insist that the police conduct their inquiries in the full glare of publicity is to hamstring their efforts.
>
> ... Legally at least, the police are subjected to serious risks in the pursuit of criminals. They have to go armed not only with guns, but with law books. If they engage in search or seizure without proper warrant, or delay the arraignment of a prisoner to question him, or tap wires to secure evidence of crime, or otherwise violate the constitutional rights of suspects, they make themselves legally liable to civil action for damages, or even to criminal prosecution. Such remedies, to be sure, are rarely successful when invoked by professional criminals; but the police owe their relative immunity not to the law but to the lawlessness of their superiors, who fail to prosecute them for their offenses. The police constantly find that the only way they can enforce the laws in the criminal code is by disregarding the higher law of the constitution. The legal has to be countered by the extralegal. On the rare occasion when the officers of the law achieve efficiency, they disregard the law and indulge in such methods as the third degree.[3]

That the police are forced to violate the law because of the limitations imposed upon them is doubtful. As a matter of fact, many police illegalities do not involve overzealous attempts to *catch* criminals at all. There is reason to suspect that many police violations are related to helping criminals *evade* the law. Consequently there seems to be no basis for assuming that these police violations will decrease when the police are given *more* power. The possibility that they will use this increased

[2] William Seagle, *Law, The Science of Inefficiency* (New York: The Macmillan Company, 1952), p. 106.
[3] *Ibid.*, pp. 109–110.

power to be more corrupt is just as likely, and more in agreement with experience.

Setting aside the question of corruption, does it follow that giving the police broader powers will inspire them to be more *efficient*? How discriminating, how careful would the police have to be if they could seize and interrogate suspects at will, if they could conduct general searches without warrants, if they could detain witnesses for long periods without fear of legal reprisal? Under these easier conditions it might well be that the police could dispense with efficiency almost entirely and rely on the much surer totalitarian technique of intimidation. These considerations cast serious doubt on Seagle's underlying assumption that higher standards of law enforcement may be achieved by lowering requirements and lifting limitations.

To the doubts about the increased efficiency that might be gained by increasing police powers and immunities may be added certain graver doubts concerning the continued protection of civil rights. Those advocating increased powers for the police usually give assurances that they will not be employed against the rights of the innocent. This casual assurance carries the implication that it is quite permissible to violate the rights of the guilty. On the face of it, this innovation may not appear startling until it is recalled that guilt and innocence are not questions for police adjudication at all. Innocence and guilt are matters for judge and jury to decide; until that decision is made, the accused, under our system, is presumed to be innocent. This presumption of innocence has been attacked as placing heavy obstacles in the way of attempts to prove the guilt of the guilty. Although this fact must be acknowledged, it should be recalled that the presumption itself was adopted as a reaction against methods *of prosecution that made it even more difficult for the innocent to prove their innocence.*

This fact is the source of the skepticism concerning assurances about the preservation of civil rights. Civil rights consist precisely in those limitations of State and police power under criticism. Almost without exception they are negative in character—prescribing what the State is *not* permitted to do.[4] To assert that civil rights shall be preserved in the absence of these limitations is, in effect, to assert a contradiction, since these rights are neither more nor less than the aforementioned limitations.

In the face of these logical, practical, and historical considerations, the assurances of the advocates of increased police power become highly

[4] As in the first ten amendments to the Constitution.

questionable. In a way, they resemble the assurances whispered by the lover to his young sweetheart: "I would love you even if your hair were gray and your face were wrinkled and old." Despite these protestations the young lady would be well advised not to neglect her complexion.

Police Functions

Patrol

All police services were originally performed by men on patrol. The patrol division is to the police force what the infantry is to the army. The patrolman is responsible for police services in a prescribed area. Some idea of the range and diversity of these services is given by Wilson, who has divided them into three classes—*services called for, inspectional services,* and *routine patrol:*

> 1. Services called for are the police actions taken in dealing with incidents. The remaining two categories are primarily preventive and deal with conditions rather than incidents. Incidents requiring police action may be reported by a victim or witness, or they may be discovered by a patrolman or another member of the force. Services called for include the disposition of violations in every field of police control by warning, citation, or arrest; the investigation and disposition of miscellaneous complaints; the investigations of accidents; the preliminary investigation of crimes; the recovery of stolen property; searching for, interviewing and investigating suspects and witnesses; the arrest of criminals, both with and without warrants; the raiding of criminal hide-outs and vice establishments; spot jobs; intensive searches of public garages, parking lots, and streets for stolen automobiles and for automobiles involved in hit-and-run accidents and other crimes; the intensive checking of commercial establishments and the interviewing of persons residing in an area or in the entire community in search of witnesses and information useful in the investigation of a crime.
>
> 2. Inspection services are directed at lessening the potency of identifiable hazards. These services include the routine examination of the doors and windows of business premises and vacation homes likely to be burglarized; the inspection of public garages, where stolen automobiles may be stored or temporarily parked; and the inspection and supervision of places under license, of questionable establishments such as taverns, bars, and cocktail lounges, and of parks, pool halls, skating rinks, dance halls, and other recreational places.

3. Routine patrol includes all patrol operations not included in the first two classes and is directed primarily at diminishing less tangible hazards that are not readily isolated and identified. Areas that contain less tangible hazards include business sections, poorly illuminated areas, poverty-stricken tenement districts, locations where large numbers of people congregate, roadways carrying heavy traffic, and districts containing cheap amusement resorts or currently experiencing a more than usual amount of crime. The officer lessens opportunity for misconduct by the observation and supervision of persons and things during his routine movement from one point to another on his beat, especially when he gives particular attention to areas in which incidents calling for police service most frequently occur.[5]

Criminal Investigation

Although the patrol division remains the backbone of most police departments, the complexity of modern tasks and responsibilities requires further specialization. The first specialized police division was the criminal investigation or detective division. This division is responsible for the investigation of designated crimes. When a crime is committed, the preliminary investigation is the responsibility of the patrol division. If the crime is not solved by the patrolman, it is referred to the detective division, which then assumes responsibility for the apprehension of the criminal and the recovery of stolen property. The detective division is also responsible for the preparation and collection of the information that will be used in court by the prosecution. Within this division there may be additional specialization, certain types of crime being assigned to one detective or group of detectives. For example, all crimes involving bad checks may be assigned to one detective, who is able to concentrate all his attention and energies on this type of offense. He becomes an expert on forgery and familiarizes himself with the habits and idiosyncrasies of known forgers in his area as well as their friends, enemies, places of recreation, etc.

Traffic Control

The advent of the automobile forced the police to develop methods of traffic-law enforcement. In the twenties and thirties there developed in many police departments a specialized traffic division responsible for

[5] O. W. Wilson, *Police Administration* (New York: The McGraw-Hill Company, 1950), p. 92.

traffic control. The effectiveness of the traffic division is reflected in Table XXIII, which shows reductions in the motor vehicle death rate in cities having a specialized traffic division.

TABLE XXIII

MOTOR VEHICLE DEATH RATES IN CITIES WITH SPECIALIZED TRAFFIC DIVISIONS

City	Year of adoption	Death rate per 10,000 registered motor vehicles	
		Year of adoption	1952
Los Angeles	1941	8.9	4.1
Detroit	1937	6.9	3.1
Atlanta	1938	7.3	4.5
Chattanooga	1938	10.5	2.4
Chicago	1948	7.0	5.2
Cincinnati	1936	13.3	3.8
Cleveland	1937	10.2	3.8
Oakland	1939	7.5	2.4
Portland, Ore.	1940	6.1	2.8

Source: Franklin M. Kreml, "The Specialized Traffic Division," *Annals of the American Academy of Political and Social Science*, 291: 65, January 1954.

Crime Prevention

In recent years it has become fashionable for police departments to develop specialized units for the prevention of crime and delinquency. These units are usually defended on the grounds that the police have primary responsibility for prevention, that they are the first to know of individuals or situations needing community attention, and that they can secure the cooperation of groups and agencies to give this needed attention. Those who object to police activities in the area of prevention maintain that police are not qualified for the work of prevention and that specialized agencies are necessary. Whatever the outcome of this controversy may be, the active juvenile aid bureaus of many police departments and the work of police athletic leagues reflect police willingness to assume welfare functions.

The Vice Squad

Many large police departments have a specialized unit concerned with law enforcement in areas of human behavior prohibited as immoral.

This unit reports directly either to the police chief or to the head of the detective division. The behavior covered in most jurisdictions includes gambling; prostitution; illegal use, possession, or sale of narcotics and liquor; and condemned sexual behavior.

The history of many vice squads suggests that the temptation of "easy money" offered by organized criminal vice is too great for most ordinary persons. The effectiveness of special vice squads is debatable, and Donal E. J. MacNamara of the Law Enforcement Institutes of New York University has stated:

> The Vice Squad in its traditional form is an undesirable, unnecessary and frequently dangerous appendage to a modern law enforcement organization. At its best it does little or nothing that can't be done by the regular uniformed police force. At its worst—which is usual—it is a continual source of departmental corruption, blackmail and a police-criminal alliance that destroys the efficiency, good name and morale of the entire Squad.[6]

The problem of vice control is complicated by our ambivalent attitudes toward illicit sexual behavior. These attitudes place the police in the position of having to decide, in each case, which value to honor: the universal preachment against vice, or the widespread private practice of it. August Vollmer has commented:

> The unwillingness of the people to face the facts about vice and their faithful and reverential devotion to the idea that the problem can be solved with the passing of repressive laws have been the greatest handicaps to an intelligent treatment of vice as one of the most important problems of society.[7]

Until the public meets this challenge, there seems every reason to believe that the problems of police corruption and commercialized vice will continue to perplex police administrators.

Police Corruption and Brutality

Reports of the corruption of police and other law-enforcement officials have become commonplace. The Special Committee to Investigate

[6] Cited in Albert Deutsch, *The Trouble with Cops* (New York: Crown Publishers, 1954), p. 77.
[7] *Ibid.*, p. 95.

Organized Crime in Interstate Commerce reported evidence of the widespread connivance of police officials in the promoting of crime. The evidence indicated corruption on all levels of government—local, state, and federal. The committee summarized its findings as follows:

> 1. Direct bribe or protection payments are made to law-enforcement officials, so that they will not interfere with specific criminal activities.
> 2. Political influence and pressure of important officials or political leaders is used to protect criminal activities or further the interests of criminal gangs.
> 3. Law-enforcement officials are found in the possession of unusual and unexplained wealth.
> 4. Law-enforcement officials participate directly in the business of organized crime.[8]

If one aspect of police lawlessness concerns cooperation and leniency with respect to criminals, another aspect relates to mistreatment of the public—especially of those social and minority groups without significant protection by status or adequate political representation. Although police corruption and brutality do not necessarily imply each other, they both indicate a common attitude of contempt for citizens' rights and a readiness to play fast and loose with the rules. In a series of reports on crime in the United States, *Life* reported the following incidents of police corruption, inefficiency, and brutality:

> In Chicago, which probably has the worst department of any sizable city, many officers try to get on the traffic detail because of the money they can make by taking bribes from traffic offenders. They are often helped to such jobs by Chicago politicians, who can wield a greater influence on any cop's career than his record as a crime fighter.
>
> In Nashville, as in the rest of Tennessee, it is forbidden to sell liquor by the glass. But some 20 bars operate openly in the downtown area, many within a half dozen blocks of police headquarters (with possible patronage from policemen, some of whom occasionally come to work drunk).
>
> Detroit's current police commissioner is regarded as the city's best in many years, but he cannot halt the motor city's numbers business, estimated at $40 million a year. Nor do his men ever seem able to find a top numbers operator to arrest.
>
> The police of many parts of Hudson County, N.J. make the old silent movies' Keystone Cops look like Scotland Yarders. Last year the

---

[8] U. S. Senate, *Third Interim Report of the Special Committee to Investigate Organized Crime in Interstate Commerce*, 82d Congress, Senate Report No. 307 (Washington, D. C.: Government Printing Office, 1951), p. 184.

county prosecutor raided a handbook in Union City without notifying the local police. As a result he bagged a police lieutenant, a city detective, an aide of the mayor and a father and a cousin of the deputy police chief. A Hudson County theater once sent the night's $1,800 box-office receipts to the police station for safekeeping. It was stolen from the desk sergeant's desk.

In Miami some members of a special squad set up to combat burglaries were recently suspended for committing burglaries.

Omaha police officials also are frequently embarrassed by citizens' charges that they are being burglarized by the police.

In Hialeah Gardens, a Florida hamlet and speed trap of only 60 registered voters, there is a police force of seven men. It exists primarily to prey on passing motorists since the fines thus collected pay 90% of the town's operating expenses, including the police salaries.

In Tulsa the police commissioner, the chief of police and six policemen, some of whom were members of the vice squad, were recently convicted of conspiring to import liquor into dry Oklahoma.

In New Orleans a conspiracy that operated several years ago was recently revealed. Dozens of officers were paid in nicely graduated steps for protecting vice and lottery operators: $50 a week went to captains, $30 a week to lieutenants, $15 to sergeants, $2 to patrolmen.

In Baltimore, where an officer can wear Argyle socks, strapwork sandals and Elvis Presley sideburns while on duty if he is so disposed, the police are also given wide latitude in handling prisoners. Beatings are common and a favorite technique is to break a man's arm by smashing it with a nightstick.[9]

The use of third-degree methods to secure confessions from arrested persons, together with excessive brutality at the time of arrest and the use of wire-tapping devices in securing evidence of illegal acts, are police practices that cut squarely across the rights and privileges guaranteed the individual by the basic law of the land. Writing about these police practices, one observer has written:

> These practices have extremely serious implications. They invade the historic rights and freedoms of every American: the right to trial by due process of law, defense against unlawful searches and seizures, and such correlative rights as freedom from assault, from false imprisonment, and from protracted detention, the right to bail, and the right to counsel. To the extent that they are indulged in they turn the police—the sworn defenders of the law—into prime lawbreakers. Their continued use by

[9] Herbert Brean in *Life,* 43:71, September 16, 1957.

some law enforcement officers accounts in large part for the low esteem in which police in this country are quite generally held.[10]

Third-degree methods range from physical brutality to various forms of mental torture, all of which are aimed at coercing the accused into making damaging admissions to the police. Not only do these devices hurt the victim, but they brutalize the police and breed contempt for the law. In addition, most outstanding police administrators would agree that they are not only vicious but useless.

Probably the most active force in the curtailment of third-degree methods by the police has been action by the federal courts. The United States Supreme Court has consistently held that convictions based on coerced confessions constitute a denial of due process under the Fourteenth Amendment. In addition, the federal government, through the Civil Rights section of the Department of Justice, can and does prosecute local police infringements of civil rights.

Attitudes toward Police

In an effort to determine what citizens think of their police, a study of citizens' attitudes was conducted in Los Angeles in 1954.[11] Older people (fifty-five and over) were most favorably inclined toward the police, while the severest critics were between eighteen and forty-four years. Men generally expressed more favorable attitudes than women. There was a definite tendency for people with the least schooling to look most favorably, and for college graduates to look least favorably, on police. Whites were more favorably inclined than Mexicans, and both these groups were more favorable than Negroes. The study found unskilled workers most favorably inclined toward the police. This group was followed closely by skilled workers, with the lowest vote of confidence being expressed by professional groups. The following are listed as the outstanding conclusions emerging from the survey:

1. There is an appalling lack of information on the part of the public concerning the caliber of their police and concerning the conditions under which they operate.

[10] Audrey M. Davies, "Police, the Law and the Individual," *Annals of the American Academy of Political and Social Science,* 291:145, January 1954.
[11] G. Douglas Gourley, "Police Public Relations," *op. cit.,* pp. 138–141.

2. Women, especially, are lacking in information about their police.

3. Current relations between the police and minority groups leave much to be desired.

    a. Recruit and in-service training in race relations should be improved and intensified.

    b. Actual performance of police in dealing with members of minority groups must be critically scrutinized, and improved if improvement is indicated.

    c. The police should publicly cooperate whenever possible in movements to advance understanding and harmony between persons of all races and creeds.

4. Public attitudes (both good and bad) toward the police are primarily the result of personal contacts between individual citizens and individual policemen.

5. In order to obtain the greatest possible approval for the police, the following things must be discouraged by effective selection, training, and supervision:

    a. Attitudes of discourtesy, prejudice, superiority, and indifference.

    b. Actions of unjustified arrests or citations, rough treatment, and inconsistency of traffic law enforcement.

6. The following things must be encouraged:

    a. Attitudes of courtesy, co-operation, sympathy, helpfulness, and tolerance.

    b. Actions of honesty, competency, promptness, and assistance of all kinds.

7. The things of which the public most need convincing are that their policemen

    a. Have a high professional interest in their work.

    b. Are selected for personal merit and ability.

    c. Operate under excellent discipline.

    d. Apprehend criminals indiscriminately, without regard for pressure brought by influential persons.

    e. Operate independent of newspaper publicity.

    f. Usually apprehend criminals in difficult cases.

    g. Respect the constitutional rights of suspected criminals.

    h. Are usually fair in dealing with minority groups.

    i. Are careful not to arrest innocent persons.

    j. Are directed by competent supervisors and top administrators.[12]

As the survey indicates, the police, like other public agencies, are spending considerable time and thought on matters of public relations.

[12] *Ibid.*, p. 141.

In the case of the police, the problem is complicated by the nature of their duties and by the existence of negative public stereotypes. Since the police have a duty to enforce laws that restrict our behavior, they are frequently the object of private and public resentment.

Police Policy as a Reflection of Social Conflicts

At the moment he decides to make or fails to make an arrest, the policeman is determining public policy around lawbreaking. If observations of police behavior suggest that this behavior is inconsistent and contradictory, one explanation may lie in the conflicting public attitudes that exist around lawbreaking and lawbreakers.

The basic conflict embodied in the criminal law, which must protect the individual against society at the same time that it protects society from the individual, has already been referred to. But there are additional conflicts that must be resolved by the policeman. One of these has been dramatically illustrated by William F. Whyte in his *Street Corner Society:*

> There are prevalent in society two general conceptions of the duties of the police officer. Middle-class people feel that he should enforce the law without fear or favor. Cornerville people and many of the officers themselves believe that the policeman should have the confidence of the people in his area so that he can settle many difficulties in a personal manner without making arrests. These two conceptions are in a large measure contradictory. The policeman who takes a strictly legalistic view of his duties cuts himself off from the personal relations necessary to enable him to serve as a mediator of disputes in his area. The policeman who develops close ties with local people is unable to act against them with the vigor prescribed by the law.
>
> It is not only the officers who are in the pay of racketeers who stress the importance of using discretion in enforcing the law. A police captain who was well known for his incorruptibility once said to me:
>
> "We don't judge the efficiency of an officer by the number of arrests he makes. There are so many arrestable offenses committed even by the law-abiding citizen that if the officer made all the arrests that he could, he would be a very, very busy man. If a man makes too many arrests, he isn't doing his job right. Of course, if he doesn't make any arrests at all, we know something is wrong. We rate the efficiency of the man as a variable considering the character of his route and how

quiet he keeps it. If a man has a difficult section and he keeps it quiet so that there isn't much violence, places aren't being robbed, and the women aren't being bothered, then we know he is doing a good job."[13]

Whyte continues his analysis of the relation of police power to ecological and social realities:

> Observation of the situation in Cornerville indicates that the primary function of the police department is not the enforcement of the law but the regulation of illegal activities. The policeman is subject to sharply conflicting social pressures. On one side are the "good people" of Eastern City, who have written their moral judgments into the law and demand through their newspapers that the law be enforced. On the other side are the people of Cornerville, who have different standards and have built up an organization whose perpetuation depends upon freedom to violate the law. Socially, the local officer has more in common with Cornerville people than with those who demand law enforcement, and the financial incentives offered by the racketeers have an influence which is of obvious importance.
>
> Law enforcement has a direct effect upon Cornerville people, whereas it only indirectly affects the "good people" of the city. Under these circumstances the smoothest course for the officer is to conform to the social organization with which he is in direct contact and at the same time to try to give the impression to the outside world that he is enforcing the law. He must play an elaborate role of make-believe, and, in so doing, he serves as a buffer between divergent organizations with their conflicting standards of conduct.[14]

A third conflict highly significant for the policies of law enforcement has been discussed in Chapter 7. There, it was pointed out that in various ways and for various reasons, society systematically cooperates in violations of the criminal law. Because the policeman must accommodate these conflicting attitudes toward sin—e.g., no gambling, but a bookie just around the corner—we may now state the corollary of an earlier axiom: Just as society gets the crime it demands, so does it get the police it deserves.

[13] William F. Whyte, *Street Corner Society*, 2d ed. (Chicago: The University of Chicago Press, 1955), pp. 136–137.
[14] *Ibid.*, p. 138.

The Disposition of Criminal Cases

THE WORK OF THE CRIMINAL COURT MAY BE DIVIDED INTO TWO DISTINCT stages: *adjudication* and *disposition*. In the first stage, adjudication, the court examines all material evidence bearing on the critical question, *Is the accused guilty of violating the law?* Except in cases of *mistrial* (a failure of the court, for any reason, to reach a verdict), the first stage of the court's work can end in only one of two ways: (1) The accused is found innocent, at which point he is discharged as a free man, or (2) he is found guilty, at which point the court must deal with the further question of what to do about him.

Unresolved Issues in the Adjudication and Disposition of Criminal Cases

In modern times the question, *What shall be done with the guilty?* has grown extremely complex. This is largely the result of an increasing awareness of the complexity of the concept of guilt itself. In societies with relatively primitive legal systems, guilt was a more or less clean-cut issue. To be guilty meant little more than having committed the forbidden act; the accused was guilty if he had, in fact, committed the act, and innocent if he had not.

In time, however, the concept of guilt lost its purely objective character and took on an increasingly psychological flavor. The transition from an objective to a psychological definition is evident in English law in which, at an early point, guilt became virtually synonymous with *mens rea*—literally, "evil mind." From this time forward it was necessary to prove not only that the accused had *acted* in an illegal way but that he had acted with malicious intent.

Once a *motive to do evil* had found general acceptance as an indispensable criterion of guilt, it was perhaps inevitable for thinking men to raise the even more basic question: What of those people who lack the wit or will to form motives in the first place? In order to show that the accused had an evil mind, must it not first be known that he had a *sound* mind? Pursuit of the logic of a psychological definition of guilt in this way forced judge and jury to come to grips with the fundamental question of the sanity of the accused.

When the question of sanity had become a material issue in the stage of adjudication, another question, equally compelling, emerged as an issue in the stage of disposition. If it is guilt alone that is punishable, and if a man must be sane in order to be capable of guilt, is it rightful for the State to exact punishment for the uncontrollable behavior of an unsound mind? Put another way, if sanity is a test of guilt, then insanity must be a test of innocence; *to punish the insane is to punish the innocent.*

The issues raised by the shift from an objective to a psychological conception of guilt have not yet been resolved; in our own time they have become more difficult to resolve than in any former period. The psychological sciences, in opening new continents of the mind, uncovered more enigmas than they found solutions for; to the urgent demand of the law for clear answers to its age-old question, the specialists could do little else than answer, "There are more things here than are dreamt of in your philosophy." Almost from the first, psychiatrists objected to the law's logically satisfying dichotomy, "sane-insane," and showed reluctance to answer a question whose simplicity violated their sense of the issue's complexity. For many psychiatrists the dividing line between sanity and madness could no longer be drawn with the clearness and cleanness the law demanded. If there was a line to be drawn at all, it was more likely to be a continuous rather than a dividing line—a line which a person might traverse in either direction, and one upon which it might be difficult to locate him at a given time. Moreover, for many psychiatrists, insanity was not merely a question of degree but a question of type as well, a question to which they could not answer "Yes" or "No" but merely how much, or in what way.

The implications of the new psychological knowledge soon became apparent in a mounting criticism of punishment as the major form of disposition. If there are different types and degrees of criminal responsibility, it becomes readily arguable that there should be correspondingly different forms of disposition. However, with the relatively recent exception of probation (shortly to be discussed), the only available legal disposition for the guilty has been punishment. Limited to punishment as its only recourse (short of clemency or outright pardon), all the law could do in dealing with obvious differences in criminal culpability was to parse and calculate within the feeble limits of its only instrument: so many more years of imprisonment, so much heavier a fine for the more culpable, so much lighter a sentence for the less culpable—but, in any case, a single disposition, punishment for all. In attacking this general condition of the criminal law, the critics could lay hold of the most basic legal principle of all: the principle, inherent in the definition of justice itself, that the reaction of the law be somehow set in balance with the culpability of the offender. In this context, the psychological definition of criminal responsibility as an individual and variable condition lends itself powerfully to the argument that the only true justice is individualized justice.

At this juncture a wide range of technical issues arise. If the forms of legal disposition are to be fitted to the requirements of individual cases, who is best qualified to determine these? At present these determinations are made largely by judges, working within the relatively narrow limits of legislation passed by the political representatives of the people—a group whose numbers include very few professionally trained behavioral scientists. To what extent and in what ways may it be necessary or desirable to modify established legal procedures in the direction of providing greater power and discretion for the professionally trained? And what limits and qualifications shall be set on the exercise of these broadened powers?

These considerations form part of the context of the controversies now taking place among those concerned with the disposition of criminal cases, and they provide part of the background against which proposals for change must be weighed. However, since these proposals are aimed at changing legal arrangements already in use, it is also necessary to consider these arrangements in their historical context and in their present form.

The Issue of Criminal Responsibility

Early legal thinkers were aware of the internal, mental coercions and disabilities that may force people to actions beyond their rational control. "This shall be no felony," runs a 1616 decision, "if a lunatick kill a man, or the like, because felony must be done *animo felonico*" (in a felonious spirit). Idiots, imbeciles, and other obvious mental defectives were immune from prosecution. The fine modern discriminations were lacking, but the community provided a rough diagnostic consensus: If a number of neighbors or townspeople reported the defendant "witless," the law would not exact its penalty. The earlier doctrines of insanity and mental defect were, in their rough-and-ready looseness, even more liberal and, in that sense, more "modern" than the more precise and legalistic doctrines to follow. It was, in fact, precisely this quality of liberality in the older doctrines of non-responsibility that inspired the more stringent insanity tests of modern times.

In 1843 one Daniel McNaghten murdered the secretary of Sir Robert Peel under the misapprehension that the secretary was Peel. At his trial it became evident that McNaghten was laboring under a number of misapprehensions sufficiently grave to persuade the jury that he was insane. McNaghten was committed to an asylum, and the consternation that had followed the crime was exceeded by that which greeted the verdict. The House of Lords appointed a committee of superior justices to re-examine the legal criteria of insanity. The result was the famous "McNaghten Rules," which became the prevailing test of the insanity plea in Anglo-American criminal law.

THE MC NAGHTEN RULES. The defendant, McNaghten, had gained acquittal on the doctrine of insanity based on the inability to know right from wrong. The new formulation restated the "right and wrong" test in more precise terms and with more specific reference to the particular criminal act:

> ...to establish a defense on the ground of insanity, it must be clearly proved that, at the time of the committing of the act, the party accused was labouring under such a defect of reason, from disease of the mind,

as not to know the nature and quality of the act he was doing; or, if he did know it, that he did not know he was doing what was wrong.[1]

Jerome Hall has pointed out that the judges who formulated the McNaghten Rules did not regard them as innovations but rather as restatements of laws of long standing. Nevertheless, though they were widely adopted on both sides of the Atlantic, they were almost immediately subjected to criticism by medical men and psychiatrists. Largely because of these criticisms and the clarifications and defenses they stimulated, the McNaghten Rules have become the principal focus of the continuing controversy over the adequacy of the legal tests of insanity.

THE "IRRESISTIBLE IMPULSE" TEST. Shortly after the formulation of the McNaghten Rules, critics centered proposals for their reform around an alternative rule—the so-called "irresistible impulse" test. The immediate historical antecedents of the new test have been traced to the work of the pioneer French psychiatrist Philippe Pinel (1745–1826), who had diagnosed cases of insanity without loss of intellectual function. On the basis of this approach, it seemed possible for persons to be clinically and behaviorally insane while still able to distinguish between right and wrong in intellectual terms. Toward the middle of the nineteenth century several prominent psychiatrists endorsed this orientation, which became the basis for a new classification of mental disease known as "moral insanity." In a work attacking the McNaghten Rules, the new insanity classification was proposed as the basis of reform:

> ...this should be the test for irresponsibility—not whether the individual be conscious of right and wrong—not whether he had a knowledge of the consequences of his act—but whether he can properly control his action.[2]

It was in America rather than in England that the new test first received judicial recognition. Three years after the formulation of the McNaghten Rules, the instructions of a Pennsylvania judge clearly suggested the irresistible-impulse test as an acceptable alternative to the right-and-wrong test:

> Insanity is *mental* or *moral;* ...there is a *moral* or *homicidal* insanity, consisting of an irresistible inclination to kill, or to commit some other particular offense. There may be an unseen ligament pressing on the

[1] Lord Chief Justice Tyndal, quoted in Jerome Hall, *Criminal Law and Procedure* (Indianapolis: The Bobbs-Merrill Company, Inc., 1949), p. 595.

[2] Knaggs, quoted in Jerome Hall, *General Principles of Criminal Law* (Indianapolis: The Bobbs-Merrill Company, 1947), p. 506.

mind, drawing it to consequences which it sees, but cannot avoid, and placing it under a coercion, which, while its results are clearly perceived, is incapable of resistance.[3]

The extent to which the irresistible-impulse test has been adopted by the courts as an alternative of the right-and-wrong doctrine of McNaghten is difficult to ascertain. Hall cites a claim that seventeen American states have used the new rule, but he doubts the correctness of this estimate, pointing out that it depends on an interpretation of judicial decisions. Certain of these decisions have not used the irresistible-impulse test as an *alternative* to the right-and-wrong test but rather as a *component* of it, indicating a view that the power to control conduct is a *phase* of normal intelligence rather than an independent ability. In any case, applications of the irresistible-impulse doctrine or variations of it have become increasingly widespread, especially in American courts, and have become the principal instruments of attempts to supersede the older rule.

THE CONTROVERSY OVER LEGAL CONCEPTS OF INSANITY. The controversy over legal concepts of insanity has been conducted mainly by those who consider the two approaches irreconcilable. There is a considerable body of somewhat less articulate opinion which does not consider them irreconcilable. Significantly, those holding this middle position have included jurists whose decisions have, in fact, merged the two doctrines by treating the intellectual and volitional (emotional) aspects as interdependent rather than separate aspects of the mind. This trend has been especially apparent in critical decisions delivered during the last thirty years, of which the following is an example.

A defendant had admitted killing a girl but had offered a plea of insanity. Convicted, he appealed, alleging errors in the trial judge's instructions to the jury. The appellate court, sustaining his appeal, wrote:

Apart altogether from the question whether "irresistible impulse" caused by disease of the mind can, consistently with McNaghten's Case, be regarded as a complete defense, it is quite obvious that proof of the existence of disease causing such impulse may at least afford evidence in proof of the existence of such a defect of reasoning as may cause the absence of knowledge necessary for establishing the defense of insanity under the rule in McNaghten's Case. For this reason it was wrong for the trial Judge to suggest and emphasize an antithesis between diseases of the mind leading to irresistible impulse and the conditions described

[3] Justice Gibson, quoted in Hall, *General Principles of Criminal Law*, p. 509.

in McNaghten's Case, for the latter might not only accompany, but even be inferred from, a disease of the mind producing an "irresistible impulse." It is quite out of accord with modern research in psychology to assert an absolute gap between cognition and conation.[4]

In the light of the trend toward judicial reconciliation of the right-and-wrong and the irresistible-impulse doctrines, an exhaustive review of the controversy between their adherents seems unnecessary. Nevertheless, in spite of this integrative trend, the controversy has continued —and has, in fact, produced a new judicial departure, shortly to be discussed. In view of this, the following brief outline of the arguments pro and con is indicated.

The McNaghten Rules have been criticized as (a) untranslatable into psychiatric concepts; (b) unintelligible to psychiatrists; (c) setting up a special and specious kind of "intellectual insanity" rarely found in actually insane people; (d) neglecting the emotional aspect of insanity in favor of the rationalistic aspect, and, consequently, (e) unjustly subjecting actually insane people to punishment.

The irresistible-impulse doctrine has been attacked as (a) being even more difficult to prove than the right-and-wrong test (thus: "We do not know that the impulse was irresistible, but only that it was not resisted"); (b) relying too much on unvalidated psychiatric opinion; (c) failing to differentiate between the insane and the merely impulsive, and thereby (d) opening the door to the escape of many persons who are sane and should be prosecuted as criminals.

Proponents of each doctrine have criticized their opponents for adherence to an outdated "faculty" psychology, which incorrectly divided the mind into separate compartments. The defenders of the McNaghten Rules (the judicial critics) have replied that more recent decisions have not done this but, on the contrary, have recognized the inseparability of the intellectual and the emotional aspects of mental disease. They hold that it is the irresistible-impulse doctrine that makes this false separation by maintaining that a person can simultaneously be rational intellectually and yet irrationally out of control. They point out, further, that when the psychiatric critics are not defending the irresistible-impulse doctrine they are, themselves, the most insistent that the intellectual and the emotional aspects of experience cannot be divided—and that psychiatry itself has insisted on the unity of the mind. For this reason, the judicial critics point out, the psychiatrists' refusal to recognize the recent

[4] Judge Evatt, quoted in Hall, *Criminal Law and Procedure*, pp. 612–613.

"integrative" trend of judicial decisions represents a kind of intellectual bad faith—a determination to attack a straw man.

RECENT DEVELOPMENTS IN THE LEGAL TEST FOR INSANITY. Despite the judicial evidence of the McNaghten test's responsiveness to modern interpretation, the attacks on it have not diminished. One of the most articulate critics has asserted that testimony by psychiatrists under the rule are violations of psychiatric principles and the medical oath, and he has urged the profession to go on a virtual strike against it.[5]

The principal proposal of the psychiatric critics has been the substitution of an entirely psychiatric definition of criminal responsibility for the legalistic definition. It is against this proposal that the defenders of a legal definition have waged their most determined opposition, pointing out that the legal rules, however rigid, ought not to be abandoned in favor of diagnostic interpretations which are themselves matters of controversy within the psychiatric profession. This impression of controversy can be verified by anyone observing two psychiatrists—one for the defense, the other for the prosecution—offering their dissimilar diagnoses of the same defendant.

Largely because of these frequently conflicting diagnoses and the difficult-to-interpret phraseology in which they are often expressed, judicial usage has tended to insist that psychiatric testimony relate itself decisively to the admittedly rigid legal questions: Was the accused able or unable to control his behavior, was he or was he not aware of the character of his act or aware that it was wrong? Unless the psychiatric testimony addressed itself solely to these questions, it was feared that neither judge nor jury could profit from it.

This usage has recently been overturned. In his decision in the Durham case in 1954, Judge Bazelon of the District of Columbia Circuit Court of Appeals established a new legal test of responsibility and insanity and, in addition, a new policy concerning the introduction of

---

[5] Gregory Zilboorg, *Mind, Medicine, and Man* (New York: Harcourt, Brace and Company, 1943).

The often conflicting state of psychiatric opinion lies close to the heart of the opposition to the proposed psychiatric reforms. When the legal scholars are asked to defer to the psychiatric position, they have frequently felt impelled to inquire, "Which psychiatric position?" Similarly, when psychiatric critics accuse the lawyers and jurists of rejecting the findings of the science of psychiatry, the lawyers and jurists have tended to raise questions about the scientific status of psychiatry. Thus Hall: "The severe criticism of the criminal law by various psychiatrists has spread the illusion that the chief difficulty, the major obstacle in the way of adequate adjudication, is a traditional legal indifference to science. But the plain fact is that the chief limitation on any solution of the problems arising from mental disease is the lack of medical and psychiatric knowledge of mental disease." (Hall, *General Principles of Criminal Law*, p. 486).

psychiatric testimony. The new test based the determination of criminal responsibility on the answer to two questions: (1) Is the defendant suffering from a mental disease or defect? (2) If so, was his crime a product of the mental disease or defect?

In order to find the defendant *not guilty by reason of insanity*, both of these questions must be answered in the affirmative, beyond reasonable doubt, in the opinion of the jury. If the defendant were suffering from a mental disease or defect that had not produced his criminal act, he might still be found guilty.

The Durham decision not only rejected the McNaghten Rules but also liberated psychiatric testimony from the requirement that it fit its evidence into any legalistic framework whatsoever. The psychiatrists could now testify as psychiatrists and not as psychiatric interpreters of legal formulas. On one question, however, the expert witness would still be required to give a discriminating *yes* or *no* answer: Was the crime a product of the disease or defect?

The Durham decision has been widely approved by critics of the McNaghten Rules, and widely deplored by the supporters of the older doctrine. As might have been expected, some of the severer critics of the new test are lawyers and legal scholars. In a critical article Edward De Grazia, a member of the bar of the District of Columbia, has raised a variety of questions concerning the possible consequences of the new decision. According to the older doctrine, when the defense entered a plea of *not guilty by reason of insanity,* the burden of proof rested with the defense; the accused was assumed to be sane until it was proved, beyond a reasonable doubt, that he was not. One of the effects, if not the intention, of the new ruling (contends De Grazia) will be a shift of the burden of proof of sanity to the prosecution:

> The introduction of any evidence of insanity—any testimony on behalf of the defense that the defendant suffers from a mental disease—will apparently cast not only the burden of proving sanity beyond a reasonable doubt, but also the burden of proving lack of connection between disease, and crime, beyond a reasonable doubt—upon the prosecution. Moreover, the average psychiatrist's attitude toward criminal behavior seems to embody, as a basic assumption, that such behavior is prima facie evidence of mental disease. It can, therefore, be expected that few psychiatrists will hesitate to find the necessary causal connection between the crime and the disease, once they have determined the disease to exist, knowing that a crime has been committed.[6]

[6] Edward De Grazia, "The Distinction of Being Mad," *University of Chicago Law Review,* 22:342–343, Winter, 1955.

In citing this and other reservations concerning the new rule, De Grazia acknowledges that its actual consequences will become apparent only after it has been in operation over a period of time. Only after it has been winnowed through the courts of appeal can the final complexion and further consequences of the new doctrine be expected to emerge.[7] In the meantime, the ultimate decision still rests with the jury. As before, the psychiatrist for the defense and the psychiatrist for the prosecution may be expected to present their individual interpretations to the jury, which, as before, will retire to ponder the newer versions of the old, old question.

The Issue of Punishment

In addition to the issue of sanity and criminal responsibility, there is one further grand question on which legal scholars and jurists have produced searching theory. This is the question of punishment: its purpose, its operation, and its consequences. As in the case of the issue of sanity and criminal responsibility, the major instrument of clarification has been a debate, prolonged and unterminated. Again, the lawyer's most articulate antagonist in this debate has been the psychiatrist.

There have been innumerable discussions and arguments about the intentions or stated purposes of *punishment* and about those of its declared antagonist, *treatment*. Few of these discussions have inquired whether the actual operations given as examples of punishment do, in fact, punish (in the sense of causing pain), whether the measures de-

---

[7] Though the Durham Rule has not yet been accepted by state and federal courts outside of the District of Columbia, sufficient time has elapsed for its preliminary evaluation within the District. In an article in *The New Yorker* (April 19, 1958, pp. 82–83) Richard Rovere writes as follows:

It has tended to increase greatly the number of defendants who plead insanity and the number of insanity acquittals.... Once it has been established—or has even been *asserted* by a reputable psychiatrist—that a defendant has a mental illness, it becomes very nearly impossible to prove beyond a reasonable doubt that his illness was *not* the cause of his crime.... The Durham Rule calls for acquittal in the event of a causal mental "defect" as well as in the event of a causal mental disease.... The word "defect" opens a Pandora's box for the courts and a vast hope chest for defendants in criminal cases.... Several defendants who have not been able to stake a claim to paranoia, schizophrenia, or any of the other recognized abnormalities of the mind have claimed simple "defects"—one of the most interesting of which has been the "sociopathic personality"... At least two defendants —one a rapist and one a mugger—have recently been acquitted on the ground that they were "sociopaths." The rule also leads to extreme difficulties in the case of a defendant whose only identifiable mental defect is—as it was put not long ago in a speech ... by Representative Kenneth Keating, of New York—"a morbid propensity for crime."

scribed as treatment do, actually, treat (in the sense of bringing ease, relief, or healing) in whatever conventional or technical senses the words may be used. Yet these questions—the objective effects of these operations—are issues beside which all others pale.

ARGUMENTS OPPOSING PUNISHMENT. Again, as in the case of the debate about sanity tests, it seems necessary to give no more than a brief outline of the argumentation. Those opposing punishment have cited the following major objections: First, its motives are seen as vindictive and harmful rather than helpful. Second, its effects are viewed as destructive. Third, it is considered ineffective both in deterring others and in teaching the individual to abandon the punished activity.

The core of the dominant psychiatric position is that the criminal is basically *a sick person,* differing in no fundamental way from other persons suffering from mental or neuropsychiatric diseases.[8] All of the additional views and proposals of those taking this position flow from it. Since the *criminal act* is a result or symptom of disease, it cannot be viewed as a willfully immoral act. The laws and social attitudes defining crime as willful immorality are not only mistaken but, in themselves, immoral, since they are collectively deliberate, vengeful, and controlled, whereas the criminal act is nonvolitional and beyond the control of the individual offender.

The judicial handling of offenders is viewed not only as mistaken, immoral, or in itself neurotic but as ineffectual as well, because the law still bases its disposition largely on the *criminal act* rather than on the *actor.* Since the cause of any crime lies in a condition within the criminal, all social measures against crime should be directed toward the prevention and treatment of the psychological conditions that produce crimes. Of these measures, punishment is seen as the most mistaken and the most ineffectual, for a variety of reasons. In the first place, the amount of punishment is determined by the nature of the crime. Actually, however, a man committing a minor crime may be suffering from a more serious mental condition than one committing a major crime, and may be far more dangerous. He may, therefore, require a longer period of more intensive therapy than a person who incidentally committed a graver crime but is not equally ill. In consequence, many psychiatrists

[8] The school of psychiatric thinking most closely identified with this view has been the psychoanalytic school, as represented by such writers as Abrahamsen, Zilboorg, Alexander, and Lindner, among others. Though not all psychoanalysts are in accord with their views, their position has been sufficiently articulated to become identified as the prevailing psychiatric orientation toward crime and criminals.

favor a completely *indeterminate sentence* (one year to life), with the decision to release left in the hands of psychiatrists, who alone are competent to determine the extent of improvement. Under this proposed system, the function of judge and jury would be restricted to findings of law and fact, while the sentence would be left entirely in the hands of competent medical experts. Any man convicted of an offense would be placed under enforced psychiatric treatment until it had been determined that he had improved sufficiently to be safely released.

ARGUMENTS IN DEFENSE OF PUNISHMENT. Rather than review the equally comprehensive argumentation in defense of punishment, it would perhaps be more appropriate to confine discussion to issues about which the disputants most clearly and fundamentally disagree. Of these, one of the most crucial is the nature of criminality itself. Those favoring the retention of punishment as a form of disposition deny that criminals, as a group, are necessarily sick, and that crime, in all or most cases, is a symptom of mental disturbance. On the contrary, they point out, for many criminals crime is a skill and an occupation, rationally pursued and realistically rewarding. Like the followers of many other occupations, those who pursue a career of gainful crime will tend to persist in their occupation so long as it remains rewarding, and will tend to desist when it ceases to become rewarding.

If this view is correct, it would seem to follow that criminals are unlikely to abandon their illegal behavior until they learn to view its consequences as frustrating rather than rewarding. In defining punishment as an instrument for producing changes in behavior, its defenders may appeal to a principle basic to most psychological learning theories: the withholding of reward for behavior that is inappropriate or incorrect.[9] Curiously enough, this learning principle, under another name, is widely accepted by psychoanalytic psychiatrists, among whom may be numbered many critics of punitive correctional practices. According to psychoanalytic theory, individuals attain maturity when they cease to be dominated by the "pleasure principle" (surrender to immediate instinctual demands) and learn to govern their behavior by the "reality principle," adjusting to the requirements of necessity. The principal instrument of this learning process is the experience of pain. Freud has written:

[9] In experimental psychology the relationship between learning and success (reward) and failure (frustration or punishment) has long been established. It is often referred to as the "law of effect," a term used by the psychologist Thorndyke in the report of a learning experiment published in 1898. Cf. Edwin G. Boring, *A History of Experimental Psychology*, 2d ed. (New York: Appleton-Century-Crofts, Inc., 1950), p. 562.

Under the influence of necessity ... they soon learn to replace the pleasure-principle by a modification of it. The task of avoiding pain becomes for them almost equal to that of gaining pleasure; the ego learns that it must inevitably go without immediate satisfaction, postpone gratification, learn to endure a degree of pain, and altogether renounce certain sources of pleasure. Thus trained, the ego becomes "reasonable," is no longer controlled by the pleasure-principle, but follows the REALITY-PRINCIPLE. . . . .

The transition from the pleasure-principle to the reality-principle is one of the most important advances in the development of the ego.[10]

POSSIBLE AVENUES OF RECONCILIATION FOR THE OPPOSING VIEWS. The foregoing citation from the founder of psychoanalysis suggests that the gap between the "treatment approach" and the "punitive approach" may not be as broad as might have been supposed. The ultimate objective of each is the same: the abandonment by the offender of his criminal behavior patterns. Each approach, moreover, seeks to attain this objective by a procedure which is essentially psychological: a learning process. Disagreement arises over the question of the most efficient means of promoting the desired learning. Those favoring the use of punishment insist that the offender cannot ordinarily achieve insight unless he is confronted with the realistic consequences of his behavior. Those opposing punishment assert that the criminal is too sick to be able to profit from painful consequences—and may, on the contrary, be worsened by them. In effect, then, the controversy boils down to a highly theoretical dispute concerning the "nature" of criminality.

Setting this issue aside, the more practical question remains: Which of these approaches and what variations of them are most *efficient* in what kinds of cases? Scientific evaluations of the actual results of procedures of either type have been few and far between; the over-all impression left by them suggests scant support for a categorical "either-or" conclusion. It may well prove true that there are certain cases which cannot profit from exposure to painful consequences—and certain other cases which cannot profit *without this exposure*. Should this conclusion gain support from future research, we may find ourselves confronted with an unexpected and paradoxical hypothesis with which to account for the disappointing results obtained so far.

Is it conceivable, for example, that certain cases which might have profited from punitive modes of treatment failed to profit because, in

[10] Sigmund Freud, *A General Introduction to Psychoanalysis* (New York: Liveright Publishers, Copyright [R] 1948, Susie Hoch), p. 312.

one way or another, the treatment was not punitive enough?[11] An analogous question arises with respect to nonpunitive modes of treatment. Is it possible that certain procedures, though described as non-coercive, failed because, as a matter of fact, they were not permissive enough? It is clear that the *effect* of any form of treatment cannot be anticipated merely from a description of its procedures or objectives. In questions of this kind, the old saying about the pavement of Hell may at times be distressingly appropriate. For the moment, however, these issues, like so many others in the field of correction, must await the verdict of future research.

THE MORAL ISSUE. There remains one further aspect of the "treatment versus punishment" controversy which cannot be resolved by appeal to values of sheer efficiency. The issue raised is moral rather than practical, and it poses the question: Regardless of the possible advantages of punishment, is it justifiable for society deliberately to inflict pain on any of its members? If it is wrong for criminals to inflict hurt on others, is it not equally wrong for the social group to respond by hurting the criminals?[12]

Here again, however, and in spite of the almost rhetorical nature of the question, it is essential to distinguish statements of intentions from descriptions of actual effects. Despite the fairly generalized social attitude favoring punitive treatment for offenders, there is one category of violator for whom humane and nonpunitive treatment is widely accepted: the criminal insane. With few exceptions, offenders of this type are considered in the same category and deserving of the same considerations as others who are mentally ill; they are to be treated rather than punished. In this connection, however, De Grazia has a disquieting comment:

> It is generally assumed that a convicted criminal will be "punished" through confinement to a prison. Yet the day is surely gone when the prison whip and chain, or the rack and wheel, promised unquestionable pain for the prisoner. The day is behind, too (gone, it seems, with the

[11] Considerable support is lent this possibility by observations of offenders in and out of prison. Inmates sent to the "hole" (solitary confinement, usually on bread and water) frequently view this punishment as a test of their toughness. In the delinquent culture, the boy who has been "sent up" gains in status. He is no longer a "kid"; he has been recognized as too tough to be coddled. The psychological processes operating to transform these "punishments" into rewards may go far to account for the noneffectiveness of punitive procedures for certain groups of offenders.

[12] For a searching and stinging presentation of the moral case against the punishment of criminals, see George Bernard Shaw, *The Crime of Imprisonment* (New York: The Philosophical Library, 1946).

coming of the writ of habeas corpus), when the prison held that awful terror of being "left to rot," of being forgotten by the world. And, it would seem, the day has also passed when the prisoner could not hope for a clean bed to sleep on, room to stretch his legs, or sufficient food and medical care to keep himself alive. The prisoner today is deprived of many liberties and much freedom, deprived of the opposite sex, and forced to wear a crown of thorns constructed of community fear and distrust.

But what of the insane? The insane criminal, by definition, is to be treated and not punished. This means he will go to a mental institution instead of to prison. This does not mean he will retain his liberties or his freedom. Rather may he be deprived of them, not for a fixed term of years, but possibly for life—for he may be obliged to "rot" in a mental hospital until "cured." It may matter not that his only offense, his "forgiven" crime, was not grievous,—but possibly only a forged check or shop-lifting or some homosexual act. It may not matter that he is incapable of cure. He may yet be incarcerated for the rest of his natural life.

The insane criminal will, of course, not be permitted to enjoy the company of the opposite sex. He will be forced to wear his own crown of thorns—constructed of community fear and disgust. But more than this, his hospital may be so overcrowded that he will find himself in the company of "many wild and violent insane persons" who are wont to beat him with their shackles and eat excreta at dinner.[13]

It is not our intention to attempt to resolve the relative morality of psychiatric treatment as contrasted with correctional treament. In an effort to give balance and perspective to a frequently heated debate, Judge Flood of the Pennsylvania Court of Common Pleas has written:

Perhaps the dominant factor in the history of criminal law in the first half of the twentieth century is the unrelenting pressure of the new science of psychiatry for the recognition of its claims in the administration of that law. The impatience of psychiatry with the unscientific premises of the criminal law has led to extravagant claims for psychiatry's ability to solve the problems of crime. Popular annoyance and judicial outrage when some of these claims were not borne out have seriously hampered those who seek to make psychiatry a major participant in the administration of the criminal law.[14]

In the same review, the Judge continues:

[The book] exposes equally, with clarity and without heat, the judge

[13] Edward De Grazia, op. cit., pp. 349–350.
[14] Gerald F. Flood, Review of Psychiatry and the Law, by Guttmacher and Weihofen, Annals of the American Academy of Political and Social Science, 287: 191, May 1953.

who holds to a precedent against solid scientific evidence of its invalidity and the psychiatrist whose claims outreach his performance. A lawyer's regard for the value of decision by precedent and the danger of sudden breaks with tradition makes for a sympathetic treatment of those judges who keep the pace of the march toward scientific procedure too slow for fear of vague harms, a fear which they feel but cannot always justify.[15]

The Nonpunitive Disposition of Criminal Cases: The Suspended Sentence and Probation

We turn now to the consideration of a subject which renders much of the previous discussion academic. There exists, and has for some time existed, a form of criminal disposition which is entirely nonpunitive and quite irrelevant to systematic theories of treatment or punishment. Though its antecedents had long roots in judicial procedure, its development was largely independent of judicial sponsorship and the pressure of the new ideas of criminal treatment. Its period of greatest expansion occurred, in fact, at the height of the controversy just discussed—a controversy which scarcely noted its existence.

The instrument of this nonpunitive form of disposition is the *suspended sentence,* a procedure by which the convicted offender is legally sentenced and then excused, provisionally, from undergoing his sentence and set free under such conditions as the court may impose. Unless he violates these conditions, he may remain at liberty until his sentence would ordinarily expire, when he is fully discharged. The term *probation,* sometimes used synonymously with *suspended sentence* and sometimes, more technically, as one of its special conditions, refers either to the legal status of the person under suspended sentence or to some form of supervision during the period of suspension. Though probation may, in many instances, impose relatively stringent restrictions on the behavior and mobility of the probationer, it does not remove him from the community. It therefore provides an alternative to imprisonment.

Historical Antecedents of Probation

The direct antecedents of probation are rooted in criminal procedure. English tradition had long recognized the local magistrate's right

[15] *Ibid.*

to "bind over" (release) a defendant in his own recognizance to keep the peace. A modified form of this procedure was absorbed into the common law, which granted the court the right to suspend punishment while the defendant appealed or applied for pardon. The powers of the court to suspend sentence were gradually broadened and eventually confirmed by legislation.

Though one essential element of modern probation—suspension of sentence—has early roots in the criminal law, the other—supervision—is relatively recent and unrelated to official procedures.[16] Credit for the introduction of the idea of supervision is generally given to John Augustus, a Boston shoemaker, who voluntarily embarked on a career of bailing out drunks and prostitutes from the Boston Municipal Court in 1841 and, in effect, became the court's unofficial probation officer. Within a short time Augustus' philanthropic work came to include almost every aspect of modern probation. A familiar figure at court, the old man would carefully select his candidates, secure their release on bail, obtain from them a pledge of good conduct, and, when needed, find them medical help, jobs, and lodging. On occasion he lodged as many as fifteen under his own roof; eventually he organized a "Temporary Home" for girls. In the course of his work he made thousands of personal visits to prospective employers and other interested citizens; and, at the time of his death, he had bailed 1,152 men and 794 women. His record of successes and failures was probably better than that of most official agencies since.

After Augustus' death in 1859 his work was taken up by Rufus Cook of the Boston Children's Aid Society. Ten years later, in 1869, the Massachusetts legislature authorized a state visiting agency to place selected juvenile offenders with private families; within that year 23 per cent of the juveniles convicted in Boston were so placed. The first statute providing a publicly paid probation officer was delayed until 1878. Though limited to the city of Boston, this law vested the municipal court with discretion to place offenders on probation without restriction as to age, sex, or previous record. In 1880 a state law granted all state courts permission to authorize probation, adding the requirement that probation officers also supervise offenders released from jail. At this point the probation officer became a parole officer as well. In 1882 the

[16] Though Grunhut mentions a practice of consigning young offenders—usually servants or apprentices—to the care of the prosecuting employer. (See Max Grunhut, *Penal Reform*, New York: The Clarendon Press, 1948, p. 299.)

appointment of probation officers was made mandatory for all courts in Massachusetts.

The spread of probation to other states was slow and cautious. By 1900 only nine states had adopted it on a state-wide basis, and in all but three of these states it was limited to juveniles. During this period of relative legislative inaction, individual courts in the various states began to take the initiative. Despite the lack of legislative authorization, many state and federal judges suspended sentences and put defendants on their "good behavior" without supervision. This practice led to the complaint that the courts were actually exercising the executive's power to grant reprieve, and in 1916 the United States Supreme Court ruled that federal judges could grant *temporary reprieves* but could not "refuse to enforce the law" by granting permanent suspensions.[17] This decision, which dramatized the conflict between legislative conservatism and judicial progress, spurred the enactment of state and federal laws authorizing judges to suspend sentences and grant probation. By 1917 twenty-one states had provided machinery for adult probation. In 1925 Congress authorized the setting up of a federal probation system under the Bureau of Prisons; in 1941 the system was placed under the administration of the federal courts.

Though the use of probation as a form of disposition has steadily increased, there is considerable variation in the extent to which it is used by different courts. In discussing this aspect of probation, Meeker has written:

> In one state only 12 per cent of all offenders found guilty on criminal charges are placed on probation; in another state the figure is 70 per cent (and in the federal courts the recent average is 40 per cent).[18]

The Organization of Probation

The administration of probation is primarily a local responsibility. Acknowledging the difficulty of establishing mutually exclusive groups, the Attorney General's Survey of Release Procedures has listed the following five general classes of probation agencies: (1) centralized state probation departments; (2) centralized county organizations; (3) metro-

[17] Attorney General's Survey of Release Procedures, Vol. II: *Probation* (Washington, D. C.: Department of Justice, 1939), pp. 9–10.
[18] Ben Meeker, "In-Service Training for Probation Officers," *1952 Yearbook of the National Probation and Parole Association* (New York: The Association, 1953), p. 170.

politan and large urban agencies; (4) smaller urban and rural departments; and (5) federal units.[19]

Wide variations exist in the procedures used by probation agencies. Variations are to be noted in the quality and quantity of probation personnel, the investigating practices of departments, the offenders eligible for probation, and the conditions of release. The general practice is to recommend a pre-sentence investigation of the offender's personal and social history. The information gathered serves as a guide to the court in determining whether or not to place the individual on probation. Though there are statutory provisions defining the conditions of probation in some states, the present trend is to allow the probation department wide discretion. Many of the statutory provisions relate to costs, restitution, and support, and contemplate money payments by the probationer. The probation department thus frequently serves as a collection agency for the courts.

Supervision during probation varies from virtually no supervision at all to efforts to individualize the treatment process for each probationer. During supervision the courts, acting usually on the advice of the probation department, may revoke the suspension of sentence and order incarceration. This termination of probationary status occurs when the probationer, in the opinion of the probation department, has become involved in either sufficiently serious or sufficiently frequent violations of the conditions of probation to warrant return to the court. If the probationer satisfies the conditions of probation his status as a probationer may be terminated even before the date on which his suspended sentence would expire.

Since 1907 the National Probation Association has been engaged in an effort to improve and extend probation services. In 1921 it became an incorporated agency with a paid staff. Later its functions expanded to include parole. The objectives of the Association are as follows:

> To study and standardize methods of probation and parole work, both juvenile and adult, by conferences, field investigations, and research;
> To extend and develop probation and parole systems by legislation, the publication and distribution of literature, and in other ways;
> To promote the establishment and development of juvenile courts, domestic relations or family courts, and other specialized courts using probation;
> To cooperate so far as possible with all movements promoting the scientific and humane treatment of delinquency and its prevention.[20]

[19] Attorney General's Survey of Release Procedures, p. 450.
[20] 1952 Yearbook of the National Probation and Parole Association, p. 233.

Penal Incarceration

In most jurisdictions employing probation, it is now customary for the judge to receive a *presentence report* on the convicted offender. The purpose of this report, which is usually prepared by a probation officer attached to the court, is to provide the judge with information that may assist him, first in determining an appropriate sentence and, second, in deciding whether the sentence shall be carried out or suspended. Unless probation is granted, pronouncement of the sentence is followed by an order committing the prisoner to the jurisdiction of the penal authorities.

Fixed and Indeterminate Sentences

Sentences to penal confinement are of two types. The first is a *fixed minimum and maximum,* and is usually limited in its application to sentences to state prisons. The minimum and the maximum cannot be identical except in those situations where the maximum period of confinement is one year. (Confinement to a state prison cannot be for less than one year.) It has been strongly urged by paroling authorities that sentences imposed by the courts should have a sufficient spread between minimum and maximum to permit them an opportunity to observe a period of adjustment on parole. If the minimum and the maximum are almost identical, there is little opportunity to observe the prisoner under parole supervision prior to the expiration of his "maximum" while on parole.

The second type of sentence, which is known as *indeterminate,* results in the commitment of the prisoner to a reformatory. Though the court does not fix or limit the duration of indeterminate sentences, the period in confinement and on parole may not exceed the statutory maximum for the offense.

Consecutive and Concurrent Sentences[21]

A series of sentences imposed at the same time may run *concurrently* or *consecutively.* If no specification is made by the court, all sentences imposed are deemed to run concurrently.

[21] The authors were assisted in compiling this information by Deputy Attorney-General Eugene Urbaniak, Chief of the Bureau of Legal Affairs, Department of Institutions and Agencies of the State of New Jersey. Though the procedures outlined follow the laws and practices of New Jersey, they are basically—and in many details—similar to procedures in several state jurisdictions.

It has been said that consecutive sentences and their interpretation have caused as much litigation in appellate courts as any other legal problem relating to the confinement of prisoners. The reason for this litigation has been the court's failure to make its intention plain at the time of imposing the sentences. Since a series of sentences imposed at the same time may be handled in many different ways (some may be consecutive and others concurrent, for example), it is imperative that the court make its intent clear and that this intent be accurately reflected in the court record.

In order to reduce the administrative problems inherent in consecutive sentences, some states have adopted statutes making it possible to *combine* such sentences, provided the prisoner himself is willing to serve the aggregate sentence rather than the separate ones. Under these statutes, the minimum of the aggregate sentence is the total of the minimum limits of the separate sentences; the maximum, the total of the maximum limits of the separate sentences. To understand the great advantages of "lumped" or "aggregated" sentences to the prisoner, consider the following examples. If a prisoner has three consecutive sentences of one to three years each, he would in New Jersey receive 72 days' "good-time" credit toward the reduction of his sentence on each one-year minimum, or a total of 216 days' credit for the three sentences. If, on the other hand, he elects to aggregate the separate sentences into a sentence of three to nine years, he would receive 252 days' credit on the aggregated minimum and 876 days on the nine-year maximum (instead of 756 days if the sentences are served individually.) Another benefit conferred by the single "lumped" sentence is that the inmate becomes eligible for parole at an earlier date. In New Jersey, for example, a first offender serving three consecutive sentences of two to four years each would not be eligible until he had served nine years—i.e., the maximum of his first two sentences and one half of the maximum of his third sentence. By aggregating the three sentences into one sentence of six to twelve years, he becomes eligible for parole after six years.

Parole Eligibility

Parole is the conditional and supervised release of a prisoner from a penal institution in which he has served a part of his maximum sentence. Like probation, it requires the person to maintain good behavior during the period of his supervision and until a final discharge is granted.[22]

An inmate's parole eligibility is determined by the length of his sentence, by his previous criminal record, and by his accumulation of time-credits for good behavior and the performance of work assignments. On longer sentences these credits may be substantial, as the schedule of "good-time" credits in the State of New Jersey reveals. In addition to "good-time" credits, credits for work performance ("work-time") are deducted from the length of the inmate's original sentence. Usually the requirement is that the work must actually be performed. If work is not available—or if the inmate, for any reason, is not suited for it—he does not secure these credits. The inmate usually "works off" one day from his original sentence for each week of work performed. Occasionally, the credits per work week may be increased for special work assignments—e.g., for assignments outside the walls.

In general, a first offender has an earlier parole eligibility than second or subsequent offenders. The statutes usually provide that second and subsequent offenders must serve progressively longer periods of their sentence in confinement. Consequently, for second, third, and subsequent offenders, the minimum of the sentence may be meaningless, since the prisoner must serve a fixed period—one half, two thirds, four fifths—of his maximum sentence before he is even eligible for parole consideration.

It should be noted that this delay of parole consideration for recidivism is not related in any way to the provisions of habitual-offender statutes, which establish increased penalties for repeated offenders through *judicial* proceedings. The courts have ruled that the withholding of parole consideration does not enhance punishment nor violate due process.

If the prisoner commits a crime while on parole, the most recently imposed sentence must be served first; then the prisoner is required to serve the balance of time remaining on the earlier sentence. The sentence to which the inmate is "reverted" is often calculated from the date of his release on parole, and no credit is given for so-called street time—i.e., time spent outside the institution on parole. The court, after learning how much time remains on the prior parole sentence, may believe that the prisoner should not be punished additionally and therefore shorten or suspend its own sentence. The prisoner then is returned to confinement as a *parole violator*.

[22] Parole is discussed in greater detail in Chapter 26.

"GOOD-TIME" CREDITS (NEW JERSEY)

A Minimum and maximum sentences in years	B Progressive credits for minimum and maximum sentences in years (days)	C Credits for each full month of fractional part of a year in excess of Column A (days)
1	72	7
2	156	8
3	252	8
4	348	8
5	444	8
6	540	8
7	636	10
8	756	10
9	876	10
10	996	10
11	1,116	10
12	1,236	11
13	1,368	11
14	1,500	11
15	1,632	11
16	1,764	11
17	1,896	12
18	2,040	12
19	2,184	12
20	2,328	12
21	2,472	12
22	2,616	13
23	2,772	13
24	2,928	13
25	3,084	15
26	3,264	15
27	3,444	15
28	3,624	15
29	3,804	15
30	3,984	16

For every year or fractional part of a year of sentence imposed upon any person ... for a minimum-maximum term there shall be remitted to him from both the maximum and minimum term of his sentence, for continuous orderly deportment, the progressive time credits indicated in the schedule herein. When a sentence contains a fractional part of a year ... then time credits ... shall be calculated at the rate set out in the schedule for each full month of such fractional part of a year.... No time credits shall be calculated ... on time served ... in custody between ... arrest and the imposition of sentence....—*Laws of New Jersey, N.J.R.S. 30:4—140.*

Allowance of Jail-Time Credits

Some states have provisions which require that in any custodial sentence the prisoner shall receive credit for the time spent in jail between arrest, conviction, and sentence. This is eminently fair, since the prisoner who cannot secure bail might otherwise be obliged to serve his full sentence in addition to the time already spent in jail. Where there are no procedures to cover this contingency, the courts may exercise their discretion in granting jail-time credits to reduce the sentence. Lack of fixed rules on this matter can, however, create situations of inequitable treatment. It should also be noted that *good-behavior credits* are frequently not available to the prisoner for the time spent in jail awaiting trial.

One of the most significant developments in modern penology is the increasingly critical attention which has been focused on the disposition of convicted offenders. Under the influence of new psychological and social conceptions, the law has progressively increased the range of its alternatives in the direction of greater responsiveness to the individual case. One reflection of this general trend is the development of more flexible doctrines of criminal responsibility. Another is the growing use of the indeterminate sentence.

By far the most revolutionary development is the increasing use of an alternative to imprisonment itself: probation. Though the origin and spread of probation cannot be credited to a general social acceptance of the idea of nonpunitive treatment as an alternative to penal incarceration, the existence of probation offers wide possibilities for the development of approaches unlimited by former conceptions and traditions of correctional procedure.

THE INSTITUTIONALIZATION
OF OFFENDERS

••

Correctional Institutions
in the United States

THE PENOLOGIST RECOGNIZES THAT HISTORICALLY, PRISONS WERE NEITHER universal nor inevitable. Of all the physical structures raised by society, they are perhaps the most obvious symbols of social improvising and expediency. In no other structures created by men have so many conflicting attitudes, contradictory motives, and intellectual uncertainties been grafted onto each other in steel and concrete.

In a typical large state prison the visitor can walk from the prison hospital to the gas chamber. These extremes define the gap between two social attitudes toward the offender, who has on more than one occasion been saved in one facility for the purpose of assuring his destruction in the other. At each of these polar points intention and procedure converge: the public demands vengeance for murder and medical treatment for the ill. Between these extremes, however, the convergence is less exact, the translation of objectives into actions more uncertain, and the gap between intention and reality filled with irresolution and conflict. The study of the institution as reality and as intention is the continuing preoccupation of the penologist.

Local, State, and Federal Institutions

Detention and Short-Term Facilities

In a nation where almost everything else has been counted and recorded, the total number of municipal and county jails and lockups is not even approximately known. The American Prisoner Association lists 4,850—3,100 county jails plus one additional facility for each of the approximately 1,750 municipalities of more than 5,000 population.[1] Sutherland has set the figure at about 14,000—an estimate including about 11,000 police and village lockups.[2] A recent estimate by Roy Casey, superintendent of the Alaskan jail system of the Federal Bureau of Prisons, puts the number at a round 10,000.[3]

Short-term and detention institutions fall roughly into four categories: (1) municipal or village lockups operated by the police department or village marshal; (2) city lockups maintained by the city police department or municipal court; (3) county jails operated, usually, by the county sheriff; and (4) specialized detention facilities for women, children, and persons held for various reasons by district attorneys. This last category occasionally includes hotels, where material witnesses may be held in protective custody under conditions of secrecy for varying lengths of time without benefit of so much as a *lettre de cachet*.

The opportunity to count the number of people held in jails and lockups occurs once every ten years—during the month of the census. The 1950 census revealed 86,492 people under municipal lock and key in March of that year. It has been estimated that between 500,000 and 2,000,000 men, women, and children pass through jails and lockups annually. The larger estimate is probably more nearly correct. Thus, during the course of a given year, one out of every eighty-five citizens may take his breakfast, lunch, or supper inside a jail. The quality of the meal will vary greatly, as will the quality of the other guests. Roy Casey observes:

> Some perhaps remain only long enough to be booked and to post bond, if their offenses are minor, or if they have money or influential friends. Others stay locked up with the usual "catch" of the police dragnets:

[1] *Manual of Correctional Standards* (New York: The American Correctional Association, 1954), p. 96.

[2] Edwin H. Sutherland and Donald R. Cressey, *Principles of Criminology*, 5th ed. (Philadelphia: J. B. Lippincott Company, 1955), pp. 362–363.

[3] Roy Casey, "Catchall Jails," *Annals of the American Academy of Political and Social Science*, 293:28, May 1954.

drunks, prostitutes, sex deviates, murderers, rapists, dope addicts, dope peddlers, embezzlers, gamblers, insane, juvenile delinquents, first offenders, highjackers, confidence men, ex-convicts, chronic alcoholics, kidnapers, amnesia victims, traffic law violators, disturbers of the peace, bums, vagrants, victims of economic reverses "without visible means of support," suspects held for investigation (illegally, in many instances), detained witnesses (when frequently the criminal himself has money for bail and a smart lawyer, and is free on the outside), immigration detainees, bank robbers, white slavers, procurers for prostitutes—all thrown together or only nominally segregated. Some stay in ... a day, a week, a month, a year, or sometimes longer, to await trial ... or while serving sentences for misdemeanor violations, or perhaps awaiting a new trial or an appeal.[4]

At a citizens' conference on the Cook County Jail the assistant superintendent, Hans W. Mattick, pointed out that the jail, designed for 1,032 inmates, housed a population of 1,600 to 2,400 persons, with an annual turnover of 16,000 to 17,000. He described this population as follows:

In the single building that constitutes the Cook County Jail is housed the most heterogeneous inmate population ever congregated under one roof. The inmates can be classified in any number of ways. The jail houses both male and female adults and juveniles of both sexes. Jurisdictionally speaking, it houses municipal, county, state and federal prisoners. In terms of legal status, it houses both sentenced and non-sentenced inmates. In terms of offense categories, the jail houses persons charged with everything from committing a public nuisance to murder. Sentences range from a few hours in custody to death in the electric chair. In terms of time served, the range is from one day to five years. Women constitute about 7 per cent of the population (100 to 130) and juveniles, that is, persons under 21 years of age, constitute about 15 per cent of the population. Ages range from 15 to 85. Sentenced prisoners comprise two-thirds of the population. Ten men are awaiting death by execution.

The distinguishing feature of the non-sentenced population, except for those charged with capital offenses, is that they are *indigent* and cannot afford bail. If they had the money they would be in the free community. That is, roughly one-third of the inmates are incarcerated in a maximum security prison, legally "innocent until proven guilty," but nonetheless confined like convicted offenders for lack of bail resources.[5]

[4] *Ibid.*, p. 29.

[5] Hans W. Mattick, "The Cook County Jail; Where We Are," *Searchlights on Corrections in Cook County* (Cook County Jail, 2600 So. Calif. Ave., Chicago 8, Ill., November 19, 1956), pp. 4–5.

At the same conference, which had as its theme "Searchlights on Corrections in Cook County," the sheriff of Cook County, Joseph D. Lohman, a sociologist and criminologist, pointed out the worst aspects of this situation both for the individual so confined and for society:

> The county jails, as presently constituted, are for all practical purposes agencies for the creation of a community of interest on the part of those who violate the law. They establish contacts and continuing association among law violators. They afford a machinery for perpetuating and transmitting the culture and tradition of crime. They produce attitudes of hostility and cynicism toward the machinery of justice which houses them together in idleness, as it does. And they insure the maturation of delinquent and criminal attitudes as well as professional criminal skills among the neophytes by the indiscriminate lodging of all types of persons (men and women; young and old; felons and misdemeanants; unsentenced and sentenced petty offenders and serious offenders; the professionals and the amateurs; the compulsive offenders and the situational offenders; the maximum security risks and the minimum security risks) under one framework of concrete and steel.[6]

Though any over-all survey of correction at municipal and county levels would be discouraging, Myrl E. Alexander, assistant director of the Federal Bureau of Prisons, who has devoted many years to this problem, believes some progress is being made not only in smaller towns and cities but in some large metropolitan areas as well. Alexander has offered several conclusions—based on a study of county detention systems—as guides to future planning:

> (1) Only prisoners with short sentences, of less than one year at most, should be retained in county institutions. As in California, New York and other states, felons and those sentenced to more than one year should be sent to state institutions. (2) The traditional and expensive security equipment—cell blocks, walls, grilles, locking devices, and bars are simply unnecessary for the majority of short-term misdemeanants. As a matter of fact, they actually promote tensions and distrust. (3) One large jail can provide nothing more than enforced detention with only token treatment programs. Diversified facilities: camps, farms, and workhouses are needed for effective and economical treatment and training. (4) Misdemeanants are usually less serious offenders who are more amenable to special treatment services. They are more likely to present less aggressive behavior patterns. Yet we usually make few services available to them as contrasted to the intensive programs in major prisons and reformatories. The large city and county can meet that

[6] Joseph D. Lohman, "Prospects for the Future," *Searchlights on Corrections in Cook County,* pp. 3–4.

need because of the heavy misdemeanant load. (5) Trained career personnel, recruited and promoted on the basis of merit and high performance standards, is indispensable to the creation and professional development of correctional services. (6) Inmate incentives and flexibility in sentence operation must be provided through full work opportunities, the use of good time, and controlled supervised release. (7) The intensive study of aggravated problems found frequently in jails must be one major goal of the system. Alcoholism and drug-addiction are two prime examples. And, finally, (8) The development of a new and broadly conceived county correction system, especially in a large metropolitan county, is dependent upon widespread public understanding and support. A thorough public relations program helps create that support.[7]

An awakened local interest and a willingness to give financial and moral support to corrective measures may result in improvements in this neglected area. Unless local political and civic leaders are willing to take the frequently unpopular steps necessary to "clean up" local jail conditions, little will be accomplished. When the general climate of public opinion supports this action, it will be politically expedient to take it.

There are two exits from the short-term detention institution: one leads to the street, the other to the correctional institution. Though many metropolitan communities maintain their own correctional institutions for misdemeanants sentenced to terms up to one year, the "correction" of convicted felons serving sentences varying from a year to life is a state and federal responsibility. Because they are concerned with the more serious and dangerous offenders, correctional institutions and their inmates have received more penological attention than detention institutions and short-term offenders.

Federal Correctional Institutions

The Federal Bureau of Prisons operates twenty-eight institutions for civilian federal offenders. The United States Public Health Service administers three additional federal institutions with specialized medical facilities. Nine disciplinary institutions are maintained by the Department of Defense: four by the Army, three by the Navy, and two by the Air Force.

The average number of all types of federal prisoners is shown in Table XXIV.

[7] Myrl E. Alexander, "Trends in Jail Administration in Metropolitan Counties," *Searchlights on Corrections in Cook County*, pp. 11–12.

TABLE XXIV

AVERAGE NUMBER OF FEDERAL PRISONERS, FISCAL YEARS ENDED JUNE 30, 1953 AND 1954

	1953	1954	Increase or decrease
All federal prisoners	22,444	24,499	2,055
Federal Institutions, total	18,757	20,114	1,357
Bureau of Prisons Institutions, total	17,931	19,245	1,314
Penitentiaries, for:			
Intractable male offenders			
Alcatraz, Calif.	235	273	38
Habitual tractable male offenders			
Atlanta, Ga.	2,267	2,341	74
Leavenworth, Kans.	2,289	2,458	169
Older improvable male offenders			
Lewisburg, Pa.	1,201	1,252	51
McNeil Island, Wash.	988	1,093	105
Terre Haute, Ind.	1,086	1,189	103
Reformatories, for:			
Agricultural-type improvable male offenders			
Petersburg, Va.	669	704	35
Younger improvable male offenders			
Chillicothe, Ohio	1,056	1,161	105
El Reno, Okla.	959	958	-1
Englewood, Colo.	363	387	24
Female offenders			
Alderson, W. Va.	511	527	16
Institutions, for:			
Male juvenile offenders			
National Training School for Boys, D. C.			
Federal cases	210	227	17
District of Columbia cases	177	205	28
Natural Bridge Camp, Greenlee, Va.	62	70	8
Correctional institutions, for:			
Short-term male offenders			
Ashland, Ky.	577	543	-34
Danbury, Conn.	411	512	101
La Tuna, Texas	649	725	76
Milan, Mich.	638	633	-5
Seagoville, Texas	419	460	41
Tallahassee, Fla.	428	506	78
Texarkana, Texas	492	511	19
Prison camps, for:			
Minimum-custody improvable male offenders			
Allenwood, Pa.	66	101	35
Avon Park, Fla. (Closed October 16, 1953)	97	32	-65
Florence, Ariz.	154	285	131
McNeil Island, Wash.	179	254	75
Mill Point, W. Va.	172	216	44
Montgomery, Ala.	162	188	26
Tucson, Ariz.	188	248	60
Tule Lake, Calif. (Closed May 22, 1953)	53	–	-53
Wickenburg, Ariz. (Closed May 22, 1953)	86	–	-86
Detention headquarters, for:			
Males awaiting trial or with short sentences			
New York, N. Y.	157	174	17
Medical Center, Springfield, Mo., for:			
Physically and mentally maladjusted male offenders			
Hospital	763	799	36
Maintenance unit	167	213	46
Public Health Service Hospitals, total	826	869	43
Fort Worth, Texas *(for male narcotic addicts)*	259	222	-37
Lexington, Ky. *(for narcotic addicts)*	551	630	79
St. Elizabeths, D. C. *(for mental patients)*	16	17	1
Non-Federal Institutions, total	3,687	4,385	698
State, county, city, and private institutions	3,058	3,670	612
Alaska jail system	197	180	-17
Other territorial jails	432	535	103

Average populations, including those of prison camps closed, computed by dividing inmate days by the number of days in the respective full years.
Source: *Federal Prisons, 1954* (Washington, D. C.: Federal Bureau of Prisons, 1955), p. 11.

State Correctional Systems

The American Correctional Association lists 395 state correctional institutions of all types: prisons, reformatories, training schools, and work-camps. With certain exceptions, the number of institutions maintained by each state varies with its population. Six states—Arizona, Idaho, New Hampshire, Nevada, South Dakota, and Utah—maintain two correctional institutions; New York maintains twenty-three; and California, thirty-five. New Jersey, with a population in excess of five million, maintains an adult prison with two branches, three reformatories, two training schools, and two specialized institutions; a diagnostic facility and center for the short-term treatment of youthful offenders.

Types and Designations of Correctional Institutions

The designations identifying different types of penal institutions illustrate the influence of public sentiment on nomenclature. The terms used to designate juvenile institutions are minimally graphic and maximally aspirational, and this tendency toward wishful nomenclature increases as the age of inmates decreases. Thus, modern public policy has generally decreed that penal institutions for eight-, ten-, and twelve-year-olds be called *homes*—for example, "The New Jersey State Home for Boys." Similarly, for juveniles in their early and middle teens, a frequent designation is *training school*—a term reflecting the public's insistence on viewing the teen-age delinquent as an errant schoolboy. The term *reformatory* is frequently applied to institutions for older juveniles, and for women of all ages. Despite the fact that these institutions are essentially similar in their basic policies and structures, none of the aforementioned designations reflects the fact that their inmates are being confined by coercion. It is only in the term used to identify the adult male institution that the terminology finally becomes graphic and realistic: *prison* accurately describes a place where people are imprisoned.

Just as the term *prison* more frankly expresses the public's acknowledged pessimism about the adult male criminal, so does the physical structure of the prison more accurately reveal the basic essentials of the penal process: authoritarian control and enforced isolation from the community. Since these principles are common to all correctional institutions, adult and juvenile alike, their processes and effects are most clearly observable in the situation where they are least disguised: the adult male prison.

The Isolation of the Correctional Community

Physical Isolation

The physical isolation of the correctional community is maintained by (1) the use of physical obstacles and (2) the use of nonphysical obstacles. An example of the first type is the armed, manned wall. An example of the second type is the reliance on regulations, threats, and incentives, which is characteristic of the "open" institution. All correctional installations may be ranged along a continuum bounded by these extremes: they are conventionally broken down into maximum-, medium-, and minimum-security institutions.

The choice of obstacles is essentially related to the public's expectations regarding the purposes of the institution. These expectations, in turn, are related to a complex series of historical and ideological values in the society. In most western societies these values have been in conflict since earliest times, alternating between an orientation based on forgiveness and an orientation based on retaliation. The maximum-security installation reflects the public's punitive orientation; the open institution, its mood of forgiveness and indulgence. Forgiveness and indulgence, however, have their limits, and the public requires any person, whether he be committed to a "treatment" institution or a "punishment" institution, to remain there, even if against his will, until he is officially released.

Where expectations are so highly conflicted, they cannot be housed under the same roof without some damage to the interior. The conflict is at its keenest in minimum-security institutions for juveniles. For a variety of reasons centering around ambivalent attitudes toward offending children, society will not tolerate the same forbidding, dreary wall around its dangerous juveniles that it demands around its dangerous adults. Yet, because of the unstable character of many of their young charges, some of whom are in their physical prime, the administrators of training schools and reformatories must find some other means of restraining them. The methods vary widely and are relatively less publicized than the institutions' sports and educational programs.

The administrator of a minimum-security installation can rely on one or a combination of two nonphysical restraining techniques. The first of these, which might be termed the "incentive approach," makes use of all of the rewards and privileges for good behavior; these vary from going to the movies to going home. The second, which might be called the "threat approach," makes use of hidden custodial devices and the inmate power structure. Most minimum institutions rely on an uneasy accommodation between these modes of control. Hidden custodial devices range from the civilian cottage parent casually strolling on patrol around the cottage to tool-proof steel in place of wooden lattice on the cottage—which also has imposingly heavy doors, and modern locks.

Psychological Isolation

The isolation of any institutional population extends further than the mere physical separation of inmates from members of the outside community. It has, in addition, certain profoundly significant psychological aspects, which, like the physical isolation, are enforced both by conditions deliberately imposed by the institution and by other conditions which the institution is powerless to prevent. Here again, as in the case of physical isolation, two opposed sets of values are in conflict—and, again, the institution is confronted by the dilemma created by its attempt simultaneously to achieve both.

The formal measures employed by the institution to ensure the psychological isolation of its inmates takes four general forms: (1) control and limitation of visits; (2) control, limitation, and censorship of correspondence; (3) restriction of the ways in which inmates and personnel are permitted to relate to each other; (4) routinization of daily behavior (including such measures as requiring inmates to wear special uniforms, walk from place to place in ordered files, etc.).

In justifying these additional isolation measures, institutional authorities have felt the need to defend themselves against the criticism of unnecessary severity. They point out that uncensored correspondence and unsupervised visits would facilitate the importing of contraband—including hacksaw blades, which could be passed by hand in visits or sent through the mails in unexamined packages. By limiting and formally defining the interaction between inmates and officials, prison administrators have tried to reduce the vulnerability of their employees to manipulation by inmates.

That these precautionary measures are not merely capricious is demonstrated both by the long and colorful history of escapes and by the fact that the measures themselves are most rigorous in maximum-security institutions. The tragic fact seems to be that the more society insists that a man be physically isolated, the more carefully his psychological isolation must be maintained in order to cut down his chances of escape. Conversely, the minimum-security inmates and the short-termers, men relatively less in need of the stimulation of communication with the outside world, are permitted it with much more freedom. Thus the unsupervised, face-to-face visit is the exception in a maximum installation; it is the rule in minimum institutions.

In recent decades there has been increasing recognition of the pernicious effects of the psychological isolation of the physically confined. A wide variety of what might be called socially reintegrative measures has been undertaken in order to neutralize these effects; the measures are limited only by considerations of custody.

The increasing tendency to move away from walls, cell blocks, and bars—all that is traditionally associated in the public mind with prisons—has been rationalized in terms of a therapeutic goal of decreasing or concealing the differences between the institutional environment and life outside. In many modern reformatories—institutions housing older juveniles and young adults—the attempt is made to simulate something of the campus atmosphere. For a while, dormitories replaced cell blocks. Critics of the dormitory system have pointed out that congregate quarters not only facilitate but encourage all manner of abuses between inmates, including forced homosexuality. Nevertheless, dormitories are established in many institutions.

The clothing worn by inmates has undergone striking changes during the last decades, with greater latitude given to individual preference and personal comfort. In some institutions the movement from stripes to sports shirts has reached the point where only the guards wear a standard uniform.

Increasing the frequency and liberalizing the conditions of visiting has brought the inmate into closer contact with the outside community. Kenyon J. Scudder, the superintendent of one of California's most popular institutions, has described a typical family visit:

> When you visit at Chino, you can bring the children and a picnic lunch. Over the loudspeaker a voice calls:
> "Will Mr. Johnson come in and meet his guest?"
> As Mr. Johnson appears, his little girl runs across the room and jumps into her daddy's arms; while he holds her closely, the wife comes up with the food basket. He embraces his wife and picks up the basket.
> "Come on out to the visiting grounds."
> His wife looks around and says: "But where are the guards?"
> "There are no guards, honey," he replies. "Come on. I'm the host."

And for four hours the little family can visit undisturbed with no one listening in to the conversation.[8]

The modern institution invites a wide variety of lay groups to visit and, occasionally, to participate under supervised conditions. Groups invited include outside sports teams—and it is not unusual for the inmate players to be matched against a team composed of police officers from the local community. Thus it is not inconceivable for an inmate shortstop to complete a double play on the officers who arrested him.

Administrative Structure and Functions

The prison's isolation from the larger community, however modified in recent years, makes it necessary for the institution to function as a self-sufficient social island, duplicating many of the essential services to which prisoners are denied access in the world outside. The organizational chart shown on page 469 relates the administrative division of functions and services to the formal lines of authority and communication in an adult institution.

The number of different types of correctional employees provides some indication of the relative emphasis on the various functions and services. Though the ratio of employees to inmates varies from one correctional system to another and from one type of institution to another, it is generally highest in specialized treatment institutions and lowest in adult prisons and work-camps. In the most general terms, the ratio is approximately 1 employee to every 1–3 inmates at the training school level, 1 employee to every 2–5 inmates at the reformatory level, and 1 employee to every 5–8 inmates at the adult prison level. Of these employees, the largest number is custodial, ranging from 60 to 80 per cent in reformatories and adult prisons to 40 to 60 per cent in training schools. The ratio of the remaining employees in correctional institutions follows a pattern of 1 medical and 1 food service worker to every 150–200 inmates; 1 administrative-clerical employee to every 35–50 inmates; 1 maintenance employee (carpenter, plumber, etc.) to every 50–75 inmates; 1 psychologist to every 150–300 inmates; 1 educational employee to every 100–300 inmates; and 1 psychiatrist to every 300–2,000 inmates.

[8] Kenyon J. Scudder, "The Open Institution," *Annals of the American Academy of Political and Social Science*, 293:83–84, May 1954.

SKELETON ORGANIZATION CHART FOR A
CORRECTIONAL INSTITUTION FOR ADULTS

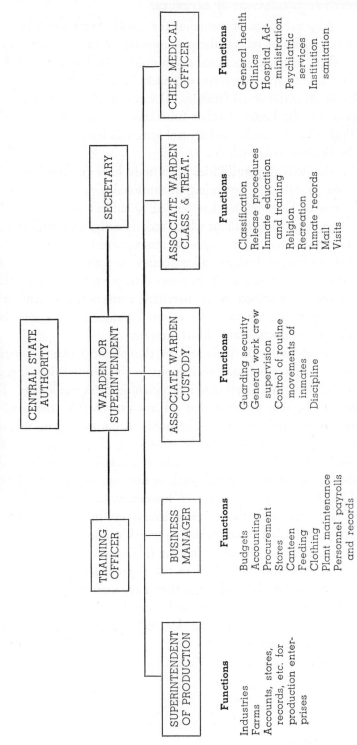

Source: *Manual of Correctional Standards* (New York; The American Correctional Association, 1954), p. 58.

The preponderance of custodial personnel over every other single category of employees reflects the pre-eminence of the custodial function over all others in the correctional community. Though most marked in adult institutions for long-term offenders, the custodial emphasis is pervasive in all correctional facilities. Because its character in any given institution sets the limits of other functions and services, a knowledge of the institutional security and control system is basic to an understanding of the institution as a whole.

The manifold responsibilities of custody have become increasingly burdensome in an era of expanding institutional populations. The sheer unwieldiness of large masses has tended to subject inmate and official alike to a regimentation without which orderly activities would be impossible. The result has been a general atmosphere of depersonalization, which reduces the sensitivity of all concerned to personal individuality—except when it expresses itself in some disruptive form. This characteristic of human relations in the oversized correctional institution continues to impede efforts to make prison administration responsive to the needs and problems of individual inmates.

Because of the wide variations in the physical plants, programs, and personnel of correctional institutions in the United States, general statements about correctional practices are subject to qualification. There does seem to be one problem that all institutions face; the conflicted orientation of the public. When the public is not expressing its insecurity about escapes, it is likely to be expressing attitudes of commiseration, which take the form of demands for increased liberality. These demands may be expressed in an attack on the custodial safeguards which the public, in its opposite mood of insecurity, demanded in the first place. Confronted with these contradictory pressures, correctional personnel frequently must decide which to translate into practice and which to honor in public statements. They are like repertory actors, who must vary their performance according to the expectations of a moody and unpredictable public. By and large, they have attempted to resolve this problem by satisfying the more fundamental demands of security by means of concrete action and the demands for increased liberality by means of public statements.

Correctional Procedures and Services

ANY DESCRIPTION OF PROCEDURES AND SERVICES IN CORRECTIONAL INSTI-tutions must be prefaced by a brief discussion of the objectives at which they are aimed. In general, the correctional institution has responsibility for (1) secure safekeeping of all inmates and personnel; (2) maintenance and improvement of the welfare of inmates; (3) achievement of these two objectives with a maximum of efficiency and economy.

These objectives, though capable of separate analysis, are very intricately related. Indeed, it is precisely this mutual relatedness which must be grasped before a clear analysis becomes possible. One of the best examples of this basic reality is the close relation of custodial efficiency to individual inmate welfare.

Custodial Functions: Security and Control

The Manual of Correctional Standards lists the following provisions as essential to a sound custodial program:

    1. An adequate system of classification of prisoners. Careful study

diagnosis and recommendations for treatment documented into case histories give prison workers the knowledge they need to handle inmates.

2. Inspection of security facilities. Regular, formalized inspections reinforced by constant observation of physical plant, help assure its best use.

3. An adequate system of counting inmates to make certain "all are present and accounted for."

4. A plan for firearms control specifying their purpose, use, safety precautions, proper inventory, storage and standardization.

5. A plan for gas control specifying its purpose, use, safety precautions, proper inventory, storage and standardization.

6. A plan for the control of contraband defines such items and provides for their regulation.

7. A plan for the control of keys so that all are accounted for and under control of free personnel.

8. A plan for control of those tools and equipment items that pose a threat to persons or to the physical security of the plant.

9. A comprehensive and up to date job analysis for all posts to aid employees in understanding their tasks.

10. Proper lock devices kept in good operating condition.

11. Proper cell equipment designed to minimize the necessity of permitting custodial risks to leave their cell after lock-in.

12. Emergency doors into housing and to areas where prisoners are congregated.

13. Plans for operation during special emergencies:
   a) Escapes
   b) Riots
   c) Firefighting[1]

In addition to the items listed, an accurate, moment-to-moment knowledge of and control over the whereabouts and destinations of all inmates is essential to the operation of a correctional institution. These twin objectives, knowledge and control, are mutually indispensable, since it is impossible to achieve either without the other. But it would be a narrow view to consider the control of movement a purely custodial objective. No matter how irksome and petty it seems to the inmates whose activities are curtailed, there is probably no other single goal which is more crucially tied up with inmate welfare.

The overriding emphasis on security and control has been explained, attacked, and defended many times and in many quarters. Critics have argued that the custodial emphasis is inimical to treatment, that it

[1] *Manual of Correctional Standards* (New York: The American Correctional Association, 1954), pp. 197–198.

creates an atmosphere of coercion, that it transforms the prison into an autocracy. And they have questioned whether men can be prepared for a free life in a democratic society by methods more typical of a police state. Defenders of custody have pointed out that a certain degree of repression is indispensable so long as the public continues to insist on its own protection from prisoners—which means that the prison authorities must, above all, prevent escapes. Moreover, they point out, a certain degree of repression is necessary so long as the public continues to demand that inmates themselves be secure and protected—which means that the authorities must prevent and punish internal violence. These two objectives—protection of the community from prisoners and protection of prisoners from each other—make security and control the pervading and dominating requirement it has become.

Analysis of this controversy leads to a curious finding. Those opposing the custodial emphasis base their opposition on its *harmfulness*. Those defending it base their defense on its *indispensability*. Actually, these arguments do not conflict; they do not even collide. The possibility arises that *both may be correct*. It may well be that the overriding demands of security are both harmful and necessary in correctional institutions as they exist today.

The traditional contrast between custody and welfare, disfigured by bias and half-truth, misses the central reality of the inmate's life in prison. The reality is this: The welfare of the individual inmate, to say nothing of his psychological freedom and dignity, does not depend primarily on how much education, recreation, and consultation he receives but rather on how he manages to live and relate with the other inmates who constitute his crucial and only meaningful world. It is what he *experiences* in this world: how he attains satisfactions from it, how he avoids its pernicious effects—how, in a word, he survives in it—which determines his adjustment and decides whether he will emerge from prison with intact or shattered integrity. Because this is true, an evaluation of the institution's contribution to the welfare of its inmates cannot realistically be made in terms of institutional statistics about hours of recreation, treatment, and education. The evaluation must rather be made in terms of how the prison authorities are affecting the total social climate—how successfully they are enabling the less hostile persons to advance themselves, how vigorously they are protecting these people from intimidation or exploitation by the more anti-social inmates, how effectively they curb and frustrate the lying, swindling, and covert violence which are always under the surface of the inmate social world.

The institution's custodial security system is thus directly related to inmate welfare. Most inmates will admit and even require the institution to assume this function. They understand that the metal detector which uncovers a file intended for an escape attempt will also detect a knife intended for the back of a friend. Inmates will privately express their relief at the construction of a segregation wing that protects them from the depredations of men who are outlaws even in the prison world. Much as they may complain of the disciplinary court which punishes them for their infractions, they are grateful for the swift and stern justice meted out to inmates who loot their cells. In short, these men realize, sometimes dimly, sometimes keenly, that a control system which is lax enough to permit widespread thievery and intimidation must eventually rob them of dignity and self-respect.

Relations between Welfare, Treatment, and Custody

Having emphasized the integral relationship between custody and inmate welfare, we must now clarify the distinction between welfare and treatment. This distinction, which is basic to understanding institution activities, has been summarized by the authors elsewhere:

> It is the tragedy of modern correction that the impulse to help has been confused with treatment and seems to require defense as treatment. One of the more ironic difficulties with this position is that when one makes "rehabilitation" the main justification for the humane handling of prisoners one has maneuvered oneself into a position potentially dangerous to the humanitarian viewpoint. What if humane treatment fails to rehabilitate—shall it then be abandoned? The isolated survivals of flogging and other "tough" techniques which still disgrace American penology remain to remind us that this is no mere academic question. The bleak fact is that just as the monstrous punishments of the eighteenth century failed to curtail crime, so the mere humane handling of the twentieth century has equally failed to do so.[2]

Correctional administration takes the position that the humane and decent handling of inmates is a distinct and independent end in itself and a moral obligation fully equal to that of treatment and rehabilitation,

[2] Lloyd W. McCorkle and Richard Korn, "Resocialization within Walls," *Annals of the American Academy of Political and Social Science*, 293:94–95, May 1954.

with which it ought to be neither linked nor confused. It is a right of the incorrigible as well as the reformable prisoners. This position draws further justification from the demonstrated fact that neither the misery of prison life nor the amelioration of it appears to have any reliably demonstrated effect on recidivism.

There are additional reasons for making the distinction between treatment and welfare. The expectations built around the welfare concept have in common the idea of easing distress and promoting pleasurable feelings. Though this purpose exists as an ultimate goal of treatment, it is recognized that the treatment process involves periods when the person treated must undergo stress and tension. During these transitional periods, when the individual is aided in the abandonment of his old ways of adjustment—ways to which he frequently clings with an irrational tenacity—his feelings are frequently the reverse of pleasurable and reassuring. Experience has demonstrated that people do not abandon long-established modes of adjustment, however inadequate, because of exhortation and reasonable argument. On the contrary, it is now recognized that individuals are able to abandon faulty behavior patterns only after repeated demonstrations of their failure. These demonstrations of failure inevitably generate anxiety and hostility, and a universal tendency among those treated is to blame those failures on others.

Whatever the personality disturbances or problems of repeated offenders, it may be agreed that their social adjustment is most often characterized by exploitation of and devious dealings with other people. It therefore becomes the goal of treatment to assist them in abandoning these ways of dealing with people—ways they bring with them into the prison. This process of abandoning old ways and learning new ones involves repeated demonstrations of the failure of those old ways, and it is indispensable that the treatment situation be one in which these ways are made to fail. In other words, the treatment situation must be one in which the devious are frustrated and exposed and the exploiters defeated in their attempts to exploit.

This objective is difficult to attain in a correctional institution, where the entire inmate society is organized to defend and perpetuate precisely those anti-social values and behaviors which the offenders bring into prison, and against which treatment must be aimed. This "organization against treatment" takes many forms—including the most aggressive and persistent attempts to have the treatment personnel behave as if their chief job were to make inmates feel happy and self-satisfied. If the treatment personnel violate this expectation—which, unfortunately, is frequently shared by other institutional officials and, on occasion, by the treatment personnel themselves—they bring down upon themselves the organized hostility of the inmate society. Should they, on the other hand, accept this inmate definition and organize their activities toward the superficial objective of making inmates feel contented and self-satisfied, they would not only defeat the objective of treatment but actually contribute to the further fixation of the anti-social behavior.

Given these requirements and the disadvantages ranged against them in the prison setting, it is possible to make some specific statements about the conditions under which a program of treatment is possible in a correctional institution:

1. Since detection, exposure, and frustration of anti-social behavior are essential to treatment, custodial control and vigilance are required.

2. Since the treatment process involves the generation of frequently intense anxieties, tensions, and hostilities, it is necessary for the institution as a whole to be strong and stable enough to tolerate these stresses without disruption.

3. Since custodial efficiency and treatment are therefore necessarily related, it is essential for the custodial and professional personnel to understand and support their respective roles and operations.

The Maintenance of Internal Discipline

Internal discipline in its positive sense may be defined as the orderliness and harmony of daily face-to-face relations. In a correctional institution it is as symptomatic of stability as the pulse rate is of the health of a living organism. The explanation of this symptomatic character of discipline is not far to seek. Orderly, harmonious relations between individuals and groups require the sharing of similar expectations about causes and effects, about how things are done, and about what will follow what in the ordinary sequence of daily events. These shared expectations are, in turn, dependent on the smooth running of the routines and procedures that first created them.

It is at this point that the relation between general efficiency and discipline becomes apparent. Any breakdown, any unannounced or senseless change in routine in any area of operation, must inevitably disrupt expectations and create confusion and ill-feeling. In a penal institution there are many pressures on officials to deviate from established routine, to take short cuts, to cut red tape, and to grant "special consideration" to "worthy cases." Widespread yielding to these influences replaces orderly functioning with a kind of haphazard day-to-day improvising and throws the door open to a chaos of competing pressures in which discipline, a product of reliable expectations, cannot long survive.

The maintenance of discipline in a penal institution requires, in addition to adherence to orderly procedures by officials, a relatively uniform conformity to these procedures by inmates. When inmates fail to conform, it is necessary for discipline to operate in its negative aspect as an inhibitor of deviations introduced by inmates. The *disciplinary court* is responsible for the disposition of reports of conduct infractions made against inmates by officials. The actions of the court are crucial to the disciplinary usages of the institution, and its procedures reflect the soundness of other operations. Efforts to "individualize" these procedures and to relate them to individual treatment programs may have the unanticipated consequence of weakening the social structure of the institution. The eyes of all inmates and custodial officers are on the disciplinary court, and loose, vague, contradictory, and inconsistent dispositions of charges preclude a stable atmosphere of inmate expectations around the definition and limits of orderly behavior.

Furthermore, unless the correctional officers have confidence in the court, they may apply their own informal punishments or rely on powerful inmates to assist in the maintenance of order. Both officers and inmates need to know that the same offense will result in the same punishment without regard for the status of the inmate charged. Only when these expectations have been confirmed and the uniformities in punishment clearly defined can due regard be given by the disciplinary court to the peculiarities of individual cases.

The Classification of Inmates

Most correctional institutions have a committee whose function is the classification of inmates. Usually inmate classifications are related to a program based on assumptions about why the inmate is in the institution and about the ability of the institution to change his behavior. The *Manual of Correctional Standards* defines classification as "the organized procedure by which diagnosis, treatment, planning and the execution of the treatment program are coordinated and focused on the individual case."[3] In general, classification proceeds by the following steps:

1. *Quarantine Period.* This period, which is sometimes called an admission-orientation period, may vary, but it usually extends over the first thirty days of the inmate's confinement. During this period he is interviewed by various staff members, from the identification officer to the psychiatrist. The impressions of these staff members are forwarded to a classification officer, who initiates a classification summary on the inmate. This summary, which contains identification data; a social history; and impressions and recommendations by medical, religious, educational, psychological, industrial, custodial, and psychiatric personnel, becomes a basic document on the inmate. Attached to it is a record of his activities in the institution—that is, custodial classification, job assignments, transfers, visits, etc. This section of the summary is often referred to as a progress report.

2. *Assignment to Job and Quarters.* After the initial quarantine period the inmate receives his *first classification* by the classification committee, which consists of representatives of all the major institutional departments and treatment services. At this time, after a discussion of the material in the *classification summary,* and possibly an interview with the inmate, a program is prescribed for the inmate by the assembled specialists. This program consists primarily of a determination of where the inmate will be assigned to work and what quarters he will occupy. The committee may, in addition, assign him to school, to see a counselor, etc.

3. *Reclassification.* Most institutions have a standard procedure for reviewing an inmate's program at stated intervals, usually six months or one year. Most have a procedure whereby inmates may request a change in their program. This phase of the process is called *reclassification.* Finally, the committee may review the summary and various conceptions of the inmate's progress and make a recommendation to the paroling authority. This phase of the program is called *planning for release.*

The *Manual of Correctional Standards* summarizes the goals of classification as follows:

As a systematic process, Classification implies three basic, interrelated

---

[3] *Manual of Correctional Standards,* p. 262.

procedures: (1) a complete evaluation of the individual with an analysis of the factors which influenced his development; (2) the use of this information as a basis of a realistic, integrated program; and (3) the organization of staff and establishment of methods whereby the rehabilitative facilities of the institution may be directed more effectively towards a solution of the individual's problem.[4]

Because operational guides are lacking, these objectives are easier to realize in manuals than in reality. Since much of this text has been devoted to the difficulties involved in the "complete evaluation of the individual" and to the "analysis of the factors which influenced his development" comment seems unnecessary. The danger of using these phrases is that they will be believed. When this happens, aspirations are discussed as realities and articles of faith replace the quest for knowledge.

The observations above are not intended to discount either the value of correctional classification or its contribution to the management and operation of institutions. The classification committee functions in many ways as the nerve center of the institution. Its functioning determines whether the institution is actually operating under integrated and centralized control or whether it is partially or wholly paralyzed.

The committee must make decisions that bear directly not only on the safekeeping and welfare of the inmates but also on the safety of the surrounding community. It is the committee which decides the custody status of the inmate, thereby determining whether or not the inmate shall be allowed outside the walls or be placed in a minimum-security institution, where opportunities for escape are multiplied. In deciding where an inmate shall work and live, the committee makes a decision that bears directly on the safety of all other inmates in the shops and cell blocks. Finally, after the initial decision has been made, it is the speed and accuracy of the committee's response to altered conditions— how quickly it becomes aware that a certain classification requires change, and how promptly this change is made—which decides whether the institution is actually determining events or is merely being carried along by them.

The importance of the committee as a focus of decision may be indirectly gauged by an analysis of inmate attempts to neutralize it. One technique of neutralization is a practice known as "assignment pending classification." Under this system an inmate is placed in a cell and given a job assignment—on the initiative of various combinations of

---

[4] *Ibid.*

persons known and unknown—often before his case comes to the attention of the committee. When the committee belatedly considers the case, its sole remaining function may be to ratify a decision already in effect. This practice opens the door to the decisive participation by sophisticated inmates of high status in the running of the institution. Indispensable or "key" inmates in various prison departments become, in effect, employment agents, with the power to recommend and effect the placement of friends and paying clients in jobs and quarters. The cumulative results of these practices became painfully apparent in the analysis of events leading to the prison riots of 1952–1955, when it was discovered that in some institutions the most dangerous and aggressive inmates occupied jobs affording them the greatest degree of mobility and access to strategic materials. A report from one institution, which was the scene of several riots, lists four decisive steps taken to restore the integrity of the classification process. These measures reflect the ways in which the process had been rendered ineffective:

1. All departments responsible for contributing information to the classification committee were required to report on inmates within thirty days of their arrival at the institution. This requirement eliminated backlogs and delays, the existence of which had provided formidable rationalizations for the practice of "assignment pending classification."

2. The practice of "assignment pending classification" was abolished.

3. The concept of "key man," which served to protect high-status inmates from loss of jobs, was repudiated. The committee now exercises the power to remove any inmate for any cause acceptable to itself, despite any claim of "indispensability" made on the inmate's behalf by an overly dependent or complacent official.

4. The classification committee, composed predominantly of civilian specialists, is independent in its decisions. Neither the warden nor the chief deputy has a vote on the committee, but either may take emergency action.

Employment Services

Institutional work programs were originally designed to teach inmates habits of industry while they were being disciplined. "Hard labor," it was argued, not only punished the inmate but aided his reformation, and the products of his industry contributed in some measure to his support. The history of prison labor reflects the rise and fall of various systems that have been used by the states and the federal government to employ prisoners. These systems have included contract labor, piece-price, lease, public account, state use, and public works.

Under the *contract* system the labor of prisoners was contracted for by an outside contractor, who supplied the raw materials and work supervisors and distributed the completed product. Under the *piece-price* system the contractor furnished the raw materials and paid the institution for the finished product. Under the *lease* system convicts were leased out to employers who (within statutory and regulatory limits) assumed complete control over them. Under the *public-account* system the state supervised the inmates and their labor and the product was sold on the open market. Under the *state-use* system, which has almost everywhere superseded these earlier systems, the state itself controls and supervises the employment of inmates, but the products of their labor may be sold only to government agencies. The public works system utilizes inmate labor in the construction and repair of public works, usually highways and roads.

External pressures to restrict prison labor have been a constant factor in its development. Most people agree that prisoners should work. People who own or work in a shoe manufacturing plant agree that they should make clothing—but not shoes. People who own or work in clothing manufacturing plants agree that they should make shoes—but not clothing. This is one area in which both capital and labor have been able to develop a common interest. With such powerful pressure groups interested in the restriction of prison labor, it is not surprising to find that useful employment for prisoners is one of the more serious problems faced by correctional administrators. The obvious evils and abuses of the contract, lease, and piece-price systems were responsible for much of this pressure. The continuance of this pressure is more difficult to understand at present, when most states have adopted the state-use system. Even within this system administrators have made many accommodations. In general, they have diversified correctional industries so as to supply only a fraction of the state's requirements in any one area, thus avoiding competition even with state business. (One exception to this is the manufacture of auto license tags.) Most state-use systems continue to operate unprofitable industries either as a service to state agencies or for the purpose of training inmates. But even these concessions have failed to satisfy pressure groups, and almost yearly attempts are made in the state legislatures to place some additional restrictions on the employment of prisoners.

In addition to industrial shops, most institutions operate farms. Farming has expanded as a result of the restriction of industrial opportunities, and it is likely to continue to do so in the future. The vegetable crops, milk, meat, etc., produced on prison farms can be consumed by the inmates and may reduce the institution's food budget. Prisoners are also employed in institutional maintenance programs. The prison community, like any other community, needs plumbers, painters, etc. Inmates must be fed, their clothing must be laundered and repaired. These activities account for the employment of large numbers of inmates.

Despite the best efforts of correctional administrators, prison idleness remains one of the most serious problems they face. Whether or not one agrees with Sanford Bates' conclusion that inmate idleness is a direct cause of riots, there is little reason to object to the remainder of his observation on inmate inactivity:

> The enforced idleness of a substantial percentage of able-bodied adult men and women in our prisons is one of the greatest anomalies of modern prison administration. It militates against every constructive element of a prison program. It is one of the direct causes of the tensions which burst forth in riot and disorder.[5]

The problems associated with the provision of adequate work opportunities have resulted in a general deterioration of the prison work situation, with important consequences for the inmate, the prison official, and society. This deterioration has been graphically described in the *Manual of Correctional Standards*:

> Unless we can contrive to solve the prison labor problem we must abandon the idea that we are operating institutions of correction and reform and that adult prisoners can be released from such institutions better and not worse than when they entered. Unless a large portion of the sentence of the prisoner can be utilized in plain hard work with habit-forming and other training values, the expenses of his detention, education, medical care, and other services will have been largely wasted; he is almost certain to continue as a parasite or as a menace to society instead of the self-respecting and self-supporting citizen he might have become.
>
> Prison industries have, generally speaking, been a dismal failure in realizing their fundamental purpose, that of fitting the released prisoner to take his place in society as an industrious citizen, by developing in him firm habits of work and self-support and giving him the knowledge

[5] *A Statement Concerning Causes, Preventive Measures, and Methods of Controlling Prison Riots and Disturbances* (New York: American Prison Association, 1953), p. 10.

and skill of a trade. Surveys have shown the almost total inefficiency of the industrial system of our institutions: one hundred prisoners crowded into shops where forty to sixty would more than adequately perform the required tasks; two or three hours of work spread over an eight- or ten-hour day with the balance spent in idleness, unsupervised handicraft activities, and "conniving" against the policies and regulations of the institution; workmanship not comparable to that found in even the poorest quality merchandise; and a financial statement which clearly indicates the waste of material, equipment, man power, and other resources.[6]

The following comment on the prison work situation is also relevant:

> The freedom from the necessity of earning a living in prison introduces a striking difference between the requirements of material success within and without the walls. A significantly different configuration of traits and aptitudes acquires value, some of which represent direct reversals of those developed outside. In prison the direct relationship between work done and material value received has largely broken down. The relationship between individual productivity and personal status is even more markedly broken down. From a sophisticated inmate's point of view this relationship seems to become a negative one. Strategic placement and effective informal connections rather than individual productivity are the crucial methods for the attainment of material goods.
>
> As a consumer-producer, the inmate lives and trades in two economic worlds: he is a barterer in the informal and illicit inmate market and a wage earner in the prison work system. The contrast between his behavior in these two worlds is most revealing. As a trader in the informal inmate barter system, he is resourceful, ingenious, and usually cooperative: there is a kind of "Better Business Bureau" tradition which is generally effective in encouraging the liquidation of debts. As a wage earner in the prison labor system he is, by contrast, encouraged to be nonproductive, dilatory, and contentious, articulating his work relations with the institution in terms of declarations of rights and grievances. In many modern institutions, the "workers' rights" of inmates go beyond the most extreme of those advanced by organized labor on the outside.
>
> The following is a summary of the sophisticated inmate's view of his economic rights—those attitudes and values concerning work most frequently articulated to institutional officials by leading spirits of the inmate social system:
>
> The fundamental authority in defining the inmate's job obligation is tradition. Inmates are to be required to work only so much as the tradition conerning given jobs requires. Any departure from these

[6] *Manual of Correctional Standards*, p. 273.

traditions—especially those departures in the direction of increased work for the same pay—are violations of the inmates' work rights and justify obstructionism. (In a certain penal institution, for instance, "tradition" had established that one inmate lay out all the salt cellars on the mess tables while a different inmate was required to lay out the pepper.)

Increases in the amount of time or output may only be required under extraordinary circumstances and merit increased pay or special benefits, since these added efforts are "favors" extended by the inmates. The inmates have a right to resent and take reprisals against any of their number who "show the rest up" by doing more than the traditional amount of work. These hostile attitudes toward more energetic inmates effectively condemn them to the deteriorating work patterns enforced by the group. Any inmate who performs more than the usual expectation must prove that he has received a special award—usually food or informal permission to evade some institutional rule.

The providing of jobs is a duty of prison officials and a right, rather than a privilege, of inmates. Once assigned to a job, there are only a limited number of legitimate reasons for which an inmate may be "fired." None of these legitimate reasons includes adherence to the accepted job tradition. Thus an inmate rarely feels that he may rightfully be dismissed for laziness, if he performs only the usual amount of work traditionally required, despite an increase in institutional needs, since the tradition protects him from any definition of himself as lazy. Inmates generally feel that the fact that they are paid less than comparable civilian workers entitles them to produce less.

The total result of the prevalence of these attitudes has been to reduce "imprisonment at hard labor" to a euphemism existing chiefly in the rhetoric of sentencing judges and in the minds of the uninformed public. The inmate social system not only has succeeded in neutralizing the laboriousness of prison labor in fact, but also has more or less succeeded in convincing prison authorities of the futility of expecting any improvement in output. Responding to a multitude of pressures within and without the prison, most institutional work supervisors have adopted patterns of expectations which are largely supportive of the inmate position.[7]

Educational Services

Most state, federal, and many county correctional institutions provide some type of academic instruction. In the absence of a separate

[7] McCorkle and Korn, op. cit., pp. 91–92.

school on the grounds, a section of the institution may be designated as a school, or areas in the institution may be used as classrooms. Frequently correspondence courses are offered. The same institution may combine several of these features in its educational program. In addition, institutions may have classroom instruction related to trade or vocational training. Recently there has been a trend to offer classroom instruction in human relations, social adjustment, etc. The type, quality, and quantity of these programs vary from one type of institution to another. There is also considerable variation among institutions of the same type, apparently related to the individual institution's philosophy and tradition. In general, the correctional school programs attempt to provide literacy training for illiterates, primary schooling, and, in some cases, high school courses. In addition, special courses of various kinds are offered to inmates with specific academic or vocational interests.

Most institutions also provide library services for inmate use. These services vary with the institution and the funds available to buy books. In connection with this service "Great Books" discussion groups are often formed.

The education department may also have responsibility for producing inmate shows directed and acted by inmates. Also, and frequently in connection with these shows, various instrumental and choral combinations are formed. Music courses which are aimed at developing inmate aptitudes in the reading, understanding, and playing of music are very popular.

Much has been written about, and many hopes have been expressed for, educational programs in correctional institutions.[8] These hopes seem more related to the American faith in education than to any objective analysis of the impact of these programs on the lives of inmates. Most inmates are school failures, have unrealistic conceptions of their potentialities as students, and, after their initial enthusiasm for correctional education diminishes, drop out of school if permitted to by the institutional authorities.

Counseling Services

Most institutions have some type of formal counseling services. These services are usually located in the social service department, the psychology department, or a special counseling department. The persons

---

[8] For a comprehensive survey of the history and present status of education in correctional institutions, see Chenault Price, "Education," in Paul Tappan, ed., *Contemporary Correction* (New York: McGraw-Hill Book Company, Inc., 1951), pp. 224–237.

who function as counselors have a wide variety of backgrounds and perform a wide range of activities. The background requirements and activities of persons in this position reflect local traditions, the organizational structure of the institution or department of correction, and the philosophy, program, age group, etc., of the institution. In general, counseling services have as their objective the direct and confidential handling of inmate problems of personal adjustment. The counselor seeks to provide a positive human relationship to which the inmate can turn. Because the wide range of problems presented to counselors defies any but the most general classification, the following categories provide only a rough outline of counseling objectives.

1. *Chronic Problems of Institutional Adjustment.* There is a numerically small group of inmates whose chronic personal difficulties create a disproportionately large and preoccupying need for official attention. Falling uncertainly between that group of inmates requiring psychiatric attention and another group which requires constant disciplinary handling, these inmates may be able to make a marginal adjustment without drifting into psychotic outbreaks or flagrant breaches of conduct. One mission of the counseling service is to maintain these inmates, however precariously, between one and the other of these points. In many cases this may be accomplished merely by providing a readily sympathetic ear for the outpouring of grievances. In some cases, as few as one or two interviews a month are sufficient.

2. *Problems Arising Out of Personal Conflicts between Inmates.* The tight physical compression of institutional life lends a tension to human relationships which is somewhat analogous to the agitation of gas molecules under pressure. The inevitable frustrations of imprisonment and the relative lack of safe channels for venting emotion frequently cause minor problems of personal interaction to expand into violent crises. This inherently difficult situation is aggravated by the inmate "code," which invariably weighs the advantage in favor of the stronger, more criminally acculturated inmates, and tends to prevent the weaker inmates from appealing to the world of officials.

The noncustodial character of the counselor's role, together with the assured privacy of his mediations, can provide an effective channel for the handling of these disputes before they reach an explosive stage. When the counselor is able to reach the disputants before either has committed an "intolerable" act or reached out for help from other inmates, it is often possible to settle the problem.

3. *Problems Connected with Work and Housing.* The counseling service is frequently called upon by the classification committee to make

special studies of inmates who present work or housing problems. The usefulness of this aspect of the counselor's job is increased if inmates realize that the counselor cannot be used as a device through which to avoid work responsibilities or attain devious goals.

Other Services

In addition to the services already described, correctional institutions provide religious, psychological, medical, and dental services for inmates. Most institutions have either organized or unorganized recreational programs. Recreation may be under the supervision of a special department, but it is most likely to be a part of the education department. Various volunteer agencies, some of which provide financial help, may supplement the activities through which correctional institutions hope to attain their objectives.

Evaluations of general correctional programs as well as specific services or procedures often make the assumption that the important and significant relationships of inmates are with the formal institutional program and official personnel. When this belief is replaced by an awareness that it is the inmates' relationships with one another that determine the meaning of the correctional experience, a different type of evaluation becomes necessary. Institutional programs and services must then be evaluated in terms of their total effect on the world in which the prisoner lives—that is, on the inmate social system.

Evaluations of correctional programs that proceed from this assumption are more difficult to make, and their results are frequently less comforting both to the specialist in correction and to the public. This type of evaluation has, however, one important advantage. The specialist and correctional administrator is relieved of his commitment to unrealistic promises about the "rehabilitative" value of a specific program. The defense of correctional programs can rest, instead, on the more secure ground of general social values. The door is then open for new experiments and critical appraisals.

It is difficult, of course, for the specialist to confess his ignorance in the face of public pressure for simple answers to vague questions. Unfortunately, unless a state of dissatisfied and self-confessed uncertainty is acknowledged, progress in correction is likely to be measured by efforts to give new labels to historical slogans.

The World of Officials

The Inadequacy of Formal Descriptions
of Correctional Functions

THE FORMAL ADMINISTRATIVE STRUCTURE OF A CORRECTIONAL INSTITU-
tion can be comprehended in a brief glance at its table of organization
(see p. 469). This table reveals a series of bureaucratically arranged
positions, with the warden at the top and the formal lines of authority
radiating downward from his position. A more penetrating glance at
the social structure of this organization reveals an ongoing complex of
processes that can be neither described nor remotely anticipated by a
static enumeration of formal roles and powers. In addition to their formal
tables of organization, most institutions provide their employees with
manuals of operating procedures, which describe the duties and functions of each category of personnel. Again, any attempt to base an
understanding of *what these employees actually do* exclusively or largely
on the formal manual of operations is highly misleading.

Operational Goals and Personal Objectives
of Correctional Workers

The operational goals of the various categories of correctional personnel are quickly stated. The custodian has aptly been called a *keeper;*

it is his mission to keep the inmates inside the institution and to keep them there safely and securely, in a manner compatible with current social values concerning humane treatment of prisoners. The professional personnel—doctors, dentists, nurses, psychiatrists, psychologists, social workers, educators, etc.—are charged with the primary responsibility of maintaining the medical and psychological welfare of the inmates. The maintenance and service personnel are charged with the upkeep of the institution's physical plant and with the supply of essential goods and services at standards set by higher authority and general public policy. The work supervisors are formally charged with the responsibility of training and supervising the inmate workers assigned to them.

These official objectives more or less define the minimal public demands made upon the various types of institutional employees; they define what the public expects and must, at all events, be told. In this last sense, they also define the safe limits of official candor, since no official can safely admit neglecting or violating them.

In addition to these objectives, correctional workers have personal goals which cannot be left out of the analysis. In common with most workers elsewhere, correctional employees want to get ahead. The guard looks forward to his raises and promotions; the work supervisor may seek to advance himself to director of prison industries, the file clerk to the position of chief clerk. Again like most employees elsewhere, the correctional worker tries to make his job more pleasant, less laborious, more endurable. There have always been two general ways of accomplishing this: by becoming more efficient or by shirking and becoming slipshod and neglectful of unpleasant chores. The choice between these general modes depends on the personality of the individual worker, on the effectiveness of supervision, and on the general morale of the organization. Finally, the correctional worker, like any other human being, must defend himself against threat. The existence of dangers severe enough to threaten the physical or psychological integrity of the individual can force him to subordinate all other goals to the primary one of self-defense.

To this list of personal objectives there must be added another, which is simultaneously so fundamental and so subtle as to interpenetrate all the others. For every individual there is a group of other people whose opinion of him is extremely important—whose way of looking at him vitally affects the way he views himself. The need of a person to be liked, respected—to be considered important by those who are important to him—probably is universal. To ask the question: *Why* does John do this? is, in part at least, to ask: For *whom* does he do this—whose approval does he desire, whose disapproval does he want to avoid? Admittedly, this question is more critical in personal relations than it is in relations between employer and employee, where the primary bond is economic. Nevertheless, in those occupations which are hazardous and in which the employee may at any time be called on to take risks or undergo stress for which economic reward alone provides insufficient motivation, the character of the employee's "primary audience" instantly becomes important. It is on these occasions that the worker asks: Whom am I doing this for?

The correctional worker, like the fireman, the policeman, the soldier, and others in stressful or hazardous jobs, may at any time be placed in a situation where decision-making suddenly becomes dependent on the way this question is answered. Conclusions emerging from wartime research in problems of military morale have suggested that in dangerous situations, the individual's most important "audience" is to be found among his immediate associates.[1]

Now, it frequently happens that the institutional correctional worker is in most continuous working contact with inmates. Unlike the soldier, the individual guard, shop supervisor, or prison doctor works more or less by himself, in his own local area of assignment—one to a section of a cell block, one to a shop, etc. He sees his fellow workers in the dining room, at the end of his shift, at meetings—or during emergencies when the situation gets "too hot" for one man to handle by himself. In the ordinary course of events—including merely "routine" emergencies—he is expected to function more or less alone, and any tendency to depend on his superiors or colleagues is noted as a deficiency in self-reliance. Thus his isolation is further enforced by a tradition that places relatively greater stress on personal accountability than it does on cooperation and collective responsibility. Unfortunately, however, if the correctional worker ordinarily cannot permit himself to depend on the help of his colleagues, he cannot dispense with the cooperation of his inmates. It is this condition that renders his work situation inherently paradoxical.

On the one hand, he is called on to enforce regulations many of which are objectionable to the large majority of inmates. His success as

---

[1] It was found, for example, that the battlefield morale of the individual American soldier was much more dependent on his relations within his own small unit than on his more formal, remote relations with superior officers or larger military units or on his impersonal commitments to the war effort. See S. A. Stouffer *et al., The American Soldier,* Studies in Social Psychology in World War II, Vols. I and II (Princeton: Princeton University Press, 1949).

a correctional worker will in large part be measured by his effectiveness in producing compliance with these regulations. On the other hand, unless he is able to elicit the cooperation of the inmates, he cannot effectively perform the essential nondisciplinary functions of his job. (In most institutions, the "housekeeping" responsibilities of the prison guard far outnumber his purely custodial functions.) In order to obtain cooperation, he must gain the respect and good will of a working majority of inmates in his local area. Failure to do this makes him dependent on the threat of force and punishment—which immediately decreases his reputation not only among the inmates but among his colleagues, who may be called on to "pull his chestnuts out of the fire."

Thus, even his status among his fellow-workers is largely dependent on his relations with his inmates. Again, of the two possible sources of his "primary audience"—the society of his colleagues and the society of his inmates—the correctional worker is significantly more dependent on the latter. In effect, in order to succeed with his co-workers, he must first succeed with the inmates. This dependency, moreover, is less than mutual. In order for inmates to succeed with each other, it is not at all necessary that they win the cooperation of officials. There are many occasions on which defiance or covert exploitation of the authorities is much more advantageous socially. The situation boils down to this: The inmate can frequently win points in his social world by refusing to cooperate. The correctional worker who withholds his cooperation and good will wins points nowhere.

Conflicts between Personal and Operational Goals

The work behavior of employees is crucially related to the harmony or conflict of their operational objectives with their personal goals. Efficiently run organizations owe their efficiency to their success in relating these goals harmoniously, motivating the employee to seek both personal satisfaction and vocational advancement through sound job performance. Conversely, most organizational inefficiency may be traced to the conflict of operational goals with one or more of the several personal objectives we have discussed. The conflict may express itself in various ways: by the emergence of cutthroat rivalry between employees struggling for favor, by the emergence of large-scale shirking and "on-the-job-absenteeism," by the emergence of anxiety, with resulting buck-passing and a progressive paralysis of decision among those whose behavior has become dominated by motives of self-protection. The prison work situation is peculiarly vulnerable to each of these forms of breakdown.

A primary focus of conflict has been the relationship between custodial and professional personnel. This conflict, which has a long history, has virtually become a standard fixture on the contemporary correctional scene. It will be described in greater detail in the chapter dealing with problems of treatment; at this point we shall merely cite its probable major causes. McKendrick has discussed these in the following terms:

1. Members of the professional staff fail to recognize the essentially totalitarian structure of the prison community. The nature of the community limits and challenges professional services. The custodial and administrative personnel fail to recognize the limitations which a totalitarian community places upon the professional employees and expect the therapist to be successful despite the restrictions of the prison community.

2. Professional personnel fail to accommodate their techniques to the prison community. It may require a considerable expenditure of time and effort to develop techniques for the application of specializations such as education, mental treatment, and vocational training in prison communities. When professional personnel fail to grasp the significance of the prison community and seek to adapt the prison to their own specialization, conflict always results. Custodial and administrative personnel fail to make changes suitable for the full inclusion of rehabilitative programs.

3. The professional employee is frequently contemptuous of customs and traditions without understanding their utilitarian role in security. The experienced custodial employee is inclined to be cautious in his acceptance of new and unproved technologies for reform.

4. The professionally trained employee often underestimates the intelligence of custodial employees who have been less exposed to formal education, and the custodial employee often looks upon the professional employee with suspicion, in much the same way that the worker looks at management.

5. The professional employee frequently approaches his prison assignment with a deterministic theory of behavior. This leads to an impractical emphasis on positivism unsuited to the classically constructed prison community. The custodial employee is often limited by retributive concepts which do not mix well even with the most conservative principles of reformation.[2]

[2] Charles McKendrick, "Custody and Discipline," in Paul Tappan, *Contemporary Correction* (New York: McGraw-Hill Book Company, Inc., 1951), pp. 159–160.

The Correctional Worker as an Employer of Inmates

The custody-treatment controversy has been widely discussed in the literature, but other sources of friction between correctional employees have received almost no attention. One of the most significant of these arises because of the peculiar situation of the institutional worker in his role of employer. Though the extent varies, most prison officials are in one way or another employers of prisoners. The chaplain needs his clerk and his altar boys. The prison doctor requires attendants and nurses' aides. The supervisor of maintenance needs inmates to help him with repair work. The cell-block officer needs his assistants. Each of these officials is to some extent in competition for efficient and dependable employees, and each, in one way or another, dangles certain inducements and informal advantages before desirable inmates.

The inmates, for their part, are well aware of the informal competition for their services. From the prisoners' point of view, all institutional jobs are ranged along a scale of personal advantage. Foremost among these are assignments involving opportunities to affect the decision-making process. The inmate asks: Who are the most influential officials? How open are they to manipulation? Even if he is not actually in a position to influence an important official, the inmate's mere working contact with him may be a source of advantage, especially if the job permits access to confidential information or advance knowledge of moves affecting other inmates. Prisoners working in key jobs are constantly being approached to "fix something up" and they frequently sell their "influence," taking credit for moves about which they have advance knowledge.

Every assignment in the institution has special advantages and disadvantages with reference to specific objectives. Inmates bent on escape, for example, will try to get jobs giving them access to strategic locations or materials. The special opportunities inherent in desirable jobs may be divided into two general categories: (1) opportunities for "legitimate" graft; and (2) opportunities for illegitimate graft.

Inmates working in the prison kitchen and dining room are usually somewhat better fed than other inmates (legitimate graft) and are in a strategic position to steal food for sale (illegitimate graft). Similarly, inmates working in the prison laundry or clothing storeroom rarely need worry about the fit, cleanliness, or quality of their clothing. Inmate clerks are traditionally good sources of stationery, office supplies—and information.

Depending on the efficiency of institutional control measures, the possibilities for illegitimate graft may outweigh the special privileges ("legitimate" graft) which are informally tolerated. Inmates working in the prison hospital are in a strategic position to steal drugs and other valued medical supplies. Inmates working with hard metals are good sources of knives. The most pernicious kind of special privilege, however, is psychological in character and has little directly to do with anything material.

Ultimately the most valued and negotiable commodity obtainable from an official is the status and reputation of being a valued "key man." In order to achieve this status, the intelligent inmate will attempt to make himself indispensable to his official employer, relieving him of burdensome tasks, advising him on delicate matters, working overtime—and showing every other indication of devotion and trustworthiness.

Not the least unfortunate result of this dependency is that it permits the official to rationalize his abdication of authority as a therapeutic measure. He is "showing the inmate he can be trusted," he is "getting the inmate used to responsibility." Neither of these general objectives is open to dispute, especially if the official comes to believe them himself and is able to defend his irresponsibility with sincerity. Once enmeshed in a personal relationship with "his" inmate, the official may quickly become blind to the fact that his own authority is being used by his employee for personal advantage. Others, outside the charmed circle, may call this fact to his attention, earning his resentment as their reward. Observers outside the institutional situation are little aware of the large extent to which conflicts between correctional personnel are caused by arguments over favored inmates. Once committed to his "key man," the official comes to identify him with his own department and may interpret any criticism of the inmate as a personal attack on himself. At this point, defense of the inmate becomes something of a psychological necessity. In the process, any vestige of real authority and therapeutic influence over the inmate is lost.

At bottom, then, the principal hazard of institutional employment for the correctional official is the danger that his "primary audience" may shift from the collective of his colleagues and superiors to selected members of the inmate population. Whether this result is brought about by his overdependence on inmates, by his fear of them, by his naive acceptance of their simulated support, or merely by his personal warmheartedness, the consequences are usually the same. At some point, his evaluations of himself and his job functions cease to reflect the definitions of the larger society and come, instead, to reflect the opposed purposes of the inmate social system.

The Custodian

The guard-inmate interact situation is one of the most vehemently discussed and least explored areas in penology. There has recently been a beginning in research in this area. Walter Reckless had several of his graduate students explore the attitudes of inmates toward prison personnel.[3] In one of these studies, E. J. Galway worked out a standardized terminal interview which he held privately and individually with 275 consecutively released inmates just prior to their release from the U. S. Reformatory at Chillicothe. Among other questions, Galway asked the departing inmates to indicate by name which staff member knew them best. The 275 inmates nominated a total of 125 different staff members, who constituted 40 per cent of the entire staff on the payroll at that time. The inmates' nominations were distributed by branch of service as follows: custody—108; trade-training—39; farm—32; industry—18; maintenance—18; classification and parole (social workers)—14; clerical—13; education—9; medical—5; chaplain—2. Galway concluded: "It is significant that the personnel which the subjects choose as knowing them best came by and large from that portion of the personnel known in less progressive correctional institutions as the guard."

Bright, in a study of inmates at the Ohio Penitentiary, found evidence to support the proposition that lower-paid nonprofessional staff members have more impact on inmates than do the higher-paid professional staff members. This conclusion was supported by the inmates' nomination of the staff members they liked best and of the staff members who had done something for them.

Information about the prison guard usually derives from two sources: the writings of inmates and the works of criminologists and penologists, whose impressions seem to be largely colored by inmate reports. These sources have contributed to the creation of a stereotype which is highly resistive to modification by fact. In order to realize the resistance of this picture to change, one need only turn to the pages of

[3] The authors are indebted to Professor Walter Reckless for making available this unpublished material.

a representative contemporary textbook. In spite of the fact that most prison guards are now selected by civil service examination, a widely used text asserts the following in a section dealing with the modern prison:

> Books by students of the prison problem and by prison inmates attest to the fact that most prison posts fall to a rather inferior grade of men, usually through the spoils system of politics. To make matters worse, salaries are low and the nature of the work is most unattractive to persons with any ambition at all, so that few competent persons apply for custodial jobs.[4]

The Guard as a Historical Figure in Penology

Present conceptions of the guard are inextricably involved with the history of penal reform; in the strictest sense, the present status of the guard cannot be understood without detailed reference to its historical origins.

Late in the nineteenth century the public became increasingly aware of the vile and brutalizing conditions obtaining in its prisons. A target figure in this mobilization of public opinion was the prison guard. The picture of the sadistic and illiterate guard tyrannizing over the hapless inmate captured the public imagination, and by the late 1880's and early 1890's the reaction in this country finally reached the levels of official government action. Within a generation, public sympathy for prisoners and public abhorrence of brutality brought about a revolution in thinking, requiring enlightened men to demand that their prisons be centers of treatment rather than places of punishment. In the gathering momentum of social indignation, prisoners were more and more viewed as the martyrs—rather than the enemies—of society, while bars, walls, and guards became symbols of social injustice. In time, the custodial safeguards designed for the protection of the citizenry fell into disrepute, and a reversion of thinking tended to view them as unnecessary repressions or, at best, necessary evils. So vivid was the picture, so effectively did it begin to transform the reality, that within another generation the picture was largely outmoded. However, in the curious way that pictures have of capturing men's minds, the image tended to persist—and persists still, long after the reality has changed. Despite the administrative revolution which increasingly liberated prisoners within the walls while

---

[4] Harry Elmer Barnes and Negley K. Teeters, *New Horizons in Criminology*, 2d ed. (New York: Prentice-Hall, Inc., 1951), p. 427.

simultaneously reducing the power of the custodian, the vivid image of the brutal guard persists. The persistence of this prejudice, which has reduced the prestige of the custodial officer not only in the public mind but in the prisoner's as well, is doubly tragic in view of the fact that prestige has become, in many institutions, the major remaining resource of intramural control.

One of the consequences of the liberalization of prison conditions was a gradual shift of internal control from the official authorities to the organized inmate population. During the period in which this transfer of actual internal authority was taking place (accelerated here and there by such officially sanctioned power transfers as the Inmate Welfare League and various other "self-government" movements), two ominous developments in the society outside the walls combined to worsen the situation within. During the past fifty years, the rate and the violence of crime have increased markedly. Each year society has sent increasing numbers of more violent and more professional recidivists into its increasingly overcrowded prisons. This development has been matched by another equally disquieting one. Despite the fact that enlightened social leaders insisted on defining their prisons as centers of treatment, the decades which saw a marked increase in the rate of crime and recidivism brought forth no effective theory or techniques of rehabilitative treatment. Nevertheless, in an era which actually accomplished the virtual neutralization of the custodian, many professional penologists continued in their books and articles to inveigh against the "repressions" of prison life and against the stubborn obstructionism of unyielding, excessively coercive guards and wardens. Actually, the custodian had yielded and accommodated more completely than the early reformers had ever dreamed, and more than the modern custodian would ever admit.

Aspects of the Guard-Inmate Relationship

Numerous factors, tangible and intangible, go into the many-sided relationship of the guard and the inmate. The tangible determinants are quickly stated: both in space and in time, the prisoner and his guard are inseparable—they are never free of the surveillance of the other.

In many ways, the guard is a prisoner of the special necessities and tensions of his custodial mission. Unlike the prisoner, the custodian's confinement carries with it an added burden of responsibility. While the inmate can relax into prison routine, the guard must constantly keep alert for the nonroutine emergency; he must, if he is to be efficient, respond not only to the actual but to the possible. In a sense, he must maintain himself in a state of artificial tension geared to the possibility of crises in which the initiative is in the hands of the inmates. This artificial tension is maintained, in part, by imposing on the guard an hour-to-hour activity schedule built largely around potential emergencies. He must continually count inmates he "knows" are present; he must continually check for fire hazards in the absence of fires; he must examine cells as if every nook and cranny were bulging with contraband. Thus his entire attention is geared to escape, violence, and violation of rules; and he lives in a world defined by frightening as-ifs. As a human being, with certain human limits to the tolerance of tension, he must make some personal, individual compromise between taking these possibilities too seriously—and not taking them seriously enough.

In addition to the tangible determinants of the guard's situation—the times, places, physical conditions, and rules of work—there is a host of highly complex intangible factors with which he must deal:

> In order to preserve his status as a symbol of authority, the custodian must surround himself with a social distance which prevents the realities of his weaknesses from becoming apparent to the inmates. The realities of his situation are most unfavorable. He is dependent in part on inmate personnel for the physical mechanics of operating his wing. He is also continuously exposed to numerous techniques of deception. However, these tangible weaknesses do not form the main hazards threatening his effective functioning. These are more intangible and, as such, difficult to detect and even more difficult to control.
>
> The inmate social system has developed techniques to exploit the custodian's psychological as well as his physical vulnerability. These techniques are aimed at a reduction of the social distance protecting his role as guard, outflanking it with a personal relationship, and exploiting that relationship for the inmates' own purposes. Once the relationship between keeper and inmate is on a man-to-man basis, the dependency and vulnerability of the custodian become apparent. "Obeying orders" becomes transformed into "doing the guard a favor." When obedience undergoes this transformation, reciprocity becomes operative, "one favor deserves another." Should a keeper now refuse to return the favor, the inmate feels it within his right to become hostile because of the keeper's "ingratitude." Once the Pandora's box of special favoritism is open it cannot be shut again without a painful and dangerous demonstration of how fickle are the personal relations between those improbable "friends"—the keeper and his prisoner. Neither can be loyal without violating the principles and risking the rejection of the groups which define their roles and set the limits of mutual accommodation. Once

these limits are passed, and it is usually the inmate who attempts to pass them, one or the other must balk. This is interpreted as a "betrayal" which terminates the relationship and transforms the friends into enemies. In the process, both become discredited by their own groups—which have now victoriously redemonstrated the insurmountability of the mutual antagonism.

It thus becomes apparent that a breakdown of the social distance between the inmate and his keeper must, sooner or later, result in the exploitation of one by the other and the ultimate degradation of one or both. It is at this point that the most hazardous consequences of this breakdown emerge. Having lost, through a personal relationship, a large measure of the control which had previously been protected by his formal, impersonal role, the keeper is far less able to cope with the powerful and eventually antagonistic emotions which that personal relationship unleashed. A violent resolution of the conflict now becomes increasingly probable, unless harmony can be re-established by a new capitulation or coerced by a convincing show of force.[5]

Gresham Sykes, in an illuminating article dealing with the corruption of authority and rehabilitation, has listed three general modes by which this corruption takes place:

Corruption through Friendship

There are many pressures in American culture to "be nice," to "be a good Joe," and the guard in the maximum security prison is not immune. The guard is constantly exposed to a sort of moral blackmail in which the first signs of condemnation or estrangement are immediately countered by the inmates with the threat of ridicule or hostility. In this complex interplay, the guard does not always start from a position of determined opposition to "being friendly." The cell-block officer holds an intermediate post in a bureaucratic structure between top prison officials—his captains, lieutenants, and sergeants—and the prisoners in his charge. Like many "unlucky" Pierres always in the middle, the guard is caught in a conflict of loyalties. He resents many of the actions of his superiors—the reprimands, the lack of ready appreciation, the incomprehensible order—and in the inmates he finds willing sympathizers; they too claim to suffer from the unreasonable caprice of power. Furthermore, the guard in many cases is marked by a basic ambivalence towards the crinimal under his supervision. Although condemned by society through its instrument the law, many criminals are a "success" in

[5] Lloyd W. McCorkle and Richard R. Korn, "Resocialization within Walls," *Annals of the American Academy of Political and Social Science,* 293:93–94, May 1954.

terms of a mundane system of values which places a high degree of prestige on notoriety and wealth even though won by devious means; the poorly paid guard may be gratified to associate with a famous racketeer. This ambivalence in the correctional officer's attitudes towards his captives cuts deeper than a discrepancy between the inmate's position in the power structure of the prison and his possible status in a *sub rosa* stratification system. There may also be a discrepancy between the judgments of society and the guard's work-a-day values as far as the "criminality" of the inmate is concerned. The bookie, the man convicted of deserting his wife, the inmate who stridently proclaims his innocence and is believed—the guard often believes that these men are not seriously to be viewed as criminals, as desperate prisoners to be rigidly suppressed.

Corruption through Reciprocity

To a large extent the guard is dependent on inmates for the satisfactory performance of his duties and, like many figures of authority, the guard is evaluated in terms of the conduct of the men he controls—a troublesome, noisy, dirty cell-block reflects on the guard's ability to "handle prisoners" and this forms an important component of the merit rating which is used as the basis for pay raises and promotions. A guard cannot rely on the direct application of force to achieve compliance, for he is one man against hundreds; and if he continually calls for additional help he becomes a major problem for the short-handed prison administration. A guard cannot easily rely on threats of punishment, for he is dealing with men who are already being punished near the limits permitted by society; and if the guard insists on constantly using the last few negative sanctions available to the institution—the withdrawal of recreation facilities and other privileges, solitary confinement, or loss of good time—he again becomes burdensome to the prison administration which realizes that its apparent dominance rests on some degree of uncoerced cooperation. The guard, then, is under pressure to achieve a smoothly running cell-block not with the stick but with the carrot, but here again his stock of rewards is limited. One of the best "offers" he can make is ignoring minor offenses or making sure that he never places himself in a position to discover infractions of the rules.

Aside from winning routine and superficial compliance, the guard has another "favor" to be secured from inmates which makes him willing to forego strict enforcement of prison regulations. Many prisons have experienced a riot in which the tables are momentarily turned and the captives hold sway over their *quondam* captors. The guard knows that he may someday be a hostage and that his life may turn on the settling of old accounts; a fund of good will becomes a valuable form of insurance.

Corruption through Default

Finally, much of the guard's authority tends to be destroyed by the innocuous encroachment of inmates on the guard's duties. Making out reports, checking cells at the periodic count, locking and unlocking doors—in short, all the minor chores which the guard is called on to perform during the course of the day—may gradually be transferred into the hands of inmates whom the guard has come to trust. The cell-block "runner," formally assigned the tasks of delivering mail, house-keeping duties, and similar jobs, is of particular importance in this respect. Inmates in this position function in a manner analogous to that of the company clerk in the Armed Forces and at times they may wield great power and influence in the life of the cell-block. For reasons of indifference, laziness, or naivete, the guard may find much of his authority whittled away; nonfeasance, rather than malfeasance, has corrupted the theoretical guard-inmate relationship.

Authority, like a woman's virtue, once lost is hard to regain. The measures to break up an established pattern of abdication need be much more severe than those required to stop the first steps in the corruption of authority. In the first place, a guard assigned to a cell-block in which a large portion of control has been transferred in the past from the correctional officer to the inmates is faced with the weight of precedent; it requires a good deal of moral courage on his part to face the gibes and aggression of inmates who fiercely defend the legitimacy of the status quo established by custom. In the second place, if the guard himself has allowed his authority to be subverted, he may find his attempts to rectify his error checked by a threat from the inmates to send a "snitch-kite"—an anonymous note—to the guard's superior officers explaining his past derelictions in detail; this simple form of blackmail may on occasion be sufficient to maintain the existing balance of power.[6]

Problems of Recruitment and Training

Not the least of the evils of the old prison system was the political method of recruiting personnel. The use of prisons as feeding grounds for the smaller fish of the victorious party was traditional. As one of the many victims of the universal spoils system, however, the penal institu-

[6] Gresham Sykes, "The Corruption of Authority and Rehabilitation," *Social Forces*, 34: 257–262, March 1956.

tion was especially unfortunate in that it received those whose low political enthusiasm or performance had entitled them to only the mealiest scraps in the public trough. The more ambitious bell-ringers and ward heelers went elsewhere.

PRESENT METHODS OF RECRUITMENT. Here and there, in smaller localities and municipalities, the old practices of appointment still persist; nevertheless, the decline has been accelerated in recent years. In all but a few states today some form of civil service appointment has succeeded the political method of selection. Applicants are usually required to pass an examination consisting of three parts: a physical screening, a written test (usually of the objective type), and an oral interview administered by experts selected by the civil service commission. In some states the oral examiners now include a high-ranking custodial officer; on the whole, however, both the written and the oral examinations are made up by examiners who are dependent on the works of professional criminologists or penologists.

Applicants receiving a passing grade on each of these three examinations are placed on a list from which appointment or certification is made. Rank on this list is not determined exclusively by test grade; most states provide for the addition of some form of bonus for veterans or others thought to be deserving of preferment. These departures from a strictly construed "merit system" of appointment are not vulnerable to misuse by personal favoritism since the "bonus" provisions apply to *classes* of persons rather than individuals.

Appointment to an institution is usually provisional for the first several months; successful completion of a probationary period entitles the appointee to the full rights and immunities of a state civil servant. These rights include a variety of pension and retirement benefits, compensation in case of injury or death, regularly defined working hours (with extra pay for overtime), and vacation and sick-leave benefits. The immunities, though more complex, are no less clearly defined; they include a guarantee of freedom from political pressure, open and protected channels of appeal from abuses, and distinct limits on the extent to which and the reasons for which the employee may be disciplined by higher institutional authorities.

EVALUATING THE EFFICIENCY OF THE CUSTODIAN. In the field of correction, standards for the evaluation of personnel are still largely on the level of clichés. Manuals continue to recite that prison officers should be courteous and respectful, cooperative but firm, understanding but not indulgent, kindly but not familiar. The conditional "and-but" character of many of these injunctions reflects the ambivalence of the correctional objective; in the absence of clear statements of the ends to be attained, descriptions of the means to be used are correspondingly vague. Nevertheless, there exist certain rough empirical standards for the evaluation of custodial performance; these may be found in two measures: the custodian's civil service standing on examinations and his periodic merit rating.

Ideally, the perfect civil service examination should predict subsequent on-the-job performance. Those scoring higher on the examination lists should also tend to receive better merit ratings; those scoring lower, inferior ratings. In an effort to cross-evaluate these two measures of custodial efficiency, the authors compared the examination performance of custodial officers scoring high and low on the periodic rating scales currently in use at a maximum-security prison. This comparison produced a curious and unanticipated finding. A surprisingly high number of the guards and higher officers who had generally distinguished themselves in routine and emergency situations had *failed* to distinguish themselves on civil service examinations. Conversely, an unexpectedly large number of officers and guards whose inefficiency and personal defects had rendered them liabilities rather than assets had received a high standing on examination lists.

In addition to their tendency to score only average or below average on examination—and often lower than the inefficient or mediocre officer—the outstanding custodians tended to be significantly less verbal in interpersonal relations, even in their interactions with each other. In some, this characteristic verged on inarticulateness. Another widely shared trait of the outstanding guards was a relatively high degree of reserve and formality; again, this trait tended to pervade their personal as well as their official relationships. In any convivial social group these men would tend to stand out as somewhat withdrawn and difficult to absorb into the general hilarity. Associated with this trait, and as difficult to define as it is impossible to avoid sensing, was a certain perceptibly lower degree of emotional liability and interpersonal empathy— an absence of those traits which the Spanish summarize in the word *simpático*.

In the shops and wings supervised by these guards there was uniformly less violence, less chicanery, and less exploitation of inmate by inmate than in the shops and wings supervised by other guards. We will shortly explore the possibility of a correlation between the socially disadvantageous traits of these men and the socially positive effects these same individuals had on their specialized human environment; for the moment, however, it may be interesting to speculate about the possible reasons for their low test performance.

In the discussion of the usual civil service examination, it was pointed out that both the oral and the written parts of the tests are usually made up from the writings of professional experts and only occasionally and in part by custodians. The background, experience, and penological orientation of the majority of these experts may have a significant influence on the test results. Analysis of the tests themselves strengthens this conclusion.

Exclusive of those questions which test general knowledge, those dealing with prison matters tend to be weighted in the direction of the history and aims of progressive penology, as defined in modern textbooks; the testers seem to want assurance that the applicant shares a knowledge of and a sympathy with the principles of humane penology. In the oral examinations—on which the outstanding guards frequently received low scores—this emphasis may be accentuated. Applicants may be asked to give their views on the meaning and importance of convict rehabilitation and the role they will play in the attainment of this objective. Dilating on this broad theme presents great difficulties for the nonverbal, excessively fact-oriented mind. Many applicants whose later custodial careers are less distinguished may do better on the oral examinations. Generally more outgoing, more responsive, and distinctly more empathic to the feelings of the interviewer, these applicants have far less difficulty in dilating on broad social themes than do their less verbal colleagues.

The observations fortify the suspicion that the abilities needed to obtain high scores on custodial examinations may not be the same as those required to be an effective custodian. The qualities of emotional responsiveness and openness to the feelings and wishes of others, the capacity for ready verbal interaction—traits so highly valued in the culture generally and in oral examinations specifically—are precisely those traits which increase the custodian's vulnerability to verbal manipulation. The applicant who is eager to please the interviewer with a far-ranging discourse on rehabilitation is frequently the same custodian who becomes the target of the inmate delegated to divert his attention from some antirehabilitative behavior currently going on in some other part of his cell block.

IN-SERVICE TRAINING. Recently there has been a growing recognition of the importance of social distance in the maintenance of discipline and good order. This recognition was by no means spontaneous or easy to achieve among men whose interpersonal habits, formed in an easy-going egalitarian society, have poorly prepared them to act as the foundation supports of a frankly authoritarian social structure. Continual reminders, both in the form of personal conferences and group lectures, are necessary for the preservation of this culturally abnormal way of relating. The following are excerpts from an in-service training lecture prepared for custodians at the New Jersey State Prison:

1. Avoid becoming involved in the personal problems of inmates. This inevitably results in having to take sides *for* some and *against* others, a procedure which directly paves the way for favoritism. Do not give any form of personal advice that is not directly connected with your running of the wing. Refer all other problems to the chaplain, the psychologist and the counselors.

2. In your conversation with inmates, never engage in or permit personal familiarity. The old adage that "Familiarity breeds contempt" was never more apt than in a prison. The inmates who are able to call Officer X by his familiar nickname "Bill" when they are feeling "friendly" toward him are just as apt to call him by equally familiar but less affectionate names when he is forced to crack down on them. Nothing is more corrupting to good discipline than this process of reducing an officer to the inmate level by the use of first names or nicknames.

3. Never discuss other institutional officials—or reveal in any way your favorites or dislikes among your brother officers or superiors. Inmates will attempt to ferret these feelings out and use them to play on your sympathies. Worse—they will attempt to blame their own violations on people they know you dislike since "even *you* have to admit that so-and-so is no good."

4. Do not become identified with or dependent upon any inmate or group of inmates—especially your runners [inmate assistants]. The whole wing will be watching you, testing you, trying to identify your "special" men. Favoritism is deadly in prison. Not only does it make it difficult to say "No" to the favorite, but it gives him power to push other inmates around. Above all, do not become overreliant on inmate sources of information, even if that information is usually correct. The inmates whose opinion you depend on will eventually hold your confidence in them as a club over the heads of other men. They will be able to say to other inmates: "Do what I want or I'll give you a rap with the keeper." In this way the officer becomes not a keeper, but a *tool* of the wing "con men."

5. This next point might be called the keystone of the whole arch of good discipline. *In all of your relations with inmates, never give*

any sign that you are becoming emotionally involved. Never lose your temper or show personal anger. Men instinctively realize that the basis of anger is fear, and the man who easily loses his temper and "throws his weight around" is quickly revealed as weak and unstable. The man who has to raise his voice and use profanity in order to get a job done is telling everybody that he feels too weak and insecure to get the same job done quietly and calmly. He is, in fact, telling everybody: "Don't take me seriously until I get excited." The good officer is above and beyond any personal involvement. When an inmate commits a serious infraction or does something which requires prompt action, that action should be carried out smoothly and unexcitedly. The officer should never act as if the offense were a personal affront to him. The truly forceful person rarely has to display his force in any obvious way. By acting methodically and calmly, he is expressing his confidence in himself and creating that confidence in others.[7]

The conception of the guard as a kindly friend and adviser is based implicitly on the assumption that the basic problem faced by the individual prisoner is rooted in his relationship with official authority. Essentially, this view maintains that the confined individual is suffering from the coldness, callousness, and abuse of society and its surrogates, and that, consequently, the major aim of all relationships in confinement is to substitute the expectation of mistreatment with the reality of sympathetic understanding. The opposing view asserts that the sufferings of inmates are largely due to oppression by other inmates, and that, consequently, a major aim of custody should be to prevent and check that oppression.

The conflict between these opposed conceptions of the custodian's role is thus based on a more fundamental difference between underlying views of the inmate's major problem in prison. One view sees him as requiring protection *against* prison authority; the other sees him in need of protection *by* the prison authorities *against* other inmates.

The Work Supervisor

The general neglect of the importance of the civilian supervisor of prison labor may to some extent be ascribed to the influence of terms and labels on thinking. The civilian work supervisor has rarely been

[7] Excerpt from an in-service training lecture, New Jersey State Prison, 1954.

included in the list of institutional treatment personnel. Just as it is "natural," when considering the mental hospital, to think of the psychiatrist and to forget the ward attendant, so it is natural, when thinking of treatment in prison, to consider the professional staff to the neglect of other personnel. Nevertheless, in the mental hospital, though the patient may not see the psychiatrist more than a few minutes every week, he lives day and night with the nurses and ward attendants. Similarly, the prisoner, who may see the professional personnel even less frequently, is in continuous daily contact with his civilian work supervisor. If improved interpersonal relations and the learning of new social roles mean something more than talking about them in a counselor's office—if it also means living them out in actual situations—then the experiences with the work supervisor are a critical part of the prison treatment program.

Needless to say, the civilian work supervisor is rarely conceptualized in this way by other staff members, and consequently he does not conceptualize himself in this way. He usually views his job in terms of fulfilling his work quotas, which is the way his job is ordinarily viewed by his superiors. If he is the supervisor of the prison tailor shop, his job is to turn out a certain number of pants and shirts and coats every month. To do this he needs inmates who can be trained to be good tailors, and who can be motivated to produce. At this point a whole series of problems may arise; the variable ways in which they are resolved may have a critical impact on several levels of institutional life.

The work supervisor's problems may be broken down into the following areas: (1) obtaining efficient inmate workers and getting rid of inefficient or troublesome ones; (2) motivating his inmates to work; (3) accommodating and relating these objectives to other institutional goals and to the desires, attitudes, and personal characteristics of his inmates.

Problems of Recruitment

In most institutions the classification committee decides where the inmates will work. The extent to which the individual work supervisor participates in these decisions, and the manner in which he does so, vary greatly. Often it is necessary to distinguish between his overt, formal and his covert, informal participation. Individual work supervisors are often represented on the classification committee by a single individual—usually the head of the prison industries division. It is through this person that the various work supervisors make their needs and wishes known. Since these wishes are usually related more or less exclusively to the supervisor's own work requirements, they must be accommodated to various other objectives, including custodial objectives. Occasionally these objectives clash.

Frequently an inmate who is vocationally suited for a given job is not considered a good custodial risk in that particular work situation. Conversely, inmates who are unsuited vocationally or by interest for a given work situation may be good custodial placements in that situation. When conflicts of this type arise, the custodial and the industrial representatives on the classification committee may find themselves in the role of opposed lobbyists, with the particular inmate occupying a critical position between them. On occasion the inmate, who, in a formal sense, seems to be merely a pawn in this chess game, may acquire a much more decisive role. At this point a wide range of covert forces may come into play.

Inmates have their own work preferences and their own reasons for them. In many cases, these preferences and reasons may be entirely compatible with the vocational, custodial, and treatment objectives of the institution. In other cases, they may not be. For example, an inmate with a real—or simulated—work history as a metal worker might desire placement in the prison tool shop for a variety of unrevealed personal reasons. These reasons may include a planned escape attempt, the stealing of metal for the making of weapons, and a wide variety of purposes unconnected with rehabilitation. If the inmate is successful in convincing the metal shop supervisor of his high ability and good intentions, the supervisor may be tempted to bring all sorts of formal and informal pressures to bear in order to obtain him, thus becoming an unwitting collaborator in the inmate's plans.

Problems of Incentive

Though most institutions provide some form of wage and "work time" benefits (so many days' reduction of sentence for each month of work), these incentives are frequently unrelated to the quality of the work done. Incentives granted as a matter of course cease to be incentives and come to be regarded as matters of right. Consequently, for many inmates, "work" becomes a matter of "pulling time" in the shop rather in the cell. Faced with this tendency toward inertia, the institution has three alternatives: (1) to accept the simulated work situation as unchangeable and reduce production goals; (2) to institute a real incentive system by means of individual work ratings that tie wages to actual work performance; or (3) to tolerate an informal incentive system, by which the supervisors reward certain inmates with special favors in exchange for real work.

In institutions where there is no official pressure to maintain production goals, the tendency toward inertia is enhanced. Where outside pressure is exerted, one of the other two alternatives is the rule. The more desirable of these—the formal system of evaluation—is difficult to maintain in institutions where the informal incentive system has been traditional. In one institution where an attempt was made to replace the informal system with a system of evaluation, all inmates were regularly given a grade of "good" on the rating sheets. In most institutions, informal incentives are probably the rule.

Problems of Relating Production Objectives to Other Institutional Goals

It is unnecessary to point out that production objectives, treatment goals, and custodial safeguards would be difficult to accommodate even in an ideal institutional situation. In less than ideal situations, one or more—sometimes all three—are usually quietly sacrificed in a tacit acceptance of simulated effort. As a central figure in this pattern of accommodation, the work supervisor tends to be cynical and defensive when discussing "rehabilitation through constructive work habits." He is an unlikely contributor to discussions of reformation—and his silence on the subject can be verified by a glance at the indexes of most works in the field.

The Professional Worker

Ambiguity of Role

Of all the people at work in the prison, the professionals—specifically, the nonmedical professionals—are charged with the most far-reaching and socially urgent responsibilities. At the same time, of all the people at work in the prison, they are assigned roles and functions defined in the most ambiguous and uncertain terms. This fact has a significance that has never been fully evaluated.

The new custodial officer, entering into his duties, comes into a situation defined by sharply articulated standards and traditions. His role is planned out for him in advance and is supported by definite expectations on the part of all levels of the prison community. Almost everyone he meets has a more or less clear expectation of what his behavior ought to be in practically every situation, and these expectations set distinct limits to individual deviation. In well-run institutions, the very uniform he wears is a kind of insulation against the effects of personal failings; it is understood that the security and discipline of the prison require the whole official community to organize its responses around the role rather than the man. Consequently, it is universally acknowledged that the institution will support the uniform, within limits, whatever the personal characteristics of the individual wearing it. A comparable situation exists in the case of administrative and maintenance personnel. Here, too, objectives are limited, well-defined, and matched with reasonably effective tools for their achievement.

This picture is thrown radically out of focus when we consider the psychologists, psychiatrists, social workers, counselors, and classification specialists—those to whom the larger society has assigned the mission of treatment. One looks in vain for the unified body of theory and practice which is to guide their operations, for the traditions that will unify expectations around their efforts and provide standards protecting the quality and continuity of their work from the disruption of individual idiosyncrasy. They do not exist. In the more than a century that has passed since the days of Howard, after hundreds of volumes and scores of textbooks, the correctional therapist is still working in a field of treatment as crude and personalized as was medicine in the days of the barber-doctors.

The professional entered penology through the breach forced in the wall by the zeal and indignation of the nineteenth-century prison reformers. Having been carried into the prison on a wave of social protest against prison conditions, the professional, in one sense, has most creditably remembered his heritage of indignation. In another sense, he has remained curiously limited by it. His forebears, the religious reformers, moved by a profound faith in the direct educability of human beings, sincerely believed that the problem of crime could be solved by a combination of decently treating and religiously exhorting confined criminals. The earliest systematic form of this uncomplicated approach was that of the Quakers, who believed that meditation in a solitude uncontaminated by contact with other inmates, and broken only by occasional preaching, would reform the convict. A more modern example of this approach was that of Osborne, who held that decent human relations might be taught to criminals by means of a program combining self-government, indoctrination, and abolition of bad physical conditions. Despite advances in the theory and method of psychological treatment in other areas, professional treatment in the field of correction has remained, by and large, limited to these two historical techniques: assistance in the relief of hardships, and various forms of verbal suasion.

Isolation from the Inmate Community

The physical isolation of the professional, and his limited involvement in the total activity of the prison community, must be taken into account in any evaluation of his significance in the institutional program. The professional meets the inmate at some physical point outside the inmate's daily routine—usually in an office, where privacy can be assumed. Moreover, his interaction with the inmate is almost wholly limited to verbal exchange; he almost never relates to the inmate in some activity in which both are participating, and he rarely observes the inmate in action.

HIS ISOLATION FROM THE OFFICIAL COMMUNITY. This situation exists with the tacit if not overt approval of many professional workers. It has become one of the canons of correctional treatment that the therapist should attempt to maintain his independence of institutional authority. Besides fortifying his isolation from the institutional stream of activity, this position has two additional drawbacks. The first is that the inmate sees through it. He is aware that the professional is a paid employee of the state and cannot actually remain aloof from the limiting conditions of institutional policy. The second difficulty is that inmates inevitably attempt, in one way or another, to induce the professional to intervene in institutional policy on their terms. The result is that, having asserted his independence from the institution and refusing to act as its representative, the professional is vulnerable to a loss of his independence when he is maneuvered into functioning as a representative of the inmate.

The World of Inmates

ALTHOUGH BIOGRAPHICAL AND FICTIONAL ACCOUNTS OF PRISON LIFE
have appeared since early literary periods, the scientific study of the
prisoner community is less than a generation old. Previous to this time,
public conceptions of prison life were dominated by considerations of
sympathy for the prisoner's lot. Though more than amply justified by
deplorable prison conditions, these feelings have tended to stereotype
public attitudes toward prison life in a manner difficult to influence by
more objective information. The core assumption underlying these
attitudes is the belief that the misery of prison life is chiefly the result
of confinement and official repression and mistreatment. Neglected in
this partial analysis is the possibility that much of the misery of prison
confinement is due to the fact that prisoners are confined with individuals who are criminals.

The neglect of this possibility has had unfortunate consequences
for penology—and, consequently, for the prisoners themselves. It has
tended to direct efforts at prison reform almost exclusively toward the
improvement of physical conditions and the expansion of official services.[1] These efforts might be effective if the exclusive causes of suffering

[1] Cf. the sociologist Clarence Schrag ("Leadership among Prison Inmates,"
The Sociological Review, 19:38, No. 1, 1954):
  The ineffectiveness of our penal institutions as therapeutic agencies is usually
  explained in terms of inadequate treatment facilities ... inferior qualifications of
  administrators or the criminogenic characteristics of inmates. The social climate of

in prison were, in fact, largely limited to the physical and psychological consequences of confinement and official mistreatment. If, on the other hand much of the travail of prison life is the result of life among criminals, these efforts may not only fail to alleviate it but actually increase it —by providing greater freedom for the mistreatment of prisoners by each other. It is probable that this has actually been the result in many institutions—especially juvenile institutions. An offender who underwent much suffering at the hands of other prisoners once posed the problem in this way: "If I wanted to set out to reform Hell, I would do something more than free the poor devils from their chains and their hell-fire. The first thing I'd do for them is free them from the other devils."

One of the problems complicating the study of the inmate social world is the difficulty of seeing the life of the inmate community whole. Some of the complexities of that community may be suggested in the following account of the activities of four inmates in a maximum-security prison:

Half a Day in the Prison [2]

It is one o'clock in the prison. The inmates have finished their noon meal and are gathered in their wings [living quarters], waiting to be sent to their shops. The officer in the Center [institutional control point] calls out each shop in turn and the men file past. The inmate band is playing a military march—yet the step of the inmates is something less than martial. All except one, who walks with a certain jaunty decisiveness. The officer points him out:

"See that man? He's one of our worst. He's just gotten out of lock-up. And if I know anything about the type, he'll be back there in a week."

We follow the inmate. He works in the kitchen—one of the few assignments from which he has not yet been "fired." But we shortly find out that, though he works *in* the kitchen, he is not working *for* it. He works only for himself—and for his friends. At the end of the work day he will file past the Center again, heavier by about a pound of "swag" beefsteak hidden under his shirt. Tonight, in his cell, he will cook that steak; a tiny, homemade stove will materialize out of a bulge in his bunk and, together with a few merry companions, he will risk

---

the prison and the interpersonal relations among inmates have received less attention. . . . Failure to investigate more thoroughly the dynamic interactions among prison inmates may be a serious theoretical and methodological omission.
[2] Impressions of a member of the counseling staff, New Jersey State Prison.

days in "lock-up" for the privilege of gulping down a few mouthfuls of badly seared meat. The fare will be poor, the eating precarious—but the spices of danger and defiance will make it a feast. At that moment we would be hard pressed to find a group of men more satisfied with themselves.

There is, perhaps, at that hour in the early evening, another man at peace with himself: old M_____, the inmate art instructor, hurrying to the inmate school with his load of paints and brushes. In civilian life M_____ was an engineer of considerable standing; unfortunately, he did not have the same control over his own inner workings that he had over his machines. Behind a façade of professional dignity, he hankered after the unfettered life of Gauguin: a few wild evenings with young girls in the distinctly non-Tahitian woods of southern New Jersey brought him to prison. But old M_____ is not wholly exiled from Tahiti. On the walls of his cell, in bright tropical colors, the belles of Polynesia are dancing still—and tonight old M_____ will go out and teach art to the aborigines.

A phone call from the Center:

"A fish [new inmate] is crying and making a fuss in quarantine. Do you want to come down and hold his hand?"

We send for the man. An old, stooped figure hesitates at the doorway, then pours into the room:

"Forgive me...I had to talk to somebody. I heard that you talk to new...inmates." (He says the word "inmate" with a kind of incredulous revulsion; it is himself he is talking about, yet he cannot quite bear the word.) He tells his story; he was a minor politician—"really, a very minor one—just a sardine among the sharks." He had an accounting job. There was a scandal. Somebody had to take the rap. They picked on a little man...one who couldn't fight back.... What will become of him?

The counselor asks a few questions, more to distract the man than to get information. He answers through tears:

"The other inmates? They're fine. They're *wonderful* to me. I never thought criminals could be so kind, so understanding. The things you hear about them. I thought they hated decent people. What did I ever do for them? What did I ever do for anybody?" (More tears; he is off on another incoherent tirade of self-recrimination.)

The pattern becomes clearer. The judge gave this offender only two years. But he himself was more severe: even among rapists and murderers, he feels himself an outcast. And they, case-hardened as they are, can still recognize a death sentence when they see it; they offer the consolation that the luckier extend to the less fortunate. But he cannot take their offer. He cannot be one of them; he cannot be one of anybody. He has lost the society that defines him as a person; hence, he has lost himself.

Another urgent message reaches us, this time from the observation tier. One of the institution's "wild men," currently under observation, is talking suicide again—probably winding up for another attempt. We go down.

The inmate does not wait for us to speak. "Why should I want to live? Everybody knows I squealed on those guys. I'm a rat. Let's face it, I'm a rat. But it's not my fault. You people made me do it. How can I go out there and live with those men? I'm finished—you people finished me, so why don't you let me die?"

We listen and we realize the man's urgent need to divert his self-hate to us. He too has lost his society and has internalized the rejection of his group. His only chance is to find another group in which he can be a person again—and this chance no longer exists for him.

Here are four men—two of them long-standing members of the "good" society, two of them long-term members of the bad. What factors unite the two who are surviving in prison? What factors differentiate them from the other two, who are "cracking up"?

The old artist and the young steak-thief have one thing in common: they accept themselves and are able to *actualize* themselves in the minds of those around them. The kind of person each wants to be is accepted. The reverse is true of the two miserable men. They can no longer realize themselves in their preferred human environment. Like cast-off repertory players, they have been thrust out of the only roles they knew; the audience has turned sour.

Our discussion of the inmate social system will be guided by the hypothesis that it is an adaptation to social rejection and punishment. Its usage patterns provide for a "style of life" which enables inmates to avoid the devastating psychological effects of internalizing and converting social rejection into self-rejection. Rather than reject himself, the inmate attempts to build and operate under a value system enabling him to reject his rejectors—courts, police, law-abiding people generally.

The Social Structure of the Inmate Community

Attempts to reduce the complexities of social stratification in a prison to a series of simple formulas are likely to be misleading. Many professional analysts fall into the trap of relying too heavily on convicts' observations, unaware that these are almost invariably tailor-made to fit the purposes of the inmate social system and the biases the professional observer brought in with him. Nevertheless, the testimony of inmates regarding their own social experiences is indispensable, provided they are regarded as presentations of a point of view rather than as an unquestionable rendering of facts. The sociologist Donald Clemmer, whose classic work *The Prison Community* inaugurated the scientific study of the inmate social world, has cited an inmate's description of the major social roles of prisoners. This is how the inmate viewed his fellow prisoners—or, at any rate, how he wished Clemmer to believe he viewed them:

Prison Friendships[3]

I will tell you about some friendships I have known in prison that have been put to the acid test and have been found not lacking in those sterling qualities of honor, loyalty, esteem, affection, and unselfishness, the five component parts so necessary to lasting friendship. In speaking of my friends I shall discuss them as a group. First let me see if I can chronicle the different other groups in their respective order.

Group one: Composed of politicians, semi-politicians, and those aspiring to be politicians; group two: composed of trustees, semi-trustees, and those aspiring to be trustees; group three: composed of gang runners, water boys, tool boys, individual gang "stools" and their ilk; group four: composed of the fellatio boys and the homosexual girls; group five: composed of those who try to be neutral, mind their own business, and do their own time; group six: for comparison's sake I am going to list my friends as group six, which is composed of fellows who have shown by action their friendships through loyalty, honor, mutual esteem and unselfishness. More of a personal nature of group six later. Please bear in mind that there are exceptions to each of these groups.

Speaking of the groups, let's see in what qualifications group one is superior or better than group six. Are they more intelligent as intelligence is rated? Yes. Does their academic or educational intelligence better qualify them for a success in the chosen branch of the profession for which they were convicted and incarcerated here? I think not. I have seen college graduates starving to death trying to make a living stealing. I don't class embezzlement as stealing. In other words, it takes more than academic intelligence to make a successful thief—if there is such an animal.

Are the friendships of group one more binding than those of group six? For example, are they more honorable? Do they honor each other? No! emphatically, no! There is no honor among them; they hide behind a veneer and make a pretense of honoring each other for what they probably call friendship's sake. They cultivate this false pretense of

[3] Donald Clemmer, *The Prison Community* (New York: Rinehart and Company, 1940), pp. 125–127.

friendship, not because they honor each other, but because they fear each other. Hence, the cultivation of false friendships with the idea always in mind that their false friendships will keep their false friends from "stooling" on them individually.

Are they loyal? Hell, no! Neither to themselves, their own group, the officials who advance them, or to the other convicts whose good will they covet. They are like an unskilled harpist forever strumming his instrument trying to strike a chord that will better appease that little streak of vanity he probably calls his soul. Some are so egoistical they even think they have struck a perfect balance and so have pleased everyone. They "stool on," and pretend to despise the officials to the "cons," and likewise "stool" on the "cons" to the officials, figuring, of course, that they are deceiving both sides—what colossal ignorance— or is it intelligence? Of course there is no such thing as genuine affection or esteem among them. They are forced for falsity's sake to pretend affection or esteem merely to safeguard that subconscious fear that they will unleash their unethical machinery on each other. For they instinctively recognize in each the counterpart of the other. They are at least unique in one manner: they recognize no known standard of ethics, but each in his own individual way manufactures his own ethics to meet his own individual requirements. That is, at least, something. Please remember, C., that when you are telling your attentive audience about the flourishing and beautiful friendships of the penitentiary politicians that I believe (granting you do tell them, or believe it yourself) you are telling them a lie about something that never existed. For how can there be friendship where there is no honor, loyalty, principle, or ethics?

Now for group two, composed of trustees, semi-trustees, and those aspiring to be trustees. First, have they honor? No! They sign away their honor, if they ever had any, when they sign the prison roll that pledges them to inform the authorities at once if they see anything untoward about their fellow "cons." They pledge their honor (my God what a sacrilege on the word) to the officials that if at any time they see any of their fellow cons escaping or preparing to escape they will immediately inform the proper authorities. They further pledge their word of "honor" that they will report any other "con" whom they observe committing an infraction of the prison regulations. Are they loyal? No! A man who sells his honor couldn't possibly be loyal even to himself. They stool on half of the cons and traffic in contraband articles smuggled in under the veneer of official loyalty, to the other half. Needless to say, there is very little true affection, no esteem, and very few friendships that are not pretended.

Group three: Composed of gang runners, water boys, tool boys, individual gang stools, and their ilk. There is no honor or loyalty among them. They each in their own individual way are trying to advance their own interests, and in order to do this they must find constant excuses for trampling on their fellow cons. Their aspirations, of course, are "politician" jobs. I think it is needless to say that there is no esteem, very little affection, and no true friendships among this group.

Group four: composed of the fellatio boys and the homosexual girls. Are they honorable? No! Not according to the recognized standards of honor. Is there honor among them? Yes. Are they loyal? I can't say. I should hate to bank too heavily on their loyalty, although I have seen them do some very loyal deeds. Are they affectionate? Yes, very. Are there any true friendships among them? Yes, according to their own standards. Have they a code of ethics which they recognize? Yes, more or less.

Group five: Composed of those who try to be neutral, mind their own business, and do their own time. Some of them have the qualifications necessary to form true friendships. This group is a minority group. (The Negro group I didn't mention because I think it unnecessary. They are all in the same category with possible exceptions interspersed here and there.)

Group six: Composed of fellows who were the best of friends or who were the cleverest, most deceitful actors imaginable. Fellows I have known from four to twelve years; some are dead, some are out, and some are still in. (He names eight men, three of whom are no longer in prison.) The fellows mentioned had a very finely drawn code of ethics that they tried to live up to. I don't know how to begin chronicling the many friendly deeds I have seen the above mob do. I have seen them suffer the greatest indignities possible for each other. I have seen them do everything from risk their lives to splitting their last bag of "Durham" with each other. I have seen them stand and get their heads knocked in, in preference to being disloyal to each other. I have seen them go to the hole and do each others' "time." I have seen them take thousands of chances to help each other escape. In fact, I have seen them tested in every conceivable way and I can safely say I believe they always came up to standard. Just how many daily newspapers that mob read, I can't say for sure, but four daily would be a conservative estimate for an average in English. Then, there was an Italian and a Spanish paper. Any unusual news feature or sensational piece of journalism was always commented upon and discussed. I have seen those guys willingly commit sacrifices that your ordinary man wouldn't do. I know of literally thousands of little and big unselfish things they have done and not talked about. If they weren't friends to each other I don't know the meaning of friendship. There is more or less of number six group in each department—kitchen, tailor shop, in each quarry gang, etc. The good, bad, indifferent are everywhere,

I suppose. I don't imagine this is exactly what you wanted, but it is the best I can do.

Classification by Social Status

As suggested in the foregoing discussion by an articulate prisoner, inmates are classified by other members of the inmate social system according to a variety of positions. The terms used to describe these status positions vary from institution to institution. For instance, in one training school the status with most esteem is "take of cottage"; in another, an inmate occupying the same status is referred to as a "big wheel." Though any general classification of status positions in the inmate social system is confronted by problems of overlapping, the following classification is an attempt to rank groups of inmates on the basis of general esteem.

1. The highest rank of general esteem is occupied by a very small number of inmates whose reputations are simultaneously so well established and so individualized that they are immune from the inmate status system. The social roles and functions of these inmates are characterized by a high degree of self-determination. They can "call their own shots," and their decisions are usually unquestioned. They have a more or less unlimited option in choosing how they will relate to others. They are, in effect, the heroes and myth-makers of the system, and they personify its most cherished values and illusions.

2. *Right Guys:* The activities of inmates occupying this status are less self-determined than those of the higher rank, but they still have a wide option in their choice of functional roles. Though still relatively independent, their independence is limited by duties and obligations to the values of the inmate group viewed as a whole. They are "right guys" because they can always be depended on to "do right" by the "inmate code." They are expected to be uncooperative with the officials and incorruptible by them. They must be willing to undertake risks and undergo punishments in behalf of the inmate community. Their continued status is dependent on their willingness to undertake these obligations; when called on, they cannot refuse.

3. *Buckers:* Individuals involved in a struggle for status and position. They are frequently younger inmates who are, to use the expression of one prisoner, "bucking to be bad men."

4. *Squares* and *Honest Johns:* A heterogeneous noncriminalistic group without honorary status in the inmate social system. In this group

are the accidental offenders who make a superficial adjustment to the inmate social system.

5. *Ball Busters:* A fairly large group of misfits, irritants, unpredictable and socially disattached inmates. They constitute a group of unorganized troublemakers not only for the official but also for the inmate social system.

6. *Punks:* A group of identified passive homosexuals and physically and psychologically weak inmates who cannot be trusted.

One can, if he chooses, add to these classifications "rats" (informers) and "bugs" (overtly psychologically disturbed inmates). There are also, of course, inmates who have almost no association with others.

Classification by Functional Role

Another approach to analyzing the inmate social structure is to classify prisoners according to their functional roles in the inmate social system—"the big shots," "politicians," "tough guys," "business men," "operators," etc. Still another approach is to relate roles to a specific activity—e.g., sex. If sex is utilized for discussion, there seem to be four major roles: "wolf" (always masculine); "pancake" (an inmate who plays both masculine and feminine roles); "punk" (an inmate who plays an institutionalized feminine role, usually for economic considerations); and "fairy" (a passive homosexual who played a feminine role prior to entering the institution). Another classification could be made in terms of relationships with the world of officials: the aloof inmate who refuses to have any dealings with officials; the "tough guys," who heroically resist officials; the "con men," who manipulate officials; the "politicians," who work out accommodations with officials; the "state man," who more or less passively accepts official direction; and the "rat," who informs on other inmates for personal considerations.

In the discussion above, reference was made to social roles around sex activity. The deprivation of normal sexual outlets for inmates has been the subject of considerable speculation and a large number of "corrective" proposals has appeared. Though it is doubtful whether anybody can do more than guess at the extent of homosexuality in places of confinement, informed opinion places the percentage fairly high (estimates of 80 per cent are not uncommon). The number of inmates involved and the frequency and form of involvement vary among institutions and seem to be directly related to the control resources of the institution. Regardless of the extent or frequency of homosexuality, much of the conniving, manipulation, and overt violation of inmate rules can be traced to "inmate love affairs." One could, in fact, analyze the world of prisoners on the basis of its patterned sex activity. As indicated elsewhere in this chapter, techniques of intimidation and seduction vary from gifts to threats of violence. In some instances physical violence is employed. In most cases, however, homosexuality seems to be a matter of mutual accommodation. In discussing their sex activity, inmates are no less hypocritical than most people; and frequently the men who complain the loudest about homosexuality are the worst offenders.[4] Most correctional administrators would agree that inmate activity in this area causes more interpersonal difficulties and violations of rules than any other activity, including gambling.

Social Stratification According to Race and Nationality

In general, the racial and ethnic attitudes of inmates tend to duplicate the biases and prejudices of the community at large. Nevertheless, since the formal living arrangements of prisoners are under official control, the social relations of inmates of different racial and ethnic backgrounds are subject to pressures of change that may reflect broad governmental policy rather than local community attitudes.

Thus, for example, the doctrine of "separate but equal" characterized the living arrangements of most non-Southern institutions well before the principle was anywhere operative as a social reality in the external community. In most modern penal institutions outside of the South, formal segregation is now limited largely to sleeping quarters—and even in this area there is a rising trend toward integration. White and Negro inmates work together, go to school together, and participate in recreation together to an increasing extent, though differentials in job opportunties still exist in many places.

Members of the Negro group, though in general accepting the principle of continued separation in living quarters, have pressed, with increasing success in some areas, for greater equality of opportunities and facilities in work and recreation. The two groups have, in general, worked out accommodations that simultaneously recognize the Negro's demands for equality and the white's insistence on separation.

These accommodations are continually under threat from deviates of both groups, especially in the area of sex relations. In prison the

[4] In this respect the inmate value system, like most value systems, is adjustive and comforting.

competition for passive homosexual partners is intense, and it is this intensity of competition which endows the status of the passive homosexual with a highly special character. As a class, the passive homosexuals of both races occupy the lowest status in the inmate hierarchy. As individuals, they are viewed as worthless; but as *possessions* they are highly prized, especially by their present and aspiring protectors. Viewed both by himself and by members of his own race as a pariah, the white passive homosexual, as a rule, is both less able and less committed to maintain a social distance between himself and the Negro group. He has, in effect, little to lose by "crossing the line," since his status is already at the lowest. Serious trouble may arise, however, when competition for him occurs between whites and Negroes; it is at this point that "racial rights" are asserted—interestingly, not in behalf of the passive homosexual, but in behalf of his white exploiter. The passive homosexual may then become a pawn, subjected to pressures which each of his aspirant exploiters defines as protection from the other; and the institution may be presented with the unsavory spectacle of known intimidators appealing to racial prejudice to support their unseemly protests against the principle of intimidation. Unless calmer and more candid heads prevail, one or two incidents of this sort can develop into a racial conflict involving large numbers of both groups—inmates having no original interest in the specific cause of the conflict but considerable involvement in the now broadened question of racial supremacy. Strong custodial control is the only safeguard against serious eruptions at this point.

Within the white population there is some splitting along ethnic lines, the most noteworthy of these splits occurring among second-generation descendants of foreign-born parents, usually from the same large urban locality. The importance of these splits is vitiated by the presence of a large Negro population and enhanced by its absence. As the Negro population becomes more evenly distributed over the entire country, the significance of national groups as determinants of group membership continues to diminish.

Within each of the racial groups, social stratification is largely determined by factors not dissimilar from those operating in the external community: the differential possession of the same prestige symbols that are valued on the outside. The peculiar social realities of the prison situation lend additional complexities to the picture, however. The problem of analysis is enormously complicated, for example, by the fact that physical detachment from the external community is not always paralleled by a similar degree of psychological detachment. There are wide differences in criminal acculturation among inmates in the same prison population. Previous group membership, length of sentence, type of offense, and various psychological factors determining the individual's feeling of personal adequacy—these and numerous other factors determine individual alignments within the walls.

Characteristics and Values of the Inmate Social System

The most obvious characteristic of the inmate social system is the *absence of escape routes* from it. The offender is not only incarcerated in a physical prison without exit; he is also enmeshed in a human environment and a pattern of usages from which the only escape is psychological withdrawal. Related to this is *loss of self-determination*. The individual in confinement has lost his control over his environment. The most important choices have been made for him—his place of living, his intimate associates, the people he sleeps with and eats with. His world *lacks privacy*, and the individual's need to withdraw in order to recuperate is severely curtailed in confinement.

Hierarchical Structure

Another characteristic of the inmate social system is its rigidly *hierarchical structure*, in which there is almost no vertical mobility. The number of roles an individual may play is severely limited; and, once roles are assigned, they are maintained—particularly at the lower status levels—with enormous group pressure. The degree to which the individual can participate in the selection of his role is similarly limited. From the moment the new inmate arrives from the court or the county jail, he is exposed to a series of very direct defining experiences. It is of interest to note that the inmates who participate in and administer these experiences are frequently those who recognize the inmate as being somewhat near their level—a perception that stimulates anxiety in them. For example, an obviously tough professional hoodlum will create no special problem for the majority of the lower-status inmates, who, responding to minimal clues, will either avoid him or immediately acknowledge his higher status. The arrival of this inmate, however, will pose a threat to the wing's chief "bad man," who will be expected to challenge the newcomer to a battle of mutual definitions.

Social Vulnerability

Still another characteristic of the inmate social system is *trial by public opinion*. The prison grapevine operates at variable speeds; it is not as fast as the speed of sound. It is as fast as this: One man tells two; two men tell four—and as fast as men can casually walk from one point to another (apparently doing something else), the rumor spreads.

Everything that happens to individual inmates is discussed, evaluated, and made the basis of an assessment; every man's reputation is exposed. In prison, reputation is like life insurance. Only the power-elite are immune from what might be called the *status undertow*—a general tendency to put the worst interpretation on events, to assume the least flattering assumptions and the worst motives. Thus men live in the fear of events that will drag down their names—and much of the tension in correctional institutions is related to this sensitivity about reputations. The situation is worsened by the fact that one of the biggest status-gainers is *knocking* someone else down: the higher the person, the greater the increase in status for the attacker. Thus men are often measured by whom they can resist and whom they can knock down. The number of people one can dominate, the number one can hold off— and the number of friends one numbers among the immune power-elite —these are what add to a man's reputation.

Interpersonal Conflict

Thus, any casual interaction between two complete strangers can turn, in an instant, into a deadly conflict. A little jostling while waiting in line—a tone of voice a little too loud and irritating—can precipitate the insult that must be avenged. If it is not avenged, the insulted party immediately becomes the target of every low-status inmate out to make a reputation. The following incident is an example: In a prison mess hall, an aggressive inmate called out to a selected target, "Hi, sweet-tail." This act achieved several objectives: (1) It identified the subject as the private stake of the aggressive inmate. (2) It publicly branded him as a "punk," with the object of breaking his morale. (3) It isolated him from possible "respectable" friends, who were, by this act, challenged either to defend the target or abandon him to the aggressive inmate. The inmate's sole alternative to submission was an equally public attack on the "wolf." Result: He stabbed the "wolf" in the mess hall.

Hunger for Status

Men deprived of the sense of personal significance, of importance and recognition, are inevitably hungry for status. One might, in fact, write this chapter in terms of the preoccupation of the members of the inmate social system with the *search for symbols of status*. This need of inmates for overt symbols that satisfy the need for personal significance to counteract the prevailing feeling of not mattering takes many forms. Inmates' requests for special consideration in dress, visits, etc., are often related to this quest.

Authoritarianism

The role-defining conflicts carried on by inmates on or near the same status level shed light on another charactertistic of the inmate social structure—namely, its *extreme authoritarianism*. Any situation of equality in a situation of threat, which must be resolved into a relationship of superordination and subordination. However vehemently inmates in groups demand equal treatment and condemn favoritism, inmates as individuals continuously press for special personal advantages. Where demands for increased permissiveness have been granted by authorities, the rigid authoritarian patterns have almost invariably not been destroyed but merely transferred to a new and less stable center of gravity. The history of inmate self-government reveals that the yielding up of power by the external ordering authority usually generates patterns of internal group coercion more punitive, more rigid, and incomparably more discriminatory than those they supplanted. The authoritarian character of inmate relationships suggests that members of the system afford no exception to the general psychological observation that the victims of power tend to regard its possession as the highest personal value.

We come now to one of the paradoxes of the prison community. Though identified as the main source of power in this community, the group of officials exercises far less actual authority over individual inmates than does the informal inmate social system. This fact becomes apparent when the punitive and coercive resources of inmates and officials are compared. More important, the psychological damage capable of being done by inmates is much greater than that which officials are able to inflict. Punishment by officials is frequently a source of status and prestige.

AVAILABLE SANCTIONS OF OFFICIALS AND INMATES

Officials	Inmates
Transfer	Blackmail
Loss of prison employment	Social ostracism, insults
Loss of privileges	Physical violence
Loss of "good time"	Death (to "squealers")
Segregation	Various forms of mental torture, including threats of the above
	Abasement

The number of points at which each group can exert pressure on the individual is highly disparate. The inmate lives, eats, sleeps, and works with other inmates. His necessary relations with officials are fewer and much less intimate. The officials go home at night. Their interest in inmates is largely negative; little or no attention is paid to them unless they become involved in disciplinary misbehavior or the focus of overt and obvious trouble with other inmates. This aspect of the world of inmates was dramatically revealed in letters written by a prisoner in a large Eastern medium-security institution who was subsequently murdered by other inmates. He wrote:

> Antagonisms here have no recognizable basis. [They] spring from nothing more than inability of many men here to feel any sense of personality unless they can integrate their feeling of self around some good solid hatred....
>
> Surprising to me how many pride themselves on being "bad"— as claim to distinction and compete in demonstrating how "bad" they are....
>
> The shocking thing is that the administration has either so little knowledge or such inadequate means of control that such "bad" cliques take over effective sway even in honor quarters....
>
> Ordinarily, any man detests the idea of being under surveillance. Here, in many quarters, the relatively decent element often wishes to goodness there were more.[5]

[5] *New York Post*, December 8, 1955, p. 4.

Power as a Supreme Value

The dominant value of the inmate social system seems to be the *possession and exercise of coercive power*. There are probably no social interactions that have escaped the influence of this factor. Even usages of mutual aid have been contaminated by and made subservient to it. To illustrate: One way to proclaim possessive rights over another inmate is to help him in some way, usually by material aid. New inmates, unaware of the subversive motivations behind these services, are quickly apprised of their coercive character. Once an inmate has accepted any material symbol of service, it is understood that the donor of these gifts has thereby established personal rights over the receiver. Aggressive inmates will go to extraordinary lengths to place gifts in the cells of inmates they have selected for personal domination. The intended victims, in order to escape the threatened bondage, must find the owner and insist that the gifts be taken back. Should the donor refuse to take them back, the receiver may be forced to fight him then and there.

One measure of the inherent cohesive strength of any social system is the degree to which behavior controls have been individually internalized, thereby obviating all but a minimal degree of interpersonal coercion. Since the basic values of the inmate social system, personal power and exploitation, are inimical to cooperative group living, enormous pressures are required to prevent the inherently centrifugal forces from disintegrating the system. These pressures are supplied in part by the external control and punitive threats of the official world. In the absence of these external unifying forces, order can be maintained only by the most tyrannical inmate rule.

There are two small groups of inmates who effectively control the prison population. Those holding key positions in the administrative offices are able to dispense special privileges. Because of their power they often become "racketeers" and extort money and services from less powerful inmates. These operators are often hated and envied by other inmates for their self-seeking behavior and general disinterest in the general inmate problems. In any conflict they may be counted on to side only with themselves. The other group consists of the "right guys"—inmates whose behavior is patterned according to the criminal and prison code. Though not classified as trouble makers, they take every opportunity to get what they can from the officials, whether it be a better job or freedom, by standing up for their rights as convicts. They can usually be trusted never to abuse their fellow inmates and are reputed to be steadfastly loyal to their class—the convicts. These are the real leaders. Because of their "upright" conduct they are able to impose their definition of proper behavior on the other convicts.

Like every other social organization, the inmate system provides not only rules and sanctions for their violation but also methods for evading those rules and escaping the sanctions. The disruptive forces inherent in the basic values of the inmate social system have generated techniques for violating the most fundamental ordinances in support of group unity. The power of these disruptive forces is indicated by the fact that even the most sacred rule of the inmate code, the law against "squealing," is daily violated and evaded with impunity. Contrary to the propaganda disseminated by the more solemn of the inmates in defense of their code, informers and betrayers require little or no seduction by prison officials. Actually, the main administrative problem presented by informers is not gaining them but avoiding them, since they come as volunteers from all levels of the inmate hierarchy.

The Impact of the Inmate Social System on Prison Administration

In the face of these weaknesses and internal contradictions, the question arises: How does the system avoid breaking down, and why have prison officials generally failed to exploit its weaknesses? A part of the answer may lie in the fact that prison officials have generally tended to use the inmate power structure as an aid in prison administration and the maintenance of good order, not realizing that in this attempt to manipulate the structure they themselves are more used than using. Far from systematically attempting to undermine the inmate hierarchy, the institution generally gives it covert support and recognition by assigning better jobs and quarters to its high-status members, provided they are "good" inmates. In this and in other ways the formal institution buys peace with the informal system by avoiding battle with it.

In institutions which are publicly committed to maintaining control without the overt use of negative sanctions the accommodation process takes its most characteristic form. The officials of these institutions are caught in an agonizing dilemma. On the one hand, they are publicly committed to more "liberal" policies of correctional administration. These policies dictate that they create an atmosphere of greater inmate freedom and individual expression. Under these conditions, the inherently intolerant and nondemocratic character of the inmate social system expresses itself in the interpersonal relations of inmates, which, uncontrolled, result in violence and anarchy. If this occurs, two courses are open to the administration: It can restore internal order by the use of negative sanctions, or it can adjust to a new power relationship with inmates. Attempts to revive sanctions are likely to meet with opposition from inmates, guards, other government officials, and the public. There are many risks in attempting to restore internal order, riots being the most serious. Avoiding this problem leaves the institution with little choice but to permit the inmate social system to resolve its conflicts in its own characteristic way. This "way" involves the emergence of dominant inmate groups and personalities who develop a vested interest in the appearance of order and, as a result, can bargain with the administration from several positions of strength.

Having demonstrated that they can "keep the peace," these individuals and groups have a convincing argument for enlisting the support of institutional authorities in attaining their personal objectives. Depending on the degree of mutual candor, this argument can take various forms. The cliques can present themselves to the administration as supporters of institutional policies and defenders of these policies against "bad" inmates. In this form the pill is less difficult for officials to swallow. The cliques can also point out that any weakening of their alliance with the authorities would inspire the "bad" inmates to hostilities, thereby bringing on "trouble." It is then argued that the institution's best interests lie in furthering "good inmates' " objectives.

Should inmates in these dominant groups at any time become dissatisfied with the administration's concessions, they can instantly withdraw their pretense of support and redefine themselves as champions of the "mistreated prisoners." This is the conventional role of inmate leaders during riots and other prison disturbances. Most of the leaders of prison disturbances, up to the time they turned their violence against their keepers, had engaged in repeated offenses against other inmates.

The accommodations reached by institutional authorities and dominant inmates go far toward explaining why the inmate social system does not disintegrate under the pressure of its own divisive forces. When they have been maneuvered into a position where they are largely dependent on the inmate hierarchy for the maintenance of order, the authorities find themselves trapped in a virtually inescapable community of interest with the most criminalistic and authoritarian inmate elements. The irony of the situation lies in the fact that what may have begun as a movement toward greater emancipation has led to a condition of greater subjugation, in which virtually every inmate has been assigned his position in the pecking order and the institutional rackets have been distributed to the clique members.

Many investigators of the correctional community have viewed inmate behavior as being preponderantly related to the behavior of the official community. Viewed in this way, the behavior of inmates is interpreted largely as a reaction to influences emanating from *outside of their own group*. This orientation obscures the possibility that most inmate behavior is independent not only of the actions of officials but also of the specific confinement situation.

Researches undertaken during the last two decades have tended to confirm the suspicion that the significant conditions of prison life are related more to conditions within the inmate social system than they are to efforts of correctional officials. Confirmation of this impression would require a drastic shift in the emphasis of correctional reform, with greater effort directed toward combating inmate social processes that neutralize correctional efforts at their source.

Research in this area is confronted not only by methodological difficulties but by long-standing prejudice as well. An atmosphere of emotionality unique in the social sciences has pervaded penologist writing. Much of this emotionality seems to be related to a history of protest. Though protest and indignation have been and are valuable weapons in the struggle for social progress, it is important to maintain the distinction between the armaments for social change and the tools of scientific analysis. The failure to distinguish between the pulpit and the laboratory leads only to wasted indignation; its proper target is missed because of faulty observation and inadequate field intelligence.

CORRECTIONAL TREATMENT: TRENDS AND ISSUES

Problems, Issues, and Alternatives
in Correctional Therapy

ANY DISCUSSION OF CORRECTIONAL THERAPY INVOLVES THE CONSIDERA-
tion of two subjects, each of which is highly controversial. In the field
of treatment the most basic questions, *whom to treat, how to treat,* and
whether to treat are largely unresolved; the mere enumeration of opposing schools and methods would require several pages. Similarly, in the
entire field of correction there is probably no issue more controversial
than *institutionalization.* Again, the critical questions, *whom to confine,
how to confine,* and *whether to confine* are still unresolved. In any discussion fusing these controversial areas, the amount of common ground
inevitably shrinks even further. Controversies without a common ground
are inherently interminable, the disputants lacking any point of contact,
and the disputes over therapy and institutionalization have given every
promise of becoming interminable. Nevertheless, it would be too pessimistic and too early to assert that no common ground exists; if it does
not exist on the level of communication, then at least it exists on the
level of action. Despite the controversies about institutions, they exist—
and describable events take place in them. Despite a profound deficiency
in communication and shared definitions, many people are engaged in
activities which each calls treatment. If it is not yet possible to reconcile
their conflicting theoretical accounts of these activities, it is at least
possible to describe them as events.

Toward a Shared Definition of the
Therapeutic Process

Perhaps the two terms most commonly used by therapists and penologists are *therapy* and *rehabilitation*. They are also among those least clearly defined. What activities, events, or situations are referred to when these terms are used?

The term *rehabilitation* is used in at least three different senses: to describe an objective or aspiration in the mind of the rehabilitator; to describe his activities; and to describe an effect or condition produced in the person rehabilitated. The term *therapy* is likewise used in these various senses. It is something the therapist *intends*; it is something he *does*; finally, it is something that *happens* to the person treated.

A survey of present treatment theories and methods revealed the following requirements and procedures common to all techniques, from the most superficial brief counseling to the most intensive and extended depth analysis:

1. The person must somehow be brought to an awareness that his difficulties are related to motives and patterns of perception within himself. His attempts to account for these difficulties by blaming a hostile or unfavorable human environment must be analyzed as deriving at least in part from a natural tendency to avoid guilt and self-rejection. He must be assisted in the gaining of an awareness and a motivation for the taking of present initiative toward change and growth within himself, and he must be shown the fruitlessness of evading this responsibility by futile attempts to change merely his environment.

2. This assistance toward understanding comes about through some relationship with the therapist (or therapeutic situation) in which the individual actually attempts to make his faulty modes of perception and behavior work. Repeated demonstrations of this failure may be necessary before he is able to abandon them. It is important that these failures be not interpreted by him as indicating that he is a worthless or helpless person.

3. Finally, the individual must be provided with opportunities for the learning, testing, and fixating of newer, more effective modes of perceiving and relating to his human environment. As these new patterns emerge and are found rewarding in terms of increased success in relations with the self and others, they tend to become more and more established in the individual's total pattern of adjustment.[1]

[1] Lloyd W. McCorkle and Richard R. Korn, "Resocialization within Walls," *Annals of the American Academy of Social and Political Science*, 293:96–97, May 1954.

It is widely agreed that the therapeutic changes based on these processes are critically dependent on the person's taking the first step by acknowledging that he is in difficulty—that "something is wrong with *me.*" The first step is usually implied when the individual seeks out help.

Differences between Institutional and Noninstitutional Treatment Situations

In addition to agreeing on a common core of treatment requirements, most therapists would agree that there are crucial differences between therapeutic situations in and out of institutions (both penal and noncorrectional), and that these differences render exact comparisons invalid. A brief statement of these differences is an appropriate preface to further discussion.

1. Most patients on the outside come to therapy on their own initiative as a result of an awareness that their adjustment has, in ways crucial to them, broken down. Most of them are further aware that at least an important part of their difficulties stems from causes *within them* and cannot be blamed entirely on others. Without this awareness it is doubtful whether they would come at all. Though they are almost always hostile toward and apprehensive about others and desire them to change, they realize—dimly and frequently inaccurately—the need for changes within themselves. They are able, that is, to make the significant observation, "Something is wrong with me."

In contrast to the outside patient, individuals do not voluntarily come to prison for treatment. Within the institution, therapy may or may not be available; where it is available, it may or may not be compulsory. In those institutions where it is mandatory it is, of course, involuntary by definition. In those institutions where inmates voluntarily request treatment, the therapist would do well to avoid premature interpretation.

The majority of patients who pay for private treatment on the outside are in some degree aware that their difficulties are internal; this awareness is, in general, a favorable prognostic sign. In the case of inmates there is reason to believe that a request for treatment is an *unfavorable* prognostic sign. Of these requests, "I want to be rehabilitated," "I feel that you can understand me, I feel that you can help me," are most foreboding. If these statements are made with enthusiasm and without anxiety, embarrassment, or chagrin, the unfavorable prognosis can be made with more certainty. (If this conclusion seems surprising, let the reader try to recall whether he ever went enthusiastically to a doctor for a case of ulcers, a broken leg—or a neurosis.) People truly seeking psychological help are, for the most part, obviously unhappy when describing their problems and their needs for aid. For these and other reasons to be discussed later, the correctional therapist should not infer that a request for treatment necessarily implies an acknowledgment of psychological difficulties.[2]

2. Noninstitutional therapy almost always requires some material contribution by the patient to the therapist. This commonly takes the form of financial payment, and involves some degree of inconvenience and sacrifice. Even in clinics this form of participation by the patient is now recognized as therapeutically valuable, and many clinics charge a fee proportionate to the client's ability to pay.

By contrast, institutional treatment is given free and is not purchased by the patient at any financial or other cost. In many cases, especially in correctional institutions, counseling sessions are held during working hours and the patient is excused from his job without any loss of work credits. In one institution an attempt was made to reproduce something of an outside treatment situation by scheduling counseling sessions after working hours. This change in procedure required inmates who wanted counseling to come during their free time, as is the case on the outside. The requirement that inmates contribute a part of their recreation period in exchange for counseling resulted in a marked drop in the case-load and succeeded to some extent in differentiating those who really wanted treatment from those wanting a pause in the day's occupation.

3. A patient in therapy on the outside is able to leave the treatment situation at the close of his sessions and resume his ordinary activities. It would be difficult to exhaust the significance of this fact in a brief presentation; the following aspect is especially noteworthy here.

Though the patient leaving the therapist's office takes out most of the same tensions and problems he brought in, he is able—in fact compelled—to leave behind much of his role and status as a patient. When

[2] The more sophisticated inmates of "treatment-oriented" institutions are well aware that requests for help are looked on favorably and may result in earlier recommendations for parole.

he gets out into the street he is expected to relate to others in many different ways; he must relate to people who will not see him as a patient or "sick person" but as a "normal" individual. Though this situation may have its disadvantages, it has one extremely important advantage. Therapeutic changes in the personality relieve certain tensions, but they are invariably accompanied by other tensions and anxieties—at least until very close to the end of a successful treatment. Effective psychotherapy involves processes which are both "catabolic" and "anabolic"; frequently the growth process is as painful as the breaking-down process.[3] Because of this, it is almost as important for the patient to "get away" from the treatment atmosphere from time to time as it was for him to get into it in the first place.

Unlike the patient on the outside, the correctional patient cannot actually leave the treatment environment. His visits to the therapist quickly become a matter of general knowledge and comment, and he is in continuous close association with others receiving treatment.

The difficulties that may arise from this situation are outlined in an article dealing with group therapy in a correctional setting:

> One of the supportive conditions of group therapy on the outside is the patient's ability to escape from the group. In the correctional institution, the inmate cannot really leave the group. He is involved in numerous other activities and living experiences with the same people with whom he has shared intimate revelations, frequently against his will and in spite of all attempts at control and disguises. These individuals include his peers, his competitors, his enemies, or friends of his enemies—persons continually on the watch for signs of weakness and vulnerability.
> The inmate ... has one of two unhappy alternatives at this point. The more healthy of these alternatives is to abandon his compensatory defenses and accept the more realistic image of himself. But this ideal alternative has many difficulties in correctional institutions where the wearing of socially appropriate masks is frequently the condition of personal survival.[4]

4. Some observers have cited the presence or absence of regimentation as the crucial difference between treatment situations in and out of institutions. In an important external sense, great differences may exist,

---

[3] Though treatment may include reassurance and support, these alone do not constitute therapy. Neither can wholly anesthetize the anxiety involved in the dismantling of defenses which took years to develop and which, however crippling, represented at least quasi-solutions to the patient's problems.

[4] Lloyd W. McCorkle, "Guided Group Interaction in a Correctional Setting," *International Journal of Group Therapy*, 4:201–202, April 1954.

especially in a correctional institution. Nevertheless, it should be remembered that the distinction is not between "regimentation" and "no regimentation," but merely a difference in degree. Many people in the "free" community live under conditions of extreme regimentation, as witness the child of tyrannical parents, the wife of a jealous husband, the employee of an overbearing employer. There are, moreover, forms of internal regimentation that are largely unrelated to the external environment—the compulsions, obsessions, and phobias of the emotionally disturbed.

The Alternatives in Correctional Therapy

Among therapists who treat delinquents and adult offenders both in and out of institutions, there is currently a dispute between those advocating permissiveness and those advocating more authoritarian methods for achieving the universally undisputed objective of rehabilitation. A full description of that controversy is neither necessary nor possible here.[5] For practical purposes, the action alternatives available to cor-

[5] The following two views of authority and treatment reveal some of the issues involved in this dispute. Carl Rogers has written:

Is it possible for the college counselor to set up a satisfactory treatment relationship if he has the authority to say that a student shall be retained or sent home? Is it possible for the probation officer to be a counselor... if he is responsible for deciding whether the individual has broken probation and hence is to be sent to an institution?
...It seems to the writer that the counselor cannot maintain a counseling relationship with the client and at the same time have authority over him. Therapy and authority cannot be co-existent in the same relationship.... There cannot be an atmosphere of complete permissiveness when the relationship is authoritative. ...If the delinquent accepts a counseling relationship with the probation officer and tells him of further delinquencies, the worker must at once decide whether he is therapist or officer.... The counseling relationship is one in which warmth of acceptance and absence of any coercion or personal pressure on the part of the counselor permits the maximum expression of feelings, attitudes, and problems by the counselee.... This therapeutic relationship is distinct from, and incompatible with, most of the authoritative relationships of everyday life. (*Counseling and Psychotherapy*, Boston: Houghton Mifflin Company, 1942, pp. 109–110, 113–114.)

The views of Rogers are in sharp contrast with those of a group of writers dealing with similar problems of psychotherapy for delinquents:

The tendency of the delinquent to act out his conflicts is the chief obstacle to psychotherapy. The coercion effected through imprisonment... is directed at the antisocial acting out impulses of the individual. Since the delinquent's ego does not sufficiently integrate his antisocial tendencies, these measures, though crude, must be substituted by society for his own inadequately functioning ego.
...Providing they are freed of the vengeful, retaliatory features too often asso-

rectional administrators and correctional therapists can be discussed with reference to three general methods:

1. *The Method of Permissiveness:* This method aims at allowing the offender to define how he will live, work, and relate to others in an atmosphere where imposed rules are held to a minimum. The expectation is that he will spontaneously become aware of his maladaptive trends as they involve him in difficulties with other group members.

2. *The Method of Authority:* This method defines acceptable and unacceptable modes of behavior and aims at restricting to the vanishing point any power of the offender to engage in the unacceptable modes. It not only defines but seeks to enforce the values of the defining authority.

3. *The Method of Authority-with-Choice:* This method authoritatively defines the *consequences* of different forms of behavior but permits the individual more or less voluntarily to commit himself to a line of action. It is made clear, however, that taking certain lines of action will result in a restriction of his freedom of choice. The individual is permitted to exercise this freedom so long as he does not interfere with the free choice of others or endanger or exploit them in defined ways.

Each of these orientations is based on a theory of anti-social behavior and each attempts to justify itself with reference to its theory. The authoritarian theory asserts that offenders cannot be allowed free choice because they have already demonstrated that their choices are anti-social. It points out that the socialization of the young—who are initially nonsocialized—takes place in an authoritarian setting, where free choice is restricted. It holds that both conformity and nonconformity are essentially learned habits and that the way to socialize the offender is to establish the habit of conformity by the repeated practice of exercises in conforming behavior. This must be done in a situation where nonconforming behavior cannot be practiced; unless this precaution is

---

ciated with them, these controls are not in opposition to the true interests of the delinquent. They do not in themselves represent a hostile infringement of his rights nor are they an unjustified interference with the satisfaction of his usual needs. Ideally, the delinquent is provided with a choice: to modify his actions (not his feelings) in accordance with the requirements of society, or to lose a large measure of his self-determination.

... This entails the clarification of all courses of action from which he may choose, with the probable and possible consequences of each openly and thoroughly discussed. It means the alternate choices and their consequences are spelled out at appropriate times with neither retaliatory nor guilty overtones, but simply as a definition of his reality. (M. Kaplan, J. F. Ryan, E. Nathan, and M. Bairos, "The Control of Acting Out in the Psychotherapy of Delinquents," *The American Journal of Psychiatry,* 113:1,110–1,111, June 1957.)

taken, the individual will, by the same repetitive learning process, merely reinforce his anti-social behavior patterns.

Each of the other two positions takes sharp issue with the authoritarian view on several grounds. They point out that, in the socialization of the young, the correct objective is not to compel conformity from without but rather to bring the individual to the point where he internalizes social values and voluntarily enforces them upon himself. External compulsion is used only in the beginning and then progressively relaxed as the child learns to exercise choice within self-enforced limits. While agreeing with the theory that both conforming and nonconforming behavior is *learned,* they argue that unrelaxed authority can inculcate only the habit of *submission to external force,* and that, in the absence of this external force, the habit becomes irrelevant and nonoperative. They further point out that the treatment experience should prepare the individual for living conditions that obtain outside, and that life in a situation where obedience is compelled cannot prepare him for adjusting to a situation where choice is much freer.

A further objection brought forward by the permissive school is that coercion and restriction actually create profound resentment and that, consequently, *the "habit" which is learned is hatred of authority.* All during the time the individual is mechanically going through the motions of conformity he is actually reinforcing the motive to rebel and retaliate—a motive he will carry out at an early opportunity after release.

Advocates of the permissive approach argue that awareness by the individual of his own maladaptive behavior should be the goal of treatment. This process can take place only in a situation where the tensions created by the awareness cannot be diverted into rebellions against authority. They further point out that, in order to become aware of his problems, the individual must be permitted to get into difficulties. Rigidly restricting his behavior will artificially prevent the emergence of these problems and awareness will not take place. Should they happen to emerge in spite of the attempted restrictions, the individual, unwilling to blame himself in the first place, will grasp the opportunity to blame authority for his problems. In doing this, he will be behaving in a psychologically appropriate manner, since his anti-social behavior was, in the first instance, *an uncontrolled aggressive response to frustration.* Continued frustration by authority will only perpetuate this pattern of aggression and thereby contaminate the healing process at its source.

Those advocating free choice within limits defined by authority agree that the major objective of correctional treatment should be the internalization and self-enforcement of social values by the individual. They would also agree that this process cannot be enforced by an external authority to which the individual is hostile, and that the person will only internalize the values of a group with which he can identify. Their advocacy of authority is, consequently, based on other grounds entirely.

Their major argument for the need of a defining authority is based on the characteristics of uncontrolled offender groups. They point to the need for an external ordering authority to control the inmate patterns of group coercion and to cope with the authoritarian character of inmate relationships. They also point to the high status with which the inmate social system rewards its most aggressive, criminalistic, and least improvable members.

The Problem of Accessibility to Treatment

It is axiomatic that any treatment based on the variables of an interpersonal relationship requires some channel of communication and some nexus of need or mutual interest between the participants. In the case of the neurotic, the motive force for treatment is the patient's anxiety and his awareness of his failure to cope with his problems. In contrast to the neurotic, whose experiences have confirmed his inadequacies, the adaptive delinquent[6] has had experiences which have confirmed the *effectiveness* of his adjustment. He has learned that people can be intimidated or manipulated. He has learned a contempt for authority as ineffectual or dishonest—or both. In effect, he has succeeded in establishing a picture of himself and others which is based on a feeling of his own superiority and greater strength.

Thus, while the neurotic comes to the therapy as a consequence of his failure and with a desire to have his adjustment *changed*, the

[6] The terms *adaptive delinquency* and *maladaptive delinquency* used in this discussion follow the distinction made by Dr. Richard Jenkins:

> Delinquency as an adaptation differs from other behavior, which we praise, or at best, condone, only in its illegality. It is goal-oriented, and at its highest level combines careful planning with skillful, calculated, resolute action. There is another kind of delinquency which implies a grosser deviation in personality and in adjustment. It represents not an adaptation but a maladaptation, not the selection and pursuit of a goal so much as the renunciation of any real goal, and a minor disorganization punctured by violence. ("Adaptive and Maladaptive Delinquency," *The Nervous Child*, 2:9, October, 1955.)

adaptive delinquent comes with a relatively undiminished confidence in his success and with the intention to continue his adjustment, in spite of environmental obstacles. This crucial distinction in the motivation for therapy determines how the therapist is perceived. Whereas the neurotic seeks to find a person who will assist him in the modification of uncontrollable feelings and reactions, the adaptive delinquent seeks, in the therapist, a person whom he can maneuver and exploit for the purpose of attaining situational objectives with greater efficiency. Thus, in striking contrast to the neurotic, whose desire for treatment is an outcome of his sense of failure, the adaptive delinquent's request for "psychological help" is frequently the outcome of the reverse motivation: an expression of confidence in his ability to manipulate human relations.

All of the foregoing suggests that the therapeutic process must be continuously related to the offender's degree or *stage of accessibility*. The stage of accessibility determines not merely the character, evolution, and progress of the treatment relationship, but, at all times, the level at which the therapist can work. It is of little use for the therapist to *inform* the offender about what his difficulties "basically" are or to tell him how he "really" feels about himself. From a diagnostic point of view, the therapist may well be correct, but unless the problem is one about which the offender himself is concerned, the information is useless. It may do no more, in fact, than make him aware that the therapist is disturbed about something concerning which the offender is not troubled at all. An offender under treatment with a young new counselor once told about his "progress in treatment" in the following words: "Everything is fine with me and Mr. ——— (the counselor). The only thing is, he's a little upset because I hate myself so much."

Failure to recognize the true stage of accessibility leads to a standard approach which frequently involves the therapist in answering the right questions at the wrong time. Thus, for example, it is fruitless for the therapist to offer warmth and affection to an offender engaged, at that moment, in deceiving or defying him. The inmate may well be in need of affection, but he is clearly not accessible to it. The question he is consciously asking is not, "Do you love me?" but "Can you stop me?" Should the therapist ignore this conscious question and attempt, prematurely, to answer the unconscious one, he will not succeed in reaching the offender on any level. The relationship of accessibility to the treatment process is illustrated in the following synoptic description of the progress of a representative, adaptive, integrated, nonneurotic offender.

The Treatment Process at Successive Stages
of Accessibility

The adaptive offender usually comes to the treatment situation at his most superficial stage of accessibility. He has already defined the therapist in his own mind and has prepared defenses to cope with that definition. Accordingly, the adaptive offender's typical first move in a treatment relationship, which is essentially one long, continuous battle of mutual definition, is to gain control of the situation by means of a favorable definition of mutual roles.

Stage I: The Struggle for Control
("Can I dominate you?")

The initial attempt to gain control is typically disguised as an appeal for help with some immediate environmental problem. The offender represents himself as put upon or abused by persons in his immediate or recent environment. He may appear angry and indignant or helpless and pathetic, depending on his information about the most effective "pitch" to use with the particular therapist. If he has heard that the therapist is easily intimidated, he will hint darkly at desperate measures and appeal for help in controlling his just rage in order "to protect everybody concerned." If the therapist is known to react poorly to this kind of pressure, the offender will represent himself as lost and hopeless. He is at the end of his rope; he "can't take it any more." He may even do away with himself unless "somebody takes the pressure off" him. Of these two approaches, simulated rage and simulated helplessness, the latter is more typical among the more intelligent and devious; both can seem quite convincing.

Nevertheless, it usually requires only a little casual probing to establish the simulation and to unmask the underlying, unverbalized purpose. If the offender seems to be on the verge of some violent and desperate act, a little quiet and detached questioning about *precisely* what he is planning to do, and to whom, will have a remarkably calming effect. Noticing that the therapist is neither alarmed nor impressed, he will quickly shift the emphasis from what he is going to do to others to what others are going to do to him—attempting, now, to mobilize sympathy where he could not stimulate alarm. As in the case of the "violent" offender, so in the case of the "helpless" one. After a few suggestions, it quickly becomes evident that he is not quite so helpless. In fact, far from being solely dependent on the therapist's advice, he has excellent solutions of his own. He knows not only what he himself should do, but what others should do. When one comes right down to it, he even knows what the therapist should do, and is able to point out how his own solution is far superior. Then, with a little encouragement, he will usually spell out the therapist's correct program for him in considerable detail, informing him whom to see, what to say, and what to insist upon, in the interests of justice and the welfare of his client.

This behavior is typical of the adaptive offender and helps to differentiate him from the truly disturbed and maladaptive type. Having evidenced his lack of interest in self-examination by his reticence in discussing his own specific behavior, he shortly manifests his lack of interest in the therapist's suggestions by insisting on "better" solutions of his own. Should the therapist have any lingering doubts about *who* is actually advising *whom,* these doubts may be readily dissolved. If the therapist, in a testing maneuver, continues to question the wisdom of the offender's proposals, a characteristic sequence of reactions takes place. Eliciting these reactions is, in fact, the therapist's next move.

The therapist need only continue in his detached, questioning mode. Gradually, the drift of his questions conveys the fact that the therapist is not only unimpressed by the simulation but is aware of its underlying motives. Failing to get the therapist to aid him—i.e., to help him succeed as an inmate—the inmate will accuse the therapist of not helping him at all. Having been unable to maneuver the therapist into the role of the dupe ("sucker"), the offender now attempts to define him as an oppressor ("son-of-a-bitch"). Since there is no need to simulate friendliness any longer, the offender's hostility becomes overt. This hostility may well be intense now that the offender's earlier definition of the *therapist-as-an-opportunity* has been replaced by an image of the *therapist-as-a-threat.* At this point, the therapist might as well settle back for a long and bitter denunciation of "bug doctors" who think they can "see through people." It is unlikely that the therapist will be able to induce the offender to master his anger sufficiently to continue the relationship at this time. Any attempt to mollify the anger will probably only worsen it, since the offender, already smarting under his failure to define the therapist as a dupe, has a diminished picture of his powers of manipulation and now needs to convince himself that the therapist is a devious, sinister, and hostile person. Conceptualizing the therapist in this manner is much more reassuring to his own self-esteem and the therapist's casual mention of this fact is unlikely to change it.

Stage II: Overt Rebellion
("Can you stop me?")

Once he realizes that the therapist has seen through his attempted deception, the inmate's next question is, in effect, "Can you do anything about it—can you stop me?" which is a more personalized version of his general orientation toward society. Since the offender will almost invariably suspend therapy at this point, it is essential that the therapeutic situation now broaden to include the entire institutional environment. This is indispensable. Failure to deceive the therapist will be of little therapeutic value if, after leaving the therapist's office, the inmate is able successfully to deceive and manipulate his work supervisors, his house parents, or the custodial personnel. His defiant question, *"Can anybody stop me?"*, must be answered in the affirmative, and probably repeatedly.

It is impossible to detail the requirements of an institution capable of accomplishing this objective; a few general points can be made. The inmate's living environment must be sufficiently permissive to enable him to attempt the same kind of adjustment that characterized his anti-social behavior outside. If the environment is too repressive and rigid, he cannot do this. An institution that commands a mechanical compliance through sheer repression merely forces the offender into a behavioral state of suspended delinquency. Underneath this surface compliance, however, his basic attitudes are unchanged; moreover, if the institution is too harsh, it merely gives his hostility a rational and realistic basis.

Though the institution must enable the offender to behave "like himself," it must be sufficiently strong to detect and thwart the adaptive inmate's pattern of manipulation and exploitation. Unless this is done, the institutional experience will merely reinforce the pattern. For the adaptive offender there can be no further therapeutic progress except through repeated environmental failure and frustration. The continued failure is necessary in order to weaken those aspects of the inmate's self-picture which are dependent on his image of himself as a successful manipulator. This weakening process is accompanied by mounting anxiety and—in the case of the healthier and better integrated inmates —will not proceed without several attempts at reprisal and counterattack.

The necessity for these moves is not only internal. In the inmate social system, continued prestige is dependent on success; the inmate who is always "getting caught" invariably falls in social esteem.

Having focused institutional attention on himself, the offender now finds himself "getting caught" with increasing frequency. The point is reached where the offender, no longer in a position to recoup his fortunes by quiet and devious manipulation, must either "give up" and accept a lower status or attempt a bold and dramatic stroke. The decision to take this step transforms his social role from that of the *devious manipulator* to that of the overt and *heroic rebel,* and makes detection and punishment a foregone conclusion in the type of institution just described.

Stage III: Heroic Suffering ("You can't break me.")

In embracing the role of the heroic sufferer by compelling the institution to take drastic disciplinary action against him, the inmate has merely exchanged one acceptable social role for another. If he can demonstrate that he can take "the worst those bastards can throw at me," his continued prestige among the inmates is assured. It is in his interest, now, to bring down on his head whatever forms of mistreatment the institutional personnel can be provoked into committing, thereby enabling him to demonstrate his fortitude. Inmates in this stage of treatment are likely to be dangerous, especially where institutional traditions forbid the kinds of mistreatment most appropriate for enhancing the spectacle of martyrdom. In institutions of this type, the offender may be compelled to go to extreme lengths in order to create this spectacle.[7]

Now, more than ever, the institution cannot afford to grant the inmate victory. The most effective means of frustrating it is to deny the inmate his audience. Unless this is done, he is likely to precipitate and endure continued punishment, content that the eyes of the other inmates are on him as he proves that he cannot be cowed into submission or repentance. Under such conditions he may prolong his commitment to the martyr role to a point dangerous to his physical endurance and safety.

One of the most effective ways of achieving the simultaneous objectives of denying the audience and securing the physical well-being of

[7] Needless to say, the foregoing is not an argument for institutional brutality but rather for extreme caution and rigor in avoiding brutality.

offenders in this stage is the *method of segregation*. The offender is physically and socially isolated in a special section of the institution, cut off from other inmates who are not being similarly disciplined. No other form of punishment is either necessary or desirable. Quarters should be equal to those provided for other inmates; and all other institutional privileges *except* contact with other inmates permitted. Facilities for individual recreation and exercise should be provided. The inmate should be permitted his normal quota of visits and letters and have virtually unlimited access to members of the professional staff, *provided he formally requests their visits*. Since a crucial requirement for satisfaction in his new role is the endurance of suffering before an appreciative audience, extreme care must be taken to protect him from any form of mistreatment by the prison personnel, who must be especially prepared to endure the abuse to which he will subject them.

Even under these conditions, the experience is rigorous enough. Continued separation from the other inmates has the eventual effect of depriving his sacrifice of its most important meaning. This is the most distressing aspect of his segregation and, before long, it has a profound effect. The reactions of offenders under this form of treatment typically pass through three phases, which might be described as the phase of active complaint, the phase of stoicism, and the phase of desperation. The length of each of these phases varies with the personality, strength, and emotional stability of the individual.

At the outset the segregated offender typically preoccupies himself with an ambitious program of protest. Intensive legal activity frequently characterizes this period; the offender busies himself with the search for an effective way to combine the expression of his resentment with a method of obtaining release. Following the failure of legal appeals, there are attempts to appeal to higher administrative authorities; and the inmate may deluge all manner of public officials with a lengthy recital of complaints. As a matter of sound correctional administration, these complaints should be fully and routinely investigated. In addition to providing a precaution against actual injustice, the investigation of unfounded complaints serves a therapeutic purpose. Once again the inmate is provided with a demonstration of failure of his manipulative techniques. Moreover, in view of the fair and impersonal manner in which his complaints are handled, it becomes increasingly difficult for him to sustain the conviction that he has been singled out for mistreatment.

The manner in which these complaints are answered can be of great assistance in bringing about the offender's accessibility to the next stage of treatment. Again and again, the following points should be made: "You alone are responsible for your present situation. You alone are capable of working your way out of it." In this and in other ways, it should be made plain to the segregated offender that, just as he was responsible for his present plight, so he will have to be responsible for his emergence from it.

Stage IV: Despair
("Does anybody give a damn?")

As time passes the inmate will feel a growing sense of abandonment and futility. In spite of his continued refusal to ask for help, the injunctions, "Find out what's wrong, straighten yourself out," will increasingly preoccupy him, especially after he realizes that the doors are closed to any other approach. The knowledge that all authorities are united and in complete earnest concerning his program will have an increasingly sobering effect, and his mood will become pervaded by a deepening despair.[8]

His first request for help should be granted, but little may be expected from it at the outset. The inmate will typically allude to the severity of his situation and the enormity of his punishment as compared with his offense. The therapist will agree that the conditions are severe and, beyond a brief reminder that morality is a two-way affair, will accept no further invitation to debate general problems of ethics. He will continue to pose the questions: "How did you get yourself in here? What led up to it? What were you trying to do? Why did it fail? How can you help yourself?" All of these statements are to be made in the interrogative form, with the therapist carefully resisting any personal temptation—or any invitation from the inmate—to preach and lecture. The offender, glad to be relieved of any responsibility to think himself out of his own troubles, would welcome such an intervention. All of his attempts to elicit this intervention should be refused. The therapist points out: "It is *you* who must find the answers; I can only help you with the questions. By asking me what *I* think, you are still only talking

[8] It should be recalled that the entire purpose of this phase of treatment is to create a mood of defeat and self-doubt in the shortest possible time and in a manner minimally destructive. For this reason, the greater the impact at the beginning, the better. The stimulation of false hopes and the resulting invitation to the inmate to resume his manipulation of officials would be senselessly brutal and antitherapeutic.

about other people, not about yourself. That is what you did before. Anyway, telling you what I want wouldn't work. In the end, you will only do what *you* want to do."

In refusing to lay down a rule of conduct for the inmate, the therapist is doing two essential things. By telling the offender that only he can control himself, the therapist is asserting that it is right and proper for people to be in charge of their own behavior and wrong for them to be under the domination of others. In taking this position, the therapist is further asserting that the responsibility for behavior cannot be shifted from the person himself.

Stage V: The Emergence of Self-Doubt
("This is getting me nowhere.")

In order to remain continuously hostile and defiant over a long period, a basically healthy individual requires fresh experiences of mistreatment. Unlike the neutrotic or paranoid person, who is continually able to manufacture external irritants out of his own abundant internal problems, a relatively well-adjusted individual cannot continue to restimulate his indignation in the absence of actual injury or abuse. Eventually, the segregated adaptive offender, almost against his own will, begins to find that his attempts to remain self-righteously hostile are beginning to suffer from a kind of law of diminishing returns. In effect, his basic soundness and sheer sense of reality start to betray him.

The struggle against this break-through of reality may be long or short, depending on many factors, including the relative success of his attempts to provoke mistreatment. In a secure and humane segregation setting, these attempts should uniformly fail. Verbal abuse, the threat of physical attack against the guards, the petitions to higher authorities —none of these have availed. The guards refuse to return the abuse. The bars and walls are secure against the inmate's threats and plans of attack or escape.[9] Every petition and complaint has been scrupulously investigated and courteously answered. The inmate is visited regularly by the doctor, and the most groundless claim of illness is seriously examined. Visiting privileges are preserved; he is permitted the same number

---

[9] The safety of guards and inmates requires that the segregation cell block maintain conditions of extreme custodial security. This requirement by no means implies the solitary dungeons of the "Siberia" type. Perhaps the most antitherapeutic effect of these discredited penal devices lay in the fact that they made heroes and martyrs of those confined in them.

of contacts with family members, legal advisers, and other authorized visitors as those allowed to nonsegregated prisoners. More important still, he is continuously aware of the fact that other segregated inmates— often with "worse" records than his own—are being released from time to time.

For these and other reasons, the relatively well-adjusted segregated offender cannot indefinitely prolong his mood of righteous indignation and self-justification. Just as it failed to pay off with the authorities, the role of martyr begins to pall on the offender himself. Eventually, he begins to be troubled by the insistent question: "Can it be *me?*"

This illumination, it should be stressed, comes rarely in the form or as a result of a conversion to newer values and moral principles. On the contrary, any protestations by the inmate that he has "seen the light" and is "now a new man" should be regarded with skepticism. True feelings of futility and self-doubt are not accompanied by enthusiasm, especially toward those responsible for stimulating the doubt. If anything, the offender truly undergoing this process is often *more* rather than *less* hostile to the authorities at this point. Already appalled by the futility of his efforts, he is now likely to be even more upset by the uncontrollable waning of his own hostile *élan*—a condition that, almost invariably, leads to a self-distrust verging hazardously on self-disgust. It is the emergence of this self-distrust and internalized hostility that marks the next stage of the offender's accessibility to therapeutic progress. This emerging mood may take one or more of various forms, including depression, loss of interest in activities, and increased irritability toward friends among the other segregated inmates.

Despite the fact that it may be disguised by intensified hostility toward the authorities, the offender's accessibility is now at a high point. Nevertheless, the therapeutic situation is extremely delicate and fraught with opportunities for bungling. Now, more than ever, the therapist must avoid any temptation to moralize. Statements implying an "I-told-you-so" attitude will merely divert the inmate from his crucial job of resenting himself. His achievement of self-distrust is precious to the therapeutic situation and should not be diluted by any well-grounded disgust with the therapist. For these reasons, it is quite unnecessary to observe that the inmate has "now seen the error of his ways." He is well aware of what will be expected of him on release from segregation; declarations of intention, promises to "behave," should be neither solicited nor accepted. The inmate should not be required to acknowledge any newly discovered obligation to the institution. He never had one in the first place. His only obligation was to himself—and this was the obligation he violated.

Thus, the only promise the offender can be expected to make is a promise to himself—the more silent and nonrhetorical, the better. Empathy and silent sympathy at this point are much more valuable, and valid, than words. The therapist should convey his awareness of the fact that the inmate is engaged in a violent internal struggle, a struggle into which the therapist will not intrude unless invited. He will probably not be invited; nonetheless, his silent understanding is participation enough.

There is another reason for avoiding any exchange of hopeful platitudes at this point. Ideally, the release of the inmate from segregation should come as a complete surprise to him. It should not come until he has given up all hope of effecting it by any manipulation of his own. Rhetorical exchanges are dangerous invitations to simulation; the offender should never be able to feel that he has achieved his release by finding the right words to say to the right person. The mood of self-doubt must not be corrupted and allowed to degenerate into a "pitch."

The decision to release should be made by agreement among custodial and treatment officials. However long and painfully deliberated, it should occur suddenly and without expectation by the inmate; it should have something of the aspect of a miraculous and incomprehensible deliverance.

Stage VI: Testing
("Can I make it?")

The treatment has now reached the stage where the inmate's new orientation must be tested. Because it is essential that this test be as realistic as possible, it is desirable that emergence from disciplinary status be followed by a "probationary period" during which the offender lives among the general inmate population.

The probationary period should be deliberately designed to reproduce significant aspects of the offender's future parole environment. Returning the segregated inmate to the general inmate population anticipates, in many ways, his eventual return to the street. During his future parole period the released offender will meet acquaintances associated with his former criminal career. Many of the personal and social pressures for a return to the criminal pattern will be present. His former criminal associates will be well aware of his knowledge of their contacts and techniques. So, too, will the police. As a continuing criminal he would be "safe"; as a reformed criminal he would be a decided risk. The one reasonably sure way of guaranteeing his loyalty—or, at least, his silence—is to reinvolve him in crime.

Similar pressures play on the returned segregated offender. As one of the institution's former "bad men," he has a wide knowledge of prison rackets and contact men. He knows the identity of the corruptible guards. Thus, in returning to the prison population, the segregated offender undergoes his first experience of balancing on the tightrope that leads back to a noncriminal existence. This rehearsal can be uncomfortably realistic; it is in society's interest to make it as lifelike as possible.

Any thoroughgoing change in the offender's attitudes must inevitably bring him into conflict with acquaintances who have not undergone a similar attitudinal evolution. The emergence of this conflict in some form is the one indispensable symptom of a true change; unless it appears, the therapeutic results are doubtful. This conflict is, moreover, not merely a symptom of improvement but one of the most important processes by which it is achieved. Consequently, the creation of this conflict and the resulting alienation of the individual from the core values of the inmate social system is essential.[10]

Stage VII: Fixating the Therapeutic Results and Terminating Institutional Treatment

The fact that the offender has made his choice may be evidenced by the outbreak of conflict with inmates whose values remain unchanged. It is now that the inmate social system, formerly the greatest obstacle to therapy, becomes its greatest asset. Previously a source of security and status, it now becomes a source of derogation and threat. The decision to transfer the probationer to another facility should be made when the inmate has successfully negotiated the hazards and temptations of his probationary period. The new institution should be minimum in custody and reserved entirely for inmates in the final stages of treatment. As such, it represents the last stage in a kind of correctional Pilgrim's Progress which began in the wilderness of this world and went the full route.

[10] Cf. McCorkle and Korn, op. cit., p. 88:
As the concept "socialization" implies group membership, so the derivative concept "resocialization" implies changes in group memberships. Many findings in the social origins of individual behavior suggest that the problem of reshaping the antisocial attitudes and values of offenders is related to the possibility of altering the patterns of group membership which they bring with them into the prison.

The major purpose of the foregoing discussion was to relate one conception of a total institutional treatment program—from which there would be many local deviations—to the critical question of the adaptive offender's capacity for positive change. It was pointed out that the adaptive offender's typical self-picture, supported by a self-confirming pattern of interpersonal manipulation, usually insulates him effectively against the anxiety and self-doubt essential for true accessibility to treatment. Accordingly, the initial objective of a therapeutic program must be to stimulate this anxiety and self-doubt and then to utilize it constructively. Needless to say, this procedure is not indicated in the case of maladaptive offenders, whose treatment is more likely to involve a reduction in anxiety and frustration.

Specific Treatment Techniques

IN THE PREVIOUS CHAPTER AN ATTEMPT WAS MADE TO OUTLINE A general course of treatment procedures under more or less optimal institutional conditions. It is now necessary to turn from the ideal to the actual and from the general to the specific and technical. How are the treatment conditions and resources of various institutions to be evaluated? What specific therapeutic techniques are available for use in correctional institutions in this country?

Difficulties Confronting Estimates of Treatment Resources and Conditions

It is almost impossible to estimate the actual treatment conditions in an institution without being personally on the scene. Institutional reports dealing with treatment facilities usually confine themselves to two kinds of descriptions: (1) statistical data about the number of treatment personnel or hours of treatment available, compared with the number of inmates; and (2) general statements about the institution's treatment policies and objectives. Neither of these methods is particularly informative; both may seriously mislead.

Statements about the ratio of treatment personnel to inmates are related to standard reporting practices of hospitals, in which the ratio of doctors and nurses to patients provides some index of the intensiveness of the medical care available. In general, the lower the ratio of patients to personnel, the better. Since medical procedures are more or less standardized, this method of reporting is informative; knowing the number and specialties of the medical staff provides a rough picture of what is being done. Moreover, hospital reports usually provide data on number of admissions, number and types of operations and their outcome, releases, deaths, etc., which provide additional bases for evaluating the effectiveness of the work being done.

The reporting practices of most correctional institutions usually do not and probably cannot meet these standards. In the first place, information about the number of treatment personnel and hours tells little about what the treatment staff is doing. Since correctional treatment procedures are largely unstandardized, this deficiency can hardly be avoided. Furthermore, even if it were found possible to describe the treatment routines in detail, these descriptions would not indicate *what else was happening in the institution.*

This is the critical issue. In a correctional institution, unlike a hospital (where patients are largely immobilized in beds and relate only superficially to each other), these "other" happenings may be much more relevant to actual treatment conditions and consequences than the formally described "treatment activities" themselves. Studies of the inmate social system underscore the fact that the individual's total adjustment is much more dependent on his relations with other inmates than it is on his interactions with staff members. Consequently, any description of the "treatment situation" which emphasizes inmate-staff relations to the neglect of inmate-to-inmate relations is necessarily biased and incomplete.

Public and private correctional agencies are dependent on the confidence of those who supply funds for their maintenance. They must justify their operations to budgetary committees and various supervisory boards. For these reasons, it is perhaps inevitable that institutional reports serve a public relations as well as a descriptive function. Saul Alinsky has described how this function distorts the reports of agencies working in the area of delinquency; his comments are applicable to the correctional field at large:

All agencies operating in the field of delinquency prevention are armed with a fool-proof approach which guarantees them success regardless of what happens. These agencies have a magic formula. This formula can best be described in that American colloquial statement, "Heads I win and tails you lose."

If... the agency is armed with statistics then it is truly in an invulnerable position. If after it comes into a community the rate of delinquency goes down the workers can always say, and do say, "See, figures don't lie.... We came in and the rate of delinquency went down." If the rate remains constant they can say, and do say, "We have held the line—since we have been working here there has been no increase in juvenile delinquency." If the rate of delinquency goes up they say, "See, crime is on the increase and if it weren't for our work just think how much higher it would be. This proves we need more money."[1]

The inherent tendency toward distortion in institutional reporting is encouraged by another condition. In this country treatment facilities tend to be concentrated in agencies and institutions for juveniles. But juvenile offenders also have the highest failure (recidivism) rates. Consequently, it is possible to compile statistics showing that the rate of failure increases with the increase of treatment personnel and decreases with their absence. In itself, this finding may signify nothing more than that juvenile offenders tend toward recidivism much more frequently than adult offenders. For analogous reasons, one would expect to find a higher death rate in hospitals specializing in diseases of the aged than in those dealing, say, with obstetrical cases. The higher death rate in hospitals of the first type implies nothing about the efficiency of the medical staff, though it does indicate that, because of the nature of the conditions treated, the treatment is not generally efficacious.

The general tendency of correctional treatment institutions to stress their successes and minimize or rationalize their failures is probably related to the current public demand that they either "produce or close up." The "heads I win, tails you lose" argument described by Alinsky is designed to cope with this public relations problem. Its effect is to render official reporting of treatment results practically valueless. For this reason, a survey of treatment resources and conditions must confine itself largely to a description of techniques and objectives rather than an evaluation of consequences.

[1] Saul Alinsky, "Heads I Win and Tails You Lose," *National Probation Association Yearbook, 1946* (New York, The Association, 1947), p. 41.

Techniques of Individual Treatment

Variations in Treatment Techniques

The number and variety of treatment techniques in use with individual patients is great, though somewhat less than the variety of theoretical orientations they reflect. The following brief review will confine itself to the methods themselves.

Therapeutic techniques may vary along several dimensions: (1) the extent to which the therapist actively participates in the treatment interaction; (2) the extent to which the therapist intervenes in the patient's activities or environment; (3) the technical procedures comprising the treatment method; (4) the average length of time required for the course of treatment.

EXTENT OF THERAPIST'S ACTIVE PARTICIPATION IN THE TREATMENT INTERACTION. The usual distinction made is between *directive* and *nondirective* techniques. The term *directive* identifies any technique in which the therapist deliberately uses persuasion, suggestion, or any form of personal influence to affect the patient's attitudes or behavior, or the flow and direction of his productions during the interaction. The use of interpretations is usually considered directive. In the most general sense, *directive* refers to the extent to which initiatives are taken by the therapist rather than the patient. The term *nondirective* applies to techniques which deliberately and rigorously avoid intervention by the therapist. All initiatives are to originate with the patient; for this reason, nondirective therapists speak of their method as "client-centered." The nondirective therapist attempts to create an entirely accepting, nonchallenging, and nonjudging atmosphere and does not offer criticism or advice of any kind.

EXTENT OF INTERVENTION IN THE PATIENT'S ACTIVITIES OR ENVIRONMENT. The variation along this dimension extends from absolute nonparticipation to virtual management of the patient's activities. Many therapists insist on maintaining an exclusively dyadic relationship, refusing to see or consult with any other figures in the patient's life. Other methods involve a varying degree of environmental manipulation by the therapist. In some forms of social casework—of which parole supervision is sometimes cited as an example—the caseworker attempts to exploit all possible personal and social resources of potential benefit to his client. He may assist in setting up living arrangements, aid in securing employment, obtain medical care, etc. These activities involve the caseworker in a multiplicity of relationships not only with his client but with other persons actually or potentially involved with him.

DIFFERENCES IN THE TECHNICAL ASPECTS OF TREATMENT. One broad distinction in the technical aspects of treatment involves the use or nonuse of special techniques or physical procedures to stimulate the patient's responses. Hypnosis or the administration of hypnotic drugs (e.g., sodium amytal) may be employed to elicit material that might otherwise be repressed. In cases of unmanageable anxiety or hyperactivity, drugs (tranquilizers) may be indicated. In the treatment of children or others for whom verbal interactions would be inadequate, the use of various play materials is common; these may include plastic clay, finger-paints, dolls, etc. The aim here is to enable the patient to express in activity feelings and ideas it would be difficult or impossible for him to express verbally.

For adult patients, the method favored by most psychoanalysts is *free association*. The patient is induced to relax, usually in a reclining position, and encouraged to let his thoughts drift with no attempt at conscious control, direction, or censorship. Because this approach attempts to reach processes below the ordinary level of conscious awareness, it is sometimes called a "depth" method. In contrast with this technique, which deliberately avoids the mutual stimulations and distractions of ordinary conversation, other methods deliberately attempt to approximate the usual face-to-face conversational situation. This is the approach used in most forms of counseling, where the purpose is to deal directly with the individual's total response patterns, including his conscious attitudes, as these are expressed in his usual interpersonal relations. The psychiatrist Harry Stack Sullivan has pointed out that this more casual procedure is equally, if not better, suited to reach depth levels in certain cases—especially with disturbed patients, where direct probing would stimulate too much anxiety.[2]

AVERAGE TIME REQUIRED FOR FULL COURSE OF TREATMENT. One of the most frequent questions asked by patients is, "How long will the treatment take—how long before I get better?" The answer to this question depends on the nature of the therapeutic objective and the time and effort both patient and therapist are prepared to devote to its pursuit. Classical psychoanalytic therapy required five one-hour visits per week and a minimum of two hundred hours. Relatively few patients are able

[2] Harry S. Sullivan, *The Psychiatric Interview* (New York: W. W. Norton and Company, Inc., 1954), p. 83.

to follow so intensive a schedule and, consequently, it is not unusual for analysis to continue for two-, three-, and four-year periods. In an extremely candid study called "Analysis Terminable and Interminable,"[3] Freud, the founder of psychoanalysis, called attention to the difficulties involved in defining and measuring cure.

In response to a widely felt need for shortening the term of a psychoanalysis, analysts have experimented with variations designed to intensify and thereby accelerate the treatment process. One of these variations is the technique called "hypnoanalysis," a well-known example of which is reported in Robert Lindner's *Rebel Without a Cause*,[4] the record of a series of hypnotic interviews with a prisoner. Franz Alexander has experimented with a short-term technique called "Briefer Psychoanalysis," a method described as more flexible and including a relatively greater degree of intervention and environmental manipulation by the therapist.[5]

Because their objectives tend to be more limited and more specific, counseling procedures require considerably less time. Therapists employing counseling methods have claimed thoroughgoing achievements of insight and relief of neurotic symptoms from five to ten sessions—sometimes even fewer.[6] The relatively limited objectives of vocational counseling and academic counseling are frequently achieved in one or two meetings. In the case of problems involving clarification of attitudes—in family counseling, for example—the period is longer but rarely exceeds a few months, with, on occasion, sporadic revisits.

Treatment Objectives

Since the criteria of cure are still largely—and perhaps inherently—subjective, it is more realistic to speak of treatment objectives in terms of intentions and directions rather than end-results. The problem is frequently complicated by the fact that the goals of the patient and the therapist may differ. In discussing failures with psychoanalytic treatment, Oberndorf has pointed out:

[3] Sigmund Freud, "Analysis Terminable and Interminable," *International Journal of Psychoanalysis*, 18:373–405, Part 4, October 1937.

[4] Robert Lindner, *Rebel Without a Cause* (New York: Grune and Stratton, Inc., 1944).

[5] Franz Alexander, Thomas M. French, *et al.*, *Psychoanalytic Therapy: Principles and Applications* (New York: Ronald Press, 1946).

[6] Carl R. Rogers, *Counseling and Psychotherapy* (Boston: Houghton Mifflin Company, 1942).

...The goal which the patient aims to attain...does not always coincide with that which the psychoanalyst hopes to achieve and neither of these estimates may correspond to that which the patient's family or friends would consider a desirable outcome. Also, various psychoanalysts may differ in what they consider a satisfactory result in a given case.[7]

Therapists usually distinguish between two broad purposes of treatment: *support* and *reintegration*. As the term suggests, *supportive therapy* aims to bolster the patient, to hold him up, on the basis of the resources and defenses he has already mobilized against his problems. The purpose is not so much to resolve the problem by attempting to alter its underlying determinants but rather to reduce its effects, to insulate the person against it. *Reintegrative therapy*, on the other hand, involves an attempt to deal more or less radically with the underlying determinants, many or all of which may be below the level of conscious awareness.

Though any therapeutic relationship is to a certain extent supportive, the choice between support and reintegration involves real differences in risks, in the time required, and in the potential consequences. In order to deal with the underlying determinants of his behavior, it is necessary for the patient to abandon the defenses he has erected against facing them in the first place. Consequently, the main emphasis is on breaching defenses rather than supporting them. In the most general sense, where supportive therapy tries to enable the patient to live with his problems by means of a better organization of his defenses, reintegrative therapy attempts to bring the patient to reject his defenses and grapple with his problems so that he can live without either. This latter form of treatment requires the utmost skill and patience on the part of the therapist, and a willingness to spend considerable time where necessary. Moreover, since reintegrative treatment involves an inevitable disruption of aspects of the individual's former adjustment, its choice involves a willingness to take calculated risks. The degree of risk is related to the character of the problems, to their centrality in the person's total adjustment, and to their relative force in comparison with that of the individual's other psychological resources. Thus, the decision between these two modes is related to a variety of practical and diagnostic factors requiring careful analysis in the individual case.

[7] Clarence P. Oberndorf, "Failures with Psychoanalytic Treatment," in Paul Hoch, ed., *Failures in Psychiatric Treatment* (New York: Grune and Stratton, Inc., 1948), p. 14.

Suitability of the Various Treatment Techniques
for Correctional Institutions

As has previously been pointed out, the lack of objective criteria defining cure and the absence of objective comparisons of the effectiveness of the various treatment methods renders a truly objective choice among them virtually impossible. To say that one method is better than another is, at this point in the development of psychotherapeutic techniques, to make a value judgment based on subjective impressions or theoretical bias. Consequently, the selection of one or more of the various treatment methods for institutional programs must be based on practical considerations. In effect, the choice is not between methods which are more or less likely to succeed, but between methods which are practical or impractical to use.

LONG-TERM METHODS. On the basis of a thirty-hour weekly treatment schedule and a minimum of three weekly sessions per patient for a two-year period, one psychoanalyst can treat ten inmates every two years. Employing the briefer method outlined by Alexander, the same analyst might conceivably increase his patient load to forty inmates a year. Since the populations of most correctional institutions are usually reckoned in the hundreds rather than in tens or scores, the widespread institutional use of long-term techniques is a practical impossibility.

SHORT-TERM METHODS. The practical realities cited above virtually limit the choice of treatment methods to those requiring a shorter period of time, of which various forms of counseling and brief analysis are the major alternatives. The way in which these techniques are used may vary according to the several dimensions described above: they may be directive or nondirective, they may or may not involve environmental manipulation. In most cases, the choice of techniques is more or less suggested by the character of the problems themselves. The following report of the activities of a two-man counseling staff over a six-month period suggests something of the range and variety of problems presented in a maximum-security prison with approximately 1,000 inmates:

Analysis of Counseling Contacts [8]

Between September, 1952 and May, 1953, the Counseling Service made an approximate aggregate number of 1,625 contacts with inmates or members of their families. A breakdown of these contacts follows:

[8] Unpublished report of the Department of Education and Counseling, New Jersey State Prison, 1953.

Contacts Initiated by Officials

The Classification Committee: Approximately 150 inmates presenting special problems of work and housing assignments were referred, formally or informally, by members of the Classification Committee. Approximately 90 per cent of these were finally placed in jobs.

Institutional Parole Recommendation Committee: Approximately 105 inmates were referred by the institutional Parole Recommendation Committee for a pre-parole report on their personal, institutional and social adjustment.

The Disciplinary Court: The Disciplinary Court has recently made increasing use of the Counseling Service in the cases of inmates whose infractions are thought to be related to severe emotional problems. These inmates, referred prior to the passing of sentence, are interviewed by the counselors who then report back to the court. Five cases have been formally referred; in each case the action of the court has followed the recommendation of the counselor. (Note: the counselors have, on rare occasions, made reports on their own initiative to the court; in a majority of these cases, the action of the court has conformed to the counseling recommendation.)

Inmates Referred by Various Institutional Officials
(Exclusive of the Court and Classification Committee)

The counselors have made approximately 400 contacts based on information or initiatives supplied by various institutional officials. This information usually concerned personal problems within or without the institution.

Contacts Initiated by Inmates

The largest number of contacts have been initiated directly by inmates, without the mediation of any intervening officials. A breakdown of presenting problems and dispositions follows:

Problems Concerning Work Assignment: Approximately 175 contacts have been initiated by inmates desiring changes in their work assignment. Approximately 70 per cent of these contacts have resulted in changes in classification; the remainder resulted in no recommendation for change. The Classification Committee has followed the recommendation of the counselors in approximately 80 per cent of the cases. The largest single cause for rejection of any recommendation has been custodial.

Problems Concerning Quarters: Approximately 150 contacts have been initiated by members desiring transfers or changes in quarters. The counselors have made favorable recommendations regarding these requests in approximately 65 per cent of the cases; the Classification Committee has concurred in approximately 80 per cent of these.

Personal Problems Unrelated to the Institution: Approximately 400 contacts have been initiated by inmates for counseling in regard to personal problems of adjustment. Approximately 350 of these contacts were handled in no more than five interviews; the remainder have been placed on a basis of fairly continuous counseling. At this writing, six inmates are receiving continuous psychotherapeutic counseling.

Personal Problems with Other Inmates: Approximately 150 contacts involved problems with other inmates; roughly 25 per cent were of a serious character, involving highly explosive situations frequently concerned with homosexuality.

The large majority of these problems were resolved directly with the inmates concerned and without any intervention by the custodial authority. Custodial intervention, initiated by the counselors, was required in most of the serious cases for the purpose of making rapid transfers and taking other emergency preventive action.

Contacts with the Families of Inmates

The counselors have had approximately 75 direct contacts with members of the inmates' families and approximately 20 contacts by mail.

Contacts with Social Agencies

The Counseling Service has had contact with 5 social agencies; these chiefly concerned economic problems of inmates' families.

In addition to the formal contacts and interviews itemized above, the counselors have had innumerable brief contacts with inmates in the shops and wings; these contacts consumed approximately 25 per cent of the working time of the staff.

Application to a Specific Counseling Situation

The problems and methods discussed in the previous pages may be concretely illustrated by the record of a fairly typical first counseling session with a nonneurotic delinquent of average intelligence who was transferred, as a disciplinary case, to an adult institution.

The counselor opened the session by asking why the inmate had come to see him.

Inmate: Well, I've been talking to a few of the guys.... They said it might be a good idea.

Counselor: Why?

Inmate (In a fairly convincing attempt to appear reticent): Well—they said it did them good.... They said a guy needs somebody he can talk to around here...somebody he can trust. A...a friend.

Counselor: And the reason you asked to see me was that you felt that I might be a friend? Why did you feel this?

Inmate (A little defensively): Because they told me, I guess. Aren't you supposed to be a friend to the guys?

Counselor: Well, let's see now. What is a friend supposed to do? (Inmate looks puzzled.) Let's take your best buddy, for example. Why do you consider *him* a friend?

Inmate (Puzzled and a little more aggressive): I dunno.... We help each other, I guess. We do things for each other.

Counselor: And friends are people who do things for each other?

Inmate: Yes.

Counselor: Fine. Now, as my friend, what is it you feel you'd like to do for me?

Inmate (Visibly upset): I don't get it. Aren't you supposed to help? Isn't that your job?

Counselor: Wait a minute—I'm getting lost. A little while ago you were talking about friends and you said that friends help each other. Now you're talking about my job.

Inmate (Increasingly annoyed): Maybe I'm crazy, but I thought you people are supposed to help us.

Counselor: I think I get it now. When you said "friends" you weren't talking about the kind of friendship that works both ways. The kind you meant was where I help you, not where *you* do anything for me.

Inmate: Well...I guess so. If you put it that way.

Counselor: Okay. (Relaxing noticeably from his previous tone of persistence.) Now how do you feel I can help you?

Inmate: Well, you're supposed to help people get rehabilitated, aren't you?

Counselor: Wait. I'm lost again. You say I'm supposed to do something for *people.* I thought you wanted me to do something for *you.* Do *you* want me to help *you* get rehabilitated?

Inmate: Sure.

Counselor: Fine. Rehabilitated from what?

Inmate: Well, so I won't get in trouble anymore.

Counselor: What trouble?

At this point the inmate launched into a vehement recital of the abuses to which he had been subjected, from his first contact with the juvenile authorities to his most recent difficulties with his probation officer immediately prior to the offense (stealing a car) leading to his present sentence. During the entire recital he never referred to any offense he had committed but, instead, laid exclusive emphasis on his mistreatment.

The counselor heard this account out with an expression of growing puzzlement which was not lost on the inmate, who continued with increasing vehemence as his listener appeared increasingly puzzled. At length the counselor, with a final gesture of bewilderment, broke in:

> *Counselor*: Wait...I don't understand. When you said you wanted me to help you stop getting into trouble I thought you meant the kind of trouble that got you in *here*. Your difficulties with the law, for example. You've talked about your troubles with different people and how they get you angry but you haven't talked about what got you into jail.
>
> *Inmate* (Visibly trying to control himself): But I am talking about that! I'm talking about those bastards responsible for me being here.
>
> *Counselor*: How do you mean?

The inmate again repeated his tirade, interspersing it with frequent remarks addressed to the counselor. ("What about this? Do you think *that* was right? Is that the way to treat a young guy?", etc.) The counselor once more looked puzzled, and broke in again.

> *Counselor*: I still don't see it. We'd better get more specific. Now take your last trouble—the one that got you into the reformatory. This car you stole....
>
> *Inmate* (Excitedly): It was that —— P.O. (probation officer). I asked him if I could get a job in New York. He said no.
>
> *Counselor*: What job? (The inmate admitted that it wasn't a specific job, just "any job in New York.")
>
> *Counselor*: But I still don't follow. The probation officer wouldn't let you work in New York. By the way—don't the regulations forbid probationers from leaving the state?
>
> *Inmate*: Well, he could've given me a break.
>
> *Counselor*: That may be—but I still don't follow you. He wouldn't let you work in New York, so you and a few other guys stole a car. How does that figure?

(Here the inmate "blew up" and started to denounce "bug doctors who don't help a guy but only cross-examine him.")

> *Counselor*: Wait a bit, now. You said before that you wanted me to help you. We've been trying to find out *how*. But so far you haven't been talking about anything the matter with *you* at all. All you've talked about are these other people and things wrong

with them. Now are we supposed to rehabilitate *you* or rehabilitate *them?*

Inmate: I don't give a —— who you rehabilitate. I've had about enough of this. If you don't mind, let's call the whole thing off.

Counselor: But I do mind. Here you've been telling me that my job is to rehabilitate you and we haven't talked five minutes and now you want to call the whole thing off. Don't you want to be rehabilitated? (Inmate is silent.)

Counselor: Let's see if we can review this thing and put it in the right perspective. You said you wanted to be rehabilitated. I asked you from *what* and you said, from getting into trouble. Then I asked you to talk about your troubles and you told me about this probation officer. He didn't give you what you wanted so you stole a car. Now as near as I can understand it, the way to keep you out of trouble is to get people to give you what you want.

Inmate: That's not true, dammit!

Counselor: Well, let's see now. Have I given you what you wanted?

Inmate: Hell, no!

Counselor: You're pretty mad at me right now, aren't you? (Smiles. Inmate is silent, looks away.)

Counselor (In a half-chiding, half-kidding tone): Here, not ten minutes ago you were talking about what good friends we could be and now you're acting like I'm your worst enemy.

Inmate (Very halfheartedly, trying not to look at the counselor's face): It's true, isn't it?

Counselor: C'mon now. Now you're just *trying* to get mad. You won't even look at me because you're afraid you'll smile.

(Inmate cannot repress a smile. Counselor drops his kidding tone and gets businesslike again.)

Counselor: Okay. Now that we've agreed to stop kidding, let's get down to cases. Why did you come to see me today?

(Inmate halfheartedly starts to talk about rehabilitation again, but the counselor cuts in.)

Counselor: Come on, now. I thought we agreed to stop conning. Why did you come?

Inmate: Well . . . I heard you sometimes see guys . . . and . . .

Counselor: And what?

Inmate: Help them

Counselor: How?

Inmate: Well, I tell you my story . . . and . . .

Counselor: And then? What happens then? (Inmate is silent.)

Inmate (Finally): You tell *them* about it.

Counselor: Who do I tell?

Inmate: You know—people who read them.

Counselor: Should I write a report on this session?

Inmate: Hell, no!

Counselor: What do you think we should do?

Inmate (Looking away): Maybe I could ... (falls silent).

Counselor (Quietly): Maybe you could come and talk to me when we really have something to talk about?

Inmate: Yeah ... Aw, hell ... (laughs).

This interview illustrates the problems and possibilities inherent in the crucial first counseling session with an adaptive offender of average intelligence who attempted to conceal his true feelings and his motive to manipulate under the disguise of a request for friendly help.

Any hope of therapeutic contact with this individual was dependent on the counselor's ability to unmask his actual attitudes and develop the counseling relationship with dignity and candor. Failure to pierce the disguise—which, characteristically, was designed to tempt the counselor by flattering him—would have foredoomed the counselor to a relationship with a mask. Behind this mask the delinquent, entirely untouched and unreached, would merely be congratulating himself on his success in deceiving and manipulating the naive adult world. Needless to say, the antitherapeutic consequences of this relationship—involving, as it did, an "expert" in rehabilitation"—would have been severe.[9]

The special character of the adaptive delinquent's motivations concerning treatment requires a special counseling technique. The usual methods of permissiveness, nondirection, and acceptance require modification. To have permitted the delinquent to "define the relationship" would have been disastrous, since that definition would have left the counselor no alternative to the roles of dupe or oppressor ("sucker" or "s-o-b"). Similarly, to have encouraged this adaptive delinquent to "solve his problems in his own way" would have been merely to collaborate with him in the continuation of his anti-social pattern: the manipulation of personal relationships for the purposes of self-aggrandizement and exploitation.

The first job of the counselor was to convey the fact that he was aware of the delinquent's underlying motive and his attempt to control the counseling situation. This accomplished two objectives: (1) it unmasked the attempt to manipulate; and (2) it uncovered the delinquent's true feelings of hostility. This job had to be done casually and without

---

[9] This inequality in the potentialities for good and bad effect is one of the more depressing facts of psychotherapy with offenders. The damage that can be done by the inexperienced in this field almost invariably overweighs the often meager, always hard-won results that may be achieved by the skillful. For this reason it is a mistake to assume that "some treatment is better than none."

condemnation, the counselor conveying the impression that the delinquent's behavior was entirely "natural" and to be expected. The absence of a condemning attitude is essential, for, though the delinquent's hostility must be laid bare, he must not be given any realistic basis for it. In effect the therapist says: "You are angry at me not because I have hurt you but because you weren't able to con me. You're also angry because I haven't given you a real reason to be angry."

The subsequent course of a counseling relationship initiated in the manner described above will depend on many factors, not all of which are under the direct control of the counselor. In many instances—perhaps in the majority of cases—the experience of failure in manipulating the counselor will not be enough to modify the pattern, and the counseling situation will require broader support from the total institutional environment.

Techniques of Group Therapy

In recent years correctional administrators and therapists have given increasing attention to the use of group methods. Many of the methods employed can be traced to early reports of a Boston physician who developed a new method of treatment for patients with psychosomatic ailments. He referred to his techniques as the "class method" and used conversational groups.[10] This method was later introduced into other treatment situations. During World War II the group psychotherapy movement (as it is generally referred to now) was greatly expanded. Treatment personnel were in short supply, and military patients with psychological difficulties increased as the war continued. The use of group methods was not limited to psychiatric patients, however, but was expanded to include delinquent soldiers sent to rehabilitation centers in an effort to restore them to full duty.

To determine the status of group therapy in current programs of United States correctional institutions, the Committee on Group Psychotherapy in Correctional Institutions and Agencies conducted a survey of penal and correctional institutions during November and December

[10] J. H. Pratt, "The Class Method of Treating Consumption in the Homes of the Poor," *Journal of the American Medical Association*, 49:755–759, August 1907.

of 1950. Questionnaires were mailed to 312 institutions; 109, or 35 per cent, responded.

1. It was found that 35 per cent of the institutions are currently using some form of group therapy and another 9 per cent are planning to start this kind of program soon.

2. Group therapy programs are a relatively recent addition to the treatment programs of our penal and correctional institutions. This observation is borne out by the fact that almost half of them, 41 per cent, have been in operation for one year or less.

3. There appears to be some tendency to redesignate existing activities with names currently in vogue. Evidence to support this contention rests on the fact that 75 per cent of the institutions [using group therapy] incorporated [it] into established, existing programs such as occupational therapy and activity programs and orientation programs. Only 25 per cent of [these] institutions reported that group therapy was considered as exclusively a part of the general psychotherapy program.

4. Although largely administered by professionally trained personnel, psychiatrists were responsible for operating group therapy programs in only 10 per cent of [these] institutions. Other therapists included psychologists (23 per cent), psychiatric social workers (9 per cent), and others such as teachers, occupational therapists, counselors and educational directors (58 per cent).

5. The level of therapy varied somewhat: 53 per cent of the institutions used the lecture-discussion method, 9 per cent used the psychoanalytic approach, 9 per cent used the repressive-inspirational technique, and 29 per cent used other types of group therapy such as music, athletic and analytic-oriented programs.

6. The number of sessions per month varied from 12 to 72 and the number of participants in each group from 8 to 20 inmates. There was some fluctuation in the number of inmates reached by the group therapy program. The range was from 53 to 102.

7. The majority of institutions relied on voluntary participation and on recommendations by members of the staff. However, there was no standardized procedure for selecting persons for the therapy groups. Also, it seems that group therapy helped "neurotic offenders," "normal inmates," and "minor behavior disorders," and that it was of little value to the feeble-minded or psychopathic inmate.

8. When asked whether they would be interested in receiving assistance in establishing a group therapy program, 27 per cent expressed a desire for aid. Of these institutions, 15 per cent sought training for their own personnel and 12 per cent preferred to employ qualified personnel.[11]

[11] Lloyd W. McCorkle, "The Present Status of Group Therapy in United States Correctional Institutions," *International Journal of Group Psychotherapy,* 3:85–86, January 1953.

Forms of Group Therapy[12]

From a survey of the literature, one might surmise that there were as many forms of group therapy as there are practitioners in the field. In an effort to order this chaos, Giles Thomas in 1943 ranged the work of selected practitioners along a continuum bounded by two antithetical abstractions: repressive-inspirational and analytical. Thomas says, in defining one of his ideal types: "The general trend in repressive-inspirational psychotherapy is to urge the patient to control himself, to suppress asocial or worrisome thoughts and wishes and to find an interest or inspiration in life, work, the community, religion, etc." Defining the other ideal type, he says: "Analytical therapy urges the loosening of repression, the conscious recognition and analysis of unconscious asocial wishes. It aims to free energy bound in needless repression and does not direct the patient's activities toward specific goals but holds that once the energies are free the patient will himself find suitable outlets."[13] After pointing out that most psychotherapy contains elements of both ideal types, Thomas cites Alcoholics Anonymous as an extreme example of the repressive-inspirational type and the work of Schilder as an extreme example of the analytical type.

Group Techniques in Correctional Institutions

In an effort to introduce into civilian correctional institutions the experiences of correctional therapists with group methods during the war, the New Jersey Department of Institutions and Agencies made an attempt to apply the technique to reformatory populations. As a result of their experiences, the therapists setting up the program elected to call the application of group methods to correctional populations "guided group interaction":

> To avoid confusion with the use of group psychotherapy as practiced by psychiatrists, and to avoid any implication that inmates are mentally abnormal and unbalanced, we decided to call the application of group-therapy principles to inmates "guided group interaction." Guided group interaction is defined as the use of free discussion to reeducate the

[12] The following discussion is derived from Lloyd W. McCorkle's article "Group Therapy," in Paul Tappan, *Contemporary Correction* (New York: McGraw-Hill Book Company, Inc., 1951), pp. 211–223.

[13] Thomas W. Giles, "Group Psychotherapy: A Review of the Recent Literature," *Psychosomatic Medicine*, 5:166–180, April 1943.

delinquent to accept the restrictions of society and to find satisfaction in conforming to social norms.[14]

In discussing group therapy in correctional institutions, Lloyd W. McCorkle, who assisted in the development of guided group interaction in the New Jersey System, states:

> To develop a group-therapy program with the above implications for the customary ways of behaving in the institution means that the administration must be ready actively to support and maintain the program. In correctional institutions this means that with anything less than the wholehearted support of the warden or superintendent the program will be at best ineffectual and at worst a dangerous failure. It is a truism in correctional institutions that whatever the warden is interested in succeeds and whatever he does not participate in fails. Since the group-therapy program will conflict sharply with established programs and practices, it is necessary to have the intelligent, sympathetic support of the warden and also to initiate a staff training program.
>
> In-service training of both custodial and professional personnel at the institution, regarding the goals and methods of group therapy, is important because they all become involved in the program. Inmates may use their attendance at group-therapy sessions to threaten or intimidate personnel of the institution. After the program is established the inmates will at first use it to threaten the personnel with exposure if they do or say things the inmates do not like. Unless the staff members have received training, such threats make them insecure and antagonistic to the program.
>
> Group therapy may also bring hostilities to the surface that inmates had previously suppressed. Feelings may overflow in other relationships, and members may get into difficulties with the institutional rules and regulations as a result of this. Unless personnel are aware of why this happens, they may become suspicious of the program and decide that "it does more harm than good." One humorous illustration of the kind of problems the establishment of a group-therapy program may make for the noninmate members of the prison community occurred at the Fort Knox Rehabilitation Center. The inmates, utilizing words learned in group sessions, would refer to angry guards as "frustrated." This would be laughingly picked up by an inmate who would "offer a group-therapy explanation for his frustration." The guards were totally unprepared for this type of response, and when the inmates learned that this disturbed them even more than curses, they became eager and enthusi-

---

[14] F. Lovell Bixby and Lloyd W. McCorkle, "A Recorded Presentation of a Program of Guided Group Interaction in New Jersey's Correctional Institutions," *Proceedings of the Seventy-eighth Annual Congress of Correction of the American Prison Association*, Boston, 1948. Mimeographed.

astic "auxiliary egos." It was finally necessary to establish an orientation program that was in effect a disguised group-therapy program for the personnel of that installation.

The question of who should attend group sessions and what types of inmates should be specifically included is an area in which there is considerable disagreement. Frequently, selection of inmates for group therapy is discussed in relation to psychiatric diagnosis, and some leaders would exclude certain categories: psychopaths, alcoholics, mental defectives, and homosexuals. Others would include these categories, provided they were in homogeneous groups; and still others would deal with these in heterogeneous groups. The decision as to who should attend group sessions can only be made after a definition of the form of group therapy to be employed has been made. After this has been decided the selection of individuals for participation becomes less of a problem. Regarding reformatory inmates, it would seem that if the group-therapy program is to achieve maximum effectiveness, all should attend some form of group session. If this ideal cannot be reached the decision of who should attend can best be determined by the leader. Dr. Lewis Wender's observation that "Any individual who does not disturb the equilibrium of the group should not only be allowed to come to group therapy but should be encouraged to do so" is an excellent guide. It would seem advisable to make selections on the basis of reaction to group life rather than on categories such as psychopath, psychoneurotic, etc. It is an invaluable experience for all to learn the essential similarity of their ways of meeting problems. This also allows for a considerable amount of flexibility in dealing with individuals in groups and makes for maximum utilization of group pressures, supports, and influences.

The actual time spent in sessions and the number of sessions per week an inmate participating in the program should attend vary with the number of personnel available, the availability of inmates, and the institution's work, recreation and school programs, etc. Arbitrarily, sessions usually last from fifty minutes to one hour. It would seem preferable, initially at least, to make the time actually spent in sessions quite fluid, since often the group does not get "settled" for at least an hour. Later, the group should be encouraged to impose definite limits upon itself and to hold to a rather rigid pattern.

Group sessions have the implication that the material discussed will come from the revealed preinstitutional and institutional experiences of participants. Some leaders have found it useful to have a schedule around which they integrate the program. While this may be useful in didactic sessions, it is doubtful how much practical value such a schedule would have in more analytically oriented group therapy. Some practitioners have also attempted to guide the process into phases, usually following the sequence of preliminary or orientation, analytical, and synthetic. The goals for these phases vary in the emphasis and method employed by each leader and the nature of the activity of the group. Often, starting with more or less formal lectures on human behavior in which the "class method" is employed, there is increased "ventilation" of feelings by members, and discussion becomes more personalized. As group members become increasingly active in the discussion, the emphasis shifts from intellectual understanding of human motivation to analysis of relationships, with a final synthesizing of material.[15]

In the same article McCorkle presents several excerpts from recorded group interaction sessions with inmates. One of these excerpts, in which a young reformatory inmate tells of his brother's death and his own feelings of guilt, is included here. At best, such excerpts afford only an inadequate description of what actually takes place in group sessions, where the infinite variety of events escapes even refined mechanical recording efforts.

Leader: What about that? Why do you feel you spent so much time with your brother? That is the question he asks.

W.: Epileptic, spells, well anyhow, any place he went I was with him in case he took sick or anything. I looked out for him and he looked out for me. If I got in trouble he would help me out, like fighting or anything he would break it up or step in front of me and stop me from fighting. And after he died I felt as if I was responsible for his death or something. You know, I feel I was responsible for his death.

Leader: How is that, you are telling us you feel somewhat responsible for your brother's death?

W.: Well, he and I went to Philadelphia from Elizabeth, New Jersey, for a recreation trip and the truck left to go back at eleven o'clock and he wasn't there so I left without him. I don't know where he was or where to find him so I go back to camp and Monday morning, back in March, 1942, they come out and got me at work taking me back and my company commander told me they found my brother on the road dead. Well, I couldn't believe it. It seemed unreasonable and after I seen it was everything was backwards, you know, and everything went black for me. And I figured if I had stayed with him it probably wouldn't have happened.

Leader: What did he die from, or of?

W.: They claimed that he fell in a ditch as a result of this spell, and died of drowning.

Leader: I see, he fell in a ditch as a result of this spell. You say when you went back to the morgue everything went black?

[15] McCorkle, "Group Therapy," pp. 216–218.

W.: Yes.

Leader: Anything else? How long were things black?

W.: For a couple of days.

Leader: For a couple of days and since that time you have felt somewhat guilty for this?

W.: Yes.

F.: Well, I mean when he said there, like Bob said, he should be able to get along with people, be able to get himself accustomed to different people—to associate with them and go along with them, not to be kinda shy or afraid of them in any way, and if he wants to be by himself then he is okay. Well, like myself, I like to be alone but I can be in a crowd of people and get along as well with a hundred as I can with one but I'd rather be by myself altogether.

Leader: Yes.

E.: Well, in this case, wouldn't that be he took on a responsibility at a small age when his brother had those epileptic fits?

Leader: He did, yes. He said he felt responsible since he can remember, responsible for his brother. He took care of his brother when he had those seizures and he feels now somewhat guilty about the fact that he was not with his brother when his brother had the seizure that resulted in his death. Don't you think that is a very important thing with him, that he had this strong feeling toward his brother and then was not with his brother when his brother died. As he told us about it, it was so strong that for several days after his brother's death he doesn't even remember what happened.

Leader: Yes. What were you going to say?

B.: I think he felt so toward his brother that he couldn't be friends to other people, just like a blind man with a dog he can't get along without it.

H.: He said something about he tried all the different fellows who were around and couldn't seem to find a companion who saw his way or anything like that. Did that go for the female part of it too? You didn't find a girl you could depend upon?

W.: I am married.

Leader: You are married, you say?

W.: Yes.

Leader: How do you get along with your wife?

W.: Fine.

Leader: Fine, no trouble with her.

W.: No trouble with her.

Leader: Children?

W.: One.

Leader: One child.

N.: That part of the male situation, that could be centered on hero worship too. He may have worshipped his brother to such an extent that he couldn't find anybody to replace him—nobody would come up to his standard.

H.: Sure.

Leader: Nobody could meet his brother's standards.

Leader: He says "I still feel it." Well, what about that?

F.: Well, I mean he feels that he was responsible for it himself and he is doing a lot of things that ordinarily wouldn't come naturally that he wouldn't do.

Leader: Yes.

P.: Well, I think the thing for him to do when he is by himself—kind of feel himself out, think back and figure out just how far he is carrying it—is he carrying it too far—is he taking everything to blame on himself. Spread it out and find out that some things he could be responsible for that he could probably have prevented and some things that he couldn't. Carry that feeling that far and maybe he would get rid of some of it anyway and go along like that, maybe he would feel better.

Leader You think he might lose some of it in this group today?

F.: Yes, he might.

Leader: What do you think about that?

Leader: Well, you have been rather tense telling us about it. It made you a little uneasy to tell us about it. Yet he wanted to tell us about it. I wonder why?

W.: If I was to relax, think it over probably.

M.: Get it off his chest.

Leader: Wanted to get it off his chest?

H.: Give him a little relief.[16]

In a later article McCorkle likened effective guided interaction groups in correctional institutions to a manufactory of human projectiles in a social situation that already has all the aspects of a human arsenal. Because this is true, the therapist is morally obliged to give serious consideration to the control elements available in the institution and to the adequacy with which they will be able to cope with the multiple tensions generated. Failure to anticipate the effects of this added source of instability in an already unstable situation will defeat the objectives of the group therapy program.

The Highfields Project

In order to explore the potentialities of guided group interaction in an informal, free, but loosely structured situation, the State of New

[16] *Ibid.,* pp. 221–223.

Jersey and the New York Foundation in 1950 established an experimental, short-term residential treatment center for twenty adjudicated delinquent boys aged sixteen to eighteen. In 1952 the State of New Jersey assumed full financial responsibility for the project and in 1957 it was given formal legal recognition. Ernest Burgess, who acted as chairman of a scientific advisory committee established to evaluate the effectiveness of the project, has raised seven important questions concerning the experiment and has offered partial answers based on the staff's research and experience:

1. The Feasibility of a Residential Center

Highfields opened with its first group of boys and a staff of four persons. The boys were not committed but came as a condition of probation. There was faith but not certainty that the Center could be operated successfully without guards and without the other precautions against escapes of the large custodial reformatory. There was nothing to prevent all the boys from running away and thus putting an end to a noble experiment.

The idea of permissiveness was carried still further. There was a minimum of regulations. The boys were privileged to spend their free time in informal association. They were told on admission that no effort would be made to prevent their leaving the Center. The one deterrent was their knowledge that an escape was a violation of probation and would result in a new appearance before the juvenile court judge who had sent them to Highfields.

2. Creating an Atmosphere of Rehabilitation

How could an atmosphere of rehabilitation be created? It is generally agreed that in a reformatory, institutional patterns of thinking and acting tend to develop which array the boys against the staff of the institution.

A central problem of a reformatory is the difficulty of establishing an atmosphere favorable to rehabilitation. Yet this is, or should be, the chief objective of a reformatory if it is to live up to its name. Many factors operate against such an atmosphere. First, there is the large size of the institution which focuses attention on the mechanics of administration rather than on interpersonal relations of the residents. Then there are rules and regulations which emphasize regimentation and which have to be enforced.

Also, there is the development of institutionalized patterns of behavior by which the boy seeks to evade or break the rules and regulations.

Finally, as a result of these influences, the group influence operates to maintain and even to intensify delinquent attitudes. Accordingly the reformatory, instead of rehabilitating the boy, tends rather to provide further education in delinquency.

3. The Nature of Guided Group Interaction

Rehabilitation begins with changes in attitudes. But how can these be brought about? The boys entering Highfields have for years identified themselves as delinquents. Their close friends are delinquent. Group pressure has generally pushed and pulled them into delinquency and prevented their rehabilitation. Most delinquents feel rejected and discriminated against by their parents. They generally manifest strong emotional reactions, particularly against their fathers, but often against their mothers, brothers, and sisters. By the time they are confronted with law-enforcing agencies they have developed strong ego defenses. They do not take the responsibility for their delinquency. Instead, they tend to blame others—their parents, their associates, and society.

The whole Highfields experience is directed toward piercing through these strong defenses against rehabilitation, toward undermining delinquent attitudes, and toward developing a self-conception favorable to reformation. The sessions on guided group interaction are especially directed to achieve this objective.

Guided group interaction has the merit of combining the psychological and the sociological approaches to the control of human behavior. The psychological approach aims to change the self-conception of the boy from a delinquent to a nondelinquent. But this process involves changing the mood of the boy from impulses to lawbreaking to impulses to be law-abiding.

To accomplish rehabilitation, the sociological approach is also needed. The insight of sociology is to reverse the process by which the group inducts a boy into delinquency and compels him to continue in it. In guided group interaction, the influence of the group is directed to free the boy from being controlled by delinquent association and to give him the desire and inner strength to be autonomous.

4. The Process of Guided Group Interaction

Guided group interaction is based on psychological and sociological conceptions. But psychological and sociological terms are not used in the sessions.

Only two concepts are voiced by the boys. The first is that of "problem." What is my problem? How did I become a problem to myself and others? How can I go about to solve my problem?

The second concept is that of "progress." Have I made progress in understanding my problem? Am I making progress in solving my problem? ...

5. Time as a Factor in Rehabilitation

How long does it take to obtain changes in attitude that may be expected to persist after the boy returns to his community? Highfields has operated on the assumption that three to four months would be adequate. Most reformatories adhere to a minimum residence of twelve months.

The experience of Highfields seems to justify the value of a short period. The boys sent to Highfields are, in general, normal except for their delinquency and antisocial attitudes. Only a few are admitted unintentionally who have deep-seated psychological difficulties.

It can therefore be concluded that the short period of residence in Highfields is adequate for the changing of attitudes of the normal delinquent boy.

6. Evaluation of the Success of the Project

Studies by the Gluecks in Massachusetts and by Shaw and associates in Illinois have revealed the high rate of recidivism of boys after their release from reformatories and industrial schools. It seemed, therefore, desirable to compare the percentage of recidivism of boys with Highfields experience with those who had been released from Annandale, the New Jersey State Reformatory. This comparison was pertinent because the boys sent to Highfields would presumably have been committed to Annandale had Highfields not been founded.

The Highfields story presents a telling account of the much lower percentage of boys with three to four months' Highfields experience who became delinquent after return to the community than of the boys with twelve or more months' residence at Annandale.

The findings are all the more convincing because of the careful control of the factors which might have been responsible for the more favorable outcome of the Highfields boys. The boys in both groups are from Essex County, in which Newark, the largest city in the state, is located. The lower recidivism rates for Highfields as compared with Annandale still hold when the following factors are held constant; number of years of schooling, marital status of parents, residence, race, and age of admission to Highfields or Annandale.

The findings... confirm those found by Dr. Ashley Weeks in his comparative evaluation of the lower recidivism rates for Highfields than for Annandale, reported in a separate volume.[17] Weeks' conclusions, however, were open to the criticism that judges selected cases for Highfields which were more likely to succeed, while sending those more likely to fail to Annandale. This objection was met in the other evaluation by choosing boys from Annandale who were committed there before Highfields opened, but who were of the type that the juvenile court judge would later send to Highfields. The results of the two independent evaluations greatly strengthen the conclusion that Highfields is much more effective in the rehabilitation of delinquents than is the conventional reformatory.

7. Change of Superintendents

At the end of two years' service, Dr. McCorkle resigned as superintendent of Highfields. Mr. Albert Elias, who had served as intern at Highfields for three months while on leave of absence from the Sheridan reformatory in Illinois, was appointed to succeed him.

The change in superintendents was a clear-cut test of the objection that the success of Highfields might be due to the personality of the first superintendent rather than to the ideas embodied in the project. The continued success of Highfields under the new superintendent demonstrated that the project was not dependent on one personality. The success was due to basic principles and techniques that were communicable and could be learned by other persons.[18]

[17] Recidivist rates for both groups were tabulated for intervals of 12, 24, 36 and 60 months after release. The total recidivism for both groups over the entire 5-year period is given in the table below:

TOTAL RECIDIVISM AMONG DELINQUENTS RELEASED FROM
ANNANDALE AND HIGHFIELDS
(Uncorrected for Exposure Time)

	White	Negro
Annandale		
No. cases	25	24
Recidivists	18	21
Highfields		
No. cases	25	25
Recidivists	9	11

(Source: *The Highfields Story, op. cit.,* p. 144.)

[18] Ernest W. Burgess, Foreword in Lloyd W. McCorkle, Albert Elias, and F. Lovell Bixby, *The Highfields Story* (New York: Henry Holt and Company, 1957), pp. iv–viii.

Correction at the Crossroads[1]

Historical Phases in the Response to Offenders

THE HISTORY OF SOCIAL REACTION TO UNTOLERATED DEVIATION MAY BE roughly divided into three great epochs, the first stretching from remotest antiquity to relatively recent times, the second beginning only a century ago, the third, still struggling to be born. The fact that many elements of later eras were anticipated earlier, the fact that many aspects of the earlier periods persisted well into the later ones, renders generalization misleading. The following brief review is given with this caution in mind, and with the added awareness that each of these epochs was the result of indescribably complex social, economic, and historical factors.

Punishment Unconcerned with the Offender

From earliest recorded times to approximately the middle of the eighteenth century, the social reaction to the offender was exclusively in terms of the welfare of the victim and the community. Whether the major emphasis was on retaliation, deterrence, disablement, or social

[1] The title of this chapter is adapted from Professor George Vold's article, "Criminology at the Crossroads," *Journal of Criminal Law and Criminology*, 42: 155–162, August 1951.

defense, the attitude toward the offender was relatively undeviating: he was a person who, by the act of offending, had forfeited his claim to social concern. Unchallenged for centuries, this unconcern with the offender was not seriously disturbed until that mighty intellectual and moral upheaval known as "The Enlightenment," when it came under sustained attack by isolated individuals. By the middle of the eighteenth century these isolated voices had blended into a rising chorus of protest against the undiminished barbarity of the older forms of punishment. At first this protest took the negative form of an indictment of the older methods; it was not until the demand for reform had produced a practical alternative that the movement was able to progress from the stage of protest to the stage of a positive program.

Punishment as a Method of Reformation

This program had two significant effects, one technical, the other ideological. By the end of the eighteenth century, the reformers had generally agreed on a platform favoring penal incarceration as the humane and effective alternative to earlier forms of punishment. To this technical solution was added a more significant ideological development: the conception that punishment, in addition to protecting the community, should serve also to improve the offender. By the second decade of the nineteenth century this movement had resulted in widespread replacement of the older forms of punishment by the single method of imprisonment. This replacement was neither total nor universal as yet. Many of the old forms of corporal punishment persisted into the new era, undergoing a redefinition as disciplinary techniques within the prison. The single most important survival of the old period was capital punishment, a method which persists still, though widely curtailed.

At its inception the new technique of imprisonment was widely hailed by men who had the vivid contrast of the old brutalities freshly before their eyes. As time wore on this basis of comparison faded, and there was an increasing tendency to view imprisonment itself as a barbarity. Coupled with this was the growing awareness that the prison was falling far short of achieving the universal deterrent effects hoped for by the reformers. This rising criticism was given its strongest impetus by a new theory of criminality, which attacked the core of the doctrine on which the eighteenth-century reformers (collectively known as the "Classical School") had built their hopes.

The heart of the Classical doctrine was the idea that crime is a deliberate act based on the criminal's rational estimate of gains against risks. By nicely calculating the length of imprisonment to be assessed against each offense (a longer period for graver offenses, a shorter period for lesser), and by making sure that punishment was swift and certain, the eighteenth-century reformers felt they would achieve a maximum of deterrence and a minimum of injustice. Pointing to the undiminished recidivist rates, the new theorists (known as the "Positivists") advanced the doctrine that the criminal act is both nonrational and, at bottom, nonvolitional as well, and that the criminal is actually suffering from some form of disease that prevents him from taking rational advantage of the careful calculations framed for him by the Classical School. Since crime is a form of sickness, it cannot be expected to respond to punishment; one might as well expect to cure an epileptic by beating him. The only cure for the disease of crime is some form of treatment—treatment based not on the character of the offense but on the condition of the offender. The widespread acceptance of this doctrine may be said to have ushered in, at least on the ideological level, the third major epoch: the era of treatment.

The Era of Treatment

By the end of a century that had seen a virtually world-wide abolition of slavery, there remained only two classes of persons under the complete domination of the State: the hospitalized insane and the institutionalized criminal. For the members of free societies increasingly aware of problems and responsibilities of social welfare, it was inevitable that the presence of these captives would become an increasingly acute moral problem. In the case of hospitalized mental patients, the problem was ameliorated considerably by the growing professionalization of treatment and the liberalizing of laws. In the case of the confined criminal, no similar solution seemed to present itself, and the persistence of the age-old attitude that the malefactor deserved his suffering only worsened the moral dilemma.

A necessary tenet of this traditional view was that the criminal was in full voluntary control of his behavior. This position was well established in the criminal law, which had made it the basis of criminal responsibility. It had also been accepted by the early prison reformers. Neither Beccaria, Voltaire and Howard earlier, nor Bentham and the Quakers later, had ever challenged this doctrine. Their indictment of

the older forms of punishment had been based on the idea that the infliction of suffering should be made more deliberate, more scientific, and
more uniform, and less personally degrading and physically destructive.

In an intellectual atmosphere increasingly skeptical of all philosophical simplicities, including ethical ones, the uncomplicated doctrine
of moral culpability began to weaken under inquiry. Denied this formidable prop, the "ruthlessness of the pure heart"[2] began to appear, to
many, more ruthless and less pure. At this juncture the simple moral
issue was further complicated by a new doctrine from the dawning
science of psychiatry: the idea that disease as well as immorality was
involved in criminal behavior.

From this point the history of educated thinking about the criminal
revolved around the attempt to accommodate the new and nonmoralistic
concept of disease with the older idea of moral culpability. An excerpt
from a widely valued contemporary textbook on psychiatry reveals this
accommodation at a time when the transition to a nonmoral view of the
criminal still involved much heart-searching. The uneasiness in the
writer's mind is clearly expressed in the following lines:

> Crime is not then in all cases a simple affair of yielding to an evil
> impulse or a vicious passion, which might be checked were ordinary
> control exercised; it is clearly sometimes the result of an actual neurosis
> which has close relations of nature and descent to other neuroses....
> There is a borderland between crime and insanity, near one boundary
> of which we meet with something of madness but more of sin, and near
> the other boundary of which something of sin but more of madness.
> ... With a better knowledge of crime, we may not come to the practice
> of treating criminals as we now treat insane persons, but it is probable
> that we shall come to other and more tolerant sentiments, and that a
> less hostile feeling towards them, derived from a better knowledge of
> defective organization, will beget an indulgence at any rate towards
> all doubtful cases inhabiting the borderland between insanity and crime;
> in like manner as within living memory the feelings of mankind with
> regard to the insane have been entirely revolutionized by an inductive
> method of study.[3]

Once the unitary doctrine of moral responsibility was undermined,
the possibility arose that those who inflicted the pain rather than those

[2] An aseptic comment by George Bernard Shaw in *The Crime of Imprisonment* (New York: Philosophical Library, 1946), p. 63.

[3] Henry Maudsley, *Responsibility in Mental Disease* (New York: D. Apple-
ton and Company, 1878), pp. 32–35.

who endured it were morally culpable. By the early years of the twentieth century this possibility had become a certainty for some of the profoundest contemporary thinkers. In his book, *The Crime of Imprisonment*, George Bernard Shaw has this to say in a section provocatively titled, "Most Prisoners No Worse Than Ourselves":

> We may take it, then, that the thief who is in prison is not necessarily more dishonest than his fellows at large, but mostly only one who, through ignorance or stupidity, steals in a way that is not customary. He snatches a loaf from the baker's counter and is promptly run into gaol. Another man snatches bread from the tables of hundred of widows and orphans and simple credulous souls who do not know the ways of company promoters; and, as likely as not, he is run into Parliament. You may say that the remedy for this is not to spare the lesser offender but to punish the greater; but there you miss my present point, which is, that as the great majority of prisoners are not a bit more dishonest naturally than thousands of people who are not only at liberty, but highly pampered, it is no use telling me that society will fall into anarchic dissolution if these unlucky prisoners are treated with common humanity. On the contrary, when we see the outrageous extent to which the most shamelessly selfish rogues and rascals can be granted not only impunity but encouragement and magnificent remuneration, we are tempted to ask ourselves have we any right to restrain anyone at all from doing his worst to us. The first prison I ever saw had inscribed on it "Cease to Do Evil: Learn to Do Well"; but as the inscription was on the outside, the prisoners could not read it. It should have been addressed to the self-righteous free spectator in the street, and should have run "All Have Sinned, and Fallen Short of the Glory of God." ... Much of the difference between the bond and the free is a difference in circumstances only: if a man is not hungry, and his children are ailing only because they are too well fed, nobody can tell whether he would steal a loaf if his children were crying for bread and he himself had not tasted a mouthful for twenty-four hours. Therefore, if you are in an attitude of moral superiority to our convicts; if you are one of the Serve Them Right and Give Them Hell brigade, you may justly be invited, in your own vernacular, either to Come Off It, or else Go Inside and take the measure you are meting out to others no worse than yourself.[4]

Shaw's refusal to admit any real difference between the confined criminal and his unconfined brother illustrated a major transformation of attitude among increasing numbers of influential men. For centuries

[4] Shaw, *op. cit.*, pp. 69–70, 71–74.

the punishment of offenders had been justified by a conviction that the criminal was basically different from other people.[5] With this difference repudiated, both the factual and the moral basis of punishment appeared to become untenable. It would be difficult to overestimate the importance of this transformation, which amounted to a virtual reversal rather than a shift of attitudes. The moral indignation that had previously been mobilized against the offender as an enemy of society now became, itself, an immoral attitude. It was the prisoner rather than his victim who merited the sympathy and concern of his fellow-men. In effect, the prisoner was now the victim, and those who punished him were the true offenders.

These twin conceptions of the *prisoner-as-victim* and the *society-as-oppressor* have become increasingly popular. Equally important, they became more and more the attitude of the articulate prisoner himself, providing him with an almost invincible moral argument against his jailors. Moreover, by encouraging him to divert his attention from his own guilt to the guilt of the society that had confined him, it gave him an unparalleled opportunity to reverse the moral roles. Where before, he himself had been called on to reform, it now became his turn to call on society to repent. In a book written by the prisoner Julian Hawthorne in 1914, the manifesto of the new convict is presented in stirring and prophetic terms:

> My business in this book was to show that penal imprisonment is an evil, and its perpetuation a crime; ... that it does not protect the community but exposes it to incalculable perils.... Men enfeebled by crime are not cured by punishment, or by homilies and precepts, but by taking off our coats and showing them personally how honest and useful things are done. *And let every lapse and failure on their part to follow the example, be counted not against them, but against ourselves who failed to convince them of the truth, and hold them up to the doing of good.*

[5] With characteristic acuteness, Shaw did not outrightly repudiate the popular conception of the "criminal type" recently criticized by Goring and other English critics of Lombroso. Pointing out that the data of criminal typology had been derived from studies of men in prison, and asserting that "nobody who has ever visited a prison has any doubt that there is a prison type," Shaw goes on to argue:

> What this means is that the criminal type is an artificial type, manufactured in prison by the prison system. It means that the type is not one of the accidents of the system, but must be produced by imprisonment no matter how normal the victim is at the beginning, or how anxious the authorities are to keep him so. The simple truth is that the typical prisoner is a normal man when he enters the prison and develops the type during his imprisonment. (*Op. cit.,* p. 108.)

Had we been sincere and hearty enough, we would have prevailed.[6] (Italics supplied.)

In this passage Hawthorne sets forth the doctrines that have since become commonplace in the publications of offenders both in and out of prison. Similar views may be found in every institutional newspaper where free expression is permitted. The emphasis is largely on the crimes committed by society; if the crimes of the prisoners are mentioned, they are immediately attributed to the evils of the social order. The principal social evil is the system of imprisonment, which has inexcusably reduced free men to the status of slaves.

Society's justifications for these abuses are dismissed by Hawthorne as hypocritical rationalizations. The offender's anti-social acts are called flimsy excuses for the greater enormities of prison conditions, particularly since many prisoners are "victims of tricks and legal technicalities." In any case, the responsibility for the crime is attributed not to the criminal but to society.

Having driven the prisoner to crime, society is accused by Hawthorne of complicating its own original criminality by punishing him. This manifest evil cannot long continue; it is an offense not only against man but against God as well. Yet it is unlikely that either God or man will intervene soon enough. Hawthorne is pessimistic about the acceptance of his "radical and astounding" proposals by the public; it may be that the prisoner will have to help himself. In a passage ominously prophetic of the era of riot and bloodshed shortly to commence in the 1920's, Hawthorne speaks of the appeal to force, should reason fail:

> The proposal toward which the book points ... is so radical and astounding ... nothing less than that Penal Imprisonment for Crime be Abolished ... that the author can hardly escape the apprehension that the mass of the public will dismiss it as preposterous and impossible. And yet nothing is more certain in my opinion than that penal imprisonment for crime must cease, and if it be not abolished by statute, it will be by force.[7]

Highly successful in their re-education of the public, somewhat less successful but still enormously influential with public officials, the program of the reformers has largely missed its principal target: the inmate himself. The ominous hostility voiced by the prisoner Hawthorne when the prison reform program was already under way has been

---

[6] Julian Hawthorne, *The Subterranean Brotherhood* (New York: McBride, Nast and Company, 1914), pp. xvii–xviii.

[7] *Ibid.*, pp. xi–xii.

exceeded in virulence by two new generations of convicts, each living under progressively improved prison conditions. If one were to draw graphs charting the rise in prison improvement, the increase and liberalization of parole, the extension of freedom and conditions of dignity within the walls, and if one were to compare these graphs with the rise in recidivism and the increase in riots and prisoner violence, the factual conclusion would be inescapable. Side by side with the slow fulfillment of the dreams of the reformers there has rapidly grown up a penological nightmare.

"Progressives" and "Traditionalists"

With regard to this situation, two extreme and simple theories have continued to dominate public debate. As is typical of two-sided controversies, the two theories, in addition to their oversimplifications of the problem, have the unfortunate effect of polarizing social attitudes and preventing a dispassionate search for alternatives in the middle ground. One is either "for" or "against" the prisoner, and correctional progress; one is either on the "side of society" or on the "side of the criminal." Each "theory" is simple enough to be stated briefly.

The most popular version of the extreme "progressive" school would argue that the failure of the reform program is due to the fact that it did not go fast or far enough. This position—which is also the view of the articulate inmate—ascribes the increased violence of modern prison populations to the continued rigor and harshness of prison life. Recidivism is similarly explained: having been demoralized in prison, the convict re-emerges into a society which continues to reject him and to deny him the essentials of a fruitful and law-abiding life.

The rebuttal offered by the "traditional," "custodial," or "reactionary" school—the name varies with the describer's own orientation—might answer these arguments as follows: The criminal was violent and dangerous when he was on the street—long before he got into prison. The effect of the modern reforms has been to make prison life more and more like life on the street, where the criminal was at his worst. What, then, is more natural than for the criminal in prison to behave more and more as if he were outside? He was "bad" before he came in—largely because he had been spoiled and pampered. He will be "worse" when he comes out, after being spoiled and pampered even more. The essential thing to do is to stop spoiling him, to get tough with him, to "teach him his lesson," to show that "prison is no picnic," and that he "can't get away with pushing people around."

Pressed to acknowledge that many people are criminalistic prior to any contact with law enforcement, the extreme progressive will accept this fact and turn it to good account in support of his cause by asserting that the criminal "got that way" in the first place by being mistreated. Continuing to mistreat him will only make him worse. On the other hand, treating him well, especially in modern minimum-security institutions, will make him better. The progressive points with pride to the absence of violence and the "good results" of such institutions as Chino and Seagoville.

The "traditionalist" is not in the least convinced by this rebuttal. Acknowledging the rarity of known violence in minimum-security institutions, he points out that the inmates selected for these establishments are almost invariably nonviolent criminal types in the first place. Being mostly "con-men," "swindlers," "racketeers," and accidental offenders to begin with, they know a "good thing" when they see it. In any case, behind the famous nonwalled institution at Chino stands the highly walled and equally famous institution known as San Quentin. If the "progressives" are so confident that kind treatment is what reforms the criminal, why don't they tear San Quentin down or, better still, transfer the San Quentin population to Chino, and vice-versa? As for the "good results" of these minimum-security institutions, the "traditionalist" is in a disturbingly advantageous position when he demands "facts and figures instead of platitudes."

Confronted by the theory that criminals on the street "got that way" because they were mistreated by society, the traditionalist would ask, "Which criminals, and how do you propose to treat them on the street?" Is it proposed that such unfortunates as Al Capone, Joe Adonis, Lepke Buchalter (to name a well-known few out of a well-known multitude) should have been treated more leniently and understandingly? Shall the professional racketeer, the builder of criminal syndicates, the systematic swindler and embezzler, the corrupt politician, be preserved from the demoralizing influences of prison life? Shall mercy and enlightenment be shown to some and not to others?

Part of the problem outlined above derives from a critical difference between the great reform movement ushered in by the Classical School and the new movement spearheaded by the Positivists. The earlier reformers possessed not only a new theory but a new method by which to effect it: imprisonment. While the later reformers also presented a new theory, they were not able to achieve a sound or a popular method for carrying it out. Thus, whereas the Classical reformers had succeeded in presenting an acceptable alternative to the barbarities they attacked, the new theorists have not yet been able to offer a radical alternative to imprisonment. Despite many internal reforms and the redesignating of old and new institutions as reformatories, training schools, etc., the major method for the treatment of offenders remains basically the same as that proposed by the earlier reformers: mass incarceration.

Though not yet succeeding on the technical level, the advocates of treatment have succeeded overwhelmingly on the ideological and educational level. Due to these educational efforts, the general public, by and large, no longer regards reformation merely as a desirable humanitarian adjunct of social defense but rather as an indispensable element of it. This new development—public clamor for rehabilitation in the absence of a sound reformative technique—has raised an entirely new and unanticipated complex of problems at all levels of correctional administration. It has created rifts among correctional workers, presenting irresistible temptations to substitute verbal solutions for dispassionate experimentation. It has increasingly diverted correctional administrators from correctional problems to problems of public relations. Finally— and this is, perhaps, the gravest consequence of all—it has laid the correctional apparatus open to wholesale manipulation by that group of offenders who are, statistically, its least likely beneficiaries: long-term habitual criminals. For these and other reasons, and despite the premature announcements by its many heralds, the Era of Treatment remains stalled at the threshold, an age still clamoring to be born.

Implications of the Controversy

In discharging his duties, the correctional administrator must in theory respond simultaneously to the expectations of at least four different groups: his official superiors in the state government, his own employees, the people of his state or locality, and the inmates confined in his institution. Without a certain minimal level of harmony among these groups, it would be impossible for him to function. In practice, however, the problem of relating to each of these groups is considerably more complicated than would appear on the surface.

Despite increasing recognition of the importance of keeping prisons "out of politics," any department of correction is, potentially at least, "in politics" by virtue of the fact that it is a part of the state administration, under control of the political party in power at any given time. Since the "outs" are against the "ins," it follows by the remorseless logic of politics that the minority party will continually seek out opportunities to embarrass the administration. Few prison systems fail to present these opportunities. Disaffected employees, with or without the connivance of inmates, can make the most efficient and conscientious administration "look sick." In those institutions where the compromises necessary to survival have reduced standards somewhat below ideal levels, a little malice in the right place can magnify a small blemish into a large scar.

In a public relations situation, where standards of judgment are at best ambiguous and at worst contradictory, the correctional system, as a politically vulnerable organization, feels an irresistible compulsion to "look good." This compulsion increases geometrically with the number of institutional difficulties officials are fearful of sharing with a critical press and a hostile political opposition. *This situation offers unparalleled opportunities for blackmail at all levels of the correctional structure, from the inmates to the higher supervisory officials.* Once an institution has made the common error of committing itself to maintaining appearances at all costs, it is vulnerable to extortion by anyone who can threaten to smudge the pretty picture with real or imaginary evidence. The more unrealistic and idyllic the public image, the easier the blackmail; in many cases the extortionists need not even use lies in order to pose their threat —a fact which lends a certain moral flavor to an otherwise matter-of-fact business transaction.

The Problem of Control

It is an administratively necessary assumption that prison officials are responsible and are to be held accountable for whatever takes place in their institution. The extent to which this assumption is increasingly inadequate as a description of actual events has not been fully understood. The reasons for this misunderstanding are obvious: to the public, the idea that their prison officials are in waning control of their institutions would be intolerable; to the officials themselves, any public acknowledgment would therefore appear as an admission of failure. Nevertheless, there seems reason to believe that the role of all members of the official hierarchy, their power both for "good" and "evil," has become increasingly neutralized. This appears to be true of the wardens and guards as well as the psychologists and social workers. What seems to have taken place is a multi-determined trend, the cumulative effect of which has been to reduce the impact potential of *all* officials, whatever their formal roles and powers. It has placed the fate of the individual inmate increasingly in the hands of the inmate society.

To a large extent, this shift of actual authority was promoted by correctional officials themselves, especially in the early stage of the process. Stimulated by the example of Osborne's Mutual Welfare League—a movement that attempted to influence the inmate social system by giving it formal recognition and status—many institutions experimented with what came to be called "prison democracy" as an adjunct to treatment. The final subversion of the movement to the inmate social system came about as a result of unanticipated and, eventually, uncontrollable forces; what began as a voluntary grant of power ended in a grudging and demoralizing accommodation to coercion.

In a prison the duties of a guard frequently require him to report the behavior of inmates who deliberately violate prison rules. These violations usually involve offenses against prison order, prison property, and, very often, abuse of other inmates. Whenever prisoners have been successful in forcing higher authorities to yield to violence they have, simultaneously, served notice on the lower prison authorities that it is no longer safe to enforce the rules. At this point the guards and prison workers have one of three alternatives: they can quit; they can decide to become martyrs—risking their safety and their jobs; or they can become lax, permitting the powerful inmates to take control.

Correctional Goals and Values

The attempt to understand the dilemma of contemporary correction now involves us in a more basic problem. According to one definition of his function, the work of the scientist should be limited to theory. Because of his social obligations as adviser and consultant, however, the criminologist and penologist is rarely permitted to define his role so narrowly. Unlike the theoretical physicist, who is not called on constantly to "do something" about the behavior of his atoms and molecules, the criminologist and penologist is constantly under pressure to intervene in the behavior of his objects of study: actual and potential offenders. He is, in fact, called on to do little else. Should the inmate be paroled?

Should we construct a maximum or a minimum institution? Should capital punishment be abolished? Thus, in addition to his heavy and difficult obligation to report on what *is* happening, the criminologist is continually required to give advice about what *should* happen; in a word, he must make not only factual judgments but value judgments as well.

In attempting to fulfill these dual obligations, the criminologist is confronted with at least three major problems: (1) How can his theoretical purposes and goals be tied down to concrete activities? Unless he can define his objectives in ways that indicate certain procedures and *not others*, there may be a wide difference between what is originally intended and what is actually done. (2) How shall the major values guiding these activities be determined? How shall he go about selecting his goals? Is there any scientific way of choosing between competing or conflicting alternatives? (3) How, finally, can his objectives be translated into actual achievements?

The Problem of Definition:
Linking Objectives to Concrete Procedures

In 1929, in the State of Iowa, a juvenile offender was committed to the State Industrial School for Boys as "a delinquent and incorrigible." At no time in the course of the proceedings was he accused of any crime. Nevertheless, neither the case nor the manner in which it was handled was in any way unusual. In Iowa and in several other states having special juvenile statutes, hundreds of minors had been committed to similar institutions under similar circumstances. The absence of a criminal accusation and other elements of criminal procedure—including a public trial—was deliberate. The whole purpose of the statute was to protect the juvenile from the stigma of the criminal and from the usual consequences of a criminal conviction.

In the particular case under discussion, however, something unusual did happen. Acting through attorneys, the boy appealed. In their appeal, the lawyers pointed out that both the state and the federal Constitution forbade the punishment of any person who had not been charged with a crime. The State Supreme Court denied the appeal, upheld the constitutionality of the law, and reaffirmed the right of the state to confine juvenile offenders without a criminal accusation. In explaining their decision, the judges made certain comments which are pertinent to the problem of linking correctional objectives with correctional procedures.

In the first place, they denied that the child was being punished. The boy was being committed "not to jail for punishment but to a reformatory for its care, education and training." The judges supported this decision by citing several other cases in which similar juvenile laws had been upheld as progressive and humanitarian. Some courts, for example, had referred to them as "paternal and benevolent." "Such statutes are not criminal or penal. They are not intended as punishment, but are calculated to save the child from becoming a criminal." [8]

In returning the boy to the reformatory, the judges were not merely asserting a social objective but taking an action that would lead to certain procedures and to certain eventual consequences for him and for society. The question arises, what procedures, and what consequences? More fundamentally, how could these be inferred or predicted from the assertion that their *purpose* was "benevolent" rather than "punitive"? All lofty aims and purposes aside, would the boy, *in fact,* be educated rather than punished? And how could we know this without knowing more about what would happen to him once he reached the reformatory?

In our previous discussion of problems of language and communication, we concluded that factual statements were meaningful only insofar as they clearly indicated recognizable things or events. The same principle applies to statements dealing with objectives. Unless we know precisely what operations we mean when we speak of "treatment," we are merely using words to create an illusion of shared meaning. Worse, we are licensing all manner of persons to employ all manner of procedures simply by affixing a common label to them. To lay exclusive emphasis on purposes and intentions is merely to invite the continuation of old procedures under new names. Many of the institutions designated as "reformatories" and "industrial schools" were merely old penal institutions under new names. The old punitive procedures were retained, despite the new fashion in correctional values. When challenged to produce proof of their progressive orientation, administrators of these institutions had only to cite the new law, which, literally by a stroke of a pen, had transformed them into "benevolent, paternal reformatories," designed to save the child from a life of crime.

Vagueness and neglect of procedural detail in the definition of correctional objectives is not confined to legislators. Many of the technical

[8] Wissenberg *et al.* v. Bradley, Supreme Court of Iowa, 1929. Cited in Jerome Hall, *Cases and Readings on Criminal Law and Procedure* (Indianapolis: Bobbs-Merrill Company, 1949), p. 97.

instructions provided for treatment personnel are scarcely less vague. Sutherland and Cressey have pointed out:

> The objective in probation work is to change the attitude of probationers. A scientific technique for the modification of attitudes has yet to be worked out. Instead of descriptions of techniques we find such statements as "by gaining the confidence and friendship of the young man, through friendly admonition and encouragement," "by stimulating the probationer's self-respect, ambition and thrift," and "by relieving emotional tensions." It is necessary to know how confidence is secured, or how ambition is stimulated, or how tensions are reduced, and also to know how these processes produce reformation.[9]

Stripped to their essentials, these "instructions" boil down to exhortations to treat, to befriend, and to encourage. In effect, our treatment personnel are often told little more than *to go out and rehabilitate somehow*—precisely how is not indicated. A military commander who confined his strategic orders to the commands, "Be brave, be careful, and be victorious!" would be laughed out of uniform. Often, however, the technical directions given to correctional workers are scarcely more specific.

We are thus presented, in the definition of value statements, with the same problems that confronted us in the definition of factual statements. In both cases, it is possible to speak grammatically without speaking meaningfully; in both cases it is possible to communicate without being informative.

The Selection of Values to Guide Correctional Activities

The problem of determining what values and goals to strive for in correction is closely related to the problem of defining objectives concretely. Unless goals are spelled out specifically, we cannot know what objectives we are actually pursuing; unless our activities are related to carefully chosen goals, we are doing little more than improvising without direction and control.

The possibility of finding a truly objective way of selecting or "verifying" values has long been debated by philosophers. The problem is acute in criminology and penology, where the choice of objectives has more than purely philosophical implications. Most civilized societies today believe that it is better to treat than to punish, better to deter than

[9] Edwin H. Sutherland and Donald R. Cressey, *Principles of Criminology,* 5th ed. (Philadelphia: J. B. Lippincott Company, 1955), p. 434.

to avenge. But is there any scientific way of verifying these positions? Or are they merely matters of faith and opinion?

One approach to this problem is to make an objective decision concerning a value by making that value a contingent member of a hierarchy of values and then demonstrating factually that the application of the first value will lead to certain verifiable events. We say: If this is done, this desirable (or undesirable) event will happen. It would appear, then, that the scientific selection of a value requires two steps: the linking of a value to other values and, secondly, the determination of specific consequences. Without both of these requirements, a scientific determination is impossible.

Now consider the question: Should criminals be punished or rehabilitated?

Our first task is to relate this value question to other values. Any one of a number of universally accepted objectives will suffice. We might select the following: It is desirable that all men live cooperatively and harmoniously together so that they will fulfill their needs without preventing others from fulfilling theirs. In order to reach this objective, it is necessary that offenders be motivated to accept the values of their fellow-men. To do this they must be re-educated or, to use a more common term, *rehabilitated*.

Before we go further, we must discover what we mean by rehabilitation. What are the activities to which we can point and say: "When these occur, that which we call rehabilitation is taking place; when these do not occur, there is no rehabilitation."

This, it will be recalled, was the problem posed by the decision of the Iowa Supreme Court judges cited earlier. In effect, the judges were saying: We assume that no punishment is taking place because it is the clear and stated intention of the law that the child be educated and not punished.

How specifically and objectively, then, can we define a term that has become a byword for ambiguity and windbagging in the field of correction?

1. Rehabilitation is first, an *intention* in the minds of those attempting to achieve it. It is a *motive*, a *desire* to attain certain objectives, which may be defined both in positive terms, as the resumption of acceptable social living, and in equally valid negative terms, as the refraining from illegal behavior.

2. Rehabilitation is also a pattern of activities engaged in by the

correctional agent. In this sense of the term, rehabilitation *consists of things done to the offender*.

3. Rehabilitation, finally, is a *changed condition within the offender,* as manifested by his concrete and specific behavior and by his relations with others. It is what he feels, what he says, and, most important, *what he does* in the incidents of his subsequent daily life. In short, it is what follows the correctional activities.

A complete description of *rehabilitation* requires specific coverage of all of these aspects of the total process; omission of any one of them makes the use of the term unwarranted as a description of a purposeful and deliberate correctional activity. This will be evident in the following illustrations.

1. *Inmate A* served a long sentence in a chain gang under conditions everywhere denounced as barbarous. Subsequent to his release, however, he settled down. For the past ten years he has been productively employed and has not again offended.

2. *Inmate B* spent several months in a modern reformatory. The intentions of the staff were entirely oriented toward his reformation, and he participated cooperatively in the intensive activity program directed to that end. All diagnostic reports being favorable, he was released. Within a few days he was involved in a series of grave crimes.

3. *Inmate C* spent the same amount of time in the same reformatory, participated in the same program, received favorable reports, was released, and has not again offended.

4. *Inmate D* underwent the same activities for a similar period of time at the same reformatory. He participated unwillingly and minimally in the activity program and received unfavorable reports. Held until the completion of his sentence, he was released and has not again offended.

5. *Intimate E* was in constant difficulty in the same reformatory. Within five months it was found necessary to transfer him to the state's adult maximum-security institution as an "incorrigible." At the prison he shortly became involved in a series of disciplinary infractions and was removed to the prison's segregation wing, where he lived under markedly rigorous conditions. After a period of several months he was released to the general prison population and again violated prison rules within a short time. He was returned to the segregation wing, where he served out the remainder of his sentence. Since his release three years ago he married, held a steady job, and has not again offended.

6. *Inmate F* at the same prison was quartered in the institution's

"Honor Wing" during most of his sentence. His excellent disciplinary record and willing cooperation with officials earned him a job involving trust and responsibility, and he was given the most "minimum" security classification. Recommended for an early parole, he was released and shortly thereafter committed a serious crime.

In the illustrations cited above, *Inmates B* and *F* were "correctional failures." In which of the other four cases did "rehabilitation" occur?

Viewed exclusively in terms of results, all four of these prisoners might be said to have been "rehabilitated." Unfortunately, we cannot tell whether their subsequent good behavior was because of their prison treatment, in spite of it, or largely irrelevant to it. Each of the institutions would probably claim these successes as vindications of their good penological *intentions*. But their *activities* in pursuit of these intentions surely varied—from the brutalities of the chain gang to the considerate treatment of the reformatory. One of the successes received highly unfavorable reports at the reformatory, and his subsequent good behavior could scarcely have been predicted. On the other hand, one of the two failures received good reports, and his poor behavior was not anticipated. Yet he underwent similar reformative activities and appeared to respond favorably.

These instances—which could be multiplied indefinitely—demonstrate the difficulties that arise when vaguely defined values are defended by the results achieved in isolated cases.

Determining the Extent to Which Goals Are Translated into Achievements

Certain methodological conclusions emerge from a consideration of these illustrations:

1. Findings based on a few or on isolated cases are valueless for the evaluation of any project in criminology. In view of the large number of books and articles claiming success for this or that project or point of view, this caution is highly necessary. However impressive the results achieved with a few or with small numbers of cases, one cannot exclude the possibility that the same successes might have occurred in the absence of treatment or even under diametrically opposite conditions.

2. Objective evaluation is possible only through the use of *groups* of subjects that have in one way or another been validly equated. Moreover, the conditions of the experiment must be carefully controlled to

assure, so far as possible, the exclusion of factors unanticipated by the researchers.

3. Finally, the standards of success and failure must be objective and behavioral, and formulated with sufficient clarity to avoid ambiguous interpretation. In the end, the results must be boiled down to certain things the subjects either *do* or *do not do* following the experiment and after given periods of exposure to the stresses of ordinary life.

The twin goals of the criminologist and penologist—the gaining of reliable knowledge and the translation of correctional goals into achievements—presuppose a situation in which the scholar is given sufficient scope of observation and experimentation. To the extent that this scope is lacking, its attainment becomes a prerequisite for the achievement of any other objective. At present the scope is limited by certain intrinsic and historical conditions.

In contrast to other social scientists, the criminologist is confronted with a number of conditions that enforce a peculiar, almost unbridgeable remoteness from his field of study. Secrecy and immunity from observation are virtual requirements of criminal behavior; the criminal becomes available to observation only after he is caught. Even at this point the criminologist's access to him is severely restricted. The treatment of criminals has always been a matter of predetermined state policy. Until very recent times, those enforcing penal policies have neither sought nor welcomed observation by outsiders, have traditionally resisted their recommendations, and have attempted to prevent their interference. As a result, the criminologist, as a specialist in the treatment of criminals, has been in a position similar to that of a doctor who cannot even locate his patients until they reach the hospital—only then to be denied access to the wards.

The inevitable effect of this enforced remoteness has been to deny criminological theory its vital contact with the phenomena of crime and penal treatment. As a result, criminologists have generally been more concerned with theories than with the relation of theory to specific problems as they arise in a naturalistic setting. Since they were not formulated with reference to specific problems, these theories have tended to be unproductive of solutions. This condition has led to a marked divergence between the criminologist's role as an objective scientist and his role as a penal reformer. In making their historic contributions to the reform of barbarous penal methods, criminologists have been forced to rely more on appeals to sentiment than on empirical evidence.

They have had to learn the art of extracting a maximum of persuasion from a minimum of data.

In the article which suggested the title of this chapter, George Vold has aptly characterized the situation of the modern penologist, standing midway between a tradition that is largely repudiated and a future that is still largely an aspiration:

> The middle of the century is a natural crossroads as we reckon time. The traveller coming to a crossroads needs to look around and choose his direction of further travel. This is the way, also, with universities on their recurring anniversaries. Neither the traveller nor the institution dares assume uncritically that he will get to his destination merely by continuing to go on as before he came to the intersection.[10]

[10] Vold, *op. cit.*, p. 162.

Release and Parole

IF ALL THE EVENTS OF THE PRISONER'S INSTITUTIONAL CAREER WERE TO be ranged in order of personal importance and broader social significance, it is likely that two incidents would compete for a high place on the list: the day of the offender's entry into prison and the day of his release. From the day of his imprisonment the offender begins to dream and speculate about the time of his release. For most offenders, fantasies about the past before prison and the future after it provide essential psychological escapes from the realities of the present. These fantasies and recollections vary from inmate to inmate and from mood to mood. Nevertheless, for most offenders, the period of confinement is a time of surviving and a time of waiting, much of it filled with thoughts and conversations about past and future achievements.

For society at large, the offender's release is no less important. Since more than half of all past crimes were committed by offenders who had previously been imprisoned, it is an almost certain prediction that more than half of all future crimes will be perpetrated by those now waiting for release. Nevertheless, in spite of these bleak statistics, a society which has asserted its determination to let ten guilty men escape rather than punish one who is innocent refuses any hard-headed advice about locking criminals up and throwing away the keys. The over-all decline of institutional populations in the face of rising crime rates is one manifestation of this moral decision in defiance of statistical probabilities. The steady increase and wider use of techniques of conditional release is another. In view of the persistent refusal by a democratic society to penalize most offenders because many fail to reform on release, the scientific study of release procedures and their effects acquires high priority in correctional research.

Numerous difficult questions suggest themselves. How do offenders react to their release? To what extent do different release policies and the attitudes toward them influence the inmates' future behavior? To what extent can release procedures be related to the objectives and techniques of treatment?

Executive Powers of Release and Mitigation

In the federal and state constitutions the executive is delegated various forms of discretionary power to terminate, suspend, reduce, or delay the execution of sentences imposed by the courts. As defined by law and tradition, these powers may be exercised in the form of pardons, amnesties, commutations of sentence, and reprieves.

Pardon

A pardon is an executive order excusing a convicted person from undergoing a penalty imposed by a court. It may be granted only after the individual has been convicted, and at any time prior to or during the serving of the sentence. Although, with certain exceptions, the decision to pardon is entirely discretionary with the executive authority, pardons are traditionally granted for one or more of the following reasons: (1) rectification of errors of justice not remedied by the courts; (2) recognition of some special merit, service, or extenuating circumstance; (3) the extending of clemency to an individual thought to be sufficiently punished for his offense.

Court decisions have established that an act of pardon wipes away guilt and restores civil rights. Pardons may be absolute or conditional. An absolute pardon nullifies the penalty permanently and unconditionally and imposes no restrictions. A conditional pardon stipulates certain requirements or restrictions to which the individual must adhere under threat of a reactivation of the penalty. One of the most common stipulations of conditional pardons is that the individual leave the state or country.

In order to go into effect, a pardon in the United States must first be accepted by the person to whom it has been granted. Pardons have, on occasion, been refused by those who prefer or insist that their innocence be established by a court of appeal. In cases where criminal conviction resulted in the loss of property or the forfeit of office or other rights, this distinction may be important. Though pardon has been interpreted as "wiping out the conviction," it does not automatically involve restitution of losses or reinstatement to a former position, nor does it, in all cases, remove the public stigma of guilt.

In twenty-seven of the forty-eight states the pardoning power of the executive is final and unrestricted except in cases of impeachment. In slightly more than half of these states, the governor employs some type of board which investigates pardon petitions and makes recommendations. Though the function of the pardon boards in these states is officially advisory, their authority, in practice, is determined by the consistency with which the governor accepts their recommendations. In the remaining twenty-one states the governor no longer has sole and exclusive authority to grant pardons and must share this power with some form of board on which he votes merely as another board member. Under the federal Constitution the President retains sole and full responsibility for the pardoning of all offenders convicted by federal and territorial courts.

Amnesty

Occasionally pardon is extended to an entire group or class of offenders; this mass release by executive order is known as an *amnesty*. Though the power of amnesty is generally considered to be included in the power to pardon, the conditions and objectives of the two methods of release differ. A pardon is granted to a single person in recognition of some individual merit or circumstance related specifically and exclusively to him. The particular offenses for which prisoners are pardoned vary; in each case, however, the focus of decision bears more on the man than on his crime.

Where amnesty is granted to a class of offenders, the focus is more on the crime than on the individual offenders composing the group.

Thus, for example, when the British government granted amnesty in 1953 to several thousand wartime deserters it was, in effect, saying: "We choose now to forgive this particular offense or to cease exacting further punishment for it." By contrast, when a prisoner convicted for burglary is pardoned, the state is saying, in effect: "We are pardoning this particular individual; we are by no means forgiving the general crime of burglary." In the most general terms, a pardon represents a decision to show clemency to an individual, while an amnesty represents a more lenient mood toward a particular kind of offense. Historically, amnesty has been associated with political or wartime violations, offenses which arouse a more or less temporary indignation during a limited period of special danger. Pardon is associated with the more conventional felonies, around which public attitude is relatively stable but where the correctness of the verdict or the punishment is open to grave question in the individual case. Both pardon and amnesty have the effect of a full restoration of civil rights.

Commutation of Sentence

Commutation is the reduction or mitigation of a sentence by the executive authority. As in the case of pardon, it is applied to specific offenders and is based on individual considerations. Unlike pardon, however, it does not legally cancel guilt and it does not restore civil rights. As such, it represents an act of clemency more or less unmixed with questions about the correctness of the original verdict and exclusively concerned with mitigating the severity of the punishment. Commutation is generally used for two purposes: to reduce terms and to mitigate the death penalty, usually by substituting a sentence of life imprisonment. In some jurisdictions, prisoners whose sentences of death have been commuted are not eligible for release on parole.

Reprieve

Though it is usually cited in the list of executive powers dealing with the mitigation of sentences, a reprieve is in no sense a method of release or a reduction of penalty. It is merely a temporary stay of the execution of a sentence, usually for a strictly defined and brief period. Reprieves are largely restricted to the granting of temporary delays in the execution of death sentences. Though reprieves are in capital cases mainly granted for the purpose of providing further reviews of evidence

or to enable the condemned man to pursue still unused procedural remedies, they may be allowed for other reasons. A condemned woman who
is pregnant will be reprieved until after the birth of her child. By legal
rule a condemned person cannot be executed while insane; the usual
method of delaying sentence in these cases is by reprieve until sanity
can be re-established. Occasionally, reprieves are granted for sentimental
reasons, as when the date of execution falls on a holiday or on the
prisoner's birthday.

Evaluation of the Executive Powers of Release and Mitigation

The exercise of the executive powers of pardon, amnesty, and commutation has been criticized in a variety of quarters for a number of
reasons. It has been charged that public officials have used pardons and
clemency to pay off political debts, and it has been argued that the
frequent alliance between crime and politics makes the pardoning power
a potential source of corruption. Certain proponents of a purely "scientific" penology have decried the intrusion of sentimental considerations
into matters which, they argue, should remain entirely within the province of objective correctional experts. Finally, it has been pointed out—
occasionally by governors themselves—that a thorough review of all
pardon petitions would so preoccupy the conscientious executive that he
would have little time for his other duties. One overburdened governor
suggested that his state ought to have two chief executives, one to review
pardon or clemency requests, the other to attend to all the other functions of his office.

None of these objections is without point. By the very act of
pardon, the governor may not only be canceling the program of the
penologists but is actually annulling the verdict of a judge and jury and,
at least in the specific case, canceling the effect of a law passed by the
legislature. Nevertheless, it is precisely this which constitutes the major
rationale of the pardoning power.

Judges and juries may err; laws may be misapplied in specific instances; and the real existence of these possibilities makes some form of
prompt remedy essential. The decision to vest certain of these remedies
in the executive authority is compatible with the theory of separation of
powers which underlies the American form of government. Each of the
three branches of government possesses certain checks and balances
against the others in the administration of justice. The courts retain the
power of overturning laws which unconstitutionally deny the rights of

the accused defendants. Against the abuses of false arrest and imprisonment, provinces of the executive, the court holds the powerful weapon
of habeas corpus. In a sense, the pardoning power is a kind of executive
counterpart to habeas corpus. Hamilton, in Number 74 of the Federalist
Papers, has provided one of the briefest and most definitive arguments
for vesting the pardoning power in the executive:

> Humanity and good policy conspire to dictate, that the benign preroga-
> tive of pardoning should be as little as possible fettered or embarrassed.
> The criminal code of every country partakes so much of necessary
> severity, that without an easy access to exceptions in favor of unfortu-
> nate guilt, justice would wear a countenance too sanguinary and cruel.
> As the sense of responsibility is always strongest, in proportion as it is
> undivided, it may be inferred that a single man would be most ready
> to attend to the force of those motives which might plead for a mitiga-
> tion of the rigor of the law, and least apt to yield to considerations
> which were calculated to shelter a fit object of its vengeance.[1]

Decline in the Use of Executive Powers of Release and Mitigation

The use of pardon, amnesty, and commutation as methods of
release has gradually declined, especially with the increased application
of parole. Table XXV analyzes the methods by which prisoners were
released in 1954. Of a total of 124,930 prisoners released from state and
federal institutions in that year, only a fraction were liberated by direct
executive action.

Release by Direct Action of the Courts

A large number of prisoners in confinement prepare and send docu-
ments to trial courts requesting new trials, correction of illegal sentences,
or vacating of judgment. Some of these result in the correction of sentences or in the granting of other relief, which either shortens the
prisoner's term of confinement or remands him for a new trial.

Petitions from inmates are, in most states, heard by the Appellate
Division of the State Superior Court or by the State Supreme Court.
Appeals cannot in general be taken directly, as a matter of right, to the

[1] Alexander Hamilton, *The Federalist*, Number 74 (New York: Random
House, 1937), p. 482.

TABLE XXV

MOVEMENT OF SENTENCED PRISONERS, BY TYPE OF INSTITUTION AND SEX, FOR THE UNITED STATES: 1954

Movement of sentenced prisoners	All institutions			Federal institutions			State institutions		
	Total	Male	Female	Total	Male	Female	Total	Male	Female
Prisoners present:									
January 1, 1954	172,729	166,059	6,670	19,363	18,743	620	153,366	147,316	6,050
December 31, 1954	182,051	175,057	6,994	20,003	19,305	698	162,048	155,752	6,296
Per cent increase	*5.4*	*5.4*	*4.9*	*3.3*	*3.0*	*12.6*	*5.7*	*5.7*	*4.1*
Admissions, total	134,252	128,910	5,342	22,959	22,318	641	111,293	106,592	4,701
Admitted, except transfers	97,497	92,604	4,893	18,568	17,937	631	78,929	74,667	4,262
Received from court	79,946	76,010	3,936	16,685	16,103	582	63,261	59,907	3,354
Returned as a parole or conditional-release violator	10,355	9,876	479	902	893	9	9,453	8,983	470
Returned from escape	2,243	2,097	146	142	134	8	2,101	1,963	138
Other admissions*	4,953	4,621	332	839	807	32	4,114	3,814	300
Transferred from other institutions	36,755	36,306	449	4,391	4,381	10	32,364	31,925	439
Discharges, total	124,930	119,912	5,018	22,319	21,756	563	102,611	98,156	4,455
Discharged, except transfers	88,116	83,539	4,577	17,930	17,391	539	70,186	66,148	4,038
Releases	78,184	74,193	3,991	16,743	16,253	490	61,441	57,940	3,501
Conditional	42,247	39,851	2,396	6,917	6,657	260	35,330	33,194	2,136
Parole	37,961	35,738	2,223	4,410	4,199	211	33,551	31,539	2,012
Conditional pardon	42	42	—	—	—	—	42	42	—
Other conditional release	4,244	4,071	173	2,507	2,458	49	1,737	1,613	124
Unconditional	35,937	34,342	1,595	9,826	9,596	230	26,111	24,746	1,365
Expiration of sentence	33,101	31,592	1,509	9,825	9,595	230	23,276	21,997	1,279
Pardon	94	94	—	—	—	—	94	94	—
Commutation	2,742	2,656	86	1	1	—	2,741	2,655	86
Escape	2,542	2,382	160	154	147	7	2,388	2,235	153
Death, except execution	682	669	13	52	50	2	630	619	11
Execution†	82	80	2	1	1	—	81	79	2
Other discharges*	6,626	6,215	411	980	940	40	5,646	5,275	371
Transferred to other institutions	36,814	36,373	441	4,389	4,365	24	32,425	32,008	417

* Other admissions and discharges include discharges by court order, and prisoner movement incidental to authorized temporary absence in court and for other purposes.

† Includes two executions carried out under local jurisdiction.

Source: *National Prisoner Statistics*: "Prisoners in State and Federal Institutions, 1954" (Washington, D. C.: Federal Bureau of Prisons, 1955), p. 2.

Supreme Court except when matters heard and determined by the Appellate Division of the Superior Court involve a constitutional question or when there is a dissent in the Appellate Division. In capital cases, appeal can be taken directly from the trial court without intervention of the Appellate Division. The remaining cases heard on appeal by the Supreme Court are those where the court, on a proper application, certifies that it will hear the appeal.

The majority of appeal cases are heard in the Appellate Division of the State Superior Court. In most states the court is extremely lenient concerning matters of procedure, waiving formalities in an effort to provide substantial justice.

It would be difficult to estimate the number of appeals to the courts from inmates in confinement. Though the number released by the courts is fairly small, appeal has become increasingly popular among inmates as a possible escape route. Many institutions provide easy access to a fairly complete law library, and one of the most industrious groups of prisoners is that of the "jailhouse lawyers." The members of the "inmate bar association" often become "experts" in technical aspects of the law, and their briefs are frequently well prepared. Some writers have argued that inmates should have access not only to a law library but to typewriters, papers, and inmate typists as well. It has also been pointed out that when the means for legal escape are made available, there will be fewer efforts to "go over the wall." Whatever one may think of some of these recommendations and their justification, there will be general agreement that the civil rights of all persons, inmates included, should be assured. This is not possible unless there is easy access to the courts.

Parole

Parole is the conditional release of an offender who has already served a portion of his sentence in a correctional institution. While on parole, the released prisoner remains in the custody and under the supervision of the paroling authority. The period of parole may be as long as the time the prisoner would otherwise have served in the institution, or it may be terminated earlier. At any point during this period, parole may be revoked for a violation of parole regulations and the violator returned to the institution to serve the remainder of his sentence in confinement.

Though they are historically related and, in some places, administered by the same authorities, parole must be differentiated from probation on the one hand and from pardon on the other. Probation involves the conditional release of a convicted offender without commitment to an institution. Unlike parole, which follows a period of institutionalization, it is an alternative to confinement. While both pardon and parole are powers exercised by the executive branch of government, the decision to grant probation is essentially a judicial function; it is the judge who must decide whether or not to grant probation—i.e., whether or not the sentence is to be executed or suspended. While a pardon may fully restore civil rights and cancel out the conviction, neither parole nor probation carries these implications.

The distinctions among parole, probation, and pardon may be illustrated by the following hypothetical example. Jones is tried and convicted for burglary and given a sentence of three to five years. On the recommendation of the probation officer attached to the court, the judge suspends sentence and places Jones, a first offender, on probation. At this point Jones, though a convicted felon, is permitted his freedom under the supervision of his probation officer and returns to his home. Shortly thereafter, Jones commits a technical violation of probation regulations, is returned to the court, where his probation is revoked, and is remanded to prison. After two years of confinement he is granted a parole. After six months of parole he violates one of his parole conditions and is returned to the institution to serve the balance of his sentence behind bars. While in prison, Jones, who has persisted in asserting his innocence, appeals to the governor for a pardon. His appeal is rejected. In the meantime, however, the police apprehend a burglar who confesses committing the offense for which Jones was convicted. On the basis of this confession, Jones again appeals for a pardon; on this occasion his appeal is endorsed by the state attorney-general and the governor grants a pardon. Jones is freed with full restoration of civil rights.

Derivations, Origins, and Development of Parole

Although the term *parole* was not used in a correctional context until 1846, the practice of conditional release has a long history. The word itself derives from the French noun meaning "word" or "promise," and reflects the long-standing military practice of releasing certain prisoners after they had given their word that they would not again take up arms against their captors. The military use of parole embodied many of the purposes and characteristics of its later adaptation to a civilian setting. These included (1) a release from captivity; (2) the promise by the prisoner that he would not resume hostilities; (3) the return of the released soldier to his ordinary civilian pursuits; (4) the threat of reprisal in the event he resumed offensive action.

The release of captured soldiers served a variety of military and extramilitary objectives. It lightened the economic burden of maintaining the captives. It increased the number of soldiers available for direct action against a still resisting enemy by reducing the number required to guard those who no longer resisted. It was an expression of clemency which looked toward an eventual reconciliation with the vanquished. It underscored the confidence of the victors in their own strength, and it offered an inducement to the enemy to abandon resistance in the hope of humane treatment. Each of these objectives has its parallel in the modern correctional use of parole.[2]

Despite its long establishment in military tradition, parole had no counterpart in a penal system which employed confinement principally as a means of detention before trial. Though there are recorded instances of the conditional release of prisoners of the Inquisition, it was not until after the widespread, systematic use of confinement as the major penal method that parole became a logical and practical expedient. Prior to this development in the late eighteenth and early nineteenth centuries, a variety of isolated practices anticipated some of the later features of parole. One of these was the English practice of "indenturing" offenders to employers who would house, board, and supervise them in return for their labor. Those who misbehaved were subject to a return to confinement. First used for juveniles in the early houses of refuge, the practice was extended to adults during the period of colonization; there were many offenders among the early colonists who bound themselves to work as indentured laborers for periods up to seven years in exchange for their eventual freedom. Out of this practice there developed another feature which anticipated an additional element of modern parole methods. Following reports of the mistreatment of inden-

---

[2] Among instances of the expedient use of military parole, the surrender terms granted to Lee at Appomattox are notable for their effective exploitation of military and supramilitary objectives. The Confederate officers were permitted to keep their sidearms and horses; each of the enlisted men was allowed a mule to "help with the Spring plowing." The clear understanding was that defeated Confederates had exchanged their swords for plowshares.

tured juveniles, special visiting agents were appointed to discourage their exploitation.

Another precursor of modern parole methods was the development of private philanthropic organizations devoted to the aftercare of released prisoners. One of these was active as early as 1776; it is still active today. This organization, known now as the Pennsylvania Prison Society, was followed by others in the first decades of the nineteenth century. In 1845 the State of Massachusetts recognized these private examples by the appointment of a state agent to disburse public funds for the purchase of food, clothing, tools, and transportation for needy ex-convicts. Within a short time other states had made similar provisions for the assistance of discharged prisoners.

The basic principle of parole, conditional release, had several fore-runners. In 1788 a patent of Joseph II of Austria provided that prisoners who had served one half of their sentence with good behavior might be discharged if they showed signs of permanent reformation. In 1790 Governor Arthur Phillip of the British colony of New South Wales was authorized to grant conditional pardons to transported criminals; under later governors selected ex-prisoners were given tickets of leave and grants of land.

In 1838 Captain Alexander Maconochie, colonial secretary of Van Diemen's Land, published his *Thoughts on Convict Management,* a work which contained one of the earliest systematic proposals for relating the prisoner's length of sentence and conditions of servitude to his improved behavior. Grunhut has summarized Maconochie's proposals:

> The whole discipline should be based on four principles: the duration of sentences should be measured not by a definite time to be served, but by a certain amount of labour to be performed, so that the prisoner's liberation would "depend on the consequent character evinced by him rather than on the quality of his original offense." The progress of his performance should be made evident by a mark system as an impressive way "to place the prisoner's fate in his own hands." These checks and stimulants should obtain not for the individual prisoner, but for a working group of six men in order to "create an *esprit de corps* in all towards good." And, finally, all this should be worked out with as little direct force as possible.[3]

In 1840 Maconochie was given the opportunity to apply his program at the Norfolk Island Prison Colony. Unfortunately, however, the

[3] Max Grunhut, *Penal Reform* (New York: The Clarendon Press, 1948), pp. 78–79.

prevailing policy of fixed sentences prevented the implementation of the core of the plan—readjustment of sentence for good behavior—and in 1844 Maconochie returned to England without having given his program a full test. Ten years later the opportunity came again. In 1854 Sir Walter Crofton was appointed chairman of the board of directors of convict prisons for Ireland and set up a program based on the principles outlined by Maconochie. His program, known both as the "Irish System" and the "Progressive Stage System," employed not only the flexible sentence but a network of separate institutions to house prisoners at each new phase of progress:

> The initial or probationary stage was regularly nine months of solitary confinement at Mountjoy near Dublin. The second stage consisted of public works at Spike Island in Cork. Here, by an elaborate system of marks and figures, the prisoner rose through five classes with the chance that by good behavior and exemplary zeal and industry he could shorten the specific terms for the particular classes. The various classes did not differ in the sort of work to be done but in the prisoner's clothes and the amount of the award; the main stimulus being the shortening of the whole prison term by a speedy progression. Then came the intermediate stage at Lusk and Smithfield. This "filter between prison and community" was the main characteristic of the Irish System. The idea was that the employment of convicts "under circumstances of exposure to the ordinary temptations and trials of the world where the reality and sincerity of their reformation may be fairly and publicly tested, will present the most favorable chances for their gradual absorption into the body of the community." Therefore, prisoners worked without supervision or went to work unattended. There were no disciplinary measures but the possibility of recommitment to a former stage. The last stage was conditional release, with strict regulations for good behavior, which might be enforced by a recommitment to prison.[4]

Though it stimulated intense opposition as well as fiery partisanship, the example of the Irish System was widely emulated in Europe. Within a decade reform agitation in the United States resulted in the establishment of a parole system at the Elmira Reformatory in New York in 1869. In 1884 Ohio became the first state to extend parole to all prisons within its borders. Adoption of parole by other states progressed rapidly. In 1910 the federal prison system inaugurated parole, and in 1944 the passage of a parole law by the State of Mississippi made the roster of states complete.

[4] *Ibid.,* p. 84.

The Organization of Parole

The administration of parole has tended to evolve through three stages of increasing centralization. During the first stage the paroling authority was localized in the various institutions and administered by institutional staffs. In the course of the movement to unify penal administration in centralized state departments, there developed a trend to transfer the paroling power from individual institutions to state departments of correction. The most recent trend has been toward the creation of parole boards independent of state correction departments. A majority of the states employ one or the other of the more centralized forms of parole administration.

The trend toward centralization of parole administration has been both defended and attacked. Parole involves two distinct, though related, functions: selection and supervision. *Selection* of inmates to be paroled involves a range of decisions dealing not only with whom to parole and when to parole but with the effects of the release on the inmate, the institution, and the community. *Supervision* of paroled inmates involves a different range of decisions and responsibilities and requires personnel who are trained to deal with the paroled offender in a looser, freer situation and who are equipped with knowledge of the local community to which he will return. These different responsibilities and functions must be recognized as underlying any discussion of parole administration.

The argument in favor of local authority stresses the importance of relating parole selection to the inmate's adjustment and behavior and to the institution's specific treatment program. Because of their personal observation of and contact with the inmate, members of the institutional staff are in the best position, it is argued, to evaluate his readiness for conditional release. Even if the central parole board utilizes institutional reports and recommendations, it is always difficult to transmit the full flavor, wealth of detail, and implication of personal observations in the form of written communications. Moreover, the writing of such reports is a time-consuming task for members of institutional staffs.

The counter-argument to this line of reasoning acknowledges that local authorities are in the best position to relate parole selection to institutional policies. But one may question whether this is always an unmixed advantage. In a situation where the officials who administer the institution also determine parole selection, there are strong incentives to use parole as an adjunct to discipline. There is also strong pressure to resolve questions about the advisability of parole in a given case on the basis of institutional expedience. The proponents of centralization point out that chief executives of correctional institutions should not have such unchecked authority and power. Because irrespective of the institutional committees responsible for deciding recommended parole dates, the subtle or overt influence of the warden or superintendent of the institution tends to permeate these decisions. This, in fine, is the heart of the argument for an entirely independent parole board: the danger that the parole responsibility may become secondary to other expediencies and objectives.

Selection of Offenders to Be Paroled

Selection for parole is based on two separate considerations, the first more or less arbitrary because it is usually fixed by statute, the second entirely discretionary, involving a decision and a calculated risk by the parole board. The first consideration is the offender's parole *eligibility;* the second, his *suitability* for parole. To these considerations, which are explicit, there may be added others which are no less decisive because they are less tangible. Of these, one of the most important is the parole board's responsiveness to its own estimate of public reaction to parole policies and decisions. The order in which these questions arise is usually the following: The parole board first asks, Is the offender eligible for parole? If he is eligible, is he now ready for parole? Finally, assuming that he is both eligible and ready, what is the probable public reaction to his parole? In practical terms, this last question asks: How will the public react if the offender violates his parole or commits a new crime?

PAROLE ELIGIBILITY. Parole eligibility is usually fixed by statute. According to most state parole laws the offender becomes eligible (i.e., becomes a parole candidate) after serving a certain portion of his sentence in the institution. The determination of parole eligibility is thus purely a matter of mathematical calculation. Shortly after the offender enters the institution the appropriate department calculates his earliest date of parole eligibility. This date determines the time at which the parole board must actively consider the inmate's parole suitability. The offender is then informed of this date as a kind of target to shoot at. (For a discussion of the factors in parole eligibility, see Chapter 18, pages 452–453.)

PAROLE SUITABILITY. As the date of the offender's earliest parole eligibility approaches, the parole board begins to gather and to evaluate the information that will bear on its decision regarding his suitability for parole. The kind of information used, the way it is evaluated and interpreted in reaching a decision, are too dependent on local situations, on local personnel, and, finally, on individual parole board members to permit any meaningful detailed discussion.

For the present purpose it is more pertinent to ask: What are the basic elements of any decision to select or reject an eligible prisoner for parole? What are the questions the board members ask themselves when they open the files on inmates X, Y, and Z? And why might they select X for parole now, "lay Y over" (postpone decision) for a year, and decide that Z should not be granted parole at all?

In the discussions of parole selection which appear in professional journals there is frequent mention of the desirability of discovering the right time to release the offender on parole. The idea is advanced that this time of maximal advantage may differ for each individual, and that if the moment is not seized the usefulness of a later parole is diminished. Accordingly, it is argued, the process of parole selection should center on the attempt to discover, for each offender, the point of greatest readiness, at which point, other things being equal, the offender should be paroled. Apart from its transparent plausibility, this idea is of interest for two separate but ultimately related reasons. In the first place, it illustrates a fairly typical technique of seeming to solve a complex problem by means of a kind of intellectual slogan. Though much attention is given to the importance and the fruitfulness of finding the "right moment," little is offered in the way of explaining how this may be accomplished. In effect, one is urged, rather vehemently, to do something considered very important, but one is not told how. In what way does this assist the parole board member? One suspects that it provides a way of rationalizing, by means of a popular slogan, what is essentially an informed leap into the dark. Accordingly, John Smith may now be paroled not because a majority of the members combined a guess with a prayer but rather because they had "concurred in their estimate that John Smith had reached his point of maximal readiness for a trial on parole."

This type of advice and rationalization, popular in the literature, is interesting for another reason. It suggests that parole board members, in their actual deliberations, do, somehow, concern themselves with this issue, vague and hard to determine as it may be. It seems to imply that what the board members are trying to do when they consider the case of John Smith *is*, somehow, to estimate or to guess at whether parole now or later is better for him. Since it would be difficult to argue that they should *not* do this (i.e., that they should not do what is best for John Smith), the procedure is rendered not only plausible but comforting.

But is this what they do? If the private discussions and actual decisions of parole boards may be taken as guides to how the members make up their minds, the proposition is rendered doubtful or, at best, revealed to be a misleading half-truth.

An examination of parole decisions suggests a different conclusion. It suggests that parole selections tend to be made less in terms of guesses or estimates about the offender's readiness or chances for success on parole and more in terms of guesses about the likelihood of failure. This distinction involves something more than a shift of emphasis from the positive to the negative. For one thing, it suggests that parole decisions are related to a range of considerations some of which are significantly unrelated to the individual offender's personal adjustment. It implies, furthermore, that the basic objective may be to minimize the risks and percentages of failures rather than to increase the number of offenders potentially able to profit from parole.

The effect of this emphasis can be demonstrated by a hypothetical example. Let us assume that experience in a given institution has shown that, over a period of years, an average of 40 per cent of the inmates selected for parole have failed, either through technical violations or by committing new crimes. Imagine further, that in response to public criticism of this failure rate, the parole board determines to better its average. The most immediate and practical way of doing this is to reject a number of doubtful cases in which the decision might have gone either way. By this method the parole board reduces the total number of inmates paroled in a given year from four hundred to three hundred. With the more questionable cases eliminated, the failure rate in the following year drops from 40 to 30 per cent.

However, among the hundred cases now considered unsuitable, there is a considerable number of prisoners who, if paroled, would have succeeded. In other words, by decreasing its failure rate, the board denied parole to an unknown number of inmates who would have made a successful parole adjustment. It is in this sense that suitability for parole, as defined by the operations of the parole board, requires redefinition as an *attempt to minimize and avoid failures* rather than an attempt to maximize successes. Viewed in these terms, the parole decision becomes an estimate of the likelihood that a given inmate will or will not increase the failure rate beyond a margin that the board feels it can afford. As a result, the decision to parole a given inmate may have more to do with the parole board's confidence in its own predictive ability and with its satisfaction in its own record than it does with the records of the inmate and the board's confidence in them. In such a situation, "parole suitability" becomes largely a measure of the parole board's personal sense of adequacy or lack of adequacy.

PAROLE PREDICTION. Although parole had been in effect in the United States for some time, it was not until shortly after World War I that an interest developed in providing authorities with statistical information as a guide in selecting offenders to be paroled. The assumption was that a reliable prediction could be made of the probable failure or success of a paroled inmate by employing information about factors associated with the success or failure of past parolees. This information was organized into experience tables, which classified each inmate according to his risk category.[5] The goal in parole prediction is to increase the number of paroles granted to offenders who are likely to succeed and to reduce the number of paroles granted to those who are likely to fail.

The first systematic effort to establish a statistical relationship between the success or failure of paroled offenders and selected factors that were known in advance was made by Sam Warner in 1923.[6] Warner attempted to determine whether there were any marked differences between three hundred prisoners who were successful on parole and three hundred who failed, with respect to any of sixty-seven different items of information available to the parole board. He concluded that though some differences did exist, only one item—the report of the alienist classifying the prisoner as an *accidental offender*, a *recidivist*, or a *feeble-minded offender*—would appreciably reduce the number of parole violations if used by the board as a guide in granting parole.

It was not until 1928, however, that the first successful construction of a prognostic instrument was reported by Ernest Burgess.[7] Then, in

[5] Lloyd E. Ohlen has pointed out that "there is a close parallel between the part played by experience tables in the parole selection process and the use of life tables in establishing premiums" (*Selection for Parole, Russell Sage Foundation,* 1951, p. 69). Ohlen's study presents a systematic description of how prediction tables are constructed and used in the Illinois parole system.

[6] Sam B. Warner, "Factors Determining Parole from the Massachusetts Reformatory," *Journal of Criminal Law and Criminology,* 14:172–207, August 1923.

[7] Ernest W. Burgess, "Factors Determining Success or Failure on Parole," *Journal of Criminal Law and Criminology,* 19:241–286, May 1928.

1930, the Gluecks published the first of their series of follow-up studies of a group of inmates paroled from the Massachusetts Reformatory, whose parole had expired during 1921–1922.[8] Their criterion of success was not the absence of any violation of parole but whether their case study of the individual, in the community where he was located five years after release from the reformatory, revealed that he had been pursuing a constructive, law-abiding life. Their conclusion was that 80 per cent were unsuccessful, though only 20 per cent had technically been considered parole violators.

The contrast between the Burgess and Glueck studies lies not only in different scoring methods but in different underlying concepts, which determined the type of question which they addressed to the data. The Gluecks' viewpoint has an individualistic orientation. The seven pre-parole factors which they attempted to correlate with success or failure on parole are (1) type of offense; (2) previous arrest record; (3) previous imprisonment experience; (4) industrial habits; (5) economic responsibility; (6) mental abnormality; and (7) behavior in the reformatory. Each of these they considered rooted in the inmate's "nature" whenever their case analysis indicated anything abnormal in the subject's mental traits, abilities, temperament, appetites (as for sex or alcohol), or family background (criminals among blood relatives). Burgess, on the other hand, brought a sociological point of view to the prediction task; and, in addition to factors similar to those studied by the Gluecks, he investigated such factors as the social type represented by the subject, the community from which the offender came, the cultural group with which he was identified, his associates in crime, his age at commission of first offense, his marital status and community mobility.

Other studies have attempted to modify these methods in certain respects, but all of them involve the same principle of attempting to predict parole outcome on the basis of past experience. Moreover, attempts have been made to extend the use of prediction tables to juveniles in public and private correctional institutions and to probation as well.

Parole prediction has been attacked on a number of grounds. Major criticisms have centered on the following considerations:

1. Prediction methods do not really predict. Parole prediction tables are based on the personal and social characteristics of those who have failed or succeeded on parole at some point in the past. Theoretically, unless conditions have drastically changed, prospective parole can-

[8] Sheldon and Eleanor Glueck, *Five Hundred Criminal Careers* (New York: Alfred A. Knopf, Inc., 1930), pp. 278–296.

didates manifesting the same characteristics as previous parole successes and failures might be expected to have similar parole outcomes. In practice, however, the predictive accuracy of these measures has been very disappointing.

2. Interpersonal and attitudinal factors, which are ignored by prediction methods, may be more fundamental in affecting outcome than the factors which are considered.

3. Prediction methods do not offer a standard for selecting offenders for parole; they can only provide data regarding the estimate of success or failure.

4. Shifts in economic and social conditions over a period of time tend to invalidate experience tables.[9]

Supervision of Paroled Offenders

The state's legal control over the paroled offender is not diminished by the fact that the offender is no longer in physical confinement. In law and theory, it may be as complete as that exercised over him while he was in the institution, even though, as a matter of practical possibility, the state's realizable resources of control are diminished by the offender's greater freedom.

In the course of this discussion it will become clear that between the state's actual and its theoretical power over the paroled offender there exists a gap that may work much mischief. It is this gap, this difference between the control which the state is called on to exercise and that which it may expect to exercise—or may expect in terms of the paroled offender's compliance—which underlies one of the most fundamental problems of parole. The problem is this: On the one hand, the paroling authorities are called on to take responsibility for the conduct of persons over whom they can exercise only the most tenuous actual control. On the other hand, the paroled offender is expected to respond to influences and controls which are at best inadequate and at worst may be wholly outweighed by contrary pressures in his actual living situation.

This gap between what is publicly expected and realistically pos-

[9] Critical analyses of the parole prediction literature may be found in M. Allen, "A Review of Parole Prediction Literature," *Journal of Criminal Law and Criminology*, 32:548–554, No. 5, 1942; Michael Hakeem, "Prediction of Criminality," *Federal Probation*, 9:31–38, No. 3, 1945; and Lloyd E. Ohlen and Otis D. Duncan, "The Efficiency of Prediction in Criminology," *American Journal of Sociology*, 54:441–451, No. 5, 1949.

sible in parole supervision has led to a series of curious official and unofficial expediencies. What is curious about these arrangements is that the actors—parolee and parole officer—respond to the gap not by attempting to close it but by widening it even further.

When the paroled offender leaves the institution, he takes with him a document setting forth the rules and regulations he must agree to observe in order to continue in good standing. In most states these regulations consist of certain general rules and restrictions plus, in certain cases, special requirements added by the parole board. These regulations tend to reflect aspirations concerning personal conduct that would severely test the "best of us." As a result, what is called parole "supervision" cannot fail, in many instances, to create a situation in which both the paroled offender and his supervisor are engaging in a kind of deliberate, cooperative ritual in which the offender agrees to pretend that he is observing the letter of the supervisory regulations while the parole officer agrees to ignore the fact that he is not. This is accomplished, in practice, by a tacit agreement by which the paroled offender avoids telling his parole officer things he should not officially know while the parole officer avoids finding out things that would constitute technical violations and require official action.

Parole Regulations

The official, formal expectations around the behavior of conditionally released prisoners have remained virtually unchanged for over a century. The "license to be at large," developed in connection with the Irish System, contained the following conditions:

1. The holder shall preserve this license and produce it when called upon to do so by a magistrate or police officer.

2. He shall abstain from any violation of the law.

3. He shall not habitually associate with notoriously bad characters, such as reported thieves and prostitutes.

4. He shall not lead an idle and dissolute life, without means of obtaining an honest livelihood.

5. If the license is forfeited or revoked in consequence of a conviction of any felony, he will be liable to undergo a term of penal servitude equal to that portion of his term which remained unexpired when his license was granted.

6. Each convict coming to reside in Dublin City or in the County of Dublin will, within three days after his arrival, report himself at

the Police Office,... where he will receive instructions as to his further reporting himself.

7. Each convict residing in the provinces will report himself to the constabulary station of his locality within three days after his arrival and subsequently on the first of each month.

8. A convict must not change his locality without notifying the change to the locality to which he is about to proceed.

9. Any infringement of these rules by the convict will cause it to be assumed that he is leading an idle, irregular life and thereby entail a revocation of his license.[10]

The license also contained this significant comment: "This license is given subject to the conditions endorsed upon the same, upon the breach of any of which it will be liable to be revoked, whether such breach is followed by conviction or not." Compare this with the terms, conditions, and limitations of a present-day certificate of parole in use in the State of New Jersey:

1. From the date of your release on parole, and until the expiration of your adjusted maximum sentence(s), you shall continue to be in the legal custody of the Chief Executive Officer of the Institution from which you are released.

2. You shall be required to abide by the rules and regulations formulated by the State Parole Board for the supervision of persons on parole.

3. While on parole, you shall be under the direct supervision of the Bureau of Parole....

4. As a condition of your being on parole, you are required to:

A. Obey all laws and public ordinances;

B. Abstain from the use or sale of narcotics and the excessive use of intoxicating beverages;

C. Refrain from association with persons of bad character or those who are considered by the Parole District Supervisor or his designated representative, to be undesirable companions;

D. Reside in a place approved by the Bureau of Parole....;

E. Report to or notify your Parole District Supervisor or his designated representative:

1. As soon as possible but in any event within forty-eight hours after your release on parole from the institution;

2. Whenever you are in any kind of trouble or in need of advice;

[10] Quoted in N. R. Arluke, "A Summary of Parole Rules," *National Probation and Parole Association Journal*, 2:6–7, January 1956.

3. Immediately, if you are arrested on any new charge;

4. Whenever you are instructed to report by the Parole District Supervisor, his designated representative, or other competent authority;

F. Obtain permission from your Parole District Supervisor or his designated representative:

1. Before marrying or applying for a divorce;

2. Before purchasing a motor vehicle, obtaining a learner's permit, a driver's license, or applying for a motor vehicle registration;

3. Before entering any form of conditional sales agreement or securing a loan;

4. Before entering any business, changing your place of residence, or changing your employment;

5. Before leaving the state of your approved residence, or changing your employment;

6. Before paying any fine or attempting to obtain bail.

7. Before applying for a permit to carry a firearm, securing a hunting license, or carrying a firearm for any purpose.

5. Having accepted the action of the State Parole Board in determining your eligibility date for release on parole at this time on the sentence, or consecutive sentences if any, imposed upon you, it is understood and agreed that you shall remain under parole supervision until the expiration of the aggregate of your maximum sentence(s), less proper credits, except as provided in the following paragraphs.

6. If you violate any of the conditions of parole set forth herein, this parole may be revoked without notice and, at the discretion of the State Parole Board, you may be required to serve the time remaining on your sentence(s) as of the date you are declared delinquent on parole.

7. If you violate any of the conditions of parole by being convicted of a crime while on parole, this parole may be revoked without notice and, at the discretion of the State Parole Board, you may be required to serve the time remaining on your sentence(s) as of the effective date of your release on this Certificate of Parole.

In a suggestive survey of parole rules, Arluke observes:

In a few states the number of stipulations about parolee behavior and parole board administrative policy exceeds twenty. How many of these a parolee can reasonably be expected to remember is a question. Because of this, one of these states includes a regulation requiring the parolee to read the regulations periodically during the entire parole period![11]

[11] *Ibid.*, p. 10.

The same survey reveals the lack of uniformity in parole regulations. In six states paroled offenders are required to be home at a "reasonable hour"; Illinois has a 10:30, and Maine an 11:30 curfew; but forty states are silent on this issue. Two states, Kansas and Nebraska, require regular church attendance, while the other forty-six states believe this is unnecessary. However, the absence of a regulation in an area does not necessarily indicate that the paroled offender has discretion, since the state may require him to agree to "abide by such special conditions of parole as may be imposed on him by his parole officer." The most unrealistic expectation is the complete prohibition of the use of liquor by forty-one states.

Another potential for mischief in regulations of this type exists in the procedures by which paroled offenders are adjudged technical violators. Since the offender may be returned to confinement for a violation of the conditions of his parole, wide discretion must rest in the paroling authorities. The paroling authorities determine whether or not to revoke parole on the basis of reports submitted by parole supervisory personnel. Certainly only a small fraction of parolees who violate the conditions of parole are returned. The process by which the determination is made to return a parolee to confinement requires careful study. Phrases such as "failed to adjust," "chronic troublemaker," "did not respond to supervision," which rationalize the return of the parolee to confinement, are vague and elusive. Not only are such terms difficult to define operationally, but they conflict with conceptions of the individualized treatment of offenders. Assume for a moment that the paroling agency has decided that only "chronic violators" will receive violation reports and that the agency has defined in precise terms—say four violations—what constitutes "chronic" violation. These definitions are communicated to parole officers in the field, and a parole officer attempts to apply them to two cases—John, a "chronic violator" who "needs one more chance," and Bill, who will be a "chronic violator" after the "one more job" the parole officer "knows" he is planning. The parole officer is likely to file two reports explaining why the definitions do not apply to these cases. In whatever review of the parole officer's action is provided for by the procedures of the parole agency, it is likely that considerations of individualized treatment would outweigh formal considerations. To operate, however, parole agencies must have either formal or informal procedures that set limits on the discretion of parole officers, supervisors, and parole boards.

Conflicts of Role and Orientation among Parole Officers

A serious problem in parole supervision is the parole officer's conflict concerning his role. Is he primarily a law-enforcement officer, responsible for the careful surveillance of former criminals likely to repeat, or a social worker who utilizes friendly guidance and supportive counseling to assist a former offender in achieving his potential usefulness in society? Though this dilemma—control vs. treatment—has received considerable attention, it can hardly be described as resolved. There are claims, made largely by social workers in the correctional field, that probation and parole are treatment processes that can best be achieved by casework methods. There are other professional social workers who claim that it is impossible to implement sound casework methods within the "restricted" agency requirements of correction.[12]

One popular approach is to suggest that control and treatment are part of one process, and that if the "proper conditions" exist, the conflict can be accommodated. This approach usually leaves unanswered some rather difficult questions. After a discussion of this problem, Lester W. Ervis concluded:

> Professional parole agents will continue to make advances in applying treatment methods to the end that there will be wider and wider acceptance of their services as therapists. To be sure, surveillance will continue to be a necessary aspect of parole supervision, but it should become a positive force in rehabilitation, applied with objectivity and friendliness. The parole agent must continue to check addresses, inspect conditions of home and employment, examine bank accounts, investigate ownership of property and explore information concerning misconduct. Yes, and on occasion he must even count empty liquor bottles. This will be obligatory since effective guidance depends upon full knowledge of all significant factors. However, the spirit with which this work will be done will not be that of a law enforcement officer seeking evidence to support the arrest and prosecution of a wrongdoer, even though in some instances the result may be the same. The surveillance work of a parole agent will be carried out in the same spirit that a physician watches a polio patient make this first attempt to walk alone. The spirit of this watchfulness is marked by a sincere interest in assisting the patient to continue on the road to recovery and certainly not finding an excuse to send the victim of this dread disease back to the hospital.

[12] For a discussion of this problem in relation to community expectations, agency organization, and types of clientele, see Lloyd E. Ohlen et al., "Major Dilemmas of Social Workers in Probation and Parole," *National Probation and Parole Association Journal*, 2:211-225, July 1956.

The skilled parole agent of tomorrow will maintain this same professional attitude in supervising parolees. Even in the negative aspects of surveillance, he will seek opportunities for positive and constructive guidance.

The work of the parole agent must be fortified by the development of consultant professional services in the community, such as out-patient psychiatric clinics where individual and group psychotherapy may supplement the casework of the parole staff.

Finally, it is not sufficient that the parole agent merely be appropriately indoctrinated with the point of view of constructive and helpful treatment. Success will only crown his efforts when parolees recognize and accept the philosophy that all phases of parole supervision are treatment when administered by a competent and properly motivated parole counselor. The leadership for this accomplishment must come not merely from the heads of parole bureaus themselves but also stem from the basic philosophy of the correctional authorities governing the institutions and from those who are responsible for the release of inmates from the prisons.[13]

It seems unnecessary to review the inadequacy of these aspirations as resolutions of a concrete problem. It is safe to assume that this problem will be around to trouble parolees, parole officers, parole agencies, and the general public for some time to come.

Termination of Parole

After he leaves the institution, the paroled prisoner is still under the custody and control of the state. This period of continued control may be terminated in one of three ways: (1) At the expiration of the original sentence; (2) earlier, by decision and certificate discharging the parolee from further custody; (3) by recall to prison for a violation of parole regulations or the committing of a new offense.

Termination of parole custody at the end of the original sentence is automatic; the state no longer has any juridical authority. An earlier termination discharging the offender from his obligations and restrictions is a matter of recommendation and decision by the paroling authorities. A paroled prisoner who has satisfied his parole officer that further supervision, guidance, or surveillance is unnecessary may be granted a *certificate of discharge from parole,* an action having the effect of termi-

[13] Lester W. Ervis, "Parole Treatment and Surveillance—Which Should Dominate?" *Proceedings of the American Prison Association,* Atlantic City, 1952, p. 60. Mimeographed.

nating his sentence and, simultaneously, ending the parole board's authority over him. In some jurisdictions termination by certificate is conditional; in others, absolute. In either case, the effect and intention is to restore the offender to his full civilian status.

Termination of parole custody by certificate of discharge from parole is entirely discretionary. It is up to the paroling authorities to determine when the offender is ready to be entirely "on his own." It usually follows a period of progressively relaxed supervision, during which the intervals at which the paroled prisoner must report to his parole officer are gradually lengthened. Toward the end of this period the parole officer may see the paroled offender no more than once or twice a year; under these conditions he is considered to be a purely formal or "inactive" case. The eventual complete termination of control by a certificate of discharge represents a reward and, in effect, a vote of confidence in the continued good adjustment of the offender.

Evaluation of Parole

The fact that parole is one of the youngest and best-loved children of modern correction has had an inevitable effect on evaluations of the subject. When parole is discussed, it is frequently assumed that (1) it will function as an incentive to inmates to improve themselves while in confinement; (2) it will provide a bridge over which the offender can negotiate his way to a good personal and social adjustment; (3) it enables a correctional system to implement the individualized treatment process; (4) it provides protection for the public against the criminal and at the same time increases the likelihood that social resources will be constructively utilized in his behalf.

Little concrete evidence exists to demonstrate which, if any, of these hopes and aspirations have been realized. The lack of research in this area should be a source of concern to every citizen. Discussing parole and probation statistics, Raymond C. Davidson notes:

> Correctional statistics is a tough field as a whole, with all of its variables, and probation and parole are the youngest of the most generally used methods of treatment in the correctional area. Some of the reasons for the lack of advance in our statistics can be laid at the doorstep of people who work in, or close to, the area of probation and parole. Some of them may, once they become sufficiently acquainted with the work, have no question as to its value. Of these, many recognize the human

values involved and benefits obtained; from then on, since they have no questions, they have no interest in statistical proof.[14]

When the case-study method is utilized, it is easier to find cases in which the "parole process" has been ineffectual than it is to find those in which it has clearly been beneficial. It would not be difficult to find cases in support of the thesis that parole treatment is largely negative, and that the individual may make a "better adjustment" without it.

The most reasonable justification for parole seems to be related to the values on which it rests: hope and charity. Like many other correctional devices, it represents an attempt to introduce these values into a field long barren of them.

[14] Raymond C. Davidson, "Probation and Parole Statistics," *National Probation and Parole Association Journal*, 3:263, July 1957.

Issues in Treatment and Prevention

Treatment and Prevention Defined, Contrasted, and Related

ONE STATEMENT FREQUENTLY HEARD IS THAT IT IS BETTER TO PREVENT crime and delinquency than to treat it: "An ounce of prevention is worth a pound of cure." How are treatment and prevention to be defined? To what extent do they imply similar, and to what extent different, operations?

The treatment of any condition implies the prevention of its further spread or damage. Thus, to treat a venereal disease means to halt its further inroads. In this sense, treatment carries with it the idea of prevention. Prevention, however, does not necessarily include the idea of treatment. The basic implication of prevention is the forestalling of a situation that will require later treatment. In practice, however, this objective often requires treatment procedures for the sources of infection, which might create a treatment problem for the uncontaminated. Thus, in order to prevent B's involvement with delinquency, it may be necessary to deal therapeutically with those factors that might contaminate B—and these may include treating A.

Prevention does not invariably require treatment procedures. Any program that fosters healthy conditions is, by definition, preventive of sickness. To teach Junior how to walk is, simultaneously, to teach him how to avoid falling over his own feet. Good drivers prevent bad accidents. In a positive sense, prevention implies the maximizing of all motivational and situational factors for the learning of legitimate modes of need fulfillment, legitimate modes of interaction.

The term *crime prevention* is as ambiguous and ambitious as the term *crime treatment*. In general, these terms are used to describe the following activities, which are believed to be related:

1. To prevent a crime from succeeding.
2. To prevent the development of criminal motivation.
3. To facilitate the channeling of motives in legitimate directions.
4. To prevent the development of criminal opportunities.

In one sense, *crime prevention* may be defined as any effort that tends to reinforce society's control over its members. From this point of view, *treatment* implies the restoration of the group's social control over the individual. Although medical analogies are particularly dangerous in correction, prevention is to correction what sanitation and immunization are to public health. The failure of sanitation and immunization in public health may result in the *sick* person; in correction, the analogous result is the *delinquent* or *criminal*. The close interdependence of treatment and prevention suggests at least three related objectives:

1. "Curing" the individual criminal.
2. Preventing a spreading of the criminal influence to susceptible or corruptible persons.
3. Protecting society (including potential victims) during the period of "criminality."

Programs of Treatment and Prevention

The evaluation of prevention and treatment programs is complicated by the problem of defining what is to be prevented and treated. Lohman has grouped various programs in the following categories:

1. Programs oriented toward the delinquent as an individual, apart from the local community and the wider social processes.
2. Programs oriented toward the delinquent as a member of natural and informally organized groups, primarily organized in leisure-time activities.
3. Programs oriented in terms of local community processes and treat-

ing the community as a whole for addressing the youth problems which arise therein.[1]

The immediate discussion will be limited to a brief description of a program in each category.

Child Guidance Clinics and Diagnostic Centers

The use of psychiatric guidance clinics in delinquency prevention can be traced to the work of Dr. William Healy, who in 1909 established, in connection with the Chicago Juvenile Court, the first psychiatric clinic for delinquents. Later Dr. Healy moved to Boston to head the Judge Baker Guidance Center. With the development of demonstration clinics under the general impetus of the mental hygiene movement, the use of clinics spread rapidly. Today there are mental hygiene and child guidance clinics in most parts of the United States.

The orientation of these clinics is toward the individual or, more precisely, toward the child-parent relationship. Clinics make use of a professional team (usually a psychiatrist, a psychologist, and a social worker) and employ the "staff conference" method to develop a treatment-referral plan for the individual. The clinic may also have its own treatment program for selected cases.

There have been some evaluations of the effectiveness of child guidance clinics. Of these, the most intensive were made in connection with the work of the Judge Baker Guidance Center. The Gluecks made a study of the subsequent court records of 1,000 boys referred by the courts to the Center and found that 88 per cent continued their misconduct.[2] A comparable group of 1,000 boys processed by the courts but not seen by this clinic were evaluated by the Center's research staff, and the percentage of recidivism was found to be approximately the same. The result was called "the close of another chapter in criminology."[3] The Center staff shifted its emphasis from diagnostic study-recommendations to the court toward a more active therapy program. Another, more impressionistic evaluation was made, and better results were reported.[4]

[1] Joseph D. Lohman et al., Juvenile Delinquency—A Proposal for Action (Office of the Sheriff, Cook County, Illinois, 1957).

[2] Sheldon and Eleanor Glueck, One Thousand Juvenile Delinquents (Cambridge: Harvard University Press, 1934).

[3] William Healy, Augusta F. Bronner, and Myra E. Shimberg, "The Close of Another Chapter in Criminology," Mental Hygiene, 19:208–222, October 1936.

[4] Helen Witmer and Edith Tufts, The Effectiveness of Delinquency Prevention Programs, Children's Bureau, Department of Health, Education, and Welfare (Washington, D. C.: Government Printing Office, 1954).

Cambridge-Somerville Youth Study

The possibilities of using friendly counseling by interested adults to prevent youngsters "in trouble" from drifting into delinquent patterns have continued to tantalize thoughtful persons. Between 1935 and 1949, Dr. Richard C. Cabot, a Boston physician, developed and financed a project, known as the Cambridge-Somerville Youth Study, to put this sort of program to the test. In a foreword to *Five Hundred Criminal Careers*, by Sheldon and Eleanor Glueck, Dr. Cabot formulated his basic hypothesis: "That someone should come to know and to understand the man in so intimate and friendly a way that he comes to a better understanding of himself and a truer comprehension of the world he lives in." [5]

To test this hypothesis, Dr. Cabot conceived of a program that would employ friendly counselors to work with a selected group of boys over a long period of time. The effectiveness of the program would be measured by comparing the treatment group with a control group which did not receive help.

Two groups of 325 carefully matched boys were formed from a large number of referrals from schools. Each group contained the same number of "problem boys" judged to be "predelinquent" by teachers and a committee of experts. The children in both groups were between the ages of nine and eleven; the median age at the start of treatment was ten and a half years. The counselors worked with the treatment group in the role of intelligent, knowledgeable adult friends, and the boys remained in treatment for a median period of five years. No treatment was given to the other group, known as the control or "C" group.

In their analysis of why the project failed to produce a marked lessening in the incidence of delinquency and poor social adjustment among the "T" (treatment group) boys compared with the "C" boys, Powers and Witmer state:

> The answer, it seems clear, is to be found largely in the fact that the kinds of boys who usually become persistent delinquents or otherwise seriously maladjusted individuals are not the sort whose difficulties, largely emotional in nature, can be reached by the kinds of service the Study provided. In other words, Dr. Cabot's hypothesis (that what is needed to prevent delinquency and to foster good character development is the presence of an adult "friend" who will stand by the boy

[5] Richard C. Cabot, Foreword in Sheldon and Eleanor Glueck, *Five Hundred Criminal Careers* (New York: Alfred A. Knopf, Inc., 1930), p. ix.

through thick and thin and make available to him the opportunities and the moral guidance that parents normally supply) appears to be disproved. The hypothesis was not rendered wholly invalid by the Study, however, for although this kind of work seldom prevented delinquency it has been shown that in certain kinds of cases "friendship" of the type Dr. Cabot envisaged did prove to be valuable. What we seem to have discovered, then, is the kind of "feller" that needs this kind of friend! What kind of "feller" that is and what the friendship must be like have been described in considerable detail above.[6]

In a foreword to the Powers-Witmer study Gordon W. Allport cites various departures from the original research design and questions whether Dr. Cabot's hypothesis received a fair test. While he does not attempt a conclusive answer to this question, he expresses the belief that the trends and indications are "in the right direction." The importance of this study, apart from its findings, is, as Allport has pointed out, "a bold and significant conception of social research, faithfully executed in spite of many obstacles, rich in conclusions, and foreshadowing future developments of greater importance both for social science and social policy."[7]

The Chicago Area Projects

The Chicago Area Projects were organized in 1934 in order to test the thesis that "the behavior of the child reflects not only the social experiences encountered in the home, but those encountered in the playgroup and neighborhood as well." These projects were established in areas of the city of Chicago, which had for many years been characterized by disproportionately high rates of delinquency. The projects, which are continuing, seek to utilize the "natural leadership" in these areas through organized "citizen committees" that would assume responsibility for a broad program of cooperative neighborhood "self-help." The late Clifford Shaw, long-time executive director of the Area Projects, based this procedure on three propositions:

1. That the problem of delinquency in low-income areas is a product of the social experiences to which children and young people are exposed;

2. that effective treatment and prevention can be achieved only in so far as constructive changes in the community life can be brought about; and,

[6] Edwin Powers and Helen Witmer, *An Experiment in the Prevention of Delinquency* (New York: Columbia University Press, 1951), p. 572–3.
[7] Gordon W. Allport, Foreword in Powers and Witmer, *op. cit.*, p. xxix–xxx.

3. that in any enterprise which is likely to be effective in bringing about these changes, it is indispensable that the local residents, individually and collectively, accept the fullest possible responsibility for defining objectives, formulating policies, providing financial support, and exercising the necessary controls over budgets, personnel, and programs.[8]

The work of the citizens committees in each of the areas is organized around a neighborhood center. This center serves as a recreational and educational facility, with a small paid staff drawn from the local neighborhood and augmented by volunteers. The activities of these committees include educational projects, summer camps, dances, etc. In addition, the committees may directly supervise probationers and paroled offenders and function as a referral agency for all sorts of neighborhood problems. The organization is loose and informal, and the method employed to achieve objectives natural and "unprofessional."

Shaw and his associates have been cautious in interpreting their findings. The statistics compiled on delinquency for the 1930–1942 period indicate a decline in three out of four areas where projects were active. After a review of the work of the projects, John B. Martin observes:

> Perhaps the results of the Project should not be measured by the rate of juvenile delinquency alone. There seems little doubt that the residents of these low-income areas have demonstrated that they can and will organize to make their neighborhoods better places in which to live. The Project has uncovered latent talent within the communities not heretofore channeled toward civic betterment. The committees have improved parent-teacher relationships and shouldered responsibility for school attendance and school improvement. They have brought to bear effective public opinion on specific contributors to juvenile delinquency. They have succeeded in leading children away from crime and in reincorporating parolees into the neighborhood.[9]

A survey of prevention and treatment programs would be incomplete without mention of settlement houses, group and casework agencies, coordinating councils, police athletic leagues, etc. In general, these private or public agencies rely on the use of semiprofessional or profession group or caseworkers to manipulate either the delinquent, his peer

[8] Clifford R. Shaw, "Methods, Accomplishments, and Problems of the Chicago Area Projects," *A Report to the Board of Directors of the Chicago Area Projects,* September 1944.

[9] John B. Martin, "A New Attack on Delinquency," *Harpers Magazine,* 188:512, May 1944.

632 · CORRECTIONAL TREATMENT

groups, his environment, or a combination of all of these. Questioning the effectiveness of these programs, Witmer and Tufts conclude:

> All this, taken together, suggests that we are on our way toward learning what does and what does not prevent delinquency, but we still have far to go. Progress toward that objective will call for close cooperation between practice and research, with both parties looking hopefully to theory and to experience for ideas about the direction in which to move next![10]

Framework for a Description of Prevention and Treatment Programs

The foregoing review of formal prevention and treatment programs suggests that perhaps at this stage in the development of theory and method, meaningful questions are more important than recommended solutions. The following questions are offered as a framework for the description of preventive and therapeutic techniques:

1. With what factors in the causal matrix does the program purport or attempt to deal? Motivational? Situational?

2. How does the program purport to deal with the problem of personal commitment?

3. How does the program purport to deal with the problem of the person's accessibility?

4. How does the program deal with the problem of ongoing delinquency? Does it attempt to intervene at the level of activity? Does it tend to ignore the activity and concentrate on the individual and his group attachments?

5. How does the program deal with the question of defining the individual as a delinquent? Does it attempt to avoid official definitions? Does it attempt to avoid unofficial definitions as well? Or does it deliberately or nondeliberately isolate the individual as a person with a problem?

Processes Related to Delinquency and Criminality

All the questions listed immediately above point up the fact that any treatment or prevention program must be related to a theory of

[10] Witmer and Tufts, *op. cit.*, p. 50.

criminality. Accordingly, we must again summarize several basic themes relating criminalization to other social factors and processes.

Given a situation where the possibilities for upward mobility are restricted, the selection of illegal modes for attaining social goals may be related to: (1) the individual's level of aspiration; (2) the relative availability of legal and illegal modes; (3) the availability of targets or victims; (4) the individual's personal abilities and disabilities; and (5) the balance between inhibitory and facilitating psychological and social factors.

This last and critical requirement is related to the person's group memberships. Group membership always involves a complex of inhibitory and facilitating orientations toward a variety of activities. Clergymen, for example, tend to be more inhibited in certain activities than do salesmen, longshoremen, businessmen, etc. Each role and status carries with it certain positive, negative or neutral orientations toward almost every conceivable activity. The forces contributing to these orientations are many and varied, but the period of adolescence seems critically related to learning delinquent and criminal roles.

The Decline of Parental Authority and Influence

In sociological terms, the period from infancy to young adulthood may be viewed as a preparation for the playing of various interpersonal and vocational roles. The young child's "preparation" consists largely in developing patterns of relating to others. His capacity for personal and social initiative, cooperation, and frustration tolerance, his ability to cope effectively with problems of object-relations and person-relations, is developed or stunted. He establishes patterns of dealing with peers, subordinates, and superordinates. He attends school, learns the language, develops his mechanical, numerical, and verbal abilities, etc. The kind and number of roles an individual will occupy depend on a variety of factors, including (1) the availability of the roles; (2) their formal and informal requirements; (3) access to role-preparations; and (4) personal qualifications.

The period between middle adolescence and young adulthood has involved different expectations in different cultures and at different historical periods within the same culture. These expectations may or may not be shared by the adolescents themselves. The adult members of most societies view the period as one of preparation for adult responsibilities—the attitude expressed in the Biblical admonition: "When I was a child I acted as a child, but when I was a man I put away childish things." In societies structured around a family economy—the farm, the home industry or craft—adolescence was conceived as a period of intense preparation for adult roles. The young man helped his father in the fields, he went out in the fishing boat, he learned to cure leather, to use his father's tools—and, like his father, he came to accept, at an early age, the idea that the day was to be spent in work.

The Industrial Revolution, the specialization of labor and the resulting decline in family industry forced the family unit to yield some of its functions in the preparation for adulthood, sharing them with outside agents. The importance of education and its increasing availability was recognized as a valid justification for postponing the child's direct participation in work. In time, the amount of education thought necessary to prepare the child adequately increased, deferring the child's actual participation in productive work even further. During the first decades of this century the agitation against child labor provided a powerful moral support for this principle of deferment, and most states enacted legislation requiring children to remain in school until middle adolescence (fourteen to sixteen years).

During this same period, the dispersion of adult labor from the farm or home to outside places of work was accelerated; the father tended to be away at work; the child, away at school. The total result was a situation that produced an increasingly sharp cleavage between the activity patterns and the activity models of the child and those of the adult during the period assigned to preparation for adult responsibilities. The child spent more of his time with other children at school and at play; the society of children and youths rather than the society of older working adults became more and more the source of his behavior and activity models. What some commentators have called the "youth culture" emerged.

This cleavage was sharper in the case of boys than in that of girls, a fact of some suggestiveness in view of the statistical disparity in delinquency between the sexes. Parsons has pointed out:

> It seems to be a definite fact that girls are apt to be relatively docile, to conform in general to adult expectations, to be "good," whereas boys are more apt to be recalcitrant to discipline and defiant of adult authority. There is really no feminine equivalent of the expression "bad boy." It was the suggestion that this is at least partially explained by the fact that it is possible from an early age to initiate girls directly into many important aspects of the adult feminine role. Their mothers are continually about the house and the meaning of many of the things they

do is relatively tangible and easily understandable to a child. It is also possible for the daughter to participate actively and usefully in many of these activities. Especially in the urban middle classes, however, the father does not work in the home and his son is not able to observe his work or to participate in it from an early age. Furthermore, many of the masculine functions are of a relatively abstract and intangible character, such that their meaning must remain almost wholly inaccessible to a child. This leaves the boy without a tangible meaningful model to emulate and without the possibility of a gradual initiation into the activities of the adult male role.[11]

The shift of the major preparatory function from the family to the school and to the society of other students was bound to have consequences difficult to anticipate at the time but somewhat clearer now that more time has elapsed. As an adult model, the schoolteacher is much more diffuse a figure than the parent. As an authority figure, he or she is not only less forceful and realistically powerful but less looked up to as well. Moreover, where the father, in his role of disciplinarian and conformity-enforcer, has to deal with only a relatively small number of individuals, the teacher must face the larger and more or less unified body of students, in a situation where "resistance" is traditionally more tolerated than resistance to a parent would be. Thus, in a society where a major part of the burden of preparation and socialization had shifted from a relatively cooperative parent-child situation to the relatively "antagonistic" teacher-child situation, any weakening of the authority of the school was bound to shift the axis of real authority increasingly toward the society of children. Progressive education, in deliberately relaxing the authority and directiveness of the teacher was derived from and had a further stimulating influence on this larger development.

The Expansion of Nonproductive Leisure Time

One of the fruits of the Industrial Revolution was a vast expansion of available leisure time. Because of their ejection from the labor force, this expansion has been most marked in the case of children and adolescents. Several writers have commented on the relationship between leisure and delinquency. McKay, for example, has written:

> In the Old World or in rural America the leisure-time problem was not serious because the child was part of the economy. He did his

[11] Talcott Parsons, "Age and Sex in the Social Structure of the United States," in Parsons, *Essays in Sociological Theory, Pure and Applied* (Glencoe, Ill.: The Free Press, 1949), p. 219.

share of the family work and by so doing earned his share of the family income. But in the city, he is not part of the income-earning group, and as a result he is free from income-procuring activity a large proportion of the time.

Since the problem did not exist before arrival in the city, no institutional forms were brought by the groups into the inner city areas to meet these particular needs. Likewise, the city has not developed adequate institutions for this purpose, since the large city in America is comparatively new. The result has been that children, especially boys, do not have any meaningful or acceptable way of employing their leisure time. And in gaining leisure time, they have lost the devices through which, historically, they have established themselves in the neighborhood. Children now have freedom, but they are not important in the economy. As the late Professor Reuter has pointed out, the lack of any real function leaves the urban adolescents in a position of tolerated parasitism.[12]

Denney and Riesman are more emphatic in asserting a causal relationship between the expansion of unproductive leisure, the deferment of work, and delinquency:

> The same forces which have reduced the work-week have lengthened the lifespan—and have made it compulsory for the young to wait it out in school until the labor force will make room for them. For many of the young, this turns out to be simply a prison, with rather inefficient and wholly unhappy jailors. The denizens of these jails have little more pleasure in their free time than prisoners usually do who exercise their ingenuity in outwitting and tormenting their guards.
>
> One set of responses to this situation is labeled by the society as "juvenile delinquency," activities in which gregarious theft and gang warfare by the boys and gregarious sex by the girls appear to be channels for the playful, sociable and conformist impulses of the lower-class youth. If, in many urban areas, we find a lower-class boy or girl who is not delinquent in this sense, we can be fairly sure that he or she is either headed up the class ladder or is psychologically deviant or both, being unwilling or unable to join in the group activities sanctioned by his peers.[13]

In the foregoing comment the analogy between leisure and a jail and idle adolescents and prisoners may be intended more as colorful illustration than as an explanation of juvenile delinquency. Nevertheless,

---

[12] Henry D. McKay, "The Neighborhood and Child Conduct," *Annals of the American Academy of Political and Social Science,* 261:35, January 1949.

[13] Reuel Denney and David Riesman, "Leisure in Urbanized America" in Paul K. Hatt, *Reader in Urban Sociology* (Glencoe, Illinois: The Free Press, 1951), p. 471.

the use of these images is suggestive, especially in the underlying context of attitudes toward leisure. Not many years ago most students of child welfare were defending the "right of play" against the threat and abuses of industrial child labor. The relationship between leisure and delinquency was viewed in terms of the inadequacy of the one leading to indulgence in the other. The belief was popularly held that providing children with better play space, playgrounds, etc., would solve many of the problems of delinquency. The significant assumption underlying this approach was that the more or less exclusive preoccupation with play and diversion by adolescents was desirable and beneficial. Whether or not the proponents of this solution actually had sixteen-, seventeen-, and eighteen-year-old children in mind when they proposed playgrounds is difficult to determine. In any case, it seems clear that the sophisticated adolescent has, by and large, accepted this adult tolerance of play as his legitimate preoccupation but has not, by and large, accepted the typical adult versions of what constitutes wholesome adolescent play. Nothing in this approach to delinquency implied any concern by adults over the fact that hundreds of thousands of individuals on the threshold of adulthood had no other responsibility than that of amusing themselves.

The Deferment of Adult Responsibilities

The revolutionary redefinition of the rights and obligations of young people has had describable effects on the general attitudes of adolescents toward the appropriate function of their particular phase of life. In the most general terms, these attitudes, reflecting and in many cases going beyond those of their parents, have tended to define their activities predominantly in terms of rights and minimally in terms of obligations.[14] In many instances, this has resulted in a thoroughgoing redefinition of the

[14] The overindulgence and overconcern of many modern parents seems at least partly related to a trend in child psychology which was highly critical of parental authority in its restrictive forms and which laid great stress on the importance of permissiveness in child-parent relations. Recently this thinking has encountered criticism on the part of psychologists themselves. Thus, for example, Alfred Farau:

> Psychology as a whole has gone much too far in preaching "adjustment," thus only too often leaving the man in the street more confused than he already is. It is true that children and students are treated better today than in the days of their parents' own youth and that is good, but parents and teachers today are, in exchange, treated worse. The *victims* have changed, but *not the authority principle*. And, unfortunately, authority has shifted to the less experienced ones. (Alfred Farau, "The Challenge of Social Feeling," speech delivered at the Adlerian Congress, New York, May 1957.)

"period of preparation" into a period of more or less indefinite postponement and avoidance. Thus, Parsons:

> Perhaps the best single point of reference for characterizing the youth culture lies in its contrast with the dominant pattern of the adult male role. By contrast with the emphasis on responsibility in this role, the orientation of the youth culture is more or less specifically irresponsible. One of its dominant rules is "having a good time." Negatively, there is a strong tendency to repudiate interest in adult things and to feel at least a certain recalcitrance to the pressure of adult expectations.[15]

In a similar vein, the child psychiatrist Erik Erikson speaks of the adolescent period as a kind of "psychosocial moratorium":

> A moratorium is a period of delay, granted to somebody who is not ready to meet an obligation or forced on somebody who should give himself time to do so. Here I mean a delay of adult commitments, and yet, not only a delay. I mean a period that is characterized by a selective permissiveness on the part of society and of provocative playfulness on the part of youth....
>
> Each society and each culture institutionalizes a certain moratorium for the majority of its young people. For the most part, these moratoria coincide with apprenticeships and adventures that are in line with the society's values....
>
> ...It seems quite possible...that juvenile delinquency, especially in its organized form, could and should be considered an attempt in itself at the creation of a psychosocial moratorium. In fact, I would assume that delinquency has been a relatively institutionalized moratorium for a long time in parts of our society, and that it forces itself on the awareness of society now only because it proves too attractive and compelling for too many youngsters—from the better neighborhoods as well.[16]

The period between early and late adolescence is a period of waiting. For some, the waiting is spent in preparation for adult responsibilities; for others, it is a period of postponement or flight. It is significant that most of the gang members described by Whyte in *Street Corner Society* were over twenty-five.[17]

For children of the lower classes, especially of minority groups, the

[15] Parsons, *op. cit.*, p. 221.

[16] Erik Erikson, "Ego Identity and the Psychosocial Moratorium," *New Perspectives for Research in Juvenile Delinquency*, Children's Bureau, Department of Health, Education, and Welfare (Washington, D. C.: Government Printing Office, 1955), pp. 5–7.

[17] William F. Whyte, *Street Corner Society*, 2d ed. (Chicago: The University of Chicago Press, 1955).

prospect of responsible and conventional occupational life may appear increasingly calamitous. The children of the slums, like the children of the wealthy and the middle class, see the same movies, the same television programs, are exposed to the same aspirational pressures. This standardization of aspiration in the face of increasing inequality of actual opportunity has occasioned concern among social commentators.

The lower-class adolescent sees his father, a factory worker, tired and insecure, come home to argue with a wife who, similarly exposed to the consumption pressure of television, makes his life miserable with her demands. In effect, the young gang member is asked to exchange his heroic, exciting, and independent life, his pattern of free-and-easy sexual exploration, for what seems to him the existence of a wage slave mated with a shrew. For the underprivileged child, viewing life from this perspective, the juvenile gang may represent something very close to a realistically satisfying alternative to a frustrating and subservient social and economic status.

The Peer Group as a Socializing Agency

For the delinquent gang member, play has virtually superseded life. It is rooted in reality; it has realistic consequences. No one objects when the cowboys and Indians kill each other in play; no one complains very much when the children destroy each other's property. But when the delinquent "plays" at violence, it is no longer so playful, no longer so distant from reality. When he destroys property, it is often adult property. The adults become hostile, and this hostility is a new impetus for unity among the delinquent group. Rejection by the adult world does several things: (1) it isolates the child from the socializing influences normally contributed by interaction with adults; (2) it isolates him from the emulation goals held out by adults; (3) it involves him in continuous, consequential conflict with adults.

The important point is that in the conflicts of nondelinquents with adults there are cutoff and shutoff points. The children are noisy, the adults become angry; there is an argument, possibly a spanking; then relations become normalized again. This distinction is crucial: With the nondelinquent child it is the conflict that gets cutoff; normal relations are re-established. In the delinquent child's conflicts with adults, the normal relations are cut off while the conflicts become established. Rather than friendly and cooperative relations, mutual hostility and conflict become the norm. When this mutual hostility is generalized to the larger social group, few, if any, avenues for reconciliation with its values remain open. Instead, both internal and external pressures are on the side of the values of the gang.

One of the distinguishing signs of personal and social maturity is the ability to defer immediate gratification. But the juvenile gang is distinctly a vehicle for the more immediate gratification of impulses. The school, the job, the family, on the other hand, increase the situations in which deferment of gratification must be practiced. In any social situation where the behavior of the actors is determined with reference to mutual obligations, duties, and performances, behavior tends to become routinized and regularized. Certain things must be done which exclude other things that might be done. These things must be done in a certain manner, and according to a certain schedule. The school situation is above all a learning experience in the submission of impulses to the control of routines. There are long periods during which one must remain in a certain place, doing a certain task. There are periods where one may not talk, must listen to others, and accommodate immediate impulses to the consent of others. There is the spelling period, the history period, the gym period, etc.

The Multiplication of Prerequisites

This multiplication of barriers between impulse and immediate satisfaction is further illustrated by the fact that the attainment of goals is increasingly made conditional on certain prerequisites. In order to obtain certain gratifications, one must first obtain things which are not immediately gratifying but which are absolute requirements. The young child may obtain his mother's adulation merely by walking across the room or by acting out an impulse. The high school boy who desires the same adulation from others may have to work hard in the gym or in the scrimmage lines; in order to become a football hero, one must sweat. The occupational world is especially organized with reference to requirements which may not in themselves be gratifying but which are prerequisites of later gratification.

In psychological terms, most crimes may be distinguished from most legitimate activities by the extent to which the actor observes or ignores the social prerequisites of gratification. Theft involves the obtaining of valued objects without observing the social prerequisites established for the transfer of property; in our society these include the consent of the owner and some form of value in return, either labor or goods. The crime of rape involves the obtaining of sexual gratification without observing the prerequisite of consent.

In more general terms, every crime involving a victim involves the violation of consent, the gratification of a wish against the wishes of others. There are three general methods by which this is accomplished: intimidation (the use of threat or force), deception, and stealth. Any offense involving a victim requires one or a combination of these techniques.

A failure to obtain the prerequisites that ordinarily make possible the gratification of individual needs by the consent, cooperation, or at least tolerance of the social group requires the individual to: (1) accept a frustration of his desires, and (2) relinquish his aspirations, or (3) attempt to gratify them by unconventional or illegitimate means. The juvenile gang and the adult criminal combination function to provide support and training in the carrying out of techniques of intimidation, deception, and stealth and to foster attitudes that rationalize and justify these techniques.

Two interacting processes seem to be operative in the social and psychological realities of the developing criminal. A failure to participate in the activities leading to the prerequisites of legitimate goal-attainment results in a narrowing of the legitimate channels of gratification. The young adult without schooling or training is confined to the lowest and most insecure occupations. This process may be called the shrinking of legitimate alternatives.

Participation in the activities of delinquent or criminal groups has the further effect of setting up social and psychological barriers against intimate relations with those engaged in legitimate occupations. These barriers, some but not all of which are conscious and deliberate, are of various kinds; the criminal rarely can spare the time and effort required to pursue a full-time "legitimate" occupation while engaging in gainful crime.

This failure to participate in the workaday world of legitimate members of his own socioeconomic class tends to prevent the development of the subtle social controls, arising out of the intimate social relations created by close contact and common interests and problems. The possibility of intimate social relations is further diminished by the difficulty of discussing such questions as how one earns a living, what happens on the job, etc.

The process of criminalization, defined in these terms, is one by which the individual increasingly views himself and is viewed by others as a person expected, by himself and others, to behave in a certain way. As such, it differs in no basic respect from the process by which a person "becomes anything"—from a doctor to a plumber.

The Reinstitution of Social Control

The theory of individualized treatment views criminal behavior as an outcome of certain personal attitudes, habits, needs, or problems. In line with this theory, the focus of therapeutic attack is the person's commitment to or involvement with these attitudes, problems, etc. The attempt is to liberate the person from his commitment to the anti-social orientations he has acquired.

The group-centered approach takes strong issue with the view that the individual's basic or binding commitments are to ideational orientations. While acknowledging the role of symbols and concepts in the channeling of motives, the group-centered theory maintains that the person's basic commitment is to human figures, whether existing in the actual environment or as a kind of "internal audience" in his mind. Its adherents argue, moreover, that the person's symbol-systems arise and are maintained by his group identifications and are not basically changed unless his group attachments are changed.

This issue, the question of *what must be changed in order that behavior may change,* is at the core of the controversy. All other differences flow from it and are essentially secondary. They are, in fact, occasionally exaggerated. Both methods rely on human relationships as instruments of treatment. The individual method relies on manipulating the relationship between a patient and a therapist, as, in earlier periods, it employed the relationship between the offender and the judge, the convict and his keeper, the punished and the punishing. What this method historically ignored, however, was the relationship between the offender and his reference group. The group-centered approach, by contrast, deals primarily if not exclusively with the individual's group attachments and tries to avoid a treatment or preventive situation that contributes to isolation and mutual alienation.

In advocating this relative de-emphasis on the details or motives of the anti-social acts, the group-centered approach appeals to some of the commonplace insights of human experience. The frustrations of parents in trying to get their male youngsters to dress neatly and observe minimal rules of personal cleanliness are well known. Up to a certain age most boys are highly resistant to such customs as brushing the hair, cleaning the nails, and wearing clean clothes, and many parents have gone to their wits' end in trying to bribe or coerce their otherwise obedient youngsters into conformity to these rules. Certain wiser parents, remembering their own childhood, understand that this resistance to conformity to adult rules is actually based on the child's conformity to a group whose expectations in these respects are much more important at this stage. Among the collective of "regular guys," to be overly combed, washed, and clean-nailed may be an intolerable sign of effeminacy. Consequently, to be well-groomed may mark the youngster down as a sissy or, equally intolerable, as one who is overly interested in those alien creatures known as girls.

So the wise parents wait. They do not imperil their own relationship with their child by bringing irresistible coercion to bear, and they do not endanger his critically important relations with his peers. They wait for the normal biosocial processes which, in a short time, will transform the group of young hoboes into a collection of fashion plates, all desperately interested in those delightful creatures known as girls. Once again, the reliance is on a range of subtle control processes, operating through the group and infinitely more powerful than any coercion from an adult figure beyond the child's critical social world.

Important secondary differences in method and emphasis derive from the core difference just cited. The individualized approach emphasizes the offense. As the individual was formerly punished for his offense, he is now to be treated for his offense. He is to be cured, say, from picking pockets or from burglarizing houses or from stealing automobiles. Despite the fact that the more sophisticated theories of individualized treatment lay less stress on the overt criminal act than on underlying motivational determinants, the basic orientation is similar: the offender is to be cured for something he *is,* which leads to something he *does.*

The group-centered approach is, of course, concerned that the criminal behavior be terminated, but its stress is less on the offender's acts, which may vary widely, and more on the group attachments and interactions that made these acts personally attractive or gratifying. The relative unconcern with the particular delinquencies is based on the expectation that, once the individual's group attachments are changed, the major impetus toward these particular activities will no longer exist.

This impetus is *conformity*, the identical impetus which impels the law-abiding toward legal behavior. Thus, according to the group-centered approach, the main motive toward most forms of delinquency, as toward most forms of behavior generally, is conformity, a term labeling the total of pressures motivating individuals to respond to the expectations of others. Accordingly, the most effective way of changing behavior is to replace the individual's commitment to the lawbreaking social group to which he has been conforming with a commitment to a law-abiding group to which he will conform in the future.

If it is true that the individual's group provides the most powerful source of social control, this fact has significant corollaries for treatment and prevention. It suggests that the intactness of the group provides powerful insulation against external attempts to reach and to change the individual. It implies further that the most effective way of influencing the individual is to alter the objectives or activities of the intimate small group to which he conforms. It also suggests that a way must be found whereby the *larger* group accepts the delinquent as a person while it disapproves of certain of his specific behaviors. Without this, it is not likely that the delinquent will find a way to achieve identification with the larger group, and submit himself to informal, nonforceful methods of social control.

How may this change in identification be achieved? Identification seems to be related to processes bringing about a personal commitment to others. When a personal commitment exists, a kind of interpersonal communication and control takes place. The actors influence and respond to each other by means of processes which are called "empathic"—i.e., not involving or requiring direct verbal communication. Empathy is the name for a condition of communication which takes place without verbal interaction.

What is our current state of knowledge concerning this process? In a discussion of value conflicts in delinquency areas, George Vold observed:

> Contemporary social psychology has continued to be inadequate in accounting for this phenomenon of empathy or identification. The same problem is fundamental in the explanation of delinquency. It is not residence, location, or physical propinquity in an area that makes the individual identify himself with the delinquent pattern of behavior, any more than in the case of the lone Democratic family in a strong Republican neighborhood. It is rather a much more basic and funda-mental social psychological fact of identification with a world and with

a way of life. Why that identification is made continues to be the principal problem.[18]

Vold's observations suggest a point from which we may chart a course for the future. In a sense, both treatment and prevention are relatively recent and are to a certain extent "experimental." The term *experimental* has, however, little relevance to a more scientific connotation. Most "experiments" in treatment and prevention have been in the nature of an evaluation of activities described as "successes." This has been true not only because of the biases and preconceptions behind such programs but also because of public opinion and the need to justify expenditures. It is not good business to admit failure. Consequently, these experiments have been novel but not experimental. Future progress depends on our being truly experimental, which means not only "trying out" something but testing it under conditions that permit observation and verification.

[18] George Vold, "Discussion of Kobrin's Findings," *American Sociological Review*, 16:661, October 1951.

INDEX

Index

Lindner, Robert, 558
liquor laws, offenses against, 13
Livingston, Edward, 213
Llewellyn, Emma, 283
Llewellyn, Karl, 71
lock step, 413
Lodge, Sen. Henry C., 225
Lohman, Joseph D., 246*n.*, 461, 627-628
Lombroso, Cesare, 145, 294
  constitutional theories of crime of, 213-215
Lonely Crowd, The, 134
Lottier, Stuart, 18
Lunt, Paul S., 8

McBoyle *v.* United States, 103
McCorkle, Lloyd W., 182*n.*, 474, 484, 533, 536, 551, 568, 570-572
McKay, Henry D., 351, 635-636
McKendrick, Charles, 492
McKenzie, R. D., 283
McNaghten Rules, 435-439
MacNamara, Donal E. J., 425
Maconochie, Alexander, 609-610
Maestro, Marcello, 380-381
Males, involved in crime, *see* sex ratio
Malinowski, Bronislaw, 128-130
manslaughter, 19, 20
Manual of Correctional Standards, 471-472
Manual for Courts-Martial, 178*n.*, 477-479, 482-484
marijuana, 168, 175
Martin, Clyde E., 166
Martin, John B., 631
mass communication and crime, 71*n.*
Mattick, Hans W., 460
Maudsley, Henry, 582
May, M. A., 268
Mayhew, 146
Mead, Margaret, 330
Meeker, Ben, 449
mens rea, principle of, 104-105, 433
mental disorders, as cause of crime, 252
Mercier, Charles, 309
Merriam, C. E., 84*n.*
Merton, Robert K., 125, 127, 130-133, 258, 280*n.*
mesomorphs, 220
methadone, 170
milieu, 291-292
milieu studies of crime, 284-288
military offender, and military law, 176-178
  punishments of, 180-181
  rehabilitation centers for, 181-182
  trial for, 179-180
military offenses, 176-178
  extent of, 182
misdemeanor, definition of, 100

mobility
  of criminals, 136-137
  social, 123-124
model, 142-143
Moloccan settlement, delinquency in, 287
Montagu, Ashley, 199-200, 218, 222, 223
Moore, Maurice E., 291
morality, of prisoners, 266-267
morals, offenses against, 13
Moreau, M., 146, 148
morphine, 175
Mosaic legal tradition, 378-381
motion to quash, 110
motivation
  for criminal behavior, 296-297
  importance of group in, 336-339
murder, 11, 18
  rural rates of, 20
  urban rates of, 16, 17, 19
Murder Incorporated, 154
Murphy, Gardner, 292
mutilation, as punishment, 378, 379, 383, 396
Myrdal, Gunnar, 236*n.*

nalorphine, 170
narcotic drug laws, offenses against, 13
Nathan, E., 538*n.*
National Prisoner Statistics, 54, 236, 240, 241
National Probation Association, 450
nativity, and crime, 224-227
natural law, 88, 93
neglect, of family and children, 13
Negroes
  arrests and offenses of, 232-236
  crime rate of, 24
  culture of, 247-248
  differential crime rate of, 9
  hypothesis about crime rate of, 243-248
  prison commitment of, 236-244
  racial mixtures in, 230, 231
  status of, in prisons, 521, 522
  validity of crime statistics of, 231-232
neurosis, 252
  contrasted to crime, 257-258
New England, crime rate of, 16, 17
New Jersey Commission on Narcotic Control, 173
New Jersey Juvenile Statute, 183
New Jersey State Prison, training lecture for custodians at, 505-506
New Jersey State Reformatory, 577-578
New Jersey Youth Commission, 184
nolo contendere, 110
non vult, 110
non support, 13
norms, 278-280, 297
  see also social control *and* socialization